Academic Governance

Research on Institutional Politics
and Decision Making

Compiled and Edited by

J. Victor Baldridge

School of Education
Stanford University
Palo Alto, California

McCutchan Publishing Corporation
2526 Grove Street
Berkeley, California 94704

Preface

As any half-awake observer will testify, the academic community is in turmoil and its events are now center stage among the major concerns of the society. Countless observers are turning their attention to the affairs of the academic world. Journalists, newspapermen, TV newsmen, amateur sociologists, and average citizens are "explaining" the events on the campus with an overflowing stream of verbiage. The pounds of pages and miles of videotape on this subject would now fill a warehouse, and they still pour forth each day. Countless books pass across my desk each day, to the point that nobody can possibly keep up with the volume. In the midst of all this outpouring of wisdom—and nonsense—a man had better have a darn good reason for adding to the already overwhelming body of material. This book, I believe, has such a justification.

After several years of trying to teach sociology courses about organizational characteristics of colleges and universities, I am extremely unhappy with the quality of material that is being written about academic governance. Most of the literature is journalistic, armchair philosophy, and very little empirical research is available. If a person wants to study government agencies, industrial organizations, or business firms, there is plenty of solid social science research to guide him. However, if a man wants to know something about the organizational and administrative features of universities—the home of all those researchers—then by and large there is a great vacuum of information. To be sure, there are thousands of pages of material at hand, but it is remarkable that the social sciences dealing with administration and organizations simply have not looked seriously at the university.

Out of a sense of frustration with the available literature, I decided to undertake a search for a collection of articles that might help fill the vacuum of knowledge about academic governance. This book tries to:

1. Gather material from sociology, psychology, and other social sciences that have direct relevance to the academic decision-making process.

2. Assemble some of the best *empirical* research—work based on social scientific analysis done in the field.

3. Avoid armchair philosophy that so dominates current commentaries on higher education.

4. Provide a systematic framework that binds the research together in a coherent theme, not just a random collection of articles. The Introduction to the book explains the basic framework in some detail.

Of the 26 articles included in the book, the vast majority are the direct result of carefully planned social science research projects, while the remaining few are classic statements from national study commissions, institutional self-evaluations, and union leaders. About 35 percent of the articles have never been published for the general public before, and many were especially written for this book. Several of the articles come from research in progress, and were made available through personal contacts with the authors. Although the research is primarily empirical social research, it tries to avoid overly technical jargon, and hopefully it is readily understandable.

Part 4: The Student Revolution's Impact on Governance

Part 5: The External Environment

Part 6: Conflict and the Dynamics of Policy Making

INTRODUCTION: MODELS OF UNIVERSITY GOVERNANCE—BUREAUCRATIC, COLLEGIAL, AND POLITICAL

J. Victor Baldridge

There are many different ways to study "academic governance," but this book has a definite bias, a way of looking at the problem that largely determines what articles are selected and how they are arranged. The reader should clearly understand that bias. Basically, this book views the university as one of a class of social systems that social scientists term "complex organizations." Consequently one of the critical tasks of this book is to draw material from sociology, social psychology, and administrative theory that bears on the operation of complex social systems. In addition, the whole volume tries to interpret academic governance as a "political" process, the interaction of various academic interest groups as they try to shape and mold the destiny of the university. In many ways this is a very different view from traditional understandings of academic governance, and the introduction explains why this particular way of looking at the problem might make sense. There are three major objectives in the introduction:

1. Two of the dominant images of university governance, the "bureaucratic" and the "collegial" models, are examined and criticized.

2. A new "political" image is offered as a alternative model for understanding the dynamics of decisionmaking.

3. The organization of articles within this book is discussed, and their relation to the overall "political" theme is suggested.

Traditional Models of Academic Governance

One of the critical first steps in analyzing the university's administrative processes is adopting a basic framework from which to view the processes. Thomas Kuhn (7) suggests that all scientists adopt analytic models from which they view their problems. In other words, they mentally construct "models" or "paradigms" that reconstruct reality on a miniature scale. The model that a scientist selects is critical to his research, for it greatly influences his choice of problems, his overall theoretical perspective, the research methodologies that he uses, and the types of evidence that he will accept as valid. This model-building may be conscious or unconscious, but in either case, it greatly affects a scientist's view of his world.

The fundamental argument of this article is that sociologists and administrative theorists have not yet constructed appropriate intellectual models for analyzing academic administration and that the lack of an adequate framework is hindering research. Let us turn first, then, to a brief description of the two models that have been commonly used to describe university administration, and after they have been reviewed we will propose a new model. One of these commonly used models is the "bureaucratic" image, while the other is the "collegial" model.

The University as a Bureaucracy

There can be little question that one of the most influential descriptions of complex organizations was Max Weber's monumental work on bureaucracies (see 1, chap. 8; 14, pt. 3; 3, pt. 3). Weber tried to describe the characteristics of bureaucracies that separated them from other, less formal, types of work organizations. In skeleton form he suggested that bureaucracies are networks of social groups dedicated to limited goals, and organized for maximum efficiency. Moreover, the regulation of the system is based on the principle of "legal-rationality," as contrasted with informal regulation based on friendship, loyalty to family, or personal allegiance to a charismatic leader. The structure is hierarchical and is tied together by formal chains of command and systems of communication. Weber's description involves such characteristics as tenure, appointment to office, salaries as a rational form of payment, and competency as the basis of promotion. Most of his ideas are well known and need little elaboration.

Several authors claim that university governance may be most fruitfully understood by applying the bureaucratic paradigm. For example, Herbert Stroup (see 13, chap. 4) points out some characteristics of colleges and universities that fit Weber's original discussion of the nature of bureaucracy. Some of Stroup's conclusions about colleges include the following:

1. Competence is the criterion used for appointment.
2. Officials are appointed, not elected.
3. Salaries are fixed and paid directly by the organization, rather than determined in "free-fee" style.
4. Rank is recognized and respected.
5. The career is exclusive; no other work is done.
6. The style of life is centered around the organization.
7. Security is present in a tenure system.
8. Personal and organizational property are separated.

Stroup is undoubtedly correct that Weber's paradigm can be applied to universities and most observers are well aware of the bureaucratic factors involved in university administration. (For example, see 6, chap. 15 and 1 p. 17). Certainly there are many bureaucratic elements in the university, and they cannot be ignored. Among the more prominent features are the following:

1. The university is a complex organization chartered by the state, and in this respect it is like most other bureaucracies. This seemingly innocent fact has major consequences, because the university is thus a "corporate person" with public responsibilities.
2. The university has a formal hierarchy, with offices and a set of bylaws that specify the relations between those offices. Professors, instructors, and research assistants are bureaucratic officers in the same sense as deans, chancellors, and presidents.
3. There are formal channels of communication that must be respected, as many a student or young professor finds out to his dismay.
4. There are definite bureaucratic authority relations, with some officials exercising authority over others. In a university the authority relations are often blurred, ambiguous, and shifting, but no one would deny that they exist.
5. There are formal policies and rules that govern much of the institution's work. The library regulations, budgetary guidelines, and procedures of the university senate are all part of the system of regulations and procedures that hold the university together and control its work.

6. The bureaucratic elements are most vividly apparent to students in the "people-processing" aspects of record-keeping, registration, graduation requirements, and a thousand other routine, day-to-day activities that are designed to help the modern university handle its masses of students. Of course, students often cry that this results in impersonality and callousness, but it makes the operation of the university possible as it struggles with an overwhelming influx of students. Certainly the university's structure and many of its daily operations suggest that a bureaucratic image is helpful for studying it.

In addition to these rather obvious features, it is also true that the decision-making processes are often highly bureaucratic, especially when rather routine types of decisions are at stake. Any observer of the decision processes on the campus cannot escape the fact that most decisions are routinely made by officials who have been given the responsibility by the formal administrative structure. The dean of admissions has been formally delegated the task of handling admissions actions, and routinely does exactly that; the procedures for graduation are routinely administered by a group of officials who have been designated to do that task; the research policies of the university are routinely supervised by officials specified in the rules of the university; financial activities are usually handled in a bureaucratic manner by the finance office. To be sure, the vast majority of the daily decisions in a university are routinely handled in a very bureaucratic fashion, and it would be folly to ignore the importance of these activities.

On the other hand, there are many ways that the bureaucratic paradigm falls short of explaining university governance, especially if one is primarily concerned with the decision-making processes. First, the bureaucratic model tells us much about "authority," that is, legitimate, formalized power, but not much about the other types of power based on nonlegitimate threats, the force of mass movements, expertise, and appeals to emotion and sentiment. The Weberian paradigm is weak when it attempts to deal with these nonformal types of power and influence. Second, the bureaucratic paradigm explains much about the formal *structure* but very little about the *processes* that give dynamism to the structure. A description of the static institutional arrangements may be helpful but it does little to explain the institution in action. Third, the bureaucratic paradigm deals with the formal structure at any one point in time, but does not explain how the organization changes over time. Finally, the bureaucratic model does not deal extensively with the crucial task of policy-formulation. The paradigm explains how policies may be carried out in the most efficient fashion *after* they are set, but it says little about the process by which policy is established in the first place. It does not deal with political issues, such as the struggles of groups within the university who want to force policy decisions toward their special interests. In these ways, then, the bureaucratic paradigm falls far short of explaining decision-making in the university.

The University as a Collegium

Many writers have consciously rejected the bureaucratic image of the university and instead have declared that the university is a "collegium," or a "community of scholars." This is a rather ambiguous concept when it is closely examined. In fact, there seem to be at least three different threads of argument running through this type of literature:

1. *A description of a collegial university's management.* The supporters of this approach argue that a university should not be organized like other bureaucracies; instead, there should be full participation of the members of the academic community—especially the faculty—in its management. There are few actual examples of such "round table" democratic institutions outside of a few small liberal arts colleges, but the image persists. Under this concept the "community of scholars" would administer its own affairs, and the bureaucratic officials would have little influence. The image of the college as a collegium has been the subject of several essays (see 8). John Millett (see 9, pp. 234-235), one of the foremost proponents of this model, has stated his views quite succinctly:

> I have already expressed my own point of view in so far as the organization of a college or university is concerned. I do not believe that the concept of hierarchy is a realistic representation of the interpersonal relationships which exist within a college or university. Nor do I believe that a structure of hierarchy is a desirable prescription for the organization of a college or university . . . .
> I would argue that there is another concept of organization just as valuable as a tool of analysis and even more useful as a generalized observation of group and interpersonal behavior. This is the concept of *community* . . . .
> The concept of community presupposes an organization in which functions are differentiated and in which specialization must be brought together, or coordination if you will, is achieved not through a structure of superordination and subordination of persons and groups but through a *dynamic of consensus.*

2. *A discussion of the faculty's "professional" authority.* Talcott Parsons (10) was one of the first to call attention to the difference

between "official competence" derived from one's office in the bureaucracy, and "technical competence" derived from one's ability to perform a given task. Parsons devoted most of his attention to the technical competence of the physician, but others have extended this logic to other professionals who hold authority on the basis of what they *know* and can *do*, rather than on the basis of their official positions. The scientist in industry, the military advisor, the expert in government, the physician in the hospital, and the professor in the university are all examples of professionals whose influence depends on their knowledge rather than on their formal positions.

The argument for collegial organization is given strong support by the literature on professionalism, for it emphasizes the professional's ability to make his own decisions and his need for freedom from organizational restraints. Consequently the argument is that a collegium is the most reasonable method of organizing the university. Parsons (10, p. 60), for example notes that when professionals are organized in a bureaucracy,

there are strong tendencies for them to develop a different sort of structure from that characteristic of the administrative hierarchy ... of bureaucracy. Instead of a rigid hierarchy of status and authority there tends to be what is roughly, in formal status, a company of equals . . . .

3. *A utopian prescription of how the educational process should operate.* There is a growing discontent in contemporary society with the impersonalization of life, as exemplified in the massive university with its thousands of students and its huge bureaucracy. There is growing concern about the "alienation" of students in the midst of this tangled educational jungle. The hundreds of student revolts have been symptoms of a deeply felt chasm between the average student and the massive educational establishment. The discontent and the anxiety are well summed up in the now-famous sign worn by a Berkeley student: "I am a human being—do not fold, spindle, or mutilate."

In the midst of this impersonal bureaucratized educational system many critics are calling for a return to the "academic community," with all the accompanying images of personal attention, humane education, and "relevant confrontation with life." In recent years the student revolutionaries often lifted this banner as they sought to reform the university. Paul Goodman's (5) work in the *Community of Scholars* appeals to many of these same images, citing the need for more personal interaction between faculty and students, for more "relevant" courses, and for more educational innovation to bring the student into existential dialogue with the subject matter of this discipline. The number of articles on this subject, in both the mass media and the professional journals, is astonishingly large. Most observers can appreciate the call being raised by sensitive social critics. Indeed, this view of the collegial, academic community is now widespread as one answer to the impersonality and meaninglessness of today's large multiversity. Thus conceived, the idea of the collegium and the academic community is more of a revolutionary ideology and a utopian projection than a description of the real shape of governance at any university.

How can we evaluate the three themes tied into the collegial model? To begin, there are many appealing and persuasive aspects to this approach. The emphasis on the professor's professional freedom, the need for consensus and democratic consulation, and the call for more humane education are all legitimate and worthy goals. Few would deny that our universities would be more truly centers of learning if we could somehow implement these objectives. However, there is a misleading simplicity about the argument that glosses over many of the realities of a complex university. Several of the weaknesses of the collegial model should be mentioned.

There is often a confusion between the *descriptive* and *normative* enterprises in the collegial literature. Are the writers saying that the university *is* a collegium or that it *ought* to be a collegium? Frequently it is obvious that the discussions of collegium are more a lament for paradise lost than a description of present reality. Indeed, the collegial discussion of a round-table type of decision-making is not an accurate description of the processes at many levels in the university. To be sure, at the department level there are many examples of collegial decision-making, but at higher levels this usually does not hold true except in some aspects of the committee system. Of course, the proponents of the collegial model may only be proposing this as a desirable goal rather than a present reality. This may be a good strategy of reform, but it does not help much if our aim is to understand and describe the actual workings of universities.

Finally, the collegial model fails to deal adequately with the problem of *conflict*. When Millett emphasizes the "dynamic of consensus" he fails to see that much consensus occurs only after prolonged battle and that many decisions are not consensus but the prevalence of one group over another. The collegial proponents are correct in declaring that simple bureaucratic rule making is not the essence of decision-making, but in making this point they take the equally indefensible position that major decisions are reached primarily by consensus. Neither extreme is correct, for decisions are rarely made by either bureaucratic fiat or simple consensus. What is needed is a model that can include consensus factors and bureaucratic processes, and that can also grapple with power plays, conflict, and the rough-and-tumble politics of a large university.

Both the bureaucratic and collegial models offer some helpful suggestions about the organizational nature of the university, but at the same time each misses many important features. Certainly it would not be fair to judge tham as completely bankrupt models, for their sensitivity to certain critical issues is quite helpful. However, by themselves they gloss over many essential aspects of the university's structures and processes. Without abandoning their insights we will try to develop another approach that offers some ideas about otherwise neglected features of academic governances.

The Development of a Political Model

Since both the bureaucratic and collegial models have serious flaws, a new "political model" of academic governance was developed during an analysis of decision-making at New York University. During 1968 interviews were conducted with 93 key members of the university's administration, faculty, and student body. Moreover, a mail questionnaire about participation in decision-making was sent to the entire faculty and administration. The researcher also observed and coded dozens of decision sessions and analyzed nearly a hundred written documents. This section only reports on the general theoretical framework of that research; the bulk of the empirical findings are reported elsewhere (2).

When we look at dynamic processes that explode on the modern campus today we see neither the rigid, formal aspects of bureaucracy nor the calm, consensus-directed elements of an academic collegium. On the contrary, student riots cripple the campus, professors form unions and strike, administrators defend their traditional positions, and external interest groups and irate governors invade the academic halls. All these activities can be understood as political acts. They emerge from the complex, fragmented social structure of the university, drawing on the divergent concerns and life styles of hundreds of miniature subcultures. These groups articulate their interests in many different ways, bringing pressure to bear on the decision-making process from any number of angles and using power and force whenever it is available and necessary. Once articulated, power and influence go through a complex process until policies are shaped, reshaped, and forged from the competing claims of multiple groups.

All this is a dynamic process, a process clearly indicating that the university is best understood as a "politicized" institution.

To get some of the flavor of the political nature of the university let us turn to an interview with a dean at New York University. Toward the end of the interview he made the following comments:

Dean: Do you have an organization chart? O.K. Well you can just throw it away. Forget it, those little boxes are practically useless. Look, if you really want to find out how this university is run you're going to have to understand the tensions, the strains, and the fights that go on between the people. You see, this is a political problem of jockeying between various schools, colleges, departments, and individuals for their place in the sun. Each school, group, and individual pressures for his own goals, and it's a tough counterplay of groups struggling for control. You've really got to understand the "politics" if you want to know how the place works.

Interviewer: Do you realize how often you've used the term "political" or "politics" in the last few minutes? Is that a deliberate choice of words?

Dean: I'll say it is—most deliberate. I think the imagery of politics is very helpful in understanding the operation of this place. Of course, this doesn't necessarily imply "dirty" politics. I simply mean that you've got to understand the political forces—both inside and outside—that are trying to control this place. There are pressures impinging on the officials of the university from all directions, and in a real sense the management of this university is a balancing process. It's a task of balancing the demands of various groups against each other and against the university's resources. People often call the university administrators "bureaucrats," implying that they are red-tape specialists, but that is a childishly naive understanding of our role. Sure, there are indeed some lower level administrators who are paper-pushers and bureaucrats in the old sense of the word, but the men in the critical roles are not bureaucrats, they are *politicians* struggling to make dreams come true and fighting to balance interest groups off against each other. This place is more like a political jungle, alive and screaming, than a rigid, quiet bureaucracy.

This comment and dozens of similar observations suggested that a study of the political dynamics surrounding decisionmaking would help unravel some of the difficulties in studying academic administration. It will be wise to outline the basic assumptions that undergird this political analysis:

1. Conflict is natural, and is to be expected in a dynamic organization. Conflict is not abnormal, nor is it necessarily a symptom of a breakdown in the university community.

2. The university is fragmented into many power blocs and interest groups, and it is natural that they will try to influence policy so that their values and goals are given primary consideration.

3. In the university, as in other organizations, small groups of political elites govern most of the major decisions. However, this does not mean that *one* elite group governs everything, but the decisions are divided up with different elite groups controlling different decisions.

4. In spite of this control by elites, there is a democratic tendency in the university, just as there is in the larger society. Thus, junior faculty and students are increasingly demanding and receiving a voice in the decision councils of the university. Much of the current unrest in the university is symptomatic of this healthy current of democratization and should be promoted rather than suppressed.

5. Formal authority, as prescribed by the bureaucratic system, is severely limited by the political pressure and bargaining that groups can exert against authorities. Decisions are not simply bureaucratic orders, but are instead negotiated compromises among competing groups. Officials are not free simply to order decisions; instead they have to jockey between interest groups, hoping to build viable compromises among powerful blocs.

6. External interest groups have a great deal of influence over the university, and internal groups do not have the power to make policies in vacuum.

With these as background assumptions, let us examine a political model more closely. Since there is no available framework in organization theory to analyze these activities, it is necessary to build a primitive sort of "political model," a framework for study that may provoke some insights about the nature of the political processes in organizations. This is basically just a set of questions that can be used to get a hold on complex processes. It might be helpful to examine the parts of the analytical system and the processes that hold it together.

The political model has several stages, all of which center around the policy-forming processes. Policy formation was selected as the central focal point, for major policies commit the organization to definite goals, set the strategies for reaching those goals, and in general determine the long range destiny of the organization. Policy

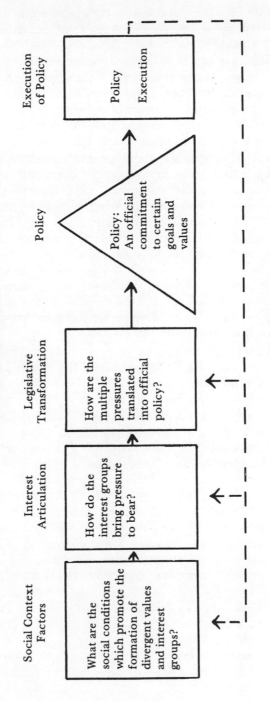

Figure 1. Policy formulation in the university: a simple political model

Social Context Factors

What are the social conditions which promote the formation of divergent values and interest groups?

Interest Articulation

How do the interest groups bring pressure to bear?

Legislative Transformation

How are the multiple pressures translated into official policy?

Policy

Policy: An official commitment to certain goals and values

Execution of Policy

Policy Execution

Feedback Processes:

The generation of new political conflicts

decisions are not just any decisions; they are decisions that have major impact—that mold the organization's future. In short, policy decisions are "critical," not merely "routine." Of course, in any practical situation it is often difficult to separate the two types, for issues that seem minor at one point may later prove to be decisive, or vice versa. In general, however, policy decisions are those that bind the organization to important courses of action.

Since policies are so important, people throughout the organization try to influence them in order to see that their special values are implemented. Policy becomes a major point of conflict, a watershed of interest group activity that permeates the life of the university. In light of its importance, policy becomes the center of the political analysis. Just as the political scientist often selects legislative acts in Congress as the focal point for his analysis of the state's political processes, organization theorists may select policy decisions as the key for studying organizational conflict and change.

The sociologist wants to know how the social structure of the university influences the decision processes, how political pressures are brought to bear on decisionmakers, how decisions are forged out of the conflict, and how formulated policies are implemented. Thus, our political model has five points of analysis:

1. *Social structure.* The university is splintered into many different social groups that have basically different life styles and political interests. The crucial point is that the differences often lead to conflict, for what is in the best interest of one group may damage another. It is important to examine the social setting with its fragmented groups, divergent goal aspiration, and conflicting claims on the decision makers. The university has a particularly complex, pluralistic social system because many groups inside and outside are pushing in various directions according to their own special interests. One need only glance at the various outside "publics" of a university to see its external social context, and the same glance turned inward would immediately reveal the internal social structure with its fragmented interest groups. Many of the current conflicts on the campus have their roots in the complexity of the academic social structure, and in the complex goals and values held by these divergent groups.

2. *Interest articulation.* Groups with conflicting values and goals must somehow translate these into effective influence if they are to obtain favorable action by decision-making bodies. How does a powerful group exert its pressure, what threats or promises can it make, and how does it translate its desires into political capital?

There are many forms of interest articulation at work on the policy makers from every quarter, and they assume a multitude of shapes. Attempts at political intervention come from external groups, faculty groups, student groups, staff groups, and administrative groups. In this political tangle the articulation of interests is a fundamental process.

3. *The legislative stage.* The legislative bodies respond to pressures, transforming the conflict into politically feasible policy. In the process, many claims are played off against one another, negotiations are undertaken, compromises are forged, and rewards are divided. Committees meet, commissions report, negotiators bargain, and powerful people haggle over the eventual policy. Not only must we identify the types of interest groups and the methods they use to bring pressure, but also we must clarify the translation process by which all of these pressures are negotiated into a formal policy.

4. *Formulation of policy.* The articulated interests have gone through conflict and compromise stages, and the final legislative action is taken. The policy is the official climax to the conflict and represents an authoritative, binding decision to commit the organization to one set of possible alternative actions, one set of goals and values.

5. *Execution of policy.* The conflict comes to a climax, the battle is at least officially over, and the resulting policy is turned over to the bureaucrats for routine execution. Of course, this is oversimplified, but it is remarkable that yesterday's vicious battle may indeed become today's boring bureaucratic chore. However, this may not be the end of the matter, for two things are likely to happen. First, the major losers in the conflict may take up their arms again for a new round of interest articulation. Second, the execution of policy inevitably causes a feedback cycle, with the policy generating new tensions, new vested interests, and a new cycle of political conflict.

In summary, the broad outline of the university's political system looks like this: there is a complex social structure that generates multiple pressures, there are many forms of power and pressure that impinge on the decision-makers, there is a legislative stage that translates these pressures into policy, and there is a policy execution phase that finally generates feedback with the potential for new conflicts.

This approach will bring several factors under close scrutiny. First, it should be evident that we will be addressing ourselves primarily to problems of *goal setting* and the conflict over values rather than to problems of maximum efficiency in carrying out goals. Second, the analysis of *change processes* and the adaptation of the university to its changing internal and external environment will naturally be a critical part of a political study of university governance. The political dynamics are constantly moving, pressuring the university in many directions, and forcing change throughout the academic system. Third, the *analysis of conflict* and conflict resolution must be a critical component of a political study. Fourth, the role that *interest groups* play in pressuring decision-makers toward the formulation of certain types of policy must be an important element in the analysis. Finally, much attention should be given to the *legislative and decision-making* phases—the processes by which pressures and power are translated into policy. Taken together these emphases are the bare outline for a political analysis of university governance. Figure 2 compares the new political approach to the more traditional bureaucratic and collegial frameworks.

Empirical Research Using the Political Framework

This political framework has now been used in several empirical investigations. In the 1968 study at New York University, the author investigated the nature of the political processes in a number of critical decisions (see 2). Major changes in the composition of the student body left private NYU in a noncompetitive situation vis-à-vis the local public universities, and this critical shift in the university's social structure prompted a period of intense conflict in which old philosophies were destroyed. The balance of power shifted away from traditional interest groups in the university's schools and colleges. Instead, influence moved increasingly to the central administration, which was taking the lead in restructuring the university to meet the threat of the public universities.

A second empirical investigation using this political framework was a study of the elevation of Portland State College to university status (11). This time the analysis focused more on shifts in the *external* social structure of the groups that surrounded Portland State. In addition, the study concentrated on the conflict generated between the rising aspirations of Portland State and the traditional stronghold of the older University of Oregon. In this case the political dynamics occurred on the boundaries between the university and its external environment, rather than internally. Thus, the utility of the political model was demonstrated for handling external political conflicts, as well as the internal activities for which it was originally designed.

In a third study the political model was used to study the growth of the April Third Movement, a radical student movement at

Figure 2. Comparison of three images of university governance

	Political	Bureaucratic	Collegial
Basic Image	Political System	Hierarchical Bureaucracy	Professional Community
Change Processes	Primary Concern	Minor Concern	Minor Concern
Conflict	Viewed as normal: Key to analysis of policy influence	Viewed as abnormal; to be controlled by bureaucratic sanctions	Viewed as abnormal; eliminated in a "true community of scholars"
View of Social Structure	Pluralistic; fractured by subcultures and divergent interest groups	Unitary; integrated by the formal bureaucracy	Unitary; united by the "Community of Scholars"
Basic Theoretical Foundations	Conflict Theory Interest Group Theory Open Systems Theory Community Power Theory	Weberian Bureaucratic Model Classical Formal Systems Model	Human Relations Approach to Organizations Literature on Professionalism
View of Decision-Making	Negotiation, bargaining, and political influence processes	Rationalistic, formal bureaucratic procedures	Shared, collegial decisions
Goal Setting and Policy: Formulation or Execution?	Emphasis on Formulation	Emphasis on Execution	Unclear: Probably more emphasis on Formulation

Stanford University (12). In this case the political framework was refined, and interrelated propositions were linked to show the relationship between political attitudes, objectives, and tactics. This study considerably expanded the theoretical framework of the political model, and demonstrated that further empirical research would lead to a clarification of the major ideas in the model.

At the present time the Stanford Center for Research and Development in Teaching, a research center funded by the United States Office of Education, is supporting further work on the application of the political model to university governance. The first stage of that work has been a continued refinement of the model and the generation of a series of propositions that link interest group theory, political attitude research, and tactical considerations into a theory of organizational policy formulation. Presently the revised political model is being employed in a major field research project entitled the Stanford Project on Academic Governance. During the spring of 1971, 18,000 questionnaires were mailed to a random sample of all college faculty and administrators in the United States. Results from this survey will hopefully expand on the theoretical framework, and will give reliable information about the political decision dynamics in a wide spectrum of colleges and universities.

Organization of the Book

This whole book is based on the idea that political interpretations will be helpful for understanding academic governance. The articles have been selected and arranged to maximize that particular viewpoint. Hopefully, however, that viewpoint has not completely pushed out other ideas, and many articles are included whose authors would genuinely be surprised that the overall emphasis of the book is on political processes. There are six major sections.

Part One deals with some general features of the university as a complex organization. In a sense this section provides a background by discussing a number of related issues, such as the goals of academic organizations (Gross), the relation between organizational size and the way the decision structure is arranged (Boland), and the forms of change and innovation in academic systems (Clark). While these articles do not deal directly with a political interpretation of governance they nevertheless set the stage, for the nature of the goals, the organizational decision structure, and the process of change are all critical elements that determine the shape of political struggles within the politicized university.

Part Two looks at the overall administrative processes that frame the political dynamics in an academic organization. Political processes are not isolated events, for they occur within a definite organizational structure. It is senseless to talk of political issues as if they had no relation to the "formal" system, for they are obviously intertwined and interrelated. The formal structure generates conflict, regulates activities, and negotiates settlements of conflicts. Surely it is critical to analyze the formal decision system if one is to understand the political processes that occur within it. Henderson and Harnett offer two different studies of the role of the trustees—the governing boards in which all the formal authority of the college or university is vested. Litchfield looks at administrative practices that are current in higher education and suggests some of their failures, while Rourke and Brooks discuss some of the innovations and changes that are reshaping academic administration. Finally, the departmental structure and its decision-making processes are discussed in Hass and Collen's article on departmental administration, and in Hill and French's article on the power of department chairmen.

Part Three examines the role of the faculty in governance. As every organizational theorist knows, the university is almost archtypical of the professionally dominated class of organizations. Along with the hospital and the law firm, the university is one of the major organizations in which the professional staffs have major responsibilities for setting long term goals and determining operating priorities. Consequently any serious discussion of academic governance must take into account the critical role of the faculty. Clark's classic article on faculty authority has influenced the thinking of many students on academic governance, and it leads the list in this section. Lewis discusses the issue of "conditional loyalty" that is, the problem of managing an organization when many of the staff have more loyalty to their disciplines than to their current school. Another article on the professional organization of the university is Hind's analysis of the evaluation system and its impact on the authority roles of the faculty. Baldridge asks about the distribution of decision-making power and the role of different faculty groups in that process. Finally, both Lieberman and Marmion confront a very different type of question: What are the structural mechanisms (e.g., faculty senates) and organizations (e.g., unions) that enhance the power of professional faculties?

Part Four opens the issue of the student as a political force in the academic community. Of course, this is the hot topic of the day and thousands of pages have now been written on the issue. No small sampling of articles can possibly cover the multitude of issues, but the four included here at least raise a number of critical points. Both Keniston and Flacks raise the question's that are on everybody's mind: What is at the root of the current student unrest, where did it come from, and what are the social and psychological forces that are promoting it? Trent points to some of the impact that the student revolution has had on academic governance, and suggests some of the likely developments that might come in the future. Finally, Scott and El-Assal show that organizational features such as size, composition of the student body, and the quality of the university are major factors in generating student unrest. (The Stam and Baldridge article on student revolution and unrest has been included in Part Six because of its special role in illustrating the political framework for conflict analysis.)

No analysis of power and power blocs would be complete without considering the *outside* political forces that impinge on the college or university and influence its policies. Unfortunately this is the least well-developed area in organizational theory and very little work has been done on the external environment of the academic community. However, the three articles in Part Five at least open the discussion and strike a few bold outlines about the impact of external forces on the university. Clark shows how the "open door" community colleges are extremely vulnerable to pressure from the local community, especially in the form of student selection of courses. Lazarsfeld and Thielens examine a more direct form of deliberate political influence, the pressure that came to bear on liberal professors during the McCarthy era of the 1950s. Finally, Baldridge proposes a theoretical statement about the link between environmental pressures and professional autonomy in the academic community.

Part Six is, in some sense, a review for it presents two articles that were specifically written to show how the "policical" analysis could be useful for studying conflict and policy making in the university. The political orientation guided the entire book, but these articles directly review that approach and apply it to empirical research.

References

1. Anderson, F. Lester. "The organizational character of American colleges and universities." From Terry Lunsford, *The Study of Academic Administration*. Boulder, Colorado: Western Interstate Commission for Higher Education, 1963.
2. Baldridge, J. Victor. *Power and Conflict in the University*. New York: John Wiley & Sons Inc., 1971.

3. Bendix, Reinhard. *Max Weber: An Intellectual Portrait.* Garden City, N.Y.: Doubleday & Co., Anchor Books, 1962.
4. Gerth, Hans and Mills, C. Wright. *From Max Weber.* New York: Oxford University Press, 1958.
5. Goodman, Paul. *The Community of Scholars.* New York: Random House, 1962.
6. Henderson, Algo. *Policies and Practices in Higher Education.* New York: Harper & Row, 1960.
7. Kuhn, Thomas. *The Structure of Scientific Revolutions.* Chicago: University of Chicago Press, 1962.
8. Martin, Warren B. "The University as Community." *The Educational Record* (Fall 1967): 320-326.
9. Millet, John. *The Academic Community.* New York: McGraw-Hill, 1962.
10. Parsons, Talcott. "Introduction." In Max Weber, *The Theory of Social and Economic Organization.* New York: Free Press, 1947.
11. Richardson, John. "The Evolution of a University: Case Study of an Organization and its Environment," Ph.D. dissertation, Stanford University, 1970.
12. Stam, James. "Revolution at Stanford: Theory and Research in the Dynamics of Interest Group Conflict. Ph.D. dissertation, Stanford University, 1970.
13. Stroup, Herbert H. *Bureaucracy in Higher Education.* New York: Free Press, 1966.
14. Weber, Max. *The Theory of Social and Economic Organization.* Translated by Talcott Parsons and Algo Henderson. New York: Free Press, 1947.

Part 1

Organizational Features of Academic Systems

UNIVERSITIES AS ORGANIZATIONS:
A STUDY OF GOALS

Edward Gross

Universities are usually not viewed as formal organizations. The extant literature in the field (41; 31; 32; 3; 14; 10; 48) tends to see them in one or both of two major ways: (1) as institutions, that is as being concerned with performing something essential for the society, such as educating the youth, passing on the cultural heritage, providing lines of upward mobility, and the like; (2) as communities, that is, as providing "homes" or "atmospheres" in which persons may set their own goals, such as self-fulfillment, the pursuit of truth, the dialogue at the two ends of the log, and other traditional ivory-tower values. It is those who follow this latter view who feel disturbed at the "intrusion" of government money into the presumably sacred confines of the university, sacred referring here to the value of "disinterested pursuit of the truth."

However, neither of these two approaches seems to have told us much about the university, though they often reveal how professors and administrators in the university feel. Apart from the sheer paucity of research, our view is that a part of the reason is that much of what goes on in universities is not "caught" by either model, though they each explain some things. Perhaps, it was our judgment, light might be shed on universities by seeing them as organizations. In so doing, we do not mean to imply that this model should supplant the others, for a single-minded view of universities as

From the *American Sociological Review*, Vol. 33, No. 4, August 1968, pp. 518-544. Reprinted by permission of the American Sociological Association and the author.

"bureaucracies" (see 43) is as one-sided as viewing them only as institutions or only as communities. This paper is an attempt to test the usefulness of an organizational model in accounting for structural variables in universities.

Nature of the Organizational Goals

As Parsons (38, Chap. 1 and 39 pp. 38-41) has noted, the distinctive feature of organizations that marks them off from other kinds of social systems is that the problem of goal attainment has primacy over all other problems. . . . In spite of the central impor-tance of "goal" in organizations, it is surprising how little attention has been given to developing a clear definition of what is meant by "goal" (42). Etzioni (21, p. 6) defines an organizational goal as "a desired state of affairs which the organization attempts to realize." But this definition immediately raises the question, pointed to by many, of *whose* state of affairs it is that is desired. Theoretically, there could be as many desired states for the organization as there are persons in it, if not more. What appear to be goals from the point of view of the top administrators may not be goals at all from the point of view of those further down.

But even before one can talk about different perceptions of organizational goals, it is essential to distinguish private from organi-zational goals. A private goal consists of a future state that the individual desires for himself. Such a notion comes close to the psychologist's conception of a motive. This meaning may be distin-guished from what a particular person desires *for the organization as a whole* (13, pp. 308-311). The latter comes closer to the notion of an organizational goal, although it still consists of something that the particular person wishes and may not at all correspond to the organization's goals. . . .

Thompson and McEwan (47) and Parsons (38, p. 17) have attempted to define goals in terms of system linkages. Both have seen a goal as involving some type of output to a larger society. In this sense organizations are always subsystems of larger systems, the goal of one subsystem being a means or input of a different subsystem. In the simplest case the production of automobile batteries is a goal to the firm that manufactures them but will be a means or input to the automobile manufacturing firm. Such an approach has the great value of emphasizing the need to relate organizations to one another and to the surrounding society. Furthermore, when goals are defined in this manner, it becomes clear that those within organizations have only a limited amount of freedom to set the goals of the organization. They will be constrained by what outsiders can be persuaded to accept. . . .

No organization can spend all of its energies on goal attainment. At least some of these energies, and perhaps a great deal, must be spent on activities which cannot easily (if at all) be shown to be contributing to goal attainment. One of the first to point this out was Bales (2) in his studies of task-oriented small groups under laboratory conditions. He found that two major sets of processes were in operation in these groups. The groups, on being assigned a particular task or goal, would typically begin by giving their attention to the most efficient way of moving towards that goal, which consisted of solutions to various problems which he posed to them. Very early, however, it was discovered that other kinds of activities began to make their appearance. When someone would make a proposal that a given approach be tried, others had to agree, disagree, or take no stand, and this activity began to divide the group on the basis of their estimates of the most worthwhile procedures. The consequence of such cleavage was the development of feelings toward one another or toward the solutions proposed, irritation at not having one's own views taken properly into account, as well as ordinary fatigue. It became necessary, Bales found, for the group to stop its goal-directed activity and give some attention to repairing the social damage that was being done as the group attempted to move towards the solution of the problem. A kind of "maintenance" activity was necessary, with certain persons assuming the role of "maintenance engineers," as it were, in giving attention to what Bales came to speak of as "social-emotional" needs. . . . The paradox may be stated as follows: an organization must do more than give attention to goal attainment in order to attain its goals. . . .

In our conceptual work, we speak of goals which admit of clear outputs as "output goals." For the university, these involve the usual goals of teaching, research and community service (further subdivided, as shown below). Those which do not involve clear outputs turn out to be what we speak of as "support goals." These involve a variety of activities designed to help the organization survive in its environment, those activities which ensure that the university is run in desired ways, those designed to ensure motivated participation, and those designed to ensure the university's position in the population of universities. Further, we found it useful to list a large number of goals, assuming that all of them would be present at a given university but in differing degrees. The extent of emphasis on given goals would be our measure of the importance of that goal at a university.

Defining a University's Goals

A serious problem in studying any organization's goals is that of devising a way of describing them that will avoid the usual tendency of participants to "gloss" their own organization's goals (the confounding of ideological elements, as mentioned above), as well as get some measure of degree of emphasis (rather than the common assumption that something either is or is not an organization goal). For the case of the university, we wanted, furthermore, a measure which was not dependent on specific measurable outputs (which, as noted previously, are only available for some goals). Our solution was the use of the model indicated by the sample question in Figure 1.

The special features of this approach are: (1) It does not ask the subject to volunteer a goal statement himself. Hence it is possible to

---

Figure 1. Sample Goal Question

One of the great issues in American education has to do with the proper aims or goals of the university. The question is: What are we trying to accomplish? Are we trying to prepare people for jobs, to broaden them intellectually, or what? Below we have listed a large number of the more commonly claimed aims, intentions or goals of a university. We would like you to react to each of these in two different ways:

---

(1) How important *is* each aim at this university?
(2) How important *should* the aim be at this university?

of absolutely top importance	of medium importance	of no importance

of great importance	of little importance	don't know or can't say

Example: to serve as substitute parents	Is	☐	☐	☒	☐	☐	☐
	Should be	☐	☐	☐	☐	☒	☐

A person who had marked the alternative in the manner shown above would be expressing his perception that the aim, intention or goal, "to serve as substitute parents," *is* of medium importance at his university but that he believes it should be of no importance as an aim, intention, or goal of his university.

Note: "of absolutely top importance" should only be checked if the aim is *so* important that, if it were to be removed, the university would be shaken to its very roots and its character changed in a fundamental way.

measure degree of consensus on a particular goal statement. Asking the subject to compose a verbal statement invites the "ideological confounding" referred to above. (2) It keeps separate the subject's *perception* of what is from his *feelings* about what should be. It asks the respondents to serve as informants as it were, and tell the investigators how they see the university separately from the question of how they would like it to be. These are not entirely separate, of course, but it was our feeling that degree of consensus would constitute a partial control on such biases. We decided to include a goal only if the standard deviation of the scored perception was less than 1. For over half of the goals we finally used, the standard deviation is actually 0.80 or less. A given respondent may be cut off from opportunities to observe the actual importance of a goal. But not everyone is, and it is a fair assumption that the average is a reasonable estimate of what the goal really is. One can, of course, quote Samuel Johnson's famous remark that an average of the opinions of gossips is still gossip, but we do not believe we are in the presence of gossip. We do not ask for opinions, but for perceptions. In effect, we ask Professor X or Dean Y at the University of A to act as our eyes. We say: "We cannot come to the University of A to check on how you actually spend your time. So we ask you to look for us and give us a report on what you have seen." The procedure can, perhaps, be compared to asking several astronomers each to look through a telescope, and then each report what he has seen. We require consensus, not because we are sure that the average is near the truth, but because it is probably closer to the truth than any other estimate.

Finally, the "score" which a given goal received at a university provided us with a measure of the degree of emphasis it receives, whether the outputs are clearly visible or not. In any case, in the last analysis, outputs are not only measures of goals but of *success* in goal realization, a factor which confounds considerations of efficiency and effectiveness in goal measurement.

Through examination of literature on university goals by the investigators and members of the research staff, and through pretesting among administrators and colleagues at the University of Minnesota, the 47 goal statements listed in Figure 2 were secured. They are presented there in the order in which we conceptualized them. On the questionnaire, the descriptive summary statements were not, of course, present, and the goal statements were presented in a random order. . . .

The data on goals were related to a variety of other measures,

Figure 2. University Goals

(A) Output Goals

Output goals are those goals of the university which are reflected, immediately or in the future, in some product, service, skill or orientation which will affect (and is intended to affect) society.

1. *Student-Expressive:* Those goals which are reflected in the attempt to change the student's identity or character in some fundamental way.

    1.1 Produce a student who, whatever else may be done to him, has had his intellect cultivated to the maximum.

    1.2 Produce a well-rounded student, that is one whose physical, social, moral, intellectual and esthetic potentialities have all been cultivated.

    1.3 Make sure the student is permanently affected (in mind and spirit) by the great ideas of the great minds of history.

    1.4 Assist students to develop objectivity about themselves and their beliefs and hence examine those beliefs critically.

    1.5 Develop the inner character of students so that they can make sound, correct moral choices.

2. *Student-Instrumental:* Those goals which are reflected in the student's being equipped to do something specific for the society into which he will be entering, or to operate in a specific way in that society.

    2.1 Prepare students specifically for useful careers.

    2.2 Provide the student with skills, attitudes, contacts, and experiences which maximize the likelihood of his occupying a high status in life and a position of leadership in society.

    2.3 Train students in methods of scholarship and/or scientific research, and/or creative endeavor.

    2.4 Make a good consumer of the student—a person who is elevated culturally, has good taste, and can make good consumption choices.

    2.5 Produce a student who is able to perform his citizenship responsibilities effectively.

3. *Research:* Those goals which reflect the dedication to produce new knowledge or solve problems.

    3.1 Carry on pure research.

    3.2 Carry on applied research.

4. *Direct Service:* Those goals which reflect the provision of services directly to the population outside of the university in any continuing sense (that is, not faculty, full-time students, or its own staffs). These services are provided because the university, as an organization, is better equipped than any other organization to provide these services.

    4.1 Provide special training for part-time adult students, through extension courses, special short courses, correspondence courses, etc.

    4.2 Assist citizens directly through extension programs, advice, consultation, and the provision of useful or needed facilities and services other than teaching.

    4.3 Provide cultural leadership for the community through university-sponsored programs in the arts, public lectures by distinguished persons, athletic events, and other performances, displays or celebrations which present the best of culture, popular or not.

    4.4 Serve as a center for the dissemination of new ideas that will change the society, whether those ideas are in science, literature, the arts, or politics.

    4.5 Serve as a center for the preservation of the cultural heritage.

(B) Adaptation Goals

Those goals which reflect the need for the organization to come to terms with the environment in which it is located. These revolve about the need to attract students and staff, to finance the enterprise, secure needed resources, and validate the activities of the university with those persons or agencies in a position to affect them.

1. Ensure the continued confidence and hence support of those who contribute substantially (other than students and recipients of services) to the finances and other material resource needs of the university.
2. Ensure the favorable appraisal of those who validate the quality of the programs we offer (validating groups include accrediting bodies, professional societies, scholarly peers at other universities, and respected persons in intellectual or artistic circles).
3. Educate to his utmost capacities every high school graduate who meets basic legal requirements for admission.
4. Accommodate only students of high potential in terms of the specific strengths and emphases of this university.
5. Orient ourselves to the satisfaction of the special needs and problems of the immediate geographical region.
6. Keep costs down as low as possible through more efficient utilization of time, and space, reduction of course duplication, etc.
7. Hold our staff in the face of inducements offered by other universities.

(C) Management Goals

Those goals which reflect decisions on who should run the university, the need to handle conflict, and the establishment of priorities on which output goals are to be given maximum attention.

1. Make sure that salaries, teaching assignments, perquisites and privileges always reflect the contribution that the person involved is making to his own profession or discipline.
2. Involve faculty in the government of the university.
3. Involve students in the government of the univerisity.
4. Make sure the university is run democratically insofar as that is feasible.
5. Keep harmony between departments or devisions of the university when such departments or divisions do not see eye to eye on important matters.
6. Make sure that salaries, teaching assignments, perquisites and privileges always reflect the contribution that the person involved is making to the functioning of this university.
7. Emphasize undergraduate instruction even at the expense of the graduate program.
8. Encourage students to go into graduate work.
9. Make sure the university is run by those selected according to their ability to attain the goals of the university in the most effective manner possible.
10. Make sure that on *all* important issues (not only curriculum), the will of the full-time faculty shall prevail.

(Figure 2, continued)

(D) Motivation Goals

Those goals which seek to ensure a high level of satisfaction on the part of staff and students, and which emphasize loyalty to the university as a whole.

1. Protect the faculty's right to academic freedom.
2. Make this a place in which faculty have maximum opportunity to pursue their careers in a manner satisfactory to them by their own criteria.
3. Provide a full round of student activities.
4. Protect and facilitate the students' right to inquire into, investigate, and examine critically any idea or program that they might get interested in.
5. Protect and facilitate the students' right to advocate direct action of a political or social kind, and any attempts on their part to organize efforts to attain political or social goals.
6. Develop loyalty on the part of the faculty and staff to the university, rather than only to their own jobs or professional concerns.
7. Develop greater pride on the part of faculty, staff and students in their university and the things it stands for.

(E) Positional Goals

Goals which serve to help maintain the position of this university in terms of the kind of place it is in comparison to other universities, and in the face of attempts or trends which could change its position.

1. Maintain top quality in all programs we engage in.
2. Maintain top quality in these programs we feel to be especially important (other programs being, of course, up to acceptable standards).
3. Maintain a balanced level of quality across the whole range of programs we engage in.
4. Keep up-to-date and responsive.
5. Increase the prestige of the university or, if you believe it is already extremely high, ensure maintenance of that prestige.
6. Keep this place from becoming something different from what it is now; that is, preserve its peculiar emphases and point of view, its "character."

---

especially the power structure of universities, as well as materials on university characteristics secured from other documentary sources, as will be described below.

Methods of Data Collection

The original motivation for the research extended beyond the simple desire for reliable knowledge about universities as organizations. As educators ourselves, we were concerned by the oft-made claim that there is a widening gulf in values and interests between academic administrators and members of the faculty. . . . Because of these interests, we deliberately decided to limit our attention to educational organizations highly likely to exhibit a range of conditions of such conflict and difference. One could find many schools, e.g., a small, church-controlled liberal arts school for men only, in which there may be almost complete consensus on organizational goals and values. Hence, we deliberately exclude all colleges which were dominated by some single point of view or a commitment to a uniform task which is of such a nature as to severely limit the goal variation that can exist. Not included in our original plans, therefore, were church-controlled schools, liberal arts colleges, teacher's colleges, and technical insititutions.

Our population consisted of the nondenominational[1] universities in the United States. It is these universities, with their graduate and professional schools, that seemed certain to exhibit the kind of goal variation we were interested in. It is further in this kind of educational institutions that the "support functions" are claimed to have increased greatly and in which administrators are often accused of having attained positions of considerable power. The universities are also distinguished by the importance in them of the graduate school and, for our purposes, a graduate school is necessary to provide assurance that the goal of research will be well represented in the university.

The institutions were selected on the basis of the following criteria:

1. The Ph.D. degree must be granted in at least three of four fields (humanities, biological sciences, physical sciences, and social sciences).

2. Ph.D. degrees granted in the two least emphasized fields must come to ten percent or more of the total degrees conferred. This provision was designed to overcome any undue concentration in one field, and thus help insure the kind of diversity of goals that we were interested in.

3. There must be a liberal arts undergraduate school or college with three or more professional schools.

4. The institution must have conferred ten or more degrees during the years 1962-1963. This conservative rule enabled us to keep the number of universities studied to manageable size in view of the large number of new universities that have appeared in recent years.

We secured the data for making the above decisions from *American Colleges and Universities,* ninth edition, 1964 (appendix IV and VI).[2]

It turned out that there were seventy universities defined in this way, and we decided to include all but two of them. These two exceptions were the University of Minnesota and the University of Washington, since these were the home institutions of the investigators. . . .

The securing of accurate data on numbers of faculty and administrators at the 68 universities proved to be an exceedingly difficult task, owing to inadequacies of catalogue information (multiple listings, variations in inclusiveness, mixing in of part-time with full-time, problems of "clinical staff," members of institutes, laboratories, and other semi-autonomous portions of universities, overseas branches, and so forth), description of duties, date of materials and other problems. We had to telephone university officers and friends at particular universities to secure many of these data. Finally, on the basis of the best information we were able to get, there were, in the spring of 1964 when our study began, the following numbers in the 68 universities: 8,828 administrators and 67,560 faculty. Although the focus of the research was on administrators, we desired a sample of faculty to serve as a basis of comparison, particularly with reference to the question of whether administrators differed, as a group, from faculty, but also to examine differential career patterns, self-conceptions, and other variables not being reported on in this paper. Because of the desire to make rather detailed comparisons among administrators, we attempted to get all of the academic administrators.[3] On the other hand, since we planned only very broad groupings among the faculty (e.g., social sciences, humanities, etc.), we felt that a 10 percent sample would suffice. Hence, the total number surveyed consisted of 8,828 administrators[4] plus 6,756 faculty members, for a total of 15,584.

The questionnaire was very long (300 questions, requiring a minimum of 1½ hours to fill out, and often—some of the respondents wrote—requiring 3 hours), and faced the usual problems of mailed questionnaires. A variety of devices was used to stimulate response: (1) the enlistment of the endorsement or assistance of accrediting bodies and professional societies; (2) an earlier study of Deans of Business Administration at 101 universities resulted in offers from approximately one-half of the deans to stimulate interest at their own universities; (3) the president of the University of Minnesota at the time (Meredith Wilson) wrote to all presidents of member universities of the American Association of Universities that fell in our sample (approximately one-half of them) asking for their assistance. In addition, it must be remembered that we were contacting a highly literate, questionnaire-sophisticated group, on a subject of direct, immediate interest to them—their own jobs. It is also, a subject, as we have said, on which there are few data of any validity. We therefore offered the *quid pro quo* of a copy of the findings, if desired, or at least the general results which would later be published. (To our dismay we received well over 1500 requests.) Offsetting such obvious interest is the clear fact that this group is continually the target of surveyors, to the point, we were told by several, that their secretaries had standard instructions to file all questionnaires unless otherwise advised ahead of time.[5] Our final response rate for the entire questionnaire of usable replies was 50.9 percent for administrators and 40.4 percent for the faculty. A short form of the questionnaire, dealing only with careers, was sent out to non-respondents. It resulted in a total response rate for that portion of the questionnaire of approximately 76 percent. A variety of tests was employed to test the likelihood of bias. They left us with confidence that the response group was not appreciably biased at least with reference to dimensions of interest to us. The main reason for the lower than desirable response rate (actually high by usual mail questionnaire standards) appears to be the length of the questionnaire.[6]

Major Findings

The following findings are limited only to the goal analysis, the relationship of goals to the power structure, and the implications of those findings for the empirical characterization of universities in organizational terms.

In Figure 3, an overall, composite ranking of the 47 goals at all 68 universities is presented. The scores there are based on unweighted means. However, subsequent analyses of the same goals making use of various weights (response rate, treating universities equally, use of single scores for entire university) produce no important shifts in goal position. As presented in Figure 3, however, they do reflect the somewhat lower response rate of faculty; that is, they reflect somewhat more the perceptions and views of administrators. The column labelled "is" refers to the ranking of goals on the portion of the question (as illustrated in Figure 1) that represented the answers to the "is" row (the respondent's report on his perception of how important the goal in fact is); the column labelled "should," in turn, refers to the ranking in terms of respondent's conception of how important he thought the goal *should* be.

As can be seen, the top goal at the 68 universities is perceived as being that of protecting academic freedom. Furthermore, not only

Figure 3. Ranking of the Goals of American Universities

"Is"	Goal	"Should"
1	Acad Freedom	1
2	U Prestige	11
3	Top Qual Imp	7
4	Ensur Confidence	26
5	Keep up to Date	6
6	Train Scholarship	2
7	Pure Research	16
8	Top Qual All	4
9	Mntn Fav Apprsl	34
10	Ensure U Goals	9
11	Dissem Ideas	5
12	Applied Research	30
13	Stud Careers	32
14	Stud Intellect	3
15	Hold Our Staff	18
16	Comm Cult Ldshp	28
17	Stud Inquire	10
18	Encour Grad Wk	27
19	Preserve Heritage	20
20	Stud Good Citzn	14
21	Well Round Stud	17
22	Max Opprtunity	25
23	Stud Objectivity	8
24	Keep Costs Down	35
25	Fac U Govt	19
26	Reward Prof	21
27	Stud Activities	43
28	Stud Success	33
29	Run U Demo	22
30	Affect Stud Perm	15
31	Assist Citizens	36
32	Just Rewd Inst	13
33	Devlp Pride Univ	23
34	Sat Area Needs	42
35	Mntn Bal Qualty	31
36	Will of Fac	24
37	Special Training	38
38	Stud Character	12
39	Educ to Utmost	37
40	Accp Good Stud Only	39
41	Stud Pol Rights	40
42	Devlp Fac Lylty	29
43	Keep Harmony	41
44	Undrgrad Inst	44
45	Stud Univ Govt	46
46	Pres Character	47
47	Stud Taste	45

do the respondents see it as in fact the top goal, but they believe that it should be the top goal. As will be shown below, this finding is of the first importance in our ability to characterize universities in organizational terms. It should further be noted that if we had elected to restrict our attention only to the usual output goals (teaching, research, service), we would never have made this discovery since we would not have thought of "protecting academic freedom" as a goal.

Paying attention, for the moment, only to the "is" list (that is the goals as listed on the table), one can characterize the "top" and "bottom" goals by the simple device of ranging the actual average scores in a single distribution, marking the distribution off in standard deviation units (from the overall mean), and asking which goals fell in the top standard deviation (of 6) and which in the bottom.

The *top goals*, then, turn out to be:

1. protect the faculty's right to academic freedom;
2. increase the prestige of the university;
3. maintain top quality in those programs we feel to be especially important;
4. insure the continued confidence and support of those who contribute substantially to the finances and other material resource needs of the university;
5. keep up-to-date and responsive;
6. train students in methods of scholarship and/or scientific research and/or creative endeavor;
7. carry on pure research.

At the other end, the *bottom goals* are seen to be:

44. emphasize undergraduate instruction even at the expense of the graduate program;
45. involve students in the government of the university;
46. keep this place from becoming something different from what it is now;
47. make a good consumer of the student.

What is most striking about the list of top goals is that practically all of them are what we have called support goals and only one of them in any way involves students. Even that one refers to training students for research or other creative endeavors which is, after all, closely associated with what the professors consider to be important and represents a possible output to them, or to the academic field. This squares with the goal of carrying on pure research, which is also rated very high. The singular scarcity of any emphasis on goals that have anything to do with students is all the more remarkable in view of the fact that of our total of 47 goals among which respondents could choose, 18 involved direct reference to students in some way.

Thus there was ample opportunity, and a result so striking as this could hardly have been produced by chance or by a sampling bias.

Supporting this general finding is the fact that students are mentioned more frequently among the goals at the bottom. The goal fourth from very bottom involves undergraduate instruction. This is quite consistent then with the finding that pure research and preparing students for research or creative careers are emphasized as top goals in American universities.

No particular pattern among the support goals is evident among the top goals although three of them are positional (increasing prestige of the university, maintaining top quality in programs felt to be important, and keeping up-to-date and responsive). As a general finding one can say that American universities, taken collectively, emphasize only pure research as an output, but put it seventh to a variety of other goals which are more concerned with the position of one's own university and the programs that it offers and with efforts to maintain a high quality at the university. At the very top they put academic freedom as a goal. Such a goal appears to be of first importance in American universities and refers to the importance in them of autonomy from outside interference of any kind. One must remember also that these findings do not refer to what people think ought to be the case, but rather to their perceptions of the way things are. The administrators and faculty at American universities believe that actually, right now, universities *do* protect the faculty's right to academic freedom more than they do any one of 46 other possibilities.

What Persons Feel the Top and Bottom Goals Ought to Be

We utilized the same procedure in selecting a top and a bottom group—one standard deviation in the distribution of means at the top, and one standard deviation at the bottom. When we did so, we found the following to be those goals that persons felt *ought* to be at the top in the American university.

1. protect the faculty's right to academic freedom;
2. train students in methods of scholarship and/or scientific research, and/or creative endeavor;
3. produce a student who, whatever else may be done to him has had his intellect cultivated to the maximum;
4. maintain top quality in all programs we engage in;
5. serve as a center for the dissemination of new ideas that would change the society, whether those ideas are in science, literature, the arts or politics;
6. keep up-to-date and responsive;
7. maintain top quality in those programs we feel to be especially important;

8. assist students to develop objectivity about themselves and their beliefs and hence examine those beliefs critically;

9. make sure the university is run by those selected according to their ability to attain the goals of the university in the most efficient manner possible.

On the other hand, those goals felt to belong at the very bottom are:

45. make a good consumer of the student;
46. involve students in the government of the university;
47. keep this place from becoming something different from what it is now.

When we examine this distribution we see that although students come out a little better, the student goals are far from being prominent. Persons felt that the faculty's right to academic freedom not only was the most important goal (as shown above) but that it ought to be the most important goal. In this list, however, two student goals came in second and third places: one referred to the same goal as had occurred in the previous table (training students in research and related activities); in addition persons felt that the goal dealing with cultivating the student's mind deserved a high amount of emphasis (although it was not perceived as in fact given that emphasis). In other words, respondents' conception of the way things ought to be is different from the way they actually are. In their view more attention should be given to cultivating the student intellect than is in fact being given.

One other student goal also was present in this top group of nine, namely the goal dealing with assisting students to develop objectivity about themselves. This goal, which did not rank high among the goals actually being emphasized was felt to be one which ought to be emphasized.

At the other end there was a feeling that involving students in the government of the university ought to be of very little importance. It would seem that those students seeking a greater share in decision-making power at the university will not receive much support from administrators and faculty. On the other hand, students might take some consolation from the fact that there is no particularly strong feeling that the faculty should be involved in the government of the university either. In general, then, students as a group are not felt to be particularly important, nor is there any strong feeling that the situation in that respect is different from what it ought to be (with one or two exceptions—training a student in research and cultivating his intellect, and assisting him to develop objectivity about himself). Nor is there evidence, either in what the goals are or what they should be, to suggest that it is an important goal of the university to prepare a student for a useful career, to assist him in upward mobility, to assist him to be a good consumer, or to become a good citizen.[7]

Goal Congruence

In the case of seven goals, there is congruence between the actual position and the position that persons feel they ought to be in. Four goals are perceived to be important and our respondents feel they ought to be important. These are:

1. protect the faculty's right to academic freedom;
2. maintain top quality in those programs we feel to be especially important;
3. keep up-to-date and responsive;
4. train students in methods of scholarship and/or scientific research and/or creative endeavor.

The following three are at the bottom and our respondents feel that that is where they belong:

1. make a good consumer of the student;
2. keep this place from becoming something different from what it is now;
3. involve students in the government of the university.

On the whole the above is rather impressive evidence that, at least at the top and bottom, there is a fairly strong sentiment that things are the way they ought to be. Four out of the seven top "is" goals and four out of the nine top "should" goals are congruent with one another. Practically all of the goals at the bottom are congruent with one another.

This generally happy[8] situation does not seem to prevail throughout the distribution. One way of examining the lack of general congruence is through "sins of goal commission" and "sins of goal omission." That is we can compare those goals which seem to be out of line with one another on the two scales. For example the goal, "to develop loyalty on the part of the faculty and staff to the university, rather than to their own jobs or professional concerns," is very low on the list of the way goals are perceived to actually be (being actually 6th from the bottom). On the other hand, when we look at the list of what persons think goals ought to be we find that this goal is considerably higher up (19th from the bottom). Such goals, which persons feel ought to be given more attention than they are being given ("sins of goal omission") include in order of discrepancy of ranks:

1. produce a student who, whatever else is done to him, has had his intellect
cultivated to the maximum;
2. make sure that salaries, teaching assignments, and perquisites always reflect
the contribution that the person involved is making to the functioning of the
university;
3. assist students to develop objectivity about themselves and their beliefs and
hence to examine those beliefs critically;
4. make sure the student is permanently affected by the great ideas of the
great minds of history;
5. develop loyalty on the part of the faculty and staff to the university, rather
than to their own jobs or professional concerns.

Looking over this list we see a relative dissatisfaction with goals
which tend to be pushed to one side when the personal ambitions
and the research careers of the faculty become dominant interest.
There seems to be some feeling that top faculty (who are likely to be
most mobile) do not have sufficient loyalty to the university. In the
second neglected goal, there is probably being expressed a feeling on
the part of persons who serve on committees and attempt to do their
jobs that they are not sufficiently well recognized. We also see the
familiar plaint of the liberal arts person that not enough attention is
being given to the student's mind or to the attempt to get the
student to develop insight into himself.

The "sins of goal commission" involve goals felt to be emphasized
too much. Those goals, in order of discrepancy of ranks, are:

1. insure the favorable appraisal of those who validate the quality of the
programs we offer;
2. insure the continued confidence and support of those who contribute
substantially to the finances and other material resource needs of the university;
3. prepare students specifically for useful careers;
4. carry on applied research;
5. provide a full round of student activities.

We see that although providing a full round of student activities is
not emphasized as a goal (as we can see again by looking at Figure 3),
nevertheless there is a feeling that it is emphasized more than it
ought to be. In addition persons resent the apparent emphasis on the
need to satisfy outside organizations that validate programs. There is
similar resistance to what might be construed as pressure from the
outside in the emphasis on carrying on applied research. On the
whole these are entirely consistent with the emphasis that we have
already noticed on academic freedom, and on the needs and the
concerns of the faculty and their own professional careers. In
addition we note again that the only way in which students come
into the picture here is that, while there is a general feeling that not

much attention is being paid to them or should be, that in one area at least, mainly providing a full round of student activities, the relatively little attention paid is too much.

Goals and Global Variables

In the attempt to secure further information on the utility of goal characterization as a descriptive component of universities, we sought answers to the question of whether types of universities differed from one another in goal structure. We characterized universities in terms of the following "global"[9] components: type of control (state or private), prestige, degree of emphasis on graduate work, volume of contract research, size (measured in two ways: number of faculty and number of students), and location (regional, and rural vs. urban). Of these the most productive by far of strong relationships were type of control and prestige. The others were considerably less productive (some, in fact, being only productive because they were related to type of control or prestige). Most interestingly size (measured by either of the two indices we used) was found to be almost completely unrelated to any goals.[10] Figure 4 is illustrative of the type of analysis summed up in the gammas (23 and 24) in the tables which follow. In Figure 4, state and private universities are compared with reference to their degree of emphasis on academic freedom. To make this possible, the average score of each university on that goal is calculated, and the scores for all 68 universities arranged in order from low to high. The distribution is then cut into approximate thirds, with each third being labelled "low," "medium" or "high." As can be seen, protecting academic freedom is emphasized as a goal to a markedly

Figure 4. Illustrative Table Showing Relationship Between Degree of Emphasis on Academic Freedom and Type of Control

| | Type of Control | | |
	State	Private	Total
Low	20	3	23
Medium	13	9	22
High	9	14	23
Total	42	26	68

Gamma=.627.

greater extent in private than in state universities: over half of private universities fall in the "high" third, whereas almost half of the state universities fall in the "low" third. A quite high gamma indicates that our impression from inspection is supported by that measure of strength of association. Furthermore, the gamma is significant at the 5 percent level, as is the case for all the gammas reported in this paper.[11] The number of relationships is, in all cases, far beyond what chance would lead one to expect.

Goals Related to Type of Control

The sample relationship examined in Figure 4 deals with the question of whether one goal, protecting academic freedom, is related to type of control (state as compared to private). In Figure 5, the findings from the comparison for all goals are presented. The

Figure 5. Goals Related to Type of Control

Private	Size of Relationship		State	Size of Relationship
	(Gamma)			(Gamma)
		Student-Expressive		
Stud Intellect	(.788)			
Affect Stud Per	(.784)			
Stud Objectivity	(.741)			
		Student-Instrumental		
Train Scholarship	(.500)		Stud Careers	(.603)
		Direct Service		
Dissem Ideas	(.531)		Assist Citizens	(.837)
		Research		
			Applied Research	(.552)
		Adaptation		
Accp Good Stud Only	(.874)		Educ to Utmost	(.941)
Ensur Confidnce	(.548)		Sat Area Needs	(.718)
			Keep Costs Down	(.626)
		Management		
Encour Grad Wk	(.602)		Keep Harmony	(.688)
			Stud Univ Gvt	(.801)
			Undergrad Inst	(.599)
		Motivation		
Acad Freedom	(6.27)		Stud Activities	(.602)
Max Opportunity	(.535)			
Stud Inquire	(.566)			
		Positional		
Keep Up to Date	(.552)			
Pres Character	(.573)			
U Prestige	(.647)			

goals are grouped in the categories described above. As can be seen, 24 out of the 47 comparisons made are significantly different in emphasis at the two kinds of university, with gammas as shown. These gammas are large, suggesting large differences between the goals of private and state universities. In private universities the goals emphasized revolve about student-expressive matters such as the student intellect, affecting the student permanently with the great ideas, and helping the student to develop objectivity about himself (no expressive goals distinguish the state universities at all), training the student in methods of scholarship and creative research, serving as a center for the dissemination of ideas for the surrounding area, and encouraging graduate work. In contrast, state universities emphasize to a distinctly greater extent than the private universities preparing the students for useful careers, assisting citizens through extension and doing applied research. Academic freedom, although it is high everywhere turns out to be particularly high in the private universities reflecting their ability to maintain a greater degree of autonomy. Note that we are not speaking of how persons would like things to be but how they perceive that things actually are. There is also emphasis on the students' right to inquire into, investigate, and examine critically any idea or program that they might get interested in, in contrast to state universities, where the emphasis is on involving students in the government of the university and providing a full round of student activities. One sees here a greater degree of responsiveness to students in a direct sense.

The private universities emphasize the needs of the faculty in the form of emphasis on making the university into a place in which faculty have maximum opportunity to pursue their careers in a manner satisfactory to them by their own criteria; they also emphasize the positional goals of keeping up to date, preserving the distinctive character of the university, and increasing or maintaining their prestige.

One of the striking differences is the extent to which the goal of accepting good students only is emphasized in private universities and by contrast the goal of educating to their utmost whoever can get into the state universities. This illustrates the traditional elitist goal of the private university in contrast to the land-grant, service goals of the state university and forms also a validation for the study. We notice also that it is in the state university that there is emphasis on satisfying the needs of the local area and keeping costs down as well as keeping harmony within the university.

On the whole, the data presented here strongly suggest that state and private universities differ from one another in type of goals. The claim of some students of the university that the differences between private and state universities are disappearing as both respond to public needs and federal research grants, is not supported. Other data, not being reported here, further support this conclusion. Those data make the comparison in terms of power structure, values of faculty and administrators, internal organizational structure, and the backgrounds of personnel.

Goals and University Prestige

The second most "productive" variable was that of "quality." We made use of several measures of "quality": (1) a measure of "reputation with peers," or prestige, (2) a measure based on size and quality of library resources, and (3) a measure based on publications and other creative products of the faculty. All three turn out to be highly related to one another.[12] We shall report on our findings using the first measure only.

That measure was based on data provided for us by the American Council on Education.[13] Essentially, those data involve ratings made by peers of departments that they were familiar with. Our measure makes use of those ratings, weighted by number of areas in which a given university awards the Ph.D.[14]

A high proportion of our goals was found to be significantly related to prestige. It is one of the most distinctive characteristics of a university and may well be the one thing that marks it off from all other kinds of organizations. By this we mean that a university is judged not only in terms of any products that may come out of it (trained students, broadened citizens, solutions to research problems) nor only in terms of some job that it does for the society (socialization of the young, providing cultural leadership, symbolizing societal values), but to a great extent in terms of how it is seen by others. Universities are an excellent example of what Caplow (11, Chap. 6) has called an "organizational set," in which members watch the members of other units in the set for any sign of a decline or rise in quality. Although it may certainly be questioned whether reputation or prestige is equivalent to "quality," the members of sets believe they can detect it or at least detect any change in it. In that sense, reputation is a measure of perception of quality, if not quality itself. The basic findings are presented in Figure 6.

When we look at those universities that are in the top third—universities that might fairly be called the great American universities—we find a distinctive pattern of goals at such universities. They

Figure 6. Prestige and University Goals

Student-Expressive	Gamma
Stud Intellect	0.516
Affect Stud Perm	0.473
Stud Objectivity	0.703
Student-Instrumental	
Stud Taste	−.0.553
Train Scholarship	0.730
Stud Careers	−0.504
Direct Service	
Dissem Ideas	0.799
Preserve Heritage	0.651
Assist Citizens	−0.455
Research	
Pure Research	0.891
Adaptation	
Sat Area Needs	−0.628
Keep Costs Down	−0.448
Mntn Fav Apprsl	−0.583
Accp Good Stud Only	0.556
Management	
Encour Grad Wk	0.709
Reward Prof	0.772
Undrgrad Inst	−0.697
Motivation	
Acad Freedom	0.496
Opportunity	0.657
U Prestige	0.691
Top Qual Imp	0.756

are universities which do emphasize student expressive goals. In them attention is given to producing a student who has had his intellect cultivated to the maximum, who has been permanently affected in mind and spirit by the great ideas of the great minds of history, and who has been assisted to develop objectivity about himself and examine his own beliefs critically. However the most prestigious universities do not give any more attention than any other universities to producing the well-rounded student, nor to developing the inner character of students. This does not mean that these goals are neglected, but rather that they simply are not given any more special attention than they are given anywhere else. In a sense then one can say that the parent who is interested in having his son's mind cultivated should send him to one of the top prestige universities; if he wants to make sure that he comes out a well-rounded student, then he has the same chance at such a university as he does at any other university. On the whole therefore, this adds up to a resounding vote in favor of the top prestige universities.

Student instrumental goals are not important except in a negative sense. Outside of the predictable goal of training students in scholarship and research, the only instrumental goals that come through are those of making a good consumer of the student and preparing him for a useful career, but these turn out to be correlated negatively with prestige. This means that they are positively de-emphasized in the better universities, which in turn means that they would be emphasized in the poorer universities. Of course this does not mean that there is any necessary causal relationship between preparing students for useful careers, for example, and prestige. A university does not attain top prestige by ignoring the attempt to prepare students for useful careers. On the contrary, we would guess that the top universities simply do not have to worry about the careers of their students, perhaps because of their selectivity of students. (Note that the goal of accepting good students only is positively correlated with prestige, gamma=0.556). On the other hand the fact that there is a negative relationship rather than no relationship at all implies that this goal is always of little importance. Again we emphasize that we are talking about how goals *are* felt to be, not how people at the university feel they ought to be. In these universities in other words both administrators and faculty feel that this is a goal that is positively pushed into the background in comparison to other universities.

There is a similar lack of concern for satisfying a constituency in the negative relationship seen in the direct service goal of assisting citizens and in the adaptation goals of satisfying the area's needs, keeping costs down and maintaining the favorable appraisal of validating groups.

It is striking that the goal of emphasizing undergraduate instruction is negatively correlated (and very highly as can be seen) with prestige, at the same time the student expressive goals are positively related. The inference we would draw is that the student's mind is to be affected in ways other than through undergraduate instruction. The emphasis on pure research as well as other indications suggest to us that student expressive goals are to be reached primarily through encouraging the student to do research, through his exposure to outstanding professors and through his taking charge of a great deal of his education himself.

When we turn to the positive gammas, we see that the great universities are those concerned with disseminating new ideas, preserving the cultural heritage, training people in scholarship and research, doing pure research, encouraging graduate study, seeing to it that professors are rewarded according to their contribution to their disciplines, protecting academic freedom and providing a maximum opportunity for professors to develop in ways that they think they should develop, insisting on a student's right to inquire into things that interest him, and in most of the position goals (keeping up to date, maintaining quality in all things, and maintaining or increasing the prestige of the institution.) This last would lead us to believe that the prestige is not simply something that lasts and lasts, but must be worked at all the time. There is more concern about prestige in the great universities than there is in the lesser ones, who may be on the make.

Power and University Goals

One of the motives for undertaking the research, as was stated above, was concern for the claimed split between faculty and administration, and for data on whether differences in power of the two groups might not be affecting the goals of the university. To that end, we developed measures of power and related them to goals, as well as global variables. We shall report only on the direct relationship between power and goals that we found.

We secured a measure of power by adapting a technique used (See 46, 44, 45) in studies of labor unions. The domain of power was restricted to "the major goals of the university." A list of power-holders (positions and categories) was provided and beside each, persons were asked to check whether they felt the indicated position or category has "a great deal of say," "quite a bit of say," "some say," "very little say" or "no say at all." The positions and categories were: regents (or trustees), legislators, sources of large private grants or endowments, federal government agencies or offices, state government agencies or offices, the president, the vice-presidents (or provosts), dean of the graduate school, dean of liberal arts, deans of professional schools as a group, chairmen of departments (considered as a group), the faculty (as a group), the students (as a group), parents of students (as a group), the citizens of the state (as a group), alumni (as a group). The major findings, across all universities, are presented in Figure 7.

The findings recorded in Figure 7 are interesting in several respects. Some persons might be surprised that the regents score as high as they do (regents themselves usually were) since they rarely do more than rubber-stamp the decisions of the president. But they do

Figure 7. Who Make the Big Decisions

	Mean Score
President	4.65
Regents	4.37
Vice President	4.12
Deans of Profess Schools	3.62
Dean of Grad Sch	3.59
Dean of Liberal Arts	3.56
Faculty	3.31
Chairmen	3.19
Legislators	2.94
Federal Govt	2.79
State Govt	2.72
Large Private Donors	2.69
Alumni	2.61
Students	2.37
Citizens of State	2.08
Parents	1.91

select the president and are often perceived as a rather shadowy, mysterious group. This perception applies mainly to the faculty, hardly at all to higher administrators. Those with a conspiratorial view of the power structure (who see large private donors, alumni, influential citizens and the like pulling strings from behind) do not receive much support from the findings, as can be seen from the low ranking of such persons or groups. Of course we only have perceptions of power, but the perceptions represent the consensus of a large group of persons well-situated to perceive power, and including, surely, a large proportion of the major powerholders themselves.

Our major concern here is only to note the position of the faculty in comparison to the administrators. As can be seen, the faculty are ranked in general below all administrators, with the single exception of chairmen (and a chairman, some believe, is after all only a *primus inter pares*). The unease and concern of faculty on the question of who is running the university hence receive support from this finding. However, it is probably doubtful that most faculty are worried about power as such. Their concern is usually whether the power is being used in their interest or not. We made a number of tests of degree of consensus on the part of faculty and administrators on values, attitudes toward university goals, and various other measures. In particular, with regard to university goals, our findings suggest that there is a striking consensus on the part of administrators and faculty on what the goals are and on what they should be. By and large the split which many people have become alarmed about, and which to some extent was one of the reasons for our beginning this study, does not find support from our data. The faculty and administrators tend to see eye-to-eye. This result held both when we made gross comparisons of the faculty as a group with all administrators as a group and when we broke this down more finely and related the rank of the administrator to the point of view. That is, higher administrators tend to agree with the faculty quite as much as do lower administrators or chairmen. In sum, the findings show that although it is true that administrators in general have more power to affect the big decisions than do members of the faculty, they apparently see eye-to-eye with the faculty; consequently one might infer they will use this greater power to further the goals of the faculty, since they seem to share the same conceptions as the faculty about what the goals ought to be. However, this is only an inference.

The final type of analysis to which we turn is one in which we related the goals of universities to the power structure. The question is: whatever the administrators *said* about the university and what it ought to be, how in fact do they behave when they get the power? For example, what are universities like in which, say, deans of professional schools have a lot of power as compared to those in which the faculty do? If they are different, then we may say that, whatever the professional school deans may *say,* one does not find the same kind of goal structure where they have power and conquently they do in fact act differently.

The major findings are presented in Figures 8 and 9, which should be looked at together. What we have done is brought together those findings which are sufficiently strong to rule out chance findings. In the first column in Figure 8 (with the heading of Faculty) are listed those goals which are emphasized in those places where the faculty are perceived to have most power. That is, we took the replies on the question dealing with faculty perceived power, calculated a mean score for the university, then arranged all 68 universities in sequence. The distribution was broken into thirds, and universities compared on this dimension. The first finding shown (Stud Intellect .476) reports that the higher the average score accorded the faculty as a power group, the more likely is the goal of cultivating the student's intellect to be emphasized. The figure in parentheses is the gamma. Occasionally, a goal came *very* close to reaching significance (off by

Figure 8. Goals Related to Relative Powers Faculty and Administrators*

| | | Type of Powerholder | | |
Types of Goals	Faculty	Chairmen	Deans of Lib Arts	Deans of Prof Schools
Student-Expressive	Stud Intellect (.476) Stud Objectivity (.564)	Stud Intellect (.695) Stud Objectivity (.648) Affect Stud Perm (.605)	Stud Intellect (.603) Stud Objectivity (.585)	Stud Intellect (.523) Stud Objectivity (.528)
Student-Instrumental	Train Scholarship (.528) Stud Careers (−.544) Stud Taste (−.495)	Train Scholarship (.621) (−Stud Careers) (−Stud Taste)	Train Scholarship (.686) (−Stud Careers) (−Stud Taste)	Train Scholarship (.516) (−Stud Careers) (−Stud Taste)
Direct Service	Dissem Ideas (.537) Preserve Heritage (.452)	Dissem Ideas (.500) Preserve Heritage (.565) Special Training (−.459) Assist Citizens (−.532)	Dissem Ideas (.661) Perserve Heritage (.478)	(Dissem Ideas) (Preserve Heritage) (−Special Training) (−Assist Citizens)
Research	Pure Research (.589)	Pure Research (.544) Applied Research (−.498)	Pure Research (.568)	(Pure Research)
Adaptation	Accp Good Stud Only (.474) Keep Costs Down (−.526)	Accp Good Stud Only (.524) Keep Costs Down (−.521) Sat Area Needs (−.487) Educ to Utmost (−.489)	Accp Good Stud Only (.497) Keep Costs Down (−.510) Sat Area Needs (−.488)	Accp Good Stud Only (.579) Keep Costs down (−.443) Educ to Utmost (−.440)

Types of Goals	Type of Powerholder			
	Faculty	Chairmen	Deans of Lib Arts	Deans of Prof Schools
Management	(Encour Grad Wk)	Encour Grad Wk (.618)	Encour Grad Wk (.537)	Encour Grad Wk (.572)
	Ensure U Goals (.506)	Ensure U Goals (.565)	Ensure U Goals (.672)	Ensure U Goals (.571)
	Reward Prof (.680)	Reward Prof (.624)	Reward Prof (.811)	Reward Prof (.583)
	Will of Fac (.946)	Undergrad Inst (−.473)	Will of Fac (.750)	(Will of Fac)
	Fac U Govt (.878)		Fac U Govt (.507)	
	Run U Demo (.821)		Run U Demo (.595)	
Motivation	Acad Freedom (.803)	Acad Freedom (.664)	Acad Freedom (.593)	Acad Freedom (.509)
	Max Opportunity (.775)	Max Opportunity (.753)	Max Opportunity (.634)	Max Opportunity (.566)
	Stud Pol Rights (.656)	Stud Pol Rights (.524)	Stud Inquire (.722)	Stud Inquire (.552)
	Stud Inquire (.766)	Stud Inquire (.714)		
Position	Top Qual All (.594)	Top Qual All (.768)	Top Qual All (.641)	Top Qual All (.570)
	Top Qual Imp (.456)	Top Qual Imp (.577)	Top Qual Imp (.590)	Top Qual Imp (.489)
	Up to Date (.446)	Up to Date (.606)	Up to Date (.563)	
			U Prestige (.505)	

*Goals followed by decimal figures (Gammas) are those attaining the 5% level of significance only. In those cases where the level of significance was *very* close to the 5% (usually off in the 2nd decimal place only), the goal is listed in parentheses without any stated gamma, but with the direction shown by a minus or its absence (that is, plus).

Figure 9. Goals Related to Relative Power: Legislature
and State Government*

Type of Goals	Type of Powerholder	
	Legislature	State Government
Student-Expressive	Stud Intellect (−.704)	Stud Intellect (−.695)
	Stud Objectivity (−.628)	Stud Objectivity (−.676)
	Affect Stud Perm (−.674)	Affect Stud Perm (−.717)
		Stud Character (−.445)
Student-Instrumental	Train Scholarship (−.473)	Train Scholarship (−.602)
	Stud Careers (.566)	Stud Careers (.514)
Direct Service	Dissem Ideas (−.482)	Dissem Ideas (−.528)
	Preserve Heritage (−.496)	Preserve Heritage (−.496)
	Assist Citizens (.692)	Assist Citizens (.480)
Research	(−Pure Research)	(−Pure Research)
Adaptation	Accp Good Stud Only (−.782)	Accp Good Stud Only (−.627)
	Keep Costs Down (.546)	Keep Costs Down (.476)
	Sat Area Needs (.602)	Sat Area Needs (.506)
	Educ to Utmost (.804)	Educ to Utmost (.554)
Management	Encour Grad Wk (−.540)	Encour Grad Wk (−.615)
	Keep Harmony (.531)	Keep Harmony (.444)
	Stud U Govt (.567)	Stud U Govt (.532)
	Undergrad Inst (.605)	Undergrad Inst (.496)
Motivation	Acad Freedom (−.654)	Acad Freedom (−.583)
	Max Opportunity (−.588)	Max Opportunity (−.547)
	Stud Inquire (−.560)	Stud Inquire (−.577)
	Stud Activities (.501)	
Position	(−Top Qual All)	(−Top Qual Imp)
	(−Top Qual Imp)	Up to Date (−.483)
	U Prestige (−.656)	U Prestige (−.529)
	Pres Character (−.482)	

*Goals followed by decimal figures (Gammas) are those attaining the 5% level of significance (or better) only. In those cases where the level of significance was *very* close to the 5% level (usually off by the second decimal place only), the goal is listed in parentheses without any stated gamma, but with the direction shown by a minus sign, or its absense (for a plus).

only a point or two in the second decimal). Those goals are listed in parentheses without a gamma, but with the direction shown by a minus or no sign (for plus), as in the case, for example, of "Encour Grad Wk." The second column shows what goals are emphasized in those places where chairmen are perceived as having more power (than at other universities), and similarly for deans of liberal arts and of professional schools.

If we read down the column headed "Faculty," we can characterize those universities where the faculty have (comparatively) more power than at other universities. At such places, the intellect of the student is emphasized and the importance of the student's developing objectivity about himself is also emphasized. Students are to be trained in methods of scholarship, whereas student taste and student careers are to be de-emphasized. Direct service consists essentially of serving as a center for ideas, and preserving the cultural heritage, and not the land-grant goals. Pure rather than applied research is emphasized, and furthermore, when the faculty have power, they tend to be elitist in trying to select students. As could be expected, the will of the faculty is one of the important goals and strong effort is made to see to it that the university is run democratically and that professors themselves have a good deal to say about running the university. Predictably, academic freedom is a major goal and the rights of students to inquire and even advocate whatever they think important is emphasized. The professors are concerned with making sure that the institution is up-to-date and that high quality is maintained. They are not concerned with keeping costs down. This finding is not quite so obvious as appears at first glance because we are not talking here about the professors' opinions about what ought to be done but rather about what happens at universities in which faculty are perceived as having a high amount of power compared to the way in which they are perceived at other universities. Universities in which professors are so perceived, we are saying, are universities in which there is little concern with the university goal of keeping costs down.

When we look at the next column (in which the power of the chairmen in relation to university goals is examined), what comes through strongly is that practically the *same* set of goals is found with certain changes, though none of them is really very large. For example "Stud Careers" and "Stud Taste," while not quite reaching significance at the 5 percent level, are in the same direction (negative). This general finding also holds up when one examines the situation for Deans of Liberal Arts *and* Deans of Professional

Schools. Although in some cases some goals drop out, we find no cases of reversals, that is, situations where a goal is positive for one powerholder and negative for another. For example, places where deans of professional schools are powerful are places which tend to select only good students; the same thing is true of places where deans of liberal arts are powerful and where chairmen are powerful and where the faculty are powerful. So is the case with emphasis on graduate work, protecting academic freedom, maximum opportunity for the professor and so forth. The number of relationships is not as high but in general reversals do not occur.

It is when we turn to the relationship between legislatures and university goals, and state government and university goals (Figure 9), that a real difference occurs and here we get almost a complete reversal from the structure that tends to obtain when faculty and deans have power. Thus for example when the faculty have power the goal of student intellect receives strong emphasis. When legislatures have power, it is positively de-emphasized with a very high gamma. "Develop student objectivity" is similarly reversed when one looks at places where faculty have power. Such is also the case for training scholarship and research, student careers, disseminating ideas, preserving the heritage, accepting good students only, keeping costs down, maximum opportunity for the professors, student right to inquire, and, perhaps most disturbing, protecting academic freedom. For all of these goals there is a complete reversal of their relationship when legislatures have power as compared to the situation when faculty have power. The situation is similar where state governments are perceived as having power.

What these findings seem to add up to is that, in view of the consistency between the views and values of faculty as compared to administrators that we pointed to earlier, we now have the further result that the kind of university one has when the administrators have power is not very much different from what one has when the faculty have power (comparatively speaking, of course). What does make a difference is when legislatures and state government are perceived as having power compared to other universities where they are perceived as having less. It is in these universities that the goal structure really changes. In sum, the faculty and administrators find themselves in agreement, and with the kind of goal structure that both of them seem to find comfortable, at least it is the same goal structure whether one is talking about whether administrators or faculty are powerful. The split is between the university and outside influences particularly the state legislature and state government.

Note too that these are local influences. We did not secure findings for the influence of the federal government or for sources of endowment funds. On the whole these results support the general picture that was suggested by our finding that academic freedom was the most important of all the goals of American universities. This suggests the importance to them of autonomy in doing their job as they see it. When that autonomy is severely breached, as it is apparently when state government or legislators begin to play a significant role in the power structure of a university, the goals of the university change in a profound way and it becomes something very different.

What, finally, of the effect of the most powerful man of all, the president? Here our findings are paradoxical and not what many would have predicted. We found that when we made comparisons between those universities in which the president was perceived as very powerful and those in which he was perceived as less powerful, there were almost no differences in the goal structures of such universities. This might be interpreted as meaning that the power of the president did not make a difference in the goal structure of the university, a conclusion we found hard to accept, precisely because he was considered to be the leading powerholder. Why should the power of persons perceived as having less power, such as deans of professional schools or the faculty, make a difference when the differences in the power of the president do not? This result appears to be a statistical artifact, but an interesting one. It says something about the power of presidents. When we arrange the average scores that presidents receive, the lowest score is 4.28 and the highest is 4.92. This means that the presidents, alone of all power-holders, occupy the unique position that *everywhere* they were perceived as having very high power, well over 4.00 on a five point scale. When we split the distribution into thirds even this was not sufficient to produce any variation. This means that there simply is little variation between a person whose average score was 4.28 and a person whose average score was higher than that. They were all crowded over to the right end of the scale. Consequently our finding that the variations in the power of the president do not make any difference in the structure of university goals is simply a way of saying all presidents are so powerful that, even when one divides the presidents into the *very very* powerful, no meaningful differences in goal structure emerge because even the least powerful are very powerful indeed. In order, therefore, to examine the effect of differences in the power of presidents it is apparently necessary to move to a different kind of organization than the university as we have defined it. The president we have in the universities that we have studied is apparently so much a part of the structure of such universities that his impact cannot be detected in the general goal structure that universities share with one another.

Footnotes

1. Our study also included 10 denominational (mostly Catholic) universities, which fulfilled our test for "university" in all respects. However, preliminary findings suggested strongly that they made up a universe of their own and deserved separate tabulation and analysis. We are not reporting on them here.

2. Purdue University turned out to be an exception. It was not classified as a university by the editors of that volume, yet it was the feeling of the investigators that it was excluded by a minor technicality. Consequently, it was included. Such places as M.I.T. and Cal. Tech. are excluded by our criteria.

3. For example, since we desired to compare deans of medical schools with deans of pharmacy schools, and since there were only about 50 of each in the total population of schools, and allowing also for the likelihood of incomplete response, the actual numbers we end up with might easily be, say, 25 of each. We could hardly operate with a smaller number and make any sort of general statements about such positions. Hence, any sampling would have reduced such numbers too much to have been of any use. Of course, most of our examined relationships involve much larger categories. Again, we are not here reporting on such finer categories.

4. The term "administrator" is, in general, restricted to academic administrators only (excluding, for example, persons involved in buildings and grounds, room scheduling, dean of students office, student residences and dining halls, and the like). However, many coding problems were presented which required intensive search of catalogue descriptions, letters to chairmen of departments or other persons, occasional personal letters to the person himself, and other searches of documents. When in doubt, we usually included the individual in the sample and hoped his responses to the background questions on the questionnaire would clarify his status. Unfortunately, this procedure depended on his filling out the questionnaire. One result was that our original estimates of numbers of administrators (and faculty) had later to be revised. They were not far off, however.

5. One president of a college not on our list wrote us, expressing concern that his university had not been included. It may be that one way colleges get recognized as universities is through joining the (less and less) exclusive group that routinely get questionnaired.

6. Space forbids description of the tests of bias employed. Detailed information may be secured by writing to the author, or by examining Gross and Grambsch (27).

7. In the above discussion the term "rank" has been used loosely to refer to what is, strictly speaking, a rating on a five-point scale. In this way, we have followed the procedure in the classic North-Hatt study of occupations, and for much the same reason, persons cannot rank a list of 47 items by comparing each with all others at the same time.

8. "Happy" in the sense implied in the Durkheimian conception of social

integration as a state of a society in which people do willingly what they must do. For an organization, such a state is approximated when the actual goals are what members think they should be. It is obvious that we are speaking only of administrators and faculty. We have no data from students, and the possibility, for example, that assigning them a low place in university government is "happy" for them is quite dubious, according to the news of student campus activities at the time of this writing (June, 1968).

9. As the term is used by Lazarsfeld and Menzel (34). See also Allen H. Barton (4) for illustrations from available research.

10. The role of size, as a determinant of organizational variation, is the subject of some controversy at present. See, for example, Blau, Heydebrand and Stauffer (7) and Hall, Haas, and Johnson (28). I do not believe that our non-findings on size are evidence one way or another on this controversy. We did get a large range: the smallest university had about 3,500 students, the largest well over 40,000. It may be, however, that there is a "critical mass" phenomenon operating such that, once a university passes, say, 2,500, further increases are not correlated with other variations. Or perhaps a "university" in the full sense (by our definition) requires some minimum number which is already very large. Peter Blau, in personal conversation, expressed the view that size *is* important in all organizations, but that it must be "washed out"; that is, it is a reflection of other changes. If these other changes are examined, the impact of size as an independent variable may disappear.

11. Use was made of the description in Goodman and Kruskal (24) of tests of significance for the measures described. Actually, the test of significance we used is the conservative one proposed in that article, based on an upper bound for the variance of the sampling distribution. It was programmed for calculation on an IBM 7090-7094 computer so that it could be read as a z-score. Gamma was used since we did not feel that actual scores, being no more than averages, represented any more precision than ranks. Gamma, in particular, served us well since our data were ordinal and since we had a large number of associations we wished to compare with one another. Gamma was used since it is what Costner (15) shows is a "proportional reduction of error" measure having qualities similar to r^2; that is, a gamma of .800 can be said to be twice as strong as one of .400.

12. Partly this is due to the fact that we classified universities on four quality levels only. In effect, this resulted in an elite group of nine, a second-level group of nine, a third-level group of 21, and the remainder of 29. However, Cartter (12) made use of actual "average scores" and found a Pearsonian correlation of .794 between his measure of quality and library resources.

13. Some of those data were reported in Cartter (12).

14. Such a procedure is clearly necessary since universities in the American Council's list varied from those which gave Ph.D.'s in only 11 areas to some that gave them in 29.

References

1. Anton, Thomas J. "Power, Pluralism and Local Politics." *Administrative Science Quarterly* 7 (March 1963): 425-457.
2. Bales, Robert F. "Task Roles and Social Roles in Problem-Solving Groups," Pp. 437-447 in Eleanor F. Maccoby, Theodore M. Newcomb, and Eugene L. Hartley (eds.), *Readings in Social Psychology*. New York: Henry Holt, 1958.
3. Barton, Allen H. *Organizational Measurement*. New York: College Entrance Examination Board, 1961.

4. ————. *Organizational Measurement and Its Bearing on the Study of College Environments.* New York: College Entrance Examination Board, 1961.
5. Berelson, Bernard. *Graduate Education in the United States.* New York: McGraw-Hill, 1960.
6. Blau, Peter M. and Scott, W. Richard. *Formal Organizations.* San Francisco: Chandler, 1962.
7. Blau, Peter M., Heydebrand, Wolf V., and Stauffer, Robert E. "The Structure of Small Bureaucracies." *American Sociological Review* 31 (April 1966): 179-191.
8. Bonjean, Charles M. "Community Leadership." *American Journal of Sociology* 48 (May 1963): 672-681.
9. Buckley, Walter. *Sociology and Modern Systems Theory.* Englewood Cliffs, New Jersey: Prentice-Hall, 1967.
10. Capen, S. P. *The Management of Universities.* Buffalo: Foster and Stewart, 1953.
11. Caplow, Theodore. *Principles of Organization.* New York: Harcourt, Brace and World, 1964.
12. Cartter, Allen. *An Assessment of Quality in Graduate Education.* Washington, D.C.: American Council on Education, 1966.
13. Cartwright, Dorwin and Zander, Alvin (eds.). *Group Dynamics.* Evanston: Row Peterson, 1953.
14. Corson, J. J. *Governance of Colleges and Universities.* New York: McGraw-Hill, 1960.
15. Costner, H. L. "Criteria for Measures of Association." *American Sociological Review* 30 (June 1965): 341-353.
16. Cyert, Richard and March, James G. *A Behavioral Theory of the Firm.* Englewood Cliffs, New Jersey: Prentice-Hall, 1963.
17. Dahl, Robert. "A Critique of the Ruling Elite Model." *American Political Science Review* 52 (June 1958): 463-469.
18. Downs, Anthony. *Inside Bureaucracy.* Boston: Little, Brown, 1967.
19. Eells, Walter Crosby. "Mark Hopkins and the Log—Fact or Fiction?" *College and University* 38 (1962): 5-22.
20. Etzioni, Amitai. "Industrial Sociology: The Study of Economic Organizations." *Social Research* 25 (1958): 303-324.
21. ————. *Modern Organizations.* Englewood Cliffs, New Jersey: Prentice-Hall, 1964.
22. Georgopoulos, Basil S. and Tannenbaum, Arnold S. "A Study of Organizational Effectiveness." *American Sociological Review* 22 (1957): 534-540.
23. Goodman, L. A. and Kruskal, W. H. "Measures of Associations for Cross-Classifications." *Journal of the American Statistical Association* 49 (1954): 732-764.
24. ————. "Measures of Association for Cross-Classifications: III. Approximate Sampling Theory." *Journal of the American Statistical Association* 58 (1963): 310-364.
25. Gouldner, Alvin W. "Organizational Analysis." Chap. 18 in Robert K. Merton et al. (eds.), *Sociology Today.* New York: Basic Books, 1959.
26. ————. "Metaphysical Pathos and the Theory of Bureaucracy." Pp. 71-82 in Amitai Etzioni (ed.), *Complex Organizations.* New York: Holt, Rinehart and Winston, 1961.

27. Gross, Edward and Grambsch, Paul V. *Academic Administrators and University Goals.* Washington, D.C.: American Council on Education, 1968.
28. Hall, Richard H., Haas, J. Eugene, and Johnson, Norman J. "Organizational Size, Complexity, and Formalization." *American Sociological Review* 32 (December 1967): 901-912.
29. Henderson, A. M. and Parsons, Talcott (trans.). *Max Weber: The Theory of Social and Economic Organizations.* Glencoe: Free Press, 1947.
30. Katz, Daniel and Kahn, Robert L. *The Social Psychology of Organizations.* New York: John Wiley, 1966.
31. Knapp, R. H. and Goodrich, H. B. *Origins of American Scientists.* Chicago: University of Chicago Press, 1952.
32. Knapp, R. H. and Greenbaum, J. J. *The Younger American Scholar.* Chicago: University of Chicago Press, 1953.
33. Landsberger, Henry A. *Hawthorne Revisited.* Ithaca, New York: Cornell University, 1958.
34. Lazarsfeld, Paul F. and Menzel, Herbert. "On the Relation Between Individual and Collective Properties." Pp. 428-429 in Amitai Etzioni (ed.), *Complex Organizations.* New York: Holt, Rinehart and Winston, 1961.
35. March, James G. and Simon, Herbert. *Organizations.* New York: Wiley, 1958.
36. Merton, Robert K., et al. (eds.). "Organizational Analysis." *Sociology Today.* New York: Basic Books, 1959.
37. Miller, D. R. "The Study of Social Relation: Situation, Identity and Social Interaction." Pp. 639-737 in S. Koch (ed.), *Psychology: A Study of a Science,* Vol. 5. New York: McGraw-Hill, 1963.
38. Parsons, Talcott. "A Sociological Approach to the Theory of Formal Organizations." *Structure and Process in Modern Societies.* New York: Free Press of Glencoe, 1960.
39. Parsons, Talcott, et al. *Theories of Society.* New York: Free Press of Glencoe, 1961.
40. Price, James L. *Organizational Effectiveness: An Inventory of Propositions.* Homewood, Ill.: Richard D. Irwin, Inc., 1968.
41. Riesman, D. *Constraint and Variety in American Education.* New York: Doubleday, 1958.
42. Simon, Herbert. "On the Concept of Organization Goal." *Administrative Science Quarterly* 8 (1964): 1-22.
43. Stroup, Herbert. *Bureaucracy in Higher Education.* New York: The Free Press, 1966.
44. Tannenbaum, Arnold S. "Control and Effectiveness in a Voluntary Organization." *American Journal of Sociology* 47 (July 1961): 33-46.
45. ————. "Control in Organizations." *Administrative Science Quarterly* 7 (1962): 235-257.
46. Tannenbaum, Arnold S. and Kahn, R. *Participation in Union Locals.* New York: Harper and Row, 1958.
47. Thompson, James D. and McEwen, William. "Organization Goals and Environment." *American Sociological Review* 23 (1958): 23-50.
48. Woodburne, L. S. *Principles of College and University Administration.* Stanford: Stanford University Press, 1958.

SIZE, ORGANIZATION, AND ENVIRONMENTAL MEDIATION:
A STUDY OF COLLEGES AND UNIVERSITIES

Walter R. Boland

There has been considerable discussion and controversy over the influence of size on the structure of formal organizations.[1] Recent comment and research indicates, on the one hand, that increasing size is relatively unimportant when compared to the much greater impact of two factors: (1) the type of technology (i.e., long-linked, "people-changing," etc.) characterizing the organization; and (2) the nature of the organization's environment (i.e., its heterogenity and instability, hostility, etc.). With regard to the former, Perrow (16), Victor Thompson (20), and James Thompson (19) assume that technological differences among organizations take precedence over size considerations in understanding the degree to which decision-making power is centralized, the functional complexity of the system, the degree of autonomy enjoyed by the lower hierarchical levels, and the type of control which is used—whether by means of programs or feedback control mechanisms. Their position has been supported by the empirical studies of Woodward (23) and Harvey (11) which indicate that the technology—structural variation relation remains considerable even with organizational size controlled. Similarly, while the study of the relationship between the organization's environment and its internal structure and processes has been neglected, the theories of Lawrence and Lorsch (14), James Thompson (19), and the findings of Aiken and Hage (1) indicate that this factor has a significance which is quite independent of size considera-

This paper was prepared for presentation at the 64th Annual Meeting of the American Sociological Association, September 1969. Reprinted by permission of the author.

tions.[2] The assumption made in the present study, on the other hand, is that there is still reason to believe that size makes a difference in the ways in which formal organizations are structured to handle their technical and environmental affairs. To provide a reasonable "test" of this notion it is necessary to limit the types of organizations studied to those with similar technologies and substantively similar environments. The assumption is examined, therefore, within one class of formal organization—namely institutions of higher learning.

While there have been a number of suggestions by Kerr (13), Ridgeway (17), Wilson (22) and others as to how institutions of higher learning are structured to handle these matters, there has been little systematic effort to "explain" the particular forms that have been described. With this in mind, it seems reasonable to argue that the demands of numbers "force" these institutions to make use of an organizational model which places heavy reliance on "expertise."[3] Where this model is found, furthermore, it is argued that the faculty has considerable power to influence the institution's educational policy as well as matters of particular interest to each group of academic professionals through the faculty's governmental system and autonomous subject-matter departments. The independence of the faculty is, of course, never complete. Rather, it is dependent on the continued integrity and viability of the model. This is accomplished through organizational mechanisms devoted to the maintenance and development of institutional legitimacy and material support and the use of system-wide (i.e., "universal") standards to assure some minimal uniformity in the great variety of departments. Control over the former activity is "centralized" at the highest level while authority over the latter is delegated to the middle level of administrative officials. At a somewhat higher level of abstraction, the model defines an umbrella structure in which the topmost levels exert rather limited control over the institution's faculty, mainly through their concern with matters pertaining to the maintenance of the system. Such a conception implies that those institutions employing such a model must accomodate to the differing styles of organization in the divisions and departments.[4] Where this model is not employed—in the smaller institutions—it follows that such a loosely integrated federation of administrative and faculty subunits will be absent. Increasing size is treated, therefore, as a necessary condition for the realization of some of the important aspects of faculty self-government and collegial authority. This seems paradoxical when compared to the writings of Weber, Michels, and others who have assumed an inevitable relation between size and a "bureaucratic" and oligarchical character to organizations.

Hypotheses and Measures

The following hypotheses are examined in the present study. They are rather straightforward derivations from the foregoing discussion of the relationship between size and the type of model employed by institutions of higher learning. To insure clarity, the measures of both the independent and dependent variables are included in this section of the paper.

1. *As institutional size increases, a "center" becomes apparent which is specialized in mediating those external relations which are crucial to the maintenance and development of institutional legitimacy and material support.*[5] The center is made up of "the representative" of the institution—the president—and a variety of "mediating roles" staffed by individuals skilled in persuasion, the manipulation of public opinion, and "money-management." By implication, the development of such a mechanism highlights the increasing concern of presidents with matters of "public" relations and financial affairs and a less pressing concern with the more mundane matters associated with the coordination and/or direction of the other administrative officials and the institution's subject-matter departments. The relative distinctiveness of the center is suggested by the frequency and directness of communication between these mediating roles—that is, those roles with supervisory responsibility for public relations, "image" producing publications, alumni relations and "money-management"—and the president.[6] To measure the frequency and directness of communication, a ratio was devised indicating the percentage of externally oriented administrative functions whose supervisors report directly to the president to the percentage of all administrative functions which have direct access to the president.[7] Although it is a rather crude measure of this form of development, the ratio does allow a reasonable test of the hypothesis. In fact, given the relatively narrow range of variation allowable by such a measure, it would seem a rather severe test. For convenience, this ratio will hereafter be referred to as the MSR ratio.[8]

2. *As institutional size increases, institutions of higher learning are characterized by an increasingly powerful faculty "Senate" or governing body and a greater autonomy of subject-matter departments over matters of particular concern to them.* The contention of the faculty and administration over these matters is well expressed by Burton Clark (4, pp. 156-157):

. . . the long-term trend in American higher education has been for authority to move from external to internal sources with faculties contending with the administration about who has authority over what. The faculties march under the banner of self-government and academic freedom, emphasizing the equality of relations among colleagues and de-emphasizing administrative hierarchy. The administrations move forward under the banner of increased efficiency, united effort, public relations—and the reducing of chaos to mere confusion.

While this contention is found in varying degrees in all colleges and universities, it is expected that the conditions favoring significant faculty self-government will be contingent on size considerations.[9]

The measurement of the autonomy and decision-making power of the Senate and the subject-matter departments is rather straightforward. First of all, the power of the Senate is suggested by its ability to influence the policy decisions of the administrative officials on academic policy, appointments to official positions, etc. Moreover, the "role" of the Senate—that is, whether it is concerned primarily with the formulation of educational policy, information dissemination or the approval of recommendations from above—is examined. The reasoning behind this analysis is clear. If the Senate is mainly concerned with information dissemination, etc., then its power over educational goals through the formulation of policy would necessarily be restricted.[10] Secondly, the degree of autonomy associated with the institution's subject-matter departments is measured by whether or not the decision on the addition of new or the withdrawal of old courses from the department's offerings, promotions and merit increases for departmental faculty, recommendations for new appointments and the termination of old appointments, and the determination of the need for new personnel is made within or outside the department in question. The latter measures are supplemented through an analysis of the role of the department chairman. This analysis centers its attention on the time the chairman spends on teaching, administration, research, etc. While this measure provides less detail than the other measures of autonomy, it does suggest whether or not a department is a self-administered unit. This would be the case, of course, if the chairman spends considerable portions of his time on administrative duties.

Relatedly, the level at which departmental decisions are reviewed by administrative officials is examined. It is expected that this authority will be delegated to the academic vice president or to the dean of the college in the larger institutions. Their concern would be centered, therefore, on evaluating the degree to which a particular subject-matter department meets a set of system-wide standards.

Such a review would assure the integrity of the structural model employed while allowing for a considerable degree of variability of organizational styles and patterns within the departments.

Data Collection

The data for the present study were secured through two questionnaires. One was addressed to the presidents of publicly supported colleges and universities.[11] Data pertaining to "administrative" matters were provided by the one hundred and fifteen institutions which returned this questionnaire.[12] A second questionnaire, pertaining to faculty matters—including the power of the Senate and the autonomy of subject-matter departments—was addressed to departmental chairmen within the one hundred and fifteen institutions in the sample. Seven hundred and twenty of these questionnaires were completed and returned. As can be seen from an examination of Figure 1, the sample institutions are spread adequately through the range of student sizes, and each size category is well represented.

While the present study focuses on the effects of size, other variables may be as important in affecting the dependent variables. A variable that seems likely to be of particular importance is the degree of organizational complexity.[13] Both organizational complexity and the development of such a strategic "center," a powerful faculty government, and autonomous subject-matter departments represent aspects of organizational diversity and can be expected to vary

Figure 1. Student enrollment in Universe and sample institutions of higher education

	Number of Institutions in		Percent Sample is of Universe
Student Enrollment	Universe	Sample	
Under 1,000	62	20	32%
1,000-2,499	112	28	25
2,500-4,999	86	26	30
5,000-9,999	49	23	47
10,000 and over	47	18	38
Total	356	115	Average 32%

together. For this reason, the effect of complexity is examined and controlled. Other control variables are the rate of institutional growth over a five-year period,[14] and institutional quality.[15] It seems reasonable to expect a "lag" in organizational development to be associated with a high rate of growth. Lastly, it is assumed that structural differences, as well as the differences in organizational goals found by Gross (9), will be associated with institutional quality. It seems likely that the higher quality institutions will have faculties with greater influence over educational policy through their faculty government and greater control over those matters of particular concern to their subject-matter departments. This may be nothing more than a "professorial bias," however.

Findings

Size and the MSR Ratio

The beta weights presented in Figure 2 indicate the relatively strong association between size and the MSR ratio when the other variables are controlled. A standardized increase in faculty size is most highly associated with the ratio when organizational complexity is controlled. Although organizational complexity is related in the predicted direction to the dependent variable, the direction and

Figure 2. Beta weights among institutional size, organizational complexity, rate of institutional growth, institutional quality, and the MSR ratio

Institutional Size and the Control Variables	Zero-Order Correlations Y	Beta Weights			
		1	2	3	4
1. Institutional Size	.495	—	.665	.527	.450
2. Organizational Complexity	.395	−.201	—	.382	.289
3. Rate of Institutional Growth	−.304	.106	.072	—	−.001
4. Institutional Quality	.301	.094	.218	.311	—

magnitude of the relationship is altered when institutional size is held constant. The rate of institutional growth is also related in the predicted direction to the ratio. Its influence, however, appears negligible when the effects of size are removed. The same is true in the case of institutional quality. These results seem to attest to the relatively strong influence of size. To allow a more detailed analysis of this hypothesis, and to clarify this relationship more fully, a tabular presentation of the joint distribution of institutional size, organizational complexity, and the ratio is presented in Figure 3. The choice of organizational complexity was made because of its relatively strong relationship to the MSR ratio and the "causal" priority given it by some investigators in regard to other aspects of administrative organization.

Figure 3 provides a rather interesting bit of additional information. A "threshold" is apparent in the relationship between institutional size and the centralization of those activities and decisions concerning institutional legitimacy and material support. The rela-

Figure 3. The relationship between institutional size,
complexity, and the MSR ratio

Number of Subject-Matter Departments	Institutional Size				
	0-85	86-155	156-325	326+	Total
0-12	1.29 (15)	1.57 (5)	1.18 (1)	— (0)	1.35 (21)
13-20	1.24 (3)	1.24 (12)	1.44 (10)	— (0)	1.32 (25)
21-45	1.12 (1)	1.13 (3)	1.39 (11)	2.16 (7)	1.59 (22)
46+	— (0) (0)	.54 (1) (1)	4.00 (1) (1)	2.72 (15) (15)	2.67 (17)
Total	1.27 (19)	1.27 (21)	1.51 (23)	2.54 (22)	1.66 (85)

tively large beta weights and coefficients describing this relationship are due to the effect of the larger institutions. Moreover, when the interior cells of the table are examined, additional support is given to the validity of the hypothesis. Thus, when the effects of increasing organizational complexity are examined within categories of size (i.e., when size is controlled) the ratio is reduced in all cells except one.[16] On the other hand, when complexity is controlled, increasing size is positively associated with the magnitude of the ratio.[17] The results lend considerable support to the notion that both the degree of centralization over these strategic institutional relations and the degree of organizational complexity reflect size considerations.[18] It is apparent, therefore, that institutional size makes a significant difference in the way in which institutions of higher learning structure themselves to handle their environmental affairs.

Size and the Decision-Making Power and Autonomy of the Faculty

The analyses of the relationship between size and the manner in which colleges and universities structure themselves to handle their "technical"—academic—affairs is presented below. As was discussed in the foregoing, the primary concern is to isolate and identify the influence of size on (1) the power of the faculty government; and (2) the degree of autonomy associated with the subject-matter departments.

The results presented in Figure 4 indicate that the relationship between institutional size and the power of the faculty government to influence policy decisions is rather strong.[19] In fact, surprisingly so.[20] The faculty in the larger institutions are much more likely to develop a strong faculty government. Those in the smaller institutions, on the other hand, are more often subject to the decrees of administrative officials. In the latter, it is likely that the "role" of the faculty government would be restricted to that of a body within which information is disseminated. This is the case in 50 percent of the smallest institutions.[21] In contrast, 35 percent of the largest institutions have a faculty "Senate" which is mainly concerned with the formulation of educational policy. The analysis of the power and the role of the faculty government indicates, therefore, that the degree of centralization of control over educational policy is much less in the larger than in the smaller institutions.

When the relationship between size and the degree of autonomy associated with the subject-matter departments is examined in Figures 5—8, the results indicate quite clearly that the larger institutions are much more likely to have these decisions made

Figure 4. The relationship between institutional size and
whether the institution's academic government has
sufficient power to influence the policy
decisions of administrative officials

Sufficient Power	Institutional Size			
	−145	146-315	316+	Total
Yes	(a) 35%(57)	51%(94)	73%(219)	370
Yes and No	15 (25)	13 (23)	12 (37)	85
No	50 (80)	36 (66)	15 (45)	191
Total	162	183	301	646

(a) Many of the percentages have been rounded.

within the department. The only exception is noted in the rather
weak relationship between size and control over curriculum. It seems
that professional prerogative rather than size considerations takes
precedence here. The results reported in these tables, furthermore,

Figure 5. The relationship between institutional size and
the autonomy of the subject-matter departments
over the addition of new or the withdrawal of old courses

Level at Which The Decision is Made	Institutional Size			
	−145	146-315	316+	Total
Department	67%(91)	76%(126)	88%(249)	466
Outside the Department	33 (45)	24 (40)	12 (34)	119
Total	136	166	283	585

Figure 6. The relationship between institutional size and
the autonomy of the subject-matter departments
over promotions and merit increases

Level at Which The Decision is Made	Institutional Size			
	−145	146-315	316+	Total
Department	45%(71)	68%(126)	83%(251)	448
Outside the Department	54 (85)	31 (58)	17 (51)	194
Total	156	184	302	642

are not affected appreciably when the relationship(s) are examined
within categories of the control variables.[22] It seems reasonable to
conclude, therefore, that the larger institutions place a greater
emphasis on the expertise of their faculties whether this is indicated
by the power of the faculty government to influence educational
policy or the power of the various groups of academic professionals
over their particular subject-matter departments.

It is apparent from an inspection of Figure 9 that the largest
institutions are most likely to have self-administering subject-matter

Figure 7. The relationship between institutional size and
the autonomy of subject-matter departments over
recommendations for new appointments and the
termination of old appointments

Level at Which The Decision is Made	Institutional Size			
	−145	146-315	316+	Total
Department	28%(46)	48%(87)	72%(221)	354
Outside the Department	72 (119)	52 (95)	28 (86)	300
Total	165	182	307	654

Figure 8. The relationship between institutional size and
the autonomy of the subject-matter departments
over the determination of need for new personnel

Level at Which The Decision is Made	Institutional Size			
	−145	146-315	316+	Total
Department	25%(42)	42%(78)	67%(204)	324
Outside the Department	74 (123)	58 (106)	33 (100)	329
Total	165	184	304	653

departments. That is, the results indicate that the department
chairmen in these institutions are much more likely than those in the
smaller to spend a considerable portion of their time on the
administration of departmental affairs. It seems reasonable to conclude, therefore, that the relatively autonomous and self-administered departments found in the larger institutions have the where-
withal to fashion their own way of doing things.[23] The chairmen of
departments in the smaller institutions, on the other hand, are

Figure 9. The relationship between institutional size and
the percentage of time department chairmen spend on
departmental administration, teaching, and research

Percentage of Chairman's Time	Institutional Size			
	−145	146-315	316+	Total
Administration—40%+	26%	44%	60%	
Teaching—50%+	58%	30%	10%	
Research—10%+	30%	46%	59%	
Total	157	179	291	627

seemingly delegated little administrative authority by the institutions' administrative officials. Rather, they spend a considerable portion of their time teaching.

Lastly, the findings suggest that the larger schools are much more likely to delegate the authority to review those decisions made within their subject-matter departments. There is a very noticeable tendency for either lower ranking administrative officials (i.e., academic vice presidents, deans of the colleges) or faculty committees to evaluate the decisions in relation to an array of system-wide standards.[24] This finding complements the others reported in this section of the paper.[25]

Summary and Conclusions

This study examined the relationship between institutional size and the manner in which colleges and universities structure themselves to handle their technical and environmental affairs. It was shown that increasing institutional size was strongly associated with the development of (1) a "center" at the highest organizational level which mediates those external relations which are crucial to the maintenance and development of institutional legitimacy and material support, and (2) a considerable power on the part of the faculty to influence the institution's educational policy as well as matters of particular interest to each group of academic professionals through the faculty's governmental system and autonomous subject-matter departments. The results suggest that while the independence of the faculty in the larger universities is never complete, it is considerable indeed. It seems reasonable, moreover, to characterize these institutions as loosely integrated federations of administrative and faculty subunits. This is in contrast to the corporate structures characteristic of the smaller colleges. That these relationships were found within formal organizations with similar technologies and substantively similar environments highlights the considerable importance of numbers in understanding these matters.[26]

It seems reasonable to argue that the demands of numbers force these organizations to make use of a model which places heavy emphasis on expertise. The model itself is, no doubt, a more effective technique of handling the system's technical and environmental affairs than Weber's "bureaucracy."[27] In fact, the model eliminates many of the contradictions found in Weber's conception.[28] The larger universities, while allowing the faculty a considerable degree of decision-making power and autonomy, exert a limited control through the development of structures and procedures which maintain the integrity of the model. The "center" is one such structure. Through its actions in mediating those relations which are crucial to maintaining and developing institutional legitimacy and material support the university is prevented from becoming something created by "market" demands. Thus, departments of classics and romance languages survive and take their place beside those, such as physics and chemistry, which are granted liberal support by a variety of external sources. Secondly, this integrity is assured through the maintenance of "universal" standards. Increasingly, these are standards that "scale."[29] Lastly, the nature of these standards and the autonomy of subject-matter departments within the larger universities suggest that the success of academic subunits is measured in terms of results. There are, of course, any number of ways of accomplishing these tasks. The university becomes, therefore, an umbrella structure which accommodates itself to any number of differing styles of organization associated with the various schools and departments.

Footnotes

1. This discussion has been centered on the nature of the relationship between increasing size and the development of "bureaucratic" structures and processes. Gouldner (7), for example, has attacked the pessimism of Weber (21) and Michels (15) who view increasing size as being inevitably associated with the development of "bureaucratic" and "oligarchical" systems respectively. Gouldner's position has been supported by the work of Hall, et. al. (10), which found little or no relationship between size and the degree of functional complexity and formalization. The conclusion of Hall, et. al. 10, p. 912, however, which states that "These findings suggest that size may be irrelevant as a factor in determining organizational structure . . ." is misleading given the faculty sampling procedures employed. Blau, et. al. (3), on the other hand, find a relatively strong relation between size and structural differentiation. In a related fashion, the findings of Hawley, et. al. (12) conflict with those of Anderson and Warkov (2) . . . on the relationship between size and the proportion of administrators. The latter claim that this proportion is a result of the organization's functional complexity rather than size. (See Starbuck (18) for a review of the literature on the implications of organizational growth.)

2. Many students of organization have examined the nature and significance of organizational differences in technology and environmental settings (See Perrow (16), James Thompson (19), and Aiken and Hage (1) for recent reviews of this literature.) The present study limits itself to considering only those contributions which are concerned with the relative significance of organizational size in understanding organizational structures and processes.

3. As was mentioned in an earlier article (Hawley, et. al., (12, p. 255)) ". . . the determinants of institutional structure come to reside in a parent system, so that functions of all kinds tend to be shaped and adapted to a standard institutional structure." Which model is used, however, tends to reflect size considerations.

4. This diversity in organizational style is the subject of an article now being completed by the present author.

5. A full-time equivalent measure of faculty size is used to measure institutional size. This measure assured some independence of variation relative to the dependent variables and is comparable to measures of size used in other studies. This measure has the further advantage of being highly correlated with the size of the student body and seemed, therefore, more than adequate for the purposes of this study.

6. The latter includes the management of endowment, bequests and other investment funds, the dividends from which are used for either special or general institutional purposes.

7. Eighteen selected administrative functions were examined in a rather detailed fashion. They were Official Publications, Scholarly Publications, Student Publications, Investments, Accounting, Staff Benefits, Institutional Development, Personnel—Non-Academic, Admissions, Student Health, Religious Affairs, Student Loans, Scholarship Funds, Counseling—Academic, Counseling—Discipline, Alumni Relations, Libraries, and Public Relations. It will be noted that although admissions is an externally oriented function it is not included as one of the elements of the center. This exclusion was based on the fact that this function has only indirectly to do with matters of legitimacy and material support and is mainly concerned with the routine and technical matters of processing student applications.

8. The Mediation of Strategic Relations ratio.

9. Gross (9) shows, however, that the goals of the administration and the faculty are remarkably alike. If this is the case, it would imply a good deal less contention than might be supposed.

10. Two questions which were answered by department chairmen were used to infer this concern and power. First, the chairman's perception of the role of the Senate was assessed. Whether, that is, it is a body concerned with the formulation of educational policy or not. Second, the chairman's perception of whether or not the faculty body has sufficient power to influence the policy decisions of the administrative officials especially on academic policy was determined. It was felt that the chairman could answer these questions in a more perceptive manner than others. His role as a mediator between the administration and a group of faculty members provides him with insight into both academic and administrative activities.

11. The universe was all tax-supported institutions of higher education having, in 1961, four-year undergraduate degree-granting programs.

12. Some data pertaining to the faculty such as its size, its rate of growth, its quality, and data on the complexity of the academic component, were also provided by this questionnaire. This questionnaire was lengthy (49 pages) and covered many aspects of administration.

13. Organizational complexity is measured by the number of subject-matter departments and non-departmentalized schools. As was mentioned elsewhere (Hawley, et. al., 12), this measure has certain disadvantages. That is, it does not adequately express the total range of diverse activities present or potentially present in a modern university. For the purposes of this study, however, such an approximation seemed adequate.

14. The rate of institutional growth was measured by the rate of growth in the student body over a five-year period.

15. Institutional quality was measured by the proportion of undergraduates of an institution who later became scholars. The output of students who later received Ph.D. degrees in a 21 year period, 1936-1956, is divided by the student size of each institution for a representative year (1949) to provide a ratio of scholars produced per student enrolled. The data were acquired from *Doctorate Production in the United States Universities, 1936-1956, with Baccalaureate Origins of Doctorates in Sciences, Arts, and Humanities* (1958).

16. Cells with less than two cases are omitted.

17. Tabular analysis indicated that the negative relationship between the MSR ratio and the rate of institutional growth is due to the negative relationship between institutional size and the rate of growth.

18. The size-organizational complexity relationship is relatively strong ($r = .840$).

19. The results are based on the perceptions of the department chairmen. The chairmen were asked the following question: "Generally, do you feel that your institution's academic government (faculty body) has sufficient power to influence the policy decisions of the administrative officials (especially on academic policy," appointment to official positions such as President, Dean, etc.)? Comment.

20. When this relationship is examined within categories of the control variables, the effects of size are not reduced appreciably.

21. The chairmen were asked to comment on the role of this group. Their answers were distributed over four categories: (1) policy-making, (2) discussion and taking limited action, (3) making recommendations and giving approval to administrative suggestions, and (4) acting as a body in which information is disseminated.

22. The only exception is when organizational complexity is controlled. In this case, the relationship is reduced. This is due, however, to the strong relationship between size and complexity. When, on the other hand, the complexity—autonomy of subject-matter departments relationship is examined within categories of institutional size, the relationship is almost completely eliminated.

23. This diversity in organizational style found in universities is the subject of another investigation.

24. The coding procedure in this case was not ideal for the purpose of this analysis. The coding instructions asked the coder to code only the highest official mentioned who reviewed these departmental decisions. As a result, the influence of size is not as clear as might be expected. However, forty to fifty percent of the chairmen in the largest schools mentioned the academic vice president or the dean of their college as the highest official while only ten to fifteen percent did so in the smallest. In the latter, the president is invariably involved.

25. There is also a considerable delegation in the larger institutions of specialized administrative services. The administrative subunits charged with these services are, in the largest institutions, quite remote from the presidents. These "staff" functions merely "serve" the faculty and have no formal authority over them.

26. It certainly leads one to question the assumptions of Perrow (16), James Thompson (19), and others.

27. See Ellul's (6) interesting discussion of technique.

28. Both Gouldner (8) and Victor Thompson (20) have criticized Weber for failing to see the possible sources of conflict within an organization composed of experts where behavior is controlled by general rules and commands from above. Rules may be a source of rigidity, hierarchy, a source of status-seeking, etc.

29. With regard to personnel matters, faculty are more often than not evaluated in terms of the number of items in print, research funds brought into the institution, etc.

References
1. Aiken, Michael, and Hage, Jerald. "Organizational Interdependence and Intra-Organizational Structure." *American Sociological Review* 33 (December 1968): 912-930.
2. Anderson, Theodore, and Warkov, Seymour. "Organizational Size and Functional Complexity: A Study of Administration in Hospitals." *American Sociological Review* 26 (February): 23-28.
3. Blau, Peter M., Heydebrand, Wolf V., and Stauffer, Robert E. "The Structure of Small Bureaucracies." *American Sociological Review* 31 (April 1966): 179-191.
4. Clark, Burton R. *Educating the Expert Society.* San Francisco: Chandler Publishing Company, 1962.
5. National Academy of Sciences, National Research Council. *Doctorate Production in the United States Universities, 1936-1956, with Baccalaureate Origins of Doctorates in Sciences, Arts, and Humanities.* Washington, D. C.
6. Ellul, Jacques. *The Technological Society.* New York: Alfred A. Knopf, Inc., 1964.
7. Gouldner, Alvin W. "Metaphysical Pathos and the Theory of Bureaucracy." *American Political Science Review* 49 (1955): 496-507.
8. ————. Merton, R. K. "Organizational Analysis." *Sociology Today.* Bloom, L., and Cottrell, Jr., L. S. New York: Basic Books Inc., 1959, p. 400-428.
9. Gross, Edward. "Universities as Organizations: A Research Approach." *American Sociological Review* 33 (August, 1968): 518-544.
10. Hall, Richard H., Haas, J. Eugene, and Johnson, Norman J. "Organizational Size, Complexity, and Formalization." *American Sociological Review* 32 (December 1967): 903-912.
11. Harvey, Edward. "Technology and the Structure of Organizations." *American Sociological Review* 33 (April, 1968): 247-259.
12. Hawley, Amos. H., Boland, Walter, and Boland, Margaret. "Population Size and Administration in Institutions of Higher Learning." *American Sociological Review* 30 (April 1965): 252-255.
13. Kerr, Clark. *The Uses of the University.* Cambridge: Harvard University Press, 1963.
14. Lawrence, Paul R., and Lorsch, Jay W. *Organization and Environment.* Boston: Graduate School of Business Administration, Harvard University, 1967.
15. Michels, Robert. *Political Parties.* Glencoe, Illinois: Free Press, 1949.
16. Perrow, Charles. "A Framework for the Comparative Analysis of Organizations." *American Sociological Review* 32 (April 1967): 194-208.
17. Ridgeway, James. *The Closed Corporation.* New York: Random House, 1968.
18. Starbuck, William H. "Mathematics and Organization Theory." *Handbook of*

Organizations. Edited by James G. March. Chicago: Rand McNally and Company, 1965, pp. 335-386.

19. Thompson, James D. *Organizations in Action.* New York: McGraw-Hill, 1967.

20. Thompson, Victor R. *Modern Organizations.* New York: Alfred A. Knopf, Inc., 1961.

21. Weber, Max. *The Theory of Social and Economic Organization.* Glencoe, Illinois: Free Press, 1947.

22. Wilson, Logan. *The Academic Man: Sociology of a Profession.* London: Oxford University Press, 1942.

23. Woodward, Joan. *Industrial Organization.* London: Oxford University Press, 1965.

INSTITUTIONALIZATION OF INNOVATIONS
IN HIGHER EDUCATION: FOUR MODELS

Terry N. Clark

Institutionalization, most broadly conceived, is the process whereby specific cultural elements or cultural objects are adopted by
actors in a social system. It is thus a process basic to all social
organizations,[1] particularly formal organizations. Nevertheless, there
is remarkably little theoretical or empirical work on institutionalization of innovations in formal organizations generally, and in institutions of higher education in particular.[2] This paper begins to fill this
gap by systematizing some conceptual approaches to the problem.[3]

For present purposes, innovations are restricted to new forms of
knowledge that result in structural change. The innovations considered here are neither simply new knowledge without any structural change, nor structural change without new knowledge; both
elements are necessary for innovations as discussed here. Frequently
an innovation develops into a profession or an intellectual discipline,
and aspects of institutionalization are best analyzed by considering
this possibility, even though not every new form of knowledge
develops into a profession or discipline.

Four models for analyzing institutionalization of innovations are
presented: (1) the organic growth model, (2) the differentiation
model, (3) the diffusion model, and (4) the combined-process model.
In each model, the essential dynamic element is the growth in
complexity, systematization, and strength of the basic ideas on
which the innovation is founded. The models do not examine

From the *Administrative Science Quarterly*, Vol. 13, No. 1, June 1968, pp. 1-25.
Reprinted by permission of the publisher.

conditions that generate the most basic new ideas; they do occasionally deal with processes through which institutional structures reshape and reorient ideas. And although most of the examples given relate to universities, the four models appear to be applicable to the institutionalization of innovations in government, industry, the military, and other types of formal organizations. Such innovations as computer techniques, budgeting procedures, engineering specialties, and public health practices may be institutionalized in all these organizations, and can be analyzed using one or more of the four models. Moreover, each model is to some extent applicable to processes taking place within an institution, between two or more institutions, or in a complex system of institutions—such as a regional or national university system. The fourth model combines the essential elements of the first three and is the most comprehensive.

Organic Growth Model

The first model delineates a series of stages and processes at progressively higher levels of institutionalization. It is most applicable to innovations that develop outside of established institutional structures. Certain stages of the model parallel those followed by emerging professions.[4]

The model includes three basic processes: development of professional activities, definition of the status associated with the innovation, and the formation of institutions for teaching the innovation. Although these three processes overlap in time, they tend to occur in the order of presentation.

Development and Functions of Professional Activities

The first step toward institutionalization tends to be the development of professional activities, most essentially professional organizations and journals. Periodic meetings and circulation of journals serve to establish, often for the first time, regular social interaction among members of an emerging profession. Especially important in the early stages of institutionalization are regular meetings bringing professionals together to discuss their work, since at this point the professional organization may be the sole link for its members. Later, of course, contacts are established in teaching institutions, research bureaus, advisory-committee meetings, and the plethora of organizations that eventually follow.

Interaction at meetings and through journals fulfills an indispensable function in contributing to the development of a self-conscious, delimited professional community. Continued association with a self-conscious community constitutes in turn a major step toward the establishment of clearly defined statuses and the identification of individuals with these statuses.

Definition of the Status

In conjunction with the organization of professional activities, other social arrangements associated with the innovation tend to become clarified and regularized. The following are basic steps in the process of status definition.

Full-time activity and self-support. An important advance is made when activities associated with an innovation are undertaken on a relatively full-time basis,[5] although there may be a lag before these activities become self-supporting.[6] Financial self-support for a status tends to attract a different type of person. During the nineteenth century, for example, the gentleman scientist declined in importance as highly committed, earnest, and generally less wealthy professionals replaced the more leisurely "amateurs."[7]

Professional ideologies and utopias. In a developing field, members seeking to unite individuals of varying intellectual backgrounds, and to obtain legitimation from the intellectual community and society at large, tend to elevate their goals to near-utopian ideals. Claims are frequently hyperbolic; the stance assumed toward older, established fields is inordinately aggressive; the language is unqualified and direct. The program may well be expounded in more than one form; a simpler version, unobscured by technicalities, is directed to a general audience; a second, more precise version, is aimed at full-fledged members, or future members, of the new field.

In time, as broader segments of society grant legitimation to the field, and as institutional support grows to support its activities, utopian ideals give way to narrower claims, which represent the innovation more realistically. Fewer communications are directed beyond the profession, fewer impassioned affirmations of indispensability are made, and less concern is shown for the most fundamental conceptual and methodological problems of the innovation.[8] The result is a more closely delimited, more realistic, and less polemical ideology.[9]

Changing the name of the status and developing a specialized vocabulary. A frequent step in institutionalization is giving the status a new name.[10] Newspaper reporters become journalists; moral statisticians become sociologists. Such a renaming performs several functions. It differentiates the new status from others closely similar, which previously performed analagous activities. It loosens the ties with earlier associated statuses. It facilitates psychological identification of status incumbents with their new status.[11] And it provides a banner in disputes with related fields.[12]

Closely associated with the change in name is the emergence of a specialized vocabulary for professional communication. Whatever the scientific utility of new terminology, one consequence of its use is the social demarcation of the emerging group and the heightening of its collective identity.

Delimiting intellectual boundaries and specifying the content of the status. Overlapping with the intellectual problem of circumscribing a distinctive subject matter are the social problems associated with institutionalization. Defining the content of the roles—the patterned sets of rights and duties associated with the new status—is a central problem in early development. The pioneers must of necessity have come from other areas. Since they rarely have a common background, they may well hold conflicting views of the new field and status. For example, in the nineteenth century, various persons, all calling themselves sociologists, engaged in a wide range of activities reflecting their differing backgrounds: biological evolution, socialism, social work, moral philosophy, and others.[13]

At the outset, competition with older fields may be bitter. But with time a developing field tends to focus less on such external problems as border disputes, and to turn inward, developing more coherent conceptual schemes, creating stronger professional and research organizations, and training new members. After a period of relative isolation, however, the field may attempt to initiate closer contacts with related specialties, but not necessarily the parent fields from which it had broken away.[14]

Forming New Teaching Institutions. Since replenishment of personnel is necessary for the maintenance of all social institutions, institutionalization implies the establishment of institutions to transmit the content of the field to successors. Their development depends largely on whether the new field emerges from within the general framework of older fields, housed in the university, or in relative isolation. In the first instance, as analyzed below, research and training facilities generally evolve through structural differentiation from the established institution. In the second, the new field may create its own teaching institutions, a pattern followed by the physical and biological sciences in the seventeenth and eighteenth centuries, the social sciences in the nineteenth, and such specialties as public relations and nursing in the twentieth.

Informal training. Although initially self-training may be relied upon to pass on knowledge of a field, in time some sort of organized instruction usually develops. In the first stages, teachers are seldom more than autodidacts and amateurs; instruction may consist simply of their research reports to one another at occasional gatherings in coffee houses or a private home.

Formal, unrecognized training institutions. The next step is the organization of some kind of formal instruction: regularly scheduled lectures offered in an academic locale; examinations at the end of a course or sequence of courses, with the awarding of a certificate or degree, although at first these may not be recognized outside the teaching institution itself.

Recognition and support. Official recognition by some board of accreditation, or (especially in the continental countries) the national ministry of education, increases the social and economic value of the instruction. In becoming more integrated into the established hierarchy of academic degrees, the formal instruction is accorded more respect by other teaching institutions. Financial support is also more readily available once official recognition is secured.

Full-time teaching staff and teaching materials. More substantial financial support makes possible additional self-supporting, full-time statuses associated with the innovation. The teaching staff may prepare materials which are themselves indicators of further institutionalization: textbooks, teacher's manuals, student guides, audio-visual aids, and others.

Applicability of the Organic Growth Model. The organic growth model is particularly applicable to the development of innovations outside established institutions. Such innovations are generally not closely similar to already institutionalized bodies of knowledge, but are composed of the more radical, hence unacceptable, ideas. They may be evolved by persons within established academic institutions, but more often are the product of marginal men or outsiders; therefore, if the innovation is to survive, professional and teaching institutions must be created to transmit it to others.

The frequency with which innovations are institutionalized according to the organic growth model varies inversely with the innovativeness and penetrability of the established institutions. The British universities—Oxbridge in particular—may have been and still are among the least innovative and least open of any educational system in the world.[15] Better than most other national university systems, the British system exemplifies the process of institutionalization of innovations through the organic growth model. Innovations such as the natural sciences grew with Gresham's College and the Royal Society.[16] Applied science and technology were emphasized in founding the provincial redbrick institutions.[17] The University of London was created for the social sciences.[18] Medicine, law, dentistry, nursing, pharmacy, architecture, journalism, and many other professions developed in a variety of *ad hoc* institutions—all outside the established universities.[19] Although the organic growth model is particularly salient in the British university system, it may certainly also characterize institutionalization in other university systems and institutions.

Differentiation Model

From Adam Smith to Spencer to Durkheim to Parsons and other contemporaries, social theorists have focused on the division of labor, or structural-functional differentiation, as a process central to institutional change. This model involves specialization within a larger system, which leads to the differentiation and separation of subunits of the system. Differentiation is thus a process basic to industrialization: as societies advance, patterns of differentiation occur and recur both within and between the economy, the polity, the church, the family, and many other institutions.[20] Differentiation is also a basic process for the institutionalization of innovations within universities. An ineluctable consequence of the expansion of knowledge is a decrease in the range of materials that any individual can master. Specialization follows, and on an institutional level, this implies the creation of additional statuses.

The differentiation model seems particularly applicable to innovations that are institutionalized largely within existing academic (or governmental, or industrial, or military) structures. Innovations that are the products of persons within universities often consist of advances based largely on established—and already institutionalized—bodies of knowledge. They tend to be less radical and extreme than innovations of outsiders and men marginal to the university, and correspondingly more acceptable to university decision makers. Consequently they are more rapidly established in the university than innovations from outside.

The broader the range of knowledge institutionalized within a university system, the more likely it is that future innovations will be created and housed within universities. American universities have traditionally found room for a far more extensive and colorful range of subject matters than universities in most other countries, and consequently have developed and institutionalized a larger proportion of innovations through a process of differentiation. Within the confines of American universities—especially the land-grant variety, those distinctive institutions at once the source of greatness and of decadence of the national system—almost every conceivable type of knowledge has been created, taught, studied, applied, and stored. In recent decades, the major universities of the country have increasingly adopted the general features of the land-grant model—though with modifications.[21] Many innovations that in Britain developed largely outside the university system—the social sciences, engineering, medicine, law, nursing, and others—have been welcome in American universities.

The differentiation model is thus particularly appropriate for institutionalization of innovations in the American university system. Indeed, some writers, focusing almost exclusively on the American case, have tended to equate all institutionalization with differentiation—ignoring other possible models.[22]

Diffusion Model

At least since Gabriel Tarde, social scientists have applied diffusion models of one sort or another to a broad spectrum of phenomena.[23] Diffusion processes may be analyzed using a scheme with five consecutive stages: (1) knowledge, (2) information collection, (3) evaluation, (4) trial, and (5) adoption.[24]

Knowledge

Diffusion of knowledge about the innovation to potential adopters is essential to institutionalization. Journals, professional meetings, visiting scholars, and newsletters are a few of the many possible channels of communication. For example, such channels brought information about the developing discipline of physiology to almost all of the German universities in the first part of the nineteenth century.[25]

Information collection

If knowledge of an idea proves to be of interest, decision makers in an institution do not wait for information to arrive unsolicited, but begin to seek relevant knowledge and advice actively.

Evaluation

This stage overlaps the second stage, for it is difficult to collect information without evaluation. But evaluation is more than collecting and evaluating information. Advisors, often in special committees or advisory councils, are likely to be asked about the innovation, and their personal views are weighted heavily. The assets and liabilities of a specific embodiment of the innovation, often a single individual, must be evaluated for the particular institution considering adoption. The competence of a particular physiologist in nineteenth century Germany, and the degree to which he helped diversify the offerings (and not conflict with established interests) of a given university, would thus be discussed at length before any sort of offer would be made.

Trial

Following a favorable evaluation, an innovation is frequently given a pretest or small-scale adoption: a professor teaches a course in a new area, a visiting scholar is invited to lecture on the topic, a nontenure appointment is made, and so on. Trials of this type were used as German universities seriously considered particular physiologists.

Adoption

Generally the trial of the innovation will subsequently be evaluated, and, if deemed acceptable, will be adopted on a more permanent basis. In nineteenth century Germany, this was accomplished by the establishment of a chair. Re-evaluation continues almost indefinitely. This continued scrutiny manifests itself when competing proposals are considered for expansion of activities in various parts of a university.

Applications of the Diffusion Model

This model may be applied to innovations that develop outside university structures and diffuse into them, or that diffuse between universities. This latter pattern is illustrated by the German national university system from the mid-nineteenth century to the present (except for the Third Reich). Many innovations developed within it and became institutionalized (through differentiation) in one of its many institutions.[26] Then, younger men attracted to the innovation frequently specialized in the innovation and become carriers *(Traegerin)*,[27] thereby serving as agents for its diffusion to other parts of the national system.[28] The decentralized, loosely integrated, relatively unstratified, and quite competitive structure of the system was particularly conducive to attracting younger men from one institution to the next, and in this way, institutionalizing innovations through diffusion.

Combined-Process Model

Although each of the first three models is useful in understanding some aspects of institutionalization for some innovations in some systems, a combined-process model is frequently more appropriate. Here, innovation is seen as developing concurrently outside and inside the university. Institutionalization outside advances largely through organic growth—the professionalization dimension of the overall process is best exemplified here. But although one essential dimension of institutionalization is creation of the structures of a profession, this is generally transcended by innovations which grow into a full-fledged discipline. A second fundamental dimension is bureaucratic—we refer here to the hierarchical structure of the university, which institutionalizes innovations largely through a differentiation process. In some instances, because of the character of the particular innovation and/or the structure of the system, only one of these two processes occurs. But in many others, the two occur together, and these two parallel sets of developments complement and reinforce each other through diffusion. Similar ideas may be set forth almost simultaneously by persons both inside and outside the university system. The ideas diffuse back and forth, and versions from both inside and outside stimulate one another. If they are not institutionalized inside the university, this may reinforce institutions developing outside, since they will receive support (intellectual attention, students, financial contributions, etc.) that would otherwise have gone to the university. As time passes, if the innovation continues to show promise, pressures will be exerted on the university to differentiate, and so institutionalize the innovation.

Institutionalization in the University System

Entrance of the innovation into the university is, in most cases, the single most decisive stage in the overall institutionalization process. With entrance, a number of benefits accrue to members of the innovating group. Relatively secure (because tenured), full-time statuses permit their incumbents to devote more time to the innovation. This in turn facilitates further intellectual and social division of labor. Problems of role ambiguity are to some extent resolved, because the intellectual and social roles of university teacher and researcher are already largely defined. The prestige and legitimacy of the innovation are generally enhanced for both the intellectual community and the general public.

The university provides protection—symbolized by the institution of academic freedom—from the immediate demands of the outside world. This protection—symbolized by the institution of academic freedom—is particularly important for the social sciences, permitting more extensive questioning of basic social values. The university also assures a continuing source of new recruits for a field, in the form of students. Both teaching and increased access to publication media facilitate diffusion of results.[29]

The *timing* of university entrance can significantly influence the lines of development of an innovation. Early entrance may lead to undue emphasis on philosophical legitimation, continued development of utopian ideals, and isolation from vital outside developments. Premature closure and dogmatism, heightened by the necessity to present the innovation formally to an academic audience, can result in precipitous solutions and lead to neglect of basic problems. Delayed entrance, however, may generate alliances with groups outside the university—industry, government, the military, coffeehouse intellectuals—which channel development of the innovation along the lines of the limited concerns of such groups—immediate practical application, routine service activities, and superficial criticism. Even after university entrance, an innovation that has been in extensive contact with such outside forces may remain—for better or worse—strongly influenced by them.

Various conditions influence the timing and form of institutionalization within the university. The innovation is considered first and then the university system. Certain of the following considerations are to some degree relevant to the first three models of institutionalization, but as they are more central to the combined-process model, they are presented here. In reading them, the dictum of *ceteris paribus* should be recalled.

Innovation

A basic proposition for the discussion is that the closer an innovation is to the central values of a social system, the more likely it is to be institutionalized. In varying guises, this idea has had widespread use.[30] It focuses attention on the relativity of criteria for institutional acceptability.

Degree of development of the innovation. The degree of development of an innovation's central conceptual schemes is one of its most important properties, since intellectual excellence is one of the most basic values of universities. Consequently, the more intellectually sophisticated the conceptual schemes of an innovation, the better it conforms with university values of excellence, and the more likely that it will be institutionalized.

Personal characteristics of the innovators. In considering persons associated with ideas, it appears that the closer the personal characteristics of innovators to those valued by the university, the more acceptable the innovators.

Innovators may be brought into the institution through processes of differentiation, diffusion, or some combination of both. Differentiation is most frequent when an advanced student, having completed the requirements for a traditional university career (such as a Ph.D. in the U.S.), acquaints himself with an innovation. He may then gradually modify the traditional career pattern to encompass the innovation he has selected. Institutionalization is accomplished here through tolerating a slightly deviant member within, for example, an established academic department, and eventually permitting him to create his own differentiated substructure (course, degree, chair, department, and so on).

A second pattern is cooptation of persons from outside the university system. But "outside" is relative. The serious candidate almost certainly will have had university training in some subject and be generally acquainted with university norms and values, although he may spend several years in a nonacademic setting. The more his personal characteristics and his interpretation of the innovation are congruent with university values, the more acceptable he will be. Particularly important is his ability to contribute new knowledge about the innovation and to teach it effectively.

Leadership and organization of the innovating groups. Innovative leaders have frequently been marginal men; a large number of innovations seems to come from quasi-outsiders, persons occupying statuses in two or more institutional realms.[31] One reason for their greater innovativeness is that marginality leads to exposure to activities in more than one sphere, which makes innovation possible by applying ideas and procedures from one sphere to a second.[32] Involvement with several institutional spheres, however, generally implies a less intense commitment to any one institution, and greater difficulty in achieving changes within it. Innovation and institutionalization are distinct processes.

The role combination of researcher-administrator is of great importance for realizing institutionalization of innovations. To achieve a major organizational innovation in most universities demands commitment to much more administrative activity than most teaching and research-oriented professors are willing to invest. Founders of disciplines in many universities have of necessity frequently doubled as administrators.[33] The private foundations in the United States, along with such interstitial funding and research-coordinating organizations as the Social Science Research Council, have served as extremely influential posts for a number of researcher-administrators concerned with institutionalizing innovations.[34]

The University

Various characteristics of universities and university systems influence their openness to innovation.

Funds. The extent of financial support is basic in restricting the ability of an institution to innovate. Generally, the more extensive the financial support, the greater the institutional innovativeness. But this is a simplification. More important is the amount of support available specifically for innovations, or at least not committed in advance to particular budget items.[35] Extra-university sources of support—private foundations, governmental agencies, industry, wealthy individuals—are especially important. The openness of American universities to such outside sources is a major factor behind their innovativeness, which differentiates them from European institutions.

An increase in the total amount of funds in a system, as well as funds available specifically for innovation, implies a number of structural changes. Most evident is the freedom of higher-level individuals to experiment unhampered by small budgets. Less obvious, but equally significant, is that as funds increase, more generous support can be provided to all members of the system. This in turn changes relationships throughout the system, but the impact is particularly marked on lower-level members, who become more autonomous with increasing funds. A larger proportion of persons in the system is thereby able to engage in potentially innovative activities.

Value climate. The importance for innovation of the value climate of an institution seems to vary inversely with the availability of funds. For example, studies of school systems in the United States during the depression showed innovativeness to be highly correlated with community wealth, whereas more recently commitments of administrators and teachers to innovative norms are more important.[36]

Orientations toward innovation vary as a function of the general eminence of an institution.[37] The leading graduate schools in the United States—the "upper upper class" institutions—are very open to experimentation and innovations that contribute to the goals of advancing research or teaching: new types of laboratories, special technical equipment, research institutes, curriculum reforms—

provided that they are undertaken by well-qualified persons. The not quite so eminent institutions—the "lower uppers" that strenuously aspire to elite membership—have funds that are almost as extensive, but seem less open to ideas that have not already been accepted by the "upper upper" institutions. These institutions seem to be insecure about their status, which inhibits innovation. The broad "middle class" institutions are much slower to adopt radical innovations and those related to more basic research, but are more accessible to outside demands for service activities that provide a continuing source of institutional change: farm product laboratories, traffic control centers, contracts for development of industrial products, and others. Finally, the "lower class" institutions—neglected by almost all outside interests, scorned by more elite institutions, and highly provincial in outlook—are usually least innovative of all.

Universities also pass through cycles.[38] Very new institutions are often the most aggressively innovative. With no traditions to respect, and having been expressly founded because of the inadequacy of existing institutions, their staffs are eager to become identified with new and different ideas. The next most innovative institutions tend to be older ones, defined as stagnant and forced through reforms and changes by a top leadership anxious to "bring the institution up to date." The least innovative are generally the established and flourishing institutions, which remain open to minor innovations, but are less accessible to radical ventures.

The less strongly values—any values—are embedded in an institution, the more accessible it will be to change. Thus, innovation would seem to be most resisted by highly religious institutions, and increasingly less by moderately religious institutions, institutions highly committed to one or two goals (e.g., teaching in liberal arts colleges, teaching and research in traditional elite universities),[39] and institutions not strongly committed to any goals (the multiversity).[40]

Competition. The extent to which universities in a system are forced to compete crucially influences their innovativeness.[41] The more competitive the system, the more innovative the institutions within it. Universities compete in three major markets: the student market, the faculty market, and the fund market. The relative importance for innovation of competition within one market in contrast to the other two varies a great deal between systems and over time.

The student market was perhaps the most important of the three in eighteenth and early nineteenth century Germany and America. In

Germany, competition for students continues from one semester to the next, whereas in the U.S. barriers to competition are erected once a student enters an institution as a degree candidate. In a system with relatively free competition for students, an innovation can be immediately measured in its student drawing power, and a corps of carriers can be more rapidly created to diffuse it than in a less competitive system.

Competition in the faculty market has been radically altered in the last century as the basis for evaluation and promotion has shifted from teaching, application of knowledge, or taking examinations, to original research. This transition in criteria makes the "market commodity" more observable, communicable, and easier to evaluate objectively. A market not restricted to candidates closely affiliated with the institution that is seeking to fill a position can draw on a national or international pool of candidates. Increased market size facilitates circulation of personnel among a wider range of institutions; and increased competitiveness leads to more rapid turnover; both in turn foster more universalistic standards. And, with more rapid organizational succession by persons from throughout an extended system, opportunities increase for carriers of innovations to become institutionalized.[42] Correspondingly, the system as a whole becomes more innovative.

Competition for funds takes place in several markets. An oligopolistic and particularistic arena is that of alumni funds—far more important in the U.S. than in Europe. Slightly more competitive is the market of wealthy philanthropists, which is similar to donations from industries. But industries, especially in the U.S., also support a good deal of research, which, although generally quite applied, has engendered vigorous competition for contracts. The values, particularistic relations to institutions, and short-term interests of these three sources have, however, restricted the range of competition and led—on the whole—to the support of relatively few radical innovations.

On the other hand, those institutions established in the U.S. by wealthy individuals or industries for disbursement of their funds— the private foundations—have probably been the mosc important single source for support of imaginative and radically innovative projects in any country.[43] This still seems true, although the importance of the private foundations has been increasingly rivaled in the last decade by agencies of the federal government. To some degree, European governments have played the same role as the foundations in the U.S., serving as sources more universalistic and less narrow in orientation than alumni, philanthropists, or industry. But there is a marked difference between most university funding by European governments and that by private foundations or the federal government in the U.S. The traditional mechanism for governmental support in European institutions—found in American state universities—is the fixed annual budget, disbursed largely through the university administration.

In contrast, the most frequent vehicle for funding by private foundations and the U.S. government is the contract or grant.[44] Forcing incumbents of elevated university statuses to compete for funds instead of guaranteeing them an annual budget makes the entire system more competitive. A university system financed largely through contracts and grants tends to be more competitive and also more innovative than one financed through fixed annual budgets. With funds dependent on competition in relatively open markets outside the university, occupants of lower statuses can have a great deal of autonomy. This increased autonomy at the lower levels—i.e., autonomy for the younger and, generally, most innovative members of the system—leads to greater innovativeness throughout the system. Still, dependence on outside financing forces the university to be responsive to desires of outside funding agencies, and which may attempt to institutionalize innovations at odds with the university's goals.

Centralization of decision making. Where decisions are made by individuals, generally the more decentralized the decision making structure, the more innovative the organization.[45] For example, leaders in highly centralized university systems, except in revolutionary situations, tend to be more experienced and mature, and also more conservative, than other system members. Furthermore, their decisions are based on their particular values. Would-be innovators must consequently phrase their claims in terms of the values of these leaders. But not every innovation can be so justified. More decentralized systems, where only the consent of a few persons is needed, make more coalitions possible and innovation more apt to be institutionalized.

Centralized systems are also poorly adapted to small-scale experimentation; decisions made at the center are generally applied throughout the system. Accordingly, it is difficult to adopt innovations piecemeal; demands for change from the lower-level members or clients of the system tend to be rejected, delayed, or passed along to higher levels. Because change in centralized organizations is so long delayed, when it does come, it is often in the form of a palace revolution, which spreads rapidly throughout the system, sweeping away previous achievements. But because leaders fear just such a radical change, their resistance to change is heightened.[46]

Stages of Institutionalization

These influences can be arranged in a series of stages of institutionalization corresponding to the combined-process model.[47] As stressed at the outset, the engine driving each of the four models forward is the (1) *cumulative development of knowledge* within a discipline, between two existing disciplines, or largely outside of any established intellectual context. The continual growth of knowledge is particularly salient in the sciences, but is present to some extent in other fields.[48] Still, knowledge is neither entirely cumulative nor regular in its growth. New ideas may result in new problems and, frequently, in redefinition of older ones. The established goals within a field and the appropriate means to their attainment may be called into question by new knowledge.[49] For example, in the first part of the nineteenth century, certain philosophers in France became interested in social questions and began to examine these questions using more "scientific" methods than were characteristic of many philosophers of the period.

At the early stages, such developments are likely to lead simply to (2) *undirected discontent.* It is often difficult, even for those most involved, to specify the precise nature or source of the discontent. Individuals most affected by the new knowledge may even experience such psychic symptoms as phantasy, diffuse anxiety, or misdirected aggression. Auguste Comte's psychic idiosyncrasies are well known, and the image which he helped establish, along with others devoted to the creation of a science of society, led one of Durkheim's professors to recommend avoiding work in the area: it would almost certainly, he cautioned, lead to insanity. Eventually, (3) *deviation from established norms* is likely: "unthinkable" statements may be made; "controversial" articles and books are published exploring the implications of the new knowledge. (For instance, Alfred Espinas wrote a doctoral thesis in 1877, which elaborated some of the ideas of Spencer.) When the professional community perceives that some of its members are deviating, it will attempt to bring the deviants back into line by (4) *application of methods of social control.* At first, these may consist simply of informal sanctions applied in day-to-day interaction; eventually, however, formal institutional sanctions may be applied. Espinas, for example, reacted to criticisms of his thesis by largely abandoning the subject and working on more traditional philosophical questions.

Thus, modifications in the realm of ideas are transformed into social acts: actors embrace heretical ideas that lead them to violate social norms; they are consequently branded as deviants. Initially, sanctions may be imposed almost unconsciously, but, if continued, the deviants, if not others, are likely to begin more systematic questioning and to attempt to formulate explicitly their views about new developments. This process is facilitated when enough deviants exist to form groups, to interact, and to develop a distinctive identity. In France at the end of the nineteenth century, a number of professional societies and journals dealing with social research were founded in this way.

But as individual grievances are transformed into social protest, (5) *social conflict* is likely. The adequacy of established norms is questioned. Informal controls begin to break down; formal sanctions (for example, rejection of manuscripts and grant applications, refusals to make appointments) are increasingly invoked. The criticisms of the new social sciences by certain members of more established disciplines led to continual incidents of this sort in the last part of the nineteenth century in France.

Each of these first five stages may involve actors inside and/or outside universities. If social conflict becomes sufficiently pronounced, the lines of cleavage will tend to harden along established institutional borders; deviants will tend to become institutionally segregated. The institutional location of the deviants, and their relative unity or separateness—in conjunction with the degree of intellectual radicalism of the basic ideas—will largely determine the timing and substance of the next stage, (6) *formulation of potential innovations.* Less radical innovations may be formulated by separate individuals inside different universities. More radical ideas, however, will generally be less immediately acceptable to universities; to institutionalize them successfully, their "carriers" may be forced to create new institutional structures. Some combination of these two processes has also frequently taken place: new professional organizations, journals, conferences, institutes, etc. may be formed outside the universities, but the persons involved in these activities may be both academicians and others. The university-based persons with interests in the innovation may gradually become more involved with it, but only to the extent permitted by the limits of their home institutions. When they, as well as others in the university, become convinced of the importance of the ideas, however, potential innovations will also be formulated for the university. Thus, while such persons as Henri de Tourville or Gabriel Tarde systematized the work of others and established two possible foundations for the elaboration of the new science of sociology, these men, and their systems, were too far removed from the sort of thought current in the French university. It was young Emile Durkheim, working within the system, who built on certain ideas developed by others outside, but shaped them into a form more acceptable to the university.

The factors that determine the openness of the university to innovation also influence the type of criteria applied in the (7) *evaluation of potential innovations.* Durkheim's ideas were first evaluated by the Ministry of Education after he published several provocative articles upon returning from Germany.

A favorably evaluated innovation will be followed, generally, by a period of (8) *restricted trial*, and if the trial is considered successful, (9) *adoption of the innovation* will normally follow. Restricted trial was offered to Durkheim in 1887 when he was appointed to a temporary teaching post at the University of Bordeaux; he was called to Paris in 1902, but did not receive a permanent position there until 1906. These last three stages are similar to those in the diffusion model, and are consequently passed over rapidly here.

Applications of the Combined-Process Model

The combined-process model was initially formulated when the first three were found unsatisfactory for analyzing institutionalization in the French university system.[50] The example of the institutionalization of Durkheimian sociology, used to illustrate the various stages of the model, was only one of many similar cases. Analagous examples of new ideas initially housed in an outside institution, but which soon entered the university, are renaissance studies and the Collège de France, the natural sciences and the Acadèmie des Sciences, and experimental methods and the Ecole Polytechnique.[51]

Although the study of the French university system led to the development of the combined-process model, the model unquestionably provides a more complete and sophisticated picture of institutionalization of some innovations in the British, American, and German university systems than do the organic growth, differentiation, or diffusion models. And although this paper has essentially dealt with institutionalization of innovations in higher education, the combined-process model also seems to correspond better to many institutionalization processes in other types of organizations than any of the first three. But this last assertion, at least for the present, must remain largely programmatic.

Footnotes

1. Indeed, Talcott Parsons has even gone so far as to define sociological theory as "that aspect of the theory of social systems which is concerned with the phenomena of the institutionalization of patterns of value-orientation in the social system." Cf., *The Social System* (Glencoe: The Free Press, 1951), p. 552.

2. Some treatment, if limited, may be found in such guides as James G. March and Herbert A. Simon, *Organizations* (New York: John Wiley, 1959), pp. 173-210; Amitai Etzioni, *A Comparative Analysis of Complex Organizations* (New York: Free Press, 1961), pp. 265-313; Peter M. Blau and W. Richard Scott, *Formal Organizations* (San Francisco: Chandler, 1962), pp. 222-253; James G. March (ed.), *Handbook of Organizations* (Chicago: Rand McNally, 1965), esp. pp. 142-193, 451-533, 614-649, 1144-1170.

3. We gratefully acknowledge assistance from the Social Science Research Committee of the University of Chicago and a grant to Professor Peter M. Blau and the author from the National Science Foundation (GS-1528). The NSF grant is supporting a project investigating the impact of organizational character-istics on the eminence of research and institutionalization of innovations in about 250 American universities and colleges.

4. An unpublished compendium of materials, Bernard J. Stern, *Historical Materials on Innovations in Higher Education* (New York: Bureau of Applied Social Research, Columbia University, 1953), has stimulated two other docu-ments: R. W. Gerard, Problems in the Institutionalization of Higher Education, *Behavioral Science*, 2 (1957); and Paul F. Lazarsfeld and Amitai Etzioni, "Innovation in Higher Education," unpublished manuscript, Columbia Univer-sity, no date. Cf. also Matthew B. Miles (ed.) *Innovation in Education* (New York: Bureau of Publications. Teachers College, Columbia University, 1964).

4. Cf., for example, A. M. Carr-Saunders and P. A. Wilson, *The Professions* (Oxford: Oxford University, 1933); Everett Cherrington Hughes, *Men and Their Work* (New York: Free Press, 1958), esp. chs. 9-13; *Daedalus*, 92 (Fall 1963); Talcott Parsons, *Essays in Sociological Theory* (rev. ed.; Glencoe: Free Press, 1954), chs. 2, 17; and Howard M. Vollmer and Donald L. Mills (eds.), *Professionalization* (Englewood Cliffs, N. J.: Prentice-Hall, 1966).

5. Cf. Joseph Ben-David, The Scientific Role: The Conditions of Its Establish-ment in Europe, *Minerva*, 4 (1965), 15-54.

6. Probably the best-known case was the traditional *Privatdozent* in the German system. See Friedrich Paulsen, *The German Universities* (New York: Macmillan, 1895), pp. 126 ff; and Alexander Busch, *Die Geschichte des Privatdozenten* (Stuttgart: F. Enke Verlag, 1959).

7. Everett Mendelsohn, The Emergence of Science as a Profession in Nine-teenth-Century Europe, in Karl Hill (ed.), *The Management of Scientists* (Boston, Beacon Press, 1954), pp. 3-48; and Max Weber, "Politics as a Vocation," in Hans H. Gerth and C. Wright Mills (eds. and trans.), *Essays in Sociology* (New York: Oxford University, 1946), pp. 77-128, on professionali-zation in politics.

8. An excellent account of the movement from utopian to ideological formulations of professional goals is presented for the discipline of the history of science in I. B. Cohen, "Discussion," in A. C. Crombie (ed.), *Scientific Change* (London: Heinemann, 1963), pp. 757-780.

9. The ideology—utopia distinction is, of course, from Karl Mannheim, *Ideology and Utopia* (New York: Harcourt, Brace and World, 1936); see also

Warren O. Hagstrom, *The Scientific Community* (New York: Basic Books, 1965), pp. 211-215.

10. Cf. Theodore Caplow, *The Sociology of Work* (Minneapolis: University of Minnesota, 1954), pp. 139-140.

11. Howard S. Becker and James Carper, in The Elements of Identification with an Occupation, *American Sociological Review*, 21 (1956), 341-348, found that graduate students in philosophy had more difficulty than engineering or physiology students in identifying with their future occupation of teacher of philosophy, since its occupational title was the same as that of great original thinkers of the past: philosopher.

12. Cf. Terry N. Clark, *Institutionalization of Innovations in Higher Education: Social Research in France, 1850-1914*, forthcoming.

13. *Ibid.*

14. Cf. Robert K. Merton, "Social Conflict Over Styles of Sociological Work," in *Transactions of the Fourth World Congress of Sociology* (Louvain: International Sociological Association, 1959), Vol. III, pp. 21-46.

15. Joseph Ben-David and Awraham Zloczower, Universities and Academic Systems in Modern Societies, *European Journal of Sociology*, 3 (1962), 45-84.

16. Martha Ornstein, *The Role of Scientific Societies in the Seventeenth Century* (Chicago: University of Chicago, 1938); Robert K. Merton, Science, Technology, and Society in Seventeenth Century England, *Osiris*, 4 (Bruges, Belgium, 1938).

17. Cf. Bruce Truscott, *Red Brick University* (London: Faber and Faber, 1945); Edward Shils, The Intellectuals: Great Britain, *Encounter*, 4 (April 1955), 3-12; Sir James Mountford, *British Universities* (London: Oxford University, 1966), pp. 1-49.

18. Beatrice Webb, *Our Partnership* (London: Longmans, Green, 1948).

19. Carr-Saunders and Wilson, *op. cit.*

20. Parsons in conjunction with Shils, Bales, and Smelser, has analyzed these institutions with variations of a differentiation model. An overview is Talcott Parsons, *Societies* (Englewood Cliffs, N.J.: Prentice-Hall, 1966).

21. Cf. Laurence R. Veysey, *The Emergence of the American University* (Chicago: University of Chicago, 1965), esp. ch. 2; and the critique of Abraham Flexner, *Universities: American, English, German* (New York: Oxford University, 1930).

22. Hagstrom, *op. cit.*

23. Terry N. Clark (ed.), *Gabriel Tarde* (Chicago: University of Chicago, Heritage of Sociology Series, forthcoming); Everett M. Rogers, *Diffusion of Innovations* (New York: Free Press, 1962).

24. *Ibid.*

25. Ben-David and Zloczower, *op. cit.*; Awraham Zloczower, "Career Opportunities and the Growth of Scientific Discovery in 19th Century Germany," M.A. thesis, Hebrew University, Jerusalem. That Ben-David and Zloczower refer to more than diffusion in their discussions is fully recognized.

26. Joseph Ben-David, Roles and Innovations in Medicine, *American Journal of Sociology*, 65 (1960), 557-568.

27. Weber, *op. cit.*

28. Helmuth Plessner (ed.), *Untersuchungen zur Lage der deutschen Hochschulleherer* (Goettingen: Vandenhoeck and Ruprecht, 1953), 3 vols.; Zloczower, *op. cit.*

29. Talcott Parsons, "The Institutionalization of Social Science and the Problems of the Conference," in *Perspectives on a Troubled Decade* (New York: Conference on Science, Philosophy, and Religion, 1950); Terry N. Clark, Discontinuities in Social Research: The Case of the *Cours élémentaire de statistique administrative, Journal of the History of the Behavioral Sciences*, 3 (January 1967), 3-16.

30. This was a basic idea of Tarde's, cf. Clark, *Gabriel Tarde*; see also Rogers, *op. cit.*

31. For example, Stern, *op. cit.;* Ben-David, Roles and Innovations in Medicine, *op. cit.;* Terry N. Clark, Marginality, Eclecticism, and Innovation: René Worms and the *Revue Internationale de Sociologie, Revue Internationale de Sociologie*, forthcoming.

32. If some innovativeness is involved in original research, and if cosmopolitanism implies contacts with a wider range of persons and exposure to a larger number of spheres of activities, then the repeated findings that the more original and eminent researchers are "cosmopolitans" instead of "locals" supports the proposition presented here. Cf., for example, Paul F. Lazarsfeld and Wagner Thielens, *The Academic Mind* (Glencoe: Free Press, 1958); Lionel S. Lewis, On Prestige and Loyalty of University Faculty, *Administrative Science Quarterly*, 11 (March 1967), 629-642. This interpretation seems more appropriate to a large number of innovations than the specific consequences of a special form of marginality analyzed in Joseph Ben-David and Randall Collins, Social Factors in the Origins of a New Science: The Case of Psychology, *American Sociological Review*, 31 (August 1966), 451-465.

33. Hagstrom, *op. cit.*, p. 202; Sam D. Sieber and Paul F. Lazarsfeld, *The Organization of Educational Research* (New York: Bureau of Applied Social Research, Columbia University, 1966).

34. James A. Perkins, *The University in Transition* (Princeton: Princeton University, 1966); Logan Wilson (ed.), *Emerging Patterns in American Higher Education* (Washington, D. C.: American Council on Education, 1965).

35. On the inflexibility of budgets, see Theodore Caplow and Reece J. McGee, *The Academic Marketplace* (New York: Basic Books, 1958), pp. 136-144.

36. Matthew P. Miles (ed.), *Innovation in Education* (New York: Bureau of Publications, Teachers College, Columbia University, 1964), pp. 317-328.

37. David Riesman, in Lazarsfeld and Thielens, *op. cit.*, pp. 266-370; and Riesman, *Constraint and Variety in American Education* (Garden City, N. Y.: Doubleday-Anchor Books, 1958).

38. Lazarsfeld and Etzioni, *op. cit.*

39. Perkins, *op. cit.*

40. Clark Kerr, *The Uses of the University* (Cambridge: Harvard University, 1963).

41. Lazarsfeld and Etzioni, *op. cit.;* Ben-David and Zloczower, *op. cit.*

42. Robert K. Merton, "The Environment and the Innovating Organization: Some Conjectures and Proposals," in Gary A. Steiner (ed.), *The Creative Organization* (Chicago: University of Chicago, 1965), pp. 50-65.

43. Robert S. Morison (ed.)), *The Contemporary University: USA* (Cambridge: Houghton Mifflin, 1966), pp. 77-109.

44. On contracts and grants versus annual budgeting, see Kerr, *op. cit.;* Alexander King, Science and Technology in the New Europe, *Daedalus*, 43 (Winter 1964), 434-458; Norman Storer, The Coming Changes in American

Science, *Science*, 142 (October 25, 1963), 464-468; Jean Cuisenier, Recherche sur programme et recherche sur contrat, *Revue Française de Sociologie*, 7 (July-September 1966), 361-367.

45. More general discussions of the consequences of centralized decision-making patterns are found in Terry N. Clark, Power and Community Structure: Who Governs, Where, and When? *The Sociological Quarterly*, 8 (Summer 1967), 291-316; and Clark (ed.), *Community Structure and Decision-Making: Comparative Analyses* (San Francisco: Chandler, 1968).

46. Cf. Michel Crozier, *The Bureaucratic Phenomenon* (Chicago: University of Chicago, 1964); but contrast Amitai Etzioni, On the National Guidance of Science, *Administrative Science Quarterly*, 10 (March 1966), 466-487.

47. Contrast the stages for the differentiation model presented by Neil Smelser, *Social Change in the Industrial Revolution* (Chicago: University of Chicago, 1959); and Hagstrom, *op. cit.*, chs. 4-5.

48. Cf. Derek J. de Solla Price, Is Technology Historically Independent of Science; A Study in Statistical Historiography, *Technology and Culture*, 4 (Fall 1965), 553-568.

49. Thomas S. Kuhn, *The Structure of Scientific Revolution* (Chicago: University of Chicago, 1962); but also Joseph Ben-David, Scientific Growth: A Sociological View, *Minerva*, 2 (1964), 455-476.

50. Clark, *Institutionalization of Innovations . . .*, op. cit.

51. Stern, *op. cit.*

Part 2

Administrative Processes

THE ROLE OF THE GOVERNING BOARD

Algo D. Henderson

The College as a Corporation

A College or a University may be founded only in accordance with
the law, the usual instrument of establishment being the corporation.[1] In some states where the terms "college" and "university" are
protected by law, an institution to be founded under either name
must conform to stated criteria.[2] Before recent restrictions were
enacted, the use of both terms had been abused: many trade and
vocational schools had been given charters under the name "college"
or "university," and some small unitary colleges were chartered with
"university" as part of the name. In both instances, the institutions
have the right to continue to use their chartered terms.

Colleges and universities, as organizations in the public interest
and as creatures of the state, are subject to a degree of supervision by
the state, commonly only to the extent of seeing that the law is not
transgressed. In some states, however, they are subject to special
supervision. New York State, for example, requires that all institutions of higher education, public and private, meet certain standards
established by the Board of Regents of the University of the State of
New York—the supervising and coordinating agency of all of education within the state. Recently, many states have created commissions or boards that have similar responsibilities for the public
colleges and universities. In a few states, the state superintendent of
public instruction is authorized to approve the founding of public
junior or community colleges.

From *A G B Reports*, Association of Governing Boards of Universities and
Colleges, Vol. 10, No. 2, October 1967, pp. 3-31. Reprinted by permission of
the Association and the author.

Source and Nature of Legal Authority and Power

A corporation is a collection of individuals united by authority of law into one body under a special name and empowered to act in many respects as an individual. The laws relating to corporations differ among the states, but the legal principles are fairly uniform. As an artificial person, a corporation has only such purposes and powers as are conferred upon it. The express purposes of a corporation are enumerated in its charter, and ordinarily are stated in a general form that gives the corporation a reasonably broad scope for action. Among the express purposes granted to a college corporation is one that enables the institution to found and operate an educational program.

The powers are those granted by statute. The implied powers that characterize all corporations, by virtue of the legal form, include power to have a corporate name, to sue and be sued, to purchase and hold property, to have a corporate seal, and to make bylaws. The implied powers also include whatever actions may reasonably be necessary to carry out the express purposes.

Certain obvious advantages inhere in the corporate form of organization. The device permits a group of persons to act as a single party in the eyes of the law; thus it may make contracts. It has limited liability; thus members of its board—in the absence of fraud or misdealings—are not individually liable for the debts of the corporation. It has continuing life irrespective of changing personnel; thus it may remain as a legal entity within the term of life stipulated by the charter or as determined by law until the charter is cancelled.

A corporation may be organized by a group of individuals, usually three or more, who prepare a proposed charter and submit it to the appropriate officer of the state, usually the secretary of state, for approval. In some states—New York is an example—a board of education or the chief education officer is delegated the power to approve all requests for charters and amendments to charters of educational institutions. Most charters provide for their amendment; approval of amendments, following adoption by the board of trustees, may be secured from the state in the same manner as for the charter itself. The preparation of a charter or of proposed amendments is a technical matter that ordinarily requires the assistance of legal counsel.

The Charters and Bylaws

There are four legal devices for the creation of a college or university: (1) the constitution of the state may provide for a specific institution, (2) the legislature may, by statutory enactment, authorize the founding of an institution, (3) a charter for an institution may be granted under the laws pertaining to corporations, and (4) in some instances a taxing district may launch a college. The courts have not always been decisive whether a public college or university organized under two of the methods is a corporation because in some instances it may, from a legal standpoint, be a department of the state. Most public institutions, however, are deemed to be public corporations.

Creation by Constitutional Provision

In eleven states, one or more of the public universities have constitutional status,[3] with varying degrees of autonomy. Among those that enjoy the maximum of autonomy are the Universities of California and Michigan.

The Constitution in California provides:

> The University of California shall constitute a public trust, to be administered by the existing corporation known as "the Regents of the University of California," with full powers of organization and government, subject only to such legislative control as may be necessary to insure compliance with the terms of the endowments of the University and the security of its funds. . . . The University shall be entirely independent of all political or sectarian influence and kept free therefrom in the appointment of its regents and in the administration of its affairs. . . .[4]

The three largest universities in Michigan have constitutional status. This policy for the oldest of them, the University of Michigan, dates from 1850 when provision was incorporated into the state's constitution in the following phraseology:

> The board of regents shall have the general supervision of the university and of the direction and control of all expenditures from the university funds.[5]

The revised Constitution of 1963 alters the wording slightly, but retains the substance. Although it also provides for a state planning-coordinating board of education, seemingly it does not seriously disturb the autonomy of the regents for operations.

The members of the respective boards of these three Michigan universities are elected by the people. Hence, by virtue of their constitutional authority they are, as a body, responsible directly to the people rather than to the legislature. The board must, of course, appeal to the legislature for funds, so that, practically, a way is available for an aggressive or hostile legislature to influence the institution by threatening to cut its appropriations. The courts have repeatedly ruled, however, that once funds have been appropriated to the institution, it becomes the prerogative of the board to administer them.[6]

Constitutional provision gives a university a freedom of action in formulating educational policy and creating a program that does not prevail among all public institutions.[7] It also frees the institution from involvements with state bureaucratic operations and, to a degree, from harassments of political machinations. The principal disadvantage in the view of some is that the constitutional protection removes control too far from the governor and the legislature, who also represent the people. Legislators frequently complain that they are asked to appropriate huge sums from limited state revenues, but must make their judgments without adequate information and without legislative controls over the proposed uses of funds.

Constitutional provision for a public university is based on the theory that education should be a fourth branch of government, and, inasmuch as it underlies the well-being of the whole society, should be separated from the other, essentially political activities of government. Opponents of this theory contend that the nature and scope of all of education is a matter of public policy and, therefore, should be responsibilities of the governor and the legislature.

Creation by Statutory Enactment

The second method of creating a college or university is through statutory enactment by the state legislature. The statute may take one of two forms: the institution may be founded as a noncorporate department of the state government; or it may be created as a corporate entity by special act of the legislature. Under the first form the institution is required to follow all procedures laid down for the state government in the transaction of business, including compliance with civil service regulations, state purchasing systems, architectural planning, pre- and post-audits of accounts, and so forth. An occasional public administrator will contend that the state institutions of higher education should be a part of the executive branch of the government. Any significant advantages under this plan are difficult to conceive, and the disadvantages are obvious. In effect the several state officers or their subordinates, in their respective roles, are in position to exercise undue influence on educational policy and program. A college or university exists for purposes that are intangible in nature—the search for truth, for example. It cannot achieve them well when the operations are embedded within the bureaucracy of the state.

The majority of public institutions are corporations that are subject to the will of the governor and the legislature. Examples are many but include the Universities of Illinois, Kansas, Missouri, and Nebraska.[8] As a corporate entity, the institution has more freedom of action than if it were a department of the state. However, if the legislature desires to place restrictions upon the institution, it may do so. In addition, various state officers may deem it their prerogative to require conformity to regulations and procedures affecting state departments, and it is difficult for the university to refuse. Much, then, depends upon the precedents and the traditions that have accrued.

Before 1850, private colleges were often created by special act of a legislature, but thereafter many states adopted constitutional provisions forbidding the creation of corporations by special legislative act (because of alleged abuses in the creation of railroad and canal corporations). Today, the almost universal practice is to incorporate private colleges through petition to the appropriate state agency, usually the secretary of state.

Creation by Charter

The charter, the third form of foundation, applies to both public and private institutions, and since the middle of the last century has become the most common form. The nature of this instrument has already been discussed. Some are short and contain only the bare essentials; others are lengthy and spell out special provisions in detail.[9]

An example of a complex charter is that of Harvard University. In 1642, six years after its founding, the General Court of the Colony of Massachusetts Bay made provision for a board of Overseers for Harvard College. This board was a large, composite body designed to tighten the organization of the college. This board continues to the present day, revised, in 1865, only to permit alumni to elect the Overseers. The board proved to be unwieldy for the purpose of conducting operations, with the result that in 1650 the college was granted a charter by the General Court. This charter incorporated the President and Fellows of Harvard College. Thus, Harvard University may be said to have two boards, in a sense analogous to the two houses of a legislature.[10] The corporate powers clearly reside in the President and Fellows. Yet the Overseers have genuine influence on policy and program; they must approve appointment of personnel and proposed bylaws affecting general policies of the university; they may veto the actions of the governing board, though they rarely do so; and they have the important function of visitation which is carried on by the approximately forty visiting committees they have created. (Provision is made at many institutions for boards of visitors, often composed of alumni and distinguished citizens.) Only a few institutions have formalized dual boards. Western Reserve University, for example, recently provided for a Board of Trustees for administrative affairs and a Board of Governors of 62 for educational matters.

Function of Bylaws

Corporations have the authority to make bylaws, and most of them do so. Bylaws must be consistent with the provisions of the charter. They usually contain sections relating to the organization of the board, the officers, the committees, quorums for various purposes, time and place for meetings, and specifications relating to the operation of the institution. Inasmuch as a board of trustees has the full legal power within the institution but ordinarily adheres to the tradition that the officers and faculty shall formulate and operate the educational program, a highly important provision or series of them in the bylaws may constitute delegations of authority to officers and to the faculty. Thus, the bylaws of a large university may be a comprehensive document containing hundreds of provisions that spell out the delegations made by the board.

Creation by a Taxing District

Under the fourth form of organization, a taxing district has power to found and operate an institution of higher education. Examples are a school district that operates a community junior college, and a municipality that has a municipal college or university. For example, the New York law on community colleges provides:

Any county, city or intermediate school district acting through its local legislative body or board, or other appropriate governing agency may by local law, resolution or ordinance, and pursuant to the master plan, standards and regulations prescribed by the State University trustees and with the approval of said trustees:
   a. Establish a community college.
   b. Elect to participate in and pay an appropriate share of the expenses involved in the community college program of any other local sponsor consenting to such arrangement.
   c. Combine with one or more other local sponsors for the joint establishment and operation of a community college.[11]

Most public junior colleges are created by an existing school district or by the establishment of a junior college taxing district. The "model" phraseology suggested jointly by the Council of State Governments and the American Association of Junior Colleges for an enabling statute for the creation of public junior colleges recommends "any one or more interested cities, counties or other subdivisions of the state" may, after satisfying certain criteria, establish such a college. The national trend strongly favors the creation of special junior college districts.

The Theory of Governing Boards

The charter of a corporation is given to a group of individuals who have petitioned for it, or who have been appointed by a governor, or who otherwise have come into existence as a group. The charter creates the board, and the board thus becomes the corporation and exercises the powers of the corporation. The board operates as a unit; individual members have no authority to act for the corporation or to endeavor to direct its affairs unless the board as a whole has given specific authorization for this purpose.

The charter ordinarily gives the board complete power within the limits of its express purposes and the implied authority. Charters sometimes mention specific officers, the faculty, alumni, boards of visitors, and so forth, with some indication of duties and responsibilities. Legally, all such provisions are delegations of the authority vested in the board itself, for the state can have only one central body directly responsible to it.

Board members of colleges and universities are commonly called "trustees"—literally, because they are involved in trust relationships. Among the trust responsibilities of the body are those to manage the institution in the public interest, to account to official bodies and to the public for actions taken and funds used, to carry out the ethical responsibilities involved in the education of youth, to hold title to and to administer endowment funds, and to execute other specific trusts. In part, these responsibilities are the same for any director or trustee of any nonprofit or charitable organization: no individual may secure any personal financial advantage or benefit. In part, they represent the duties of a trustee under a legal trust: title is given to one party but the beneficial interest lies in others. The holder of the title is a "trustee" and he is responsible under the law to administer the trust faithfully in accordance with its conditions. A college receives many trust funds to administer. Members of boards whose experience has been limited to the boards of business corporations or who do not understand the legal theory of trusts sometimes fail in their responsibilities as trustees of an educational institution because they have not comprehended the nature of the trust.

The State of New York has an interesting provision under which the Board of Regents of the University of the State of New York may summon to a hearing any trustee or group of trustees who appear not to be administering their trust responsibilities faithfully.[12] In other states legal action, frequently by the attorney general, may be brought to cause trustees to account for their trust. In either instance, a trustee may be dismissed for reasons of violation of the trust provisions.

Types of Boards and Membership

Governing boards are variously named: board of trustees, board of control, board of regents, board of education, and many occasional variations. According to Wicke, about 80 percent of the independent institutions and 50 percent of public institutions use the term "board of trustees."[13]

Whatever the name, the essential characteristics of authority and responsibility for the institution are the same. Variations in scope occur, as when a board of education is responsible for the public schools as well as for the state colleges that train teachers, or when a board of regents, as in New York, is given statutory charge of licensing for the professions.

Size and Selection

Numbers of board members have varied widely—from three to 257.[14] Membership of boards of state institutions usually runs between seven and 12, but the University of North Carolina has 100, ten of whom must be women. The median size is ten for public institutions and 24 for private ones.[15] Many authorities have advocated relatively small boards. Eliot liked seven. [16] Reeves and Russell recommended from seven to nine.[17] A smaller board— between seven and 20—can be representative, is easier to get together for meetings, and incurs less expense for meetings. Its members are likely to take their individual responsibilities seriously, and the chairman can engage the group in effective discussions. A larger board, however, may have advantages accruing from wider representation of interested parties, and many institutions have found the combination of a small board of trustees and a larger board of visitors (or several such committees) to be a productive arrangement.

Boards are selected in many ways. In independent institutions it has been the custom for the board to be self-perpetuating, that is, to have the power to elect new members to fill vacancies. In church-sponsored colleges, the appropriate church body may name the trustees or control their appointment through specifying their qualifications. Among public institutions, practices vary—election by the public, appointment by the governor, selection by the houses of the legislature, or a combination of these. Over-all, it has become rather common for charters to be amended to permit alumni to select some portion of the trustees, an instance of an interest group securing representation on the board.

Views on Faculty Representation

The question has often arisen whether the faculty should be represented on the board. A few colleges and universities have done so and apparently with good results. In many foreign universities a faculty council is the board or dominates it through majority membership. The American practice is the opposite. Generally speaking, the foreign universities have not demonstrated results superior to the American plan. In some countries these institutions are really controlled by a national ministry of education.

It can be argued that the primary work of an institution is the operation of an educational program; therefore, those who know most about the job—the professors—should be represented on the board. Many faculty have thus contended. Their principal concern usually is to protect academic freedom, about which they have a better understanding and feel more zealous than do lay trustees. They may, however, influence the board in other desirable ways because of their expertness of knowledge and because they must implement many of the decisions. On the other hand, a faculty-dominated board can become highly introverted and lead the institution down the most conservative of academic paths to the point that it becomes remote from the "real world of affairs."

The opposing contentions cite the advantages of having members who are personally free from involvement, who can look at the institution and its problems objectively and disinterestedly. The infusion of faculty into the board, it is said, can lead to muddy waters in administrative responsibility. If the lay members represent a variety of occupations, civic interests, and personal backgrounds, as they should, they can bring fresh perspective to education. Some boards have solved the problem of including professional educators by electing distinguished members from other faculties and thus have gained the advantage of expert knowledge but avoided involving institutional personnel. The balance of arguments seems to favor having some professional educators on the board, whether from the inside or outside, or both.[18] Since the board of trustees represents the public interest, it seems best to provide that lay members shall be in the majority.

Charters sometimes make special provision to allocate the faculty responsibility for the educational program and for making and enforcing rules and regulations pertaining to the students, but always subject to the express or implied delegation of authority from the trustees.[19]

The author believes in the value of informal exchanges between faculty members and trustees, and in an earlier volume discussed the matter:

> Theoretically the trustees are the representatives of the public; by controlling policies and finances they insure that the institution is fulfilling its social duties and proceeding on a sound educational path. Actually this is what the Antioch trustees do. Not having to spend their two day session in minute discussion of college investments and administrative detail, they can find time to consider the real questions of the institution's role in society and its larger social usefulness . . . These men and women provide an excellent sounding board not only for the present program of the college but for contemplated changes and additions. And, finally they represent to the college a cross section of public opinion concerning how far and how fast we can advisedly go in the direction of educational change. Antioch trustees are eager to get acquainted with both faculty and students and to find out how those inside the institution feel and think. The trustees meet regularly with the administrative council; they stay in faculty homes; they meet groups of the faculty informally for discussion; and joint faculty-trustee dinners are arranged. A feature of almost every meeting of the board of trustees is a report from the community manager or from a student group, usually followed by an informal discussion and question period. Thus the trustees can form first hand judgments about the Antioch personnel who are behind the policies and can function as part of the group.[20]

Criticisms of Membership and Proposals for Reform

The composition of most boards becomes skewed in favor of the upper socioeconomic segments of society. This leads to criticisms of the American practice of using exclusively lay boards and of the composition of lay boards. It has been said that trustees do not understand higher education and that many members are not even well educated. The criticism continues along several lines: membership is biased strongly in favor of businessmen, lawyers, persons of wealth, and older people; boards, whose dealings are with problems that affect young people, have members who are too old and conservative when, instead, genuinely progressive leadership is required; large segments of the public—notably women, labor, and the lower socioeconomic classes—are not represented.

Thorstein Veblen, a voluble critic, stated the more extreme view of the faculty: "Plato's classic scheme of folly, which would have the philosophers take over the management of affairs, has been turned on its head; the men of affairs have taken over the direction of the pursuit of knowledge."[21] Veblen advocated that the professional job be left in the hands of the profession. His view has been shared widely by faculty.

The Veblen-faculty criticism has a degree of consistency with that of certain students. The students of the Free Speech Movement of the University of California in 1964 and 1965 voiced criticisms of the "establishment" along the following line of reasoning:

> Most of the Regents, FSM leaders argued, are not qualified "academically" to govern a university; moreover, they are not non-political, as the Constitution requires. Indeed, the FSM suggested, it is naive to believe that this is possible. Regents have their own views of proper social policy, and their interests are intimately bound up with those views. Since most of the Regents are associated with large and successful commercial, industrial, or financial corporations, the FSM leaders reasoned, it is to be expected that they will strongly favor preservation of the *status quo*, will opt for stability and for little change of existing "power-relations" in society. The FSM charged the Regents with pursuing such interests by systematic attempts to suppress student political action for social change.[22]

The Board and Academic Freedom

This charge by students seems to add a dimension to the age-old argument about academic freedom. Faculty who voice or publish criticisms of existing social behavior and structure invariably invoke the principles of academic freedom to protect their position. The purpose of academic freedom is to assure freedom in search for truth. Some students apparently feel that there should be complete freedom in speech and social action. The issue of freedom goes beyond this discussion, but the Berkeley controversy sheds light on the problem of maintaining the essential function of a university, which includes inquiry into controversial issues, concern with finding solutions to the unresolved issues of the day, and a search for the good life.

A prime responsibility of the board is to protect the institution from the wrath of groups that would destroy the function. The board must guard zealously the privilege of objective search and responsible advocacy regarding change in our society; it must support the administration and faculty in any endeavor to direct the motivations and energies of students of high intellectual ability and strong social sensibility into constructive educational channels.[23] At the same time, it must support the administration in avoiding impairment of freedom because of actions of individuals—faculty and students—whose minds are controlled by external groups or whose agitation is not the fruit of intellectual inquiry. The dividing line is sometimes hard to identify, but it is better to err in the direction of freedom than to stifle speech and action.

Members of governing boards have a high duty to society to acquire for themselves a thorough understanding of the essential nature of an institution of higher learning. The very existence of the problem implies the great care that should be exercised in selecting board members. It suggests that members should be open-minded on controversial issues and objective in making inquiry.

Need for Broader Representation

Hubert Beck has supplied considerable data about the representativeness of trustees, their ages, and their interests. Among his sample of 734 trustees from 30 universities of high prestige, he discovered only 36 educators of any type, including several presidents. Business and professional people held 71 percent of the posts. The clergy, who a century ago controlled privately financed American higher education, in 1947 occupied only 6.6 percent of the positions, and three-fifths of them were Catholic priests. Forty-one percent were in some social register or exclusive club; only 3.4 percent were women.[24] Forty-seven percent were sixty years of age or over. Beck concluded that ". . . the observed pattern in trustee selection was closely consistent with the high value current American society places on pecuniary success, the high prestige and power enjoyed by certain occupations characterized by high pecuniary reward, and the common tendency to identify achievement of these awards with the furtherance of the public welfare."[25] He concluded in general that trusteeships go to persons who have resources, time, and prestige.

Data that suggest that the characteristics of members have not changed were collected in 1965 by Troy Duster. The median age was sixty, and the median income between $50,000 and $75,000 per year. In his sample of 306 trustees, there were ten professors, eight clergymen, one Negro and one labor official.[26]

It is probably obvious that people with these qualifications have many contributions (other types, as well as money) to make to our colleges and universities. The question arises not in criticism of any individuals but to ask whether the boards should not be more representative than they are. Would there not be value in giving a larger representation to younger men and women who are closer in age to students and whose viewpoints would be less inhibited by acquired interest that they are accustomed to protect? Since women constitute more than 40 percent of enrollments, are women sufficiently represented on the boards? Men from organized labor are on the boards of only a handful of institutions; should they not be more widely represented? Such questions seem pertinent.

Beck suggested a number of reforms: fix a definite retirement age (with, perhaps, honorary trusteeship following); revise the method of co-optation so that the in-group would not always recruit from among its own type; use a principle of broad representation, for example, draw in—from the public—representatives of business, the professions, agriculture, and labor, and—from the universities themselves—faculty, alumni, and students: make the term of office at least four years and possibly six or eight.[27]

Beck's data confirm an impression that board members too often are selected for their ability to make gifts to the institution. Much as the money is needed, the policy seems unwise. In the first place, it does not always produce the desired results. But second, and of greater importance, it puts into the hands of persons chosen on a single criterion the governance of institutions in which there is a substantial public interest. Our colleges and universities deserve to be governed by persons who have been selected on grounds other than sheer expediency.

Functions of the Board

Legally, the board of trustees has the full authority and responsibility for the institution; there is no way in which it can avoid its charge. Customarily in higher education, however, a board delegates large areas of authority. The institution employs faculty members who have professional competence, and to them the board and president entrust the educational program—a practice that was started even before lay boards came into existence.

Basic Responsibilities

Burgess, a trustee of Northwestern University, defined the basic duties of trustees as three: (1) to select a president and to have a hand in selecting other of the officers who might logically be in line to succeed the president, (2) to declare the principal objectives and policies of the institution (with the president and other officers), and (3) to preserve and invest the assets of the institution.[28]

Hughes, a distinguished university president, divided the responsibilities of the board into two categories, those that are specific and those that pertain to policies. As specific, he listed the responsibility to "hold all property, authorize the budget and budget changes, fix policies, appoint the president, and serve as a court of final appeal in all matters." The responsibility for policy formation, Hughes saw as including size of the institution, the general admission requirements, the campus and the buildings, the scope of the work, the policies affecting the faculty, the library, the chapel, scholarships, student activities, athletics, fraternities and sororities, residence halls, the placement of students and graduates, and alumni relations. To draw the distinction between the responsibilities of the board and of the faculty, he said, "The faculty, under the board, teaches all students, determines all curricula and courses to be offered and classes to be taught, and assigns classes to teachers, determines grades, who shall graduate and who shall receive degrees, both in course and honorary."[29]

Most authorities agree that the selection—and sometimes the dismissal—of the president of the institution is the single most important responsibility of the trustees. This statement in no way implies that the trustees should not consult with the faculty and other parties concerning nominees for the position. A highly desirable procedure is to have parallel committees, frequent consultations, and final agreement on the choice. The faculty must recognize, however, that the final responsibility lies with the board.

The board's duty to declare the principal objectives and policies of the institution derives from the charter. Once formulated at the time of the initiation of the institution, thereafter the board will ordinarily consult through the president with the faculty on these matters. Policies need frequent review and reconsideration if the institution is to attain fully its objectives in education and research.

Responsibility for Fiscal Affairs and Appointments

Inasmuch as the board holds title to the property of the institution, it feels keen responsibility for its preservation and management.[30]

Money and people are two principal ingredients in the conduct of any operation. Governing boards should be kept fully informed by the president about the acquisition and status of funds and about the employment of key personnel.

An important vehicle through which to plan, implement, and control a college or university is by controlling the use of funds—the budget. Usually the board will require that the budget be submitted for its inspection and approval. Although the board does not participate in the formulation of the budget, it may have discussed and laid down the guidelines for its preparation. In general:

... it can and should ensure that the budgetary operation has been conducted in a sound fashion, that it adequately reflects the aims of the institution, that economy is being practiced, and that there is balance and good sense in the whole process. Without second-guessing the president on specific items, the board may exercise a powerful long-range influence on budgets by throwing the weight of its opinion and judgment in one direction or another.[31]

A president would be unwise not to seek the approval of his board on appointments to top-level administrative posts, especially as provost, vice-president, or dean. Boards sometimes claim the prerogative of identifying and appointing these officers. Such actions are inconsistent with the policy of acting through a single executive officer, the president; and if the president yields his own prerogative of recommendation, he is in for future trouble. Traditionally, boards have approved faculty appointments, by voting a list proposed by the president, which has been arrived at in collaboration with appropriate segments of the faculty. Under this plan, if a member of the board has any objection to an appointment, the case can be discussed by the president with the board. Board approval of appointments can be justified on two grounds: (1) the courts have held that a board may not abdicate the responsibilities that are specifically given to it; and (2) the president needs the understanding support of the board for the policies affecting faculty appointment and tenure.

During their one- or two-day meetings, boards usually are deluged with materials that relate to formal approvals. An example of one of these items might be the request to approve from 50 to 200 faculty appointments, with most of the information about each person being given in a one-page "Who's Who" memo. Formal approval, based upon confidence in the recommending officers, is about all that can reasonably be expected.

Improving the Quality of Deliberations

Some boards have endeavored to open the way for more productive use of their time in considering basic policy and long-range planning. This approach can be illustrated by an action at the University of Chicago. A trustee of Chicago, Laird Bell, expressed fresh views about functions of the governing board and described the attempt made at Chicago to delegate more complete authority to the president. He stated:

Logically the trustees as the controlling body have the right—and in fact the duty—to determine what *kind* of education shall be offered. As custodians of the property and funds they are bound to see that they are devoted to the purposes for which they were given. They are free (subject to terms of their charter and endowments of course) to determine whether the institution shall be a liberal arts college, a technical school, a professional school or teachers college, whether new projects shall be undertaken, new schools or institutes created, existing ones liquidated, and so on. They also can and should have much influence on what might be called the tone of the institution. But once overall policy is decided it *ought* to be true that the educational experts should determine how the policy is to be implemented. Curricula, personnel, promotions, tenure and the like should be prescribed by the experts.[32]

The view expressed by Bell, a trustee, is similar to a position taken by Clark Kerr during his presidency of one of the largest universities. At a meeting of the Board of Regents of the University of California on June 18, 1965, Kerr made recommendations for reorganizing some of the procedures of governance. In support of them:

He stated that his proposals assume that The Regents may be willing to reverse their historical approach to their responsibilities and delegate to the administration responsibility for all matters not specifically reserved for action by the Board. He pointed out that his proposals do not contemplate that the Regents would relinquish their traditional authority over and responsibility for the affairs of the University, but, rather, that they would devote their time to matters involving major policy decisions, major appointments, review of performance, etc.[33]

To illustrate the functioning of the board at Chicago, Bell described how the trustees passed motions giving the president authority to make all appointments to staff and faculty subject to (1) departmental approval and (2) referral to the board of cases likely to involve public criticism. As a further illustration, he described the duality of responsibility of the chancellor (president) and the council of the university senate regarding the educational program: ordinarily they arrive at agreement, but in the event of a deadlock the matter is carried to the trustees for a decision. This role for the board seems to concur with Hughes' idea of using the body as a court of appeals.

Assuming that Burgess has defined aptly the basic functions of the governing board, and the Hughes has shed light on the functions as they are usually carried out, Bell and Kerr have offered constructive suggestions for performing the functions in a manner that makes optimum use of members' wisdom and energies. The ability to operate with the degree of delegation of authority that the views of Bell and Kerr implied will depend, of course, upon the mutuality of confidence that exists between the board and its executive officer. Because the functions of trustees of a college or university differ from those of directors of business corporations—their trust responsibilities, the authority delegated to faculty for academic matters, the intangible nature of the products of teaching and of research—new members should be given an orientation to their role. Probably this should be done by the president and the chairman.

Role of the Executive Officer

The board invariably selects the executive officer, In nearly all American institutions he is given the title "president," although in a few it is "chancellor," and in a few junior colleges it is "director" or "dean." Universities of other countries use such titles as "vice-chancellor," "rector," "principal," or "president."

In one sense the executive officer is president of the educational corporation, just as he would be in any other corporation. In another sense, he is the educational leader of the institution. The point that the president is the *executive* officer must be emphasized. He is responsible for carrying into operation the policies and decisions of the board. By virtue of the board's authority, it is his duty to inform that body about the operations, the achievements, and the problems of the institution. Ordinarily he makes recommendations to the board for actions to be taken by it. It is equally the responsibility of individual board members to avoid meddling in the internal affairs of the institution.

Practice varies with respect to whether the president is a member and also chairman of the board. Eliot advocated that the president should be chairman so that he may serve as "leader and inspirer" at their sessions.[34] An additional argument is that, inasmuch as the president is the liaison officer between the board and the faculty, and if he is able to preside over the deliberations of both bodies, he is in a position to coordinate all activities effectively. This plan seems to offer efficiency, for when the board has a separate chairman, it is usually the president who must prepare the agenda (which may consist of dozens or hundreds of items) and then coach the chairman on the actions that should be taken. But it can be argued that the board employs the president and, therefore, he should report to it, rather than being in a command position or even a member of the body. A lay chairman who is a man of distinction and influence can help the institution substantially if he supports the president and also makes himself available for advice and counsel and for public contacts. Effective administration suggests that the advantage lies in having the president serve as the presiding officer, an arrangement that also avoids the occasional situation where the chairman "takes over" the prerogatives of the president.

Sometimes when the president is not the presiding officer of the board, he is designated as secretary. In this position he can help control the agenda and can insist that decisions be clearly stated and recorded. Although many boards use secretarial staff to take minutes—a practice to be commended—others require the secretary to do this. Thus the president may be kept occupied in making clerical notes when his leadership in discussion is needed. In this role, the board sometimes treats him as a flunky.

If someone other than the president is chairman of the board, it is of the highest importance that the two men have a strong personal rapport and a good working relationship. To achieve this, the president must consult the chairman frequently on important matters, keeping him fully informed, and the chairman on his part must use discretion in his actions by consulting carefully with the president. If the two men do not find much common agreement on policy formation or if they are temperamentally unable to work well together, the president may as well recognize that he is on his way out.

Although the president is dependent on the board for support, inasmuch as it has full control over his position and tenure, the board is dependent upon the president as its executive officer. Board members who meet once a month, or in some cases as rarely as once a year, cannot keep well abreast of the institution's affairs and need to have their memories refreshed at nearly every meeting. Furthermore, since members typically are not educators, they must rely heavily upon the president for leadership.

Administrative Relationships

In early practice, many boards required that the chief financial officer as well as the president report directly to them. The theory was that the board was responsible for finances and that it needed to have an officer in charge independent of the president; thus also the president would be free to devote himself to education. This proved to be unrealistic in that the president has never been able to divest himself of the principal financial responsibility. The plan also is inconsistent with the concept, now universally approved by authorities, that the board should relate to the administration through a single officer, the president. Modern accounting practices—internal audits, and post-audits by state auditors or certified public accountants—protect the board from the misuse of funds.

Having subordinate officers—the various vice-presidents, the provost, the treasurer—attend meetings of the board as assistants to the president is a different matter. Many presidents wish to bring selected principal staff officers to most of the meetings, so that their knowledge and advice will be available. These officers, in turn, gain perspective on the work of the institution and the interests of the board. This practice is to be commended, but the wise president will maintain careful control by making it clear that the officers are present, at his request, to render assistance to him in connection with his responsibilities to the board.[35]

The procedure described above relates to the administration of the institution. When the board has occasion to provide for a substantive review of policy and practice, it should seek the full cooperation of the president. It may, however, be advisable to appoint a study director who would report directly to the board.

Sometimes faculties feel that they should appoint representatives to sit in on board meetings to express the views of the faculty. The matter of having faculty serve as members has been discussed; similar arguments, pro and con, can be applied to their official attendance at the meetings. As noted above, there are other techniques which the president can use to facilitate communication between the faculty and trustees. Of course, when a board opens meetings to the public, faculty may attend as part of the audience.

Board Meetings

Customarily the president and his staff assistants prepare for meetings of the board of trustees by readying the agenda, arranged as an order of business. Also customarily agenda are supplemented by memoranda, which include analyses of problems and justifications of recommendations. Unless the board has authorized the president to handle matters without reference to it (as in the illustration from the University of Chicago given above), he must present for the board's consideration all matters pertaining to the operations of the institution—budget plans, building needs and maintenance, appointments to the faculty, authorizations of programs, recommendations for the granting of diplomas, data about financial requirements, and so forth. Clearly, the items requiring attention and the data to support recommendations become voluminous. In view of the demands on the board, it is of utmost importance that all communications prepared for its attention cover the subject matter succinctly and are readable so that members can digest the ideas in advance of the meeting.

Delegation of Responsibilities

Not many boards have had the courage shown at the University of Chicago to turn over substantial authority to the president and his staff. A simple procedure would be for the board to require the president to report on all actions that lie within its province but to relinquish the right to act separately upon each item. The president would, in effect, be given a vote of confidence or would be advised of differences of viewpoint on the part of the board. Discussions of the differences could become the basis for altered actions in the future. In genuinely serious cases, actions taken might be reversed inasmuch as the board does possess veto power. This procedure makes an appropriate and clear distinction between policy promotion, a board function, and administration, the responsibility of the president.

The handling of large numbers of detailed items can readily give rise to another difficulty. Many boards divide their work among subcommittees and many specify that a member of the administrative staff be delegated to meet with the subcommittee whose concern is in line with this function. Whether the committee meets alone or with a vice-president or dean, the president is likely left out of the discussion. Thus to a degree he loses contact with, and control over, actions being taken. A better solution suggests having a limited number of subcommittees whose meetings are held at intervals scheduled to permit the president to attend.

According to Wicke, subcommittees most frequently found are: executive, investment, buildings and grounds, and faculty, followed by budget, audit, student affairs, athletics, and nominations.[36] In each institution the board should determine the number and role of subcommittees only after it has clearly defined its own functions. Often an executive committee is appointed with power to act between board meetings subject to ratification by the board.

Some presidents have loaded the board with so much detail about campus, buildings, finances, and public relations that it can find little time to devote to the educational program. The ulterior but deliberate purpose may be to keep the board so occupied as to give the faculty a freer rein in managing the educational program. It seems questionable, however, that trustees can act imaginatively and effectively in behalf of the institution if they are kept at arm's length from the institution's main job. The best practice seems that of keeping the trustees fully informed and, indeed, inviting them to participate in discussions about educational objectives and program. Under such a policy, many presidents have been successful in persuading the trustees to leave decisions affecting educational policy and program to the faculty, subject only to review from time to time.

Open Meetings

At a number of public institutions issue has been made in recent years whether board meetings should be open to the public, including representatives of the press, faculty, and students. The contention goes: The institution uses public funds, renders public services, and engages in educational activities of great importance to taxpayers, parents, faculty, and students; these matters should be debated in public, and the public should get its news direct from the scene of action rather than from news stories prepared by the institution. Further, some faculty and student groups contend they should have the privilege of addressing the board on matters of educational and environmental concern. On the other hand, it is argued: The board members are representatives of the public, the lay board existing for this very purpose; the president should be the spokesman about all internal matters; the presence of outside parties not directly responsible for decisions damps the agenda and the discussion; and, the meetings can be conducted more efficiently when only board members are present and participating. In any event, it is said, the institution normally does publicize the principal actions taken at board meetings, and publishes annual reports detailing both achievements and finances.

The pressures for open meetings have gradually caused more public institutions to open their board meetings. In some states, the law has been revised to require that meetings be open but with the privilege retained of holding executive sessions. Often, when meetings are public, board members hold "informal" gatherings where controversial issues are discussed prior to the formal meeting. The values of public meetings have not been fully assessed. In the absence of a specific law, a possible compromise is for the board, exercising its powers to govern itself, to hold some executive sessions, opening other sessions to the public.

Informal Services of Trustees

The discussion thus far has been limited to the official duties of the members of a board. Many college presidents obtain from their trustees additional contributions of service, especially for public relations purposes. Indeed, among private colleges it is not uncommon for board members to be chosen primarily for their capacity to "deliver" in this respect. The additional activities most often involve raising money for the institution and publicizing it with parent and student groups. Some colleges rely heavily on their trustees individually and as a group to raise funds to balance the budget, to build plant, to provide scholarships, and so on. In a public institution, the members can give the president strong support in working with the legislature and governor.

A board that is composed of men of high caliber can bring to the institution advantages not necessarily implicit in their official duties. They can serve the president as a source of readily available consultation and inspiration in discussing educational problems and ideas. He may gain added perspective from their more disinterested viewpoints. The members, drawing on their experience in industrial laboratories, civic and cultural activities, the professions, and the like, may be more alert than the faculty to certain educational needs and means of implementation. A member can perform a needed function by asking questions that provoke fresh thinking. In essence, the board may serve as a "balance wheel" in the ongoing development of the institution.

Another value of a strong board lies in the support that its members can give the president, his faculty, and the institution in times of crises. Assuming that the trustees have been kept fully informed about problems, if a crisis causes the institution to become the subject of controversial discussion, the trustees can do much to stabilize the situation. As trustees, they have a responsibility to weigh the issues carefully and to consider them in the frame of fundamental objectives of an institution of higher learning. Thus, their seasoned judgment can be better grounded than the emotionally derived opinion of segments of the public. As laymen and persons of some prominence whose opinions are respected, they can do much, through appropriate statements, to allay suspicions and fears. They can also provide the president a sense of security for dealing with the problem.

A primary, but unofficial, role for trustees is to represent the institution to the public.

Interinstitutional Boards

A college or university may, under certain circumstances, be subject both to an operating board and to a high-level coordinating board. The best example among public institutions is the case where the state regards its several public colleges as constituting a system of higher education for the state. Some states have one board as the board of control of all the institutions. But in other instances each institution may continue to have its own board, and may also be subject to certain policies enunciated by a state board that performs broad roles of planning and coordination. An illustration occurs in California, where the public junior colleges have their individual operating boards but also are under the state board of education, the several state colleges have an operating-coordinating board, the state university with its several campuses has an operating board, and above all is a board that does certain over-all planning and coordinates all of higher education. This subject is too involved for detailed analysis at this point.

These complex systems of governance give rise, however, to certain kinds of problems of administration. A primary purpose of a planning-coordinating board is to project plans for the state as a whole, to allocate to particular institutions their general roles, and to take steps to avoid unnecessary overlapping. The top-level board may thus persuade the legislature to assign to a particular institution its role in the state system, within which it will be required to operate. Proposals for new programs, for additions to programs, and for new budget may be required to be approved by the coordinating board before they can be presented to the appropriate public authorities. In certain respects this protocol inhibits the actions of the individual institutions. Yet state legislatures have sometimes been so confused by the competition and bitter rivalries displayed among state institutions that they have sought a means to bring about a degree of coordination.[37]

Summary

Colleges and universities are corporations governed by boards of trustees. Some are public; others are private, nonprofit corporations. Ordinarily the boards are composed of lay personnel, the theory being that they are representative of the public who, in turn, are interested in the welfare of the institution. In legal theory, the board has complete authority and responsibility for the institution. In practice, by reason of tradition and the professional competence of the faculty, much of the authority of the board is delegated to the officers and faculty. As a rule of thumb, the faculty largely determines the program and standards for educating students, and the trustees take direct responsibility to assure that the plant is adequate, finances are obtained and well used, a president is selected, and overall policies are determined. The president becomes the executive officer of the board who works, in effect, in liaison capacity with the faculty and with the board.

The lay board as found in the United States is unique among the universities of the world. It has some advantages of involving representatives of the general public in the formation of policy, in overseeing the management of the institution, and in assisting the institution to secure adequate resources. The board, however, has not been without criticism, especially because its ranks include few educators, and membership tends to be skewed toward the high socioeconomic classes. Over-all, the board of trustees hold a vital position in the educational institution, yet its role commonly is not well understood by any of the parties involved.

Footnotes

1. As an illustration, see "General Corporation Act," *Compiled Laws of the State of Michigan,* 1948, and *Supplements,* §§ 450.1-450.696; especially §§ 450.117;450.124-450.127;450.170-450.177.

2. *Ibid.,* "Educational Corporations," § 450.171; see also *CL* 1948, 390.871, "Community College Defined."

3. Fred W. Hicks, "The Constitutional Autonomy of the University of Michigan and Its Significance in the Development of a State University" (Unpublished Ph.D. dissertation; Center for the Study of Higher Education, University of Michigan, 1963).

4. Constitution, State of California, Art. xi, § 5.

5. Constitution of Michigan of 1908, Art. xi, § 5.

6. See *Michigan Statutes Annotated* (Chicago: Callaghan & Co., 1936), I, 430-31.

7. See Edward C. Elliott and M. M. Chambers, *The Colleges and the Courts* (New York: Carnegie Foundation for the Advancement of Teaching, 1936), for details on this and the several following paragraphs.

8. For a specific instance, see Public Act No. 120 of 1960, § 15.1852, Grand Valley State College; *Michigan Statutes Annotated* (Chicago: Callaghan & Co., 1960), pp. 186-88.

9. Edward C. Elliott and M. M. Chambers, *Charters and Basic Laws of Selected American Universities and Colleges* (New York: Carnegie Foundation for the Advancement of Teaching, 1934), 640 pp. This volume sets forth the charters of a considerable number of American universities. It also gives the constitutional provisions and the statutes, as of the publication date of the book, that provided for the universities in certain states.

10. Charles W. Eliot, *University Administration* (New York: Houghton Mifflin Co., 1908), pp. 48-65.

11. New York State Laws of 1948, Ch. 696, Art. 126, § 6302.

12. The Board of Regents in New York "may remove any trustee of a corporation created by them for misconduct, incapacity, neglect of duty, or where it appears to the satisfaction of the regents that the corporation has failed or refuses to carry into effect its educational purposes." See *McKinney's*

Consolidated Law of New York Annotated, Book 16, pt. 1 (tit. 1, art. 5, § 226, ¶ 4), 1953, pp. 97-98.

13. Myron F. Wicke, *Handbook for Trustees* (Nashville, Tenn.: Board of Education, Methodist Church, 1957), 57 pp.

14. E. C. Elliott, M. M. Chambers, and William A. Ashbrook, *The Government of Higher Education* (New York: American Book Co., 1935), p. 26.

15. "The Role of the College and University Trustee" (New York: Carnegie Foundation for the Advancement of Teaching), p. 6.

16. Charles W. Eliot, *op. cit.*, p. 3.

17. Floyd W. Reeves, John Dale Russell, *et al.*, *The Liberal Arts College* (Chicago: University of Chicago Press, 1932), p. 67.

18. For recommendations from the teachers' viewpoints see the "Statement of Principles" of Committee T, American Association of University Professors.

19. For examples of such charters, see Edward C. Elliott and M. M. Chambers, *Charters and Basic Laws of Selected American Universities and Colleges*, charter of George Washington University, pp. 197-98, or charter of the University of California, pp. 64-78, Art. I, III, V.

20. Algo D. Henderson and Dorothy Hall, *Antioch College: Its Design for Liberal Education* (New York: Harper & Bros., 1946), pp. 210-11.

21. Thorstein Veblen, *The Higher Learning in America* (New York: Sagamore Press, 1957), p. 57.

22. Terry F. Lunsford, *The "Free Speech" Crises at Berkeley, 1964-1965: Some Issues for Social and Legal Research* (Mimeographed; Berkeley: Center for Research and Development in Higher Education and Center for the Study of Law and Society, University of California, December 1965), p. 126.

23. There is much evidence that students who are articulate about the ills of society and who engage in social action are high in intellectual potential. See Paul Heist, "Intellect and Commitment: The Faces of Discontent" (Mimeographed; Berkeley: Center for the Study of Higher Education, University of California, 1965).

24. Hubert Park Beck, *Men Who Control Our Universities* (New York: King's Crown Press, 1947), pp. 130-33, 168.

25. Beck, *ibid.*, p. 134.

26. Data collected by Troy Duster, Center for Research and Development in Higher Education, University of California, Berkeley, 1965.

27. Beck, *op. cit.*, p. 147.

28. K. F. Burgess, "The Trustee Function in Today's Universities and Colleges," *Association of American Colleges Bulletin*, October 1958, pp. 399-407.

29. Raymond M. Hughes, *A Manual for Trustees of Colleges and Universities* (3rd ed.; Ames: Iowa State College Press, 1951), p. 11.

30. For a more detailed discussion of the responsibilities of trustees, including a number of case studies, see Morton A. Rauh, *College and University Trusteeship* (Yellow Springs, Ohio: Antioch Press, 1959), especially pp. 17-57. See also the report of the self-analysis made by the Board of Trustees of Columbia University, *The Role of the Trustees of Columbia University* (William S. Paley).

31. "The Role of the College and University Trustee," p. 11.

32. Laird Bell, "From the Trustees Corner," *AAUP Bulletin*, October 1956, p. 354.

33. Minutes of the Regents of the University of California, June 18, 1965, pp. 1-2, as quoted in Lunsford, *op. cit.*, p. 132.

34. Charles W. Eliot, *op. cit.*, pp. 228-29.

35. For a discussion of the unit versus the multiple type of organization, see John Dale Russell, *The Finance of Higher Education* (Rev. ed.; Chicago: University of Chicago Press, 1954), pp. 12-19.

36. Wicke, *op. cit.*, p. 3.

37. For discussions of this subject, see Lyman Glenny, *Autonomy of Public Colleges* (New York: McGraw-Hill Book Co., 1959), and M. M. Chambers, *Voluntary Statewide Coordination in Public Higher Education* (Ann Arbor: University of Michigan, 1961).

TRUSTEES:
BACKGROUNDS, ROLES, AND EDUCATIONAL ATTITUDES

Rodney T. Hartnett

Introduction

American higher education is going through an uncomfortable period of soul-searching. Though the events at Columbia University during the spring of 1968 perhaps serve as the clearest highlight for this assertion, Morningside Heights is by no means an exception. Almost daily a new crisis erupts on some college or university campus, drawing still closer attention to the apparent confusion that exists within the halls of academe. The questions being raised—most conspicuously by students but also by faculty—are serious ones. Essentially, the traditional purposes and processes of higher education are being questioned or attacked. In the midst of this turmoil is the college trustee. As one who for years has been ultimately responsible for charting the course of his college, his role is now becoming uncertain. As a greater demand is made for student and faculty involvement in college and university governance, the authority of the trustee is being challenged.

Given these circumstances, it is somewhat remarkable that so little is known about who trustees are, what they do in their roles as trustees, and how they feel about current issues in American higher education. Except for a now outdated and somewhat limited survey by Beck,[1] a more recent survey by Duster,[2] and a state-wide study in New York,[3] practically nothing in the way of empirically gathered information has been accumulated for this rather elite group of people. Most of what has been written has dealt primarily, almost exclusively, with governing boards as groups of corporate entities, not as a collection of individuals. Consequently, the "literature" tells us much about the typical size of governing boards, how they are selected, the source and nature of board authority, and basic board functions but precious little about the *people* who form these boards.

In the fall of 1967, Educational Testing Service joined with Morton Rauh, Vice President for Finance at Antioch College, to carry out a large survey of members of college and university governing boards. The Campus Governance Program of the American Association for Higher Education and the Association of Governing Boards of Universities and Colleges also joined in the sponsorship of the study.

In collaboration with Mr. Rauh, who was preparing a new book on college trustees,[4] a questionnaire was developed and mailed to trustees of over 500 colleges and universities. From the responses of more than 5,000 board members, data regarding who trustees are, what they do, and how they feel about current educational issues have been compiled.

Of the 654 institutions asked to provide us with the names and addresses of their trustees, 536 (82%) cooperated. The 536 lists received from the presidents of the institutions yielded the names and addresses of a total of 10,036 trustees. On February 26, 1968 a survey package was mailed to these trustees, containing a letter explaining the nature and purpose of the survey, the questionnaire, and a prepaid return envelope. Returns were received from 5,180 trustees, for a 52.5 percent response rate. A summary presentation of the sample is given in Figure 1.

Results

Only selected highlights from the total compilation of data are presented and interpreted here. The two most important criteria employed in deciding upon what results should be included and what emphasis they should receive were relevance and freshness: relevant to the current higher education scene, preferably to an "issue" still unresolved, and fresh, in the sense that the findings must add to what has been previously known about college and university trustees.

Thus, data regarding trustees' age, sex, level of education, income and the like are treated only briefly. On the other hand, the trustees' educational and social attitudes are dealt with in considerable detail, especially those having to do with academic freedom, business orien-

Figure 1. Trustee response summary

Institutional Category*	Number of Institutions	Number of Ques. Mailed	Number Returned	Percentage Response
Public junior colleges	67	547	261	47.71
Public colleges	50	438	184	42.01
Public universities	79	914	475	51.97
Private junior colleges	45	785	419	53.38
Private colleges (excluding Catholic)	164	4,329	2,434	56.23
Private universities (excluding Catholic)	53	1,561	739	47.34
Catholic colleges and universities	78	1,462	668	45.69
TOTALS:	536	10,036	5,180	52.46%
		− 162		
		9,874 Base No.		

*Post office returns, duplicates, deaths, nontrustees.

tations, and the decision-making process. Information relating to trustees' familiarity with what has been written about higher education is discussed at some length, whereas the question of "Who shall be educated?" is, by comparison, treated very briefly, and responses to many of the questions in the survey are not discussed at all.

Biographical Characteristics

Data regarding some of the more basic characteristics of college and university trustees conform to previous findings and are not surprising in terms of the nature of the description they provide. In general, trustees are male, in their 50's (though, nationally more than a third are over 60), white (fewer than two percent in our sample are Negro), well-educated, and financially well-off (more than half have annual incomes exceeding $30,000). They occupy prestige occupations, frequently in medicine, law and education, but more often as business executives (in the total sample over 35 percent are executives of manufacturing, merchandising or investment firms and at private universities nearly 50 percent hold such positions). As a group, then, they personify "success" in the usual American sense of that word.[5]

Most are Protestants, with only four percent being Jewish and 17 percent Catholic, the majority of the latter serving on boards of Catholic institutions. Trustees also tend to identify themselves as Republicans (approximately 58 percent overall) and most often regard themselves as politically moderate (61%) rather than conservative (21%) or liberal (15%). Many of them—nearly 40 percent overall and well over half at certain types of institutions—are alumni of the institutions on whose boards they serve. Of considerable interest is the fact that for the great majority (85%) their current board membership, whether with their alma mater or not, is their only college or university trustee commitment.

Educational/Social Attitudes

Perhaps more important than biographical characteristics for understanding the college trustee is how he feels about prevailing issues that face American higher education. Indeed, the relevance of such information as occupation, income, and the like is its presumed relationship to educational attitudes. Traditionally, this relationship has been taken for granted, and some have drawn the rather reckless conclusions that because the trustee is seldom young his educational attitudes are old-fashioned, that because he is frequently a business executive he will urge that his institution be "run like a business," and so on.[6] One of our intentions in developing the questionnaire was to replace suppositions with facts, to replace easy generalities with "hard" data. To our knowledge, information regarding trustees opinions on most of these matters has never before been systematically gathered on a national scale.

Academic Freedom

One of the prime areas of interest is that of academic freedom. A number of items in the attitude section of the questionnaire were directed at this issue. These items and the trustees' responses are summarized in Figure 2.

Though the great majority of trustees favor the right to free expression by faculty in various channels of college communication, the more general impression one gets from these data is that the trustees, by and large, are somewhat reluctant to accept a wider notion of academic freedom. For example, over two-thirds of these

Figure 2. Extent to which trustees agree with statements
regarding academic freedom[a]

	Percentage Strongly Agreeing or Agreeing[b]	Percentage Disagreeing or Strongly Disagreeing
Faculty members have right to free expression of opinions	67	27[c]
Administration should control contents of student newspaper	40	51
Campus speakers should be screened	69	25
Students punished by local authorities for off-campus matter should also be disciplined by the college	49	38
It is reasonable to require loyalty oath from members of faculty	53	38

[a]Statements in table are abbreviated; for complete statements see questionnaire.
[b]Percentages rounded to whole numbers.
[c]Percentages do not add to 100 because of those responding "unable to say."

people favor a screening process for all campus speakers, and nearly half feel that students already punished by local authorities for involvement in matters of civil disobedience *off the campus* should be further disciplined by the college.[7]

These attitudes are extremely relevant to campus problems today. Those who would argue that the trustee holds no authority or influence need only to examine some of the trustee attitudes regarding academic freedom against a backdrop of trustee/faculty conflicts. In the fall of 1968, for example, the regents of the University of California voted to withhold regular college credits for a series of speeches by Eldridge Cleaver (Minister of Information for the Black Panthers, an Oakland-based black militant group, and author of *Soul on Ice*), at the Berkeley campus. The academic senate at Berkeley has recorded its opposition to the regents' "encroachment" in curricular matters, but, at the time of this writing, the trustees' decision stands. There are many cases similar to this one and none should come as a surprise in view of trustee attitudes.

Naturally, trustee opinions about these matters vary considerably, not only across types of institutions, as already suggested, but across other dimensions as well. As an example of this, the academic freedom attitudes reported in Figure 2 are presented again in Figure 3 this time arranged by geographic region. The diversity is apparent. Notice, for example, that over half of the trustees of institutions located in the South agree that the contents of the student newspaper should be controlled by the institution, whereas only about 30 percent of the trustees of New England and Mid-Atlantic institutions hold similar views. Similar comparisons suggest that, in general, trustees of southern and Rocky Mountain institutions are most cautious in these matters, whereas trustees of institutions located in the New England and Mid-Atlantic region appear to be the most "liberal." The point of this particular analysis is to underscore the fact that the total sample of trustees could be categorized many different ways—by type of control, geographic region, enrollment, and sex makeup of student body to name but a few—and differences would almost surely appear.

There is an interesting sidelight to the academic freedom data which is not presented in Figures 2 or 3. Trustees of public junior colleges appear to be the least freedom-oriented in terms of their responses to these items. At the same time we note that 42 percent of the trustees of public junior colleges are elected by the general public (item 5 in questionnaire Part III). Though such an occurrence is far too tenuous to draw any definite conclusions some speculations are hard to resist. In a recent discussion of the matter, Jencks and Riesman remark, "Publicly elected or appointed boards of trustees seem in many ways to cause more trouble than they are worth."[8] This opinion apparently stems from their belief that "budgetary support and review are the only forms of public control that make much sense" and that these functions could just as easily, and more efficiently, be performed by already existing groups (for example, the legislature). As suggested by comments of these same authors in another source, however, we may wonder if their opinion isn't also influenced by the numerous cases in which trustees have campaigned for a position on an institution's governing board on a plank opposed to academic freedom.[9] The public often does not understand the full meaning of academic freedom and is apparently suspicious of it. It is possible, therefore, that publicly elected trustees may be conservative in these matters, as suggested by the junior college data reported here.[10]

If this is true, it would suggest that publicly elected trustees may

Figure 3. Agreement with academic freedom statements by trustees of institutions in different geographic regions (in percentages)[a]

	New England and Mid-Atlantic	South	Midwest	Rockies	West
Faculty members have right to free expression of opinions	73.2	64.0	64.2	62.6	62.0
Administration should control contents of student newspaper	29.8	51.5	42.0	48.1	44.4
Campus speakers should be screened	58.3	80.9	72.0	77.8	74.5
Students punished by local authorities for off-campus matter should also be disciplined by the college	39.8	63.2	49.5	62.5	44.0
It is reasonable to require loyalty oaths from faculty members	46.4	63.6	52.2	66.1	53.4

[a]Numbers are percentages agreeing or strongly agreeing with each statement.

not be confronted with the long-standing dilemma facing other governing board members, that is, whether to adopt the role of "protector of the public interest" or that of insulator between the public and the institution. While most trustees—at least at public institutions—appear to vacillate between these two roles, the publicly elected trustee, perhaps by virtue of being elected rather than appointed, is apparently committed to the former.[11]

Education for Whom?

Another topic of recent concern to American higher education has to do with the question of "education for whom?" Until fairly recently American higher education was restricted to those of demonstrated academic ability who could afford the high costs that earning a degree required. More recently, however, we have seen a trend toward more flexible selection criteria and an "open-door" philosophy, perhaps exemplified best by the growing number of junior colleges throughout the country. Trustee attitudes toward this phenomenon are summarized in Figure 4.

For the national sample taken together, there appears to be general sympathy for the broader-access trend just discussed. Slightly

Figure 4. Trustees' views regarding who should be
served by higher education

	Percentage Strongly Agreeing or Agreeing[a]	Percentage Disagreeing or Strongly Disagreeing[b]
Attendance a privilege, not a right	92	6
Aptitude most important admissions criteria	70	24
Curriculum designed to accommodate diverse student body	63	27
Opportunity for higher education for anyone who desires it	85	11
College should admit socially disadvantaged who do not meet normal requirements	66	22

[a] Percentages rounded to whole numbers.
[b] Percentages do not add to 100 because of those responding "unable to say."

more than 85 percent agree (with almost one-third *strongly* agreeing) that there should be opportunities for higher education available to anyone who seeks education beyond secondary school, and two-thirds agree that colleges should admit socially disadvantaged students who appear to have the potential, even when these students do not meet the normal entrance requirements. Nevertheless over 90 percent still regard attendance at their college to be a privilege, not a right. In fact, 68 percent of the trustees of public junior colleges, open-door institutions if you will, also share the privilege-not-a-right sentiment. In view of the other responses indicating acceptance of the concept of wide accessibility of higher education opportunity, these latter figures seem inconsistent. Several explanations seem plausible, however. It may mean that even trustees of non-selective institutions cling to the elitist model, perhaps thinking that while *other* colleges should employ flexible admissions criteria, their own institution must "maintain high standards." Or perhaps most trustees simply interpreted the statement somewhat differently, wishing only to indicate their feeling that students should not *expect* to be in college but, rather, should feel *grateful* for the opportunity. Or finally, it could mean that trustees favor extending the opportunity for college *admission* to more and more students but, in order to protect themselves and their institutions against *unacceptable* student conduct, feel the institutions must retain the authority to decide who will *remain*.

Business Orientation of Trustees

One frequently hears the assertion that trustees tend to think colleges and universities can function best by imitating the corporation or big business model (the assumption being that such a model is inappropriate and, in the long run, damaging to higher education). Whether such a model is appropriate or not cannot be answered by these data, but we can at least get some idea of whether or not it is a model preferred by the trustees.

It has already been indicated that trustees are frequently business executives. Two additional indices should also suggest such an orientation: first, whether trustees endorse the statement that "running a college is basically like running a business," and, second, the extent to which they feel "experience in high-level business management" is an important quality to consider in the selection of a new president. These data are presented in Figure 5.

Inspection of this table makes it clear that trustees who are business executives definitely have a stronger business orientation

Figure 5. Trustee responses to items indicative of their
business-model orientation for colleges and universities (in percentages)

	Regard themselves as executives of manufacturing, merchandising or banking firm	Agree that running a college is basically like running a business		Regard experience in high-level business management as important quality for new president	
	(col. 1)	Business Executives[a] (col. 2)	Others (col. 3)	Business Executives (col. 4)	Others (col. 5)
TOTAL SAMPLE	35	49	31	49	44
Public junior colleges	33 (7)[b]	56 (2)	49	45 (6)	46
Public colleges	39 (3)	56 (2)	42	55 (1)	40
Public universities	36 (5)	45 (6)	28	51 (4)	43
Private colleges	36 (5)	48 (4)	29	49 (5)	45
Private universities	49 (1)	42 (7)	23	41 (7)	38
Catholic colleges and universities	22 (8)	56 (2)	31	54 (2)	43
Selective public	36 (5)	47 (5)	30	55 (3)	38
Selective private	43 (2)	30 (8)	14	31 (8)	25

a"Business executives" includes all those in first column, determined on the basis of their response to the occupation item (#16) in first part of questionnaire.
bNumbers in parentheses alongside percentages in columns 1, 2, and 4 are within-column ranks (excluding total sample).
Rank-order correlations (ρ) between columns are as follows:

$\rho_{12} = -.62$ (p. $<$ .05), $\rho_{14} = -.40$ (n.s.), $\rho_{24} = +.69$ (p. $<$ .05).

toward the university than trustees with other occupations. For the total sample, of the 35 percent who are business executives nearly half (49%) agree that running a college is basically like running a business, whereas fewer than one-third (31%) of the nonexecutives accept this view. In fact, of the 16 possible business executives vs. "other" comparisons (eight institutional types by two attitude items) there is only one case in which trustees who are business executives are not also more business oriented. The exception is for public junior colleges, where a slightly higher proportion of nonbusiness executives regard business management experience as an important quality for a new president. Thus, there appears to be validity to the often heard claim that because governing boards are made up of businessmen, the decisions they make about the institutions will reflect this business outlook.

Another finding emerging from the data in Figure 5, however, has to do with the relationship between the three indices and suggests that the "business outlook" hypothesis is not so simple. Note that the group having the second greatest proportion of trustees who are business executives (selective private universities) is the group which has the smallest percentage of those executives agreeing that running a college is like running a business and also the smallest proportion regarding high-level business management experience as an important criterion for a new president. Contrast this with trustees of public junior colleges, where a nearly opposite pattern occurs. In fact, the rank-order correlations between columns indicates that, across all types, the proportion of trustees holding business-executive positions is *negatively* correlated with the proportion of those executives endorsing the attitude statements in Figure 5; that is, the greater the proportion of business executives on the governing board, the *smaller* the proportion of executives who feel that "running a college is like running a business" and that high-level business management experience is an important quality to consider in choosing a new president. Consequently, even though the "business orientation" is distinctly more prevalent among business executives generally, it would be a mistake to jump to the conclusion that on boards where the proportion of business executives is high, the business orientation will be strongest.

What is the explanation for this befuddling situation? One is at first tempted to speculate about the influence of the nonbusiness trustees on their colleagues' attitudes. While such a possibility should not be lightly dismissed, a more convincing interpretation might consider the varying levels of "executiveness" represented on the boards. We suspect, for example, that the types of institutions having the greatest proportion of business executives (the private universities and selective private institutions) generally have men who are a much different kind of executive than those who serve on boards with the smallest proportion of businessmen (the junior colleges and Catholic institutions). This is probably a case of men simply not being cut from the same cloth, regardless of what may be suggested by the mutual occupational perception of "business executive." This difference, in turn, is reflected in their attitudes about "running" a college, and the high-level executive appears to be more inclined to see it as a nonbusiness undertaking when compared to his probably less prestigious executive counterpart serving on some of the other boards.

The Decision-Making Process

One of the complaints most frequently made about higher education by disenchanted members of the academic community is that the wrong people are making the decisions. Many of the campus demonstrators have been claiming, in one way or another, that the university should be run by the faculty and students, not by administrators and trustees. The following quotation, taken from a newspaper article summarizing some of the events at Columbia in the spring of 1968, is not atypical:

Speakers in buildings and on the lawn . . . called for the 'reconstruction of this university,' with students and faculty assuming the power now exercised by the president and trustees.[12]

Though the extent to which faculty and students across the country actually feel they should "run" the campus is not known, there are some indications that it is not just a radical minority who desire more participation in the decision-making process. In a survey of faculty opinion regarding participation in academic decision making at one institution, for example, 51 percent of the faculty included in the survey felt that "the faculty has too little influence on decisions; more of the decision making power should rest with the faculty," and another 44 percent agreed that "the faculty's role is not what it should be ideally, but it is about what one can realistically expect." Furthermore, 63 percent indicated that they were either dissatisfied or very dissatisfied with this situation.[13] And a recent survey of college trustees, administrators, faculty members, and students conducted by the American Council on Education, tells us that faculty are almost unanimous in wanting a larger share in academic rule, including greater participation in the selection of their president.[14] Though the former study was done at one university in the Midwest, and the faculty sample in the A.C.E. study consisted only of American Association of University Professors chapter heads (thus making neither sample "representative" in any sense), together they provide some empirical support for the claim that there is dissatisfaction with the perceived way in which decisions are reached.

With this information in mind, let us examine the trustees' views of who should have major involvement in deciding various campus issues. Several things are made quite clear by these data, which are presented in Figures 6 and 7.

First, trustees generally favor a hierarchical system in which decisions are made at the top and passed "down." For example, over 50 percent of the total sample of trustees believe that faculty and students should *not* have major authority in half of the sixteen decisions listed (that is, eight column-one percentage figures exceed 50 percent in Table 7). The proportion feeling that trustees and/or administrators alone should have major authority in making the decision exceeds 40 percent in 12 of the 16 decisions.[15] Some of these are particularly interesting. For example, 63 percent say that the appointment of an academic dean should be made with only the administrators and trustees having major authority, or, to say it another way, 63 percent feel that the faculty should *not* have major authority in the appointment of their dean. Similarly, 57 percent would exempt the faculty from major authority in the awarding of honorary degrees, and 58 percent would exempt them from major authority in policies regarding faculty leaves. To many, of course, these findings come as no surprise. But, surprising or not, they do help underscore some of the very wide differences of opinion among members of the academic community as to who should govern.

Second, there is a perceptible difference in the kinds of decisions trustees feel should and should not involve other groups having substantial authority. For example, the areas that should have greatest faculty authority are seen to be, by and large, academic matters, such as whether or not to add or delete specific courses, or what criteria should be employed in admitting students. Student authority is judged relevant in matters of student life, such as housing, student cheating, fraternities and sororities, and the like.

Third, though the trustees generally prefer an arrangement in which the faculty and students do not have major authority, neither do they want to "rule" by themselves. Notice in Figure 6, for example, that with the exception of presidential appointments, they prefer major authority for decisions to rest with the administration alone or with the administration and trustees conjointly. Thus, the "power at the top" model must be modified. Trustees prefer their own power to be singularly authoritative only when it comes to choosing the president of the institution. Having selected him, however, they like to lean heavily on him (and his administrative colleagues) for making the decisions.[16]

Finally, as seen in Figure 7, there is a great deal of variation from group to group on these matters. It would appear that trustees of selective private institutions are most inclined to include other members of the academic community in the decision-making process, while trustees of non-selective public institutions are more inclined toward a power-at-the-top sort of arrangement. Notice, for example, that 50 percent or more of the trustees feel that administrators and/or trustees alone should have major authority in deciding 13 of the 16 issues at public junior colleges, but only 4 of the 16 issues at selective private institutions. The concept of democratic governance or shared authority clearly has a more receptive audience among trustees at the latter type of institution. In fact, the ordering of institutions in Figure 7 would correspond very closely to an ordering of institutional types by educational prestige. That is, where prestige is defined by the usual (but not necessarily reasonable) indices of student ability, faculty prominence and the like, it would appear that the greater the prestige of the institutional type, the more likely the trustees are to favor student and faculty involvement in decision making.[17] It can also be seen that, with the exception of the selective public universities, there is public-private division on this question.

It would be easy to get caught in a chicken vs. egg cycle in trying to account for these relationships, and there surely is no simple explanation. But again, speculation is hard to resist, and several interpretations are compelling. The most basic reason for the public-private difference probably comes from the sources of financial support. Because they do not have to answer to a public constituency, trustees of private institutions may be more willing to maintain a looser hold on the reins. Though accountable to the alumni, parents, and "friends" of the institution, such groups are basically *for* the institution and are seldom as concerned about its actions as the general public might be of colleges supported by tax money. Thus, trustees of private institutions are less hesitant to involve the faculty and students.

The reason for the prestige difference is not as straightforward but

Figure 6. Proportion of trustees who think that certain campus groups should have major authority in making various decisions (in percentages)[a,b]

	Decision should be made by administrators alone (A), trustees alone (T) or trustees and admin. together (TA)				Decision should be made by faculty alone or in conjunction with admin., trustees or both (col. 2)	Decision should be made by students alone or in conjunction with faculty and/or A and/or T (col. 3)
				(col. 1)		
	A	T	TA	Total[c]		
Add or delete courses	11	1	4	16	65	14
Add or delete degree programs	9	6	18	33	57	3
Rules re student housing	32	2	13	47	6	37
Commencement speaker	29	4	13	46	25	22
Presidential appointment	1	64	5	70	8	1
Determine tuition	10	17	64	91	2	1
Professor's immoral conduct	29	7	28	64	27	2
Tenure decisions	27	7	30	64	30	1
Student cheating	20	0	1	21	39	37
Policy re student protests	16	6	30	52	18	22
Appoint academic dean	22	8	33	63	30	1
Policy re faculty leaves	19	8	31	58	37	0
Admission criteria	17	3	16	36	59	1
Honorary degrees	7	19	31	57	34	1
Athletic program	17	4	22	43	22	24
Fraternities and sororities	18	5	21	44	10	31

[a]Statements in table are abbreviated; for complete statements see questionnaire.
[b]Percentages rounded to whole numbers.
[c]Column 1, which is simply a total of columns A, T, and TA, can be interpreted as the percentage of trustees who feel that faculty and/or students should *not* have major authority in deciding the various issues.

Figure 7. Percentage of trustees by type of institution feeling that various decisions should be made with administrators and/or trustees having the only major authority

Decision	TOTAL	Public J.C.	Public Colleges	Public Univ.	Private Colleges	Private Univ.	Catholic C's & U's	Selective Public	Selective Private
Add or delete courses	16	31	21	17	14	10	13	13	6
Add or delete degree programs	33	56	42	32	31	25	31	26	18
Rules re student housing	47	54	55	53	46	47	37	48	40
Commencement speaker	46	52	49	46	46	48	44	39	44
Presidental appointment	70	85	72	60	69	70	70	61	63
Determine tuition	91	91	87	88	93	93	88	88	95
Professor's immoral conduct	64	74	70	67	65	60	56	63	54
Tenure decisions	64	79	67	61	67	55	54	63	44
Student cheating	21	26	27	24	19	20	20	14	19
Policy re student protests	52	64	60	61	51	54	45	63	49
Appoint academic dean	63	81	68	57	64	61	61	48	54
Policy re faculty leaves	58	70	65	60	59	54	46	57	48
Admissions criteria	36	56	50	41	33	27	33	47	25
Honorary degrees	57	64	62	48	55	51	60	43	45
Athletic programs	43	49	58	50	41	42	41	48	37
Fraternities and sororities	44	95	48	47	45	47	38	43	44
No. of issues with 50% or more trustees feeling trustees and/or administrators alone should have major authority	8	13	11	9	8	8	6	6	4

certainly no less important. There is a relationship between institutional prestige and trustee affluence. More specifically, the greater the prestige of the institution, the higher the trustees' income, level of education, occupational status, etc. Such people are probably more inclined to delegate authority and to be less concerned personally about maintaining control over things. Trustees of the more prestigious institutions, by virtue of the characteristics that led to their being selected to such boards, are simply more inclined to a laissez faire attitude regarding student and faculty involvement in campus governance.

In any event, the question "who shall govern" is obviously a very complex one and to be treated thoroughly would require far more detailed treatment than provided by the brief summary of responses reported here. Many faculty who complain about lack of participation in academic governance are actually unwilling to participate themselves and suspicious of other members of the faculty who do get involved. Furthermore, it is sometimes members of the faculty who would prefer to keep authority out of the hands of their colleagues. As one recent example of this, at an institution which is moving from a teachers' college to a large state university, one department chairman opposed efforts to give greater authority to faculty members on the grounds that there were still far too many holdovers on the faculty from the teacher-training days who were not at all interested in research and presumably would have slowed the institution's emergence as a first-rate institution.[18]

Nevertheless, it seems safe to conclude that, by and large, faculty members tend to favor a horizontal as opposed to vertical form of authority, whereas trustees prefer a hierarchical arrangement or system of graded authority, imitating, it would seem, the "bureaucratic management" model. Though neither of these forms of government actually exist in any pure sense, they still represent what would appear to be rather basic ideological differences between trustees and faculty.

Political Preference and Ideology

A summary of the trustees' political party affiliation, political ideology, and the relationship between these two variables is presented in Figure 8. Of the trustees who indicated both their party preference and ideology, over 60 percent described themselves as Republican and slightly less than 35 percent as Democrat. The majority regard themselves as moderates, 21.6 percent as conservatives, and 15.9 percent as liberals. Furthermore, there was an

Figure 8. Classification of trustees by political party
preference and ideology (in percentages)

	Conservative	Moderate	Liberal	TOTAL[a]
Republican	16.95	39.53	4.06	60.54
Democrat	3.74	20.32	10.50	34.56
Other	0.91	2.69	1.31	4.91
TOTAL	21.60	62.54	15.87	100%

Note: The correlation (contingency coefficient) between party affiliation and political ideology is .32 (p < .01), i.e., there is a tendency for those who are Republicans to also be conservative, etc.

[a]The data in this table include only those trustees who indicated both their party preference *and* ideology. Therefore it differs slightly from the data reported on page 20 and in Part II.

interaction or correlation between these characteristics. We note the tendency for Republicans to regard themselves more often as conservative than liberal (approximately 17% vs. 4%) and for Democrats to view themselves more often as liberals than conservatives (10.5% vs. 3.7%).

Contrast this profile of the trustee with that of the college faculty member. In general, one gets a much different picture, with most reports indicating that the majority of college faculty members are Democrats. Furthermore, though we can cite no research evidence for this claim, it is extremely unlikely that 22 percent of the faculty would regard themselves as conservatives (though we do suspect that conservative trustees tend to be at the same institutions as conservative faculty). With such a gap in the political orientations of these two groups, then, it should hardly come as a surprise to find disagreement over educational matters, for both party affiliation and political ideology are related to the attitude items already discussed. On the basis of correlational data, for example, we note a definite tendency for trustees who regard themselves as conservatives to endorse such statements (see Figure 2) as "the administration should exercise control over the contents of the student newspaper" (r = .37), and "the requirement that a professor sign a loyalty oath is reasonable" (r = .47).

Most academicians would probably attach a negative value to such facts, but it should be pointed out that, as with most situations of this kind, there are two sides to the coin. Jencks and Riesman, for example, offer cogent arguments that, at least until quite recently, it has been the Republican moderates, not the Democrats, who have led the struggle for more generous university appropriations.[19] These are obviously not simple matters.

The party preference data in Table 9 are also reflected in the extent to which the trustees feel that their political or social views are similar to various well-known (usually political) figures. Of the 18 persons listed in the questionnaire, only two received similarity-of-view endorsements from more than 60 percent of the total trustee sample. These were Richard Nixon (62%), and Nelson Rockefeller (68%).

Activities as a Trustee

The median number of board meetings during the 1967 calendar year was three or four, with approximately one-third of all trustees attending five or more. Attendance at these meetings was fairly faithful; over half attended all the meetings, and over 80 percent attended more than three-fourths of them. Attending these meetings was the single board activity requiring the most time, with nearly half of the trustees spending over 20 hours (including travel) attending these meetings during the year. Attending committee meetings was the only other board activity on which more than 20 percent of the trustees spent over 20 hours.

On the basis of the trustees' estimates of the amount of time they had spent on the various activities during the year, it was possible to estimate the total number of hours devoted to their trusteeships in general. These data, presented in Table 10, are arranged by institutional type, in left-to-right, high-to-low ordering on the basis of total (median) time devoted to trustee activities. The variation of total hours is substantial, ranging from a median of 115.88 hours for trustees of public universities to a median of 56.18 for trustees of Catholic institutions.[20] As already mentioned, full board meetings were the most time-consuming activity, but again the variance was considerable, ranging from 47.80 hours for public universities to 16.10 hours for Catholic institutions.

Of the activities listed, only one, soliciting contributions, reveals a systematic difference. That is, trustees of private institutions spend some of their time soliciting contributions, but, as one would expect, there is no effort in this direction among trustees at public institutions.

If the estimate of total annual hours spent on governing board

Figure 9. Median number of hours spent by trustees annually on various trustee activities

	TOTAL SAMPLE	Public U's	Sel. Pub.	Sel. Private	Private U's	Public JC's	Public Colleges	Private Colleges	Cath. C's & U's
Full board meetings	20.57	47.80	41.60	27.73	20.51	43.84	37.41	18.79	16.10
Committee meetings	16.76	33.17	37.07	36.18	26.63	15.04	18.11	15.89	12.47
Meetings of ad hoc college groups	5.19	9.90	6.83	9.00	6.94	7.41	5.61	4.51	4.84
Making speeches on behalf of college	0.00	1.19	3.48	0.00	0.00	0.00	0.00	0.00	0.00
Soliciting contributions	5.48	0.00	0.00	11.63	11.75	0.00	0.00	7.90	2.69
Conferences with college personnel	9.16	11.66	12.29	11.33	9.95	7.47	8.59	8.31	12.67
Other	6.01	12.16	12.07	9.23	7.73	8.59	7.35	3.86	7.41
Total Median Hours (Annual)	63.17	115.88	113.34	105.10	83.51	82.35	77.07	59.26	56.18

Note: Medians were calculated by assuming an equal distribution of frequencies within a range of hours. Furthermore, the computations were based only on those responding to each item. For unknown reasons, the number of respondents omitting these items was considerable (see Part II), especially for the "other" category. Thus, to the extent that omits were trustees who should have indicated "none" for that response, these data probably *overestimate* trustees' time spent; to the extent that omits were trustees who spent their time on "other" activities but didn't feel inclined to review and total it, these data *underestimate* trustees' time spent.

activities is fairly accurate, it means that, depending on the type of institution, the median time-per-month ranges from approximately five to ten hours. This is only the median or midpoint value, of course, and hence about half spend more and half spend less than the median value at each type of institution. In fact, though the data are not provided in this report, it should be noted that at certain types of institutions over 20 percent of the trustees estimate spending over 80 hours per year at board meetings alone!

The New York State survey mentioned earlier also attempted to learn how much time is spent on trustee matters. Though the slightly different form of the survey question makes a direct comparison difficult, it is worth noting that that study found 42 percent of their trustees spending fewer than 10 hours per month on board-related activities and 60 percent less than 20 hours per month.[21]

Trustees and the "Literature" of Higher Education

Though it is impossible to know what activities trustees included in the "other" category in their estimates of time devoted to trustee activities, it is safe to say that reading about higher education wasn't one of them. As a group, trustees are barely familiar with the major books and periodicals of relevance to American higher education. In terms of books, for example, only Ruml and Morrison's *Memo to a College Trustee*—a book now some nine years old—has been read completely by more than 10 percent of the trustees. In fact, of the 15 books listed, only four have been completely read by more than five percent of the trustees, and in most cases, the trustees have never even heard of the books, most of which are now regarded as "classics" in the higher education field. The same story holds for educational periodicals. Only the *EPE 15-minute Report* is read regularly by more than 10 percent of the trustees, and again, the majority of trustees are not even familiar with most of the journals listed.[22]

One might argue, of course, that this lack of familiarity with higher education books and journals is understandable because trustees are extremely busy men, caught up in the activities that led to their selection as trustees in the first place. While this is undoubtedly true, the trustees' lack of familiarity with the literature serves to underscore the peripheral nature of the trusteeship for most of the board members. What it also suggests is that the institutions are not doing enough in the way of keeping their trustees abreast of current thinking. Though there is strength to the lack-of-time argument as an explanation of why trustees do not read these materials, it would seem that some of the blame for their not even being familiar with such publications can be directed to poor communications from the officers of the institutions.

As with many other features of the survey, there was a great deal of diversity across institutional types on this matter of familiarity with the literature. This is summarized in Figure 10. It would appear that trustees of Catholic institutions are the best read trustees with those of public junior colleges, private colleges and private universities among those least familiar with the books and journals listed. Though attempts to explain data such as these are speculative at best, several reasons seem to be plausible in explaining why trustees of Catholic institutions seem to be the best read group. First, nearly 32 percent of the trustees of Catholic institutions are members of the administration and/or faculty of an institution of higher learning; this is approximately four times the proportion of trustees so employed at other types of institutions. Second, the rapid changes occurring within American Catholic higher education and widespread attention given to modifications in the governing board structure and organization at these institutions have surely prompted many trustees of Catholic colleges to carefully examine their roles. Thus, trustees of these institutions are the most attentive to the relevant literature, even though, as we have already seen, the total amount of time they contribute to formal board activities is not great.[23]

Figure 10. Number of books and periodicals read by 10 percent or more of trustees at various types of institutions[a]

	Books	Periodicals
TOTAL TRUSTEE SAMPLE	9	7
Catholic colleges and universities	12	9
Public universities	10	6
Selective public	9	5
Selective private	8	2
Public colleges	7	3
Private universities	6	1
Private colleges	6	2
Public junior colleges	5	3

[a]For books, this 10 percent includes all trustees indicating they had either read this book completely or read portions of it; for periodicals, it includes those indicating they read the periodical regularly or "read, but not regularly." For a list of the books and periodicals included in this item, see the questionnaire (appendix). Fifteen books and eleven periodicals were listed.

To Make Decisions or Offer Advice

We have already seen that, as a general rule, trustees feel that the major authority for many institutional decisions should reside with the trustees and/or administrators of the institution. The delicate balance between deciding and advising, however, remains unclear, at least as it pertains to the way the trustees and the administration together reach decisions. The trustees were therefore asked to indicate their perception of their action in terms of the decide/advise/confirm model for topics commonly considered by trustees.

Responses to this section of the questionnaire make it clear that the trustees perceive their responsibility to lie most clearly in the areas of finance, physical plant, and "external affairs." In matters of personnel, student life, and the educational program, the trustees' preferred role would appear to be one of approving or confirming a decision already made by some other, presumably better qualified, group. It is true, of course, that the distinction between making a decision and approving one already made is far from clear. Since the reverse of the "approve or confirm" option is obviously "disapprove or veto," even this latter level of involvement is (or could be) essentially a decision making function. Nevertheless, there are clearly many "rubber stamp" activities required of trustees, and our purpose here was to attempt to learn how trustees perceived their role in these terms.

In Figure 11 the percentage of trustees feeling they have *decided* on a course of action in six areas (personnel, student life, finance, plant, educational program, and external affairs) has been converted to ranks. Thus we see that the percentage of the total trustee sample who have made a decision is highest in the area of long-range financial plans, second in the area of fund raising, and so on. It would appear that trustees make most decisions in the fiscal areas, followed by physical plant and "external affairs," in that order. (The selection of the president was not included in this list of topics.) Across all types of institutions, the five topics about which trustees most often make decisions are in the three major areas of finance, plant, and external affairs, with only two exceptions: the area of personnel (wage scales for non-faculty) for junior college trustees, and student life (policies on student-invited speakers) for trustees of selective public universities. It is interesting to note that of the topics listed, the one about which most trustee decisions were made in three types of institutions was the selection of new trustees.

Figure 11 also includes an indication of the total number of topics (out of 20 listed in the questionnaire) about which 20 percent or

Figure 11. Ranking of topics in which trustees were directly involved in the decision-making process

	TOTAL SAMPLE	Public JC's	Public Colleges	Public U's	Private Colleges	Private U's	Cath. C's & U's	Selective Public	Selective Private
Finance:									
Investments	5	4a	5	2	5	4	4	3	4
Budget Analysis			4	4		5	4	5	5
Long-range Plans	1	2	1	1	2	3	3	2b	3
Plant:									
Master Plan	4	3	2	3	4		5	4	
Select Architect		1	3	5					
External Affairs:									
Fund Raising Plans	2				1	2	2		2
Select New Trustees	3				3	1	1		1
Total number of topics in which 20% or more of the trustees have been directly involved in making a decision (out of 20 topics listed):	8	11	6	6	8	6	7	4	8

Note: The ranks are based on within-type percentages and should be interpreted carefully. Thus, for example, the area of investments is ranked second at public universities (i.e., the second highest proportion of trustees made one or more decisions in this area) and fifth at private four-year colleges, yet the proportion of trustees at each type actually making a decision in this area is very close (36.8% vs. 32.3%).

aFifth rank for public junior colleges was in the area of personnel.

bFirst rank for selective public institutions was in the area of student life.

more of the trustees have made a decision. From this listing it would appear that trustees of public junior colleges make the largest number of decisions, while at the other extreme, trustees of selective public institutions more often advise or confirm the decisions of others, since 20 percent (or more) of their trustees actually made a decision in only four areas.

Footnotes

1. Beck, Hubert P. *Men Who Control Our Universities*. New York: King's Crown Press, 1947.

2. Duster, Troy. "The Aims of Higher Learning and the Control of the Universities." Unpublished paper. Berkeley: University of California, 1966.

3. *College and University Trustees and Trusteeship*. New York State Regents Advisory Committee on Educational Leadership (James Perkins, Chairman), 1966.

4. Rauh, Morton A. *The Trusteeship of Colleges and Universities*. New York: McGraw-Hill, in press.

5. Again, we caution the reader to keep in mind the purposely very general nature of these summary statements. There is considerable diversity on these characteristics across types of institutions.

6. Of course an opposite, and perhaps more dangerous, assumption has also been frequently made: that because one is a "successful" businessman, attorney, dentist, or whatever, he will therefore be a competent overseer of a higher educational institution.

7. It should be pointed out that this particular item, dealing with off-campus civil disobedience, is probably more a matter of "in loco parentis" than academic freedom. Nevertheless it is included here since freedom (though perhaps not academic freedom) *is* involved, and the item does correlate with the other four in this table.

8. Jencks, Christopher, and Riesman, David. *The Academic Revolution*. New York: Doubleday, 1968, p. 269.

9. Riesman, David, and Jencks, Christopher. "The Viability of the American College," in *The American College* (Nevitt Sanford, editor). New York: Wiley, 1962, p. 109.

10. The general question of what differences exist, if any, among trustees gaining board membership by different avenues is one of many we hope to pursue in much greater detail in subsequent analyses of these data.

11. For a more detailed discussion of these roles at both public and private institutions, see John D. Millett, *The Academic Community: An Essay on Organization*. New York: McGraw-Hill, Inc., 1962.

12. Kramer, Joel. "Does Student Power Mean: Rocking the Boat? Running the University?" *New York Times*. May 26, 1968, section IV, p. 32.

13. Dykes, Archie R. *Faculty Participation in Academic Decision Making*. American Council on Education, 1968.

14. Caffrey, John. "Predictions for Higher Education in the 1970's," in *The Future Academic Community: Continuity and Change*, background papers for participants in the 51st annual meeting of the American Council on Education, 1968, pp. 123-153.

15. Caution should be used in interpreting Table 7. It should be kept in mind, for example, that the percentages in columns two and three might also include trustees and administrators, and column three might also include faculty members. Column one, then, is the only "pure" combination. Again, the reader is urged to study Part II of this report.

16. It should be remembered that these data refer to how trustees think decisions *should* be made, not how they *are* made. They are trustee preferences. As suggested in the introduction to this report, many claim that the trustees' real authority has diminished substantially over the years to a point where the gap between "paper" power and actual power is large indeed. For a more complete discussion of this, see Ernest L. Boyer, "A Fresh Look at the College Trustee," *Educational Record*, Summer, 1968, pp. 274-279.

17. There is corroborating data for this assertion. In other research currently underway in the Higher Education Research Group at ETS, scores on the Democratic Governance scale of an experimental *Institutional Functioning Inventory* (an instrument which asks for faculty perceptions of their own institutions) have been found to correlate significantly with selectivity, income per student, proportion of faculty holding a doctorate, and average faculty compensation.

18. Rourke, Francis and Brooks, Glenn. *The Managerial Revolution in Higher Education.* Baltimore: The Johns Hopkins Press, 1966, p. 117. Readers interested in more detailed discussions of this problem should see *Faculty Participation in Academic Governance*, a report of the AAHE Task Force on Faculty Representation and Academic Negotiations, Campus Governance Program (1967), and a report of a study by Archie R. Dykes, *op. cit.*

19. Jencks and Riesman, *op. cit.*, p. 277-279.

20. It is extremely important to emphasize that these total-time-spent medians are estimates and should be interpreted with caution. The total median hours makes sense only if one assumes that the respondent lumped all time spent on activities not listed as "other." This is a somewhat dangerous assumption, especially since so many omitted the "other" option.

21. *College and University Trustees and Trusteeship, op. cit.*, p. 38.

22. The *EPE 15-minute Report* is a brief newsletter for trustees, published bi-weekly by Editorial Projects for Education, 3301 N. Charles St., Baltimore, Md.

23. It should probably also be mentioned that trustees of Catholic institutions are quite often administrators of the same institution on whose board they serve, e.g., the president and vice president(s) of the institution are also members of its governing board (*not* to be confused with the advisory board, which often has no authority). Thus, at Catholic institutions, a meeting of the executive officers of the institution may in fact be a trustee meeting, though not formally regarded as such.

ORGANIZATION IN LARGE AMERICAN UNIVERSITIES:
THE ADMINISTRATION

Edward H. Litchfield

If we are to change the congeries of faculties, clinics, and institutional hospitals which compose the large university into an organic whole, we must look carefully to the organization not only of the faculty, but also of the administration. It is unreasonable to expect individual faculties—no matter how devoted and able—to appraise the needs and minister to the continuing problems of the many diverse parts of a large institution. Even in limited areas, we have often needed more than individual faculty effort to settle major issues of academic policy. Examples of this are the early conflicts between medicine and public health, between economics and business administration. If there is to be anything approaching unity within an institution, it is essential, in my judgment, that the administration be vigorous, academically creative, well trained, and well organized. Its role should be affirmative, not merely neutral. The administration should be the source of new developments as well as the co-ordinator of existing programs. The time has come when university administrators must play more creative and responsible roles if our institutions are to deal effectively with the large tasks ahead.

Unfortunately, in the years since the growth of the large and complex university all too few institutions have developed this type of administration. The explanation may, in part, lie in the failure of recent generations to produce an Eliot or an Angell or a White, but I

Reprinted from the *Journal of Higher Education* 30 (December 1959), pp. 489-504. Copyright © 1959 by the Ohio State University Press and reprinted with its permission.

am inclined to think that the answer is more complicated. Broadly speaking, it seems to me that the explanation lies, in the first place, in our failure to understand the real nature of the administrative process per se; second, in our failure to organize the administration so that it will be able to undertake its real responsibilities; and, third, in our unwillingness to train men and women for administrative roles in university organizations. These are not superficial failures. They result from fundamental misunderstandings and misgivings.

Understanding of the administrative process is complicated by reason of the emotional overtones with which the term "administration" is regarded in many academic circles. The unhappy dichotomy of the "egghead" and the "woodenhead" reflects the chronic distrust and misunderstanding between what are loosely referred to as the faculties and the administration. If we consider the process of administration, and not persons or positions which are judged to be administrative rather than academic, it will become readily apparent that much of the administrative process is normally carried forward in any university by persons who traditionally would not be regarded as administrators. Conversely, I think a full understanding of the administrative process would suggest that those who are normally referred to as administrators must be deeply involved in purely academic questions which an arbitrary dichotomy would deny them.

We shall never fully understand administration in the university unless we are willing to look to institutions beyond the campus which may have relevant experiences to share with us. There has been far less thought devoted to the administrative process in university organizations than in any other large and complex institution in contemporary society. Careful consideration of the function of administration per se has been the work of those who have been concerned with the process in the business corporation, in the public service, in military organizations, in the church, and in other large-scale, non-educational settings. Although all of these institutional settings are different and each, therefore, modifies the process in terms of its own peculiar needs, it is nevertheless apparent as a result of the research conducted by students in this field that the administrative process has a universal content which we can identify and articulate. On the basis of what we know of administration in the whole of modern society,[1] we can, I believe, postulate the following:

1. Administration is the performance of a definable social process (the administrative process) by individuals and groups in the context of a specific enterprise functioning in its definable environment. The

performance will obviously vary with the individual (or group), with the enterprise in which it is performed, and, in turn, with the environment in which the administrator and the enterprise are situated. Thus the performing individual (or group), the enterprise, and the environment constitute variables which not only influence the performance but, indeed, significantly modify the process per se. Yet, in spite of all the modifications which these variables introduce, there are constants within the process which we can isolate and identify.

2. The administrative process (however and wherever and by whomever performed) is a cycle of action composed of the following activities:

a. *Decision-making.* We are aware, of course, that decision-making, on the one hand, may be rational, deliberative, discretionary, and purposive; and on the other hand, it may be irrational, habitual, involuntary, and random in character. However, in so far as it is rational, deliberative, discretionary, and purposive, it is performed by means of five major steps: definition of the issue, analysis of the existing situation, calculation and delineation of alternatives, deliberation, and, finally, choice. Some of these steps may be performed carefully and others in a cursory fashion. But regardless of the variation among them, depending upon time and circumstance, in one degree or another all five are present in all decision-making, whether the decision is made by an individual or a group, or, as is more often the case, some combination thereof.

b. *Programing.* Decisions become guides to action after they have been interpreted in the form of specific working plans, projects, and methods that will achieve the objective which the decision represents.

c. *Communication.* We are not speaking of all forms of communication here, for that is a larger subject. We are referring, rather, to that aspect of communication which is concerned with communicating a programed decision to those of whom action is required.

d. *Control.* All action required by a programed and communicated decision is more nearly assured if specific standards of performance are established and subsequently enforced. A combination of the setting and enforcement of standards is, in fact, "control."

e. *Reappraisal.* Decisions, even correct ones, have limited validity. The facts upon which they are based change. The goals which they serve will vary. Indeed, every decision in itself so changes the situation in which it was made as to create a new situation which will ultimately require a revision in the original decision. For all of these reasons, a decision is no sooner made than it is necessary to reappraise it. In reappraisal the process then runs full circle, and the whole group of activities begins again. This might well be referred to as the dialectic of the administrative process.

3. The process is thus a composite of the actions taken by the administrator. These are the five things he actually does. At this point we must make several observations. First, it is only in the idealized circumstance that all steps occur and are completed in this sequence. In many cases, for example, "programing" will produce "reappraisal," and "control" may precede "communication." In the second place, the administration does them with reference to different kinds of things and for the realization of different kinds of objectives. More specifically, the performer takes those actions making up that process in order to do the following:

a. *Prepare policy.* Here the administrator is concerned with defining the objectives that guide the actions of the whole enterprise or significant portions thereof. In doing so, he is making a decision, designing a program, developing a strategy of communication, devising a system of controls, and preparing the opportunity for reappraisal.

b. *Manage resources.* Five resources are available to him which he must organize and allocate and husband in every way possible, Those resources are people, money, materials, time, and authority. He manages them to the end that he may realize the institution's objectives or its prepared policies. In doing so, he makes decisions about where he will obtain these resources and how he will allocate them. He lays plans or prepares programs for securing the personnel, the material, or the dollars from the source decided upon. Likewise, each of the other steps in the cycle is performed in full or cursory fashion with reference to the acquisition, the control, or other aspects of the management of any one of these five resources.[2]

c. *Execute policy.* Here we are concerned with relating resources to policy and actually setting in motion the whole complex of objectives and resources. The performer of the process now has a prepared plan and the resources with which to carry it out. In setting it in motion, there are many things that he (or the administering group) will do. They will include providing the enthusiasm which is necessary to carry the policy forward and the constant interpretation both of prior decisions and the relationship of actual experience to policy. The administrator will need to keep the various parts of the enterprise developing in relation to time and in reference to one another. He will be constantly concerned with the interaction between the organization and its environment and with the modifications and adaptations which that interaction requires in organizational policy and behavior. He will need to resolve inevitable areas of conflict, both within the enterprise and between it and the environment within which it functions. In some instances, his own performance will be necessary to provide examples to his colleagues or his staff, and he must constantly review it in terms of the standards previously determined. Involved here are many aspects of what we commonly refer to in varying ways and with varying degrees of understanding by such terms as co-ordination, synchronization, supervision, and words derived from other fields. Here is the conductor with his prepared score, a whole complement of instruments and musicians before him, whose role it is to make audible music from the objective which the score represents and the resources which people, instruments, acoustics, and so on, make possible. As he performs, he is constantly deciding, making plans for the realization of his decision, communicating the decision to others, exercising controls over them, and revising the original decision in the light of his own experience as well as the resulting sound and, perhaps, audience and acoustical reactions. In these more artistic actions, the identity of the steps of the cycle becomes less discernible as a series of individual actions, although they are, nevertheless, present.

Thus we have a definition of administration as a process consisting of definable steps performed with reference to the functions of policy preparation, management of resources, and execution either by an individual or a group. As indicated earlier, the performance of these constants will obviously vary with the individual, with the kind of enterprise in which the performance takes place, and with the general environment within which the organization and the individual function. It must also be apparent that the cycle is performed simultaneously at different levels in an organization and in each of the different functional areas of policy, resources, and execution.

Of what value is such a theoretical concept to us in our review of what needs to be done in universities in this country to enable them to discharge their institutional responsibilities more effectively? I should say the answer is that, having defined administration, we are in a better position to review our present practice and to determine whether or not responsibilities have been appropriately assigned, whether there are parts in the process which are entirely neglected, and whether the necessary structure exists to enable us to carry on all aspects of administration as effectively as possible.

This leads directly to my second point. I question whether the "administration" of the large and complex American university is organized in such a way as to enable it to discharge the responsibilities broadly defined in this paper. Although a single article does not permit an extensive analysis of the inadequacies of our administrative organizations, I should like to describe several of what I believe to be our most fundamental difficulties as illustrations of the more general point—our need to review and overhaul our administrative organizations thoroughly if they are to undertake the university-wide role which is required of them in achieving anything approaching an organic institution. I would respectfully suggest that among our large universities, with their multiple faculties, institutions, research centers, museums, and hospitals, there are major shortcomings:

1. *Inadequacy of central structure for decision-making.* Here we encounter several basic deficiencies. In the first place, few heads of institutions have the staff organizations necessary for careful calculation of alternatives on which the administration may deliberate and among which it may ultimately choose. In the second place, such a very large number of individuals report to the president and the provost, or their equivalents, that, even with adequate staff work, deliberation is difficult because of the number and diversity of fields involved. One of two consequences results from these two circumstances. Either decision-making by the central administration is seriously delayed, or, because of that administration's general ineffectiveness the over-all decisions are, in fact, made in some one of the parts of the institution. The latter course is certainly appropriate when the individual unit is competent to make the decision. However, we are speaking here of questions of institution-wide significance that tend to be resolved below the over-all administrative levels because of the inability of those levels to organize themselves to cope with such questions. In concrete terms, the usual result of lack of proper organization is that the president and provost become essentially mechanical officers rather than academic leaders sharing gen-

uine academic concerns with their faculty colleagues. Much of this difficulty could be corrected by a combination of several simple but fundamental changes. Important among them are the following:

a. Creation of a series of academic vice-presidents who, functioning in homogeneous areas as staff officers, would extend the administration's ability to make rapid decisions based on a clearer understanding of the problems involved than the president as a single individual possesses. These officers, acting for the president, would become extensions of his office and his administrative personality. Extreme care would be required to avoid creating in them another level of authority which would weaken the role of the deans. This is a staff function intended to facilitate decision-making (our immediate point) and also to improve performance of programing, control, and reappraisal activities.

b. Establishment of formal structures to assure at least a minimum of thoughtful consideration of alternative courses of action available. In my judgment, a "cabinet" or "operating committee" (to borrow terms from other contexts) or some equivalent type of organized staff meeting at the over-all administrative level is essential; yet relatively few institutions today have regularly scheduled meetings of this kind. In our institution, the vice-chancellors and assistant chancellors in charge of primary staff and supporting areas meet several times a week to consider major decisions in almost exactly the same way that a committee in a corporate organization would function. Great care must be taken to make certain that such a group does not exercise choice, for this, in large measure, should be reserved for the chief executive, although such a group tends to develop a consensus which, more often than not, becomes the chief executive's choice. In any event, the group participates actively and significantly in the other steps in the decision-making activity, for it does assist in defining issues, in casting up alternative solutions, and in deliberating on them. Such a device, of course, has assets in respect to communication and co-ordination which are above and beyond its role in decision-making.

c. Providing the president with the types of staff assistance in the fields of budgeting, personnel, organization and methods, academic research, and total institutional planning which would normally be available to the heads of other organizations in our society that are of comparable size. Here our problem is twofold; first, to develop such staffs, and, second, to learn to use them. For some of us who are reluctant to acknowledge that a president is in fact an executive, the latter may prove the more difficult. If changes of this type can be made, relief from an infinite amount of detail will enable the president to do some of the broad thinking about the institution as a whole which is the principal responsibility of his office. He should find that the academic questions which come before him have been carefully analyzed by his vice-presidents on the academic staff, and the major issues crystallized to enable him to exercise choice. Thus consolidated and distilled, the issues become manageable, and he can again participate in academic affairs from which he tends to be excluded in the present confused organizational structure. To refer again to our definition of the administrative process, the task of achieving the types of change we have outlined becomes easier when "choice" has been recognized as a separate and identifiable aspect of decision-making. It becomes an activity which the president can undertake without having assumed all of the other steps involved in decision-making. The refinement of definition also permits others in the institution to become essential to the activity of decision-making even though they may not exercise choice. A happy and effective institution is usually one whose parts are sufficiently sophisticated in their understanding of the several aspects of decision-making so that each can participate in the appropriate aspect (be it definition of the issues, calculation of alternatives, or deliberation), and none feel neglected if it does not join equally in the exercise of choice. It is my personal opinion that more institutional conflict arises from confusion in this matter than from any other single aspect of institutional governance.

2. *Neglect of the problems of communication.* Systematic efforts to improve communication processes are important in any large organization. However, more than the usual effort must be made in universities because of several circumstances which are inherent in those institutions. In the first place, the interests of the several parts of the institution are infinitely more specialized than those of most organizations in modern society. Furthermore, they cover a wider range of subjects. In this respect there is no comparison between most large industrial corporations and a large university organization. Also, the essential but unusual individuality of thought and behavior of the academic person presents specialized problems in communication. Similar problems are often seen in hospitals, in laboratories, and in other highly professionalized areas of both the government bureau and the corporation. It is one of the tasks of administration in these large and complex universities to find ways of improving methods of

communication in order to create a reasonably cohesive total institution. As it attempts to do this, the administration must bear several things in mind. First, there are many standard devices for communication to which we resort less often than we should. The tendency is to hold staff meetings at the departmental, school, and university levels irregularly or, often, not at all. Preparation for such meetings is frequently casual at best. Again, we do not systematically insist on "concurrence" when policy papers are in the process of development. We seldom encourage the use of standardized systems for informing all interested parts of the institution of policy decisions that have been made. When used indiscriminately and by persons more concerned with procedure than with substance, these communication devices can become bureaucratic nuisances; but properly used, they become an indispensable aid in cutting through institutional complexity. They are, however, only means to an end: the need to make the administrations of our institutions constantly aware of the importance of communication within the total enterprise. It is this awareness with which we must be concerned. When it has been developed, the various mechanical devices that assure communication will follow naturally.

There is a third consideration. Having become aware of the need for communication, one must guard against permitting it to become an end in itself. One of our great difficulties, it seems to me, is that many of us as academic people feel that we must be concerned with every issue, however detailed and mechanical, that comes up in the institution. The dangers are great, and the time wasted is significant, when the professor becomes interested in elevator-operation and an individual trustee feels he must make decisions about curriculum content. Communication which goes to the extreme of informing everyone about everything on the theory that every member of the institution must be consulted on every subject is dangerous indeed. This is a confusion of ends and means that contributes to an already murky understanding of roles within an institution.

3. *Confusion regarding "control."* Unfortunately, "control" is another term which is emotion-laden in university circles. Here our problem is to handle institutional controls in a sophisticated way, not inveighing against them, on the one hand, or stupidly multiplying them, on the other. In idealizing the academic community, we visualize every individual as functioning exclusively in terms of his conscience, his sense of academic appropriateness, and his understanding of truth. In such a romanticized situation, he is subjected to no more controls by his colleagues than an individual in a society

entirely free from governmental restrictions. When the controls come, too often they are judged to be the products of an aggressive administration or a meddlesome board of trustees. Actually, they arise from the conflicting needs and interests which a complex institution develops. Thus, for example, undergraduate students may insist upon restrictions in the use of graduate assistants for classroom instruction. One area of the graduate faculty may insist on standards of residence for the Ph.D. degree which are bitterly resented by other faculties in more "applied" areas. Non-medical interests within the university, for example, may insist upon a proportionate distribution of total institutional fund-raising effort to make certain that there is some balance among the resources of the institution. Deans are constantly pressed to assure at least a minimum of uniformity in teaching loads within a given school. Many of the less well-paid faculties would like the institution to maintain at least a general uniformity in salary structures, not only within a given field, but, increasingly, between fields as diverse as philosophy and medicine. The faculty of one discipline will hold the administration responsible for the damage to the reputation of the total institution if a national accrediting organization refuses to accredit the program of another discipline within the university. The most independent of our teaching and research colleagues are the first to demand that an administration impose rigid controls upon the institution's athletic program.

Any one of us can add to this list indefinitely. These conflicting demands are resolved by policies which, in fact, are the controls of future operations. Although some obviously stem from a sense of bureaucratic tidiness, for the most part they have their origins in real conflicts of interest which necessitate the restriction of individual groups in the interest of the whole institution.

The difficult but very human aspect of this problem is that we are all interested in controls for other people but are often unwilling to concede that they should apply to ourselves. We may demand that the administration force efficiencies on one part of the university in order to avoid a disproportionate loss of funds in that area, but object to the administration's efforts to economize in centralized purchasing when they affect us. We may be sharply critical of the use of inferior personnel on someone else's faculty, and bitterly resentful of any effort by the administration to review the qualifications of persons whom we propose to appoint to our own staff. If programs leading toward graduate degrees are superficial in another field than our own, we expect the administration to do something about it. But if the administration turns on our own programs, we are inclined to consider this an arbitrary intrusion upon a field in which the administration lacks competence and in which it should be denied authority.

This confusion about the origin and functions of control leads to several practical administrative difficulties. Resistance to the notion of controls leaves us with gross inefficiencies, which are not only expensive but do nothing to create a climate of genuine academic effort. In the second place, it is too often true that the remoteness of the administration from the real academic problems of the institution makes for controls that are frequently ends in themselves. Budgetary and personnel controls are important in resolving internal institutional conflicts when they are exercised by persons who are seeking to maximize the human and financial resources of the entire institution. They become mechanical playthings when exercised by those who are not thoroughly immersed in the objectives of the academic program.

The secret lies, I believe, not in avoiding controls but in delegating their enforcement to the smallest unit which can efficiently exercise them. In making this judgment, we are obliged to recognize a further point. In each major "control area" there are varying degrees of generality of control. Specific and detailed controls, such as the control of library acquisition funds, of travel grants, and of many aspects of student aid, may thus be exercised by quite small units; whereas more general control policies having to do with broad degree requirements, basic standards of selection and promotion, the overall allocation of funds, and the determination of the fields of academic activity in which limited resources may best be invested will necessarily be charged to larger units of a total institution.

In other words, I should urge that we accept the essentiality of controls, that we endeavor to define them in both their specific and general aspects, and that we studiously attempt to place responsibility on those units within the institution which are capable of exercising the controls in their varying degrees of generality.

4. *No systematic provision for "reappraisal".* It seems to me that "reappraisal" is the part of the administrative process which is most important in assuring change in an organization and, therefore, in maintaining a dynamic institution. Although we know that a decision, once made, must immediately be reappraised, the tendency in most institutions is to make a decision and then leave it alone until it gets into trouble. This practice is the result of several factors. In the first place, our natural tendency is to standardize an activity, not change it constantly. This inclination is typical in all organizations, but particularly in universities, which lack the built-in competition

that leads to change. As individual faculty members, we are defensive about existing courses, curriculums, and programs. In addition, there is the protective role played by the alumni, a host of organized professional societies, accrediting agencies, and even the legislature, which tends to preserve the status quo. Again, and most importantly, there is no one whose responsibility it is to reappraise the program constantly. Other kinds of institutions have developed their own particular ways of assuring reappraisal. In an industrial concern, one would not expect the manufacturing division to make all decisions concerning changes in the product. Reappraisal might be stimulated by suggestions from the sales staff based on conditions in the market, by the constant efforts of the engineering staff to improve the product, or by the findings of the research and development division. In a military organization, it might well come from a planning staff, a research unit, an inspection organization, or some one of the various staff organizations immediately surrounding the commanding officer.

I am not arguing that these avenues of reappraisal are available to an academic institution. I know they are not. I am saying that other institutions than the university have found ways of building in mechanisms for constant reappraisal of their programs, and I think the university in its own way must do the same thing. I doubt that this will be achieved by suddenly establishing a planning or a research staff in the president's office or by charging business affairs with greater responsibility for the establishment of standards of efficiency, though both of these steps would be helpful. I think, rather, that, beginning at the departmental level and working through the entire institution, persons or groups of persons must be charged with the activity of reappraisal as a continuing responsibility. The chairman of any department of any size should be in a position to relieve one of his colleagues of some or all of his teaching and research responsibilities so that he can devote himself to a constant reconsideration of curriculum matters. At the school and college level, this is a matter with which several individuals should be occupied, perhaps full time, perhaps part time, perhaps in rotation, perhaps not. Here, as in the case of the other points I have made, I am not arguing for any particular method. My primary concern is to emphasize the fact that the activity of reappraisal is an important and constant aspect of decision-making and institutional growth.

5. *Absence of a concept of human-resources management.* Large-scale management in church, government, and corporate and military organizations has long since recognized the essentiality of careful

husbanding and development of its human resources. In those organizations, the management of human resources is regarded as a corporate responsibility. In the academic world, we have always maintained that our faculties are by far our most important resource, but I seriously question whether our universities have sufficiently acknowledged the importance of the executive function of selecting, encouraging, developing, and rewarding this resource. The development of the young faculty member is left largely to the individual himself. Departmental chairmen and deans seldom deliberately plan development programs for young faculty members and then attempt to assist them in the realization of the objectives of those programs. Little counsel is given them, and our compensation plans are not established in such a way as to provide systematic rewards for successful effort or penalties when effort is not forthcoming.

Criteria for promotion are not always established, and, when they are, there is often confusion as to the relative importance of research, teaching, and professional and community service as goals toward which the individual should work. Basic personnel records are meager indeed. The role of the personnel office is generally regarded as a mechanical one which relates primarily to the functions of non-academic personnel. Salary surveys, when made, are often the function of an *ad hoc* faculty committee, which is seldom in a position to secure or maintain all of the data which a central personnel office should record. In many cases, appointment, promotion, and even salary increases are the responsibility of faculty committees.

We condone all of this in the name of the independence of the individual scholar. I question whether this kind of confusion is helpful in maintaining the independence of creative effort. I would, rather, believe that we can do infinitely more for the individual and for his institution if we are willing to adopt the concept that the total institution has an administrative responsibility for the maximum growth and utilization of its human resources. Although there is no question concerning the importance of faculty participation in these activities, to me it is equally clear that no individual faculty member or committee can successfully assume responsibility for the development of individual members of the faculty over a period of years, nor can they intelligently establish, encourage, and develop a balanced staff in any broad area. Definite administrative responsibility is needed to ensure that (1) a balance exists within the staff, (2) one person complements another and is rewarded in terms of that complementary relationship as well as on the basis of absolute standards for individual performance, and (3) a suitable program of personal development is operative for the individual from the time he begins as a young member of the faculty until he has reached a level of professional maturity, when little further assistance is required. These are the responsibilities of the chairmen and the deans. They should not be left to chance, and they cannot be passed to the president's office, though effective academic vice-presidents of the type described earlier can and should make certain that administrators at the school and departmental levels are assuming these responsibilities, and can assist and encourage them in doing so.

6. *Widespread disregard of proven management tools.* Relatively few among us have a sufficient number of employees at the executive level to enable us to take full advantage of new but by no means experimental management tools. Thus, for example, there are few institutions that have a staff concerned with problems of procedural improvement or the solution of organizational problems. Few of us have staffs capable of carrying on continuous analysis of our use of equipment and space, although we are today seriously concerned about the adequacy of our capital plants for the critical years ahead. Our lack of modern methods of inventory control, the absence of centralized office services, and our failure to use machines for the essentially clerical tasks that are now too frequently performed by faculty are illustrations of the point. We tend to resist such innovations because of the mistaken notion that the introduction of "efficiency concepts" endangers the autonomy of the individual faculty member. A perceptive administration and a receptive faculty can come to understand that these are methods which, when properly employed, can do much to save faculty time and increase the use of human as well as dollar resources.

7. *Rudimentary concept of the function of execution.* In earlier pages, we have spoken of execution as the relating of resources to policy and the actual setting in motion of the whole complex of objectives and resources. In still other sections, we have commented on the tendency of the modern university to fragmentation. Implicit in such fragmentation is a certain distrust of, and even opposition to, the function of execution. To the extent that the parts regard themselves as self-contained and self-maintaining, they deny the need for an activity which relates them to one another, which assists them in the realization of their own objectives, or guides and controls their internal development.

In fact, however, the establishment of a new professional school, for example, will require that someone make certain that it grows in accordance with the purposes of its founding, that it is encouraged to establish the appropriate relationships with the related disciplinary department, that it develops its program in some consonance with others on the campus, and that it receives allocations in accordance with its need, its progress, and its relative importance in the total university undertaking. In addition, the new school will require assurance of assistance from other parts of the campus and help in securing understanding and support from the community.

The same problems will appear whenever a new series of course offerings is introduced in a single department. As an example, let us take a new teaching and research program in the field of the history of technology. Through the years, it must gradually be related to work in engineering, industry, economics, and a variety of other areas. It will need encouragement in the form of new funds and the allocation of scholarships and fellowships, and will rely on the growth of faculties in those related areas upon which it will come to depend in its rise to full maturity.

I have cited these examples to emphasize the importance of counseling, guidance, encouragement, support, and co-ordination of effort in enabling the individual part to continue to grow both within itself and in its relationship to the total institution. These are the activities which compose the function of execution. Too often they are frustrated in practice by our tendency to fragment our institutions so as to protect what we choose to regard as freedom of intellectual effort. In fact, of course, we are dealing with two separate values. The importance of maintaining the individual's freedom is pre-eminent, but the mature function of execution in relating one part to another and in encouraging each individually is essential if this freedom is to be meaningful. Here, as in other cases, it is increasingly important to understand that freedom is more than a mere negation of efforts to relate one of us to another. Stated affirmatively, it is time, in the complex academic institutions of today, that we develop a well-defined concept of execution which does not destroy the values of the freedom which we cherish.

8. *Confusion of roles within the institution.* At the turn of the century, the American university was still a relatively simple social institution. Today it is many times larger and infinitely more complex. It serves a greater variety of people, has many more students, faces infinitely more difficult public-relations responsibilities, maintains much larger capital plants, and offers a wider range of subject-matters. These changes in the size and complexity of the institution

have not been accompanied by a corresponding redefinition of the responsibilities of the administration in conducting its affairs.

In the simpler forms of university organization in the past, virtually everyone could be concerned with all problems of any consequence within the institution. Trustees concerned themselves with curriculums; faculties addressed themselves to the problems of the budget and the operation of the capital plant; and administrative officers were sometimes involved in the details of student discipline. Today, this "one big family" type of institutional management is becoming less and less practicable in our large universities. Our need now is to develop specialized roles so that each part of the institution concentrates on the areas of its greatest competence. Governing boards should limit themselves to trustee-like functions. There is no excuse for businessmen-trustees' meddling in internal institutional affairs; such an intrusion of the board of directors into the affairs of management would be considered inappropriate in commercial corporations. The need for specialization in a corporate setting must be transferred to the governance of a large academic institution. It is equally unfortunate when faculty committees take to themselves the principal responsibility for making decisions concerning matters of faculty personnel, for this usurps the authority of the department chairman and the dean. More often than not, it means that selection and promotion rest with the committee, but the control of salaries and other ways of rewarding and encouraging faculty development rests with the dean and the department chairman. Again, in a complex institution, it is equally apparent that our administrators frequently fail to devise methods for assuring over-all control of resources, on the one hand, and leave much of the responsibility for individual action in the hands of those best able to exercise it, on the other. Thus the use of line-item budgets by central administrations in complex institutions (often required by law) is an anachronism. Detailed types of personnel control belong in the same category. Effective methods of decentralization are essential if the administration is to avoid the rigidities which are destructive of the initiative that keeps an institution alive.

The problems of role definition are legion. They stem in some instances from an unfortunate competition for power which is coupled with a tendency to divide institutions arbitrarily into artificially rigid categories such as trustees, administration, and faculty, or academic and non-academic. In truth, however, the problem is not to define powers but roles and functions. It is complicated further by the difficulty of developing a sufficient understanding of the role of staff units within the university structure. A concept that has long been recognized in other institutional settings faces an uphill battle in our academic organizations. Perhaps the greatest obstacle is the widespread feeling to which I referred earlier that a person is not participating in the general administration of the institution unless he is making decisions, and he cannot be making a decision unless he is actually making the ultimate choice. A concept more consonant with the needs of a complex organization would allocate the various aspects of decision-making to the individuals and groups most capable of undertaking them. Some might participate in choice, and others might not. All might on some subjects, and few on others. Many may deliberate among alternatives, but the right of making the ultimate choice may be exercised by the trustees. On the other hand, the trustees may recognize the need for a decision, but the calculation of alternatives, deliberation among them, and ultimate choice may be exercised by the teaching staff, by a dean, or by the president. In either situation, each is fulfilling definable roles with reference to decision-making, which, in turn, is an important part of the administrative process. It follows from this that, in their special ways, all persons and groups have a contribution to make; an adequate definition of roles permits all parts of the institution to participate in an integrated administrative process, and as a result leads to a concept of institutional totality which makes the university something more than a congeries of isolated parts.

9. *Failure to train for university administration.* No large institution in our society gives less attention to the problems of training students for administration than does the university. We have developed schools of public administration, business administration, hospital administration, hotel administration, and elementary- and secondary-school administration. But we offer almost no preparation for those who will be administrators of our large institutions of higher education. The literature on the subject is modest indeed; what we have is either mechanical in character or devoid of the insight into the administrative process which the field of administrative science is bringing into other institutions in contemporary society. Beyond all of this, I think it is quite clear that most of the academic community would disapprove of the development of training programs in this field because of its suspicion of the administrative process itself. Many deans and presidents of my acquaintance are half-apologetic about being administrators, and their teaching and research colleagues leave no doubt of their distrust of the function and of those who are willing to perform it as a full-time occupation. I

doubt that we will overcome our training problem in this field until we have first established the legitimacy of the administrative process and the respectability of performing it. This is a matter of far-reaching consequence which will not be corrected by a few summer study programs for the development of university executives or by the introduction of a few more courses in educational administration within our schools of education. In a generation which has isolated the administrative process in society and subjected it to careful appraisal, we university administrators have done little to study it, are self-conscious in our performance of it, and have been almost systematic in our neglect of the necessity of training for it. As educators, we are reluctant to accept responsibility for it, but, on the other hand, we complain when business administrators are called upon to do it for us.

For years we have been reminding ourselves that universities are moving into a crucial period in the decade ahead. In doing so, we have been inclined to think that much of the adaptation to the new problems must come from taxpayers, alumni, parents, and others on whom our institutions depend for support. It is certainly, however, equally important that we re-examine ourselves in preparation for these trying times. As we do look at ourselves, I should suggest that the three questions I have raised in this and the preceding article[3] concerning the concept of the institution as an organic whole, the organization of our faculties, and the organization of our administrations are matters of far-reaching significance.

As we examine them, is it not important to develop new attitudes on a number of subjects? In the first place, I would ask whether or not our attitude toward change, or, more exactly, our resistance to change, is compatible with the responsibilities which our institutions must assume in the years ahead. There is not a reader among us who is not familiar with an institution or with a major faculty within an institution which bitterly resents change, whether suggested from without or actively urged by members from within. We know the protective attitude we adopt toward our individual courses and our individual methods of performing administrative activities. Is it not incumbent upon every responsible educator to ask himself whether or not he is as willing to consider fundamental change in his course offerings, in his department's curriculums, and in current teaching methodology as he is expectant that students will change their traditional attitudes toward borrowing, that parents will appreciably increase their interest in sacrificing for higher education, that corporations will substantially alter their attitude toward financial support of higher education, and that legislators will dramatically transform their attitudes toward the percentage of state and municipal budgets that go into higher education?

In this preparation for the years ahead we must be concerned about another attitude within university circles. I return here to a point which I have mentioned several times; namely, our attitude toward one another and toward the institution. We are traditionally and properly a skeptical profession, but we can be constructively skeptical without being constantly suspicious of one another. We should be able to articulate our differences constructively and avoid the public vituperation and personal insinuation which all too frequently characterize the atmosphere of segments of too many of our institutions. I refuse to believe that vindictiveness and recrimination are essential to scholarly creativity and the maintenance of intellectual independence. This is no plea for the rounded edge of "the organization man," but a question as to whether our attitudes toward one another and toward the total institution are as consistent with good citizenship as they might be.

If desirable changes in attitude can be achieved, we shall have some prospect of constructively appraising the three questions raised here. Finally, if those questions can find affirmative answers, we shall be better prepared to face successfully the years of pressure that are upon us.

Footnotes

1. This dicussion of the administrative process draws upon an earlier article of mine, "Notes on a General Theory of Administration," *Administrative Science Quarterly*, I (June, 1956), pp. 3-20. See also F. A. Shull, editor, *Selected Readings in Management* (Homewood, Illinois: Richard D. Irwin, Inc., 1958), pp. 368-89, which, in turn, draws heavily upon the emerging literature of administrative science.

2. This aspect of the process is often distasteful to academic administrators. (See Harold Taylor's "College President—Idea Man or Money Man?" in the *New York Times Magazine*, April 12, 1959, pp. 23, 84-85.) Yet I do not see how we can separate it from the rest of the process, or, indeed, divorce the acquisition of funds from their control and allocation, or distinguish between the acquisition of money and of personnel. They are an integral part of the administrative process.

3. "Organization in Large American Universities: The Faculties," *Journal of Higher Education*, 30 (October, 1959), pp. 353-64.

THE "MANAGERIAL REVOLUTION"
IN HIGHER EDUCATION

Francis E. Rourke and Glenn E. Brooks

Universities are the source of constant intellectual and scientific innovation for the society as a whole, and yet, as many observers have noted, university personnel are highly reluctant to accept changes in the operation of the university itself. Only in recent years have American universities shown much inclination to revise their tradi- tional organization and procedure. Even now, such changes face heavy opposition. Faculty members who constantly seek to break new ground in their own discipline may steadfastly resist any innovation in university management. Administrative officers themselves often find it difficult to accept departures from the traditional way of doing things. Somehow, university personnel, whose lives are devoted to expanding knowledge about the most elusive processes of their environment, nonetheless find it extremely difficult to accept the idea of looking into the campus itself. And yet this resistance to reform cannot simply be written off as lack of vision or a defense of vested interests, for often it is founded upon deeply felt assumptions about the purpose of higher education.

In the context of this conservative tradition, the changes that have taken place recently in the administration of colleges and universities have the appearance of a managerial revolution, for these changes have brought basic modifications in the administrative structure of educational institutions. And while the modifications are not yet as thoroughgoing as appearances indicate, they may eventually be as

From the *Administrative Science Quarterly,* Vol. 9, No. 2, September 1964, pp. 154-181. Reprinted by permission of the publisher.

significant for education as they have been in the past for industry and government, for in the years since World War II, institutions of higher learning have increasingly engaged in a conscious effort to find ways and means of using their resources with greater efficiency. In the course of this attempt to rationalize their operations, a growing number of universities are beginning to experiment with theories and practices usually identified with scientific management, or, as some would prefer, "managerial science."

These managerial innovations are scientific at least in the sense that they are characterized by much greater "explicitness, rigor, and quantification"[1] than has been the case in the past with academic administration. The new techniques of management include the operation of professional offices of institutional research, the use of quantitative analysis as a basis for making decisions about the internal allocation of resources, and a growing reliance upon automatic data-processing equipment in the everyday processes of university administration. The introduction of computer techniques is of particular importance in accelerating this development. Several universities plan to program models of their institution on a computer so that the effects of administrative decisions may be simulated in advance.

Among university administrators the wisdom of applying these new management tools to higher education is being debated on campuses across the country. Proponents of these administrative innovations feel that more rational techniques—that is, techniques which permit an objective comparison of alternatives in terms of specified goals—permit the institution to achieve greater efficiency and fairness in its internal operation. They argue that the pressures of growing enrollments, curriculum modernization, and shortages of funds no longer allow the educational institution the luxury of rule-of-thumb procedures. Under a rationalized system, inequities in teaching loads, inefficiency in space utilization, or imbalances in salary schedules are clearly revealed to the administrator's view.

It is also claimed that public universities will fare much better in their dealings with state government and the community at large if they rely on space-utilization formulas, cost analysis, and other quantitative measuring devices in justifying their requests for support. Advocates of scientific management believe that resistance to these new techniques springs mostly from men who misunderstand the nature of science, or whose positions are threatened by a rational handling of educational resources. Without these management innovations, it is felt, universities will not be able to meet the enrollment surge in the decade to come, or to handle the large and complex campus systems now needed in higher education. There is widespread agreement with the view of Chancellor Edward H. Litchfield of the University of Pittsburgh, who holds that *"administration and the administrative process occur in substantially the same generalized form in industrial, commercial, civil, educational, military, and hospital organization."*[2]

There are others—including men in objective and unthreatened positions—who recall the words of Thorstein Veblen: "Men dilate on the high necessity of a businesslike organization and control of the university, its equipment, personnel and routine. . . . In this view the university is conceived as a business house dealing in merchantable knowledge, placed under the governing hand of a captain of erudition, whose office it is to turn the means in hand to account in the largest feasible output." This concept of efficiency, said Veblen, "puts a premium on mediocrity and perfunctory work, and brings academic life to revolve about the office of the Keeper of the Tape and Sealing Wax."[3] In more recent and less vitriolic terms, John D. Millett, President of Miami University, has expressed the belief that *"ideas drawn from business and public administration have only a very limited applicability to colleges and universities."*[4]

Critics also contend that the impressive procedures of scientific management may be little more than camouflage for the prejudices of the administrator. In this sense, some educators fear that a pseudo science is emerging which will ultimately do violence to higher education as well as to any efforts to develop reliable methods of improving educational management. As compared with other organizational systems, the educational enterprise in this country has always been comparatively disorderly, undisciplined, and hostile to "bureaucracy," and there are many educators who devoutly believe that academic creativity and inspiration wither in the atmosphere of stringent administration. The perennial dream of many an academician is that of a university run entirely by professors—a citadel of learning undisturbed by the presence of registrars, business managers, or even perhaps deans and presidents.[5]

In an effort to clarify the issues involved in this dispute, we have begun a survey of managerial innovations at leading state universities across the country.[6] This study was launched with two principal objectives in view. The first is that of gauging the extent to which practices associated with scientific management have actually permeated public higher education, and the second is that of making a cautious assessment of the effects of these managerial changes on the educational process, including the position of the faculty and the handling of students, the management of the plant, and the quest for outside support by public colleges and universities.

Four areas of managerial activity have been singled out for systematic observation in this survey: (1) the establishment of offices of institutional research; (2) the growing use of automatic data-processing techniques in public higher education; (3) the development of new methods of resource allocation, both in budgeting and space utilization; and (4) changes in the character of top-level university administration which both reflect and contribute to this trend toward scientific management. We have centered our attention in this study on public institutions because the advent of scientific management is deeply affected by, and has important implications for, the position of public colleges and universities as agencies of the state. However, it is generally accepted that private universities have been as much influenced in their internal administration by the onset of scientific management as public institutions, and in some cases have been pacesetters in this development. MIT, for example, has pioneered in the use of computers for class scheduling.

Institutional Research

Institutional research occupies a position of central importance in the trend toward scientific management in higher education. Although the nature and scope of this kind of research activity still eludes precise definition, it boils down to the fact that universities are beginning to study themselves very carefully—to develop all kinds of data about their students, faculty, costs, and operations—for the purpose of making informed judgments, instead of guessing or relying on the intuitions of the administrator in making decisions.

But the growth of institutional research has an effect far beyond the accumulation of additional information. A good bureau of institutional research may probe into many dusty corners of university life, revealing, for example, that there is a much heavier work load in some departments than in others, that a high dropout rate is present among the most promising students, or that the level of faculty salaries is putting the university at a serious competitive disadvantage. Sometimes the information gathered may simply bring alterations in administrative routine. On other occasions, however, it may trigger sharp disputes among departments, or a searching re-examination by top-level administrators of a university's goals and achievements.

It is only very recently that most colleges and universities have formally established offices or bureaus of institutional research. In 1957, when the American Council on Education sponsored a nationwide conference on the subject of institutional self-study, it was hard put at first to locate individuals to whom invitations to attend such a meeting should be extended. Five years later there were over 60 people present at a national conference of institutional research officials held at Northern Illinois University,[7] and in the following year over 200 attended a similar meeting at Wayne University in Detroit.[8]

In part, of course, these swelling figures reflect not so much an increase in the actual number of individuals engaged in institutional research as they do the growing tendency of those involved in this activity to identify themselves with this new role in academic administration. For a long time institutional research was carried on at a number of institutions in at least an embryonic way as a by-product of regular budgetary preparation, or in conjunction with studies of the university's building needs, or as a result of the persistent efforts of registrars and admissions officers to analyze the kind of student an institution was attracting and the quality of the record he was compiling after admission.

Institutional research was thus a standard procedure at many institutions of higher education in this country long before it made any appearance on their formal table of organization, and it is still performed in this informal way at many schools where it has not yet gained official recognition as a separate administrative function. In a survey published in 1961 of institutional research activity at schools having an enrollment in excess of 4,000, Howell and Carlson found that less than 20 per cent of the institutions responding employed staff members who were engaged in this activity on a full-time basis.[9]

Actually there is still far from unanimous agreement in higher education as to what institutional research really is. At least two principal schools of thought on this subject have attracted considerable support. There are those who feel that institutional analysis should deal primarily with administrative or housekeeping problems, space utilization and the like, thus remaining in effect a form of operations research as applied to educational management. Others contend that it should not be confined to the buildings and grounds side of higher education but should go to the heart of the matter and appraise what is happening in the classroom. When the New England Board of Higher Education held a workshop on institutional research in 1962, it devoted its attention exclusively to the administrative aspects of campus operations. There was sharp criticism of this approach as being narrowly bureaucratic in its orientation, and in the following year the Board conducted a workshop on institutional research which was centered almost entirely on questions of academic effectiveness.

The kind of activity in which any particular bureau of institutional research chooses to engage is shaped by a variety of factors. Partly it reflects the philosophy and interests of the individual in charge of the operation, particularly when the tasks of the institutional research staff has some slack in its work schedule. One director with a background in economics has concentrated his research on cost studies and general financial problems. Another director with a particular interest in computers has devoted much of his time to the development of a comprehensive administrative system for his university based on the use of electronic data-processing equipment. Over a period of years, a successful institutional research director has an opportunity to make the office a lengthened shadow of his own figure.

External pressures also play an important role in determining the activity of an office of institutional study. Research must very often be directed at questions to which the community demands an answer, or at questions a university president anticipates will very shortly be asked. Much of the time of an office of institutional research may thus be consumed in dealing with emergencies which arise in an institution's relations with its environment. For a considerable period of time after its establishment, the bureau of institutional research at the University of Massachusetts devoted a major portion of its energy to assisting in the university's efforts to free itself from a wide range of restrictions by state agencies over its internal financial and personnel practices.

Because of the need to deal with emergency situations of this kind, an office of institutional research ordinarily has very little opportunity to develop into an instrument of long-range planning—helping a university president to look ahead and anticipate the problems which his institution may confront in five or ten years. In this respect, of course, the plight of an office of institutional research is no different from that of similar research units in other organizations, as, for example, the policy planning staff in the State Department, which has tended over the years to be distracted from its intelligence function by the need to confront crises in the everyday work of the department.

Some institutional research directors also take the view that too much of their time is taken up with repetitive projects of one kind or another—annual enrollment distributions, faculty work load studies and the like. To avoid investing too much energy in this kind of recurring task, one institutional research director in the Midwest follows the practice of relinquishing jurisdiction over any study once it becomes clear that the project will need to be undertaken on an annual or periodic basis. He feels that the chief threat to the effective functioning of an office of institutional research is the possibility that it may become a routine fact-gathering agency rather than a participant in making studies focused on the more fundamental policy decisions which arise in the life of the university.

The fact of the matter is, however, that many offices of institutional research do engage in studies that are conducted on a regular basis, and their image on the campus in some cases is that of an agency which engages in routine projects connected with the budget, enrollments, or some other recurring concern. This practice was defended by one institutional research director who pointed out that it is only through repeated studies of the same subject that important trends in academic life can be clearly identified.

Considerations of diplomacy also have a distinct effect upon the work of an office of institutional research. At some institutions there has been a tendency for such offices to shy away from research concerned with areas that have traditionally lain within the jurisdiction of the faculty—curriculum, for example, or grading practices. For many faculty members the prospect of research by outsiders into the area of the classroom is, to adopt Herman Kahn's description of reactions to the possibility of nuclear war, a matter of "thinking about the unthinkable." At one institution where the office of institutional research does in fact work in academic areas, it has proven expedient to co-opt the faculty into the institutional research operation by establishing a faculty advisory committee to guide the research projects undertaken by the bureau, thus legitimizing the results of these studies in the eyes of the academic staff.

Contrasting approaches to the handling of institutional research can be found at the neighboring universities of Washington and Oregon. At the University of Washington, most of the administrative units do their own research and analysis, and a small office known as the Office of Institutional Educational Research confines itself mostly to studies of student characteristics and performance. The registrar, the business office, the planning office, and several other agencies share, in effect, the responsibility for institutional research. This decentralization of the function prevents any single office from gaining a monopoly of critical information and fosters a lively spirit of responsibility for research among operating agencies. On the other hand, the decentralized arrangement also poses problems in the coordination of information and the duplication of effort.

At the University of Oregon, institutional research is carried on by the office of the Director of Institutional Planning and Research. The title of the office suggests the broad range of the director's responsibility. He studies long-range growth problems of the university, curriculum development (such as the question of introducing new PhD programs), and general sociological and psychological problems of the campus community (such as the role of women students and their influence on the university). In addition, the office gathers general data concerning costs, space, and university organization. Even with this concentration of institutional research in one office at the University of Oregon, several other agencies continue to do their own studies to complement the work of the central office. What the Oregon example suggests is that the presence of a highly developed office of institutional research will not necessarily pre-empt the research functions of their university agencies but may instead represent a net increase in the amount of institutional research conducted on the campus.

In any event, the question of jurisdiction is a sensitive one, and there is considerable variation among the campuses covered so far in this survey with respect to the kinds of projects considered to lie within the province of such an office. The fact that this establishment of an office of institutional research may arouse concern among faculty members should not be surprising in view of the congenital tendency of academic man to look with suspicion upon any expansion in the scope and apparent power of university administration. What is not so generally recognized, however, is the fact that such an office may also trigger opposition within university administration itself. For example, from a division of finance or business manager's office which suspects that an institutional research unit will pull some power out from under its own jurisdiction by conducting studies of fiscal administration. At two of the institutions visited there was evidence of strain between institutional research and financial administrators growing largely out of this kind of concern. While, from the remote perspective of the faculty member, university administration may appear monolithic, it is—in institutions of large size and complexity at least—as characterized by division and competition as any other bureaucratic apparatus.

There is certainly little support for the proposal made on one campus to integrate all institutional surveys in one office under the direction of an administrative vice-president for research and information. Such a proposal would go considerably beyond the centralization of, say, the University of Oregon, and would design the new office as a substitute rather than as a complement to other university agencies. Shortly after his appointment, the dean of liberal arts at one university indicated that he would now undertake to carry on his own research operation rather than rely on the university's office of institutional research. His motive in part was to counteract the trend toward a centralization of information—and administrative power—in the institutional research office.

As yet it is far from clear what effect institutional research has had upon university policy and planning at the institution at which it is being conducted. At the University of Rhode Island it can fairly be said that the bureau of institutional research and its director are at the right hand of the president and at the center of university decision making.[10] More characteristically, however, the institutional research office serves in a staff capacity, and its director is at most a technical consultant to the top levels of university policy making. And there are still some institutions where institutional research is isolated from the center of policy—its studies largely ignored by university administrators and without apparent influence on their decisions. There is a story, perhaps apocryphal, that the president of one Southern university hired a professional staff member to conduct a study of his institution's operations only to discover that he already had a bureau of institutional research on his campus specifically charged with responsibility for this kind of project. It was certainly clear in some of our interviews that university presidents put a somewhat lower estimate upon the role of institutional research directors in making university policy than the directors themselves.

The closer a bureau of institutional research is to the president's office, the more immediate and direct its influence on university policy is likely to be. Hence the Rhode Island model would have considerable appeal in some quarters. The problem that arises, however, is that a university is a dual organization in which control over decision making is shared between administrators and academicians. To the extent that an office of institutional research becomes identified as an arm of administrative authority, it may lose some of its persuasive capacity on the academic side of the campus. The dean of arts and sciences at one institution contended that the office of institutional research should scrupulously avoid any identification with the administration but should cultivate instead a reputation for neutrality and independence akin to that of the U. S. Bureau of Labor Statistics. Only in this way, he argued, would its findings ever be likely to have any substantial influence with the faculty.

It is frequently pointed out that many of the questions investigated through institutional research at individual universities today have already been answered by studies conducted on other campuses. Such duplication is, of course, widespread, but it is to a very large extent inevitable. In the system of higher education which prevails in this country, each institution tends to regard itself as having a very distinctive set of goals which sets it apart from other educational organizations. To be sure, this conception is to some extent an illusion, since American universities tend, as Riesman points out, to be "isomorphic in character"[11] —to imitate each other in their purposes and organization procedures. But the belief of educators in the uniqueness of their own institutions is a strong one, and it represents a substantial barrier against efforts to apply the findings of an institutional research project conducted in one campus setting to answer questions raised in another.

Hence, many of the studies undertaken in the name of institutional research today are not so much designed to answer questions as they are to win support for findings which administrators know about from reports published by other schools, but which they hope to see applied to their own campuses. As one institutional research director put it: "The situation is that each institutional group, whether faculty or administration, feels the need to be convinced on its own ground."[12] While the ideology of institutional research thus stresses its importance as a "basis for decision,"[13] in actual practice such research also serves as a means of implementing courses of action already decided upon. In this context, institutional research becomes part of a strategy aimed at overcoming resistance to change. It is an instrument in the hands of the decision maker rather than a source of decision.

In states in which a number of state institutions of higher education must compete for funds, each institution may be pressed to develop data which will justify the largest possible allocation of funds to the home campus. In states which use formulas as a means of distributing legislative appropriations among the state institutions, institutional research is likely to be thrown into the contest to determine the ground rules for the allocation formula. A university with large graduate enrollments, in which the graduate student carries an average of eight or ten hours in contrast to the fifteen-hour load of undergraduates, can be expected to resist any move to define a full-time student as one who carries a fifteen-hour load, particularly when this definition becomes the basis for allocating the annual appropriation for higher education. So the institutional research of the university may be geared to proving the case against a flat fifteen-hour formula. In this context institutional research is not so much a tool of internal management as it is an instrument for controlling the external environment. Consequently, in such competitive states, the legislature may assign the task of institutional research to a central coordinating body not connected with any of the individual schools in hopes that a neutral agency may come up with a more objective basis for allocating funds. Once this is done, however, the institutions may turn their energies to convincing the central research agency of the merits of their local campus data. The arena of conflict may be shifted, but the dispute itself is certainly not resolved.

Automating the Campus

Related to the emergence of institutional research, but nonetheless separate from it, is the growing use of computers and electronic data-processing equipment in the management of public colleges and universities. In some quarters scientific management has been identified with the arrival of the computer on the campus, but in point of fact the computer is more the symbol than it is the source of the new managerial innovations. Scientific management had come a long way in this country prior to the advent of electronic computers, and the computer was preceded on many campuses by the establishment of an office of institutional research, the use of budgetary formulas, space-utilization studies, or other manifestations of concern over the need to obtain reliable quantitative data in making management decisions.

The use of computers in university administration must also be separated from the establishment of offices of institutional research, since automatic data processing was highly advanced at a number of institutions even before institutional research was explicitly recognized as a university function. Conversely, there has been a lively amount of institutional research on college campuses, particularly at the smaller private institutions, even without the benefit of computers or other automated aids to management analysis. Bennington College, for example, has long conducted a very careful program of appraising faculty members through the use of questionnaires to students and alumnae—a type of research it is difficult to conceive of the larger institutions undertaking, with or without the use of computers.[14]

Nevertheless, there is a clear interdependence between institutional research and the use of computers. For one thing a recent study of the uses to which computers were being put in the administration of American colleges and universities revealed that the activity for which the highest percentage of institutions were employing computers in 1962 was institutional research. This finding was something of a surprise to the authors of the computer study, who had expected that "Payroll and Accounting . . . would be the area of greatest use" of automation in college administration.[15] The operations of a bureau of institutional research may thus be facilitated, and in some cases expanded, by the accessibility of computers. Moreover, the development and exploitation of the analytical possibilities of the computer may eventually point the way toward the establishment of a bureau of institutional research, as occurred at MIT.

But even apart from their role in institutional research, computers have come to play an increasingly important role in the day-by-day chores of university administration, particularly on the larger campuses. The computer has no peer as a device for improving the speed and accuracy with which a number of routine operations can be performed, such as student registration, grade recording, and payroll processing. Used in this way, computers need not necessarily have any substantially innovative effect upon the character of university administration. As one university official put it: "We use computers primarily to carry on at a faster pace operations that we have always performed."

This is not, however, to suggest that the use of computers to perform routine clerical tasks has had no administrative impact on higher education. Actually the introduction of computers into university administration in recent years has served as a substitute for the sizable increases in clerical staff that would otherwise have been necessary to the influx of students since World War II. Because higher education has been a "growth industry" during this period, the increasing automation of the campus has not led to any reduction in the administrative work force, as contrasted with other areas of white-collar employment where the introduction of computers has brought about a substantial amount of unemployment.[16] But without computers a substantial increase in administrative personnel would have been necessary in higher education.

While data-processing machines in higher education are still used primarily for the performance of routine clerical chores, there is growing interest in employing such equipment in the analysis and development of university policy in such key areas as student admissions, curriculum development, and the planning of physical facilities. The state university of Massachusetts is making extensive use of electronic data-processing equipment to develop more accurate criteria for the selection of students than have been available through the conventional college testing programs.[17] The University of Maryland is using information obtained through computer analysis of student records to plan for the establishment over a four-year period of a new undergraduate campus in the state. The computer is being used to determine what programs, how many faculty members, and what kind of physical facilities will be needed each year during the four-year transitional period as the new undergraduate program is phased in.

Put to these more sophisticated uses, computer analysis thus becomes an important instrument of management decision. A great deal of this kind of data was—in theory at least—always available to top-level university officials, but it would have required the assignment of a substantial number of clerical employees to gather the information, and a considerable period of time would have elapsed before it was available. By easing the task of gathering quantitative information, the computer makes it much more likely that such data will have an impact on decision. The advent of computers thus means that as a practical matter university officials now have a great deal more information available to them about their own operations than ever before.

Still largely in the drawing board stage is the possibility under study at a number of the institutions visited of programming a model of the university on the computer so as to simulate the effects of major university decisions before they are taken. At the moment this appears to be a possibility which chiefly fascinates technical experts in the field of institutional research and computer technology. It is only now becoming a live possibility on the agenda of the top-level university administrators with whom interviews were conducted. In addition, there is still considerable skepticism among university administrators as to the feasibility of using computers to make what Simon calls nonprogrammed as opposed to programmed decisions, a distinction which roughly corresponds to the difference between novel decisions for which there is no precedent and routine repetitive decisions.[18] The range and, in some cases, the intangibility of the forces that must be taken into account at the highest level of university policy would seem, to some observers at least, to outreach the present limits of the computer as a decision-making tool.

One question that often cropped up in discussions with college officials regarding the role of the computer on the campus is the extent to which the new automation contributes to impersonality in the handling of students. The notion that such depersonalization is occurring is often reflected in campus newspapers and other expressions of student opinion as we move into a day in which the computer takes over the processing of student applications, registration procedures, class scheduling, the posting of grades, and decisions on dismissal. As a matter of fact, it appears quite likely that in the university of the future virtually every routine administrative contact with the student will be channeled through electronic date-processing equipment.

With virtual unanimity the college officials surveyed in this report denied that university administration was becoming more impersonal as a result of automation. Registrars and admissions officers, for example, commonly argue that use of the computers makes it possible to deal with the student on a personal basis by freeing administrators from the burden of clerical chores that would otherwise consume an increasing proportion of their time in the face of expanding enrollments and the increased range and complexity of university course offerings. From this perspective, the computer is looked upon as a device which takes over the day-to-day chores of administration, while the college official is left free to conduct interviews in depth with students and to give close personal attention to their problems.

It can also be contended, although admissions officers did not usually argue this way, that the computer itself has certain characteristics such as speed and versatility in operation, not to mention unlimited patience, that enable it in certain areas to give each student a degree of personal concern that no system of human administration would today find feasible on a large campus. It is conceivable, for example, that criteria for the appraisal and selection of entering students can be much more complex and sophisticated when the processes are administered by a high-speed piece of electronic equipment than when they must be devised and applied by overworked admissions officers. Carried to its logical extreme, this argument would suggest that the student is more likely to have his individual and perhaps idiosyncratic characteristics taken into account in an administrative environment in which he confronts banks of computers than in one in which he deals with rows of clerks.

Nevertheless, college officials are wary of the possibility that the use of computers will give their institution a reputation for impersonality which will deter highly qualified students from applying for admission. At two of the institutions visited, where the use of computers in the selection of students is highly advanced, strenuous efforts have been made to publicize the fact that personal attention is still being given to each individual application. As one registrar put it in explaining his institution's use of automation in the admissions process:

> Electronic data processing equipment and methods have not depersonalized the admissions process. They have simplified the handling of this great volume of material and increased the time admissions personnel can devote to the careful and equitable *evaluation* and *review* of records. Time saved in information retrieval and preliminary recording can now be devoted to personal interviews, clarifying problem situations and developing more realistic deadlines. In this process the "numbering" of a candidate has been unavoidable and beneficial.[19]

So far at least, it thus appears to be highly important to some universities to avoid the public image of being unduly automated. This is not, of course, universally true. Miles and Hartford report the case of one institution where "the computer was being used to produce the President's letter of appointment to the academic staff."[20] Such a procedure may not in fact be any more impersonal than a form letter typed out by a secretary, but it is hard to conceive of a method of operation more likely to convey an image of soulless administration to the faculty.

Most literature on the application of computers to educational management is appropriately concerned with the problem of administrative efficiency. Yet the consequences of introducing computers must go well beyond the realm of managerial convenience. A computer system may influence the distribution of power in a university in subtle but distinct ways. For example at one Western university, the registrar strongly resisted proposals to convert his old-fashioned registration procedure to an automated system. Outwardly, the question was simply one of administrative efficiency: would the new arrangement register students more quickly and more cheaply? Beneath the surface, however, lay another issue. The old system permitted departments to exercise a high degree of control over the admission of any student to their courses. A centralized computer registration system would have robbed the departments of their discretion in this respect. Thus several of the departments aligned themselves with the registrar in his opposition to change, not because of antagonism to efficiency, but because they wanted to preserve their traditional autonomy. The real and largely obscured issue was not whether the new system would work faster and more accurately—it would—but whether it would take power away from some people and give it to others. With such conflicting interests at stake, the dispute could not readily be resolved in terms of narrow managerial considerations alone.

Rationalizing the Use of University Resources

Traditionally, state universities have made decisions on the allocation of their resources without very much knowledge of the productivity with which these resources were already being employed. Budgets, for example, were drawn up largely in response to the pressures mounted by individual departments as well as the hunches of university administrators as to where additional funds would be likely to do the most good. And it would probably be fair to say that this is the way in which major budgetary decisions are still being made at most public institutions of higher education today. The difficulties of measuring output in the field of higher learning have been so great as to discourage many institutions from making any substantial effort in this direction at all.

And yet, along with this traditional resort to horseback judgment recent years have seen an increasing effort to develop techniques of quantitative measurement which will, in some areas at least, provide a factual basis for administrative decision. This development has been carried furthest in the area of space utilization. As one college official commented: "If science has really entered the halls of academe it is in this field." More than anything else in higher education, the use of space is measurable, down to the last inch if necessary and a growing number of institutions have developed very precise measures of the way in which space is being employed, particularly for instructional purposes.[21]

Studies of classroom utilization are ordinarily conducted in terms either of the extent to which individual classrooms are being used for instruction at particular hours of the day, or of the percentage of maximum student capacity which is being accommodated in rooms in which classes are being held. Similar investigations have been made into the use of space for offices, laboratories, and other campus facilities. Out of such studies, a number of institutions have developed formulas governing the allocation of space for particular purposes, such as dormitory rooms and faculty offices.

Some of these studies are undertaken as a result of pressures from outside sources, particularly from state building agencies which have been trying to reduce the need for additional construction by getting better utilization of existing space. But even when a state university is more or less pushed into studying the efficiency with which it is using its buildings, it soon finds that these data can be highly useful for internal management purposes, such as weighing the conflicting demands from individual schools and departments for additional offices, classrooms, or laboratory space.

There are, however, sharp upper limits on the value of space utilization studies in making decisions on the development of a campus building program. These studies or the formulas to which they give rise are highly useful in allocating space within buildings once they are constructed, or in determining the size of buildings before they are put up, but such studies cannot automatically generate decisions on the order in which buildings are to be constructed. They do not, for example, eliminate uncertainty as to whether higher priority should be given to a new science facility or to a classroom building. Top-level decisions of this kind must still be made in terms of some rather imprecise judgment of relative need, or, as is often the case, in terms of the relative pressure which rival claimants for additional space can exert.

In some cases space management will directly affect the autonomy of academic departments and agencies. At one Western university, individual departments had, over a period of many years, acquired virtual title to certain buildings and rooms on the campus. The arrangement of office and classroom space was not particularly equitable, but the idea of letting departments control their own space was consistent with the prevailing philosophy of departmental autonomy. Under a new administration, however, the university began to develop plans to inventory all space on a central computer and to allocate space on the basis of a rationalized distribution. The plan would have provided a more efficient and equalitarian use of campus buildings. It would also have cracked many of the departmental bastions. Efficient space utilization was the public issue; the related threat to departmental discretion was a source of private dispute.

There has been a growing movement in public higher education toward the development of techniques for measuring the use of fiscal resources which will parallel in exactitude those which have been designed for space utilization. Through faculty workload studies and in a variety of other ways efforts have been made to gather data on costs which will provide a clearer picture of the manner in which the educational dollar is presently being spent, and hopefully such studies will point the way toward more efficient patterns of expenditure in the future. There is still a great deal of argument as to how cost data can be most meaningfully employed in measuring educational output. Many of the college officials interviewed in this study expressed concern over the emergence of cost-analysis techniques which provide no adequate measurement of quality of program, or of the different level of expenditures necessary in graduate as opposed to under-graduate education. But there can be no doubt about the fact that state institutions of higher education today have increasingly committed themselves to collecting data on the way in which they spend money, even when they disagree as to how this data should be analyzed.

Even administrators who are skeptical of the value of fiscal studies in making budgetary decisions within public institutions of higher education nevertheless concede that such data can be highly useful in justifying and defending university expenditures against the hostile scrutiny of the legislature, a state fiscal agency, or a taxpayers' association which is challenging university's request for increased financial support. This defensive use of statistics is almost universal in public higher education today, and there are in fact those who feel that much of what passes for scientific fiscal management in academic administration is motivated by a desire to use fiscal data not as a real tool of university management but as window dressing designed to radiate an impression of efficiency and economy around a university's handling of its fiscal resources. And there can be no disputing the fact that the gathering and dissemination of information about the way in which it spends money has become an integral part of a state university's strategy in dealing with its various publics either in promoting support or in warding off attack. Increasingly, public institutions of higher education are being required under law to conduct such studies as a condition for financial support. A statute enacted in 1960 by the Michigan legislature, for example, requires institutions in the state to furnish state officials with comprehensive data on instructional costs. This legislative demand for economy provides sufficient impetus to keep the trend toward fiscal analysis in public higher education moving forward with irresistible force, even if this data gathering eventually proves to have only limited utility in internal management decision.

Certainly it is clear that there are limits on the usefulness of cost studies as a tool for making basic decisions on the allocation of fiscal resources in higher education. Unlike many business firms, a university cannot use these studies as a method of weeding out unprofitable programs, since the mission of a university requires it to commit resources to many areas of higher learning where the students are few and the unit costs are necessarily high. A case in point for many institutions of higher education today is the study of classical languages and literature. But there are many other areas where this is also true, including, for example, medical education. Cost studies thus have only limited utility for an institution seeking to appraise the return from one academic program as against another.

They have substantially more relevance, however, in certain other respects. They are useful, for example, in comparing the costs of services which all departments use in common, including telephone or secretarial facilities. They are of considerable value in highlighting certain kinds of policy problems which might not otherwise be visible, such as the cost advantages, coupled perhaps with educational liabilities, which flow from the heavy use of graduate students in undergraduate instruction. And cost studies, conducted over a period of time, may point up gradual shifts in the direction of a university's educational efforts which might take considerably longer to observe with the naked eye. Used with discretion, quantitative analysis was thus regarded as a highly valuable instrument of management planning and decision at the institutions visited in this survey.

New Styles of University Administration

The trend in the direction of what has been called scientific management in public higher education has been accompanied by certain changes in the style of university administration. The fact that such detailed information is now collected and disseminated about the internal affairs of public institutions of higher learning means that state officals and the community at large are much more aware today than was ever true in the past of the way in which the educational dollar is being spent. Traditionally, many academic administrators were as secretive about the details of university finances as a branch of the armed forces might well be about its most cherished military secrets. Needless to say, this method of operation aroused considerable suspicion among state legislators and budget officers, and in the past it has been the source of acrimonious dispute between state and university officials.[22]

Now, however, the state university has moved into a day in which, in order to obtain adequate financial support, it must reveal details about its own operations that its president himself may not have known years ago. The barriers to the free flow of information, which as Caplow and McGee point out, are so traditional a part of the academic environment, are slowly eroding under the pressure of increased demand for precise factual data on the way in which public institutions of higher education use their resources.[24] This new age of publicity is the product not only of the increased demand for accountability, but also of the fact that more efficient machinery and techniques are now available for gathering information with the advent of electronic data processing equipment. At one and the same time institutions of higher education both need to know more and can know more about what they are doing with their resources than has ever before been the case.

The shift from privacy to publicity in the style of academic administration carries with it many potential embarrassments for college administrators. One Midwestern institution recently found that a space-utilization study it had conducted soon became a weapon in the hands of opponents of the university's plans for building expansion, since it inevitably revealed less than full use of existing capacity. Another institution in the East avoided a similar fate only by withholding the publication of a space survey which showed a very low rate of utilization of the university's physical plant, until it could improve its performance in this regard. Thereupon it conducted and released the findings of a new and much more favorable report.

To some extent, state colleges and universities push each other in the direction of being much more public than was true in the past, since cost and other quantitative studies conducted at one institution very quickly become models for the kind of reports which state officials expect to receive from other schools. While this is particularly true where a number of institutions compete for support in the same state, public institutions of higher education today are becoming increasingly subject to having their performance compared with that of schools in other states through studies conducted by regional associations to which they belong or as a result of information made available by national associations in which state officials participate. The internal affairs of public institutions of higher education thus receive greater publicity today not only in the sense of being exposed to closer surveillance within their own state, but also because they are open to scrutiny before a regional or even a national audience.

Such changes in the style of academic administration have been accompanied by changes in structure and personnel at the highest level of university administration. At the larger institutions a layer of vice-presidents or assistants to the president has become firmly fixed at the summit of the administrative hierarchy. The emergence of this intermediate layer of executive personnel parallels a similar development which took place in the management of business firms earlier in this century.[24] While the university president increasingly focuses his energies on the external relations of the institution under his jurisdiction (much as the role of the United States President is now centered on his responsibilities in the area of foreign policy), the task of managing internal university affairs has increasingly been delegated to vice-presidents in charge of business, student, or academic administration. Formally or informally, these officials are organized into an executive cabinet which meets together to handle most of the critical decisions that come before the university, including budgetary allocations, plans for campus expansion, and other matters of major importance.

While the onset of scientific management has sharpened the tools of administrative decision at most schools, its influence on the basic patterns of academic organization was quite varied in the institutions visited so far in this survey. Some universities, which have just recently emerged from a teacher training or agricultural college background and are pushing hard for improved quality in the face of bigger enrollments, tend to look upon the techniques of scientific management with great enthusiasm. One university we visited had only a few short years ago been a normal school. Its enrollments were burgeoning, and the quality of its academic program, by the assessment of its own faculty, was deficient in comparison to the major state university. At the same time, the administration radiated an image of self-confidence. Exercising a high degree of control over academic and nonacademic policies it used a full arsenal of modern management techniques to make and justify its decisions.

And yet for such an institution, the advent of scientific management may be a very mixed blessing indeed. In a context in which faculty members are less privileged and in which they often feel oppressed beneath the weight of administrative authority, the innovations wrought by the new devices of management may widen the gulf between faculty and administration and thus intensify the antagonism, latent and overt, which has traditionally existed between the administrative and the academic cultures. In this respect, the new modes of management may increase the capacity for administrative oversight only at the price of making it more difficult to attract and hold a faculty upon whose quality the institution's drive for advancement and status actually depends.

At the long-established and more prestigious institutions visited in this survey, the advent of scientific management cannot yet be said to have worked any fundamental alteration in the relationship between faculty and administration. Other innovations have generally tended to offset the effects of such managerial changes as the introduction of computers and the establishment of offices of institutional research. If the president's office has grown in administrative authority, so too has the autonomous strength of individual departments through the negotiation of research contracts which give these subdivisions a measure of fiscal independence, and the increased competition for high-quality faculty members brought on by the enrollment surge as well as the research revolution. There has in short been a simultaneous operation of centripetal as well as centrifugal forces at this upper level of higher educational institutions.

Thus, where faculties are powerful and departments virtually autonomous, scientific management has not yet brought radical changes in internal organization. But even in this setting, the new techniques of management may yet have a great deal of utility for a university administrator, for it is of vital importance that the state legislature and the taxpaying public also be convinced of the soundness of university operations. Under the pressures of competition from other state institutions, a large state university is often forced to put on a dramatic show of scientific objectivity in order to justify its requests for continued support, even though the dramatic props—elaborate formulas, statistical ratios, and so on—may have very little to do with the way in which decisions are actually made within the academic establishment. As one administrative vice-president remarked about the preparation of the university budget, "We simply use the displays that give us the best image." In this case, the image of quantitative rationality discharged the university's obligations to the state without reducing the scope of faculty control over academic policy. In such a crossfire between the demands of the academic community and pressures from the state, scientific management serves not so much to manage the university as to manage the impression that outsiders have about the university.[25]

In short, managerial innovations in higher education have consequences which are considerably more tangled than appearances might indicate. New trappings of management sometimes herald authentic changes in university operation. They sometimes conceal the fact that nothing has really changed at all. But even in the universities where scientific management is introduced primarily for its dramaturgical effects, its continued practice may well influence the internal policy of public institutions of higher education as administrators come to believe that their judgments are indeed informed by the light of science.

Footnotes

1. Edward F. R. Hearle, How Useful Are "Scientific" Tools of Management?, *Public Administration Review*, 21 (1961), 206.

2. Edward H. Litchfield, Notes on a General Theory of Administration, *Administrative Science Quarterly*, 1 (1956), 28.

3. Thorstein Veblen, *The Higher Learning in America* (New York, 1957), pp. 62, 75-77.

4. John D. Millett, *The Academic Community* (New York, 1962), p. 4. See also Amitai Etzioni, Authority Structure and Organizational Effectiveness, *Administrative Science Quarterly*, 4 (1959), 43-67.

5. Consider the words of Paul Goodman: "I am proposing simply to take teaching-and-learning on its own terms, for the students and teachers to associate in the traditional way and according to their existing interest, but *entirely dispensing with the external control, administration, bureaucratic machinery, and other excrescences that have swamped our communities of scholars,*" in *The Community of Scholars* (New York, 1962), p. 168.

6. Thus far interviews have been conducted with officials at more than a dozen public institutions of higher education located in all of the principal sections of the country. These interviews took place on the campuses of the institutions concerned or at conference and workshop meetings. The authors also interviewed

some officials with statewide jurisdiction over several institutions, as well as administrators with regional or national responsibilities in the field of higher education.

7. For the proceedings of this meeting, see Northern Illinois University Research Bulletin No. 6, *Conference on Institutional Research in Higher Education* (DeKalb, Ill., 1962).

8. The proceedings of this meeting have also been published. See L. Joseph Lins, ed., *The Role of Institutional Research in Planning* (Madison, Wis., 1963). Regional groups, such as the Western Interstate Commission for Higher Education have also conducted a number of meetings and workshops on institutional research.

9. Charles E. Howell and Milton E. Carlson, *Institutional Research* (DeKalb, Ill., 1961), p. 3.

10. See the address by the President of the University of Rhode Island, Francis H. Horn, in L. Joseph Lins, *op. cit.*, pp. 1-13.

11. See David Riesman, *Constraint and Variety in American Education* (New York, 1958), pp. 10-11.

12. See Northern Illinois University Research Bulletin No. 6, *op. cit.*, p. 23.

13. See the collection of papers on institutional research edited by L. Joseph Lins *Basis for Decision* (Madison, Wis., 1963).

14. E. P. Miles, Jr., and D. L. Hartford, *A Study of Administrative Uses of Computers in Colleges and Universities of the United States* (Tallahassee, Fla., 1962), pp. 6-7.

15. As employed here, the term "greatest use" is subject to conflicting interpretation. What Miles and Hartford were comparing was the number of institutions using computers for varying purposes. Payroll and accounting might well prove to be the prime users of electronic data-processing equipment from the point of view of the computer time these activities actually monopolize. A veteran institutional research director complained to us that "most institutional research offices have the very devil of a time getting to use the machines at all, and must accept a low priority for the use of odds and ends of machine time when the so-called bread and butter operations permit."

16. See Ida R. Hoos, When the Computer Takes Over the Office, *Harvard Business Review*, 38 (1960), 102-112.

17. For a review of the complete range of uses to which computers have been put at the University of Massachusetts, see Leo Redfern, The Calculating Administrators, *State Government*, 36 (1963), 183-188. A description of the new Massachusetts admission system may be found in William Starkweather, *Electronic Data Processing of Admissions* (Amherst, Mass., 1963).

18. Herbert A. Simon, *The New Science of Management Decision* (New York, 1960) pp. 5-7.

19. Starkweather, *op. cit.*, p. 5.

20. E. P. Miles and D. L. Hartford, *op. cit.*, pp. 8-9.

21. Space-utilization studies in higher education have been much influenced by and often follow the procedures specified in John Dale Russell and James I. Dol, *Manual for Space Utilization in Colleges and Universities* (Athens, Ohio, 1957).

22. See Malcolm Moss and Francis E. Rourke, *The Campus and the State* (Baltimore, Md., 1959), pp. 87-88.

23. For their very revealing discussion of this point, see Theodore Caplow and Reece J. McGee, *The Academic Marketplace* (New York, 1958), pp. 59-62.

24. See Alfred D. Chandler, Jr., and Fritz Redlich, Recent Developments in American Business Administration and Their Conceptualization, *Business History Review*, 35 (1961), 9-15.

25. On the concept of dramaturgy and the management of impression, see Erving Goffman, *The Presentation of Self in Everyday Life* (Edinburgh, Scotland, 1956), and Victor A. Thompson, *Modern Organization* (New York, 1961), pp. 138-151.

ADMINISTRATIVE PRACTICES
IN UNIVERSITY DEPARTMENTS

Eugene Haas and Linda Collen

Until recent years the comment by Caplow and McGee in 1958 that social scientists have been neglecting their own academic domain as a focus for research was a valid one.[1] The last few years, however, have seen an upsurge of interest in both the sociology of education and the sociology of organizations. These developments have provided the orientation and conceptual tools necessary to investigate some of the problems associated with higher education in general and the American university in particular. This paper reports on one segment of research that reflects these combined orientations.

Universities and colleges have certain organizational problems which are common to most organizations in urban societies. Among them is the recruitment and selection of professional and other expert personnel, the evaluation of the performance of such personnel once they become part of the organization, and the handling of unsatisfactory participants.

Although universities resemble other organizations in having these problems, they operate in an institutional context unlike that of many organizations. Some of the significant institutional features that are important for this study are:

1. The tendency to base major policy and procedural decisions within teaching departments on democratic processes. This tendency can be seen in departmental policies and procedures that reflect a

From the *Administrative Science Quarterly,* Vol. 8, No. 1, June 1963, pp. 44-60. Reprinted by permission of the publisher.

consensual base usually lacking in organizations patterned on the "monistic" model.[2]

2. A norm which holds that the professor's classroom is a castle which is not to be invaded by peers or higher officials of the organization. This means that direct observation of teaching performance and evaluation of teaching ability, if it is to be accomplished at all, must be done through indirect means.

3. The significance of secondary (i.e., research) activity in evaluation and promotion. Although most professors are hired primarily as instructors, their evaluation and promotion are based *primarily* on the products of their research activity.

4. The application of the concept of job tenure. This frequently means, in practice, that an unsatisfactory performer cannot be legally dismissed from his position. Extralegal techniques, therefore, may develop.

This report deals with certain administrative practices in the teaching departments of a midwestern state university. Whether this university is a typical American university, we do not know. Several of its characteristics should probably be noted. It is large, having well over 20,000 students; it is complex in that it contains over eighty departments in approximately twenty colleges and professional schools.[3] Its financial condition appears to be neither excellent nor poor when compared with other public universities. This university also has a long history of having had a central administration at the top with relatively little power vis-à-vis the colleges and departments.

While having certain bureaucratic characteristics, large universities are probably less systematically bureaucratic than many business and governmental organizations of comparable size. Several studies have indicated that the divisions or departments within a particular organization will vary in the degree of bureaucratization.[4] In a broad study of the university it became apparent that while the various teaching departments had a number of common practices, they showed considerable variation in the procedures used in selecting new faculty, in evaluating the performance of faculty, and in the techniques employed in handling the unsatisfactory performer. Some of the variation may be due to the idiosyncratic characteristics of the various chairmen or a product of the unique decisions reached by the faculty within each department, but there was reason to suspect that certain organizational factors might explain much of the variation.[5]

It is generally held in organizational theory that as an organization becomes larger, formally devised, systematic procedures will become more prevalent.[6] Policies and procedural rules are usually promulgated in an organization to offer guide lines for action when many persons have to make many decisions on a wide variety of problems.

It was hypothesized that this relation between organization size and the use of formal procedures would also apply to sub-units of the organization, that larger departments would be more likely to use formalized techniques than smaller departments. More specifically, it was hypothesized that, as the size of the department increased, the methods used (a) in filling faculty vacancies, (b) in evaluating the performance of departmental faculty, and (c) in dealing with the professor on tenure who is consistently performing in an unsatisfactory manner would be more formalized. Size as treated here deals strictly with the number of personnel in the organizational subunits.

There appears to be a related but distinctly different element which could also determine formalization: the frequency with which certain decisions have to be made. If one type of decision has to be made only infrequently, it is likely that there would be little tendency to formalize the procedure for making that type of decision. If, on the other hand, certain decisions have to be made repeatedly, we would expect some standardization to be instituted. It was hypothesized, therefore, that frequency of decision making would be associated with formalization of procedures in the following instances: During a given period of years (1) the greater the number of new faculty hired, the more formal would be the hiring procedures, and (2) the greater the number of faculty considered for tenure, the more formalized would be the methods used for evaluating the performance of faculty members of the department.

Although it has been suggested that size is related to degree of formalization used in handling unsatisfactory faculty members, this process should be seen in its broader context. If an unsatisfactory participant is officially dismissed or forced out of the department in some manner, the problem of replacement must be faced. A department which can be relatively certain of getting competent replacement because of its high prestige will have a freedom, which permits it to "sluff off dead wood," that other departments will not have. A department with a favorable supply-demand ratio would have a similar freedom. It, too, could readily locate replacements. It was further hypothesized, therefore, that departments which have a high national reputation or a favorable supply-demand ratio would have more systematic procedures (a) for determining level of performance and (b) for handling unsatisfactory performers.

A fifth factor, less frequently considered in organizational research, might be called the "humanistic orientation" of the department. It goes beyond the legalistic notion of tenure. It is a view which places high priority on the dignity and needs of the unsatisfactory performer and is reflected in a recent comment of a renowned professor: "We have to live with the living as long as they are alive." This view insists that any consideration of dismissal must take into account more than the alleged incompetence of the faculty member; it must consider the consequences of dismissal for the man and his family.

This "humanistic orientation" would be reflected, it was thought, in departmental practices. In departments where this was a dominant view, there might be formal criteria and procedures for determining level of performance, but a similar formalization would not be seen in the practices used to deal with an unsatisfactory performer. More specifically, it would be expected that there would be few, if any, formal procedures for forcing an incompetent member out of the department if the department has a strong humanistic orientation.

Procedures

The data for this study were obtained primarily through the use of a short structured interview with each of the chairmen of over eighty departments. Additional information came from departmental and university records and from interview material secured during another phase of the large research study.

Each department chairman was asked a series of questions, which included the following:

1. What is the typical procedure used to fill faculty vacancies in your department?

2. How do you tell whether or not a faculty member in your department is fulfilling his position in a satisfactory manner?

3. Have you ever had a faculty member who had tenure but was consistently performing in an unsatisfactory manner? If so, what is usually done? We are not interested in names, only in what is usually done in such a situation.

The interviewer followed each general question with probe questions wherever the response seemed ambiguous or incomplete.

The concept, "formalization of procedures," as used in this study centers on two questions: First, does the department use *some* systematic procedure when certain decisions need to be made? Is there clear evidence that it is possible to predict the general sequence of events? Secondly, if several procedures are used, is the sequence in which they are used predictable? Formalization does not necessarily imply that the procedures appear in written form—only that it is possible to predict what will occur.

Each interview transcription was analyzed separately, and the department was categorized as high, medium, or low on formalization of procedures[7] (a) for filling vacant faculty positions, (b) for evaluating a faculty member's performance, and (c) for handling a tenured faculty member whose performance was consistently unsatisfactory.

Factors Influencing Formalization

Size

Department size was taken as the number of full-time faculty who had tenure. Since these persons make up the permanent staff of any department, this appeared to be the best single measure of department size. There were 25 large departments (15 to 46 members), 29 medium departments (7 to 14 members), and 27 small departments (1 to 6 members).

When department size and formalization of departmental procedures were contrasted in a 3 X 3 chi square analysis, the following results were obtained:

1. The formality of hiring procedures and size of department are significantly related (.001 level).

2. The formality of the methods used to evaluate member performance is likewise related at the .001 level to departmental size.

3. The formality of procedures used to handle an unsatisfactory, tenured member is only moderately related to size (significance level .10).

The size factor appears to be of great importance. It apparently is so strong that even when other variables are not held constant, as in this analysis, the degree of association remains high.

Frequency of Decision Making

Information was obtained from departmental records about the number of hiring decisions and number of tenure decisions made during the most recent five-year period. The number of faculty hired by any department during this period ranged from none to twenty-eight. These were grouped into high, medium, and low categories on the basis of natural breaks in the distribution (13 high, 42 medium, and 22 low). Formalization of hiring procedures and number of hiring decisions made were found to be significantly associated (p < .01). Departments which had engaged in more hiring decisions typically had more formal procedures established for the selection of the new members.

Evaluation of departmental faculty may occur under various circumstances: (1) when a faculty member has been offered a position by another university; (2) when merit raises are being considered; (3) when a promotion in rank is being contemplated; and (4) when the question of tenure is under consideration. Investigation revealed that all departments kept systematic records only of decisions on tenure.[8] The number of times tenure was granted during the most recent five-year period was used, therefore, as the index of the frequency with which evaluation decisions took place within each department.

The number of tenure decisions ranged from none to twenty-two. When separated into three categories, there were 13 high, 20 medium, and 44 low departments. The number of tenure decisions made is clearly associated with formality of evaluation procedures in the expected direction (p < .001)—the larger the number of decisions made, the more standardized the procedure used.

Prestige of Department

Determining the relative prestige of university departments is very difficult without a nationwide survey.[9] Since such a survey was not financially possible for this study, a variety of sources was used as the basis for estimating department prestige. A composite index was developed which included the following kinds of information:

1. A study by Keniston,[10] which included a report on departmental prestige based on the ratings of chairmen in the 25 "leading" universities in the country. The ratings included only the traditional arts and sciences departments. Raters were asked to list the first five, second five, and, if possible, the third five departments within the discipline in the country.

2. The number of Woodrow Wilson and National Science Foundation fellowships awarded to students in the departments, or to students who elected to come to the department after receiving such an award elsewhere.

3. Estimates made of the national reputation of the department by the chairman of each department. Each chairman indicated whether his department was reputed to be in the top ten, second ten, and so forth.[11]

4. Evidence secured from the reports of accrediting agencies. Based

on the composite index, each department was categorized as high or low in relative prestige.[12]

High-prestige departments were found to use more formalized evaluation procedures (significant at the .02 level) than those of lower prestige. No difference between the two was found, however, in regard to the formalization of practices for handling a tenured, unsatisfactory member.

Supply-Demand Ratio
As with relative prestige, measuring the supply-demand ratio for each academic discipline is extremely difficult. The estimate used was based on the only available source which provided even reasonably adequate data, the study on teacher supply and demand by the National Education Association.[13] Two types of information were provided: the total number of unfilled teaching positions in 1959-1960 or 1960-1961 by field, and the number of institutions reporting a shortage of qualified teachers by field in 1959-1960 and 1960-1961. The data on the shortage were reported only for junior colleges, but examination of the various tables supports the conclusion that the report is essentially accurate when it says, "The many details presented . . . show that universities and colleges of the nation report conditions *closely paralleling those of the junior colleges.*"[14] It was necessary to include the data on junior colleges because these listed more disciplines separately rather than grouping them in large categories; e.g., the social sciences were listed individually *only* in the junior college tables. Even with this approach, however, satisfactory information was obtained only for 28 departments.
If the measure of the supply-demand ratio is valid, favorableness of supply-demand ratio is not significantly related to the formality of methods used in evaluation or handling of an unsatisfactory faculty member.

Humanistic Orientation
Finally, an attempt was made to ascertain whether departments with more formal procedures for dealing with an unsatisfactory, tenured faculty member were less humanistically oriented than those with less formal procedures. In order to determine the degree of humanistic orientation of the various departments, each department chairman was presented a fictional case history of a professor whose

performance was described in terms which would make it clearly unsatisfactory in any department.[15] A list of possible courses of action was provided and the chairman was asked, "Which of these, if any, would *very probably* be used in your department in the event that you had a professor as described in the hypothetical case history?" The various responses were assigned relative weights in accordance with the degree of humanistic emphasis involved in the course of action.[16] The responses were then scored, and the total score for each department was used as the basis for categorizing them into high, medium, and low in humanistic orientation.

The degree of humanistic orientation was not found to be significantly related to degree of formality of methods used in handling an unsatisfactory, tenured faculty member. Apparently, highly formalized procedures may be just as humanistic in *content* as those which are relatively informal.

Correlates of Humanistic Orientation

Some interesting patterns did emerge, however, in analyzing the relationship between humanistic orientation and formalization. First, it became evident that the orientation of a department is associated with the nature of the academic discipline of the department. Departments whose subject matter deals primarily with human beings in their social and cultural orientation are clearly (t= 3.72, 53d.f., .001 level) more humanistic in their techniques for handling an unsatisfactory member than are those whose subject matter is essentially nonsocial in focus.[17] The social sciences, humanities, and applied disciplines based on them (e.g., social work and education) are far more humanistically oriented than are the physical and biological sciences and related disciplines (e.g., engineering and medicine).

Secondly, the visibility of the training given by the department appears to be related to level of humanistic orientation of the department. In most departments the relative quality of the training provided the students majoring in the field is rather difficult to determine. The quality of the education received has low visibility, especially for persons who are not specialists within the field. In some disciplines, however, graduates are required to take standardized examinations; e.g., medicine, pharmacy, law, optometry, and nursing. Since the scores from these examinations are not confidential, it is relatively easy to determine the percentage of the graduates of a particular department that pass the examination. Comparisions can then be made between various colleges and universities.

Departments whose students take such standardized exams may be said to have high visibility.

Departments with high visibility show a significantly lower degree of humanistic orientation (p < .05) than those having lower visibility.[18] It would appear that departments with high visibility tend to make humanistic considerations secondary. The pressure resulting from visibility may force the department to make its immediate self-interest the primary or only consideration in deciding how to handle the tenured faculty member whose performance is judged to be clearly unsatisfactory.

Figure 1. Summary of findings on hypotheses

Hypotheses	Statistical test χ^2	Level of significance
Departmental size and formalization of:		
Hiring practices	39.66 (4d.f.)	.001
Evaluation procedures	33.38 (4d.f.)	.001
Handling unsatisfactory performer	8.76 (4d.f.)	.10
Frequency of decision making and formalization of:		
Hiring practices	15.84 (4d.f.)	.01
Evaluation procedures	20.68 (4d.f.)	.001
Prestige of department and formalization of:		
Evaluation procedures	8.69 (2d.f.)	.02
Handling unsatisfactory performer	1.66 (2d.f.)	.50
Supply-demand ratio and formalization of:		
Evaluation procedures	7.83 (4d.f.)	.10
Handling unsatisfactory performer	5.56 (4d.f.)	.30
Humanistic orientation and formalization of procedures for handling unsatisfactory performer	1.03 (2d.f.)	.70
Correlates of humanistic orientation: Subject matter of the department and humanistic orientation	3.72 (53d.f.)	.001
Visibility of the product of the department and humanistic orientation	3.92 (1d.f.)	.05

Discussion

The variation in formality of certain administrative practices used among departments within the university has been found to be primarily a function of department size and the frequency with which relevant decisions are made. As department size increases, there is increasing formalization of practices used in the hiring of new personnel and in the evaluation of performance of present members.

There are two major ways in which increasing size may contribute to increasing formalization. First, as organizational size increases, the number of personnel involved directly or indirectly in a certain type of activity is likely to increase. For example, in a small organization one person may make all of the hiring decisions. The standards he uses in making such decisions may not be very explicit, and they may vary from time to time. Standardization of hiring practices may be relatively low, but this will not be particularly obvious to others in the organization. As organization size increases, however, the work load will be divided, and several employees will take part in the hiring decisions. Any discrepancies or variations in the standards used in making the decisions will then become more apparent. Differences in procedures used by the different decision makers will be more readily recognized both by the decision makers and by other members of the organization. As a result, pressure for standardization is likely to develop and bring about the adoption of more formalized procedures.

Viewed in this way, size is merely an indicator of the number of members involved in carrying out a certain activity. In other organizations and where other types of activity are being investigated, the hypothesized relationship between number of employees involved in a particular activity and the degree of formalization of practices should hold true. This explanation appears, however, to be only partially applicable to the particular tasks and departments investigated here. The early phases of the hiring process do involve more members in the larger departments. More persons read the vitas and conduct interviews with various candidates. The final selection is usually a group decision, and whether the group is composed of fifteen rather than ten persons would not appear to be very crucial for level of formalization. The information available on persons concerned with tenure decisions indicates that the number of persons involved does not necessarily increase as department size increases; therefore, the increasing formalization in handling tenure decisions as department size increases must reflect the operation of another process.

Size is also reflected in the frequency with which certain decisions are made. For example, as an organization grows, the number of employees hired, paid, evaluated, and dismissed will also increase during a given period. As the number of occasions in which a decision must be made increases, the probability of standardization goes up. If a particular decision is made only infrequently, it is possible for the decision maker to view each occasion as a relatively unique one with a resultant variability in the manner in which it is performed. When that task is performed repeatedly, however, the common elements will become more readily apparent to the decision maker. He, or the supervisor, is likely to see that standardization will reduce the time and attention required for the task, and as a result some formalization of procedures is likely to occur.

In this study three types of decisions were considered: hiring, evaluation, and treatment of the incompetent employee. For hiring and evaluation procedures, formalization was found to increase with increase in size or frequency of decision making. Department size and frequency of decision making may each be viewed as an independent variable, each contributing, in part, to formalization. It is possible, however, that size might be simply a correlate of the frequency with which hiring and evaluation decisions were made.

An analysis of the association between departmental size and frequency of decision making provides support for this explanation. Department size and the number of faculty hired in the most recent five-year period are correlated .68 (p < .001), while size and number of faculty receiving tenure during that same period are correlated .71 (p < .001). This would indicate that larger departments tend to make hiring and tenure decisions more frequently than do smaller ones.

It appears that in the departments studied here, size is a reflection of the more central process which is a determiner of formalization—the frequency with which certain decisions are made. *It is the repetitiveness of decision making which tends to produce increased formalization rather than size in itself.*

It is not clear at this point why formalization of methods for handling an unsatisfactory performer is not as obviously related to size as is the case for hiring and evaluation practices. It is possible that the hypothesized relation does, in fact, exist even though statistically it is not quite significant at the .05 level. One would expect that larger departments would also have more cases where a tenured member was unsatisfactory in performance. (No data were available which would permit this hypothesis to be checked.) But the number of unsatisfactory members in any department is probably determined by more than just the size factor. If the hiring and evaluation procedures, regardless of their formality, are relatively *inefficient* in screening out the potential incompetents (who later are defined as unsatisfactory), then the number of unsatisfactory, tenured members could be as great in the smaller departments as in the larger ones. It is suggested, then, that factors such as the ineffectiveness of screening in hiring may obscure the actual relation between department size and formalization of methods for handling the unsatisfactory member and make the hypothesized relation appear invalid.

The findings on the prestige hypotheses parallel those of the size dimension. High-prestige departments rely more consistently on formalized methods in evaluating member performance. Although the data do not provide direct evidence on the point, prestige seems to be significant, for a department with high prestige has many more potential decisions to make than does a department of less prestige. As the data clearly show, high prestige departments are acutely aware of their position. They know that they can replace a member of questionable competence with relative ease; therefore, they have the freedom and motivation to set up standardized procedures for systematically evaluating those who are not contributing at an acceptable level. In this framework, formalization is viewed as a dependent variable. It may be, however, that these high-prestige departments attained their reputation in part because they first adopted standardized and effective evaluation procedures, which over the years meant that only the most competent men were retained. Thus, standardized evaluation procedures may be both antecedent and consequent in relation to the prestige of a department.

As noted earlier, the high-prestige departments do not differ from low-prestige departments in the extent of formalization in the treatment of a tenured, unsatisfactory member. We cannot offer a satisfactory tentative explanation for the lack of congruence in the findings for the two prestige hypotheses. Obviously more research is required to clarify the relationship.

The supply-demand ratio in the various disciplines apparently is not related to variation in formalization. Better indicators of the supply-demand ratio should be devised and used for a further test of this hypothesis.

Finally, degree of formalization of methods for handling an unsatisfactory member is apparently not a function of humanistic emphasis. Standardized practices may incorporate either a strong or a weak humanistic orientation. The degree of humanistic orientation evidenced in the handling of an unsatisfactory, tenured member was found, however, to be associated with the subject matter of the discipline. The social sciences and humanities use more humanistic practices in handling an unsatisfactory member than do other departments.

It should be noted that all departments in this comparison are engaged in teaching and research; they are indistinguishable in the traditional, functional sense. In one sense, however, the physical and biological science disciplines are different from the social sciences and humanities—in the consequences of their activity. Activities within an organization which appear to be identical in the formal, functional sense are not always identical, at least not in their consequences. If this finding could be generalized to the many clusters of activities found in other types of organizations, it would have significant impact on further organizational analyses. Some of the variation in organizational behavior might be explained in terms of these diverse orientations of member groups within the organization.

Humanistic emphasis may also be influenced by pressures resulting from the visibility of the "product" produced by a department. Where segments of an organization, such as university departments, have considerable autonomy in deciding how to handle incompetent members, humanistic considerations will be less prevalent when the product has high visibility. If this relationship between humanistic orientation and visibility is found to hold true for departments in other types of organizations, it might be significant for departmental efficiency. Departments with low product visibility would presumably be more prone to allow humanistic considerations to take precedence over considerations of efficiency when incompetent faculty members were involved. Administrators as well as researchers may wish to investigate this relationship more closely.

Footnotes

1. Theodore Caplow and Reese McGee, *The Academic Marketplace* (New York, 1958), p. 3.

2. Victor A. Thompson, *Modern Organization* (New York, 1961), esp. pp. 19-80.

3. In order to protect the identity of the university under investigation exact numbers have been changed to approximations.

4. See, for example, Richard H. Hall, "An Empirical Analysis of Bureaucratic Dimensions and Their Relation to Other Organizational Characteristics" (unpublished Ph.D. dissertation, Ohio State University, 1961).

5. The influence of larger organizational characteristics on subordinate units within the total organization is discussed in Allan H. Barton, *Organizational Measurement and Its Bearing on the Study of College Environments* (New York, 1961), pp. 25-28.

6. The importance of size as a determiner of organizational characteristics is discussed in Hall, *op. cit.*, pp. 38-41. See also Mason Haire, *Modern Organization Theory* (New York, 1959), pp. 274-275; Rensis Likert, *New Patterns of Management* (New York, 1961), pp. 157-160.

7. The degree of formality used in evaluating the performance of faculty was estimated in the following fashion. Techniques used to ascertain teaching performance, research performance, and other competencies considered by the department to be relevant in the evaluation process were separated into these three categories. For each category each procedure was coded as being "formal" or "nonformal." All departments employing at least one formal method in each of the three categories were classed as high on formalization. Those departments using no formal procedures in any of the three categories were classed as low, with the remainder being classed as moderately formal. A similar method with slight variation was used in estimating the formality of hiring procedures and methods of handling the unsatisfactory performer.

8. Even these records were not entirely complete. No systematic record was available of the number of persons considered for tenure and rejected. In this university, if tenure is not granted at the end of a specified period of time, the faculty member is not offered a new contract. General information indicates, however, that such rejections are relatively infrequent. Within this university the granting of tenure is a departmental decision.

9. For a discussion of the concept, "quality," as distinct from reputation, see Paul F. Lazarsfeld and Wagner Thielens, *The Academic Mind* (New York, 1958), pp. 163-167, 411-414.

10. Hayward Keniston, *Graduate Study and Research in the Arts and Sciences at the University of Pennsylvania* (Philadelphia, 1959), pp. 115-150.

11. The "aggrandizement effect" noted by Caplow and McGee was apparently operating here also (*op. cit.*, pp. 103-105). Sixty-eight percent of the chairmen placed their departments among the top ten in the country.

12. While it was established that certain departments had relatively high prestige, and others definitely low prestige, it was not possible on the basis of available data to ascertain with reasonable certainty where the remainder (45) should be placed. They were therefore excluded from consideration.

13. National Education Association, Research Division, *Teacher Supply and Demand in Universities, Colleges, and Junior Colleges, 1959-60 and 1960-61* (Higher Education Series, 1961—R 12; Washington, D. C., 1961), pp. 19, 36-37. Another general source of supply-demand information in Dael Wolfle, *America's Resources of Specialized Talent* (New York, 1954). Besides being somewhat outdated, the data in this book were too grossly categorized for our purposes.

14. National Education Association, *op. cit.*, p. 37.

15. The case history read as follows: John Doe, age 43, has been an associate professor in your department for approximately five years. During the past two years, you have been receiving many indications that his performance is clearly unsatisfactory. A number of undergraduate and graduate students have

repeatedly complained to you concerning the inadequacy of his classroom performance, his unwillingness to be available for conferences, unfair testing procedures, etc. His research or scholarly writing activity has been practically nil, and during the past two years, he has published only one article, the quality of which was unsatisfactory. He has repeatedly neglected university committee responsibility and has virtually ignored departmental duties.

Being an associate professor, John Doe has tenure. Since it is extremely difficult to establish proof of incompetency, he cannot be dismissed from the university.

16. An example of a highly humanistic course of action: "The chairman and other faculty members would work with [the unsatisfactory performer] informally, trying to find out what the problem is and suggesting ways to improve. This would be done for as long as three years." An example from the opposite extreme: "[The unsatisfactory performer] would immediately be denied the usual amenities of a professor, such as secretarial service, adequate office space, travel funds, and desired vacation time."

17. Since the nursing profession focuses on human beings as *both* social *and* biological entities, it was decided to omit it from consideration in this case.

18. When all departments were included in a 2 X 3 chi-square analysis (high, moderate, and low on humanistic orientation versus high and low on visibility), the distribution showed an association in the expected direction, but the association was not quite statistically significant. When those departments with a moderate emphasis on humanistic orientation were omitted from the comparison, however, the relationship was significant at the .05 level.

PERCEPTIONS OF THE POWER OF
DEPARTMENT CHAIRMEN BY PROFESSORS

Winston W. Hill and Wendell L. French

This study examines one dimension of college administration—administrative power—as it relates to the performance and satisfaction of the faculty. The central concerns of this investigation were to develop an instrument for measuring the power of departmental chairmen as viewed by professors, and to determine whether variations in such perceptions of power were associated with variations in the professional output, perceived productivity, and satisfaction of the departmental faculty.[1]

This study also investigates professors' perceptions of the relative influence of various groups in the authority systems of their colleges in order to determine the power position of the chairman relative both to other administrators and to the professors themselves. This aspect of the study tests the idea that the college or university is a special kind of social system, with an administrative hierarchy that has much less power than the authority systems of other kinds of organizations, such as industrial and military establishments.[2]

Research Design

Research Hypotheses
Several general hypotheses guided the investigation. The first was designed to discover how the professors viewed the authority systems of their colleges in terms of the relative power of various administra-

From the *Administrative Science Quarterly*, Vol. 2, No. 4, March 1967, pp. 548-574. Reprinted by permission of the publisher.

tive groups. Earlier studies have indicated that the real power in colleges is not centered in the administrative authority system, but in the departments, where all important decisions are made by the collegium, or community of scholars.[3] Furthermore, those who carry out the administrative tasks for this professional collectivity are sometimes seen as amateurs, functionaries, or mere paper-handlers,[4] so that, "the perennial dream of many an academician is that of a university run entirely by professors—a citadel of learning undisturbed by the presence of registrars, business managers, or even deans and presidents."[5] This leads to the first hypothesis:

Hypothesis 1. Professors view the authority systems of their colleges as relatively "flat" hierarchies, in which the professors have considerable power as compared with the administrative groups of departmental chairmen, deans, higher administrators, and boards of trustees.

The second hypothesis is based on the idea that, whatever the power of the chairmen relative to other groups, the distribution of power among department heads may vary, and such variations might be associated with differing degrees of faculty satisfaction. This hypothesis states an inverse relationship between professors' satisfaction and their chairman's power on the assumption that professors favor collegial decisions, and so will be most content with a chairman who has little power over their activities. The second hypothesis, therefore, is:

Hypothesis 2. There is an inverse relationship between the power of the departmental chairman and the satisfaction of the departmental faculty.

The level of satisfaction among participants in organizations is important to the institution because of its presumed relationship to turnover, morale, and smooth operation. And even though there may be no simple, direct relationship between satisfaction and productivity,[6] the "productivity" of professors is also important to the college. But professors' work and productivity are structured by the demands of at least two orientations, which may not be compatible: in their institutions, the orientation toward teaching in their academic disciplines and the orientation toward research. Two measures of activity seem to be necessary, therefore: one dimension for the degree to which a professor contributes scholarly works to his academic field, here designated "professional output"; another for the degree to which he contributes to the goals of his organization, here called "perceived productivity." Two additional hypotheses, arbitrarily stated in positive terms, follow:

Hypothesis 3. There is a direct relationship between the power of the departmental chairman and the professional output of departmental faculty.

Hypothesis 4. There is a direct relationship between the power of the departmental chairman and the perceived productivity of departmental faculty.

Research Sites

The sites chosen to test the four general hypotheses were five, state-supported, four-year colleges in two western states. Three are located in urban areas, one in a suburban area, and one in a rural area. Two are old and established institutions, three are relatively new.

The sample was selected for the following reasons: (a) It was assumed that the university, with its extensive graduate programs, might have somewhat different goals, therefore the study should not mix the two kinds of institutions. (b) It was assumed that the distribution of power in private colleges might be somewhat different from that in state-supported colleges. (c) The colleges in the sample were accessible. (d) Four-year state colleges are playing an increasingly important role in higher education.[7]

The organization and administration of the colleges in the sample appear to be typical of four-year state colleges throughout the United States, but care should be taken in generalizing from any findings reported here. In particular, conclusions should not be extended to the large, state-supported universities nor to privately endowed colleges and universities, which might constitute radically different samples.

The Questionnaire

Appropriate tests of the hypotheses appeared to require data from a large number of professors in a variety of disciplines to make any bias introduced by association with particular disciplines negligible, and from a large number of departments to test adequately the premise that power varies among chairmen. The mailed questionnaire seemed to be a technique suited to these requirements.

The questionnaire developed included 74 items organized in six sections. One section was concerned with the respondent's perceptions of the power of his chairman, the others were concerned with the respondent's satisfaction, his professional output, his estimate of the productivity of his department in comparison to other departments, the relative influence of various groups in the college, and general information about the respondent.

Power. For the purposes of the study, it was necessary to devise a method for measuring the power of departmental chairmen. Both the authority associated with the position of chairman and the influence of the actual individual were of interest. A broad definition of power was developed which seemed sufficiently operational to use as a guide:

Figure 1. Power instruments available to chairmen as seen by 375 professors in five state colleges*

Mean imputed power	Available power instrument
2.7	*Scheduling:* power to determine times and days of class meetings
2.5	*Influence:* power to establish contacts with higher administrators
2.4	*Committees:* power to form committees and make committee assignments
2.4	*Information:* knowledge of what is going on around the college
2.4	*Course assignment:* control over courses (field, level, number of preparations) professor is assigned
2.2	*Interdepartmental relations:* ability to sustain liaison with other departments
2.1	*Assigning additional teaching:* control over *summer* teaching opportunities
2.0	*Goal determination:* influence in setting goals of the department
2.0	*Promotion:* ability to influence promotion decisions for department members
1.9	*Curriculum:* influence over curriculum development
1.8	*Recruitment:* ability to recruit a qualified staff of professors
1.8	*Tenure:* control over awards of tenure to members of the department
1.7	*Inspiration:* ability to exert professional leadership and stimulation
1.7	*Facilities:* power to secure adequate equipment and supplies
1.6	*Student assistants:* control over amount of student help supplied to professors
1.6	*Community:* ability to maintain good contacts with community; publicity
1.5	*Teaching loads:* influence over deciding class contact hours of professors
1.4	*Counseling:* ability to counsel staff about teaching and/or research
1.4	*Paid extra teaching:* control over *extension* teaching appointments
1.3	*Academic contacts:* ability to assist professors in developing professional acquaintanceships

1.3   *Clerical work:* power to secure adequate clerical assistance for faculty
1.1   *Paid extra work:* ability to affect the acquisition of paid short courses, etc.
1.0   *Colloquia:* ability to develop stimulating academic environment through seminars, bringing distinguished visiting lecturers to campus, etc.
 .9   *Research assistance:* ability to get research assistants, supplies, etc.
 .9   *Sabbaticals:* ability to influence awards of sabbatical leaves
 .8   *Travel funds:* authority to secure funds for travel to professional meetings
 .8   *Research:* power to secure research time and facilities for faculty members
 .6   *Consulting:* contacts leading to paid consulting jobs for professors
 .5   *Speaking and consulting:* power to make unpaid "community service" assignments to professors
 .5   *Research:* ability to acquire funds for faculty research

*This table should be read with the categories of continua in mind. A score of 4.0 would indicate that the chairman had the power instrument available "To a very great degree"; a score of 3.0, "To a great degree"; a mean of 2.0 indicates "To quite some degree"; 1.0 "some," and 0.0, "Little or none."

Definition. The power of an individual in a social situation consists of the sanctions others in the situation perceive that he has available to employ in ways that will affect them.

This definition appeared comprehensive enough to encompass both authority and influence, and also permitted the measurement of power in terms of perceptions of sanctions.[8] Sanctions are the power instruments, the resources, the means of control and inducements that a person may have available to influence the behavior of others. It was assumed that department chairmen have some sanctions because of their position in the organization, but that they are able to acquire others because of their personalities and/or individual differences in carrying out their roles. For example, a chairman may build exceptionally effective relationships with his dean and so may gain control of some sanctions not ordinarily associated with the position of chairman. But a chairman may not acquire interpersonal means of control, so may lose control of some of the sanctions associated with the position.

First a list was made of sanctions that chairmen might have available to influence the professors in their departments. The 31 items, shown in Figure 1, finally included in this part of the instrument were derived from a series of interviews with state-college professors in which they were asked to name the sanctions they thought their chairman had available. A five-point modified Likert-type scale with categories varying from "To little or no degree," "To some degree," "To quite some degree," "To a great degree," to "To a very great degree" was then constructed. An index of the power of the chairman imputed to him by each professor could then be computed by using the method of summed ratings. Scale categories were numbered from zero to four, and the sum of scores of each respondent to the 31 items represented the chairman's power, in the eyes of the professor.

Satisfaction. Satisfaction was measured by using a similar scoring method for three questions dealing with the respondent's feelings about his working conditions, about relationships among faculty members, and about faculty-administrator relationships.[9] They were asked to compare their institutions with other colleges and indicate whether they felt their working conditions and relationships were "inferior," "fair," "good," "very good," or "superior," with scores of from 0—4, respectively, assigned to the categories.

Professional output. The professional output index was based on five items about the respondent's contribution to his academic field; i.e., whether he had completed his dissertation, whether the dissertation had been published in full or in part, the number of books he had published, the number of articles he had published, and the number of papers he had presented at meetings of professional associations. The values assigned in the scoring key to these measures were quite arbitrary, but seemed to discriminate well between the more and less productive.[10] The quality dimension in this index is missing, but this aspect presented insurmountable obstacles in the context of this study.

Perceived productivity. The second measure of productivity was intended to separate achievement of college goals from achievement in academic fields. In four questions, respondents were asked what they considered to be the goals of their institutions, which goals were primary and which secondary, and how well they thought each goal was being achieved, as compared with other departments in their institutions. The scale categories were "inferior," "fair," "good," "very good," and "superior," with the scoring key values from 0—4, respectively. Four goals were listed: "Teaching," "research and publication," "community service," and "service to the college," and three spaces were provided for the respondent to indicate additional goals. The index of "perceived productivity" was based on these items as scored by the key.

Relative influence of various groups. A series of 25 questions was designed, following the general method suggested by Tannenbaum and Georgopoulos,[11] to measure the relative influence of five groups

Figure 2. Questionnaire returns from various disciplines by college *

	State colleges					Total		
Discipline	1 %	2 %	3 %	4 %	5 %	Sent no.	Returned no.	%
Professional	48	68	89	36	27	172	103	76
Humanities	51	58	57	33	38	147	74	50
Science	59	42	64	55	70	190	110	58
Social sciences	51	58	74	20	37	147	76	52
Psychology	78	72	55		61	65	42	65
Total	54	59	69	36	51	721	405	56

*All figures for colleges are returns expressed as a percentage of the number of questionnaires sent, in order to protect the anonymity of the institutions. The discipline of psychology was separated from other social sciences because it is located in various divisions of the colleges in the sample.

in the colleges: faculty members, department chairmen, deans and other middle administrators, the president and other higher administrators, and the board of trustees. These groups were listed five times, and in each instance the respondent was asked to indicate how much influence one group had over all the others. The scale values were "Little or none," "Some," "Quite a bit," "A great deal," and "A very great deal." The means of responses based on a 0–4 scoring scale, were used to construct control graphs showing the influence exercised by each group over all others (active control), and the influence to which each group was subject from all others (passive control).[12]

General information questions. The last section of the questionnaire asked the respondent to record his total years of teaching experience, his years of teaching at his present college, his degrees, his academic rank, his age, and the permanency of his appointment (tenure). Answers to these six questions made it possible to assess the relationship between these variables and the criterion measures, e.g., the relationship between age and professional output.

Questionnaire returns. Questionnaires were mailed to 721 professors in 65 departments representing five classifications of academic fields. As shown in Figure 2, there were 405 replies of which 375 were complete enough to use in one phase or another of the analysis.

Results[13]

Power Distribution in the College

The first research hypothesis was suggested as a basis for exploring the organizational structure of the colleges, with particular emphasis on the relative power position of the departmental chairmen. To test this proposition, the responses to the questions on relative influence were summed in the manner outlined, the means calculated, and the results plotted on a control graph. The solid line in Figure 3 represents data from all respondents in all the colleges and indicates the relative control exercised by each level over all levels. The broken line is the "passive control" line and shows the control exercised by all levels over each level.[14]

Figure 3 generally substantiates Hypothesis 1. The responding professors see themselves as exercising considerable influence in the colleges. All the administrative levels, however, from the departmental chairmen to the state boards, are seen as having successively increasing amounts of influence, indicating that professors view the *administrative branches* of their colleges to a limited extent as hierarchies. These colleges have a mixed structure, including communities of scholars having a good deal of control compared with other groups in the college as well as a distinct but weak authority system. Professors consider departmental chairmen as having less influence than any other groups in the colleges, even less than the professors.

Although an authority hierarchy does exist, it is quite "flat." The professors wield almost as much control as the control to which they are subject, and only departmental chairmen are subject to considerably more passive control (the amount of influence to which they are subject from all other levels) than the active control (the amount of influence they have over all other levels) they exercise. The relative "flatness" of the curves indicates that each group generally is subject to considerable pressure from each other level, implying a good deal of give-and-take. Also, the curve is not only "flat," but it is also low on the four-point scale. Such a low and flat authority system may possibly indicate that an outside agency—such as the state legislature —exerts considerable control over the internal affairs of the colleges.

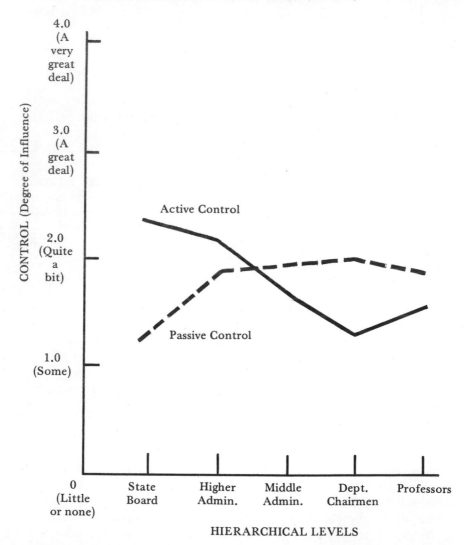

Figure 3. Amount of influence of each level over all levels
(*active control*), and amount of influence of all levels over each level
(passive control) in five state colleges ($N = 375$)

Influence of Departmental Chairmen over Various Groups

When the active and passive control measures are computed for
the chairmen, it becomes evident that the chairmen have the greatest
amount of influence over *their own* activities, and only a little less
over professors (see Figure 4). Their low-power position in the

colleges seems to be a result of their lack of influence over higher administration groups. The passive control curve indicates that they are subject to more control by the professors than they exert, but are pressured to an even greater extent by the higher and middle administrators. One may infer from these results that higher

Figure 4. Influence of departmental chairmen over hierarchical groups (active control), and influence of hierarchical groups on chairmen (passive control) in five state colleges ($N = 375$)

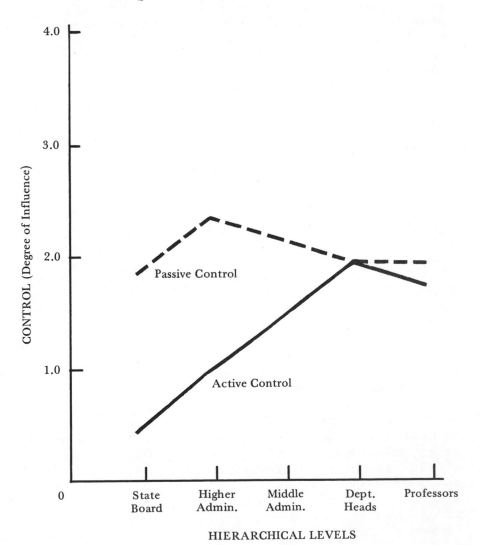

administrators are seen as directing and controlling the chairmen in carrying out the policy of the colleges, at the same time that the professors are attempting to influence them; i.e., "men in the middle," caught between two groups, both of which probably make heavy demands upon the chairmen and expect them to serve their unique needs.

Power Instruments Available to Departmental Chairman

Responses to the power instruments questions support the conclusion that the chairmen have little power in the colleges studied. One can calculate the mean degree to which chairmen are perceived to have each of 31 sanctions available, with the results shown in Figure 1.

An examination of the table indicates that the typical chairman cannot be said to have a high degree of access even to the sanction with the highest power, "scheduling," where the mean degree to which he is perceived to have power to schedule class meetings is 2.7 on a 4.0 scale, somewhat less than "to quite some degree."

Of the six highest power items, three are concerned with the chairman's formal duties of scheduling classes and establishing committees, as might be expected; but the other three are concerned with sanctions that might be available more because of the way the individual plays his role than because of the formal role alone. The typical chairman is seen as relatively high in influence with higher administrators, in knowing what is going on in the institution, and in relations with other departments. The six lowest power items are concerned with either the provision of time or money for professors. Typically the chairman may have some good contacts and be able to schedule classes, but he has little control over released time for research, sabbatical leaves, travel funds, or research monies.

Particularly noteworthy is the chairman's relative lack of control over salary administration. In one state, salary schedules are determined at the state government level, and advances within ranks tend to be automatic. For each rank, including that of full professor, specific minimum and maximum salaries are stipulated and published. There is slightly less control at the state level in the other state. In contrast, promotion and tenure awards are made by the college, subject only to budgetary provisions. These differences in authority over salary administration and promotion and tenure awards are reflected in Figure 1.

Teaching loads are also specified by state agencies in the two states, providing the chairman with only limited flexibility in deciding class contact hours for the faculty. With so little control

Figure 5. Correlation matrix: power and satisfaction (N = 371)

Power item	Satisfaction index	Working conditions	Faculty relations	Faculty—administration relations
Power index	.4165‡	.4086‡	.2298‡	.3242‡
Inspiration	.4069‡	.2703‡	.3436‡	.3198‡
Information	.3887‡	.2714‡	.3387‡	.2831‡
Recruitment	.3856‡	.3125‡	.2864‡	.2891‡
Influence	.3584‡	.1982†	.3083‡	.3129‡
Academic contacts	.3394‡	.2546‡	.2519‡	.2736‡
Counseling faculty	.3388‡	.2727‡	.2443‡	.2629‡
Community	.3344‡	.2685‡	.2498‡	.2517‡
Colloquia	.3382‡	.3201‡	.2294‡	.2323‡
Interdepartmental relations	.3118‡	.1957†	.2713‡	.2478‡
Research supplies, help	.2783‡	.2802‡	.1541†	.2094‡
Facilities	.2771‡	.3208‡	.1091*	.2132‡
Research funds	.2689‡	.2931‡	.1438†	.1866†
Curriculum	.2547‡	.2272‡	.1792†	.1816†
Paid extra work	.2484‡	.2064‡	.1562†	.2090‡
Goal determination	.2424‡	.2106‡	.1755†	.1733†
Promotion	.2352‡	.2501‡	.1174‡	.1772‡
Consulting	.2270‡	.2063‡	.1188*	.1980†
Clerical work	.2135‡	.3358‡	.0389	.1262*
Sabbaticals	.2064‡	.2008‡	.0542	.2203‡
Research time and space	.1945†	.2791‡	.0009	.1733†
Committees	.1841†	.2261‡	.1077*	.0952
Travel funds	.1717†	.2731‡	.0024	.1269*
Scheduling class times and days	.1599†	.1577†	.0658	.1456†
Teaching loads	.1388†	.2233‡	−.0214	.1229*
Scheduling course assignments	.1210*	.2161‡	.0027	.0665
Summer teaching	.1174*	.1260*	.0211	.1239*
Paid extra teaching	.1160*	.1767†	.0417	.0539
Speaking and consulting	.1151*	.0916	.0570	.1155*
Student help	.0989	.1165*	.0257	.0871
Salary increases	.0698	.1638†	−.0889	.0903
Tenure	.0682	.1352*	−.0173	.0436

No star, not significant.
*Correlation significant at .05 level or better.
†Correlation significant at .01 level or better.
‡Correlation significant at .001 level or better.

over salary administration and the structuring of professors' roles, it is not surprising to find interpersonal items ranking high among the sanctions available to the department chairmen:

The finding that the personal contacts of the chairmen provide some base of power indicates the *person* in the roles as well as the role itself may be important in the allocation and use of power instruments within an organization. Further evidence is provided by the finding that different chairmen are perceived to have differing degrees of power, even though their formal authority is presumably very similar. In summing the average power imputed to each chairman on each of the 31 sanction items, variations in power could range from zero to a maximum of 124. Based on returns from 375 respondents, the mean power index of the average chairman was 47.8, and varied from 19.6 to 65.4.

Figure 6. Professional output reported by 375 professors
in state colleges

Doctoral dissertation

	N	%
No	92	24.0
Yes	280	75.0
No answer	3	1.0

Dissertation published

	N	%
No	223	60.0
In part	103	27.0
In full	46	12.0
No answer	3	1.0

Books published

No.	N	%
0	271	72.0
1	57	15.0
2	29	8.0
3-5	8	2.0
5+	7	2.0
No answer	3	1.0

Papers

No.	Published		At professional meetings	
	N	%	N	%
0	93	25.0	118	31.0
1-2	108	29.0	120	32.0
3-5	88	23.0	74	20.0
6-10	45	12.0	36	10.0
11+	38	10.0	24	6.0
No answer	3	1.0	3	1.0

Power and Satisfaction

This differential access to resources by various department chairmen was suggested in Hypothesis 2 as being inversely related to the satisfaction of the professors. However, a direct, but positive, relationship was found when the power and satisfaction indices were correlated. The higher the power imputed to a chairman, the higher the satisfaction of the respondent, the degree of association being relatively high, with a coefficient of correlation of 0.4165 (significant at the 0.001 level).

When the relationship between the satisfaction index and the individual sanctions is examined, as shown in Figure 3, it appears that many of the factors closely related to the satisfaction of professors tend to be sanctions based on the interpersonal ability and the contacts of the chairman. For example, the first nine sanctions include the inspiration provided by the chairman, his knowledge of what is going on, his ability to recruit an able faculty, his influence, and the academic contacts he has established.

Induction can be dangerous, but on the basis of these results, it seems reasonable to infer that the power of the chairman that provides satisfaction to the departmental faculty in the organizations studied is interpersonal, not organizational. Conversely, since the chairmen in this sample had little access to sanctions pertaining to salary administration, travel funds, and research assistance, these sanctions were relatively unavailable as administrative tools and could have little influence on satisfaction. The findings do not prove that sanctions based on interpersonal relations are universally more important than those based on organizational role. They do suggest, however, that where control over formal sanctions is not great, a chairman's effective interpersonal contacts may contribute to the satisfaction of professors in the department.

When professors' satisfaction with working conditions was separated from the total satisfaction index and compared with power items (see Figure 5), it was found that the chairman's ability to secure clerical help, adequate equipment and supplies, and a competent staff appear to be especially important. Developing a stimulating academic environment by seminars, distinguished visiting lecturers, and similar activities also appeared relatively important.

Correlations between individual sanctions and satisfaction with faculty relations correspond closely with the correlations between the sanction and the total satisfaction index. The items, inspiration, information, influence, recruitment, interdepartmental relations, academic contacts, community, counseling, and colloquia, are particularly associated with satisfaction with faculty relations. The same nine sanctions available to the department chairman are also the most highly correlated with satisfaction with faculty-administration relations.

Power and professional output. Figure 4 shows the professional output reported by the responding professors: 27 percent of the faculty have published books, 72 percent have not; 71 percent have published papers, 25 percent have not; and 68 percent have delivered papers to professional societies, 31 percent have not. It is suprising that so many of the professors are engaging in research and publication in these institutions where, as is seen later, the overriding primary mission appears to be teaching.

The relationship between professional output and perceived power was suggested in Hypothesis 3. As shown in Figure 7, the basic finding is that although there is a relationship between the perceived power of the chairman and the professional output of the faculty in the department, the relationship is negative and not strong, even though it is statistically significant.

Thus, to a slight extent, the more power the faculty members impute to the chairman, the less productive they have been in their academic fields. This finding is difficult to interpret. In the first place, the time dimension confuses the nature of the correlation. Faculty members may have been selected, or their books and articles written, before the incumbent chairmen took office. Second, it may be that the professors who have achieved high productivity in their academic fields may impute less power to their chairmen because of the strength of their professional connections. It is quite likely that a professor's extra-organizational achievement weakens the power of the institution over him. On the other hand, the negative direction of the correlation may imply that the stronger the chairman, the more likely he will be to secure compliance with the primary goal of the college—teaching in this instance—while de-emphasizing other goals he may consider subordinate.

Care must be exercised, however, not to read too much meaning into the relationship; for though it is statistically significant, and the direction is clear, the coefficient of correlation is very low. Furthermore, attempts to explain the negative relationships with the specific power items shown in Figure 7 for perceived productivity were frustrating, except perhaps that the more the chairman involves the faculty in institutional affairs and successfully ties them to the reward system of the college, the less the professional output.

Figure 7. Correlation matrix: power and professional output; power and perceived productivity ($N = 371$)

Power items	Professional output index	Perceived productivity index	Power items	Professional output index	Perceived productivity index
Power index	−.1368†	.3619‡	Teaching loads	−.0916	.0835
Curriculum	−.1921†	.1800†	Research funds	−.0822	.2351‡
Community	−.1689†	.3278‡	Facilities	−.0668	.2453‡
Salary increases	−.1564†	−.0059	Scheduling class times and days	.0629*	.1129*
Sabbaticals	−.1533†	.0559	Paid extra work	.0589	.1784†
Paid extra teaching	−.1471†	.1159*	Academic contacts	−.0543	.3595‡
Information	−.1414†	.3825‡	Promotion	−.0472	.1542†
Clerical work	−.1390†	.1918†	Recruitment	−.0470	.2907‡
Speaking and cousulting	−.1343*	.1451†	Counseling faculty	−.0438	.3690‡
Colloquia	−.1263*	.2955‡	Student help	−.0396	.1551†
Research supplies, help	−.1151*	.2429†	Committees	−.0396	.2182‡
Travel funds	−.1055*	.1099*	Research time and space	−.0387	.1573†
Goal determination	−.1023*	.2496‡	Inspiration	.0323	.4770‡
Scheduling course assignments	−.0947	.0458	Interdepartmental relations	.0304	.3336‡
Consulting	−.0943	.2134‡	Tenure	−.0166	.0329
			Influence	−.0133	.3100‡
			Summer teaching	−.0046	.0033

No star, not significant.
*Correlation significant at .05 level or better.
†Correlation significant at .01 level or better.
‡Correlation significant at .001 level or better.

The question should be asked, then, what other factors, in addition to a chairman's power might account for variations in professional output?

Power and productivity. An analysis of responses to other measures of productivity confirms impressions that these colleges are primarily teaching institutions. As noted in Figure 6, 92 percent of the responding professors see teaching as a primary institutional goal, and 88 percent score the quality of teaching good or better.

Figure 8. Perceptions of productivity of department as compared with other departments by 375 professors in five state colleges

Goal	Goal			Goal achievement				
	Pri-mary	Second-ary	Not a goal	Infe-rior	Fair	Good	Very good	Supe-rior
Teaching								
Number	343	28	4	6	39	110	163	53
Percent	92	7	1	2	10	29	44	14
Research and publication								
Number	50	305	20	95	149	80	28	3
Percent	13	82	5	25	40	21	8	1
Community service								
Number	44	290	41	38	110	122	53	11
Percent	12	77	11	10	29	33	14	3
Service to college								
Number	229	105	41	14	60	125	118	17
Percent	61	28	11	4	16	33	31	5
Student counseling	8	2	—	1	4	2	2	1
Build department morale	5	0	—	1	1	0	2	1
Curriculum development	4	0	—	—	2	2	—	—
Interdepartmental relations	3	0	—	2	1	—	—	—
Live the good life through 20 years of loafing and short hours	3	0	—	—	—	1	1	1
Public relations	2	0	—	1	1	—	—	—
Professional societies	2	0	—	—	—	1	1	—

In testing Hypothesis 4 it was found that the greater the power of the chairman, the more productive its department faculty perceived themselves to be in terms of attaining organizational goals. Figure 7 shows the degree of association to be fairly high. We may infer from these results that chairmen who are perceived as having high power tend to lead the faculty to perform their functions well and/or are better able to secure resources which help the faculty to accomplish the goals of the institution.

Figure 7 also shows how the specific power items are correlated with perceived productivity. The first nine sanctions that are most closely correlated with productivity are also the nine power instruments most closely correlated with faculty satisfaction.

Additional interrelationships. Figure 9 shows the correlations between the various criteria indices. Although satisfaction with the institution shows practically no association with professional output (.0270), it is positively correlated with productivity (.4736); i.e., the degree to which professors believed their departments to be attaining their primary goals.

The positive correlation between satisfaction and productivity unfortunately, does not provide any substantiation for any causal relationship. Productive professors may be content; or satisfied faculty may consider themselves productive; or there may be unidentified outside variables causing the fluctuations in both. For example, perhaps the department chairman with high power is able to enforce organizational goals by rewarding those who fulfill them. The professors so rewarded may then feel satisfied. There does seem to be a positive correlation in this sample between (a) perceived power of the chairman, (b) perceived productivity, and (c) faculty satisfaction.

Figure 9. Summary correlation matrices

Total sample (N = 371)	Satis-faction	Professional output	Perceived productivity
Power	.4165†	−.1368*	.3619†
Satisfaction		.0270	.4736†
Professional output			.0134

No star, not significant.
*Correlation significant at .01 level or better.
†Correlation significant at .001 level or better.

Combined productivity measures. The two productivity measures, professional output and perceived productivity, were combined into one index. Because of the negative relationship between power and professional output and the positive association between perceived productivity and power, however, the two indices tended to cancel one another. There was almost no correlation between them (.0134), and it seems reasonable to infer that they are unrelated.

Influence of other variables. So far the data suggest that the power of the departmental chairman is associated significantly with such other organizational variables as faculty satisfaction and with productivity, defined in terms of primary organizational goals. Perhaps, however, the high correlations between power and satisfaction, and power and perceived productivity, can be explained by the relationship between both of these factors and independent variable or variables not included in the simple correlation studies. The high intercorrelation between satisfaction and perceived productivity gives considerable weight to this view. Furthermore, the association between professional output and power is so low as to raise the question of other variables that might more adequately explain variations between professors in terms of writing and delivering professional papers. Therefore, three multiple correlation analyses were made, successively using satisfaction, perceived productivity, and professional output as the dependent variables, to see if variations in these indices were associated more strongly with variables other than with power.

When satisfaction is taken as the dependent variable, as shown in Figure 10, the results permit a rejection of the proposition. Variations in professional output, age, rank, and degrees earned have some, but very little relation to the satisfaction of the respondents. Years of teaching appears to be related in a small degree to their satisfaction. One can conclude, therefore, that the power of the chairman fluctuates significantly and fairly closely with the satisfaction and perceived productivity of the departmental faculty.

The same close relationship was shown again when perceived productivity was taken as the dependent variable. As shown in Figure 10, neither professional output, age, rank, degrees earned, nor years of college teaching appear to have much relationship to perceived productivity. Variations in this index are most effectively explained by variations in faculty satisfaction and the chairman's power.

As could be expected, however, the relationship between professional output and years of teaching, degree, rank, and age indicates that this group of independent variables is closely related to

Figure 10. Multiple correlation coefficients using groups of items as independent variables with perceived productivity, satisfaction, professional output, and power as dependent variables (N = 371)

Power	Perceived productivity	Satisfaction	Years of teaching	Degrees	Rank	Age	Professional output	Multiple correlation coefficient
*	*	†	*	*	*	*	*	.5534
*	*	†	*	*	*	*		.5532
*	*	†	*	*	*			.5531
*	*	†	*	*				.5528
*	*	†	*					.5524
*	*	†						.5417
*		†						.4165
*	†	*	*	*	*	*	*	.5283
*	†	*	*	*	*	*		.5267
*	†	*	*	*	*			.5257
*	†	*	*	*				.5180
*	†	*	*					.5180
*	†	*						.5070
*	†							.3619
*	*	*	*	*	*	*	†	.6006
*	*	*	*	*	*		†	.6005
*	*	*	*	*			†	.5500
*	*	*	*				†	.4413
*	*	*					†	.1688
*	*						†	.1651
*							†	.1368
†	*	*	*	*	*	*	*	.5087
†	*		*	*	*	*	*	.4205
†	*		*	*	*	*		.4154
†			*	*	*	*		.1973‡
†				*	*	*		.1935‡
†				*		*		.1402‡
†						*		.0741‡

*Items used as independent variables.

†Dependent variable.

‡ All correlations are significant at the .001 level except that .1973 and .1935 are significant at the .01 level or better, .1402 is significant at the .05 level or better, and .0741 is not significant.

professional output as Figure 10 shows. Age does not seem to be a particularly important contributing factor, but rank attained, degrees earned, and in particular years of teaching, are closely associated with professional output. Single correlation coefficients are shown in Figure 11. This association between professional output and the

Figure 11. Correlation between indices and respondent data ($N = 371$)

	Power	Satis-fac-tion	Profes-sional output	Perceived produc-tivity
Years of teaching	.0325	.0914	.4107‡	.1475†
Years of teaching at present college	−.0276	.0564	.3233‡	.1368*
Degrees held	−.1559†	.0716	.4429‡	.0191
Permanent appointment	−.1596†	.0017	.3235‡	.0632
Completed dissertation	−.1392†	.0049	.5767‡	.0058
Publication of dissertation	−.0553	.0284	.6376‡	−.0345
Other books published	.0019	.0413	.6662‡	−.0046
Papers published	−.1820†	.0351	.8343‡	.0142
Papers delivered	−.1043*	−.0127	.7874‡	.0506
Rank	−.0506	.1002	.5340‡	.1631†
Age	.0741	.0904	.3161‡	.1155*

No star, not significant.
*Correlation significant at .05 level or better.
†Correlation significant at .01 level or better.
‡Correlation significant at .001 level or better.

variables shown in Figure 10 and 11 suggests a reason for the inverse relationship between professional output and the perceived power of the chairman. Experienced professors who hold doctorates, who are protected by tenure, and who feel somewhat insulated from institutional vagaries by strong professional reputations, are inclined to impute low power to their chairmen.

Figure 10, where power is taken as the dependent variable, generally supports this conclusion and gives further evidence of the kind of professor who tends to impute high power to his chairman. He is one who tends to be satisfied, to perceive that his department is productive in terms of college goals, to have a low rank, and whose teaching experience is likely to be limited.

Relative influence of various groups. An important purpose of this study was to assess the relative influence of other administrative groups. When influence indices (active control) are calculated for various ranks in the authority system and correlated with the indices of satisfaction, output, and other indices, some interesting patterns develop. As shown in Figure 12, the relative influence of the state boards of control is seen as having little relationship to the perceived

Figure 12. Correlation matrix: indices of relative influence with
productivity and satisfaction (N = 360)

| | Relative influence | | | | |
Output, satisfaction	State board	Higher adminis-tration	Middle adminis-tration	Dept. chair-men	Professors
Perceived productivity	−.0174	.0511	.0791	.2236†	.2484†
Professional output	.0042	−.1198*	−.0868	.0625	.0146
Satisfaction	−.1122*	−.0026	.0438	.1772†	.1848†
Power of chairmen	.0617	.2408†	.2354†	.4491‡	.0545

*Correlation significant at .05 level or better.
†Correlation significant at .01 level or better.
‡Correlation significant at .001 level or better.

productivity of professors to their professional output or to the power of departmental chairmen, but is associated negatively with professors' satisfaction, although the degree of association is low. One can infer that institutional autonomy—and the professional freedom that could accompany it—are valued by the faculty.

The relative influence of presidents and other higher administrators is negatively associated with the professional output of professors, again suggesting the possibility that the greater the influence of administrators to direct activity toward institutional goals, the less active the faculty will tend to be in their academic disciplines. But the alternative explanation again may be more valid; that professors active in their field may tend to impute little influence to administrative groups in their colleges.[15] The last column in Figure 12 shows correlations between professors' influence over various groups in the colleges and other indices. It is not surprising to find that professors' perceptions of their relative influence is closely associated with their perceptions of productivity and with their satisfaction.

Discussion

The findings reported here tend to confirm the impression of a number of students that colleges are unique kinds of organizations. Although, in the professors' eyes, an authority system does exist, it cannot be called a command system. Its aggregate influence, as shown on the control graph in Figure 1, is seen by professors to be relatively low. The influence of the administration in the colleges appears to be limited both by the state government and by the collegial norms of academia.

The administrator closest to professors is perceived by them to be the least influential of the various groups in the college. It seems likely that the professors consider their chairman the first among equals, whom they expect to carry their wishes to other administrators, but who is also subject to the demands of other administrative groups (see Figure 14). The finding that professors' satisfaction is positively correlated with the power of their chairman does not exactly confirm this proposition, but an examination of the relationship between the satisfaction of professors and various power items available to their chairman shows clearly that professors are most satisfied when the chairman has considerable personal influence. We infer that it is the power of the chairman to speak effectively on behalf of the faculty that explains the positive association between the chairman's power and the satisfaction of professors.

That the chairman's power and professional output should be negatively correlated is a surprising finding. The best explanation seems to be that the professor who has strong personal contacts in his discipline tends to impute lower power to his department head than a professor who sees himself primarily as a member of the particular college. The positive relationship between the power of the chairman and the perceived productivity of the faculty seems to indicate that teaching is the primary goal of the colleges sampled. Although research and writing are not reported as the primary goals of their colleges by most of the professors, for a number of professors the research demands of their disciplines seem to be as compelling as the demands of the teaching system. We suggest that professors who are active in their academic disciplines have adopted research norms; those who see themselves as productive in their colleges apparently have accepted the teaching and service aims of their institutions. The results presented cannot be generalized to universities, which are likely to have a heavier commitment to research, and perhaps cannot be extended to private four-year colleges; however, we think that further research will find the relationships in other four-year state colleges consistent with these results.

The present study suggests a number of questions associated with the role of the department chairman and faculty productivity and satisfaction, which may be productive areas for study. For example, how do professors in the large universities view the power hierarchy in their organizations? What goals do the university professors see as paramount? What are the relationships between variations in the power of chairmen and faculty satisfaction and productivity? If the chairmen have less power than the departmental faculty and the dean in colleges and universities, how do the chairmen handle the associated stresses? What is the impact on the chairmen of various organizational sanctions? Are there any counterparts to this role in other types of institutions?

The findings in this study suggest that it is feasible to investigate differential availability of power instruments to individuals in organizations and to relate this to important organizational outcomes. Knowledge of such relationships in colleges and universities, as well as in other kinds of organizations, would seem to be valuable.

Footnotes

1. The case for needed research about academic institutions has been made elsewhere. See, for example, T. R. McConnell, "Needed Research in College and University Organization and Administration," in Terry F. Lunsford (ed.), *The Study of Academic Administration* (Boulder: Western Interstate Commission for Higher Education, October, 1963), p. 113.

2. This notion is implicit in the typology of organizations advanced by Daniel Katz and Robert L. Kahn, *The Social Psychology of Organizations* (New York: Wiley, 1966), pp. 132-133.

3. For example, see Ben Euwema, The Organization of the Department, *The Educational Record*, 24 (January 1953), 38.

4. For an analysis of this view, see G. Lester Anderson, "The Organizational Character of the American Colleges and Universities," in Lunsford, *op. cit.*, pp. 10-14.

5. Francis E. Rourke and Glenn E. Brooks, " 'The Managerial Revolution' in Higher Education," *Administrative Science Quarterly* 9 (September 1964), 156-157.

6. See Victor H. Vroom, *Work and Motivation* (New York: Wiley, 1964), pp. 181-187, for a review of the literature relating to job satisfaction and productivity, and confirmation of this point.

7. Although the enrollment in private colleges and universities in the United States was 1.7 times larger in 1965 than in 1955 and the enrollment in public universities was 2.2 times as large, the enrollment in publicly supported four-year colleges multiplied by 2.9 times during the same period. Derived from tables on "College and University Enrollments (4-year Institutions)," U. S. Department of Health, Education and Welfare, Office of Education, *Opening Fall Enrollment of Higher Education* (Washington, D. C.: U. S. Government

Printing Office, published annually). The issues for 1955-1966 were consulted for this paper.

8. Defining power in terms of sanctions is generally consistent with recent thought. See Peter M. Blau, *Exchange and Power in Social Life* (New York: Wiley, 1964), p. 117, who defines power as "the ability of persons or groups to impose their will on others despite resistance through deterrence either in the forms of withholding regularly supplied rewards or in the form of punishment." Both are negative sanctions, which we define in terms of subordinates' expectations. As defined by Blau, "sanctions" seem similar to the "resources" of the agent discussed by Dorwin Cartwright, in "Influence, Leadership, Control," in James G. March (ed.), *Handbook of Organizations* (Chicago: Rand McNally, 1965), pp. 5-7.

9. These questions were suggested by those used by Paul F. Lazarsfeld and Wagner Thielens, Jr., for their study of social scientists in 165 colleges and universities. See Lazarsfeld and Thielens, *The Academic Mind: Social Scientists in a Time of Crisis* (Glencoe, Ill.: The Free Press, 1958), pp. 22-24, 390-391. The "Satisfaction" results of the two studies are not comparable because the scale categories are quite different.

10. This method of measuring productivity was similar to that used by Lazarsfeld and Thielens, *op. cit.*, pp. 7-10, 402-406, 397-398, but the continua categories were different so that the results are not comparable.

11. Arnold S. Tannenbaum and Basil S. Georgopoulos, The Distribution of Control in Formal Organizations, *Social Forces*, 36 (October 1957), 46.

12. *Ibid.*, 44-45.

13. Some of the conditions that affect the confidence that can be placed in the conclusions should be noted. There are statistical limitations, based primarily on the well-known problems of correlations, especially of indices derived from attitude scales. There are sampling limitations; the conclusions may apply only to the particular state colleges in the sample. This limitation may not be serious since the schools were of varying sizes and ages and represented two separate state jurisdictions. Finally, the questionnaire may be unreliable or invalid in certain key respects. However, considerable care was taken in its preparation, and a split-half reliability test of the power measure, after correction by means of the Spearman-Brown formula, yielded a reliability coefficient of .9526. A power index was derived for each of 35 chairmen and from the "relative influence" questions a "chairman's influence" index was derived for the same group. When these two indices of the chairman's power were correlated, the result was a validity coefficient of .7438, which is statistically significant at better than the .001 level. The other section of the questionnaire had considerable face validity, but the reliability and validity were not checked because a criterion measure would have made the instrument too long. We must assume that the respondents correctly reflected their attitudes as requested. We have no evidence that they did not.

14. When graphs were constructed for each of the colleges separately, the results were markedly similar. Neither size, location, nor state jurisdiction seemed to affect the general pattern shown in Figure 3.

15. Table 10 shows again the close association between the influence of department heads and the perceived productivity and professional output of professors. The difference between the "relative influence" and "power"

measures comes about because the two are not precisely symmetrical. "Power" of the *chairman* is measured according to perceptions of the degree of his access to various sanctions; "influence" is based on the degree of influence *chairmen in the aggregate* have over other groups. The influence of department heads is correlated .4491 with their power. The difference between this and the validating correlation noted in note 13 is due to the fact that the validity test was based on the correlation of *means* of power and influence imputed to department heads by members of 35 different departments.

Part 3

The Faculty and the Governance Process

FACULTY ORGANIZATION AND AUTHORITY

Burton R. Clark

As we participate in or study various faculties in American higher education, we observe decisions being made through informal interaction among a group of peers and through collective action of the faculty as a whole. Formal hierarchy plays little part, and we have reason to characterize the faculty as a collegium.[1] At the same time we sense that what we now observe is not a counterpart of the collegiality of the days of old. The modern faculty in the United States is not a body to be likened to the guilds of the medieval European university,[2] or to the self-government of a dozen dons in a residential college at Oxford or Cambridge,[3] or to the meagre self-rule that was allowed the faculty in the small liberal arts college that dominated American higher education until the end of the last century.[4] The old-time collegium has modern reflections, as in the Fellowships of the colleges at Yale, but for the most part it is no longer winningly with us, and the kind of collegiality we now find needs different conceptualization. We also observe on the modern campus that information is communicated through formal channels, responsibility is fixed in formally-designated positions, interaction is arranged in relations between superiors and subordinates, and decisions are based on written rules. Thus we have reason to characterize the campus as a bureaucracy. But, at the same time, we sense that this characterization overlooks so much that it becomes misleading. Though the elements of bureaucracy are strong, they do not dominate the campus; and though they grow, their growth does not mean future dominance if other forms of organization and authority are expanding more rapidly.

The major form of organization and authority found in the faculties of the larger American colleges and universities, and toward which many small campuses are now moving, is now neither predominantly collegial nor bureaucratic. Difficult to characterize, it may be seen as largely "professional," but professional in a way that is critically different from the authority of professional men in other organizations such as the business corporation, the government agency, and the hospital. To approach this unusual pattern, we will first discuss trends in the organization and culture of the campus as a whole and then turn to the related trends in the organization and authority of the faculty.

We begin with broad changes in the nature of the campus because they condition the structure of authority. Authority is conditioned, for example, by the nature of work, the technology of an organization. The mass assembly of automobiles does not allow much personal discretion on the part of the worker; surgery in the hospital operating room requires on-the-spot judgment and autonomous decision by the surgeon and one or two colleagues. To understand faculty authority, we need some comprehension of what academic work has in common with work in other settings and how it differs from work elsewhere. Authority is also conditioned by patterns of status. Status comes in part from formal assignment, hence men called deans usually have much of it, but status is also derived in academia from one's standing in a discipline, and this important source of status is independent of the official scheme.[5] Authority is also conditioned by traditional sentiments. Legends and ideologies have a force of their own. Conceptions of what should be are formed by what has been or by ideals handed down through the generations. The stirring ideologies of community of scholars and academic freedom are forces to be reckoned with when one is dealing with faculties and in understanding their organization. Thus, the work itself, the status system, the traditional sentiments, all affect authority.

Trends in the Social Organization of the Campus

Four trends in the campus, closely related, are as follows: unitary to composite or federal structure; single to multiple value systems; non-professional to professional work; consensus to bureaucratic coordination.

Unitary to Federal Structure

The history of American higher education is a history of movement from unitary liberal arts colleges to multi-structured colleges and universities. The American college of 1840 contained a half dozen professors and fifty to a hundred students;[6] in 1870, average size was still less than 10 faculty and 100 students. All students in a college took the same curriculum, a "program of classical-mathematical studies inherited from Renaissance education."[7] There was no need for sub-units such as division and department; this truly was a unitary structure. In comparison, the modern university and college is multi-structured. The University of California at Berkeley in 1962-63, with over 23,000 students and 1,600 "officers of instruction," was divided into some 15 colleges or schools (e.g., College of Engineering, School of Public Health; over 50 institutes, centers and laboratories; and some 75 departments (including Poultry Husbandry, Romance Philology, Food Technology and Naval Architecture). In three departments and three schools, the sub-unit itself contained over 50 faculty members. Such complexity is not only characteristic of the university: a large California state college contains 40 or so disciplines, grouped in a number of divisions; and even a small liberal arts college today may have 20 departments and three or four divisions.

The multiplication of sub-units stems in part from increasing size. The large college cannot remain as unitary as the small one, since authority must be extensively delegated and subsidiary units formed around the many centers of authority. The sub-units also stem from plurality of purpose; we have moved from single- to multi-purpose colleges. Goals are not only more numerous but also broadly defined and ambiguous. Those who would define the goals of the modern university speak in such terms as "preserving truth, creating new knowledge, and serving the needs of man through truth and knowledge."[8] The service goal has a serviceable ambiguity that covers anything from home economics for marriage to research and development for space. A tightly integrated structure could not be established around these goals. Organizational structure accommodates to the multiplicity of goals by dividing into segments with different primary functions, such as liberal arts and professional training, scientific research and humanistic education. The structure accommodates to ambiguity of goals with its own ambiguity, overlap, and discontinuity. We find some liberal arts disciplines scattered all over the campus (e.g., statistics, psychology), residing as components of professional schools and of "other" departments as well as in the appropriately named department. No neat consistent structure is possible; the multiple units form and reform around functions in a catch-as-catch-can fashion. Needless to say, with a multiplicity of ambiguous goals and a variety of sub-units, authority is extensively decentralized. The structure is federal rather than unitary, and even takes on some likeness to a loosely-joined federation.

Single to Multiple Value System

Most colleges before the turn of the century and perhaps as late as the 1920's possessed a unified culture that extended across the campus,[9] and this condition still obtains in some small colleges of today. But the number of colleges so characterized continues to decline and the long-run trend is clear: the campus-wide culture splits into sub-cultures located in a variety of social groups and organizational units. As we opened the doors of American higher education, we admitted more orientations to college—college as fun, college as marriage, college as preparation for graduate school, college as certificate to go to work tomorrow, college as place to rebel against the Establishment, and even college as a place to think. These orientations have diverse social locations on campus, from fraternity house to cafe espresso shop to Mrs. Murphy's desegregated rooming house. The value systems of the students are numerous.

The faculty is equally if not more prone to diversity in orientation, as men cleave to their specialized lines of work and their different perspectives and vocabularies. Faculty orientations differ between those who commit themselves primarily to the local campus and those who commit themselves primarily to their farflung discipline or profession; between those who are scientists and those who are humanists; between those who think of themselves as pure researchers or pure scholars and those who engage in a professional practice and train recruits. The value systems of the faculty particularly cluster around the individual disciplines and hence at one level of analysis there are as many value systems as there are departments.

Nonprofessional to Professional Work

Intense specialization characterizes the modern campus; academic man has moved from general to specific knowledge. The old-time teacher—Mr. Chips—was a generalist. He covered a wide range of subject-matter, with less intensity in any one area than would be true today, and he was engaged in pure transmission of knowledge. In the

American college of a century ago, the college teacher had only a bachelor's degree (in the fixed classical curriculum), plus "a modest amount of more advanced training, perhaps in theology. . . ." [10] There was no system of graduate education, no reward for distinction in scholarship, and the professor settled down into the groove of classroom recitation and the monitoring of student conduct. We have moved from this kind of professor, the teacher generalist, to the teacher of physics, of engineering, of microbiology, of abnormal psychology, and to the professor as researcher, as consultant, as professional-school demonstrator. We have moved from transmission of knowledge to innovation of knowledge, which has meant specialization in research. Taking the long view, perhaps *the* great change in the role of academic man is the ascendance of research and scholarship—the rise of the commitment to create knowledge. This change in the academic role interacts with rapid social change: research causes change, as in the case of change in technology and industrial processes; and such changes, in turn, encourage the research attitude, as in the case of competition between industrial firms, competition between nations, competition between universities. In short, the research component of the academic role is intimately related to major modern social trends.

In his specialism, modern academic man is a case of professional man. We define "profession" to mean a specialized competence with a high degree of intellectual content, a specialty heavily based on or involved with knowledge. Specialized competence based on involvement in knowledge is the hallmark of the modern professor. He is pre-eminently an expert. Having special knowledge at his command, the professional worker needs and seeks a large degree of autonomy from lay control and normal organizational control. Who is the best judge of surgical procedure—laymen, hospital administrators, or surgeons? Who is the best judge of theories in chemistry—laymen, university administrators, or professors of chemistry? As work becomes professionalized—specialized around esoteric knowledge and technique—the organization of work must create room for expert judgment, and autonomy of decision-making and practice become a hallmark of the advanced profession.

Not all professional groups need the same degree of autonomy, however. Professionals who largely give advice or follow the guidelines of a received body of knowledge require extensive but not great autonomy for the individual and the group. They need sufficient leeway to give an honest expert opinion or to apply the canons of judgment of their field. Those requiring great autonomy are those who wish to crawl along the frontiers of knowledge, with flashlight or floodlight in hand, searching for the new—the new scientific finding, the new reinterpretation of history, the new criticism in literature or art. Academic man is a special kind of professional man, a type characterized by a particularly high need for autonomy. To be innovative, to be critical of established ways, these are the commitments of the academy and the impulses of scientific and scholarly roles that press for unusual autonomy.

Consensual to Bureaucratic Coordination

As the campus has moved from unitary to composite structure, from single to multiple systems of values, from general to specialized work, it has moved away from the characteristics of community, away from "community of scholars." A faculty member does not interact with most other members of the faculty. In the larger places, he may know less than a fifth, less than a tenth. Paths do not cross. The faculty lounge is no more, but is replaced by coffee pots in dozens of locations. The professor retains a few interests in common with all others, such as higher salaries, but he has an increasing number of interests that diverge. Even salary is a matter on which interests may diverge, as men bargain for themselves, as departments compete for funds, as scientists are paid more, through various devices, than the men of the humanities.

In short, looking at the total faculty, interaction is down, commonality of interest is down, commonality of sentiments is down. With this, coordination of work and policy within the faculty is not so much now as in the past achieved by easy interaction of community members, by the informal give-and-take that character-izes the true community—the community of the small town where everyone knows nearly every one else, or the community of the old small college where the professors saw much of everyone else in the group. The modern campus can no longer be coordinated across its length and breadth by informal interaction and by the coming together of the whole. Informal consulting back and forth is still important; the administration and the faculty still use the lunch table for important business. But campus-wide coordination increasingly moves toward the means normal to the large-scale organization, to bureaucratic means. We appoint specialists to various areas of administration, give them authority, and they write rules to apply across the system. They communicate by correspondence, they attempt to make decisions fairly and impartially by judging the case before them against the criteria of the rulebook. Thus we move toward bureaucratic coordination, as the admissions officer decides on admissions, the registrar decides on the recording of grades, the business officer decides proper purchasing procedures, and various faculty committees decide on a wide range of matters, from tenure to travel funds to the rules of order for meetings of an academic senate.

In sum: the campus tends toward composite structure, toward a multiplicity of sub-cultures, toward intense professionalism, and toward some bureaucratic coordination.

Change in Faculty Organization and Authority

The organization and authority of the faculty accommodate to these trends in at least three ways: by segmentation, by a federated professionalism, and by the growth of individual power centers.

Segmentation

As campuses increase in size, complexity, and internal speciali- zation, there is less chance that the faculty will be able to operate effectively as a total faculty in college affairs, less as the govern- mental body we have in mind when we speak of a community of scholars. The decision-making power and influence of the faculty is now more segmented—segmented by sub-college, by division, and particularly by department. Since the interests of the faculty cluster around the departments, faculty participation in government tends to move out to these centers of commitment. Who selects personnel, decides on courses, and judges students? The faculty as a whole cannot, any more than the administration. Indeed, as departments and professional schools grow in size and complexity, even they often do not; it is a wing of the department or a part of the professional school that has most influence. A liberal arts department that numbers 40 to 80 faculty members may contain six or eight or a dozen specialties. The day has arrived when a department chairman may not even know the name, let alone the face and the person of the new instructors in "his" department.

What happens to the governmental organs designed for the faculty as a whole? They move in form from Town Hall to representative government, with men elected from the various "states" coming together in a federal center to legislate general rules, which are then executed by the administration or the faculty committees that constitute an administrative component of the faculty. With the move to representative government, there is greater differentiation in participation; a few Actives participate a great deal; a considerably larger group constitutes an alert and informed public and participates a modest amount; the largest group consists of those who are not very interested or informed and who participate very little. The structure of participation parallels that found in the larger democratic society, and apparently is normal to a representative mass democracy. The situation is, of course, vexing to those who care about faculty government.

Professionalization

The authority of the faculty which flows out toward the departments and other units of the campus becomes located in the hands of highly specialized experts; and, as suggested earlier, takes on some characteristics of professional authority. Almost everywhere in modern large-scale organizations, we find a tug-of-war going on between administrative and professional orientations. In the hospital, the basic conflict in authority lies between the control of the non-medical hospital administrator and the authority of the doctors. In industry, a fascinating clash is occurring between management and the scientist in the research and development laboratory.[11] The fantastic expansion of research and development has brought over 400,000 scientists and engineers into industry, there to be committed to innovation and to the development of new inventions to the point of practical utility. Many of these technologists have a high degree of expertise, a strong interest in research—often "pure" research—and they press for a large degree of freedom. Their fondest wish is to be left alone; they make the point that in scientific work it seems rational to do just that, that basic discoveries stem not from managerial direction but from the scientist following up his own initial hunches and the leads he develops as he proceeds. Management has found such men difficult to deal with; their morale suffers easily from traditional forms of management, and they present unusual demands on management to change and accommodate. In this situation, professional authority and bureaucratic authority are both necessary, for each performs an essential function: professional authority protects the exercise of the special expertise of the technologist, allowing his judgment to be pre-eminent in many matters. Bureaucratic authority functions to provide coordination of the work of the technologists with the other major elements of the firm. Bureaucratic direction is not capable of providing certain expert judgments; professional direction is not capable of providing the over-all coordination. The problem presented by the scientist in industry is how to serve simultaneously the requirements of autonomy and the requirements of coordination, and how to accommodate the authority of the professional man and his group of peers to the authority of management and vice versa.[12]

The professional-in-the-organization presents everywhere his special kind of problem. He gains authority, compared to most employees, by virtue of his special knowledge and skills; he loses authority, compared to a man working on his own, by virtue of the fact that organizations locate much authority in administrative positions. The problem of allocation of authority between professionals and bureaucrats does, however, vary in intensity and form in different kinds of organizations. As mentioned earlier, advisers and practitioners need a modest degree of authority, while scientists and academics have perhaps the highest requirements for the autonomy to engage in research, in unfettered teaching, and in scholarship that follows the rules of consistency and proof that develop within a discipline.

The segmentation of the faculty into clusters of experts gives professional authority a special form in academic organizations. In other situations, there usually are one or two major professional groups within the organization who, if they are influential, substitute professional control for administrative control. This occurs in the case of medical personnel in the hospital who often dominate decision-making. The internal controls of the medical profession are strong and are substituted for those of the organization. But in the college or university this situation does not obtain; there are 12, 25, or 50 clusters of experts. The experts are prone to identify with their own disciplines, and the "academic profession" over-all comes off a poor second. We have wheels within wheels, many professions within a profession. No one of the disciplines on a campus is likely to dominate the others; at a minimum, it usually takes an alliance of disciplines, such as "the natural sciences" or "the humanities," to put together a bloc that might dominate others. The point is that with a variety of experts—chemists, educationists, linguists, professors of marketing—the collective control of the professionals over one another will not be strong. The campus is not a closely-knit group of professionals who see the world from one perspective. As a collection of professionals, it is decentralized, loose and flabby.

The principle is this: where professional influence is high and there is one dominant professional group, the organization will be integrated by the imposition of professional standards. Where professional influence is high and there are a number of professional groups, the organization will be split by professionalism. The university and the large college are fractured by expertness, not unified by it. The sheer variety supports the tendency for authority to diffuse toward quasi-autonomous clusters. Thus, faculty authority has in common with professional authority in other places the protection of individual and group autonomy. It is different from professional authority in other places in the extremity of the need for autonomy and in the fragmentation of authority around the interest of a large variety of groups of roughly equal status and power. The campus is a holding company for professional groups rather than a single association of professionals.

Individualization

When we speak of professional authority we often lump together the authority that resides with the individual expert and the authority that resides with a collegial group of experts. Both the individual and the group gain influence at the expense of laymen and the general administrator. But what is the division of authority between the individual and the group? Sometimes group controls can be very tight and quite hierarchical, informally if not formally, as young doctors learn in many hospitals, and as assistant professors learn in many departments. The personal authority of the expert varies widely with the kind of establishment, and often with rank and seniority. The campus is a place where strong forces cause the growth of some individuals into centers of power. We will review several of these sources of personal authority.

First, we have noted the expertise of the modern academy. The intense specialization alone makes many a man into king of a sector in which few others are able to exercise much judgment. Thus, *within* a department, men increasingly feel unable to judge the merits of men in specialties they know nothing about. The technical nature of the specialized lines of work of most academic men, then, is a source of personal authority. If we want to provide a course on Thomas Hardy, we are likely to defer on its content to the judgment of the man in the English Department who has been knee-deep in Hardy for a decade. The idea of such a course would really have been his in the first place; Hardy falls within his domain within the English Department, and his judgment on the need for the course will weigh more than the judgment of others.

Second, some professorial experts now have their personal authority greatly enhanced by money. Despite his location within an organization, the professor in our time is becoming an entrepreneur. It used to be that the college president was the only one on campus, other than an enterprising and dedicated member of the board of trustees, who was capable of being an entrepreneur. Many of the great presidents were great because they were great at coming home with the loot—adventurers who conquered the hearts and pocket-books of captains of industry and then with money in hand raided wholesale the faculties of other institutions. Presidents who can raise money and steal faculty are still with us, but they have been joined by professors. Kerr has suggested that the power of the individual faculty member is going up while the power of the collective faculty is going down because the individual as researcher, as scholar, and as consultant relates increasingly to the grant-giving agencies of the Federal government and to the foundations.[13] He has direct ties to these major sources of funds and influence; indeed, he participates in their awarding of grants and even has problems of conflict of interest. A professor-entrepreneur, by correspondence and telephone and airplane trips, lines up money for projects. He sometimes arranges for the financing of an entire laboratory; occasionally he even brings back a new building. Even when the professor does little of the arranging, it is *his* presence that attracts these resources. He represents competence, and the grant-givers pursue competence.

The entrepreneurial activity and resources-gaining influence of professors, which extends down to assistant professors in the social as well as the natural sciences, has had remarkable growth since World War II, and the personal autonomy and power thus achieved in relation to others in the university is considerable. A professor does not have to beg postage stamps from a departmental secretary nor a two hundred dollar raise from the department chairman nor travel money to go to a meeting from a dean or a committee if he has monies assigned to him to the tune of $37,000, or $175,000, or $400,000. His funds from outside sources may be called "soft" funds, in the jargon of finance, but they are hard enough to hire additional faculty members and assistants, to cover summer salaries, and to provide for travel to distant, delightful places.

The following principle obtains: a *direct* relation of faculty members to external sources of support affects the distribution of influence within the campus, redistributing influence from those who do not have such contacts to those who do, and moving power from the faculty as a whole and as smaller collectivities to individual professors. In the university of old, members of the faculty achieved a high degree of influence by occupying the few professorial positions available in a structure that narrowed at the top. Their source of influence was structural and internal. The source of great influence in the modern American university is less internal and less tied to particular positions; it is more external and more tied to national and international prestige in a discipline, and to contact with the sources of support for research and scholarship that are multiplying and growing so rapidly.

This individualization in faculty organization and authority excites impulses in the faculty and the administration to establish some collective control, for much is at stake in the balance of the curriculum, the equality of rewards in the faculty, and even the character of the institution. But the efforts at control do not have easy going. Collective bodies of the faculty and the administration are hardly in a position, or inclined, to tell the faculty member he can have this contract but not that one, since the faculty member will define the project as part of his pursuit of his own scholarly interests. When the faculty member feels that this sensitive right is infringed, he will run up the banners of academic freedom and inquiry, or he will fret and become a festering sore in the body politic of the campus, or he will retreat to apathy and his country house, or he will make it known in other and greener pastures that he will listen to the siren call of a good offer.

Third, personal authority of the professorial expert is increased in our time by the competitiveness of the job market. The expansion of higher education means a high demand for professors, and the job market runs very much in the professor's favor in bargaining with the administration. His favorable position *in* the market enhances his position *on* campus. He can demand more and get it; he can even become courageous. In the world of work, having another job to go to is perhaps the most important source of courage.

To recapitulate: Faculty organization and authority tends in modern times to become more segmented, more professional in character, and somewhat more individualized. We are witnessing a strong trend toward a federated structure in colleges and especially in universities—with the campus more like a United Nations and less like a small town—and this trend affects faculty authority by weakening the faculty as a whole and strengthening the faculty in its many parts. Faculty authority becomes less of a case of self-government by a total collegium, and more of a case of authority exercised department by department, sub-college by sub-college. The *role* of faculty authority is shifting from protecting the rights of the entire guild, the rights of the collective faculty, to protecting the autonomy of the separate disciplines and the autonomy of the individual faculty member.

Faculty authority in our time tends to become professional authority in a federated form. We have a loose alliance of professional men. The combination of professional authority and loosely-joined structure has the imposing function of protecting the autonomy of the work of experts amidst extensive divergence of interests and commitments. The qualities of federation are important here. The federation is a structure that gives reign to the quasiautonomous, simultaneous development of the interests of a variety of groups. Within an academic federation, a number of departments, divisions, colleges, professional schools, institutes, and the like can co-exist, each pushing its own interests and going its own way to a rather considerable extent. Professional authority structured as a federation is a form of authority particularly adaptive to a need for a high degree of autonomous judgment by individuals and sub-groups.

This trend toward a federation of professionals is only part of the story. To hold the separate components of the campus together, we have a superimposed coordination by the administration, and, as Kerr has suggested, this coordination increasingly takes on the attributes of mediation.[14] The administration attempts to keep the peace and to inch the entire enterprise another foot ahead. The faculty, too, in its own organization, also counters this divisive trend with a machinery of coordination. The very fact of diffusion of authority makes the faculty politician more necessary than ever, for the skills of politics and diplomacy are needed. There must be faculty mediators; men who serve on central committees, men with cast iron stomachs for lunch table discussions and cocktail parties, men who know how to get things done that must be done for the faculty as a whole or for part of the faculty. There must be machinery for setting rules and carrying them out impartially across the faculty. The modern campus is, or is becoming, too large and complicated for collegial or professional arrangements to provide the over-all coordination, and coordination is performed largely by bureaucratic arrangements—e.g., the rulebook, and definite administrative domains.

Federated professionalism within an organization, like many other trends, thus promotes counter-trends. Specialization and individualization seriously weaken the integration of the whole. The weakness of collegiality or professionalism in the large organization, as suggested earlier in the case of industry, is that it cannot handle the problem of order, it cannot provide sufficient integration. Thus the above trends in faculty organization and authority open the door to bureaucracy—more bureaucracy in the administration, more within the faculty itself. The modern large faculty, therefore, combines professionalism, federated structure, and bureaucracy—perhaps in a mixture never before evidenced in human history.

This combination of what seem contradictory forms of organization perplexes observers of academia. Is the faculty collegial? Yes, somewhat. Is it split into fragments? Yes, somewhat. Is it professional? Yes, somewhat. Is it unitary? Yes, somewhat. Is it bureaucratic? Yes, somewhat. Different features of the faculty strike us according to the occurrences of the week or the events we chance to observe. The ever-mounting paperwork firmly convinces us that the campus is doomed to bureaucratic stagnation. The fact that the president often gets what the president wants convinces us that he really has all the authority. The inability of a campus to change a department that is twenty years behind in its field convinces us that departmental autonomy has run amok and the campus is lacking in leadership and in capacity to keep up with the times. One observer will see the campus as a tight ship, the next will speak of the same campus as a lawless place where power lies around loose. No wonder we are confused and no wonder that outsiders are so often even more confused or more irrelevant in giving advice.

But in the combination of forms of organization and forms of authority that we find today within the campus and within the faculty itself, there are certain trends that are stronger than others and certain features that tend toward dominance. The society at large is tending to become a society of experts, and the campus has already arrived at this state. Expertise is a dominant characteristic of the campus, and organization and authority cluster around it. Because of its expertness, together with its ever-growing size, the faculty moves away from community, moves away from collegiality of the whole. The faculty moves toward decentralized or federated structure, and authority moves toward clusters of experts and the individual expert. Thus professional authority tends to become the dominant form of authority, and collegial and bureaucratic features fall into a subsidiary place. In short, when we say college, we say expert. When we say expert, we say professional authority.

Footnotes

1. A major type of collegiality is that involving collegial decision: "In such cases an administrative act is only legitimate when it has been produced by the cooperation of a plurality of people according to the principle of unanimity or of majority." Max Weber, *The Theory of Social and Economic Organization*, translated by A. M. Henderson and Talcott Parsons, New York: Oxford University Press, 1947, p. 400.

2. Hastings Rashdall, *The Universities in Europe in the Middle Ages*, edited by

T. M. Powicke and A. B. Emden, Oxford: At the Clarendon Press, 1936 three volumes.

3. C. P. Snow, *The Masters*, New York: The Macmillan Co., 1951.

4. Richard Hofstadter and Walter P. Metzger, *The Development of Academic Freedom in the United States*, New York: Columbia University Press, 1955; George P. Schmidt, *The Liberal Arts College*, New Brunswick, New Jersey: Rutgers University Press, 1957.

5. Logan Wilson, *The Academic Man*, New York: Oxford University Press, 1942; Theodore Caplow and Reece J. McGee, *The Academic Marketplace*, New York: Basic Books, Inc., 1958.

6. Hofstadter and Metzger, *op. cit.*, pp. 222-223.

7. *Ibid.*, p. 226.

8. Clark Kerr, *The Uses of the University*, The Godkin Lectures, Harvard University, 1963.

9. Hofstadter and Metzger, *op. cit.*,; Schmidt, *op. cit.*

10. Hofstadter and Metzger, *op. cit.*, p. 230.

11. See William Kornhauser, *Scientists in Industry: Conflict and Accommodation*, Berkeley: University of California Press, 1962, and Simon Marcson, *The Scientist in American Industry*, New York: Harper and Brothers, 1960.

12. Kornhauser, *op. cit.*

13. Kerr, *op. cit.*

14. *Ibid.*

ON PRESTIGE AND LOYALTY
OF UNIVERSITY FACULTY

Lionel S. Lewis

There has been little study of the institutional loyalty of university faculty; in fact, most of what is known about the general question of loyalty is impressionistic. This is perhaps because loyalty is usually "taken for granted and is, under normal circumstances, a latent social identity in a rational bureaucracy."[1] Yet, loyalty is an important condition behind the behavior of academic men or men in any organization,[2] for loyalty to the organization as a distinctive social structure and to its goals is one of the conditions necessary for organizational survival. Because there is a tension between loyalty and expertise, and because expertise is a central need to institutions of higher learning, the problem of the loyalty of faculty to a university takes on special meaning.

In one of the few systematic studies of university faculties, Gouldner has described academic cosmopolitans and locals according to their degree of loyalty, commitment to professional skills, and reference group orientation. Of the three, loyalty holds a special place. Gouldner writes:

In some measure, loyalty to the organization often implies the other two criteria, (1) a willingness to limit or relinquish the commitment to a specialized professional task and (2) a dominant career orientation to the employing organization as a reference group.[3]

This suggests that it would be useful to know more about who in a university is loyal, and some of the conditions associated with loyalty. This paper is an attempt to deal with these issues.[4]

From the *Administrative Science Quarterly*, Vol. 2, No. 4, March 1967, pp. 629-642. Reprinted by permission of the publisher.

Procedure

Sample and Method

This study is based on data from questionnaire responses of the faculty of a northeastern state university. A questionnaire was mailed to the entire full-time faculty in residence in the fall of 1964. Of the 915 persons in the sample, which was the population universe, 513 (or 56 percent) completed and returned the questionnaire, and all but four of these were usable in the analysis.[5]

The institution from which the sample was obtained is a rapidly growing, urban university, which had an enrollment of over 10,000 full-time day students in the fall of 1964. It offers degrees in as many programs as the typical state university, except that it has no School of Agriculture. Data on the respondents are given in Figure 1.

The questionnaire was designed to obtain, among other things, information about each respondent's position and duties, scholarly activities and achievements, institutional loyalty, satisfaction with various conditions at the university, and opinions regarding conditions that would lead to more satisfaction.

Formulation of Propositions

An almost unique aspect of universities, which differentiates them

Figure 1. Characteristics of the sample *

Characteristics	%	Characteristics	%
Age		*Discipline*	
Under 35	38	Science	28
36-45	36	Behavioral science	22
46-60	22	Humanities	13
Over 60	4	Professional	27
Rank		*Highest degree*	
Professor	23	Ph.D. or Ed.D.	56
Associate Professor	21	M.D. or D.D.S.	15
Assistant Professor	35	Master's degree	19
Lecturer or Instructor	16	Other, i.e., B.A., B.S., LL.B.	10
Sex			
Male	83		
Female	16		

*Because of unknowns, not all percentages total 100.

from other organizations, is their dual-prestige system. In universities, a faculty member's overall status is derived both from his position within the institution and from his standing in his professional discipline. Consequently, to be granted high prestige within a university, an individual must obtain more than a professorship; he must generally gain high prestige within his discipline. This dual-prestige system complicates any analysis of loyalty among university faculty. Nonetheless, it can be expected that, as in other institutions,

Proposition 1. Those with more prestige within the institution will be more loyal to it than those with less institutional prestige. Furthermore, to the extent that those with more professional prestige would have more extensive and intensive ties with colleagues outside their own university than those with less professional prestige, it could be predicted that

Proposition 2. Those with more professional prestige will be less loyal to their university than those with less professional prestige.

These two propositions, even if substantiated, are too simple to account for the contingencies resulting from the dual system of prestige. If for simplification, the two variables, institutional prestige and professional prestige, are dichotomized, there are four possible ways by which academicians could be characterized in terms of prestige. For at least one of these possibilities—high prestige within both the university and the profession—the crosspressures from the two systems of prestige would make it difficult to anticipate how loyal such persons would be to their university. In any case, the following proposition suggests itself:

Proposition 3. Those with high institutional prestige and low professional prestige will be the most loyal to the university; those with low institutional prestige and high professional prestige will be the least loyal to the university; those with both high institutional and high professional prestige or with both low institutional and low professional prestige will show less loyalty than the former of the two extreme aggregates, but more than the latter.

Examination of Propositions

Proposition 1

The first relationships examined were those between three measures of university prestige and loyalty: rank, age, and length of time at the university.[6] Only the first of these three measures is a direct criterion of university prestige; however, there is considerable

Figure 2. University Prestige and loyalty *

Loyalty to University	Rank			Age		Time at university	
	Asst. Prof. (N = 176) % N	Assoc. Prof. (N = 105) % N	Prof. (N = 110) % N	45 or younger (N = 364) % N	46 or older (N = 124) % N	1-6 yrs. (N = 267) % N	7 or more yrs. (N = 132) % N
Would not leave	12.5 (22)	6.7 (7)	28.2 (31)	10.4 (38)	36.3 (45)	11.2 (30)	30.3 (40)
Undecided	27.3 (48)	34.3 (36)	14.5 (16)	27.7 (101)	22.6 (28)	26.2 (70)	22.7 (30)
Would leave at a higher salary	33.0 (58)	35.2 (37)	37.3 (41)	34.9 (127)	26.6 (33)	31.5 (84)	33.3 (44)
Would leave at the same or lower salary	27.3 (48)	23.8 (25)	20.0 (22)	26.9 (98)	14.5 (18)	31.1 (83)	13.6 (18)

*Chi square values for rank is 14.18, d.f. = 2; for age is 33.41, d.f. = 1; and for time at university is 28.68, d.f. = 1. Only high loyalty and low loyalty, and not moderate loyalty, are considered in statistical analysis. In a one-tailed test, all chi square values are significant at the .0005 level.

justification for including the other two criteria in light of the widespread feeling of many faculty, particularly senior faculty, that besides being measures of mobility potential, they are valid indices. That gerontocratic principles should be operative was expressed by a department chairman from the school under study in a memorandum to the members of his department when the research was being concluded. In defending the process whereby tenure was granted in his department, he wrote:

> The criteria of age and experience ... should not be so difficult to *understand.* In American democracy there are lower age limits for senators, representatives, presidents, vice presidents, etc. The American ... Association requires 5 years post Ph.D. work to qualify as fellow, etc. The criteria merely assumes [sic] that anyone knows more at 40 or 50 than he does at 30. It does not deny that *some* people know more at 30 than others at 50. Again, we are talking about what is true as a general rule—on the *average* if you will.

To question this argument does not deny its extensive acceptance.

To ascertain loyalty, the respondents were asked whether they would take another academic position at Harvard or the University of California at Berkeley, ostensibly more prestigious institutions, at a lower, the same, or a higher salary, or whether they were undecided, or would not leave. It was assumed, partially following others who have used this question to measure loyalty to the organization, that those who would not leave had a relatively high commitment to the university and were loyal to it, that those who would leave at the same or lower salary had a low commitment and were not loyal, and those who were undecided or would leave at a higher salary had a moderate commitment and were somewhat loyal.[7] Figure 2 shows the degree to which faculty in different academic ranks and age seniority categories are loyal to the university.

It can be seen from Figure 2 that faculty with more institutional prestige are generally more loyal to the university. Professors are more loyal than associate professors. The reason a larger percentage of assistant professors than associate professors indicate that they would not leave is perhaps that more of them are new, and it is too early for some to think that their present position might prove to be unsatisfactory, so that they might possibly leave in the future. Faculty over 45 years of age are more loyal than faculty under 45 years of age; and faculty with seven or more years of service to the university are more loyal than faculty with six or less years of service. Although these relationships are not marked, chi square tests considering those with high loyalty and low loyalty produce

Figure 3. Professional prestige and loyalty *

Loyalty to university	Professional publications in the past 3 years			Highest degree			Time spent on research	
	None (N = 151)	One or two (N = 128)	Three or more (N = 207)	Bachelor's or Master's (N = 117)	Medical, Dental or other professional (N = 90)	Ph.D. or Ed.D. (N = 274)	Hardly any (N = 114)	1/5 or more (N = 346)
	% N	% N	% N	% N	% N	% N	% N	% N
Would not leave	30.5 (46)	11.7 (15)	10.6 (22)	27.3 (32)	18.9 (17)	12.0 (33)	32.5 (37)	11.0 (38)
Undecided	30.5 (46)	27.3 (35)	21.7 (45)	36.8 (43)	24.4 (22)	23.0 (63)	28.9 (33)	25.1 (87)
Would leave at a higher salary	21.2 (32)	35.2 (45)	40.1 (83)	20.5 (24)	34.4 (31)	38.0 (104)	29.8 (34)	34.1 (118)
Would leave at the same or lower salary	17.9 (27)	25.8 (33)	27.5 (57)	15.4 (18)	22.2 (20)	27.0 (74)	8.8 (10)	29.8 (103)

*Chi square value for professional publications is 22.04, d.f. = 2; for highest degree is 15.66, d.f. = 2; and for time spent on research is 39.64, d.f. = 1. Only high loyalty and low loyalty, and not moderate loyalty, are considered in statistical analysis. In a one-tailed test, all chi square values are significant at the .0005 level.

statistically significant results, so that the data clearly substantiate Proposition 1.

Proposition 2

Professional prestige was measured by number of professional publications in the preceding three years. The assumption behind the use of publications as a reflection of professional prestige is that those who were more actively engaged in scholarly writing were the most esteemed by colleagues in their discipline. This supposition is surely valid, even if one might wonder why.

Two additional, and more tenuous, measures of professional prestige used were highest degree earned and time spent in research. The premise underlying the utilization of highest degree earned, which is also an indication of mobility potential, is that this is commonly a necessary condition for full acceptance in a discipline and precedes the attainment of prestige. The premise underlying the utilization of time spent on research is that research activity is a necessary condition for professional publication. Figure 3 presents the relationship between professional prestige and loyalty.

From Figure 3 it can be seen that the higher the professional prestige of faculty, the less loyal they are to the university. Again, all relationships are statistically significant. Those faculty who have not published in the past three years, those with only a Bachelor's or Master's degree, and those who devote hardly any time to research activity clearly show more institutional loyalty than those who publish, those who have a higher degree, and those who spend more time on scholarly enterprises. These findings support Proposition 2. It should be noted that the relationships in Figures 2 and 3, and those found in data presented below were not fundamentally altered when multivariate analyses were made with other academic attributes, such as discipline or organizational unit of the university, as third variables.

Proposition 3

This was tested with a simple multivariate analysis. The simultaneous effects of what appears to be two noncomplementary systems of prestige on loyalty were studied. For this analysis, the most appropriate measure of university prestige—rank, the most appropriate measure of professional prestige—publications, and the measure of loyalty were cross-tabulated. All three variables were dichotomized: rank into professors and associate professors, on the one hand, and assistant professors, on the other; publications into those

Figure 4. Faculty expressing loyalty (in percent)

Professional prestige	University prestige	
	High (Prof. or Assoc. Prof.) % N	Low (Asst. Prof.) % N
Publications		
High (Publications)	38.0 (71*)	29.2 (33)
Low (No Publications)	76.9 (30)	57.4 (35)
Doctorate degree		
High (Doctorate)	37.2 (71)	34.2 (50)
Low (No Doctorate)	94.1 (16)	64.3 (18)

*Number indicating they were undecided or would not leave.

who had published in the past three years and those who had not; and loyalty into those who would leave, and those who were undecided or would not leave. The results of this examination are shown in Figure 4.

The relative size of the four percentages in the top half of Figure 4 lends support to Proposition 3; the relationship of one to another is in accordance with what could be anticipated on the basis of this proposition. It would appear that the most loyal faculty are those with high university prestige and low professional prestige, that the least loyal are those with low university prestige and high professional prestige, and that the moderately loyal are those who are either both high or both low in the two prestige systems.

To substantiate this finding, an additional analysis was made in which the supplementary measures of prestige introduced in Figures 2 and 3 were substituted seriatim in place of either rank or publications. The outcome of these tests, although not as convincing as the original associations, generally confirms Proposition 3. One of these calculations is given in the bottom half of Figure 4. This

Figure 5. Loyalty to the university and dissatisfaction with
university conditions (in percent)

University conditions	Would not leave (N = 83)	Unde-cided (N = 129)	Would leave at a higher salary (N = 161)	Would leave at the same or lower salary (N = 117)	Chi square (d.f. = 3)
Economic conditions					
Health insurance benefits	8.4	13.2	13.7	18.8	4.4
Life insurance benefits	16.9	17.8	17.4	15.4	0.3
Retirement policies	10.8	8.5	16.1	11.1	4.2
Funds available for professional meetings	33.7	42.6	50.3	47.0	6.4
Salary increases	15.7	11.6	23.0	19.7	6.8
Colleagues					
Interest in teaching	20.5	18.6	15.5	18.8	1.0
Interest in research	12.0	17.8	13.7	18.8	2.9
Interest in students	20.5	16.3	23.0	27.4	4.7
Integration in university life					
Participation in policies affecting students	7.2	17.1	29.8	23.9	18.7*
Participation in policies affecting promotions	18.1	20.2	21.7	21.4	0.5
Maintenance of social life among staff	13.3	18.6	15.5	26.5	8.1*
Communication between faculty and administration	16.9	27.1	28.6	44.4	19.1*

*Significant at the .05 level.

particular example is utilized because it verified, better than other distributions, two conclusions that were already evident from Figure 4. These were, first, that professional prestige is more powerful in determining loyalty for those with low professional prestige than for those with high professional prestige. When one of the less direct measures of prestige was utilized, the effect of university prestige on the loyalty of those with high professional prestige was inconsequential.

Determinants of Disloyalty

It is not uncommon to hear university faculty characterized as avaricious Philistines concerned mostly with money, power, prestige and, sometimes, security. This portrayal is the consequence of many conditions in American life—anti-intellectualism, the populist tradition, the unpopular stands that academicians sometimes take, and perhaps a partial description of some academicians. Even scholars writing about scholars have been seduced by this caricature and have let it influence their observations. For example, in their mostly creditable account of the academic marketplace, Caplow and McGee specify "prestige," "security" and "authority" as major "motives for migration."[8] This is surely an oversimplification of complex motivations.

It is clear from the study that a large number of faculty were not eager to take another position no matter what the enticement. If they were contented with their present position, they probably were not overly concerned with the need for money and prestige. Furthermore, since those with the most professional prestige, when university prestige was held constant, expressed the least loyalty, there are apparently factors other than economic ones behind disloyalty, and therefore academic migration. The present limited findings lend themselves to the interpretation that a dominant reason behind disloyalty (hence migration) is the attempt to find an environment where one feels he can better carry out his scholarly investigations.

An attempt was made to learn why faculty might be disloyal through two different types of questions. First, fifteen conditions at the university were listed, and each respondent was requested to indicate how satisfactory (from very satisfactory to very unsatisfactory) he found each to be. Twelve conditions could be classified under the generic categories of economic conditions, colleagues, and integration in university life. This classification is shown in Figure 5. Second, respondents were asked how important salary, fringe benefits, opportunities for research, and the institution's reputation would be in reaching a decision to take another position. The alternatives offered were from "very important" to "not important at all." The distribution of responses of the sample is shown in Figure 6.

Of the 12 distributions in Figure 5, statistically significant

Figure 6. Loyalty to the university and conditions considered
important at another institution (in percent)

Conditions believed very important	Would not leave (N = 83)	Undecided (N = 129)	Would leave at a higher salary (N = 161)	Would leave at the same or lower salary (N = 117)
Salary	21.7	11.6	40.4	12.8
Fringe benefits	20.5	13.2	21.7	9.4
Opportunities for research	32.5	41.9	60.2	65.8
Scholarly reputation of university	27.7	44.2	42.9	67.5

differences were found between the most and least loyal in only
three instances. Among persons differing in loyalty, there is little
variation in how satisfactory they find their economic situation or
their colleagues; there is considerable variation, however, in how
well-integrated they feel in university life. In three out of four
instances, those who could be most easily induced to move elsewhere
were most dissatisfied with their associations within the university.

For only two of the four aspects of a university in which one was
seeking an appointment, is there a distinct dissimilarity between the
most and the least loyal. The opportunities for research and the
school's scholarly reputation are factors that are important to about
two-thirds of those who would leave at the same or a lower salary,
but to less than one-third of those who would not leave. Salary and
fringe benefits were more important for those who would not leave
than for those who would, perhaps because they have estimated their
value on the academic scene, and believe that these could not be
equalled elsewhere. Notice how much more relevant salary is for
those who would leave at a higher salary only than for others. This is
a partial validation of the measure of loyalty; those who say they
would leave for a higher salary probably would do so.

Taken together, the data in Figures 5 and 6, along with the findings in Figure 4, would lead to the conclusion that rather than being concerned with economic factors, faculty are disloyal, and hence inclined to be mobile, because of feelings of alienation in their present situation and because of the possibility of becoming a part of a more scholarly environment with more chances for scholarly production.

Concluding Remarks

There are indications that there are both a "push" and a "pull" behind faculty turnover. The "push" is a perception of not adequately participating in the university community. The "pull" is the expectation of finding an academic paradise. In either case, economics is not a signal factor. For example, one assistant professor who would leave at the same or lower salary mentioned "the intellectual quality of my faculty colleagues" at his new school as being the most important pull factor that would enter into his decision. Another assistant professor categorized as disloyal, thought fringe benefits were very important, but this would "include excellent classrooms and offices, faculty club as good or better than ours, attractive campus, etc." A third assistant professor who would have been classified as disloyal felt that fringe benefits would be of consequence if they took "into consideration the cultural activity etc. of the city in which the prospective university is situated." Economic considerations entered into the decisions of those who were most ready to move only one-sixth as often as the wish for a more favorable milieu in which to do research; even when economic factors did become important, it was for reasons other than simple opportunism. Economics, then, is generally crucial neither as a push nor as a pull factor.

In the association between disloyalty, alienation, and a scholarly orientation, it is not possible to determine which is antecedent; that is, it cannot be ascertained from the data whether faculty who become professionally active do not become integrated on their own campus, or whether those who are estranged turn to scholarship to compensate for their isolation. There is some reason to believe that the first interpretation is the more accurate, although probably both are true. First of all, in spite of the fact that some faculty mentioned that "my voice in department's policies" or "the climate, atmosphere, cooperation, equity, and good will within the institution" were "very important" in evaluating a university, these were overwhelmingly faculty who were not potentially the most mobile.

Furthermore, the finding that the least loyal are those who experience a lack of consistency in prestige is relevant in the light of research in the area of social stratification, which has shown that those who are characterized by a low degree of status crystallization manifest more estrangement than those characterized by a high degree.[9] All of this would suggest that scholarly orientation is antecedent to alienation and disloyalty. Of course, the other aggregate with a lack of consistency in prestige are the most loyal and manifestly the most integrated in university affairs. Yet, just as those with high professional prestige and low university prestige are alienated from that feature of their lives which seems to be responsible for this inconsistency—that is, the university, those with high university prestige and low professional prestige may be alienated from that feature of their lives which seems to be responsible for this inconsistency—that is, their discipline.

Footnotes

1. Alvin W. Gouldner, Cosmopolitans and Locals: Toward an Analysis of Latent Social Roles—I, *Administrative Science Quarterly*, 2 (December 1957), p. 290. Gouldner also notes that "Max Weber's theory of bureaucracy seems to have taken as given, and therefore neglected, the role of loyalty needs as functional requisites of modern bureaucratic groups." Cosmopolitans and Locals: Toward Analysis of Latent Social Roles—II, *Administrative Science Quarterly*, 2 (March 1958), 465.

2. Alvin W. Gouldner, The Problem of Loyalty of Groups Under Tension, *Social Problems*, 2 (October 1954), 82-88.

3. Gouldner, Cosmopolitans and Locals . . .—I, *op. cit.*, 291.

4. I am grateful to the Office of Institutional Research of the State University of New York at Buffalo for financial support of the research on which this paper is based.

5. The incomplete return, expected for this type of survey, along with the fact that the sample is drawn from one institution, are conditions that could introduce a bias in the data and that must be taken into account in interpreting the reported findings. The findings might be limited in their generality; since this institution may be atypical, raising the possibility that idiosyncratic properties are being described.

6. Since many instructors and lecturers have nonrenewable term appointments, they are not included in the analysis of the relationship between university prestige, as measured by rank, and loyalty.

7. Gouldner, Cosmopolitans and Locals . . .—I, *op. cit.*, 305-306.

8. Theodore Caplow and Reece J. McGee, *The Academic Marketplace* (New York: Basic Books, 1958), p. 147.

9. As only one example, see Gerhard E. Lenski, Status Crystallization: A Non-Vertical Dimension of Social Status, *American Sociological Review*, 19 (August 1954), 411-413.

ANALYSIS OF A FACULTY: PROFESSIONALISM, EVALUATION, AND THE AUTHORITY STRUCTURE

Robert R. Hind

The purpose of this article is to report some of the findings of a study of faculty members' perceptions of their work and the ways in which it is evaluated, and to present some derivative interpretations about authority in universities as professional organizations.[1] These interpretations are not confined to the university setting alone, but are considered in the light of our knowledge of the behavior of other professionals in bureaucratic organizations.

Our interest is twofold. First, to add to the understanding of the ways in which professional work forces relate to their organizational settings. And second, to interpret these findings as they apply to the needs of higher education. This latter objective, addressed in the concluding section, is consistent with the responsibility of researchers to stick their necks out a bit by pointing to the ways in which their findings might be used to improve social conditions and institutions.

The article is organized in four major sections. Section I discusses some theoretical concepts about authority systems in professional organizations. Section II reports the data on a study of the Stanford University faculty of Humanities and Sciences, concentrating on their task conceptions and evaluation processes. Section III shows the implications of these data for the study of professional organizations, and Section IV suggests how these findings might bear on broader questions of university reform.

A complete report of the study is contained in Robert R. Hind, *Evaluation and Authority in a University Faculty*, Stanford University Dissertation, 1968; and in a forthcoming book by Hind, Sanford N. Dornbusch, and W. Richard Scott.

I. Background Concepts:
Professionalism, Evaluation, and Authority

Over the past couple of decades, organization theorists have become increasingly concerned about the characteristics of professional work organizations. In the early days of the study of organizations, attention was concentrated on factories, government bureaucracies, and other organizations whose workers were relatively low-skilled and nonprofessional. Recently, however, attention has been focused on high-skill, professionally dominated organizations such as the university, the school, and the hospital. By focusing on the university professor and his work, it is hoped that this article will enlarge the body of information about professional organizations.

The Concept of Professionalism

Greenwood's (7) criteria of a profession, based on a review of earlier definitions, provides us with a yardstick to determine the professional character of a faculty. He conceives of a profession as possessing:

1. Dependence on a *body of theory* derived from an extensive fund of knowledge.
2. Client subordination to *professional authority* in matters within the professional's sphere of competence.
3. *Community sanction* of authority, either formal or informal.
4. An *ethical code* regulating behavior, especially demanding affective neutrality toward clients, and support of colleagues.
5. A *professional culture* with its own values, norms, and symbols; and its formal organizations for training recruits, conducting practice, and regulating performance.

Faculty members, by and large, would seem to fall within these criteria. Close adherence to some of them seem certain to produce strains between individual professionals and the organization in which they work. A few of these points of conflict are brought out by our findings and discussed in the light of these data. Who in fact controls? If collective faculty wishes are thwarted, how does this happen? How can these conditions be altered? These are among the questions to be explored.

Another reason for concern with professionalism here is the reciprocal of the above. If faculty members strongly exhibit the characteristics of professionals, then the behavioral patterns observed in other professionally dominated organizations can be anticipated in a faculty. Thus we would be able, with some confidence, to predict faculty behavior as an application of the theory which concerns itself with professionally dominated organizations in general.

Professionalism and Issues of Organizational Authority

How does the concept of "professionalism" relate to problems of organizational authority? Much of the research in this area has shown that in organizations with many highly professional workers, normal patterns of superior-subordinate authority relations breakdown. Instead, work tends to be *peer controlled* for only the highly trained technical peers have the expertise to judge the quality of a professional's work. Professionals tend to resist strongly any interference by organizational "bureaucrats" (the administrators, those nonprofessional demons). Because of high professionalism, because of the need for expert knowledge, authority tends to be horizontal, and dominated by peer relationships.

If this is the case, then we would expect that authority relations in a university would be highly dependent on the interaction among academic colleagues, and not predominantly determined by the administrative hierarchy of the university. Our data, to be reported later, show that this is precisely the situation. Before turning to those data, however, we must clarify the concept of authority, and frame it with a theoretical approach that allows a systematic study of authority systems.

The Evaluation-Reward-Authority Concept

This analysis of faculty structure is based on a conception of organizations developed by Scott and Dornbusch which postulates that the authority structure is based upon the evaluation process that regulates, or is seen to regulate, institutional rewards.[2] On the opposite page is a schematic description of the component elements of the evaluation-reward process as described in their conception, with examples derived from two very different kinds of work situations:

Members of the authority structure are seen as those who significantly influence the distribution of *organizational sanctions* through their exercise of one or more of the four *authority rights* which constitute the evaluation process. In the case of the machinist, the evaluation process and the authority structure which derives from it are rather clear cut. For example, the superintendent might allocate, the engineer set criteria, the inspector sample, and the

Figure 1. The evaluation/reward process

AUTHORITY RIGHTS				
ALLOCATION	CRITERIA SETTING	SAMPLING	APPRAISING	REWARDS/ SANCTIONS
For a Machinist: What products will he make?	What rate of production and tolerances are expected?	Which pieces will be checked?	How good was the quantity and quality of output?	Compensation Status Independence Recognition Self-esteem etc.
For a Faculty Member: What courses will he teach and what time for other tasks?	What determines good teaching and research?	What information on performance will be used?	How well were tasks performed?	

foreman make appraisals. The relationships between these four evaluators and the machinist largely define the authority system for the job: These are the people who determine his rewards.

The faculty member, on the other hand, is part of a complex evaluation structure. As will be shown in the discussion of our study, a large number of people play a part in the evaluation process. Colleagues, students, administrators, outsiders of various descriptions are all influential. And their influence makes itself felt at various points along the authority rights sequence.

Because of the complexity of this authority structure, our study did not attempt to differentiate among the four authority rights, but rather probed the influence of the various groups in the global evaluation-reward process. Furthermore, our questioning was confined to institutional rewards such as salary and rank, although we took account of intangible and intrinsic rewards in our interpretation. Despite these departures, our study is based upon the Scott-Dornbusch concept that *the influential participants in the evaluation process are, in effect, the authority structure.* This concept has been employed in studies of a number of diverse organizations, ranging from a factory to a hospital.[3] It was found to be an effective and consistent device for determining the functional relationships among members of these organizations, thus clarifying effective organizational structure.

Applicability of the Concept

Among the assumptions underlying this research is the notion that the perception of the evaluation-reward pattern will influence individuals' behavior. Authority is seen as vested in those who are perceived as *significant evaluators*, i.e., those whose evaluations of organizational tasks influence the distribution of organizational sanctions. Further, that most participants value their performance evaluations because at least some of the attendant sanctions are important to them.

These assumptions and conditions appear to be met by a university faculty. Here rewards such as rank and salary are usually differentially distributed. They are not equal for all participants. Neither are they dispensed exclusively in accord with uncontrollable factors or status characteristics such as seniority, sex, or ethnicity. Rather rewards are dispensed on the basis of evaluations of task performances, and at least some of these rewards are valued by the participants.

Character of the Authority System

One of the purposes of this research was to determine the nature of the authority system by identifying those persons who are seen as *influential evaluators* by participants. Some of these evaluators were predicted to lie outside the institution, which raises questions about the true boundary of the faculty structure. Such an absence of clear boundaries, and the collegial character of a faculty, add to the difficulty of comprehending and describing the lines of control which operate in a university. The pyramidal bureaucratic pattern fails to describe the complex role relationships which comprise the system. The failure of the hierarchical model is vividly expressed by one writer (Guthrie, 10): The relation of a college president to his faculty is less like the relation of a general to his subordinates than it is like the relation of a watchman on the end of a dock to the seagulls circling overhead. Our study attempts to determine the perceived pattern of the evaluation-reward process, and where, as a consequence, authority lies in the university.

The Theoretical Background: A Summary

It might help to stop and summarize a moment. The purpose of this research is (1) to study a professional organization, the university; (2) to show some of the authority problems and patterns that develop in such a professional organization, especially as these relate to horizontal, peer-dominated types of authority systems; and (3) to analyze the links between the evaluation of work, the distribution of organizational rewards, and the nature of authority. In short, we want to study the role of work evaluation and authority in the university as they are perceived by the professors.

In order to accomplish this purpose we will be raising the following critical issues:

1. What are the work patterns of professors? Where do they spend their time?

2. What types of work are considered as important in the evaluation process, that is, what kinds of work are highly rewarded?

3. Who is viewed as the evaluator? Who has the right to judge work performance?

4. How is the evaluation of work tied to organizational rewards?

5. Can we learn anything about the authority system of the university by examining the evaluation process?

6. How might the evaluation-reward process be altered so as to bring about desirable changes in the university?

II. The Study and Its Findings

Since our theory predicts that the authority structure of an organization, and much of the behavior of its members, will be determined by the members' *perceptions* of the evaluation-reward system, the heart of the study was a series of structured interviews with faculty members, supplemented by information from university records.

Design of the Study

The study was planned and conducted during the academic year 1967-68, and all the data, plus the interview responses, were as of the latter part of that year. In brief, the population studied was a stratified (by rank) random sample consisting of 100 members of the Stanford University faculty of professorial rank in the School of Humanities and Sciences. This portion of the faculty was selected because it has counterparts in virtually all other institutions of higher education. Usually called a college of arts and sciences, it is the core of every major university; in terms of subject matter and background it is similar to the faculty of a traditional liberal arts college.

The subjects were asked a series of questions on the influence of evaluations of principal tasks in determining university rewards, and the identity and importance of various evaluators. In keeping with the subjective basis of our theory, questions were designed to elicit information on the individual experiences and perceptions of respondents, and not what they thought about institutional processes. The list of questions was repeated for each of the principal tasks to which respondents attached importance: teaching, research (and/or scholarship), university service (administrative and committee work, etc.), and external service. Where strong disparities or dissatisfactions were noted, we probed for causes, noting these along with volunteered comments.

Since it seems to us misleading to attempt to quantify precisely such subjective information, even when responses are made from a five-point scale, most of the results are presented in qualitative terms. We simply report that a certain number of subjects were high or low on a given characteristic, or that a certain proportion of them made a particular type of observation. Statistical tests of validity—most often chi-square computations—were made for the findings, and only differences significant at the .05 probability level are reported here.

Generalizability

In our pluralistic system of higher education, no institution is exactly like any other. Thus we would not claim any wholesale generalizability for our findings. Obviously, they would be more likely to be repeated in the score or so institutions directly comparable to Stanford. Beyond that they suggest tendencies that should apply to a greater or lesser extent to all institutions of higher education, and indeed to some other types of organizations dominated by responsible specialists.

For those who may wish to make judgments about the applicability of our results to other institutions, it seems useful to provide a brief sketch of the university we studied. Stanford is an independent, non-denominational university located on a large suburban campus in Northern California. Although tuition was free when Stanford first opened in the late 19th century, it is now among the highest in the nation, and its coeducational student body of about 12,000, divided roughly equally between graduates and undergraduates, contains a high proportion who receive scholarship or fellowship support. Admission is highly competitive.

The regular faculty numbers about 1,000, with a little over half of them members of the Humanities and Sciences faculty from which our sample was drawn; the remainder are distributed among six graduate and professional school faculties.

Stanford was recognized as a good regional university from its early days until after World War II. Following the war, an aggressive administration parlayed newly available government research grants, effective fund raising from private sources, and active faculty recruitment into constructing what is now regarded as one of the leading universities in the nation, with a strong research and graduate training program. As a result of recruitment and expansion, most of the faculty (and our sample) had been at Stanford less than ten years. It still retained, however, a sizeable proportion (15 percent in our sample) of professors who had been at Stanford over 20 years. The faculty was dominated by younger men (median age of our sample: 40) who are there primarily because of their research qualifications. The organization is strongly along disciplinary lines, each department having the right to set its instructional program and, in most cases, the principal say in new appointments. The central administrations of the university and of the school exercise their authority primarily through allocation of resources and by persuasion. Although the board of trustees and the administration of course have ultimate legal authority, the faculty possesses, as a consequence of its prestige, much of the real power to run the internal affairs of the university.

With this background on the institution and the study, the reader is free to judge the applicability to other situations of the various findings we now report.

Evaluations: What Tasks are Considered Important?

The first step in our study was to test the widely held notion that teaching and research[4] are the pre-eminent tasks for faculty members, and that research tends to dominate in the kind of institution we examined. We wanted also to see these two tasks in relation to each other, and to other important tasks which we grouped together as "university service" (committee and administrative work, advising, and other non-instructional student contacts) and "external service" (consulting, work in professional organizations and government boards, etc.). In this section we report several findings: (1) The tasks that professors actually did; (2) the reward potential of each task as revealed through faculty members' assessments of the evaluation system as it is seen to exist; (3) the difference between the existing task emphasis and the task emphasis faculty would prefer if they could change the situation; (4) the influence of other variables such as field and seniority: and (5) respondents' satisfaction with the evaluation process, both as an indicator of organizational stability and as a guide to recommended action for improvement of institutional functioning.

Allocation of Effort

We asked respondents to estimate how they distributed their time, with the following results, by rank (there were only minor variations by field):[5]

Figure 2. Median proportion of total professional
time devoted to various tasks

	Asst. Prof.	Assoc. Prof.	Full Prof.	Total All Ranks
Undergraduate classroom teaching	25%	19%	16%	21%
Grad. classroom teaching	16	19	22	19
Other Undergrad. teaching	7	2	—	1
Other grad. teaching	8	10	14	12
Subtotal: All teaching	56	50	52	53
Research (and scholarship)	33	35	29	32
University service	9	9	12	11
External service	—	5	7	4
	98%	99%	100%	100%
(N)	(33)	(33)	(34)	(100)

These results show that more time is spent on all forms of teaching than on research. Such a distribution of effort flies in the face of much of the conventional wisdom about faculty behavior in universities. It also defies the logical prediction that people will devote more effort to tasks that lead to rewards, in this case research, as our data below will show. Such a relationship is likely to produce strains and a desire for better balance, as revealed in the following table:

Figure 3. Desired changes in time allocation
(N=100, so figures read as percent across columns)

	N's Wanting Increased Time	N's Wanting No Change In Time	N's Wanting Decreased Time
Undergrad. classroom teaching	15	62	23
Grad. classroom teaching	12	65	23
Other undergrad. teaching	8	83	9
Other grad. teaching	12	72	16
Research (and scholarship)	40	44	16
University service	5	61	34
External service	7	83	10

Here we see only a minority (44 percent) satisfied with the amount of time now devoted to research; most of the rest (40 percent of the total number) would like to increase research time. Yet few wish to slight teaching in order to make time for research: A substantial majority are satisfied with the amount of time presently devoted to teaching, and those who want to decrease teaching time only slightly outnumber those who want to increase it. There appears to be a conflict between values (a professional commitment to the central task of teaching) and realities (the 24-hour day), a matter to which reference will again be made in the discussion interpreting our findings.

Perceived Influence of Teaching and Research

When asked how much influence each task has in determining university rewards, respondents ranked research and teaching at the top, in that order. Only eight percent thought that university service was very or extremely influential; just three of our sample of 100 rated external service in the same way. Thirty-five percent saw university service, and 51 percent saw external service, as "not at all influential" in the evaluation-reward process. Following, by contrast, are the results for teaching and research:

Figure 4. Influence of evaluations of principal tasks
in the determination of university rewards

Task	1 Extremely Influential	2 Very Infl.	3 Moderately Infl.	4 Slightly Infl.	5 Not at all Infl.
Teaching (96)*	5%	15%	23%	39%	17%
Research (98)	59%	19%	13%	3%	6%

*Numbers in parentheses, here and throughout, represent the number who responded to the question. Although the sample was 100 for all interview questions, some did not respond to certain questions, for one reason or another.

The median response to the question on the influence of teaching was four on the five-point scale, "slightly influential," while the median for research fell at the top of the scale, "extremely influential." Clearly research is seen as greatly more influential than teaching in determining rewards. As one full professor put it, "There is so little reward for good teaching it's hard to rate its influence. It's just assumed one is a good teacher; if you're terrible, of course, you're let go." Quite a number of respondents volunteered comments on the negative influence of teaching, that it becomes a factor only if someone's teaching is very bad. Many also echoed the view that good teaching is simply an expectation for all; its quality is a matter of self-discipline and not something for external review. The finding that research is more influential than teaching in this kind of university is of course no surprise, and has been empirically established by Caplow and McGee (3) and others.

Desired Influence of Teaching and Research

In order to determine how the faculty would like things to be we asked them how much influence each of the tasks *should* have in the evaluation-reward process. The results, for teaching and research, follow:

Figure 5. Influence that evaluations of principal tasks
should have in the determination of university rewards

Task	1 Extremely Influential	2 Very Infl.	3 Moderately Infl.	4 Slightly Infl.	5 Not at all Infl.
Teaching (99)	14%	37%	29%	16%	4%
Research (99)	32%	35%	25%	5%	2%

Research still comes out ahead, but the differential between teaching and research is markedly reduced. The median desired influence for each task falls at 2, "very influential." Although the majority saw research as having a much higher payoff at present, and would like to see the difference in rewards continue to some extent, they would nonetheless like to see a reduction in the disparity. The table on the following page breaks down the desired direction of shift in emphasis according to the influence presently perceived for each major task.

We see that a majority (53 of 96) want an increase in the influence of teaching; only three want a reduction. But looking at the lower portion of the table, we see that most do not want this shift at the expense of research. About a third want some reduction in the influence of research, but a majority (55 of 98) want it to remain as it is.

The implications of this latent faculty desire to shift emphasis toward teaching should not be overlooked when considering how to deal with contemporary problems in higher education. But it raises questions about who feels this way. Is there disparity across the faculty?

Effects of Faculty Characteristics

To find out we made a number of cross-tabulations. We found some differences across disciplinary areas, but these were relatively minor, especially for research. Eighty-two percent in the sciences (and mathematics) thought that research was "extremely" or "very" influential, against 72 percent in the humanities (including languages

Figure 6. Perceived influence and direction
of desired change

Perceived Influence		Direction of Desired Change					
		More		No Change		Less	
Teaching	1. Extremely (5)	—		100%	(5)	—	
	2. Very (14)	—		93%	(13)	7%	(1)
	3. Moderately (24)	58%	(14)	38%	(9)	4%	(1)
	4. Slightly (39)	72%	(28)	26%	(10)	3%	(1)
	5. Not at all (14)	79%	(11)	21%	(3)	—	
	(96)	(53)		(40)		(3)	

Perceived Influence		Direction of Desired Change					
		More		No Change		Less	
Research	1. Extremely (58)	—		55%	(32)	45%	(26)
	2. Very (18)	—		61%	(11)	39%	(7)
	3. Moderately (13)	31%	(4)	62%	(8)	8%	(1)
	4. Slightly (3)	33%	(1)	67%	(2)	—	
	5. Not at all (6)	67%	(4)	33%	(2)	—	
	(98)	(9)		(55)		(34)	

and arts). When asked how influential research *should* be, the gap was even narrower (73 percent in the sciences against 67 percent in the humanities responding that it should be in this high range). These minor differences may be surprising in view of the general notion that the empirical work of the sciences is more easily judged and more highly valued than the more subjective forms of scholarship and performance in the humanities that we classify under research.

In the area of teaching, the differences across disciplines are somewhat greater. Only eight percent of the scientists perceived it as highly influential, against 33 percent in the humanities. As one scientist put it, "I never heard anyone's teaching discussed when it was time for promotion." Twenty-seven percent of scientists thought that teaching *should* be highly influential, against 77 percent of the humanists. For whatever reasons, humanists appear to care more about teaching.

Different ranks do not hold substantially different views toward the existing or desired influence of the two principal tasks. Neither does age alone account for sharp differences, although younger men tend to see research as slightly more influential than do their elders. When we hold rank constant, however, sharper differences do emerge (see Figure 7).

The figures for "All Ranks" show that among older men there is greater perceived influence of evaluations of teaching, and a strong preference for an increased stress on teaching. Consistent with this, younger men in each rank appear to believe that research has, and should have, strong influence (although results are not significant at the .05 level). Older men in each rank may be those who lag in promotion because they neither do the research necessary for promotion nor see it as influential. On the other hand, younger men may see more rungs on the status ladder ahead of them and more time in which to move upward. Noting that success in research, rather than teaching reputation, is the route to higher status which is followed by the leaders in virtually every field, they perceive the influence of research as more important in their own quest for distinction and tangible rewards. This age differential may also result in part from the greater research emphasis in the past two decades which has influenced younger men during their early years in academe.

A final characteristic that was cross-tabulated with faculty views toward the influence of principal tasks was salary level—held constant by department because of the well known salary variation across disciplines. There was no consistent or significant pattern. Salary does not appear to be a factor in faculty attitudes toward task evaluations, an outcome that might be expected of a professional group.

Satisfaction With the Evaluation Process

Overall satisfaction appears to be high, with 49 percent responding that they were "extremely" or "very satisfied" with evaluations. Forty percent were "moderately satisfied," and only 11 percent were either "slightly" or "not at all satisfied." There was good correlation between level of overall satisfaction with the evaluation process and satisfaction with each of the principal task evaluations, particularly with evaluations of research—perhaps because of its greater perceived emphasis. Furthermore, those who were most satisfied tended to want the same or greater emphasis on research; those least satisfied were inclined to prefer no change or a reduction in research

Figure 7. Effect of age on evaluations with rank held constant

Rank/Age	Evaluation of Teaching		Evaluation of Research	
	Is Very or Extremely Influential	Should be Very or Extremely Influential	Is Very or Extremely Influential	Should be Very or Extremely Influential
Asst. Prof.				
Young (22) (under 35)	14%	36%	91%	73%
Old (11) (35 & over)	27%	73%	64%	45%
Assoc. Prof.				
Young (16-18)* (under 40)	19%	47%	83%	82%
Old (14-15) (40 & over)	14%	67%	64%	80%
Full Prof.				
Young (17) (under 50)	12%	24%	77%	71%
Old (16-17) (50 & over)	37%	76%	71%	59%
All Ranks				
Younger half (55-57)	15%	36%	84%	75%
Older half (41-43)	39%	72%	67%	63%

*In some cases the N's vary within the range indicated due to the failure of some respondents to answer all questions.

emphasis. No such pattern was observed on evaluations of teaching. Overall satisfaction did not vary in any consistent way with age, or with salary level.

In concluding this section it may be noted that teaching and research are clearly seen as the principal faculty tasks, and that research dominates in the eyes of faculty members under the present arrangement. They would like to spend more time on research, but not at the expense of teaching. They are reasonably satisfied with present practice, but would like to see the dominance of research reduced, although not eliminated. This inclination toward research is strongest among scientists and younger members of each faculty rank.

Evaluators: Who Does the Evaluating?

Assessing the task emphasis lays out a basic framework, but in order to employ the evaluation-reward process as a guide to the *authority structure*, one must know who are seen as evaluators, their relative importance, and subjects' attitudes toward their judgments. This is consistent with the basic theoretical premise of the research: He who holds the power to evaluate, and to dispense rewards based on that evaluation, holds the real authority in the organization.

Each member of the faculty sample was provided with a list of potential evaluators and asked to name and assess those whom they believed to have an influential part in the process of determining rewards. The Figure 8 graph summarizes the influence level of evaluators of principal tasks.

The pattern of responses was generally similar for the whole sample. One exception is the fact that full professors are simply less caught up in the evaluation-reward system, and named fewer evaluators (4.5 each compared to 6.2 each for associate and assistant professors), and regarded them as less influential. Other variations from the general pattern related to seniority and to discipline, and are reported in the discussion below.

Students as Evaluators

One finding from the Figure 8 graph that has significant implications for broadening involvement in university management is the importance attached to student evaluations of teaching. Although student influence in research judgments is seen as negligible, they are the most frequently identified evaluators of teaching, and their influence is only slightly lower than that of department heads and colleagues. Furthermore, it should be noted that, at the time this

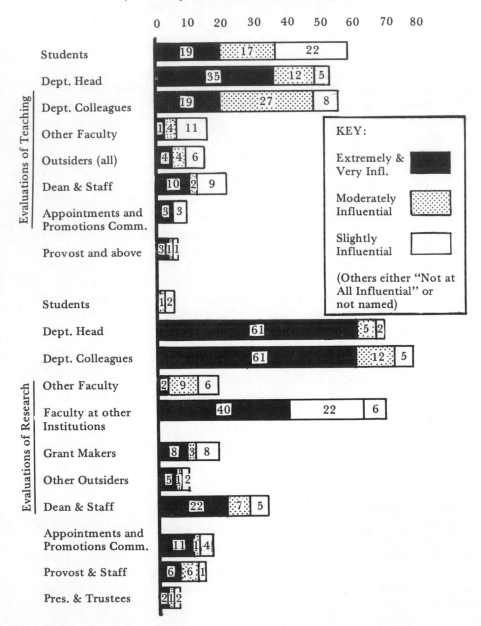

Figure 8. Perceived influence of evaluators
(N=100; figures are both numbers and percents)

study was made, the university did not conduct any systematic student evaluation program; only a few departments and individual professors used rating sheets of their own devising.

These data actually underestimated the part played by students in evaluations, since they are a principal source of information to the more influential judges. We asked respondents what sources of information they thought each evaluator relied on in making his assessments. Eighty-one percent of those who named department heads as evaluators, and 93 percent who named department colleagues, thought that students provided information that contributed to their judgments.

Despite their perceived influence, there were mixed feelings about the *competence* of students as evaluators. Twenty-eight percent volunteered comments to the effect that students are good evaluators of teaching, but 29 percent said they are poor or unreliable judges. This uncertainty about students showed up again when we asked respondents how much influence they would like various evaluators to have. Following were the results for key evaluators of teaching:

Figure 9. Comparison of "actual" and "ideal"
influence of various groups

	Percent Naming as Actually Extremely or Very Influential	Percent Saying Should Be Extremely or Very Influential
Students	19%	28%
Department Colleagues	19%	23%
Department Head	33%	35%

Although some faculty members would welcome more student participation in evaluations, there is a tendency to want the department chairmen to retain their predominant influence. Even though students are the primary sources of information about teaching for colleagues and department heads, it appears that doubts about student judgments lead faculty members to wish that their professional colleagues would weigh student opinions carefully and rely on their own final judgments.

Faculty skepticism about student evaluations have been reported by Woodburne (22) and Lehman (13). Guthrie (10) and Remmers (18), on the other hand, studied long-established student rating systems at Washington and Purdue (respectively) and concluded that students were effective and reliable judges of teaching quality. Kent (12) and Gaff and Wilson (6) report growing or high acceptance of student evaluations.

Colleagues as Evaluators

It is not surprising that faculty members would place greatest confidence in colleague evaluations. Such a peer reference group is characteristic of professionals. Respondents' conviction that trusted colleagues play an important part in evaluations may in part account for the high level of satisfaction with the process, especially in the all important area of research where 59 percent said they were "extremely" or "very" satisfied; only five percent were "not at all satisfied." For teaching, the enthusiasm was somewhat lower, but 49 percent expressed a high level of satisfaction with the total task evaluation process, with only six percent "not at all satisfied."

Knowledge of the Evaluation Process

An essential attribute of an effective organization is good communication. Figure 8 provides at least one indication that information on the evaluation-reward process is faulty. The Appointment and Promotion Committee is viewed by administrators and department heads as very influential in every promotion and tenure decision. But only 17 of these 100 faculty members selected this committee from the list as one of the agents in the evaluation process. Those who know about it recognize its importance, as demonstrated by the fact that 11 of them named the A & P Committee as "extremely" or "very influential."

Further evidence of ignorance of the system was provided by volunteered comments. Forty percent explicitly stated during the interview that they were unaware, to some degree, of the way in which the evaluation-reward system operates. One associate professor summed up with a view shared by a number of other subjects, "It's a Kafka-like structure. I haven't the vaguest idea who evaluates." As might be expected, old hands and those in higher ranks were less likely to profess ignorance. Yet 19 percent of those on the faculty more than ten years, and 26 percent of full professors, volunteered that they didn't understand the process.

Luthans (15) in a study of business school faculties reports related findings. Only 28 percent of the faculty members thought that evaluation and promotion policies were spelled out and well known, and barely half of the administrators thought so. Five percent of the faculty said there were no policies, and 26 percent responded to the effect that "the policy is nebulous and confused and could not be communicated to anyone.... Almost all faculty members who reported a nonexistent, vague or confused policy were also dissatisfied with the promotion process in general."

In our sample we found a tendency for ignorance of the system to coincide with low satisfaction toward the evaluation-reward process, but surprisingly, the relationship was not strong or statistically significant at the criterion level.

Administrators as Evaluators

Figure 8 provides evidence of behavior to be expected in a professional bureaucracy. We have already noted the strong emphasis on colleagues in evaluations. But a comparison with the perceived influence of administrators not only verifies the presence of this professional characteristic in the faculty, but highlights a problem faced by the management structure of such an institution. Only 10 see the dean and his staff as high in influence on evaluations of teaching, against 19 for department colleagues; the number naming the provost or higher management levels is negligible. For research, 22 named the dean as important against 61 for department colleagues. Faculty members at other institutions were seen as highly influential by 40 respondents. Taken together, outsiders' judgments appear important to nearly twice as many faculty members as do administrative assessments in the dominant research area.

III. Implications of the Research
for Understanding Professional Organizations

Thus far we have reported on the data gathered in the Stanford study. In this section our goal is to relate those findings to the general problem of understanding professional behavior within bureaucratic organizations.

No one would question that faculty members in a university are professionals, and that the institution in which they are located has some of the earmarks of a bureaucracy. But "professional" and "bureaucracy" are not absolute but relative terms. We discuss here some selected findings that give an indication of the extent of professional behavior of faculty members, that help define the character of the organization, and that illuminate some of the conflicts between faculty values and institutional form.

Organizational Permeability

The results reported in the preceding section included one that is characteristic of professionals: a preference for evaluation by colleagues, whether inside or outside the institution. This is but one indication of the permeability of the organizational boundaries. Offers from other institutions are another external mechanism that affects the evaluation-reward system. No questions about offers were asked, but 33 respondents volunteered comments on their importance, some even asserting that "playing the offers game" is the only way to get ahead.

These results, coupled with the findings of others that faculty members are highly mobile (Russell, 19, Marshall, 16, Brown, 2), indicate that talk of offers is not just telegram waving, and that the university is indeed a highly permeable organization. Its faculty probably finds more in common with colleagues across the discipline than with others across the campus.

Intrinsic Motivations and Professional Behavior

Cross tabulations of salary level against satisfaction with evaluations suggest that faculty members tend not to be tied to extrinsic rewards. We found virtually no difference in satisfaction between those who were in the high and low ends of the salary scale within rank. Neither did we find any association between salary level (within rank and department) and the amount of perceived or desired influence of evaluations of principal tasks. Furthermore, the 16 professors who volunteered complaints about their own salaries were equally divided between those above and below the median salary for their ranks and departments.

These results would suggest that there is little internal basis for salary complaints. One explanation is that these respondents were not comparing themselves with institutional colleagues, but with those in other institutions or nonacademic organizations, supporting the assertion of permeability. Another, of course, is that faculty members are more concerned with intangibles such as the quality of the institutions or their working conditions than they are about salary, consistent with the findings of Gustad (9), Marshall (16), Brown (2), and Lewis (14).

Interaction of Individuals and Organization

Looking back over the data reported in this and the preceding sections, we see many pieces of evidence that faculty members are professionals, and that they are operating in an organization whose formal structure is at least in part bureaucratic. The inevitable conflict results in modifications to both faculty behavior and effective structure.

In addition to the usual characteristics of a professional group, such as reliance on a specialized body of knowledge and extended training, control over admission to the profession, client subordination, and community sanction of authority, this sample of faculty members exhibited adherence to its own ethical code and values. Independence of salary from other variables supports a greater reliance on intrinsic rewards. Preference for increased attention to teaching and devotion of more time to teaching must be rooted in internalized professional values and not on a desire for extrinsic gain. Yet, although the differences reported are statistically significant for the faculty as a whole, they are far from unanimous. We found some evidence that individuals tended to devote their energies to tasks that pay off. Although there was a general tendency for faculty members to devote more of their time to teaching, a task not seen as very influential in producing rewards (see Figure 2), we found that those individuals who saw teaching as highly influential tended to devote more time to it; likewise, those who saw research as important in obtaining rewards tended to apply their energies in this direction. This evidence, plus the viewpoints of substantial numbers of respondents who did not go along with the majority position on teaching and the predominance of intrinsic rewards, suggests that compromises have been made to adjust to institutional pressures.

The views of faculty members toward the evaluation-reward process, which under our concept of organization effectively determines structure, describes a strongly collegial system. We find colleagues (and even students) to be considered far more important than the hierarchy. The extension of the colleague reference group beyond campus boundaries, and the mobility of the profession, characterize a highly permeable organization which diminishes the institutional loyalty essential to a bureaucratic structure.

Tensions between a faculty group with much of the power to control the purposeful functioning of the institution, and the formal structure that must take external responsibility and which largely controls the flow of resources, is bound to be high. Under these circumstances, achieving progress to meet changing societal needs is no simple matter. In the next section we discuss some of the implications of our findings for achieving such progress.

IV. Implications for University Reform

Many of the findings in the preceding sections provide guidelines for those responsible for bringing about improvements in higher education—trustees, administrators, faculty and student committees, alumni, and external groups. Others post warning signals, or suggest a framework for developing change mechanisms. In the remainder of this concluding section we endeavor to interpret our findings by pointing out the broad strategies for change which they suggest, and conclude by applying some of these strategies as well as the details of our findings to the teaching-research conflict, a major concern in higher education in our study as well.

Strategies for Change

An organization is not the sum of the values of individual participants. Institutions also have their values and goals based on their constituencies, legal status, and history; and are influenced by their structural pattern. Even in a collegial organization we observe the phenomenon described by Etzioni (5) as "differential peer control" wherein colleagues of different status (e.g., tenured and nontenured) have correspondingly differing influence over their nominal peers. In a bureaucratic organization, those in the supervisory levels will have more influence, and their values will carry the weight.

In a university, a professionally dominated institution with elements of a bureaucracy, strong desires for change will lie dormant if a catalyst is not introduced. The evidence from our study, wherein the faculty in its expression of latent desires, and the administration in its policy statements, call for increased emphasis on teaching while the status quo remains, suggests that nothing will happen until some impetus is applied. Everyone wants change and waits for someone else to do something.

The administrative structure of a university must press for change through such devices as it has at hand, but the change itself, especially when such change affects core functions, must be devised and carried out by the faculty. It is evident that the faculty has the power to bring about change in a university (or, of course, to thwart it). The increase in faculty powers during the present century is an outgrowth of changes in the university's character and role, and has been traced and documented by such students of the field as Burton Clark (4) and Neal Gross (8). Further, faculty reliance on a colleague reference group suggests the power to bring along the dissidents.

Complete independence of professionals, in this case faculty members, is no longer possible in a closely integrated structure striving to achieve institutional (as well as individual) goals. The university is characteristic of an evolving form of organization in which both individual and group goals can be accommodated. For such an organization to be effective, these goals must be in harmony.

Drawing upon our study, we see the evaluation-reward process as a device which can be employed by the leadership to initiate change. As predicted by the theory on which we relied, and as demonstrated in our study, members are inclined to devote their time and attention to tasks that they perceive as being rewarded. If we want more faculty emphasis on teaching, or advising, or institutional service, these tasks should receive realistic evaluation and reward.

The evidence gathered by us and by others shows that gross failures in communication occur in the absence of clearly understood evaluation criteria. One of the senior faculty members we interviewed, who had served on the key university committee dealing with appointments and promotions, commented, "I feel like a babe in the woods about the administration." And this was in the context of a discussion of the evaluation-reward process, something viewed by many as the exclusive province of "the administration." Initiative for regularizing the process and communicating it to all concerned must come from the institution's leadership. The criteria and procedures may vary from field to field, and must be worked out in a collegial setting, but whatever they are they must be conveyed to participants in a forthright manner if they are to have an influence on performance.

Communication, in this realm, must be a two-way process. Institutions must seek to determine the basic values and preferences of their members so they can identify areas of goal coincidence, and where resistance is likely. Our study demonstrates one method for probing such attitudes. It may be that simpler devices—questionnaires instead of extensive interviews, for example—would prove effective in gathering information on faculty attitudes. There is a need to develop and standardize simple instruments to assess basic goals and attitudes so that they can be taken into account in encouraging change.

In the university setting there are opportunities to involve a number of groups in the change process. Students represent a force more often felt today than in the past. Their influence is respected, as our data show, at least in the areas that touch them, and can be energized through committee membership or through formal involvement in the evaluation process.

Faculty members look well beyond the institution, and to their professional colleagues wherever they may be an influential reference group. This suggests that there may be merit in enlisting professional organizations as allies in institutional reform wherever professional values appear to coincide with institutional goals. Other outsiders, including colleagues who are now effectively involved as members of visiting committees at some universities, will be listened to. Their involvement should be sought as well.

Teaching and Research

The generally perceived imbalance between these tasks in leading universities has long been a source of discontent among students and of criticism from outsiders. Our data suggest that faculty members, who have dedicated their careers to the purposes of higher education, are just as eager to see the emphasis on research brought into better balance with teaching. What, then, is responsible for maintaining the imbalance? Certainly not the official policies of governing boards and their administrative agents. On the basis of our study, we would be inclined to blame a reward system that favors research, in part because the evaluation process takes the easy route of judging the visible products of research while substantially ignoring work in teaching.

One stratagem suggested by our results is to tie rewards more closely to the desired task emphasis. As one of our respondents put it, "I'm willing to play the game any way they want it." The key word here is "they," presumably synonymous with "the system." But our findings indicate that in the eyes of faculty members the principal "theys" are colleagues. This would point to a need for each department to decide what, if anything, is better than the current haphazard process of evaluation, especially in the area of teaching. The administration, which must lurk in faculty minds as part of the "they," can use its influence to encourage this process of clarification and communication of evaluation-reward criteria.

The institution's leadership can also demonstrate the reality of its concern about teaching by making available various clinical devices for improving teaching: videotaping lectures and class discussions for later review; encouragement of team teaching with established colleagues; and sessions on classroom techniques with teachers of recognized ability.

Care should be taken to express the institution's concern for teaching at every opportunity. For example, annual faculty report forms should allow as much space for recording development work in new courses and teaching approaches as for listing publications. Provision should be made for faculty members to use freed time to develop new courses.

Students as Evaluators of Teaching

Evidence from our study and from others cited indicate that students are accepted judges of teaching effectiveness, and in fact play a role in the evaluative process. Yet the formal use of student evaluations is limited. Astin and Lee (1) report that only 11.3 percent of the departments in a large sample of institutions they reviewed make use of student evaluations.

How students might best be involved remains a matter of lively debate. Faculty members are less than enthusiastic about the formal participation of students in the promotion process, according to our study. A representative comment, reflecting unwillingness to place one's professional career at the mercy of a transient population (also a client population), came from a full professor who said of student evaluation, "It may make one dependent on the students for promotion." Such a shift in role relationships would be seen as disturbing, at best, and as leading to unprofessional efforts at ingratiation at worst. The respondent who commented that "self-satisfaction is more important that rewards" would surely resent the presence of students on a tenure committee, yet he would probably welcome constructive feedback as contributing to his achievement of self-satisfaction.

A number of schemes for systematic course evaluation by students have been developed, notably the long-lived and routinized processes at Purdue University and the University of Washington. The most effective of these have reported results directly and only to faculty members, essentially appealing to their professional responsibility while avoiding the gestapo-like surveillance and public pillorying which can result from published evaluations. One way or another the sense of these confidential assessments of teaching effectiveness do find their way into the evaluation process: often favorably rated faculty members submit their reports into the formal evaluation process while the others do not.

There seems to be sufficient evidence of success to urge that systematic student evaluation procedures be established and supported by university administrations, both for constructive feedback to individual teachers and as a positive way of increasing the influence of teaching in the evaluation-reward system. Each faculty group should be urged to define what should be measured and to aid in the devising and administering of instruments to obtain such measures.

Closer Links Between Teaching and Research

Another approach to redressing the teaching-research imbalance lies in the promise of drawing these two functions closer together. Such a process is suggested by our finding that in the humanistic fields there is a closer balance between the influence (both perceived and desired) of teaching and research than is the case in the sciences. Research in the humanities—more properly, scholarship—is at a level of complexity that can be grasped by conscientious students. It can be introduced with little difficulty into the classroom of nonspecialists, and frequently is. Furthermore, teaching is traditionally important in the humanities. In the words of a professor in the arts, "Teaching is the primary function—the end of research." Under such circumstances, all colleague-evaluators are themselves teachers. The pattern of the humanistic fields that links teaching and research can itself be strengthened, and may serve as a model in other areas.

In conclusion, it is insufficient to rely on superficial assumptions as the framework for change, and unthinkable to yield to inertia. There are real opportunities to harness the professional values of faculty members, as well as their responsiveness to the goals expressed by the evaluation-reward system. Each institution of higher education should seek ways of determining faculty desires and perceptions and of utilizing them in the process of changing to meet shifting societal needs.

Footnotes

1. A complete report of the study is contained in Robert R. Hind, *Evaluation and Authority in a University Faculty*, Stanford University dissertation, 1968; and in a forthcoming book by Hind, Sanford N. Dornbusch, and W. Richard Scott.

2. No attempt is made here to spell out this conception in complete detail. Readers are referred to a basic paper (Scott et al., 20) that provides a full description.

3. Reports on these studies are forthcoming under the authorship of W. Richard Scott, Sanford M. Dornbusch, and their associates.

4. The term "research" as used throughout this paper includes research, scholarship, and (in the case of many in the arts) performance. This is done simply as a convenience. Whenever "research" is used, it represents any or all of the related tasks.

5. These results are similar to those reported by Parsons and Platt (1968) for institutions in their study that resemble Stanford, and compare closely to another study at Stanford of a nonoverlapping sample (Stanford 1969).

References

1. Astin, Alexander W., and Lee, Calvin B. "Current Practices in the Evaluation and Training of College Teachers." *Education Record*, Vol. 47, No. 3 (Summer 1960): 361-375.
2. Brown, David G. *The Mobile Professors*. Washington, D. C.: The American Council on Education, 1967.
3. Caplow, Theodore, and McGee, Reece J. *The Academic Marketplace*. New York: Basic Books, 1958.
4. Clark, Burton. "Faculty Authority." *AAUP Bulletin*, Vol. 47, No. 4 (December, 1961): 293-302.
5. Etzioni, Amitai. *A Comparative Analysis of Complex Organizations*. New York: The Free Press of Glencoe, 1961.
6. Gaff, Jerry G., and Wilson, Robert C. "The Relationship Between Professors' Views of the Formal Incentive System and Their Career Status." (Mimeographed.) Berkeley, Calif.: Center for Research and Development in Higher Education (Undated: issued 1969).
7. Greenwood, Ernest, "Attributes of a Profession." *Social Work*, Vol. 2, No. 3 (July 1957): 44-55.
8. Gross, Neal. "Organizational Lag in American Universities." *Harvard Educational Review*, Vol. 33, No. 1 (Winter 1963): 58-73.
9. Gustad, John W. "They March to a Different Drummer." *Educational Record*, Vol. 40, No. 3 (July 1959): 204-211.
10. Guthrie, E. R. "The Evaluation of College Teaching." *Educational Record*, Vol. 30, No. 2 (April 1949): 109-115.
11. Guthrie, E. R. *The State University*. Seattle: University of Washington, 1959.
12. Kent, Laura. "Student Evaluation of Teaching." *Educational Record*, Vol. 47, No. 3 (Summer 1966): 376-406.
13. Lehman, Irving J. "Evaluation of Instruction." In Paul L. Dressel, ed., *Evaluation in Higher Education*. Boston: Houghton Mifflin Co., 1961.
14. Lewis, Lionel S. "On Prestige and Loyalty of University Faculty." *Administrative Science Quarterly*, Vol. 11, No. 4 (March 1967): 629-642.
15. Luthans, Fred. *The Faculty Promotion Process*. Iowa City: The University of Iowa, 1967.
16. Marshall, Howard D. *The Mobility of College Faculties*. New York: Pageant Press, Inc., 1964.
17. Parsons, Talcott, and Platt, Gerald M. *The American Academic Profession*. (Multilithed.) 1968.
18. Remmers, H. H. "Rating Methods in Research and Teaching." In N. L. Gage, ed., *Handbook of Research on Teaching*, Chicago: Rand McNally & Co., 1963, 329-378.
19. Russell, John Dale. "Faculty Satisfactions and Dissatisfactions." *Journal of*

Experimental Education, Vol. 31, No. 2 (December 1962).
20. Scott, W. Richard, Dornbusch, Sanford M., Busching, Bruce C. and Laing, James D. "Organizational Evaluation and Authority." *Administrative Science Quarterly*, Vol. 12, No. 1 (June 1967): 93-117.
21. Stanford University. *Teaching, Research and the Faculty.* Vol. 8 of the Report to the University of the Study of Education at Stanford, 1969.
22. Woodburne, Lloyd S. *Faculty Personnel Policies in Higher Education.* New York: Harper & Row, 1950.

FACULTY ACTIVISM AND INFLUENCE PATTERNS
IN THE UNIVERSITY

J. Victor Baldridge

Organization theorists have long been concerned about policy formulation within complex organizations, but in general, the study of organizational policy has proceeded under a set of formalistic nonpolitical assumptions. While the community power theorists scrutinized interest group behavior, influence tactics, and power manipulation in local governments, the organization theorists have largely ignored these factors. Instead, policy formulation within complex organizations has been viewed as essentially a *problem-solving task* with clearly identified problems and rational means/ends chains. This problem-solving approach to policy formulation varied considerably, of course, from formal decision schemes such as Litchfield's (12) to Lindbloom's "muddling through" strategy (9), to computer simulations of problem analysis. Even the studies of "informal group" pressure on policy formulation, such as Dalton's (5), which appear to be analyzing political influence tactics used by informal groups, come from a nonpolitical, small group tradition rather than from the interest group literature, and they do not usually deal explicitly with issues of power, influence, and interest group activity. On the whole, organization theorists have taken a radically different approach to the study of policy formulation than the community power theorists.

This article takes the position that an explicitly political analysis would be very useful for studying organizational policy formulation. There are already a few examples of political approaches in organization theory, including Selznick's study of the TVA (15), Cyert and March's (3) analysis of the business firm as a political coalition, Clark's (2) study of the interest group activity surrounding an adult education unit, and Gross's (7) analysis of the political forces impinging on school superintendents. Thompson (16) extended several of these empirical studies in his theoretical discussion of coalition formation and political processes. The present research is an attempt to couple insights from the community power literature with insights from traditional organizational theory, applying both to the study of organizational policy formulation in a university.

Drawing on community power theory, conflict theory, and interest group theory the author proposes that organizational policy formulation can be fruitfully studied with political frameworks. Of special concern is the problem of oligarchy, power elites, and spheres of influence—all issues of major concern for political theories of decision making. Using data from a case study of New York University, three strategies were used for charting patterns of influence on a series of major decisions. *First*, respondents were categorized into policy influence groups, and the characteristics of these groups were analyzed to determine the nature of the power elites. *Second*, spheres of influence were identified and power holders vis-à-vis these issues were specified. Both political activists and inactivists tended to identify similar patterns of influence over given spheres of influence. *Finally*, intense issue-histories were used to supplement the data gathered from the cross-sectional survey, and a high degree of agreement was noted between the survey data and the intensive interviews. All in all, the picture of the power structure was very confused. Neither of the dominant theories in community power theory—the pluralist model or the power elite model—was clearly supported. Instead, there was a complex, fragmented power structure with several miniature power blocs specialized around specific issues.

Methodology

An 18-month case study at New York University analyzed the policy formulation processes surrounding three critical decisions (see 1 for further details of the study). One decision concerned the reorganization of departmental structures, another handled student participation in university decision-making, and a third dealt with the abandonment of a "school of opportunity" philosophy and the concurrent shift to emphasis on high quality admissions standards. Each decision represented a critical, long range policy issue that significantly affected the entire university.

Several research techniques were used. First, 1,748 *questionnaires* were mailed to all the full-time faculty and major administrators, with 693 returns (a return rate of 40 percent). The characteristics of respondents matched known characteristics of the faculty very closely. Second, a series of 93 intensive *interviews* were conducted with the nominated leaders on the three specific policy issues. In addition, participant *observation* and *document analysis* techniques were used to gather supplemental information about the influence patterns surrounding the specific issues. Some of the information was "hard" data that could be expressed in figures and tables, while much of it was rich impressionist feeling-tone that came from intensive analysis of complex events. When all these sources were pieced together, a complex mosaic emerged revealing some clues about the nature of organizational power.

Objectives of the Research

The distribution of power and influence has always been one of the major concerns in studying organizational policy formulation. The basic question is deceptively simple: Who has influence over what? One of the most famous formulations about influence patterns in complex organizations was Michels' "Iron Law of Oligarchy," which argued that power elites are always dominant, even in so dogmatically democratic a group as the Marxist political parties (13). Lipset, Trow and Coleman (11) applied Michels' thesis to a labor union, and suggested some factors that helped mitigate the oligarchical tendency. Michels envisioned a strong power elite, while Lipset, et. al. believed that under some circumstances democracy had a chance. In the community power literature the researchers split along similar lines. "Elitists" like Hunter (8) argue that a dominant power elite controls most of the significant decisions in a local community, while "pluralistists" such as Dahl (4) and Polsby (14) deny the existence of a dominant elite and suggest instead that different interest groups control different decisions. (See Walton (17) for a comment on the methodologies and ideological biases of the two groups of researchers.)

The objective of the current research was to study some of these theories within another organizational context. A university was chosen, for academic organizations definitely have both democratic and oligarchical tendencies, thus providing a middle ground between organizations that are rigidly bureaucratic (e.g., prisons, government bureaucracies, military units) and democratic local communities where the community power research was conducted. In many ways the university is highly flexible, with professionals making many critical decisions, outside groups exerting significant influence, and students increasingly gaining a voice. At the same time, however, there are strong oligarchical forces, for the administration and trustees still retain wide authority, and the senior faculty largely dictates the nature of the academic enterprise. With its contradictory stresses and processes, the university makes an excellent host organization for an attempt to determine influence patterns and study power structures.

More specifically, the basic research questions were:

1. How are policy influence opportunities distributed among participants?

2. Is there significant overlap between power holders at the departmental, college, and university levels?

3. Are there significant differences between those who rate high on policy influence and those who rate low?

4. Are there clear "spheres of influence" claimed by various groups, and if so does a definite pattern emerge?

5. Do those who rate high on influence see the spheres of influence differently from those who rate low?

6. How are the spheres of influence changing, and how do the influentials become involved in the changes?

Each of the questions will be considered in turn.

The General Pyramid of Influence: How Are Influence Opportunities Distributed?

One of the first research tasks was determining the distribution of political activity among the faculty and administration. One part of the questionnaire asked respondents to check as many of the following policy-influencing activities they did at the department, college, and university levels: (1) little or no participation, (2) informal contacts with decision-makers, (3) regular participation in faculty meetings, (4) serving on committees, (5) holding an official position. With option 1 excluded, the question formed a Gutmann scale, with each higher level of activity assuming all of the less active forms. Reproducibility was 87 percent.

From this question it was possible to assemble a picture of four different types of activists. First, there are the *officials* (operationally defined as those who checked option 5 and all below it) who are committed by career, lifestyle, and ideology to the task of running the organization. They constitute by far the most politically active segment of the university community and have the most influence over organizational decisions. At the second level of participation are the *activists* (operationally defined as those who checked option 4 and below); a relatively small body of people who are intensely involved in the university's politics even though they do not hold fulltime administrative posts. These activists serve as part time authorities in the official committee system and in the complex network of advisory councils. The activists are usually concerned faculty members leading dual lives as professors and as amateur organization men.

At the third step down the activity scale is the *attentive public* (operationally defined as those checking option 3 and below). These are the sideline watchers who are interested in the activities of the formal system, regularly attend and vote at faculty meetings, but usually do not serve on committees or study groups. Their rate of participation is very situationally oriented. When a "hot issue" comes along, they jump into the conflict; otherwise they are basically just active onlookers. They are potentially a very powerful bloc when aroused and therefore they have a great deal of indirect control over decision makers.

Finally, at the lowest level of participation are the *apathetics* (operationally defined as those checking option 1 or 2). These people almost never serve on committees, rarely show up for faculty meetings, and in general could not care less about the politics of the university. The apathetics come in many stripes, from the star professor who is simply "too busy to mess with this kind of nonsense" to the teaching assistant who is politically disfranchised in spite of his teaching service. The NYU survey included only full-time personnel and thus the vast majority (79.4 percent) of the 693 respondents reported official activity on some level. However, the part-time faculty, the teaching assistants, the lecturers, and other "quasi-faculties" constitute a huge group of apathetics who do not show up in a survey of full-time faculty; over half of NYU's faculty fall into this group. The apathetics probably constitute a large majority in spite of the contrary statistics found in a survey of fulltime faculty.

The number of people at each step of the activity scale varies considerably by levels in the university. Figure 1 shows that there is a very high degree of integration of the full-time faculty into the departments' decision-making structure, but at the levels of the college and the university the percentage of activists and officials decreases sharply.

Figure 1. The "activity pyramid" at different levels

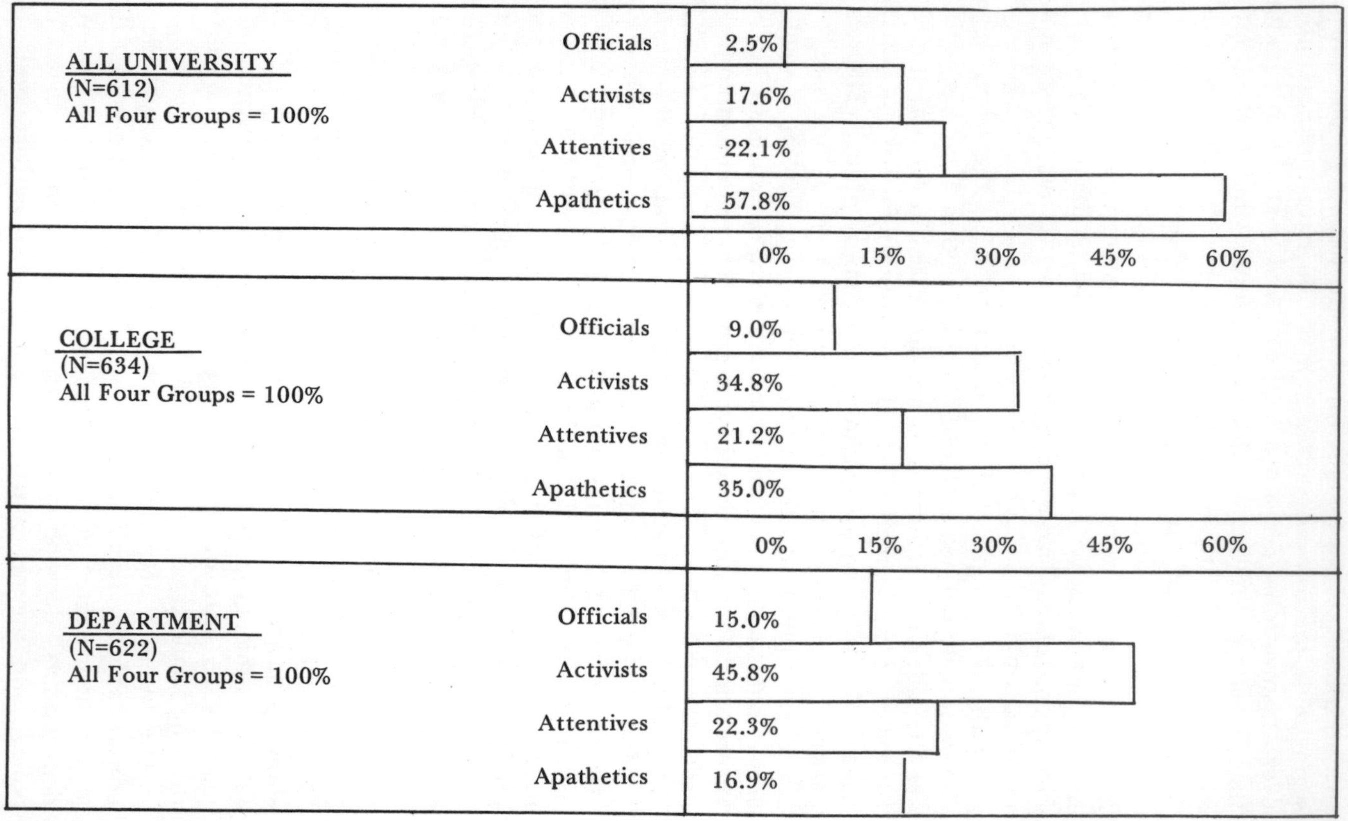

ALL UNIVERSITY
(N=612)
All Four Groups = 100%

Officials	2.5%
Activists	17.6%
Attentives	22.1%
Apathetics	57.8%

0% 15% 30% 45% 60%

COLLEGE
(N=634)
All Four Groups = 100%

Officials	9.0%
Activists	34.8%
Attentives	21.2%
Apathetics	35.0%

0% 15% 30% 45% 60%

DEPARTMENT
(N=622)
All Four Groups = 100%

Officials	15.0%
Activists	45.8%
Attentives	22.3%
Apathetics	16.9%

Overlapping Influence: Is There Significant Overlap Between Power Holders at the Departmental, College, and University Levels?

Mapping the activity scale by levels in the university gives some clues about the distribution of influence, but an even more interesting question is the *overlap* between various levels. That is, how frequently is an influential person in his department also influential in his school, and in the university councils? This is a critical question for the research, since much of the debate in the community power literature focuses on the existence or nonexistence of power elites who have amassed overlapping power.

The procedure for identifying respondents who had overlapping power was as follows. First, each respondent was rated either high or low on his influence in the department, the college, and the university as a whole. High meant the respondent was above the median on influence activities, as defined by the same question used earlier. Although the overlap was not exact, this essentially meant that officials and activists were combined into Highs, while attentives and apathetics were combined into Lows. With this procedure each respondent could be placed into one of eight cells, as shown in Figure 2. Since several of the eight cells were almost empty the eight were reduced to five. Figure 2 shows how the respondents divided into the five categories of overlapping influence, with some people having little influence over any decisions regardless of levels, and others having compounded influence at all levels. As might be expected, most people fell somewhere in between.

Several conclusions are suggested. First, there is a wide distribution of overlapping influence. 32.8 percent of the respondents (227

Figure 2. Overlapping influence patterns: eight logical combinations of influence reduced empirically to five

Department	College	University	Final Titles	N	%
Low	Low	Low —Inactives		143	20.6
High	Low	Low ⟩ Department *or* College		137	19.8
Low	High	Low ⟋			
High	High	Low ——Department *&* College		147	21.2
Low	Low	High ——University only		39	5.6
Low	High	High ⟍			
High	Low	High ⟩ All Levels		227	32.8
High	High	High ⟋			
				693	100.0

people) report that they participate in policy activities at all three levels, while only 20.6 percent (143 people) report that they do not participate in policy activities. From this it appears that influence overlap indeed does occur, but for a large number of people, not just for a small elite group. However, two factors mitigate this optimistic view. First, this was a survey of fulltime administrators and faculty only and the many parttimers who were not questioned would almost surely add up to an overwhelming majority who have little or no influence at higher levels.

Second, the researchers were extremely generous in the rating of all-university influence. Since the "high" score was simply those who were above the median in influence, many people who only participated in very minimal activities could be rated above the median at the university level. It is wise to keep this in mind when interpreting the results, since the all-university influentials are probably overrepresented because of these generous allowances. In spite of the reservations, however, the spread of influence at the various levels was rather striking.

Characteristics of Actives and Inactives

Once the categories of overlapping influence were established the next step was to analyze the contrasts between the activists and those who have little influence. Three interesting complexes of characteristics emerge from the survey. First, it seems plausible that people who serve on committees, hold seats on advisory panels, and hold official positions (our operational definition of high activity) will also have subjective feelings of personal power. This is clearly supported, for those who have these "objective" aspects of power also indicate that they feel more subjectively influential than their colleagues (see Figure 3). Moreover, these official activities are matched by informal policy influence, for the higher the official power as defined by committee membership etc., the higher the tendency to join informal interest groups (see Figure 4), although the relation is not very strong. Finally, the more official activity inside the university, the more contact a person has with influential outside power blocs. Although there was little outside contact by any group, when there was it was by activists. This conclusion points to the critical "boundary—spanning" role that such activists play vis-à-vis the environmental context (see Figure 5).

The second complex of characteristics concerns disciplinary achievement and scholarly productivity. The analysis clearly contradicts the common campus myth that activists are usually mediocre

Figure 3. Percentage of each "objective" influence group
reporting "subjective" self-report of influence at different levels

Reported Self-Perception of
Influence at Different Levels

Categories of Objective Overlapping Influence	Inactive	Influential in Department	Influential in College & Department	Influential at all Levels	Total	
					%	N
Inactives	70.6	23.1	4.2	2.1	100.0	141
Dept. or College	36.5	41.6	16.1	5.8	100.0	138
Dept. & College	18.4	46.9	28.6	6.1	100.0	149
University Only	38.5	25.6	12.8	23.1	100.0	37
All Levels	12.3	26.9	31.7	29.1	100.0	228
Total Percentages		31.9	33.2	21.2	13.7	100.0	693
Total N		221	230	147	95		

Gamma = .559

scholars who forfeit disciplinary achievement in order to gain local
influence. In fact, the data show just the opposite, for the activists
have somewhat higher professional achievement than the inactives,
including more publications (see Figure 6), more professional
memberships (see Figure 7), and more disciplinary papers read at
meetings (see Figure 8). In addition, there is a strong correlation
between degree of activism and academic rank (see Figure 9). Two
additional things should be noted. First, there are lower scholarly
achievement scores in almost all the tables for the "university only"
influence group, for these are mainly the fulltime central administrators who have become professional administrators and largely
withdrawn from scholarly activities. Second, there was a strong
suspicion that the high scholarly productivity of the activists was
because they were merely the elder statesmen who had had more
time to publish. To test this assumption all the tables were controlled
for "professional age," i.e., how long it had been since the
respondent received his highest degree. In all tables except one the
original results still held significant. The exception is Figure 10 where
professional age does make a difference on publication, but only for

Figure 4. Percentage of each "formal" influence group reporting
"informal" influence tactics* at different levels

Categories of Formal Influence	Categories of Informal Influence				Total	
	None	Dept. Only	Dept. and College	All Levels	%	N
Inactives	72.0	20.3	4.9	2.8	100.0	141
Dept. or College	58.4	29.2	10.9	1.5	100.0	132
Dept. & College	45.6	32.0	20.4	2.0	100.0	147
University Only	66.7	20.5	7.7	5.1	100.0	37
All Levels	40.5	20.7	22.9	15.9	100.0	223
Total Percentages	53.1	24.7	15.4	6.8	100.0	
Total N	368	171	107		47	693

Gamma = .342

*Informal tactics were defined as belonging to an interested clique that tried
to influence policies at each level.

the oldest group. In other words, for the oldest group the activists
were no more prolific publishers than the inactivists, but for the two
younger groups activists were still more energetic publishers. All in
all, the picture of the activists was rather uniformly one of high
scholarly achievement and professional expertise.

The third set of differences between actives and inactives is rather
surprising in light of the above information. Gouldner (6) has argued
that "cosmopolitans" in the faculty are likely to have high
disciplinary achievement, and by that standard the NYU activists are
definitely cosmopolitans. However, the NYU activists seem to
exhibit a contradictory desire to be "locals" by not wanting to move
to another university (see Figure 11) and by not having significant
outside interests (see Figure 12). However, Gouldner's research was
done on a small campus. On the massive NYU campus it is quite
reasonable that the nonactive, low rank, low productivity faculty
members will feel somewhat out of place, probably have fewer
rewards, and desire to retreat either to outside interests or to another
university. Thus, the picture of the NYU influentials is one of high
cosmopolitanism on scholarly activities, but high localism in their
commitment to the university. Coupled with their feelings of
personal influence and their objective participation in the decision-
making system, the overall picture seems to indicate that the
fragmented power elite at NYU was indeed a highly professional,

Figure 5. Percentage of each influence group that reported
contacts with outside influences*

Influence Groups	Number of Contacts With Outside Policy-Influence Groups				Total	
	No. Contacts	1 Contact	2 Contacts	3 or more Contacts	%	N
Inactives	97.8	2.2	0.0	0.0	100.0	135
Dept. or College	96.3	2.2	1.5	0.0	100.0	134
Dept. and College	93.8	2.8	2.8	0.7	100.0	149
University Only	89.7	7.7	0.0	2.6	100.0	39
All Levels	80.8	5.4	6.7	7.1	100.0	225
Total Percentages	90.6	3.7	3.1	2.6	100.0	
Total N	618	25	21	18		682

Gamma = .599

*Contact with outside influences included contact with foundations, government agencies, accrediting agencies, alumni, and professional organizations.

Figure 6. Percentage of each influence group with
different publication records

Influence Groups	Publications in the Last Five Years		Total	
	2 or Less	More than 2	%	N
Inactive	67.2	32.8	100.0	140
Dept. or College	45.3	54.7	100.0	137
Dept. and College	40.8	59.2	100.0	147
University Only	59.0	41.0	100.0	39
All Levels	32.4	67.6	100.0	225
Total Percentages	45.3	54.7	100.0	
Total N	312	376		688

Gamma = .318

Figure 7. Percentage of each influence group with
different professional memberships

Influence Groups	Number of Professional Memberships			Total	
	2 or less	3-4	More than 4	%	N
Inactives	59.8	26.1	14.1	100.0	140
Dept. or College	41.0	30.6	28.4	100.0	137
Dept. and College	23.8	37.4	38.8	100.0	147
University Only	43.7	28.9	27.4	100.0	39
All Levels	16.9	40.8	42.3	100.0	226
Total Percentages	33.5	34.5	32.0	100.0	
Total N	231	237	221		689

Gamma = .374

Figure 8. Percentage of each influence group
reading papers at professional meetings

Influence Group	Number of Papers Read in Last 2 Years			Total	
	None	1	More than 1	%	N
Inactives	79.6	12.1	9.3	100.0	140
Dept. or College	54.8	13.9	31.3	100.0	137
Dept. and College	42.9	14.3	42.8	100.0	147
University Only	51.3	17.9	30.8	100.0	39
All University	41.6	18.1	40.2	100.0	226
Total Percentages	52.1	15.2	32.7	100.0	
Total N	359	105	225		689

Gamma = .405

Figure 9. Percentage of each influence group
with different ranks

Influence Group	Academic Rank				Total	
	Other	Assistant Professor	Associate Professor	Professor	%	N
Inactives	55.2	21.7	13.3	9.8	100.0	141
Dept. or College	19.0	26.3	29.2	25.5	100.0	138
Dept. and College	16.3	27.2	25.9	30.6	100.0	147
University Only	43.6	10.3	12.8	33.3	100.0	39
All University	7.5	13.2	26.9	52.4	100.0	228
Total Percentages	23.5	20.3	23.5	32.7	100.0	
Total N	163	141	163	226		693

Gamma = .453

significantly scholarly group of influentials. Perhaps this gives some hope to those who argue that professional organizations should be dominated by professionals, and that the power elites and the professional elites should be congruent.

Spheres of Influence

Up to this point the analysis has focused on the different groups of participants who held influence in the university. However, this was only one of the ways that influence patterns were charted. A second method was to specify definite areas of activity and then ask for perceptions of the groups that control the areas.

Six groups were listed: trustees, central administration, deans, college faculty, departmental faculty, and individual faculty members. The respondents were then asked to rank the influence of these various groups on ten specific issues. Their rankings, shown in Figure 13, illustrate the patterns of influence that the respondents believed existed, though there is of course no guarantee that this is "actually" the way influence is distributed. Figure 13 lists the areas of responsibility one at a time and shows the controlling groups.

The chart suggests that instead of one dominant power elite there seems to be a fragmented system of influence, for different groups are strong in different spheres of influence and no single group

Figure 10. Percentage of each influence group scoring
high* on publication, controlled for professional age

Influence Groups	Professional Age		
	1-5 years	6-15 years	Over 15 years
Inactives	16.3	45.5	70.8
Dept. or College	41.1	69.2	57.1
Dept. and College	41.4	71.7	69.4
University Only	25.0	71.4	46.7
All University	51.9	75.9	69.5
Total % scoring High in each group	34.4	68.1	66.3
	N = 93	N = 145	N = 138
	Gamma = .368	Gamma = .265	Gamma = .069

Total N of Those Rating High on Publication = 376

*High is three or more publications in the last five years.

dominates everything. The trustees are strong on budgetary planning,
physical plant maintenance, long range planning, and public relations.
The central administration's influence is strongest in personnel
appointment, budgetary control, planning, and public relations. The
deans have very broad power indeed, with considerable influence in
all areas. By contrast, the college faculty and the individual professor
seem to have the narrowest range of influence, mostly concerned
with curriculum. Finally, the departmental faculty has fairly broad
influence on curriculum, faculty appointment and promotion, and
selection of the department chairman. All in all, the distribution of
influence appears to be very diffuse and specifically attached to
certain issues.

Spheres of Influence as Perceived by Different Activists

Now two different thrusts of the research have been reported.
First, there was the identification of groups of participants who had
different types of policy influence, depending on their participation
in committees, etc. Second, there was the specification of issues with
the groups that were perceived to control them. The next logical step
would be to compare the activity groups and their differential
perception of the issues. That is, would all-university activists see the

Figure 11. Percentage of each influence group with
different degrees of identification with the university

| Influence Groups | Identification With University | | Total | |
	Desire to Stay	Desire to Leave	%	N
Inactives	32.2	67.8	100.0	141
Dept. or College	40.9	59.1	100.0	138
Dept. and College	36.1	63.9	100.0	147
University Only	46.2	53.8	100.0	39
All University	53.3	46.7	100.0	228
Total Percentages	42.4	57.6	100.0	
Total N	294	399	N	693

Gamma = .225

Figure 12. Percentage of each influence group with
different levels of outside interests

| Influence Groups | Number of Outside Interests that Distract from University Commitments | | Total | |
	Few	Many	%	N
Inactives	53.1	46.9	100.0	141
Dept. or College	73.0	27.0	100.0	138
Dept. and College	70.7	29.3	100.0	147
University Only	56.4	43.6	100.0	39
All University	80.2	19.8	100.0	228
Total Percentages	69.8	30.2	100.0	
Total N	484	209		693

Gamma = —.276

Figure 13. Who has influence on various areas?
(Percentage of each group reported with high influence in that area)*

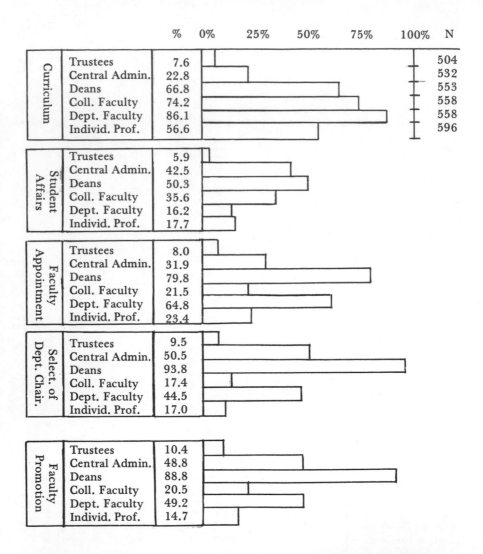

*Taking the first line at the top as an example, this chart should be read as follows: Of the 504 respondents (the N listed on the right) who answered the question, 7.6 felt that trustees have high influence over curriculum. Of the 532 respondents who answered the question, 22.8 percent felt that the Central Administration has high influence over curriculum. (Etc.) N's are same for every chart; refer back to first one.

(Figure 13, continued)

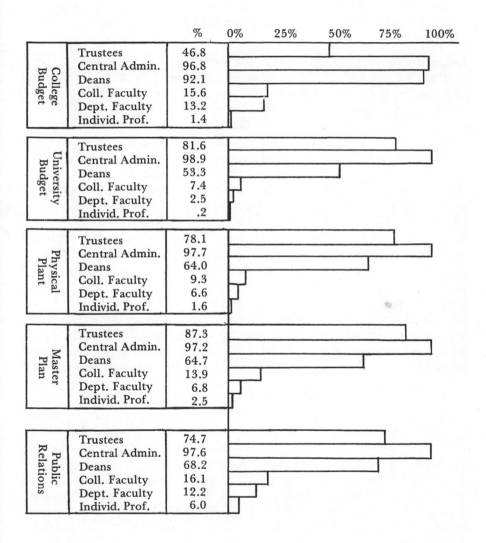

		%	0%	25%	50%	75%	100%
College Budget	Trustees	46.8					
	Central Admin.	96.8					
	Deans	92.1					
	Coll. Faculty	15.6					
	Dept. Faculty	13.2					
	Individ. Prof.	1.4					
University Budget	Trustees	81.6					
	Central Admin.	98.9					
	Deans	53.3					
	Coll. Faculty	7.4					
	Dept. Faculty	2.5					
	Individ. Prof.	.2					
Physical Plant	Trustees	78.1					
	Central Admin.	97.7					
	Deans	64.0					
	Coll. Faculty	9.3					
	Dept. Faculty	6.6					
	Individ. Prof.	1.6					
Master Plan	Trustees	87.3					
	Central Admin.	97.2					
	Deans	64.7					
	Coll. Faculty	13.9					
	Dept. Faculty	6.8					
	Individ. Prof.	2.5					
Public Relations	Trustees	74.7					
	Central Admin.	97.6					
	Deans	68.2					
	Coll. Faculty	16.1					
	Dept. Faculty	12.2					
	Individ. Prof.	6.0					

division of responsibilities on each of the ten issues differently than, say, inactives or departmental activists? The answer was rather surprising, for in 59 of 60 comparisons (10 issues by six power blocs by the scale of activism) there were no significant differences. The one significant finding was assumed to be due to random chance. Thus, the picture of the division of responsibilities among groups seemed to be relatively stable, regardless of how much a person did or did not participate in the policy formulation processes.

Influence Spheres as Examined in the Issue History Approach

The two basic blocks of data reported above (the activity groups and the spheres of influence) show the static distributions of influence as they were described in the questionnaire results. In addition when the three specific policy issues were intensely analyzed by interviews, document analysis, and participant observation, the findings in the questionnaire were largely substantiated. In each issue, whether it was student participation in decision-making, departmental reorganization, or the shift in basic program philosophy, there emerged rather contradictory statements about the power structure. On one hand, there was always a "power elite" of highly involved officials and activitists who largely make the critical decisions, thus supporting the elitist view of a power elite. On the other hand, there were very few overlaps of these elites among the different issues, with the exception of the major central administrators such as the president and the chancellor. This tended to support the pluralist's contention that power is not centralized, but fragmented with different elites having power over different spheres of influence. This rather contradictory picture had emerged from the questionnaire data, and was corroborated by the intensive studies of the three specific issues.

Another insight that emerged from the study of the specific issues that could not have been gained from the cross-sectional survey data was the nature of conflict that surrounded the various spheres of influence. While the survey indicated how groups perceived the situation at a given point in time, the intensive issue-histories indicated that vigorous battles were under way to change that picture. One young radical professor who saw the questionnaire results on the influence spheres suggested that they should not be published. "You shouldn't publish those figures" he said. "Just as sure as you say 'this is how it *is*,' people will start saying 'this is how it *ought* to be.' Listen, I don't like the way it is, and hopefully we can carve up that cake differently in the future!" Of course, there is no necessity for viewing the spheres of influence issue in static terms, for certainly the areas of influence do change.

A definite pattern of change seemed to emerge in each of the three specific issues. One group traditionally held influence in each area, but other groups began to challenge their right to make the decisions in that sphere. First, there was an "apathy breakthrough" as nonelite groups began to challenge the elite for control of the issue, and interest was mobilized among previously apathetic nonelites. Second, there was an "ideology challenge" as more or less carefully articulated rationales were developed to explain why the nonelites actually deserved control and the current elites were usurpers of power. Third, a series of "specific issue" conflicts occurred in which the nonelites challenged the elites on rather definite, concrete issues, usually quite unsuccessfully. Fourth, a "procedural attack" was mounted in which the nonelites blamed the decision procedures for their failure on specific issues, and demanded procedural reforms. Finally, an attack was mounted on the "policy-making structure" and the very machinery of governance was challenged and demands were made for restructuring the right of participation so that the elites were replaced by the nonelites, and the sphere of influence shifted. This new gain was then codified into new procedural and structural mechanisms in the stage we call the "bureaucratization of conflict." The change cycle is then completed and a new stability is established, until the next round of conflict.

This cycle was observed in each of the three issues studied at NYU, and may be a generalized cycle that accompanies conflict over spheres of influence. Thus, the rigid sphere of influence picture, with its dominant elites, must be tempered by a picture of power and influence patterns that are shifting, changing, and dynamic. Certainly this is true of the dynamic university, and probably it is true of both the more politicized local communities and the more bureaucratized hierarchical organizations at the opposite end of the continuum. However, it must be noted that the pattern of conflict over spheres of influence just described represents the *successful* revolution, and most attempts at changing influence spheres are failures. We must be on guard against what one critical reader of this paper suggested was a "revolutionary romanticism" that overstressed the ease with which influence spheres are changed. One must certainly be on guard against generalizing from successful challenges to the countless situations in which spheres remain stable over long periods of time, quite impervious to the demands for reform that come from nonelites. It is just such pent-up frustration over lost challenges that may partly account for the turmoil on the contemporary campuses.

Conclusion

Drawing on community power theory and other studies of organizational policy formulation, this research studied the distribution of power and influence within a university. The basic research question revolved around the nature of power elites and the charting of spheres of influence. Three different strategies were used. First, participants in the university were analyzed as to their participation in the policy-formulation activities. Various types of activities were identified for the departments, colleges, and university levels separately; overlapping influence patterns between the various levels were charted; and then the differences between activists and inactives were outlined. The second strategy shifted from the consideration of activity styles and instead concentrated on the spheres of influence that were claimed by various power blocs within the university. Finally, intensive studies of specific policies added confirming information to the patterns that emerged from the questionnaires, and in addition showed some of the conflicts that were surrounding the different spheres of influence.

From this research on the distribution of power and influence in a university the following conclusions are drawn:

1. Obviously the university is not "democratic," for there are clear pyramids of influence, with dominant elite groups that are highly involved and highly influential in almost every area.

2. Nevertheless, no single elite group controls most issues, for there are definite spheres of influence with their own miniature elites. This emerged both from questionnaire data on perceived spheres of influence, and from the intensive interviews that identified the participant decision makers on specific issues.

3. In light of the above information it is increasingly plausible that the "pluralism versus power elite" debate is unnecessarily polarized, and may be due mainly to ideological bias on the part of the researchers and methodological differences that tend to uncover different influence structures. In this issue, as in most social science questions, the either/or question is misleading and the more fruitful research asks about relative distribution of power, and about the patterns that emerge. This allows for coexisting elite groups, fragmented spheres of influence, and interconnected networks of power to be seen as all part of a very complex pattern, a pattern much more complicated than the simplistic dichotomies would allow.

4. Influence spheres and elite groups are constantly changing and are subject to political influence attempts. A patterned series of events seems to surround a challenge to an influence sphere, although most challenges fail to change the influence distribution significantly.

5. Perhaps the most important conclusion is that community power theory and interest group theory may indeed be useful for studying policy formulation in complex organizations.

References

1. Baldridge, J. Victor. *Power and Conflict in the University*. New York: John Wiley & Sons, Inc., 1971.
2. Clark, Burton R. *Adult Education in Transition*. Berkeley: University of California Press, 1956.
3. Cyert, R. M. and March, James G. *A Behavioral Theory of the Firm*. Englewood Cliffs, N.J.: Prentice-Hall, 1963.
4. Dahl, R. *Who Governs?* New Haven: Yale University Press, 1961.
5. Dalton, Melville. *Men Who Manage*. New York: John Wiley & Sons, Inc., 1959.
6. Gouldner, Alvin W. "Cosmopolitans and Locals: Toward an Analysis of Latent Social Roles—I, II." *Administrative Science Quarterly* 2 (1957-58): 281-306, 444-480.
7. Gross, Neal. "The Sociology of Education." In *Sociology Today*, Edited by Robert K. Merton et al. New York: Basic Books, 1959, pp. 128-152.
8. Hunter, Floyd. *Community Power Structure: A Study of Decision Makers*. Garden City: Doubleday & Company, Inc., Anchor Books, 1963.
9. Lindbloom, Charles. "The Science of Muddling Through." *Public Administration Review* 19 (1959): 78-88.
10. Lipset, Seymour M. *Agrarian Socialism*. Berkeley and Los Angeles: University of California Press, 1950.
11. Lipset, Seymour M., Trow, Martin A., and Coleman, James S. *Union Democracy*. Glencoe, Ill.: Free Press, 1956.
12. Litchfield, Edward H. "Notes on a General Theory of Administration." *Administrative Science Quarterly* 1 (1956): 3-29.
13. Michels, Robert. *Political Parties: A Sociological Study of the Oligarchical Tendencies of Modern Democracy*. Glencoe, Illinois: Free Press, 1948.
14. Polsby, Nelson W. *Community Power and Political Theory*. New Haven: Yale University Press, 1963.
15. Selznick, Philip. "An Approach to a Theory of Bureaucracy." *American Sociological Review* 8 (1943): 47-54.
16. Thompson, James D. *Organizations in Action*. New York: McGraw-Hill, 1967.
17. Walton, James "Discipline Method, and Community Power: A Note on the Sociology of Knowledge." *Administrative Science Quarterly* 12 (December 1968): 396-419.

REPRESENTATIONAL SYSTEMS
IN HIGHER EDUCATION

Myron Lieberman

The objective of this paper is to assess the major representational systems, in existence or proposed, for higher education in the United States. This objective is developed as follows: First, the paper sets forth the purposes and types of representational systems in our economy. It then outlines the characteristics of representational systems in higher education, including those proposed by various organizations and agencies active in higher education. The analysis then focuses upon some major issues characterizing representational systems in higher education. Then concluding sections are devoted to the implications of the analysis for faculty representation systems and for the leading organizations seeking to organize faculty members.

At the outset, certain limitations should be noted. Perhaps the most important is the lack of comprehensive data on the nature, number, and effectiveness of representational systems in higher education. For example, faculty senates, under a wide variety of titles, constitute a common type of faculty representational system. Nevertheless, this observer was unable to locate research data providing both a feasible definition of academic senates and a count of their frequency. Systematic research into their operations was also not available, although there are many case studies on the subject.[1]

From *Employment Relations in Higher Education*, edited by Stanley Elam & Michael H. Moskow, published by Phi Delta Kappa, Inc., 1969, pp. 40-71. Reprinted by permission of Phi Delta Kappa, Inc. and the author.

Typically the case studies deal with situations wherein the academic senate has failed to operate effectively. For this reason, the studies do not necessarily provide a balanced view of the extent or effectiveness of academic senates. The same conclusion would apply to the available material on other representational systems in higher education.

The lack of evaluative data is particularly evident. Regardless of the structure of a representational system, the results obtained under it are affected by other factors such as the ability of the persons exercising leadership roles in the system. Of course, the tendency of representational systems to produce outstanding leadership is a legitimate basis for evaluating the systems, but it may be very difficult to ascertain what is due to the system and what is due to other factors. In any case, this observer was unable to discover useful studies along these lines.

The analytical problem is to identify a basis for evaluation which is practically defensible even though limited to very gross data which may not illuminate the relationships between crucial variables in specific situations. The approach adopted here has been to assume that representational systems for professors share some of the goals of representational systems in other fields. The specific content of these goals, such as professional autonomy or enhanced professorial welfare, may vary from field to field, just as they vary from institution to institution within the field of higher education. Nevertheless, the goals will be similar if not identical in some respects. For example, any representational system, regardless of whether it applies to professional or nonprofessional employees, or public or nonpublic ones, is supposed to strive for the prompt resolution of grievances. Thus although all objectives of representational systems may not be similar, effectiveness in achieving those that are seems like a reasonable if imprecise basis for evaluation. If this is so, perhaps we can draw some valid conclusions about the effectiveness of representational systems in higher education despite the lack of detailed data on many important issues.

Purposes of Representational Systems

Professors typically participate in several representational systems. As citizens, they participate in a system of political representation. Those who own stocks participate in a system of economic representation. If professors find it necessary to employ lawyers, they participate in still another representational system, and so on.

A representational system in higher education must serve the purposes appropriate to groups of employee professionals. Despite some interesting disclaimers, professors are employees of institutions of higher education. Therefore, their representational systems at the institutional level include, but are not limited to, the broad purposes of employee organizations. These purposes include improving the terms and conditions of employment for the employees.

In mentioning this purpose first, there is no intent to prejudge the priority it receives or should receive in practice. At the same time, professors are a particular kind of employee, at least in their own eyes. Professors are concerned about their field of study, their subject-matter organizations, the goals of their employing institutions, and a wide variety of factors which are not terms and conditions of employment. These aspects of professorial concern are summed up for many by the concept of "professionalism."

For present purposes, the point is that representational systems at the institutional level can and should also be analyzed in terms of their effectiveness in serving "professional" as well as "employment" purposes. In practice, the two types overlap and are often closely interrelated. Smaller classes are an improvement in working conditions; they may also be a defensible objective strictly from the "professional" standpoint of improved student performance. Thus although our main concerns here are the representational systems relating the professors to their employing institutions, the overall effectiveness of such systems must take into account their effectiveness in relating professors to other components of higher education, such as national scientific and academic organizations, students, and so on. We shall not, for example, consider here the way in which history professors are represented in the American Historical Association or medical professors in the American Medical Association; nevertheless, we should recognize that representational systems at the institutional level are not the only ones in higher education.

Employee representational systems (as well as employee organizations) are typically initiated by the employees. Analytically, the organization is only one element in a representational system, but both system and organization are meant to serve the same broad professorial purposes. Within this context, the AAUP's statement of its organizational purposes is adequate as a statement of the purposes of representational systems in higher education:

". . . to facilitate a more effective cooperation among teachers and research scholars in universities and colleges, and in professional schools of similar grade, for the promotion of the interests of higher education and research and in general to increase the usefulness and advance the standards, ideals, and welfare of the profession."

Types of Representational Systems

The effectiveness of any representational system in higher education will ultimately depend upon the specific circumstances prevailing there. What prevails successfully or otherwise, in private enterprise, municipal employment, or other sectors may be helpful in higher education, but only to the extent that the relevant conditions in these other fields are similar to those in higher education.

Some professors insist that there is no similarity between employment conditions in higher education and in other fields. This is an ideological preconception, not an empirical fact. Reasonable men can differ about the extent to which higher education is not a *completely* unique area of employment relations. This does not mean that other experience is to be copied; undoubtedly, some of it at least is to be avoided. But to make intelligent judgments on this issue, we need to know what other representational systems have been tried and what experience has been persuant to their use. With this in mind, a few comments about representational systems outside of higher education may be in order.

In private employment, especially such as is governed by federal legislation, the predominant representational system is collective bargaining through an exclusive bargaining agent designated by a majority of the employees in an appropriate unit. As defined in federal law, and as used here, collective bargaining (or collective negotiations) is ". . . the performance of the mutual obligation of the employer and the representatives of the employees to meet at reasonable times and confer in good faith with respect to wages, hours, and other terms of employment, or the negotiations of any agreement, or any question arising thereunder, and the execution of a written contract incorporating any agreement if requested by either party, but such obligation does not compel either party to agree to a proposal or require the making of any concessions."[2] Although each of these elements raises a number of significant issues, the basic structure of this representational system is fairly clear.

Collective bargaining is in part an adversary process. Nevertheless, the rationale for it assumes that the parties involved in bargaining have common interests which outweigh their conflicting ones. The parties are not required to agree or to make any concession but to follow a procedure requiring sincere effort to reach agreement. The rationale is that if the parties follow the procedure, they will in practice arrive at a mutually satisfactory agreement because of the predominance of their common interests.

For a variety of reasons, the adversary element in collective negotiations is frequently stressed. Attitudes toward the procedure often depend upon whether one sees collective negotiations as an appropriate response to a pre-existing conflict of interest, or as a procedure which creates such conflicts, or both. Regardless, the agreement-making and community of interest aspects of collective negotiations are also essential elements of its theory and practice; inability or unwillingness to recognize this serves no scholarly purpose. Nor is any such purpose served by assuming that a rejection of invalid criticisms or assumptions about the process commits one to the proposition that it is feasible or appropriate in higher education.

For several very practical reasons, collective bargaining requires employee representation through an exclusive bargaining agent. The bargaining agent (typically but not necessarily a union) is authorized to negotiate a binding agreement for the employees in an appropriate unit. Under federal legislation and some state statutes, the bargaining agent must be designated as exclusive representative by a majority of the employees. The employees retain the right to change their bargaining agent or to go without one under specified conditions; however, once certified as the exclusive representative, the majority organization has the exclusive right to negotiate terms and conditions of employment for all the employees in the unit for a specified period of time.[3]

The vast majority of employees covered by federal labor law are represented as employees through an exclusive bargaining agent. However, such representation is an employee initiative, and this initiative is not always exercised. The reasons vary from fear of employer reprisal (though such reprisal is illegal) to the belief that exclusive representation is undesirable or unnecessary in a given situation.

State and local employment relations, including public employment relations not under federal jurisdiction, present a variety of representational patterns. In addition to exclusive representation in negotiations by a majority organization, other types of representational systems include employee councils, joint representation, and multiple representation systems. A few brief comments about each type may help to clarify the subsequent analysis.

Employee councils are representational systems in which the employees elect one or more fellow employees to represent them. Employees are thus not represented through external organizations. Only individual employees of the same employer represent their fellow employees concerning terms and conditions of employment. Employee councils are thus "internal mechanisms"; neither individuals who are not employees nor organizations serve as employee representatives in employee councils.

Under joint representation, employees are represented by organizations on the basis of membership. Unlike exclusive representation, where one employee organization represents all the employees in an appropriate unit, organizations represent their members only under a system of joint representation. The rationale is that an organization should have the right to represent its members but not the right to represent nonmembers, including those adamantly opposed to the organization.

Sometimes a system of joint representation is qualified by a requirement that an organization enroll a minimum number of employees before it is entitled to representation rights. Without any such qualification, an employer could be faced with the prospect of negotiating with a tremendous number of small organizations. To avoid such an outcome, organizations may be required to enroll a certain minimal proportion of employees before they are entitled to representational rights.

Proportional representation is a form of joint representation in which employees are represented by representatives from different employee organizations. Representation is in the form of a committee (or council). Organizations have membership in the joint committee in proportion to the number of employees enrolled by each organization; thus if organization A enrolled twice as many employees as organization B, the former would be entitled to twice as many representatives as the latter on the joint committee. Again, a minimal number of members may be required for representational rights. The procedures for allocating places on the joint committee vary, but it is not practicable to adjust such places to small variations in organizational membership.

Finally, there are situations in which two or more representational systems coexist. There may be an employee council coexisting with some system of organizational representation. Multiple representational systems present many theoretical and practical inconsistencies, but there is no doubt that such systems do exist; in fact, this appears to be the predominant pattern in higher education.

Organizational Policies on Faculty Representation

Let us turn next to organizational policies on faculty representation. The policies of the AAUP will be considered first.

The most recent statement of AAUP policy is set forth in the Association's "Statement of Policy on Representation of Economic Interests." This statement was approved by the Association's Committee on the Representation of Economic Interests in January, 1968, and by the AAUP's Council and the Fifty-fourth Annual Meeting in April, 1968. This policy statement clearly places the AAUP on record in support of internal mechanisms (i.e., employee councils) for faculty representation. Because the representational system faculties want is the one they are most likely to get, and because the AAUP is the largest professorial organization in the United States, this recent statement is worth quoting in some detail:

> Two main kinds of approach [to faculty representation] have been developed: (1) collective bargaining by an exclusive bargaining agent, patterned after union procedures in industry, and (2) professional self-representation by an internal faculty agency, based upon faculty authority of the kind which the Association supports for the handling of all kinds of faculty interests.
>
> The Association recommends that faculty members, in decisions relating to the protection of their economic interests, should participate through structures of self-government within the institution, with the faculty participating either directly or through faculty-elected councils or senates. As integral parts of the institution, such councils or senates can effectively represent the faculty without taking on the adversary and sometimes arbitrary attitudes of an outside representative. . . .
>
> . . . statutory models of general application may be ill-suited to the situation of the faculty member in higher education. As stated above, he has, or should have, access to avenues of self-government and of shared authority and responsibility. Because of these special characteristics of the academic community, professors should be especially concerned to avoid dependence on external representative agencies that diminish the opportunities of the faculty for self-government. B. The Association will therefore oppose legislation imposing upon faculty members in higher education the principle of exclusive representation derived from models of industrial collective bargaining. When legislation of this character exists or is proposed, the Association will rather support measures that will encourage institutions of higher education to establish adequate internal structures of faculty participation in the government of the institution. . . .
>
> 1. Any statute authorizing collective bargaining for public employees should permit, for faculty members of colleges and universities, some system of joint representation. In such a system, collective bargaining might be conducted by a committee composed of delegates from each of the organizations which represented a substantial number of faculty members and which were willing to take part in the system of joint representation.

2. Any such legislation should make it clear that, in higher education, a faculty-elected council or senate is eligible to represent the faculty, since such an internal representative can have the requisite autonomy and independence of the administration to carry out its functions. . . .[4]

Significantly, the Association's policy statement goes on to state that "if the faculty is considering representation through an outside organization, the Association believes itself by virtue of its principles, programs, experience, and broad membership, to be well qualified to act as representative of the faculty in institutions of higher education."[5] Thus although opposed to collective bargaining through an exclusive representative, the AAUP believes that it ought to be selected as the bargaining agent if a faculty should disregard this advice.

The American Council on Education is another organization deeply interested in faculty representational systems. The ACE is formally composed of institutions, organizations, and agencies concerned with higher education; in operation, it is controlled by college and university presidents.

The ACE's position on faculty representation is embodied in a 1966 statement formulated and issued jointly with the AAUP and the Association of Governing Boards of Universities and Colleges. The statement thus reflects the views of the major organizations of administrators and lay boards in higher education. Despite some language which could be interpreted otherwise, it seems clear that the ACE and AGB endorse faculty representation through internal mechanisms. This is not surprising since such mechanisms typically strengthen the position of the employer *vis-à-vis* the employees; what may be more significant is that the statement was jointly formulated and approved by the AAUP as well. As a matter of fact, there is nothing in this joint statement to indicate that the AAUP, or any external organization, should exist or play a significant role in the government of colleges and universities. Perhaps one reason for the omission is that the statement urges that rather broad responsibilities be delegated to the faculty:

The faculty has primary responsibility for such fundamental areas as curriculum, subject matter, and methods of instruction, research, faculty status, and those aspects of student life which relate to the educational process. On these matters the power of review or final decision lodged in the governing board or delegated by it to the president should be exercised adversely only in expectional circumstances and for reasons communicated to the faculty. . . . Faculty status and related matters are primarily a faculty responsibility; this area includes appointments, reappointments, decisions not to reappoint, promotions, the granting of tenure, and dismissal. . . . Determinations in these matters should first be by faculty action through established procedures, reviewed by the chief academic officers with the concurrence of the board. The governing board and the president should, on questions of faculty status, as in other matters where the faculty has primary responsibility, concur with the faculty judgment except in rare instances and for compelling reasons which should be stated in detail.

Agencies for faculty participation in the government of the college or university should be established at each level where faculty responsibility is present. An agency should exist for the presentation of the views of the whole faculty. The structure and procedures for faculty participation should be designed, approved and established by joint action of the components of the institution. Faculty representatives should be selected by the faculty according to procedures determined by the faculty. The agencies may consist of meetings of all faculty members of a department, school, college, division, or university system, or may take the form of faculty-elected executive committees in departments and schools and a faculty-elected senate or council for larger divisions or institution as a whole.[6]

The American Federation of Teachers is composed predominantly of teachers below the college level. Nevertheless, the AFT has recently created a staff position to implement its interest in enrolling college and university personnel. At present, about 10,000 college and university faculty belong to the AFT, including a considerable proportion of junior college personnel.

The AFT supports collective bargaining through an exclusive representative for college as well as for elementary and secondary school personnel. AFT locals have occasionally gone on strike to secure such a representational system, and in the immediate future, the success or failure of AFT college locals in achieving bargaining rights, and in negotiating good agreements from a professorial point of view, may be a crucial factor affecting the rate at which collective bargaining becomes accepted in higher education.

One other position on faculty representation should be mentioned here, even though it is not the official position of a major national organization in the field of higher education. This is the position set forth by a task force established by the American Association for Higher Education enrolling both administrators and faculty members in higher education.[7]

In many respects, the report of this task force is the best (i.e., the least confused) statement on faculty representational systems currently available. This is undoubtedly due to the fact that the task force included several members with considerable professional background and experience in employment relations; two nationally recognized authorities in public employment relations served as counsel to the task force.

The AAHE report states "a clear preference for the development of effective internal organizations as the primary instrument of faculty participation in campus government. In most cases this will mean the academic senate or its equivalent."[8] The report goes on to outline some of the requirements which an effective academic senate should meet. It then goes on, however, to support the principle of exclusive bargaining rights for any organization which gains the allegiance of a majority of the faculty. The report also urges that regardless of their legal freedom to avoid a test of faculty interest in exclusive representation, institutions of higher education follow the same basic procedures concerning representation elections and recognition that are embodied in the National Labor Relations Act and in the state statutes which follow the NLRA pattern for state and local public employees.

Faculty Senates: an Introductory Analysis

Of all the representation systems listed, it is probable that some type of faculty senate is currently the most common if not the prevailing type on U. S. campuses. This is only to be expected in view of the organizational positions previously mentioned. Given the fact that the AAUP, ACE, and AGB (the preeminent organizations of faculty, administration, and governing boards respectively) officially support the use of faculty senates, it would be surprising if they were not a common pattern of faculty representation.

Faculty senates vary a great deal. For example, faculty representatives may be elected on a departmental or a college basis or some combination of these. In some institutions, the administration appoints certain persons to the senate, or administrative appointees may preside at certain senate proceedings. Faculty below a certain rank may be unable to vote or hold office in some senates. The legal or constitutional base of the academic senate also varies widely from institution to institution.

These variations can be very important, but no attempt will be made here to explore them. Instead, let us consider faculty senates chiefly with regard to their salient characteristics as representational systems. In doing so, the analysis will consider at some length the question of whether special factors in higher education justify or require a representational system generically different from those prevailing in other areas of employment, including professional employment.

In theory and practice, faculty senates are a type of employee council. Employee councils were fairly common in private employment before the Wagner Act. In operation, they failed to provide effective employee representation for the following reasons:

1. Employee councils lacked funds needed to pursue an aggressive campaign of employee representation. Employers provided the funds, and they naturally did not wish to subsidize a strong employee representation system.

2. Employers typically regulated the internal affairs of employee councils. The more serious an issue became, the more likely that the employer would exercise his control over the representation system to impose his will on the employees.

3. Under an employee council, there is no employee appeal from an adverse decision by the employer. This is because employee councils are not organically related to higher echelons of employee organization, such as a regional or national organization. There is nobody outside the employing agency to whom the employee can appeal, at least without calling into question the basic adequacy of the employee council itself. An adequate employee representation system would envisage the possibility that employer action may have to be vigorously resisted by resort to outside assistance and that such resistance should be available within the representational system.

4. Employee councils typically put the employees at a psychological disadvantage. Under a council system, employee representatives are employees under the direction and control of the employer. Whereas the employer is or may be represented by persons who devote full time to the problems of employment relations, the employee representatives tend to be more inexperienced since they do not work full-time at representing the employees. Because the task of representing the employees is superimposed on their full-time work, the employee representatives are handicapped in preparing for representational activities.

5. If the employee representatives on the council are chosen from subgroups of employees, there is no employee representative whose constituency includes all the employees. This weakens the moral authority as well as the practical ability of the employee representatives to represent all the employees.

These and other deficiencies in employee councils are not simply matters of conjecture. They are the reasons why employee councils are, in effect, prohibited by federal labor legislation from representing employees on terms and conditions of employment. As a matter of public policy, federal law supports the principle that employees shall be represented by organizations free of employer domination.

Since employee councils are likely to be employer dominated, they are prohibited, *even if the employees are professionals and desire such a representational system.*

It seems hardly debatable that faculty senates are characterized by at least some of the objectionable features of employee councils. For example, faculty senates typically lack funds independent of those provided by the administration. For this reason, the senates are gravely handicapped in securing the services needed for effective representation. Faculty senates are not likely to have the expert negotiating, actuarial, accounting, legal, and other experts needed to maximize faculty benefits. This weakness is not routinely overcome by the expertise available from within the faculty.

In the first place, many faculties with academic senates simply lack the expertise needed for effective representation. Most faculties will not include a lawyer specializing in employment relations or an expert on pension and retirement systems. Most will not have experts in public finance or public personnel administration. Furthermore, faculty members with an expertise useful for representation do not necessarily participate in the academic senate. The individual faculty member may be unable or unwilling to devote the time to securing benefits which are diffused to the entire faculty; the effectiveness of a representational system that relies upon volunteers to perform all the specialized services required for effective representation is open to serious question.

As in private employment, it is typical for employers (i.e., administration or governing board), to regulate the internal affairs of faculty senates. In many institutions, faculties have worked diligently to get their trustees to incorporate a faculty senate into the official statutes of the institution. Such incorporation is usually regarded as a victory for a "faculty self-government." Surely, however, a strong argument can be made that faculty senates have precisely the opposite effect.

Suppose a board of trustees has approved the structure of a faculty senate and the senate is now recognized as an official component of faculty government. Suppose further that the faculty subsequently desires to change the representational system. It may want to exclude administrative officers or have faculty representatives elected at large instead of by department or college. If such changes must be approved by the trustees or by the administration, the "self-government" is obviously a matter of sufferance, not of right. Its inherent tendency is to be authorized or tolerated only to the point where it threatens no crucial interest of governing boards or administrators.

Of course, if one assumes that there is not and cannot be a conflict of interest between the faculty and those who must approve the structure of "faculty self-government," there is no problem here. In that case, however, it is difficult to see the need for a representational system in the first place. Paradoxically, a union of common laborers can change the way it selects its representatives without consulting the employers of common labor. Professors represented through academic senates cannot change the way they select their representatives without employer approval. Nevertheless, the professors supposedly have more "self-government." This is a curious conclusion, to say the least.

Perhaps the argument is that laborers have more control only over their organizational affairs, whereas the professors have more control over occupational affairs even if they are subject to employer control in ways that laborers are not. Still, it is at least as reasonable to suppose that an employee organization which operates independently of employer approval or support will press more vigorously than one which is not for joint decision making in employment relations.

Academic senates are not part of any state or national structure which can bring pressure to bear upon a recalcitrant administration. When an administration finally rejects a senate recommendation, the faculty's options are to accept the rejection or to appeal to an external organization. On its face, this situation is clearly inferior to the procedures prevailing in private employment under exclusive representation. In the latter situation, the exclusive representative negotiates a binding agreement on terms and conditions of employment. The employer administers the agreement, but he is effectively precluded from interpreting or applying the terms and conditions of employment in such a way as to deprive the employees of their rights under the agreement. This is so because the employees typically have the right to appeal to arbitration of such disputes by an impartial third party. Such appeals are part of the structure of employment relations, hence they are relatively expeditious in practice. By contrast, a faculty member or organization wishing to challenge an adverse decision by an employer must activate local and national organizations which have no legally or operationally recognized place in institutional employment relations.

Although faculty senates are clearly subject to some of the disabilities of employee councils, perhaps they are not so subject to others. For example, a major weakness of employee councils is that the employee representatives must prepare for their dealings with the employer after the normal work day or on weekends. Apart from the physical burdens involved, the employee representatives find it difficult to communicate with appropriate persons or locate appropriate resources at these times.

This weakness probably does not apply to faculty members to the same degree that it does to employees in private enterprise. Some institutions of higher education provide released time for representational duties, much as an industrial company releases union ship stewards for union duties on company time. Even without this arrangement, however, faculty members typically have more time to prepare their case than employees operating under an employee council in private enterprise. Faculties are also more likely to include personnel who would not be at a disadvantage psychologically in negotiating with institutional management. Nevertheless, on balance, it appears that the major criticisms levelled against employee councils are valid as applied to faculty senates.

Why do faculties support a representational system characterized by such basic deficiencies? The belief that faculty senates constitute a "professional" (as distinguished from an "employee") approach to faculty representation is undoubtedly part of the explanation. "Employee" is a dirty word in academe; in fact, academicians frequently assert that they are not "employees." One example of such an assertion may suffice to indicate its widespread acceptance among faculties. In the spring of 1968, Bertram H. Davis, the newly appointed general secretary of the AAUP, stated that:

"Faculty members have rightfully complained when boards or administrators have treated them as employees, and it would be ironic if they were now themselves to perpetuate the employer-employee concept through an industrial style of collective bargaining."[9]

Such professional overreactions to their employee status (including the delusion that they are not employees) is based upon the conviction that professors are professional persons and that professional status is inconsistent with employee status. This conviction is clearly fallacious, but it underlies much academic support for faculty senates.

The reason is that most professors fail to understand the distinction between an employment problem and a professional one. Employment problems should be resolved within the context of employer-employee relations; professional problems are those appropriate for action by professional organizations independently of employer action. To illustrate, suppose a physician appears late for his appointments. What is the patient's recourse—to report this to the local medical society? Ordinarily such tardiness is not handled this way. If a patient is aggrieved for this reason, he seeks an adjustment from the physician; if he does not get it, he changes physicians. But whatever he does, the matter is not ordinarily referred for action to the physician's professional organizations. It is an employment, not a professional, problem.

Suppose, however, that the physician has been supplying a dope ring at great profit to himself. In this case, the professional organization would be concerned with the physician's right to practice at all; the problem would be clearly a professional one.

A problem can be both an employment and a professional problem. For example, a physician who operated recklessly might give rise to legal action by his employer, i.e., the patient. Such reckless behavior might also justify disciplinary action by his professional organization. Without attempting a precise categorization, we can say that some actions are clearly employment problems, some are clearly professional problems, and some are both.

In higher education, however, the problem is not where to draw the line. It is the lack of awareness that there is a line to be drawn. As a result, faculties are apt to insist upon "professional autonomy" or "academic self-government" on problems which should be handled as employment problems.

For example, suppose a faculty member habitually appears late for his classes. For a faculty to regard disciplinary action, if any, as within the scope of their "professional autonomy" is to be confused. Such confusion probably stems from the fear that if jurisdiction over such matters is not "professional," i.e., within the faculty's domain, it must be an unbridled administrative prerogative. It would be possible for the faculty and the institution to negotiate a binding agreement which (1) would include the grounds and criteria for disciplinary action and which (2) would be administered by the administration with ample safeguards against administrative violation of the agreement. But this possibility simply has not occurred to most professors.

We may put the matter this way: Failure to understand how employee representation systems can and do work to serve professional employees leads many faculty members to deny that they are employees at all. Having abandoned any claim to protection as employees, these faculty members seek such protection as a professional prerogative. In doing so, however, they have thoroughly confused both employment relations and professionalism on the campus.

The idea that persons should not be appointed to administrative positions (president, dean, etc.) without professorial approval is strongly supported by many professors as an appropriate step toward "professional autonomy," "faculty self-government," and "democracy." Realistically, the idea illustrates the pervasiveness of professional confusion concerning their status as professionals and as employees.

In the first place, there is a conflict of interest on the part of faculty members who recommend persons for administrative positions (in this context, meaning those that involve making decisions or effective recommendations concerning faculty employment, retention, promotion, discipline, and so on). Professors are not likely to recommend candidates who advocate curtailing their courses or programs. Nor can we assume that a professor would knowingly recommend anyone known to harbor sincere doubts about the competence or promotional merits of the recommender. As a rule, faculty members on appointment committees tend to support candidates known or likely to have a favorable view toward the individuals on the committees or their particular academic projects and objectives.

The conflict of interest does not disappear if, as happens, the appointment committee recommends someone whose views on these matters are not known to the committee members. A college president or dean or chairman will find it more difficult to make objective personnel decisions about faculty members who vigorously supported or opposed their appointment than about those who did not participate in it.

Stripped of its academic rhetoric, a faculty appointment committee involves all the contradictions inherent in having employees choosing the representatives of the employer. The dangers inherent in this procedure extend far beyond the likelihood that faculty members will recommend on the basis of the expected impact on their own interests. The procedure itself maximizes the possibility that a managerial appointment will be made on the basis of employee interests which are not laid on the table.

It is doubtful, to say the least, whether a faculty appointment committee provides as much faculty protection as a negotiated collective agreement covering terms and conditions of faculty employment and negotiated consultation procedures on other matters of mutual concern. Theoretically, faculties might enjoy the benefits of both procedures although they are ideologically inconsistent. The selection committee approach to college administration puts great reliance upon choosing a "democratic" individual. Faculty rights are not secured by a written agreement on terms and conditions of faculty employment, regardless of the individuals occupying administrative positions at any given time. They are supposedly secured because the faculty, in its wisdom, will choose administrators who will render adversary procedures unnecessary. Because of their confusion over professional autonomy, faculty members assume that they should choose, or at least have a veto power over the selection of, employer representatives.

Apart from the fact that such participation is subject to unhealthy resolution of various employer-employee conflicts of interest, it does not provide adequate protection for the faculty. Adequate protection requires adherance to certain procedures *regardless* of who occupies particular administrative positions. To put one's faith in whoever is appointed to administrative positions while simultaneously failing to insist upon the incorporation of appropriate administrative procedures in an enforceable contract is a questionable order of priorities.

A representational system should not be evaluated solely on the basis of its effectiveness from the standpoint of the employees represented. The interests of the employer are also important, and those of the public may be decisive. For this reason, the public policy implications of faculty appointment committees cannot be ignored.

As previously pointed out, it would seem contrary to public policy, at least in publicly supported institutions of higher education, to permit public employees to select the representatives of the public employer. To whatever extent procedures permit or encourage this, they increase the probability that hidden conflicts of interest will play an unhealthy role in the selection process. Beyond this, there are additional and perhaps even more important issues to be raised.

Assume that a faculty senate exists and that a board of trustees has agreed to appoint as president only a person recommended by the faculty. Assume also no administrative interference or pressure but ample support for whatever the faculty needs to arrive at a recommendation. Assume, therefore, that the trustees pay all the expenses of faculty participation without stint while agreeing to appoint from a list submitted by the faculty. On most campuses, such an arrangement would be cheered as a great step foreward.

Suppose, however, the faculty members on such a presidential appointment committee do a very poor job. Perhaps they do not work hard at it. Perhaps they work their heads off, but their judgment is poor. What happens to them as a result?

Obviously, if they have recommended a person who turns out to be a disaster, the president so recommended is not going to press the matter. He is not going to say, to the faculty or trustees or to anyone else, that the faculty selection committee flubbed the job. Nor is it likely that the trustees on their own will cite the disastrous recommendation as a reason to deny the faculty members who made it any advances in rank or pay or privilege.

By contrast, a department chairman is held responsible for the quality of his recommendations to deans and president. If a chairman recommends weak persons for appointment or promotion, this fact is legitimately cited against him in evaluating his own performance and setting his own future level of compensation. We are, therefore, confronted by a most anomalous situation. At the lowest administrative levels there is accountability for personnel recommendations; one clearly expects the quality of staff recruited by a chairman to be a significant factor in the evaluation of the chairman. But not so for the faculty committee to recommend a president. Whoever heard of a board of trustees or university president citing the poor judgment of the faculty presidential selection committee as a reason to withhold rank or pay to the committee members?

In short, faculty appointment committees constitute an irresponsible approach to appointment, since there is no accountability for the quality of the work done. As a practical matter, it would be extremely difficult, if not impossible, to inject accountability into the procedure. Who would implement the procedure? The president who was appointed as a result of the shoddy committee performance? The trustees who accepted and acted on the recommendation? The rest of the faculty? Absurd.

It is indeed remarkable that the AAUP, which has never allowed active membership to persons whose duties are mainly administrative, should nevertheless support procedures whereby the faculty, as employees, participate in the selection of employer representatives. Perhaps some board of trustees should propose that the officers of the AAUP be selected from a list submitted by the trustees to the faculty. This would make as much—or as little—sense as having the trustees choose the president from a list submitted by the faculty. In any event, the surprising thing is not that professors confusedly support the procedure—after all, it is difficult to resist the temptation to be a president maker. It is that so many governing boards have taken this academic rhetoric as seriously as they do.

Efficiency is not a very popular concept in academe, but it is important from a public policy standpoint. With this in mind, I would like to turn next to some comments about faculty senates from the standpoint of faculty efficiency.

It is an article of faith on most campuses that professors want to share, to participate, in decision making. The very vagueness of this objective suggests the desirability of careful analysis of its operational use and implementation.

How do professors "participate" in decision making? Typically, participation means that a faculty committee must be established to deal with a problem. If there is no faculty committee, there is no faculty participation.

The upshot is a tremendous diffusion of faculty energies to administrative matters, e.g., parking or scheduling. However, the function of faculty representation should not be faculty administration of an institution. Rather, it should be to ensure that administration is equitable and efficient. The way to achieve this objective is not to have the faculty choose the administrators or to administer the institution but to incorporate equitable and efficient administrative procedures in a contractual agreement between the faculty and the governing board. A grievance procedure culminating in binding arbitration by an impartial third party should be available to process a claim that the administration has violated or misapplied these procedures. Under such an agreement, the faculty would undoubtedly devote less of its time and energies to administration than it does now under faculty senates.

In other areas of employment, the employee representation system is neither designed nor intended to shift the burden of administration from the employer to the employees. On the other hand, the rights of the employees are protected because they are spelled out in a contractual agreement with impartial arbitration as the terminal point of the grievance procedure. If, therefore, the issue is whether a dismissal was for just cause, the employees' protection is not that his fellow employees process the charges and sit in judgment on them. It is that the employer must follow the standards and procedures embodied in the collective agreement; if he fails to do so, his action can be challenged through a grievance procedure in which the employer must ultimately prove his case to an impartial third party. Similarly, the function of a faculty representation system and of faculty organization should not be to administer the institution but to achieve agreement with the employer on how administration should be carried on and to enforce such agreement where enforcement is necessary.

Despite all the talk about faculty self-government, professionalism, and so on, the vast majority of professors have not more but less protection against arbitrary and unfair employer action than the vast majority of employees under contractual collective agreements. One reason is that contractual agreements provide greater protection than delegated authority, which can be revoked or ignored under pressure. Another reason requires that we reexamine the mystique of faculty participation.

The prevailing philosophy is that faculty protection lies in faculty self-government and faculty participation in personnel decisions. However, faculties and faculty organizations and academic senates are hardly immune from prejudice and self-interest and error; these are not administrative monopolies. The issue, then, is this: If the faculty exercises final authority on personnel decisions, how are faculty members protected against unjust action by the faculty?

Under a faculty senate, such protection is virtually nonexistent. The logic of the faculty senate approach is that a decision is right because it is made by the faculty. If this interpretation seems unfair, the answer is simple. If the rightness of a decision depends upon the standards and procedures involved in making it, then those standards and procedures should be binding upon *anyone* who has to make the decision, regardless of how that person or group is selected. But this view logically leads to a contractual approach through an exclusive representative, not to a faculty senate.

The point here is simple but fundamental. If the role of a faculty organization is not one of administration but of ensuring that administration is equitable and efficient, there is, at least in theory, an organization in being whose *raison d'être* is the protection of faculty rights from arbitrary or unjust administration. But if the faculty itself is responsible for the administrative action, faculty rights are practically without protection from administrative abuse.

Because faculty members are employees, their organization should serve protective functions. These should not be its only functions, but they are important ones. However, if a faculty senate assumes the functions of the employer, where does the aggrieved faculty member go for assistance? Surely not to the AAUP, since the Association's test of due process and equity in employment relations is whether the faculty made the decision being challenged. Beyond this, the AAUP merely recommends that "the terms and conditions of every appointment should be stated in writing and be in the possession of both institution and teacher before the appointment is consummated." The Association does not, however, recommend that these terms and conditions of employment include the teacher's right of access to his personnel file, that evaluation reports about him by administrators be routinely made available to him for his information and reaction, and that complaints and criticisms about him from any source that may bear upon his status be brought to his attention. Thousands of public school teachers have these and other protections as contractual rights; meanwhile, unless a personnel decision involves tenure, the AAUP has no rationale for involvement, and not even then if the faculty made the decision challenged.

Thus far, most of our attention has been paid to faculty senates because their viability is the major issue in faculty representation now, and will continue to be in the next few years. However, there are other important issues in faculty representation which should be mentioned.

One major issue is who should be represented in a faculty representational system. Are department chairmen, deans, and central office administrators to be included among those represented by the same system that represents nonadministrative personnel? Significantly, this issue arises sometimes with respect to a faculty senate. Some faculty members believe that administrators should not be constituent members or officers of the senate; others feel differently.

It appears likely that this issue will be fought out mainly over the status of department chairmen. It is difficult to believe that deans (or higher administrators) will, ought to, or want to be represented by faculty organizations, internal or external, concerning the terms and conditions of employment for deans. On the other hand, we can expect growing controversy over the status of department chairmen. One reason is that the title actually encompasses a widely disparate group of positions from the standpoint of employment relations. One chairman may have only three members in his department and receive no time or compensation for his administrative duties; another may have a department of 25 and serve chiefly as an administrator.

There is widespread inconsistency on this issue, even on the part of those who advocate collective negotiations through an exclusive representative. For example, a proposed contract[10] between the State University Federation of Teachers and the State University of New York being disseminated by the Federation includes the following:

A. *Administrative personnel.* The hiring, retention, and separation of division heads, associate deans, deans, vice presidents, and presidents shall be done with the advice and consent of the faculty. . . .

B. *Department chairman.*
    1. *Election.* The department chairman shall be elected by full-time faculty of the department.

These proposals may be intended mainly for their propaganda value, but the fact that they were made at all suggests the popularity of the view that faculty members should choose employer representatives in institutions of higher education. Furthermore, even if the AFT strategists who propose this are doing so only for tactical reasons, the tactics themselves will reinforce the view that faculties ought to choose administrators. All such propaganda will tend to obscure the issues, including the issue of administrator membership in the faculty's negotiating unit and organizational representative. Eventually, administrative personnel above the chairman's level will be recognized as employer representatives, hence not to be chosen by the employees; in both the short and the long run, there will be widespread variation concerning the place of department chairmen in the representational structure.

Another aspect of unit determination may prove more troublesome than administrative roles, especially in the larger institutions. A college faculty includes an extremely wide range of talents. Many of these talents are in great demand outside academe; many faculty members, such as professors of medicine, tend to identify more with the organizations in their field such as the AMA than with faculty organizations interested in academic governance.

In large organizations enrolling a wide variety of occupational talents and levels of compensation, organizational leadership must respond to the wishes of its largest constituent groups. In higher education, these groups may not accept the view that faculty compensation should be geared, partially at least, to market factors. Thus a faculty representational system composed largely of faculty members in the social sciences and humanities—fields in which the nonacademic demand for personnel may not be strong—may object to large differentials for faculty in such fields as medicine, engineering, mathematics, or law, where the nonacademic demand is very strong indeed. It is difficult to visualize English and history and speech professors dying on the barricades for $25,000 salaries for their colleagues in professional schools, even though such salaries may be rather modest for the kinds of persons who teach in them.

Thus there may be tremendous heterogeneity within faculties at a single institution, in terms of (1) their identification with organizations which are primarily nonacademic, (2) the nonacademic demand for their services, and (3) their conditions of employment, such as load, research facilities, administrative organization, and level of instruction. This heterogeneity raises serious questions as to whether a single organization, internal or external, can effectively represent all the faculty.

The problem is complicated by the fact that some conditions of employment, such as retirement benefits, are institution-wide, and it would be practically impossible or extremely difficult to change this. One possible solution is institution- or even system-wide negotiations on matters that should logically affect all faculty. Yet even here there will be major difficulties if faculty from some areas conclude that they can do better apart from an institution-wide representational system.

In technical terms, this is the community of interest problem. Should all faculty members, regardless of subject or function, be part of one faculty representational system at their institution? Do all share such a community of interest that effective representation, efficient administration, and stable employment relations are maximized by a single system? Or will there be constant friction as various specialized groups come to feel their interests are being sacrificed in such a system?

At the present time, this issue is important chiefly in the smaller public institutions which have salary schedules applying to all faculty. The main effect of such schedules is to introduce rigidities in the compensation structure, but the problem is not typically regarded as an especially serious one. If faculties at larger institutions turn to collective negotiations, however, this issue will become more important to both administration and faculty. The administration will normally want to avoid negotiating with several different faculty groups. Apart from the increased demands on administrative time resulting from such multi-unit negotiations, there are some tactical advantages in requiring major faculty groups to agree among themselves on their proposed allocation of institutional funds. Under a unitary system, the administration can also avoid being whipsawed by organizations representing different faculty negotiating units.

Probably these advantages to the administration will outweigh the real disadvantages of multi-unit negotiations (e.g., by a different faculty organization representing each of the major professional schools or institutional divisions). Nevertheless, it seems safe to predict that some smaller groups within the faculty, especially in areas of highest nonacademic demand or least academic identification, will become increasingly unhappy with institution-wide representational systems. These groups may not be dissatisfied with current institution-wide systems, such as faculty senates, because these systems do not really prevent the administration from making a separate deal with subgroups within the faculty.

Summary and Conclusions

Let me now try to summarize the preceding analysis and suggest some issues and trends of future concern. Essentially, the analysis has been devoted chiefly to academic senates. Its major conclusion is that faculty senates are subject to the deficiencies of employee councils for these reasons:

1. Faculty senates rely upon the employer for funds and faculties. Thus they have inherent limitations on aggressive representation of faculty interests.

2. The structure of faculty senates is subject to approval by institutional governing boards and/or administrators. Faculties should not permit the mechanics of their representational agency to be subject to employer approval.

3. Faculty senates lack accountability. Faculty members assert that teaching and research competence should be the standards of personnel administration. Nevertheless, they wish to exercise personnel functions that vitally affect the integrity and effectiveness of their institutions. It is practically impossible for faculty senates to provide for faculty accountability in matters of personnel administration.

4. Faculty senates tend to place faculty representatives at a psychological disadvantage in dealing with institutional administrators.

5. Faculty senates increase the probability that faculties will lack experienced full-time representatives supported by the wide variety of supporting services and personnel needed for effective representation.

6. Faculty senates make no provision for appeals outside the structure of the institution. Since the senates are not part of any larger representational system, any such appeals are inherently outside the scope of institutional representation.

7. Faculty senates which exercise personnel functions tend to deprive faculty members of protection against abuse in the exercise of such functions. An employee organization is needed to protect faculty against certain kinds of employer action. If the employer delegates such action to the employee organization, no agency serves the protective functions of an employee organization.

These criticisms of faculty senates are not exhaustive. What is needed is not so much a critique of their inherent weaknesses, but an explanation of their persistence in spite thereof. The analysis has touched upon some reasons, such as befuddled faculty leadership and the large numbers of faculty who identify with, and find their greatest support in, nonacademic organizations and pressures. An additional reason for the representational vacuum in higher education relates to the organizational dynamics of the AAUP.

In electing faculty members to serve on the AAUP's Executive Council, its major governing body, there is a natural tendency to nominate and to vote for the better known professors at the most prestigious institutions. Unfortunately, employment relations for leading professors at prestigious institutions may have little in common with employment relations in other institutions, especially state college systems and struggling private institutions. The faculty at the prestigious institutions are employees, but their income levels and perquisites are so high that collective negotiations seem irrelevant, even dangerous to them. On the other hand, the faculty at state college systems are in a much different situation. The individual faculty members tend to lack bargaining power and urgently need to utilize their collective strength to improve their conditions of employment. Unfortunately, the AAUP's national leaders are more apt to be the leading beneficiaries of the status quo than the apostles of change. Eventually, pressures from the rank and file will make themselves felt, especially as the increasing size of the professoriate forces it to seek more effective ways to exert collective pressure upon the employing institutions.

This pressure will inevitably lead to an upsurge of collective negotiations in higher education. Such negotiations are advocated most vigorously by the AFT; however, professors typically do not desire identification with public school teachers or with organized labor. The present interest in collective negotiations in higher education, despite its unattractive auspices, suggests that a breakthrough may be near. One good argreement, negotiated at a moderately prestigious institution, could well set off a chain reaction that will affect a number of institutions in the near future.

In a 1967 vote at 18 state colleges in California, the combined faculties narrowly rejected a proposal for an exclusive bargaining agent (by 274 votes out of 5,756). Indeed, had eligibility to vote been determined on more rational grounds (administrators were permitted to vote on many campuses), it is quite possible that the proposal would have carried. As it was, the proposal carried in four of the six largest institutions in the state college system.

These changes will inevitably result in organizational realignments and reorientations. At present, the organizational situation in higher education is extremely fluid. A crucial issue is whether the AAUP will modify its opposition to collective negotiations before rival organizations capitalize on such opposition on a large scale. The AFT, however, is not the main national threat to the AAUP. The AFT has too many handicaps in the organizational sweepstakes, and it may merge with the NEA within the next few years. The near future will provide the NEA with its greatest opportunities in higher education; much depends on the NEA's reactions to these opportunities.

In competing with the AAUP, the NEA has some important advantages as well as disadvantages. Most faculty members are in state-supported institutions, hence representation at the state level is essential. Nevertheless, the AAUP has never been organized effectively at the state level; there is not a single full-time leader of the AAUP at the state level. By contrast, the state associations of the NEA are well organized and could use such organization very effectively in a contest for professorial membership.

More importantly, the NEA has learned some invaluable lessons regarding faculty representation in the past few years. In the early 1960's, the NEA was adamantly opposed to collective negotiations through an exclusive representative. Today, the Association provides a broad spectrum of negotiating services for its state and local affiliates. The NEA has been through all of the arguments against collective negotiations—the Association advocated them to the point of disaster. It therefore has no illusions about the rhetoric of the current debate in higher education. Also, both NEA and AFT leaders have had invaluable experience in representation elections. They are far better equipped to conduct such elections than either the weak local chapters of the AAUP or its somnolescent national office.

The major handicap confronting the NEA would be the greater prestige of the AAUP in higher education. This handicap is substantial but not insuperable, provided the NEA were to make an all-out (and sophisticated) effort to organize professors. The Association may be too preoccupied with other problems to launch such an effort. If it is not, and if it does not delay until more realistic leadership emerges in the AAUP, it could become the majority organization in higher education in the United States. After all, less than one-third of all the professional personnel in higher education are AAUP members now. This reflects something less than smashing success in organizing professors.

Recent representation proceedings at the City University of New York City are equally significant. The City University includes over 10,000 faculty members on 17 constituent campuses, including the city's highly regarded city colleges. After protracted hearings, the New York State Public Employment Relations Board divided the faculty into two separate bargaining units. One unit consisted of faculty in tenured positions or positions leading to tenure; the other unit consisted of faculty holding part-time or other positions not leading to tenure status. The organizations seeking representation rights were the United Federation of College Teachers, a higher education affiliate of the AFT, and the Legislative Conference, a faculty organization not affiliated with any state or national faculty organization.

In the first election, the UFCT won bargining rights for 6,060 nontenured faculty. The vote was 1,634 for the UFCT, 731 for the Legislative Conference, and 350 for no bargaining agent. The result in the tenured unit was inconclusive. With 5,647 eligible to vote the Legislative Conference received 2,095 votes, the UFCT 1,680 votes, and no bargaining agent 656 votes. Subsequently, the Legislative Conference won the runoff election by a vote of 2,067 to 1,774. It appears, therefore, that the UFCT would have won bargaining rights for the entire faculty had there been only one bargaining unit. The low vote for no representation and the absence of an AAUP affiliate from the ballot are other noteworthy aspects of this election.

Recent developments in New Jersey are especially significant. In 1968, the New Jersey legislature enacted legislation providing rights for state and local public employees. In vetoing the bill, New Jersey's Governor Richard J. Hughes stated, "I have been asked by administrators and by organizations representing college professors to exclude faculty members from the coverage of this act so that the evolving pattern of college senates, in which elected representatives of faculties participate on an equal basis with college administrators in developing policy, not be impeded. In view of this apparent unanimity, I am recommending such an amendment." Nevertheless, the legislature overrode the governor's veto by substantial margins, so that professors in public institutions of higher education in New Jersey now have bargaining rights. In May, 1969, the New Jersey Education Association, which conducted a vigorous campaign to achieve bargaining rights for its local affiliates in the New Jersey public colleges, was designated as the bargaining agent by almost 80 percent of the total faculty in these institutions. Developments such as these indicate that we are on the verge of widespread changes in faculty representation systems.

In fact, the organizational situation in higher education today bears a striking similarity to an earlier situation in education below the college level. In 1961, the AFT was urging collective bargaining for public school teachers. The NEA and its affiliates, which enrolled most of the country's teachers, opposed it. The NEA's reasons were identical to those urged now by the AAUP. Collective negotiations was appropriate only in the industrial sector. Teachers dealt with persons and ideas, not inanimate objects. Since public education is not carried on for profit, and there are no profits to be divided, there is nothing to negotiate about. Collective negotiations is inconsistent with professional status. The relationships between teachers and administrators would be impaired by the advent of collective negotiations, which would replace a collegial and cooperative relationship with an adversary one. Strikes or the threat of strikes are an essential characteristic of collective negotiations; since strikes by professors (at least in public institutions) would be illegal, collective negotiations would be futile.

The NEA barely averted organizational catastrophe by its belief in these pronouncements and anathemas. When the need for a more effective representational system at the local level could no longer be avoided, except at the risk of losing hundreds of thousands of teachers to the AFT, the NEA embraced collective negotiations, albeit under its own label and with never a word to indicate that its previous opposition was misplaced. Today, persons not publicly committed to collective negotiations cannot realistically aspire to a top leadership position in the NEA; a few years ago, open support for negotiations would have destroyed a person's chances for Association leadership.

All of this experience, as well as the history of employment relations in the private and other public sectors, seems completely lost on the AAUP. Its leadership does not appear to take seriously the possibility that AAUP objections to collective negotiations may turn out to have as little merit as NEA objections to it in 1961. This view does not require any uncritical view of collective negotiations or insensitivity to real differences between higher education and other fields.

Collective negotiations, culminating in a contractual agreement which is binding on the parties to it, has certain advantages to employee groups. The very fact that such negotiations are virtually always an employee initiative certainly strengthens the presumption that there are some advantages to collective negotiations. Granted, collective negotiations also involves disadvantages which may outweigh the advantages. In that case, however, the critics should explicate these disadvantages. They should be able to identify the specific conditions in higher education which render negotiation inappropriate there; generalized appeals to the notion that "higher education is different" are not enough.

Most assuredly, professors do differ from steelworkers, airline pilots, doctors, lawyers, public school teachers, and sanitation workers, to mention just a few groups which negotiate collectively. But it could also be said of any one of these groups that they differ in some important respects from others which negotiate collectively. If opposition is to rise above the cliché level, it must focus upon specific differences which are relevant to the appropriateness of collective negotiations.

It is precisely at this point that the AAUP's opposition to collective negotiations through an exclusive representative falls short. For instance, to oppose collective negotiations on the ground that it would create an adversary process where none exists is a rather pitiful argument at this stage—one expects that faculty leaders would by now understand the distinction between recognizing a conflict of interest and creating one. Similarly, other AAUP policy statements do not respond to the real issues; the Association's arguments ignore rather than respond to the basic issues in representation systems. As much as anything, its failure to confront the issues indicates that the AAUP will experience severe strains in the immediate future.

One of the most striking illustrations of the AAUP's failure to understand the issues is its policy toward legislation authorizing collective negotiations in institutions of higher education. The AAUP opposes "legislation imposing upon faculty members in higher education the principle of exclusive representation derived from models of industrial collective bargaining." As a practical matter, no one has proposed legislation that would "impose" collective bargaining on a faculty; the latter need only vote for no representative to avoid this outcome. But to oppose legislation that would authorize faculties to decide for themselves whether they want to bargain collectively is another matter.

It is doubtful whether the vast majority of AAUP members realize fully what the AAUP is doing, both in its stated policies and in the activities of its staff associates. In effect, the AAUP supports any kind of representation system except collective bargaining as long as it is chosen by the faculty; the collective bargaining alternative is so bad, however, that faculties must not be permitted to choose it.

I do not believe that the AAUP can or should survive if it adheres to this policy for very long. The NEA learned through bitter experience that it could not actively oppose the right of teachers to negotiate collectively while simultaneously urging them to vote for NEA affiliates in representation elections to choose an exclusive representative. It will be interesting to see how long it takes the AAUP to learn the same lesson.

Footnotes

1. For example, see Archie R. Dykes, *Faculty Participation in Academic Decision Making* (Washington, D.C.: American Council on Education, 1968). In a sense, the reports of Committee A of the American Association of University Professors often constitute case studies of academic senates, or of other types of faculty representational systems.

2. Labor Management Relations Act, 1947, Sec. 8 (d).

3. For a more detailed analysis of collective bargaining as well as the other representational systems discussed in this paper, see Myron Lieberman and Michael H. Moskow, *Collective Negotiations for Teachers* (Chicago: Rand McNally & Company, 1966).

4. "Policy on Representation of Economic Interests," *AAUP Bulletin*, Vol. 54, No. 2 (June, 1968), pp. 152-53.

5. *Ibid.*, p. 153.

6. American Association of University Professors, American Council on Education, and the Association of Governing Boards of Universities and Colleges, *1966 Statement on Government of Colleges and Universities*, in Louis Joughin (ed.), *Academic Freedom and Tenure*, a Handbook of the American Association of University Professors (Madison, Wis.: University of Wisconsin Press, 1967), p. 98.

7. *Faculty Participation in Academic Governance*, Report of the Task Force on Faculty Representation and Academic Negotiations (Washington, D.C.: American Association for Higher Education, 1967).

8. *Ibid.*, p. 39.

9. Bertram H. Davis, "Unions and Higher Education: Another View," *Educational Record*, Vol. 49, Spring 1968, p. 144. The fact that an individual can become the full-time executive officer of the AAUP while denying that professors are employees surely has some implications for the effectiveness of the AAUP as an employee organization.

10. The proposed contract is available from the New York State AFT College and University Council, 300 Park Avenue, New York, N.Y. 10010.

UNIONS AND HIGHER EDUCATION

Harry A. Marmion

A growing restiveness among public school teachers in certain
urban areas and the rise of unionism among them in some of the
nation's largest cities is by now familiar news in educational circles.
The summer's discontent of 1967 stretched into the autumn in such
places as New York City, Chicago, and Detroit, where strikes closed
schools. In late September of 1967, a spokesman for the union
movement in California said, "Collective bargaining by teachers and
boards is no longer coming. It is here. . . . The question which now
faces the Board of Trustees is whether it will come peacefully or with
travail." Although there is nothing particularly notable about this
statement *per se*, the fact that it was made by a professor in his dual
role as President of the American Federation of Teachers College
Council and referred to the state colleges of California and not to
public schools should cause it to elicit the concern of college and
university officials.

Too many college administrators and trustees think the issue is
confined to the elementary and secondary levels, but the problem is
theirs as well. A new labor organization affiliated with the AFL-CIO,
the Council on Scientific, Professional and Cultural Employees
(SPACE), was founded in Washington in March 1967, and plans to
push the organization of white collar professionals who, together
with public employees and service industries' employees, are now the
largest portion of a labor force heretofore considered unorganiz-
able.[1] The prominent trade unionist, Mr. Gus Tyler, writes that the

From the *Educational Record,* Winter 1968, pp. 41-48. Reprinted by permission
of the American Council on Education.

"professional associations" in the teaching professions are already unions in all but name, although educational associations cling desperately to clichés of the past when defining terms in the delicate area of collective bargaining. At the 1967 annual meeting of the AAUP in Cleveland, however, a vocal minority of union-oriented delegates were present. It is easy to overestimate the strength of a movement when a minority makes its voice heard out of proportion to its size, but the voice was there, and it came through loud and clear. The Association, after skirmishes with the union group on several issues, voted to refer to a special committee for consideration a resolution supporting the right of faculty to organize to protect group interests, or to join existing unions for such purposes, which would include the right to strike.

The history of teacher unionism follows the general development of unions in America. In 1897, the first teachers' union was formed in Chicago; in 1916, the American Federation of Teachers (AFT) was organized and the previously unaffiliated local groups became part of a national organization; in 1919, the AFT received a national charter from the American Federation of Labor. During the depression, teacher union membership grew from 7,000 in 1930 to 32,000 in 1939. This growth was exactly the opposite to the trends in general union membership at this time. In the post-World War II period of teacher militancy, union membership increased from 37,000 members at the end of the war to approximately 140,000 at the present time. The unions now comprise primarily teachers located in urban areas, with over 40,000 members in New York City.

The expansion of teacher unionism into higher education has developed very rapidly, for until the 1960's there was little known activity in this realm. In 1966, the AFT initiated an organizational change that clearly indicated the significance which the national union attaches to the recruiting of college faculty members. A separate college division having its own staff and separate college locals was formed. Until then, a college faculty member interested in joining a teachers' union had been forced by the organizational structure to join a local whose membership was composed of teachers from the kindergarten to the college level. There are now at least 70 separate college locals in the country, most of them in New York, California, Illinois, and Michigan.

Of the more than 300,000 college faculty members, approximately 10,000 now belong to unions. The AAUP has a membership of about 85,000. More than two-thirds of the total faculty population have yet to make a choice. It seems safe to assume that some will join either organization, while others will not, preferring to give their sole loyalty to a particular discipline.

Signs of Movement

The forecast of collective bargaining by teachers in the state colleges in California before the end of the academic year is not unwarranted. Early in June 1967, the 18 state colleges in California narrowly turned down (by 274 votes out of 5,756 votes cast) a question regarding the selection of an exclusive bargaining agent for the state college system. A majority of faculty voting at four of the six largest institutions in the state college system in California favored the proposal. The unionists will probably proceed in California on an institution-by-institution basis, rather than attempt to force a state-wide referendum—unsuccessfully tried last summer. In October 1966, the Board of Trustees of the California State Colleges passed a resolution rejecting the concept of collective bargaining as it applies to faculty within the California system. In Illinois the Chicago Junior Colleges Union, after a three-day strike, secured a collective bargaining agreement that, in their words, is "probably the most comprehensive union contract for college teachers in the nation." Similar examples occurred in New York and other places. Although the list is not long, it does indicate a rising trend.

Increased group action by the nation's teachers has various causes. In the public schools, issues revolve around salary schedules, fringe benefits, and work conditions. At the college level, economic security is a major factor. The real unrest, however, lies in the following areas: first, the inability of any one faculty organization to assert significant leadership; second, the status and degree of future financial support for both public and private higher education; third, the question of institutional policy making. In public institutions there is concern over the increasing layers of external control—by state-wide systems, master plans, chancellor policies, interstate compacts, and other similar arrangements and relationships. These general issues are compounded by the growth of educational institutions, the increased numbers of students, and the rapid creation of new institutions, particularly junior colleges. Increased student militancy adds a further element of uneasiness.

Specific Stances

With respect to academic freedom, *the union* strenuously opposes all loyalty and disclaimer oaths for faculty and students. It makes no distinction between secular and denominational colleges in dealing with issues concerning freedom to teach, engage in research, and publish in accordance with individual professional conscience. This position differs from that of the AAUP which allows certain limitations on academic freedom, particularly with regard to the teaching of controversial subjects by church-related institutions. The AAUP feels that as long as these limitations are clearly spelled out, it is within the province of a church-related institution to impose special restrictions on its faculty.

On academic tenure, the union holds that tenure status be conferred upon any full-time staff member not more than three years after initial appointment. In general, the AAUP position provides for a maximum of seven years before tenure is granted. The union is also concerned about the mechanics of the tenure procedure to a far greater degree than is the AAUP. It wants the institution to establish written evaluations of performance that would be available to the faculty member concerned; to submit written reasons for non-re-appointment, and to provide the opportunity for a written answer from the faculty member concerned. The AAUP, on the other hand, leaves the formalities of the tenure process to the particular institution, within a framework of acceptable practices.

Among other provisions, the union wants to do away with the rank of instructor. Faculty salaries should start at $10,000 a year and be increased by annual increments to $30,000. It is against the use of merit systems of payment, based on criteria developed by the individual institution—publications, research, grants, etc. Under the union proposal, salary schedules would be made public, and no salary privately negotiated between a faculty member and the administration. All promotions should be tied to salary increases. Once a faculty member reaches the top salary range of one academic rank, he is promoted to the next rank and to the new salary schedule during the next academic year. The union also supports sabbaticals every eighth year with full pay.

The AAUP, which pioneered the report on "The Economic Status of the Profession," supports the goal of President Eisenhower's Committee on Education Beyond the High School, which in 1957 called for the doubling of faculty salaries in the next decade. The AAUP has never, however, specified minimum or maximum salary levels, and it has never called for the abolition of the rank of instructor. It is a fact, though, that the rank of instructor is diminishing within the teaching profession because many of the duties of that position have, in some institutions, been taken over by graduate teaching assistants and part-time faculty. Finally, the AAUP position on promotions and salary increments is the traditional one accepted by most institutions and faculty members throughout the country—that of letting the institutions set up their own rules. The AAUP does not advocate automatic promotions but it believes that promotion should be granted only after deliberation by departmental chairmen, departmental colleagues, and appropriate administrators. In turn, merit increments should be granted according to whatever criteria have been established by the institution in consultation with the faculty.

Working Conditions

The union has a great deal to say about the formal and informal working conditions that should prevail in colleges and universities. It advocates undergraduate teaching loads not exceeding nine hours per week, and teaching loads of six hours per week for graduate faculty. It seeks uniform personnel policies, records of which are kept in writing and made available to the faculty member in question. It also advocates the election of departmental chairmen for definite terms by members of departments, and it favors regulating many other specific details concerning working conditions, such as adequate secretarial help, parking facilities, and the like. On some of these matters, the AAUP takes no position, preferring not to interfere in the internal operations of colleges and universities.

The unionists say they do not desire a closed shop, or a union shop, representing instead the individual rights of faculty members regarding membership. Once a collective bargaining representative is selected and agreed to by the institution, however, the position of the individual faculty member becomes meaningless because others will bargain for him. The unionist position is that faculty salaries and other conditions of employment—such as tenure and working conditions—should be attained through the collective bargaining process, leading to a written contract. It contends there is no other process that will enable them to redress the imbalance between the individual employed professional and the administration or governing body of an institution. It further states that the right to strike is a part of any collective bargaining agreement, although it should not be exercised except under the most extreme of circumstances. What are considered by the union to be extreme circumstances are not spelled out. The AAUP position on this matter is well known. Not a union, it fundamentally rejects the employer-employee relationship upon which the concept of trade unionism rests.

In a recent interview, Dr. Israel Kugler, President of Local 1460 of the United Federation of College Teachers in New York City, and an official of the new college union organization formed by the AFT, made several distinctions concerning the union position. On the question of salary adjustments or what are commonly called "merit increases," he indicated that some faculty members may get more than across-the-board increases. He cited as examples theatrical unions, newspaper unions, and television unions, in which certain "stars" receive more money than the rank-and-file members of the union. He felt a two-track system might be in order—one track of annual increments, the other above that level for merit. Kugler also admitted that the three-year tenure proposal of the teacher union may be extreme. He felt, however, that the weight of the argument was in favor of the three-year period because tenure is very intimately tied to the concept of academic freedom. To keep a faculty member in an insecure position, sometimes exceeding seven years, is a serious limitation on his right to speak out and be heard on controversial issues. Dr. Kugler was also quick to distinguish between conditions of work and the overall policy of the university. He argued strongly that the union was trying to determine work conditions, and did not seek to control the internal operations of an institution. This last point would most assuredly be debated by college administrators and trustees.

The union position is clear. The primary thrust is for increased salaries, better working conditions, the abolition of traditional methods of promotion, tenure, individual salary negotiations, and for salary increments based on a merit formula. If it is hard to visualize the triumph of unionism, it is well to remember that few foresaw, as recently as five years ago the present degree of militancy on the part of public school teachers and college students.

A Flexible Approach

Union organizers face difficulties. Currently, the strength of the union is in a few large metropolitan areas that have unique problems. Also, the past history of the union reveals little indication of any real understanding of the problems facing faculty in institutions of higher education. There is no indication that faculty members in general favor the union approach. The formation of a separate college division within the teachers' union indicates a recognition of this problem. But this move also indicates by its attempt to counteract weaknesses that the union has the organizational flexibility to facilitate change.

Much has been recently written on which segments of higher education are most susceptible to union encroachment. The June 1967 issue of *College Management* published the results of a questionnaire concerning college faculty unions. Over 90 percent of administrators questioned, in all segments of higher education, see unions on the horizon. The most exhaustive study of the subject thus far was done by a task force of the American Association of Higher Education.[2] The results confirm a widely-held belief about which segments of higher education will first be affected. Based on visitations to 34 institutions in all parts of the country, the task force concluded that junior colleges and former teachers colleges will be the most fertile institutions for union activity.

The analysis that follows must include generalizations. There will, of course, be exceptions to any general rule; so it should be made clear that not all institutions within any one segment will be affected.

Institutional Tensions

One can probably accurately predict that junior colleges will be the first significant battleground between unions and educators. The battle, in fact, has already begun in some states. All eight junior colleges in the Chicago system went on strike in December 1966. Many junior college faculty members are former public school teachers who have had experience with the bureaucratic control of school administrators and school boards, and some have also had experience with unions. The rapid growth of the junior college movement and the diversity of educational offerings within the junior colleges have thrust this movement squarely into higher education. Further, as the number of junior colleges has increased throughout the nation, systems of control have changed from local boards to district or statewide bases, thus weakening the on-campus or local community control of these institutions. Thus external authority, coupled with the junior college faculty's desire for the traditional academic status of college faculty, creates tension, unrest, and—in some cases—militant action.

The evolution of former normal schools to teachers colleges and now to multi-purpose institutions that provide educational opportunities in both teacher preparation and the liberal arts, has also created tensions which may give rise to increased faculty militancy and to possible union activity. The tensions come in part as a result of faculty divisions within the institutions. The new faculty, primarily schooled in subject matter disciplines, are hired to develop and enlarge the liberal arts curriculum, and at many institutions, this expansion comes at the expense of teacher preparation programs. Because the traditions of these institutions are still rooted in teacher education, the number of non-education majors is often small at first and may never reach a large proportion of student enrollment. Thus, newer faculty may have fewer contact hours and may teach fewer students. This uneven state of affairs is worsened by the fact that the older faculty are more apt to accept rigid administrative control. The newer faculty—in most cases, younger men and women—are self-consciously aware of faculty prerogative in matters of normal academic concern.

Finally, one may suspect (although the suspicion is not widely shared by others studying this issue) that certain church-related institutions that previously have been tightly controlled will face similar problems. St. John's University is an example of a situation in which union activity thrived as a result of administrative intransigence Laymen teaching in church-related schools usually have only the option to leave if they feel the institution is curtailing their academic freedom or if they are otherwise unsatisfied. The role of the layman in Catholic institutions, however, is changing. One vehicle in facilitating this process of change could be a resort to faculty unions.

An element common to all three of these segments of higher education—the junior colleges, the transitional normal schools, and the church-related colleges—is the lack of a deeply rooted system for faculty participation in decision making concerning the educational functions of the institution. Most junior colleges, newest members of the higher education community, have not been in existence long enough to develop patterns of shared responsibility for decision making. The emerging multi-purpose institutions have problems similar to those of the junior colleges. In the past, they have been basically administered without significant faculty participation. Now there is the added problem of the cleavage between old and new elements on the faculty. Historically, most church-related colleges have not needed to be concerned about faculty participation in administration because of the reticence of faculty members to become involved in educational decision making. In many places, however, this situation no longer holds and more and more lay faculty members desire full participation in the educational enterprise.

The Contestants

The one professional organization traditionally recognized as performing a national role in matters of educational concern has been the AAUP. This is not to say that on every campus the AAUP chapter speaks for the faculty, but to acknowledge that it is an organization to be reckoned with on at least some general matters of interest to faculties. The college faculty drive of the AFT is directly challenging the 85,000-member AAUP. It is challenging it not only for individual faculty membership, but more importantly, because the union is seeking to become the established voice of the faculty in dealing with administrators and boards of trustees on matters of educational policy as well as on salary negotiation.

In a contest with the union, the AAUP faces problems. In the late 1950's, "an objective observer would say that the AAUP was Committee A"[3]—the Academic Freedom and Tenure Committee. Although it has a wide range of committees working in various areas, the Association is still best known for its efforts in the areas of academic freedom and tenure. The censure of institutions not conforming to the standards set by the Association as judged by an investigatory committee has been in general an effective deterrent to arbitrary action by administrators. The unionists say the AAUP functions in a highly centralized manner. They are also critical of the organizational structure of the Association.[4] They cite as an example the recent action at the AAUP national meeting, which, through Committee A, reversed a decision by the local chapter at the University of Arizona, requesting by formal vote that the censure status of the institution be continued.[5] The AAUP feels that the action to remove censure was taken only after extended deliberation and after significant improvements had occurred at the University of Arizona.

"Community of Scholars"

A decade ago, the Association instituted the self-grading salary survey, which has been a highlight of its activity and a widely heralded enterprise in the academic profession. Regarding administrative relationships, the Association has taken the traditional position set forth by retiring General Secretary William Fidler in his address to the National Convention in Cleveland in 1967. He stated that the historic role of the AAUP, as a professional organization was one that views the institution as a "community of scholars" in which all faculty members participate in decision making in a democratic fashion.

"The community of scholars" approach was carried forward by the recently issued tripartite statement on the "Governance of Colleges and Universities." Formulated over a two-year period through the cooperation of the American Association of University Professors, the American Council on Education, and the Association of Governing Boards, this statement was formally endorsed by the AAUP National Convention in Cleveland in April 1967. Both the ACE and the AGB commended the document to their memberships as a significant step towards the clarification of the respective roles of the educational enterprise, spelling out (in necessarily general language) the shared responsibility for institutional control by a community of scholars, administrators, and trustees. Sharing of responsibility is advocated as an alternative to the adversary relationship that would prevail if the faculty segment of the academic community resorted to unionism.

A difficulty with the statement, aside from its generality, is that it has no real status or authority. There is also a question as to whether the document can accomplish its intended purposes, "to foster constructive, joint thought and action, both within the institutional structure and in protection of its integrity against improper intrusions"—while relegating the status of students to a cursory acknowledgement at the end of the statement. Representatives of the three organizations responsible for the tripartite statement are considering a further statement pertaining to an expanded student role in governance. There is no indication that this statement will be forthcoming in the immediate future. All the while, this question looms ever larger as the strident tones of student activism increase on campus after campus throughout the nation.

Where the Action Is

A few feel that the AAUP has the further problem of suffering from a diffusion of objectives resulting in confusion between the economic goals of the college teaching profession as exemplified by salary ratings and its more altruistic professional objective as exemplified by Committee A on Academic Freedom and Tenure.[6] The AAUP may need to decide whether to continue on the high road of professionalism or to go where "the action is," where the numbers are, and where many feel the future of higher education lies. If the Association continues to emphasize professionalism, it may become an association of established tenured faculty at generally prestigious institutions. If it chooses the latter approach, it will tend to become less professional and probably more militant, but it should survive as a viable institution. Its survival may include active participation on the part of the rapidly increasing junior college faculty. In the May 1965 issue of the *Bulletin,* there is evidence of the Association's wrestling with the problem of future membership. A minority recommendation argues against admitting junior college faculty into membership, the theory being that the AAUP was founded on a long-standing tradition of membership from institutions empowered to confer baccalaureate degrees.[7] It is obvious that if the AAUP seriously considered this recommendation regarding membership, the AFT would surely move into the breach and actively solicit junior college faculty membership. There are signs, however, that the opposite is true. In 1967, the AAUP elected a junior college member to its National Council. There is a former junior college faculty member on the professional staff of the Association in Washington, and at present, about 200 chapters of the AAUP are at junior colleges, containing a total of five to six thousand active members. This figure represents about 20 percent of the total chapters within the Association and about 6 percent of its membership.

It should be noted that in June of 1967, the National Education Association formally recognized a new professional organization to serve junior college faculties. This new body, called the National Faculty Association of Community and Junior Colleges, was developed in concert by NEA and the American Association for Higher Education. The acknowledged intention of this new organization is to give attention to the professional needs of the community college segment of American higher education.

Most of those studying the question of college faculty unionism are convinced that some type of effective faculty association will emerge on college campuses in the near future. Many also feel that some existing "professional associations" in education and in other fields are essentially unions in all but name. The proposed solutions are really already truisms. What is needed to present polarization into formal bargaining situations on a variety of issues is effective communication, both formal and informal, between faculty and administrations. The most viable means of formal communication will be some type of faculty body, democratically selected, and representing, as much as possible, the total faculty. Where such a formal group exists, it is identified by a variety of titles, e.g. faculty senate, faculty council, academic council, academic senate, or university council. It would seem that the administration should be represented on such a body by election and/or through *ad hoc* membership in a limited form. Duties, responsibilities, and policy-making functions of this formal body should be carefully spelled out. Obviously, policy should encompass only academic issues clearly within the competence of faculty to decide. The body should not become involved with details or focus on day-to-day administrative problems more readily handled by other mechanisms.

The committee system utilized throughout higher education also has a role to play in effective communications, although many in education wince when the subject of committees is discussed. Proliferation of committee work can be time-consuming and cumbersome, but it does allow interested faculty to become involved in the operation of an institution.

There are certain faculty organizations outside the formal institutional structure such as the AAUP and various other faculty associations that also provide important modes of communication. College and university administrators should take every opportunity to convey information to the various organizations present on the campus. It probably will be true that no single organization will truly represent the faculty, but the president and the administration should use all available means of communication to bring these organizations to the point at which they have the information needed to make independent judgments on matters of importance to the institution.

Informal communication is more difficult to describe. In general, it indicates an institutional atmosphere in which faculty members have access to information pertaining to the educational process. It means that administrative decisions are made after consultation with those likely to be vitally affected by the decisions. It calls for an atmosphere of mutual respect between faculty and administration. Problems of communication must be solved in a decentralized manner on an institution by institution basis. What works on one campus may not work on another. If for example, the local chapter of the AAUP does reflect the faculty constituency within one institution then it will be an important group with which the administration should work. A state-wide faculty association may not, however, provide the proper forum for meaningful communication because it is too far removed from the individual campus where the problems exist.

Senates and Bargaining

An institution with a strong faculty senate, democratically elected and functioning as a meaningful partner in the educational enterprise, will have no need for collective bargaining. Conversely, an institution that has no faculty senate or a weak faculty senate dominated by administrators, is an institution ripe for more militant action by the faculty. In the future, such militancy will probably include unions. It will not be enough for institutions to reiterate the fact that unions and collective bargaining mechanisms traditionally have no place in the college teaching profession. Viable alternatives must be provided. Effective lines of communication must be available to enable a community of scholars to share in educational decision making. If reform is not forthcoming, the results will be increased armslength dealing through the mechanism of collective bargaining. It could happen. If you don't believe it, watch California!

Footnotes

1. Gus Tyler, "Fresh Breezes in the Labor Movement," *New Republic*, May 20, 1967 (*156*), pp. 13-15.

2. *Faculty Participation in Academic Governance* (Washington: American Association for Higher Education, 1967), p. 67.

3. Walter P. Metzger, "The Origins of the Association," *AAUP Bulletin*, June 1965 (*51*), p. 236.

4. Israel Kugler, "The AAUP at the Crossroads," *Changing Education*, Spring 1966 (*1*), pp. 34-43.

5. "Report of Committee A, 1965-66, The University of Arizona," *AAUP Bulletin*, June 1966 (*52*), p. 125.

6. George Strauss, "The AAUP as a Professional Occupational Association," *Industrial Relations*, October 1965 (*1*), pp. 125-40.

7. *AAUP Bulletin*, May 1965 (*51*), pp. 202-04.

Part 4

The Student Revolution's Impact on Governance

THE SOURCES OF STUDENT DISSENT

Kenneth Keniston

The apparent upsurge of dissent among American college students is one of the more puzzling phenomena in recent American history. Less than a decade ago, commencement orators were decrying the "silence" of college students in the face of urgent national and international issues; but in the past two or three years, the same speakers have warned graduating classes across the country against the dangers of unreflective protest, irresponsible action and unselective dissent. Rarely in history has apparent apathy been replaced so rapidly by publicized activism, silence by strident dissent.

This "wave" of dissent among American college students has been much discussed. Especially in the mass media—popular magazines, newspapers and television—articles of interpretation, explanation, depreciation and occasionally applause have appeared in enormous numbers. More important, from the first beginnings of the student civil rights movement, social scientists have been regular participant-observers and investigators of student dissent. There now exists a considerable body of research that deals with the characteristics and settings of student dissent (see 37; 5, forthcoming; 21; 50 for summaries of this research). To be sure, most of these studies are topical (centered around a particular protest or demonstration), and some of the more extensive studies are still in varying stages of incompletion. Yet enough evidence has already been gathered to

From the *Journal of Social Issues*, Vol. 23, No. 3, July 1967, pp. 108-137. Reprinted by permission of the Society for the Psychological Study of Social Issues and the author.

permit tentative generalizations about the varieties, origins and future of student dissent in the nineteen sixties.

In the remarks to follow, I will attempt to gather together this evidence (along with my own research and informal observations) to provide tentative answers to three questions about student dissent today. First, what is the nature of student dissent in American colleges? Second, what are the sources of the recent "wave of protest" by college students? And third, what can we predict about the future of student dissent?

Two Varieties of Dissent

Dissent is by no means the dominant mood of American college students. Every responsible study or survey shows apathy and privatism far more dominant than dissent (see, for example, 44; 20; 51; 49; 5, forthcoming). On most of our twenty two hundred campuses, student protest, student alienation and student unrest are something that happens elsewhere, or that characterizes a mere handful of "kooks" on the local campus. However we define "dissent," overt dissent is relatively infrequent and tends to be concentrated largely at the more selective, "progressive," and "academic" colleges and universities in America. Thus, Peterson's study of student protests (49) finds political demonstrations concentrated in the larger universities and institutions of higher academic calibre, and almost totally absent at teachers colleges, technical institutes and non-academic denominational colleges. And even at the colleges that gather together the greatest number of dissenters, the vast majority of students—generally well over 95%—remain interested onlookers or opponents rather than active dissenters. Thus, whatever we say about student dissenters is said about a very small minority of America's six million college students. At most colleges, dissent is not visible at all.

Partly because the vast majority of American students remain largely uncritical of the wider society, fundamentally conformist in behavior and outlook, and basically "adjusted" to the prevailing collegiate, national and international order, the small minority of dissenting students is highly visible to the mass media. As I will argue later, such students are often distinctively talented; they "use" the mass media effectively; and they generally succeed in their goal of making themselves and their causes highly visible. Equally important, student dissenters of all types arouse deep and ambivalent feelings in non-dissenting students and adults—envy, resentment, admiration, repulsion, nostalgia and guilt. Such feelings contribute both to the selective over-attention dissenters receive and to the often distorted perceptions and interpretations of them and their activities. Thus, there has developed through the mass media and the imaginings of adults a more or less stereotyped—and generally incorrect—image of the student dissenter.

The Stereotyped Dissenter

The "stereotypical" dissenter as popularly portrayed is both a Bohemian and political activist. Bearded, be-Levi-ed, long-haired, dirty and unkempt, he is seen as profoundly disaffected from his society, often influenced by "radical" (Marxist, Communist, Maoist, or Castroite) ideas, an experimenter in sex and drugs, unconventional in his daily behavior. Frustrated and unhappy, often deeply maladjusted as a person, he is a "failure" (or as one U.S. Senator put it, a "reject"). Certain academic communities like Berkeley are said to act as "magnets" for dissenters, who selectively attend colleges with a reputation as protest centers. Furthermore, dropouts or "non-students" who have failed in college cluster in large numbers around the fringes of such colleges, actively seeking pretexts for protest, refusing all compromise and impatient with ordinary democratic processes.

According to such popular analyses, the sources of dissent are to be found in the loss of certain traditional American virtues. The "breakdown" of American family life, high rates of divorce, the "softness" of American living, inadequate parents, and, above all, overindulgence and "spoiling" contribute to the prevalence of dissent. Brought up in undisciplined homes by parents unsure of their own values and standards, dissenters channel their frustration and anger against the older generation, against all authority, and against established institutions.

Similar themes are sometimes found in the interpretations of more scholarly commentators. "Generational conflict" is said to underly the motivation to dissent, and a profound "alienation" from American society is seen as a factor of major importance in producing protests. Then, too, such factors as the poor quality and impersonality of American college education, the large size and lack of close student-faculty contact in the "multiversity" are sometimes seen as the latent or precipitating factors in student protests, regardless of the manifest issues around which students are organized. And still other scholarly analysts, usually men now disillusioned by the radicalism of the 1930's, have expressed fear of the dogmatism, rigidity and "authoritarianism of the left" of today's student activists.

Activism and Alienation

These stereotyped views are, I believe, incorrect in a variety of ways. They confuse two distinct varieties of student dissent; equally important, they fuse dissent with maladjustment. There are, of course, as many forms of dissent as there are individual dissenters; and any effort to counter the popular stereotype of the dissenter by pointing to the existence of distinct "types" of dissenters runs the risk of oversimplifying at a lower level of abstraction. Nonetheless, it seems to me useful to suggest that student dissenters generally fall somewhere along a continuum that runs between two ideal types—first, the political activist or protester, and second, the withdrawn, culturally alienated student.

The activist. The defining characteristic of the "new" activist is his participation in a student demonstration or group activity that concerns itself with some matter of general political, social or ethical principle. Characteristically, the activist feels that some injustice has been done, and attempts to "take a stand," "demonstrate" or in some fashion express his convictions. The specific issues in question range from protest against a paternalistic college administration's actions to disagreement with American Vietnam policies, from indignation at the exploitation of the poor to anger at the firing of a devoted teacher, from opposition to the Selective Service laws which exempt him but not the poor to—most important—outrage at the deprivation of the civil rights of other Americans.

The initial concern of the protester is almost always immediate, ad hoc and local. To be sure, the student who protests about one issue is likely to feel inclined or obliged to demonstrate his convictions on other issues as well (17). But whatever the issue, the protester rarely demonstrates because his *own* interests are jeopardized, but rather because he perceives injustices being done to *others* less fortunate than himself. For example, one of the apparent paradoxes about protests against current draft policies is that the protesting students are selectively drawn from that subgroup *most* likely to receive student deferments for graduate work. The basis of protest is a general sense that the selective service rules and the war in Vietnam are unjust to others with whom the student is identified, but whose fate he does not share. If one runs down the list of "causes" taken up by student activists, in rare cases are demonstrations directed at improving the lot of the protesters themselves; identification with the oppressed is a more important motivating factor than an actual sense of immediate personal oppression.

The anti-ideological stance of today's activists has been noted by many commentators. This distrust of formal ideologies (and at times of articulate thought) makes it difficult to pinpoint the positive social and political values of student protesters. Clearly, many current American political institutions like de facto segregation are opposed; clearly, too, most students of the New Left reject careerism and familism as personal values. In this sense, we might think of the activist as (politically) "alienated." But this label seems to me more misleading than illuminating, for it overlooks the more basic *commitment* of most student activists to other ancient, traditional and credal American values like free speech, citizen's participation in decision-making, equal opportunity and justice. In so far as the activist rejects all or part of "the power structure," it is because current political realities fall so far short of the ideals he sees as central to the American creed. And in so far as he repudiates careerism and familism, it is because of his implicit allegiance to other human goals he sees, once again, as more crucial to American life. Thus, to emphasize the "alienation" of activists is to neglect their more basic allegiance to credal American ideals.

One of these ideals is, of course, a belief in the desirability of political and social action. Sustained in good measure by the successes of the student civil rights movement, the protester is usually convinced that demonstrations are effective in mobilizing public opinion, bringing moral or political pressure to bear, demonstrating the existence of his opinions, or, at times, in "bringing the machine to a halt." In this sense, then, despite his criticisms of existing political practices and social institutions, he is a political optimist. Moreover, the protester must believe in at least minimal organization and group activity; otherwise, he would find it impossible to take part, as he does, in any organized demonstrations or activities. Despite their search for more truly "democratic" forms of organization and action (e.g., participatory democracy), activists agree that group action is more effective than purely individual acts. To be sure, a belief in the value and efficacy of political action is not equivalent to endorsement of prevalent political institutions or forms of action. Thus, one characteristic of activists is their search for new forms of social action, protest and political organization (community organization, sit-ins, participatory democracy) that will be more effective and less oppressive than traditional political institutions.

The culturally alienated. In contrast to the politically optimistic, active, and socially-concerned protester, the culturally alienated student is far too pessimistic and too firmly opposed to "the System" to wish to demonstrate his disapproval in any organized public way.[1] His demonstrations of dissent are private: through nonconformity of behavior, ideology and dress, through personal experimentation and above all through efforts to intensify his own subjective experience, he shows his distaste and disinterest in politics and society. The activist attempts to change the world around him, but the alienated student is convinced that meaningful change of the social and political world is impossible; instead, he considers "dropping out" the only real option.

Alienated students tend to be drawn from the same general social strata and colleges as protesters. But psychologically and ideologically their backgrounds are often very different. Alienated students are more likely to be disturbed psychologically; and although they are often highly talented and artistically gifted, they are less committed to academic values and intellectual achievement than are protesters. The alienated student's real campus is the school of the absurd, and he has more affinity for pessimistic existentialist ontology than for traditional American activism. Furthermore, such students usually find it psychologically and ideologically impossible to take part in organized group activities for any length of time, particularly when they are expected to assume responsiblities for leadership. Thus, on the rare occasions when they become involved in demonstrations, they usually prefer peripheral roles, avoid responsibilities and are considered a nuisance by serious activists (9).

Whereas the protesting student is likely to accept the basic political and social values of his parents, the alienated student almost always rejects his parents' values. In particular, he is likely to see his father as a man who has "sold out" to the pressures for success and status in American society: he is determined to avoid the fate that overtook his father. Toward their mothers, however, alienated students usually express a very special sympathy and identification. These mothers, far from encouraging their sons towards independence and achievement, generally seem to have been over-solicitous and limiting. The most common family environment of the alienated-student-to-be consists of a parental schism supplemented by a special mother-son alliance of mutual understanding and maternal control and depreciation of the father (25a).

In many colleges, alienated students often constitute a kind of hidden underground, disorganized and shifting in membership, in which students can temporarily or permanently withdraw from the ordinary pressures of college life. The alienated are especially attracted to the hallucinogenic drugs like marijuana, mescalin and LSD, precisely because these agents combine withdrawal from ordinary social life with the promise of greatly intensified subjectivity and perception. To the confirmed "acid head," what matters is intense, drug-assisted perception; the rest—including politics, social action and student demonstrations—is usually seen as "role-playing."[2]

The recent and much-publicized emergence of "hippie" subcultures in several major cities and increasingly on the campuses of many selective and progressive colleges illustrates the overwhelmingly apolitical stance of alienated youth. For although hippies oppose war and believe in inter-racial living, few have been willing or able to engage in anything beyond occasional peace marches or apolitical "human be-ins." Indeed, the hippies's emphasis on immediacy, "love" and "turning-on," together with his basic rejection of the traditional values of American life, innoculates him against involvement in long-range activist endeavors, like education or community organization, and even against the sustained effort needed to plan and execute demonstrations or marches. For the alienated hippie, American society is beyond redemption (or not worth trying to redeem); but the activist, no matter how intense his rejection of specific American policies and practices, retains a conviction that his society can and should be changed. Thus, despite occasional agreement in principle between the alienated and the activists, cooperation in practice has been rare, and usually ends with activists accusing the alienated of "irresponsibility," while the alienated are confirmed in their view of activists as moralistic, "up-tight," and "un-cool."

Obviously, no description of a type ever fits an individual perfectly. But by this rough typology, I mean to suggest that popular stereotypes which present a unified portrait of student dissent are gravely oversimplified. More specifically, they confuse the politically pessimistic and socially uncommitted alienated student with the politically hopeful and socially committed activist. To be sure, there are many students who fall between these two extremes, and some of them alternate between passionate search for intensified subjectivity and equally passionate efforts to remedy social and political injustices. And as I will later suggest, even within the student movement, one of the central tensions is between political activism and cultural alienation. Nonetheless, even to understand this tension we must first distinguish between the varieties of dissent apparent on American campuses.

Furthermore, the distinction between activist and alienated students as psychological types suggests the incompleteness of scholarly analyses that see social and historical factors as the only forces that "push" a student toward one or the other of these forms of dissent. To be sure, social and cultural factors are of immense importance in providing channels for the expression (or suppression) of dissent, and in determining *which* kinds of dissenters receive publicity, censure, support or ostracism in any historical period. But these factors cannot, in general, change a hippie into a committed activist, nor a SNCC field worker into a full-time "acid-head." Thus, the prototypical activist of 1966 is not the "same" student as the prototypical student bohemian of 1956, but is rather the politically aware but frustrated, academically oriented "privatist" of that era. Similarly, as I will argue below, the most compelling alternative to most activists is not the search for kicks or sentience but the quest for scholarly competence. And if culturally-sanctioned opportunities for the expression of alienation were to disappear, most alienated students would turn to private psychopathology rather than to public activism.

Stated more generally, historical forces do not ordinarily transform radically the character, values and inclinations of an adult in later life. Rather, they thrust certain groups forward in some eras and discourage or suppress other groups. The recent alternation in styles of student dissent in America is therefore not to be explained so much by the malleability of individual character as by the power of society to bring activists into the limelight, providing them with the intellectual and moral instruments for action. Only a minority of potential dissenters fall close enough to the midpoint between alienation and activism so that they can constitute a "swing vote" acutely responsive to social and cultural pressures and styles. The rest, the majority, are characterologically committed to one or another style of dissent.

The Sources of Activism

What I have termed "alienated" students are by no means a new phenomenon in American life, or for that matter in industrialized societies. Bohemians, "beatniks" and artistically-inclined undergraduates who rejected middle-class values have long been a part of the American student scene, especially at more selective colleges; they constituted the most visible form of dissent during the relative

political "silence" of American students in the 1950's. What is
distinctive about student dissent in recent years is the unexpected
emergence of a vocal minority of politically and socially active
students.[3] Much is now known about the characteristics of such
students, and the circumstances under which protests are likely to be
mounted. At the same time, many areas of ignorance remain. In the
account to follow, I will attempt to formulate a series of general
hypotheses concerning the sources of student activism.[4]

It is abundantly clear that no single factor will suffice to explain
the increase of politically-motivated activities and protests on
American campuses. Even if we define an activist narrowly, as a
student who (a) acts together with others in a group, (b) is concerned
with some ethical, social, ideological or political issue, and (c) holds
liberal or "radical" views, the sources of student activism and protest
are complex and inter-related. At least four kinds of factors seem
involved in any given protest. First, the individuals involved must be
suitably predisposed by their personal backgrounds, values and
motivations. Second, the likelihood of protest is far greater in certain
kinds of educational and social settings. Third, socially-directed
protests require a special cultural climate, that is, certain distinctive
values and views about the effectiveness and meaning of demonstrations, and about the wider society. And finally, some historical
situations are especially conducive to protests.

The Protest-Prone Personality

A large and still-growing number of studies, conducted under
different auspices, at different times and about different students,
presents a remarkably consistent picture of the protest-prone
individual (1; 14; 15; 17; 18; 39; 56; 62; 63; 21; and 47). For
one, student protesters are generally outstanding students; the
higher the student's grade average, the more outstanding his
academic achievements, the more likely it is that he will become
involved in any given political demonstration. Similarly, student
activists come from families with liberal political values; a disproportionate number report that their parents hold views essentially
similar to their own, and accept or support their activities. Thus,
among the parents of protesters we find large numbers of liberal
Democrats, plus an unusually large scattering of pacifists, socialists,
etc. A disproportionate number of protesters come from Jewish
families; and if the parents of activists are religious, they tend to be
concentrated in the more liberal denominations—Reform Judaism,
Unitarianism, the Society of Friends, etc. Such parents are reported

to have high ethical and political standards, regardless of their actual religious convictions.

As might be expected of a group of politically liberal and academically talented students, a disproportionate number are drawn from professional and intellectual families of upper middle-class status. For example, compared with active student conservatives, members of protest groups tend to have higher parental incomes, more parental education, and less anxiety about social status (63). Another study finds that high levels of education distinguish the activist's family even in the grandparental generation (14). In brief, activists are not drawn from disadvantaged, status-anxious, under-priviledged or uneducated groups; on the contrary, they are selectively recruited from among those young Americans who have had the most socially fortunate upbringings.

Basic Value Commitments of Activists

The basic value commitments of the activist tend to be academic and non-vocational. Such students are rarely found among engineers, future teachers at teachers colleges, or students of business administration (see 59). Their over-all educational goals are those of a liberal education for its own sake, rather than specifically technical, vocational or professional preparation. Rejecting careerist and familist goals, activists espouse humanitarian, expressive and self-actualizing values. Perhaps because of these values, they delay career choice longer than their classmates (14). Nor are such students distinctively dogmatic, rigid or authoritarian. Quite the contrary, the substance and style of their beliefs and activities tends to be open, flexible and highly liberal. Their fields of academic specialization are nonvocational—the social sciences and the humanities. Once in college, they not only do well academically, but tend to persist in their academic commitments, dropping out *less* frequently than most of their classmates. As might be expected, a disproportionate number receive a B.A. within four years and continue on to graduate school, preparing themselves for academic careers.

Survey data also suggest that the activist is not distinctively dissatisfied with his college education. As will be noted below, activists generally attend colleges which provide the best, rather than the worst, undergraduate education available today. Objectively then, activists probably have less to complain about in their undergraduate educations than most other students. And subjectively as well, surveys show most activists, like most other American undergraduates, to be relatively well satisfied with their undergraduate educations (56; 30). Thus, dissatisfaction with educational failings of the "impersonal multiversity," however important as a rallying cry, does not appear to be a distinctive cause of activism.

In contrast to their relative satisfaction with the quality of their educations, however, activists *are* distinctively dissatisfied with what might be termed the "civil-libertarian" defects of their college administrations. While no doubt a great many American undergraduates distrust "University Hall," this distrust is especially pronounced amongst student protesters (30; 47). Furthermore, activists tend to be more responsible than other students to deprivations of civil rights on campus as well as off campus, particularly when political pressures seem to motivate on campus policies they consider unjust. The same responsiveness increasingly extends to issues of "student power": i.e., student participation and decisions affecting campus life. Thus, bans on controversial speakers, censorship of student publications, and limitations on off-campus political or social action are likely to insense the activist, as is arbitrary "administration without the consent of the administered." But it is primarily perceived injustice or the denial of student rights by the Administration—rather than poor educational quality, neglect by the faculty, or the impersonality of the multiversity—that agitates the activist.

Most studies of activists have concentrated on variables that are relatively easy to measure: social class, academic achievements, explicit values and satisfaction with college. But these factors alone will not explain activism: more students possess the demographic and attitudinal characteristics of the protest-prone personality than are actually involved in protests and social action programs. Situational, institutional, cultural and historical factors (discussed below), obviously contribute to "catalysing" a protest-prone personality into an actual activist. But it also seems that, within the broad demographic group so far defined, more specific psychodynamic factors contribute to activism.

Activists—Not in Rebellion

In speculating about such factors, we leave the ground of established fact and enter the terrain of speculation, for only a few studies have explored the personality dynamics and family constellation of the activist, and most of these studies are impressionistic and clinical (e.g. 6; 10; 9; 12; 15; 43; 53; 54; 55; 67). But certain facts are clear. As noted, activists are *not,* on the whole, repudiating or rebelling against explicit parental values and ideologies. On the contrary, there is some evidence that such students are living out their parents' values in practice; and one study suggests that activists may be somewhat *closer* to their parents' values than nonactivists (14). Thus, any simple concept of "generational conflict" or "rebellion against parental authority" is clearly oversimplified as applied to the motivations of most protesters.

Activists—Living Out Parental Values

It does seem probable, however, that many activists are concerned with *living out expressed but unimplemented parental values.* Solomon and Fishman (54), studying civil rights activists and peace marchers, argue that many demonstrators are "acting out" in their demonstrations the values which their parents explicitly believed, but did not have the courage or opportunity to practice or fight for. Similarly, when protesters criticize their fathers, it is usually over their fathers' failure to practice what they have preached to their children throughout their lives. Thus, in the personal background of the protester there is occasionally a suggestion that his father is less-than-"sincere" (and even at times "hypocritical") in his professions of political liberalism. In particular, both careerism and familism in parents are the objects of activist criticisms, the more so because these implicit goals often conflict with explicit parental values. And it may be that protesters receive both covert and overt support from their parents because the latter are secretly proud of their children's eagerness to implement the ideals they as parents have only given lip-service to. But whatever the ambivalences that bind parents with their activist children, it would be wrong to overemphasize them: what is most impressive is the solidarity of older and younger generations.

Activists—Family Structure

While no empirical study has tested this hypothesis, it seems probable that in many activist-producing families, the mother will have a dominant psychological influence on her son's development. I have already noted that the protester's cause is rarely himself, but rather alleviating the oppression of others. As a group, activists seem to possess an unusual *capacity for nurturant identification*—that is, for empathy and sympathy with the underdog, the oppressed and the needy. Such a capacity can have many origins, but its most likely source in upper-middle class professional families is identification with an active mother whose own work embodies nurturant concern for others. Flacks' finding that the mothers of activists are likely to be employed, often in professional or service roles like teaching and social work, is consistent with this hypothesis. In general in American society, middleclass women have greater social and financial freedom to work in jobs that are idealistically "fulfilling" as opposed to merely lucrative or prestigious. As a rule, then, in middle-class families, it is the mother who actively embodies in her life and work the humanitarian, social and political ideals that the father may share in principle but does not or cannot implement in his career.

Given what we know about the general characteristics of the families of protest-prone students, it also seems probable that the dominant ethos of their families is unusually equalitarian, permissive, "democratic," and highly individuated. More specifically, we might expect that these will be families where children talk back to their parents at the dinner table, where free dialogue and discussion of feelings is encouraged, and where "rational" solutions are sought to everyday family problems and conflicts. We would also expect that such families would place a high premium on self-expression and intellectual independence, encouraging their children to make up their own minds and to stand firm against group pressures. Once again, the mother seems the most likely carrier and epitome of these values, given her relative freedom from professional and financial pressures.

The contrast between such protest-prompting families and alienating families should be underlined. In both, the son's deepest emotional ties are often to his mother. But in the alienating family, the mother-son relationship is characterized by maternal control and intrusiveness, whereas in the protest-prompting family, the mother is a highly individuating force in her son's life, pushing him to independence and autonomy. Furthermore, the alienated student is determined to avoid the fate that befell his father, whereas the protesting student wants merely to live out the values that his father has not always worked hard enough to practice. Finally, the egalitarian, permissive, democratic and individuating environment of the entire family of the protester contrasts with the overcontrolling, over-solicitous attitude of the mother in the alienating family, where the father is usually excluded from major emotional life within the family.

These hypotheses about the family background and psychodynamics of the protester are speculative, and future research may prove their invalidity. But regardless of whether *these* particular speculations are correct, it seems clear that in addition to the general social, demographic and attitudinal factors mentioned in most research, more specific familial and psychodynamic influences contribute to protest-proneness.

The Protest-Promoting Institution

However we define his characteristics, one activist alone cannot make a protest: the characteristics of the college or university he attends have much to do with whether his protest-proneness will ever be mobilized into actual activism. Politically, socially and ideologically motivated demonstrations and activities are most likely to occur at certain types of colleges; they are almost unknown at a majority of campuses. The effects of institutional characteristics on protests have been studied by Cowan (8) and Peterson (49). . . .

In order for an organized protest or related activities to occur, there must obviously be sufficient *numbers* of protest-prone students to form a group, these students must have an opportunity for *interaction* with each other, and there must be *leaders* to initiate and mount the protest. Thus, we might expect—and we indeed find—that protest is associated with institutional size, and particularly with the congregation of large numbers of protest-prone students in close proximity to each other. More important than sheer size alone, however, is the "image" of the institution: certain institutions selectively recruit students with protest-prone characteristics. Specifically, a reputation for academic excellence and freedom, coupled with highly selective admissions policies, will tend to congregate large numbers of potentially protesting students on one campus. Thus, certain institutions do act as "magnets" for potential activists, but not so much because of their reputations for political radicalism as because they are noted for their academic excellence. Among such institutions are some of the most selective and "progressive" private liberal arts colleges, major state universities (like Michigan, California at Berkeley and Wisconsin) which have long traditions of vivid undergraduate teaching and high admissions standards (37) and many of the more prestigious private universities.

Once protest-prone students are on campus, they must have an opportunity to interact, to support one another, to develop common outlooks and shared policies—in short, to form an *activist subculture* with sufficient mass and potency to generate a demonstration or action program. Establishing "honors colleges" for talented and academically-motivated students is one particularly effective way of creating a "critical mass" of protest-prone students. Similarly, inadequate on-campus housing indirectly results in the development of off-campus protest-prone sub-cultures (e.g., co-op houses) in residences where student activists can develop a high degree of ideological solidarity and organizational cohesion.

But even the presence of a critical mass of protest-prone undergraduates in an activist sub-culture is not enough to make a protest without leaders and issues. And in general, the most effective protest leaders have not been undergraduates, but teaching assistants. The presence of large numbers of exploited, underpaid, disgruntled and frustrated teacher assistants (or other equivalent graduate students and younger faculty members) is almost essential for organized and persistent protest. For one, advanced students tend to be more liberal politically and more sensitive to political issues than are most undergraduates—partly because education seems to have a liberalizing effect, and partly because students who persist into graduate school tend to be more liberal to start than those who drop out or go elsewhere. Furthermore, the frustrations of graduate students, especially at very large public universities, make them particularly sensitive to general problems of injustice, exploitation and oppression. Teaching assistants, graduate students and young faculty members also tend to be in daily and prolonged contact with students, are close enough to them in age to sense their mood, and are therefore in an excellent position to lead and organize student protests. Particularly at institutions which command little institutional allegiance from large numbers of highly capable graduate students (37) will such students be found among the leaders of the protest movement.

The Issues of Protest

Finally, issues are a necessity. In many cases, these issues are provided by historical developments on the national or international scene, a point to which I will return. But in some instances, as at Berkeley, "on-campus" issues are the focus of protest. And in other cases, off-campus and on-campus issues are fused, as in the recent protests at institutional cooperation with draft board policies considered unjust by demonstrating students. In providing such on-campus issues, the attitude of the university administration is central. Skillful handling of student complaints, the maintenance of open channels of communication between student leaders and faculty members, and administrative willingness to resist public and political pressures in order to protect the rights of students—all minimize the likelihood of organized protest. Conversely, a university administration that shows itself unduly sensitive to political, legislative or public pressures, that treats students arrogantly, ineptly, condescendingly, hypocritically or above all dishonestly, is asking for a demonstration.

Thus one reason for the relative absence of on-campus student protests and demonstrations on the campuses of private, nondenominational "academic" colleges and universities (which recruit many protest-prone students) probably lies in the liberal policies of the administrations. As Cowan (8) notes, liberal students generally attend non-restrictive and "libertarian" colleges. Given an administration and faculty that supports or tolerates activism and student rights, student activists must generally find their issues off-campus. The same students, confronting an administration unduly sensitive to political pressures from a conservative board of regents or State legislature, might engage in active on-campus protests. There is also some evidence that clever administrative manipulation of student complaints, even in the absence of genuine concern with student rights, can serve to dissipate the potentialities of protest (22).

Among the institutional factors often cited as motivating student protest is the largeness, impersonality, atomization, "multiversitification" etc., of the university. I have already noted that student protesters do not seem distinctively dissatisfied with their educations. Furthermore, the outstanding academic achievements and intellectual motivations of activists concentrate them, within any college, in the courses and programs that provide the most "personal" attention: honors programs, individual instruction, advanced seminars, and so on. Thus, they probably receive relatively *more* individual attention and a *higher* calibre of instruction than do non-protesters. Furthermore, protests generally tend to occur at the best, rather than the worst colleges, judged from the point of view of the quality of undergraduate instruction. Thus, despite the popularity of student slogans dealing with the impersonality and irrelevance of the multiversity, the absolute level of educational opportunities seems, if anything, positively related to the occurrence of protest: the better the institution, the more likely demonstrations are.

Nor can today's student activism be attributed in any direct way to mounting academic pressures. To be sure, activism is most manifest at those selective colleges where the "pressure to perform" (26) is greatest, where standards are highest, and where anxieties about being admitted to a "good" graduate or professional school are most pronounced. But, contrary to the argument of Lipset and Altbach (37), the impact of academic pressure on activism seems negative rather than positive. Protest-prone students, with their superior academic attainments and strong intellectual commitments, seem especially vulnerable to a kind of academic professionalism that, because of the enormous demands it makes upon the student's energies, serves to cancel or preclude activism. Student demonstrations rarely take place during exam periods, and protests concerned with educational quality almost invariably seek an improvement of quality, rather than a lessening of pressure. Thus, though the pressure to perform doubtless affects *all* American students, it probably acts as a deterrent rather than a stimulus to student activism.

Deprivation of Expectations

What probably does matter, however, is the *relative* deprivation of student expectations. . . . A college that recruits large numbers of academically motivated and capable students into a less-than-first-rate education program, one that oversells entering freshmen on the virtues of the college, or one that reneges on implicit or explicit promises about the quality and freedom of education may well produce an "academic backlash" that will take the form of student protests over the quality of education. Even more important is the gap between expectations and actualities regarding freedom of student expression. Stern (57) has demonstrated that most entering freshmen have extremely high hopes regarding the freedom of speech and action they will be able to exercise during college: most learn the real facts quickly, and graduate thoroughly disabused of their illusions. But since activists, as I have argued above, are particularly responsive to these issues, they are apt to tolerate disillusion less lightly, and to take up arms to concretize their dashed hopes. Compared to the frustration engendered by disillusionment regarding educational quality, the relative deprivation of civil libertarian hopes seems a more potent source of protests. And with regard to both issues, it must be recalled that protests have been *fewest* at institutions of low educational quality and little freedom for student expression. Thus, it is not the absolute level either of educational quality or of student freedom that matters, but the gap between student hopes and institutional facts.

The Protest-Prompting Cultural Climate

Even if a critical mass of interacting protest-prone students forms in an institution that provides leadership and issues, student protests are by no means inevitable, as the quiescence of American students during the nineteen fifties suggests. For protests to occur, other more broadly cultural factors, attitudes and values must be present. Protest activities must be seen as meaningful acts, either in an instrumental or an expressive sense; and activists must be convinced that the consequences of activism and protest will not be overwhelmingly damaging to them. During the 1950's, one much-discussed factor that may have militated against student activism was the conviction that the consequences of protest (blacklisting, F.B.I. investigations, problems in obtaining security clearance, difficulties in getting jobs) were both harmful to the individual and yet extremely likely. Even more important was the sense on the part of many politically-conscious students that participation in left-wing causes would merely show their naiveté, gullibility and political innocence without furthering any worthy cause. The prevailing climate was such that protest was rarely seen as an act of any meaning or usefulness.

Academic Support

Today, in contrast, student protesters are not only criticized and excoriated by a large segment of the general public, but—more crucial—actively defended, encouraged, lionized, praised, publicized, photographed, interviewed and studied by a portion of the academic community. Since the primary reference group of most activists is not the general public, but rather that liberal segment of the academic world most sympathetic to protest, academic support has a disproportionate impact on protest-prone students' perception of their own activities. In addition, the active participation of admired faculty members in protests, teach-ins and peace marches, acts as a further incentive to students (23). Thus, in a minority of American colleges, sub-cultures have arisen where protest is felt to be both an important existential act—a dignified way of "standing up to be counted"—and an effective way of "bringing the machine to a halt," sometimes by disruptive acts (sit-ins, strikes, etc.), more often by calling public attention to injustice.

Universalism

An equally important, if less tangible "cultural" factor is the broad climate of social criticism in American society. As Parsons (45, 46), White (64), and others have noted, one of the enduring themes of American society is the pressure toward "universalism," that is, an increasing extension of principles like equality, equal opportunity, and fair protection of the law to all groups within the society (and in recent years, to all groups in the world). As affluence has increased in American society, impatience at the slow "progress" of non-affluent minority groups has also increased, not only among students, but among other segments of the population. Even before the advent of the student civil rights movement, support for racial segregation was diminishing. Similarly, the current student concern for the "forgotten fifth" was not so much initiated by student activists as it was taken up by them. In this regard student activists are both caught up in and in the vanguard of a new wave of extension of universalism in American society. Although the demands of student activists usually go far beyond the national consensus, they nonetheless reflect (at the same time that they have helped advance) one of the continuing trends in American social change.

A contrasting but equally enduring theme in American social criticism is a more fundamental revulsion against the premises of industrial—and now technological—society. Universalistic-liberal criticism blames our society because it has not yet extended its principles, privileges and benefits to all: the complaint is injustice and the goal is to complete our unfinished business. But alienated-romantic criticism questions the validity and importance of these same principles, privileges and benefits—the complaint is materialism and the goal is spiritual, aesthetic or expressive fulfillment. The tradition or revulsion against conformist, anti-aesthetic, materialistic, ugly, middle-class America runs through American writing from Melville through the "lost generation" to the "beat generation" and has been expressed concretely in the bohemian sub-cultures that have flourished in a few large American cities since the turn of the century. But today, the power of the romantic-alienated position has increased: one response to prosperity has been a more searching examination of the technological assumptions upon which prosperity has been based. Especially for the children of the upper middle-class, affluence is simply taken for granted, and the drive "to get ahead in the world" no longer makes sense for students who start out ahead. The meanings of life must be sought elsewhere, in art, sentience, philosophy, love, service to others, intensified experience, adventure —in short, in the broadly aesthetic or expressive realm.

Deviant Views

Since neither the universalistic nor the romantic critique of modern society is new, these critiques affect the current student generation not only directly but indirectly, in that they have influenced the way many of today's college students were raised. Thus, a few of today's activists are children of the "radicals of the 1930's" (37); and Flacks comments on the growing number of intellectual, professional upper middle-class families who have adopted "deviant" views of traditional American life and embodied these views in the practices by which they brought up their children. Thus, some of today's activists are the children of bohemians, college professors, etc. But in general, the explanation from parental "deviance" does not seem fully convincing. To be sure, the backgrounds of activists are "atypical" in a statistical sense, and thus might be termed empirically "deviant." It may indeed turn out that the parents of activists are distinguished by their emphasis on humanitarianism, intellectualism and romanticism, and by their lack of stress on moralism (14). But it is obvious that such parental values can be termed "deviant" in any but a statistical sense. "Concern with the plight of others," "desire to realize intellectual capacities," and "lack of concern about the importance of strictly controlling personal impulses"—all these values might be thought of as more normative than deviant in upper middle-class suburban American society in 1966. Even "sensitivity to beauty and art" is becoming increasingly acceptable. Nor can the socio-economic facts of affluence, freedom from status anxiety, high educational levels, permissiveness with children, training for independence, etc. be considered normatively deviant in middle-class America. Thus, the sense in which activists are the deviant offspring of sub-culturally deviant parents remains to be clarified.

Psychological Flexibility

Another explanation seems equally plausible, at least as applied to some student activists—namely that their activism is closely related to the social and cultural conditions that promote high levels of psychological flexibility, complexity and integration. As Bay (1966) has argued, social scientists may be too reluctant to entertain the possibility that some political and social outlooks or activities are symptomatic of psychological "health," while others indicate "disturbance." In fact, many of the personal characteristics of activists— empathy, superior intellectual attainments, capacity for group involvement, strong humanitarian values, emphasis on self-realization, etc.—are consistent with the hypothesis that, as a group, they are usually "healthy" psychologically. (See also 18 and 59). Similarly, the personal antecedents of the activist—economic security, committed parents, humanitarian, liberal and permissive home environments, good education, etc.—are those that would seem to promote unusually high levels of psychological functioning. If this be correct, then former SDS president Tom Hayden's words (16) may be a valid commentary on the cultural setting of activism:

Most of the active student radicals today come from middle to upper middle-class professional homes. They were born with status and affluence as facts of life, not goals to be striven for. In their upbringing, their parents stressed the right of children to question and make judgments, producing perhaps the first generation of young people both affluent and independent of mind.

In agreeing with Bay (3) that activists may be more psychologically "healthy" as a group than nonactivists, I am aware of the many difficulties entailed by this hypothesis. First, complexity, flexibility, integration, high levels of functioning, etc. are by no means easy to define, and the criteria for "positive mental health" remain vague and elusive. (See 19). Second, there are obviously many individuals with these same "healthy" characteristics who are not activists; and within the group of activists, there are many individuals with definite psychopathologies. In any social movement, a variety of individuals of highly diverse talents and motivations are bound to be involved, and global descriptions are certain to be oversimplified. Third, the explanation from "psychological health" and the explanation from "parental deviance" are not necessarily opposed. On the contrary, these two arguments become identical if we assume that the preconditions for high levels of psychological functioning are both statistically and normatively deviant in modern American society. This assumption seems quite plausible.

Whatever the most plausible explanation of the socio-cultural sources of activism, the importance of prevailing attitudes toward student protest and of the climate of social criticism in America seems clear. In the past five years a conviction has arisen, at least among a minority of American college students, that protest and social action are effective and honorable. Furthermore, changes in American society, especially in middle-class child rearing practices, mean that American students are increasingly responsive to both the universalistic and romantic critique of our society. Both strands of social criticism have been picked up by student activists in a rhetoric of protest that combines a major theme of impatience at the slow fulfillment of the credal ideals of American society with a more muted minor theme of aesthetic revulsion at technological society itself. By and large, activists respond most affirmatively to the first theme and alienated students to the second; but even within the student protest movement, these two themes coexist in uneasy tension.

The Protest-Producing Historical Situation

To separate what I have called the "cultural climate" from the "historical situation" is largely arbitrary. But by this latter term I hope to point to the special sensitivity of today's student activists to historical events and trends that do not immediately impinge upon their own lives. In other nations, and in the past, student protest movements seem to have been more closely related to immediate student frustrations than they are in America today. The "transformationist" (utopian, Marxist, universalistic or democratic) aspirations of activist youth in rapidly developing nations often seem closely related to their personal frustrations under oppressive regimes or at "feudal" practices in their societies; the "restorationist" (romantic, alienated) youth movements that have appeared in later stages of industrialization seem closely connected to a personal sense of the loss of a feudal, maternal, and "organic" past. (See 31; 32; 33). Furthermore, both universalistic and romantic youth movements in other nations have traditionally been highly ideological, committed either to concepts of universal democracy and economic justice or to particularistic values of brotherhood, loyalty, feeling and nation.

Anti-ideological

Today's activists, in contrast, are rarely concerned with improving their own conditions and are highly motivated by identification with the oppressions of others. The anti-ideological bias of today's student activists has been underlined by virtually every commentator. Furthermore, as Flacks notes, the historical conditions that have produced protest elsewhere are largely absent in modern America; and the student "movement" in this country differs in important ways from student movements elsewhere. In many respects, then, today's American activists have no historical precedent, and only time will tell to what extent the appearance of organized student dissent in the 1960's is a product of locally American conditions, of the psychosocial effects of a technological affluence that will soon characterize other advanced nations, or of widespread changes in identity and style produced by psycho-historical factors that affect youth of all nations (thermonuclear warfare, increased culture contact, rapid communications, etc.).

Sensitivity to World Events

But whatever the historical roots of protest, today's student protester seems uniquely sensitive to historical trends and events. In interviewing student activists I have been impressed with how often they mention some world-historical event as the catalyst for their activism—in some cases, witnessing via television of the Little Rock demonstrations over school integration, in another case, watching rioting Zengakuren students in Japan protesting the arrival of President Eisenhower, in other cases, particularly among Negro students, a strong identification with the rising black nationalism of recently-independent African nations.

Several factors help explain this sensitivity to world events. For one, modern means of communication make the historical world more psychologically "available" to youth. Students today are exposed to world events and world trends with a speed and intensity that has no historical precedent. Revolutions, trends, fashions and fads are now world wide; it takes but two or three years for fashions to spread from Carnaby Street to New York, New Delhi, Tokyo, Warsaw, Lagos and Lima. In particular, students who have been brought up in a tradition that makes them unusually empathic, humanitarian and universalistic in values may react more intensely to exposure via television to student demonstrations in Japan than to social pressures from their fellow seniors in Centerville High. Finally, this broadening of empathy is, I believe, part of a general modern trend toward the *internationalization of identity*. Hastened by modern communications and consolidated by the world-wide threat of nuclear warfare, this trend involves, in vanguard groups in many nations, a loosening of parochial and national allegiances in favor of a more inclusive sense of affinity with one's peers (and non-peers) from all nations. In this respect, American student activists are both participants and leaders in the reorganization of psychosocial identity and ideology that is gradually emerging from the unique historical conditions of the twentieth century (34).

A small but growing number of American students, then, exhibit a peculiar responsiveness to world-historical events—a responsiveness based partly on their own broad identification with others like them throughout the world, and partly on the availability of information about world events via the mass media. The impact of historical events, be they the world-wide revolution for human dignity and esteem, the rising aspirations of the developing nations, or the war in Vietnam, is greatly magnified upon such students; their primary identification is not their unreflective national identity, but their sense of affinity for Vietnamese peasants, Negro sharecroppers, demonstrating Zengakuren activists, exploited migrant workers, and the oppressed everywhere. One of the consequences of security, affluence and education is a growing sense of personal involvement with those who are insecure, non-affluent and uneducated.

The Future of Student Activism

I have argued that no single factor can explain or help us predict the future of the student protest movement in America: active expressions of dissent have become more prevalent because of an *interaction* of individual, institutional, cultural and historical factors. Affluence and education have changed the environment within which middle-class children are raised, in turn producing a minority of students with special sensitivity to the oppressed and the dissenting everywhere. At the same time, technological innovations like television have made available to these students abundant imagery of oppression and dissent in America and in other nations. And each of these factors exerts a potentiating influence on the others.

Given some understanding of the interaction of these factors, general questions about the probable future of student activism in America can now be broken down into four more specific questions: Are we likely to produce (a) more protest-prone personalities? (b) more institutional settings in which protests are likely? (c) a cultural climate that sanctions and encourages activism? and (d) a historical situation that facilitates activism? To three of the questions (a, b, and d), I think the answer is qualified yes; I would therefore expect that in the future, if the cultural climate remains the same, student activism and protest would continue to be visible features on the American social landscape.

Consider first the factors that promote protest-prone personalities. In the coming generation there will be more and more students who come from the upper middle-class, highly educated, politically liberal professional backgrounds from which protesters are selectively recruited (40). Furthermore, we can expect that a significant and perhaps growing proportion of these families will have the universalistic, humanitarian, equalitarian and individualistic values found in the families of protesters. Finally, the expressive, permissive, democratic and autonomy-promoting atmosphere of these families seems to be the emerging trend of middle-class America: older patterns of "entrepreneurial-authoritarian" control are slowly giving way to more "bureaucratic-democratic" techniques of socialization (42). Such secular changes in the American family would produce a growing proportion of students with protest-prone personalities.

Institutional factors, I have argued, are of primary importance in so far as they bring together a critical mass of suitably protest-predisposed students in an atmosphere where they can interact, create their own subculture, develop leadership and find issues. The growing size of major American universities, their increasing academic and intellectual selectivity, and the emphasis on "quality" education (honors programs, individual instruction, greater student freedom)—all seem to promote the continuing development of activist sub-cultures in a minority of American institutions. The increasing use of graduate student teaching assistants in major universities points to the growing availability of large numbers of potential "leaders" for student protests. Admittedly, a sudden increase in the administrative wisdom in college Deans and Presidents could reduce the number of available "on-campus" issues; but such a growth in wisdom does not seem imminent.

Cultural Climate May Change

In sharp contrast, a maintenance of the cultural climate required for continuation of activism during the coming years seems far more problematical. Much depends on the future course of the war in Vietnam. Continuing escalation of the war in Southeast Asia will convince many student activists that their efforts are doomed to ineffectuality. For as of mid-1967, anti-war activism has become the primary common cause of student protesters. The increasing militancy and exclusivity of the Negro student civil rights movement, its emphasis on "Black Power" and on grass-roots community organization work (to be done by Negroes) is rapidly pushing white activists out of civil rights work, thus depriving them of the issue upon which the current mood of student activism was built. This fact, coupled with the downgrading of the war on poverty, the decline of public enthusiasm for civil rights, and the increasing scarcity of public and private financing for work with the underprivileged sectors of American society, has already begun to turn activists away from domestic issues toward an increasingly single-minded focus on the war in Vietnam. Yet at the same time, increasing numbers of activists overtly or covertly despair of the efficacy of student attempts to mobilize public opinion against the war, much less to influence directly American foreign policies. Continuing escalation in Southeast Asia has also begun to create a more represive atmosphere towards student (and other) protesters of the war, exemplified by the question, "Dissent or Treason"? Already the movement of activists back to full-time academic work is apparent.

Thus, the war in Vietnam, coupled by the "rejection" of white middleclass students by the vestigial black Civil Rights Movement is producing a crisis among activists, manifest by a "search for issues" and intense disagreement over strategy and tactics. At the same time, the diminution of support for student activism tends to exert a "radicalizing" effect upon those who remain committed activists—partly because frustration itself tends to radicalize the frustrated, and partly because many of the less dedicated and committed activists have dropped away from the movement. At the same time, most activists find it difficult to turn from civil rights or peace work toward "organizing the middle-class" along lines suggested by alienated-romantic criticisms of technological society. On the whole, activists remain more responsive to universalistic issues like peace and civil rights than to primarily expressive or esthetic criticisms of American society. Furthermore, the practical and organizational problems of "organizing the middle-class" are overwhelming. Were the student movement to be forced to turn away from universalistic issues like civil rights and peace to a romantic critique of the "quality of middle-class life," my argument here implies that its following and efficacy would diminish considerably. Were this to happen, observations based on student activism of a more "universalistic" variety would have to be modified to take account of a more radical and yet more alienated membership. Thus, escalation or even continuation of the war in Vietnam, particularly over a long period, will reduce the likelihood of student activism.

Yet there are other, hopefully more permanent, trends in American culture that argue for a continuation of protests. The further extension of affluence in America will probably mean growing impatience over our society's failure to include the "forgotten fifth" in its prosperity: as the excluded and underprivileged become fewer in number, pressures to include them in American society will grow. Similarly, as more young Americans are brought up in affluent homes and subcultures, many will undoubtedly turn to question the value of monetary, familistic and careerist goals, looking instead toward expressive, romantic, experiential, humanitarian and self-actualizing pursuits to give their lives meaning. Thus, in the next decades, barring a major world conflagration, criticisms of American society will probably continue and intensify on two grounds: first, that it has excluded a significant minority from its prosperity, and second, that affluence alone is empty without humanitarian, aesthetic or expressive fulfillment. Both of these trends would strengthen the climate conducive to continuing activism.

World Wide Protest-Promoting Pressures

Finally, protest-promoting pressures from the rest of the world will doubtless increase in the coming years. The esteem revolution in developing nations, the rise of aspirations in the impoverished two-thirds of the world, and the spread of universalistic principles to other nations—all of these trends portend a growing international unrest, especially in the developing nations. If young Americans continue to be unusually responsive to the unfulfilled aspirations of those abroad, international trends will touch a minority of them deeply, inspiring them to overseas activities like the Peace Corps, to efforts to "internationalize" American foreign policies, and to an acute sensitivity to the frustrated aspirations of other Americans. Similarly, continuation of current American policies of supporting anti-communist but often repressive regimes in developing nations (particularly regimes anathema to student activists abroad) will tend to agitate American students as well. Thus, pressures from the probable world situation will support the continuance of student protests in American society.

In the next decades, then, I believe we can foresee the continuation, with short-range ebbs and falls, of activism in American society. Only if activists were to become convinced that protests were ineffectual or social action impossible is this trend likely to be fundamentally reversed. None of this will mean that protesters will become a majority among American students; but we can anticipate a slowly-growing minority of the most talented, empathic, and intellectually independent of our students who will take up arms against injustice both here and abroad.

In Summary

Throughout this discussion, I have emphasized the contrast between two types of students, two types of family backgrounds, and two sets of values that inspire dissent from the Great Society. On the one hand, I have discussed students I have termed alienated, whose values are apolitical, romantic, and aesthetic. These students are most responsive to "romantic" themes of social criticism; that is, they reject our society because of its dehumanizing effects, its lack of aesthetic quality and its failure to provide "spiritual" fulfillment to its members. And they are relatively impervious to appeals to social, economic or political justice. On the other hand, I have discussed activists, who are politically involved, humanitarian and universalistic in values. These students object to our society not because they oppose its basic principles, but because it fails to implement these principles fully at home and abroad.

In the future, the tension between the romantic-alienated and the universalistic-activist styles of dissent will probably increase. I would anticipate a growing polarization between those students and student groups who turn to highly personal and experiential pursuits like drugs, sex, art and intimacy, and those students who redouble their efforts to change American society. In the past five years, activists have been in the ascendant, and the alienated have been little involved in organized political protests. But a variety of possible events could reverse this ascendency. A sense of ineffectuality, especially if coupled with repression of organized dissent, would obviously dishearten many activists. More important, the inability of the student protest movement to define its own long-range objectives, coupled with its intransigent hostility to ideology and efficient organization, means that *ad hoc* protests are too rarely linked to the explicit intellectual, political and social goals that alone can sustain prolonged efforts to change society. Without some shared sustaining vision of the society and world they are working to promote, and frustrated by the enormous obstacles that beset any social reformer, student activists would be likely to return to the library.

How and whether this tension between alienation and activism is resolved seems to me of the greatest importance. If a growing number of activists, frustrated by political ineffectuality or a mounting war in Southeast Asia, withdrawn from active social concern into a narrowly academic quest for professional competence, then a considerable reservoir of the most talented young Americans will have been lost to our society and the world. The field of dissent would be left to the alienated, whose intense quest for *personal* salvation, meaning, creativity and revelation dulls their perception of the public world and inhibits attempts to better the lot of others. If in contrast, tomorrow's potential activists can feel that their demonstrations and actions are effective in molding public opinion and, more important, in effecting needed social change, then the possibilities for constructive change in post-industrial American society are virtually without limit.

Footnotes

1. The following paragraphs are based on the study of culturally alienated students described in *The Uncommitted* (25). For a more extensive discussion of the overwhelmingly anti-political stance of these students, see (28) and also (32, 2, 62, and 65).

2. The presence among student dissenters of a group of "nonstudents"—that is, drop-outs from college or graduate school who congregate or remain near some academic center—has been much noted. In fact, however, student protesters seem somewhat *less* likely to drop out of college than do nonparticipants in demonstrations (17), and there is no evidence that dropping out of college is in any way related to dissent from American society (29). On the contrary, several studies suggest that the academically gifted and psychologically intact student who drops out of college voluntarily has few distinctive discontents about his college or about American society (58; 48; 66). If he is dissatisfied at all, it is with himself, usually for failing to take advantage of the "rich educational opportunities" he sees in his college. The motivations of students dropping out of college are complex and varied, but such motivations more often seem related to personal questions of self definition and parental identification or to a desire to escape relentless academic pressures, than to any explicit dissent from the Great Society. Thus, although a handful of students have chosen to drop out of college for a period in order to devote themselves to political and societal protest activities, there seems little reason in general to associate the drop-out with the dissenter, whether he be a protester or an alienated student. The opposite is nearer the truth.

3. Student activism, albeit of a rather different nature, was also found in the nineteen thirties. For a discussion and contrast of student protest today and after the Depression, see (35).

4. Throughout the following, I will use the terms "protester" and "activist" interchangeably, although I am aware that some activists are not involved in protests. Furthermore, the category of "activist" is an embracing one, comprising at least three sub-classes. First, those who might be termed *reformers*, that is, students involved in community organization work, the Peace Corps, tutoring Programs, Vista, etc., but not generally affiliated with any of the "New Left" organizations. Second, the group of *activists proper*, most of whom are or have been affiliated with organizations like the Free Speech Movement at Berkeley, Students for a Democratic Society, the Student Non-violent Coordinating Committee or the Congress on Racial Equality or the Vietnam Summer Project. Finally, there is a much publicized handful of students who might be considered *extremists*, who belong to doctrinaire Marxist and Trotskyite organizations like the now-defunct May Second Movement. No empirical study with which I am acquainted has investigated the differences between students in these three sub-groups. Most studies have concentrated on the "activist proper," and my remarks will be based on a reading of their data.

References

1. Aiken, M., Demerath, N. J., and Marwell, G. Conscience and confrontation: some preliminary findings on summer civil rights volunteers. University of Wisconsin, 1966. (mimeo)
2. Allen, M., and Silverstein H. Progress report: creative arts—alienated youth project. New York: March, 1967.
3. Bay, Christian. Political and apolitical students: facts in search of theory. *Journal of Social Issues*, 1967, 23, (3).
4. Bernreuter, Robert G. The college student: he is thinking, talking, acting. *Penn State Alumni News*, July, 1966.
5. Block, J., Haan, N., and Smith, M.B. Activism and apathy in contemporary

adolescents. In J. F. Adams (Ed.), *Contributions to the understanding of adolescence*. New York: Allyn and Bacon, forthcoming.

6. Coles, Robert. Serpents and doves: non-violent youth in the South. In Erik Erikson (Ed.), *The challenge of youth*. New York: Basic Books, 1963.
7. ————. *Children of crisis*. Boston: Little, Brown, 1967.
8. Cowan, John Lewis. Academic freedom, protest and university environments. Paper read at APA, New York, 1966.
9. Draper, Hal. *Berkeley, the new student revolt*. New York: Grove, 1965.
10. Ehle, John. *The free men*. New York: Harper and Row, 1965.
11. Erikson, Erik H. (Ed.) *The challenge of youth*. New York: Basic Books, 1963.
12. Fishman, Jacob R., and Solomon, Frederic. Psychological observations on the student sit-in movement. *Proceedings of the Third World Congress of Psychiatry*. Toronto: University of Toronto/Mcgill, n.d.
13. Fishman, Jacob R., and Solomon, Frederic. Youth and social action. *The Journal of Social Issues*, 1964, 20, (4), 1-28.
14. Flacks, Richard E. The liberated generation: an exploration of the roots of student protest. *Journal of Social Issues*, 1967, 23, (3).
15. Gastwirth, D. Why students protest. Unpublished paper, Yale University, 1965.
16. Hayden, T. Quoted in *Comparative Education Review*, 1966, 10, 187.
17. Heist, Paul. Intellect and commitment: the faces of discontent. *Order and freedom on the campus*. Western Interstate Commission for Higher Education and the Center for the Study of Higher Education, 1965.
18. ————. The dynamics of student discontent and protest. Paper read at APA, New York, 1966.
19. Jahoda, Marie. *Current concepts of positive mental health*. New York: Basic Books, 1958.
20. Katz, J. The learning environment: social expectations and influences. Paper presented at American Council of Education. Washington, D. C., 1965.
21. ————. The student activists: rights, needs and powers of undergraduates. Stanford: Institute for the Study of Human Problems, 1967.
22. Keene, S. How one big university laid unrest to rest. *The American Student*, 1966, 1, 18-21.
23. Kelman, H. D. Notes on faculty activism. *Letter to Michigan Alumni*, 1966.
24. Keniston, Kenneth. American students and the 'political revival.' *The American Scholar*, 1962, 32, 40-64.
25. ————. *The uncommitted*. New York: Harcourt, Brace and World, 1965a.
26. ————. The pressure to perform. *The Intercollegian*. September, 1965b.
27. ————. The faces in the lecture room. In R. S. Morison (Ed.), *The American university*. Boston: Houghton Mifflin, 1966a.
28. ————. The psychology of alienated students. Paper read at APA, New York, 1966b.
29. Keniston, Kenneth, and Helmreich, R. An exploratory study of discontent and potential drop-outs at Yale. Yale University, 1965. (mimeo)
30. Kornhauser, W. Alienation and participation in the mass university. Paper read at American Ortho-Psychiatric Association, Washington, D. C., 1967.
31. Lifton, Robert Jay. Japanese youth: the search for the new and the pure. *The American Scholar*, 1960, 30, 332-344.
32. ————. Youth and history: individual change in post-war Japan. In E. Erikson (Ed.), *The challenge of youth*. New York: Harper and Row, 1963.

33. ————. Individual patterns in historical change. *Comparative Studies in Society and History*. 1964, 6, 369-383.
34. ————. Protean man. Yale University, 1965. (mimeo)
35. Lipset, Semour M. Student opposition in the United States. *Government and Opposition*, 1966a, 1, 351-374.
36. ————. University students and politics in underdeveloped countries. *Comparative Education Review*, 1966b, 10, 132-162.
37. ————. and Altback, P. G. Student politics and higher education in the United States. *Comparative Education Review*, 1966, 10, 320-349.
38. Lipset, Semour M., and Wolin, S. S. (Eds.), *The Berkeley student revolt*. Garden City, New York: Doubleday, 1965.
39. Lyonns, G. The police car demonstration: a survey of participants. In S. Lipset and S. Wolin (Eds.), *The Berkeley student revolt*. Garden City, New York: Doubleday, 1965.
40. Michael, Donald Nelson. *The next generation. the prospects ahead for the youth of today and tomorrow*. New York: Vintage, 1965.
41. Miller, Michael, and Gilmore, Susan. (Eds.), *Revolution at Berkeley*. New York: Dell, 1965.
42. Miller, Daniel R. and Swanson, Guy E. *The changing American parent*. New York: Wiley, 1958.
43. Newfield, Jack. *A prophetic minority*. New York: New American Library, 1966.
44. Newsweek. Campus, 1965. March 22, 1965.
45. Parsons, Talcott. *The social system*. Glencoe, Ill.: Free Press, 1951.
46. ————. *Structure and process in modern societies*. Glencoe, Ill.: Free Press, 1960.
47. Paulus. G. *A multivariate analysis study of student activist leaders, student government leaders, and non-activists*. Cited in Richard E. Peterson, *The student Left in American higher education*. Draft for Puerto Rico Conference on Students and Politics, 1967.
48. Pervin, Lawrence A., Reik, L. E. and Dalrymple, W. (Eds.), *The college drop-out and the utilization of talent*. Princeton: Princeton University, 1966.
49. Peterson, Richard E. *The scope of organized student protest in 1964-65*. Princeton: Educational Testing Service, 1966.
50. ————. The student Left in American higher education. Draft for Puerto Rico Conference on Students and Politics, 1967.
51. Reed, M. Student non-politics, or how to make irrelevancy a virtue. *The American Student*, 1966, 1, (3), 7-10.
52. Rigney, Francis J., and Smith, L. D. *The real bohemia*. New York: Basic Books, 1961.
53. Schneider, Patricia. A study of members of SDS and YD at Harvard. Unpublished B.A. thesis, Wellesley College, 1966.
54. Solomon, Frederic, and Fishman, Jacob R. Perspectives on the student sit-in movement. *American Journal of Ortho-Psychiatry*, 1963, 33, 873-874.
55. ————. Youth and peace: a psycho-social study of student peace demonstrators in Washington, D. C. *The Journal of Social Issues*, 1964, 20, (4), 54-73.
56. Somers, R. H. The mainsprings of the rebellion: a survey of Berkeley students in November, 1964. In S. Lipset and S. Wolin (Eds.), *The Berkeley student revolt*. Garden City, New York: Doubleday, 1965.

57. Stern, G. Myth and reality in the American college. *AAUP Bulletin* Winter, 1966, 408-414.
58. Suczek, Robert Francis, and Alfert, E. Personality characteristic of college drop-outs. University of California, 1966. (mimeo)
59. Trent, James W. and Craise, Judith L. Commitment and conformity in the American college. *Journal of Social Issues* (July 1967): 34-51.
60. Trow, Martin. Some lessons from Berkeley. Paper presented to American Council of Education, Washington, D. C. 1965.
61. Watts, William Arther, and Whittaker, D. Some socio-psychological differences between highly committed members of the Free Speech Movement and the student population at Berkeley. *Applied Behavioral Science* 1966, 2, 41-62.
62. ———. Socio-psychological characteristics of intellectually oriented, alienated youth: a study of the Berkeley nonstudent University of California, Berkeley, 1967. (mimeo)
63. Westby, D., and Braungart, R. Class and politics in the family backgrounds of student political activists, *American Social Review,* 1966, 31, 690-692.
64. White, Winston. *Beyond conformity.* Glencoe, Ill.: Free Press, 1961.
65. Whittaker, D., and Watts, W. A. Personality and value attitudes of intellectually disposed, alienated youth. Paper presented at APA, New York, 1966.
66. Wright, E. O. Student leaves of absence from Harvard College: A personality and social system approach. Unpublished paper, Harvard University, 1966.
67. Zann, Howard. *SNCC, the new abolitionists.* Boston: Beacon, 1965.

THE LIBERATED GENERATION: AN EXPLORATION OF THE ROOTS OF STUDENT PROTEST

Richard Flacks

As all of us are by now aware, there has emerged, during the past five years, an increasingly self-conscious student movement in the United States.[1] This movement began primarily as a response to the efforts by southern Negro students to break the barriers of legal segregation in public accommodations—scores of northern white students engaged in sympathy demonstrations and related activities as early as 1960. But as we all know, the scope of the student concern expanded rapidly to include such issues as nuclear testing and the arms race, attacks on civil liberties, the problems of the poor in urban slum ghettoes, democracy and educational quality in universities, the war in Vietnam, conscription.

This movement represents a social phenomenon of considerable significance. In the first place, it is having an important direct and indirect impact on the larger society. But secondly it is significant because it is a phenomenon which was unexpected—unexpected, in particular, by those social scientists who are professionally responsible for locating and understanding such phenomena. Because it is an unanticipated event, the attempt to understand and explain the sources of the student movement may lead to fresh interpretations of some important trends in our society.

From the *Journal of Social Issues*, Vol. 23, No. 3, July 1967, pp. 52-75. Reprinted by permission of the Society for the Psychological Study of Social Issues and the author.

Radicalism and the Young Intelligentsia

In one sense, the existence of a radical student movement should not be unexpected. After all, the young intelligentsia seem almost always to be in revolt. Yet if we examine the case a bit more closely I think we will find that movements of active disaffection among intellectuals and students tend to be concentrated at particular moments in history. Not every generation produces an organized oppositional movement.

In particular, students and young intellectuals seem to have become active agents of opposition and change under two sets of interrelated conditions:

When they have been marginal in the labor market because their numbers exceed the opportunities for employment commensurate with their abilities and training. This has most typically been the case in colonial or underdeveloped societies; it also seems to account, in part, for the radicalization of European Jewish intellectuals and American college-educated women at the turn of the century (Coser, 1965; Shils, 1960; Veblen, 1963).

When they found that the values with which they were closely connected by virtue of their upbringing no longer were appropriate to the developing social reality. This has been the case most typically at the point where traditional authority has broken down due to the impact of Westernization, industrialization, modernization. Under these conditions, the intellectuals, and particularly the youth, felt called upon to assert new values, new modes of legitimation, new styles of life. Although the case of breakdown of traditional authority is most typically the point at which youth movements have emerged, there seems, historically, to have been a second point in time—in Western Europe and the United States—when intellectuals were radicalized. This was, roughly, at the turn of the century, when values such as gentility, laissez faire, naive optimism, naive rationalism and naive nationalism seemed increasingly inappropriate due to the impact of large scale industrial organization, intensifying class conflict, economic crisis and the emergence of total war. Variants of radicalism waxed and waned in their influence among American intellectuals and students during the first four decades of the twentieth century (1, 8, 14).

If these conditions have historically been those which produced revolts among the young intelligentsia, then I think it is easy to understand why a relatively superficial observer would find the new wave of radicalism on the campus fairly mysterious.

In the first place, the current student generation can look forward, not to occupational insecurity or marginality, but to an unexampled opening up of opportunity for occupational advance in situations in which their skills will be maximally demanded and the prestige of their roles unprecedentedly high.

In the second place, there is no evident erosion of the legitimacy of established authority; we do not seem, at least on the surface, to be in a period of rapid disintegration of traditional values—at least no more so than a decade ago when sociologists were observing the *exhaustion* of opportunity for radical social movements in America (2, 15).

In fact, during the Fifties sociologists and social psychologists emphasized the decline in political commitment, particularly among the young, and the rise of bland, security-oriented conformism throughout the population, but most particularly among college students. The variety of studies conducted then reported students as overwhelmingly unconcerned with value questions, highly complacent, status-oriended, privatized, uncommitted (11, 10). Most of us interpreted this situation as one to be expected given the opportunities newly opened to educated youth, and given the emergence of liberal pluralism and affluence as the characteristic features of postwar America. Several observers predicted an intensification of the pattern of middle class conformism, declining individualism, and growing "other-directedness" based on the changing styles of childrearing prevalent in the the middle class. The democratic and "permissive" family would produce young men who knew how to cooperate in bureaucratic settings, but who lacked a strongly rooted ego-ideal and inner control (18, 4, 7). Although some observers reported that some students were searching for "meaning" and "self-expression," and others reported the existence of "sub-cultures" of alienation and bohemianism on some campuses (12, 23, 19), not a single observer of the campus scene as late as 1959 anticipated the emergence of the organized disaffection, protest and activism which was to take shape early in the Sixites.

In short, the very occurence of a student movement in the present American context is surprising because it seems to contradict our prior understanding of the determinants of disaffection among the young intelligentsia.

A Revolt of the Advantaged

The student movement is, I think, surprising for another set of reasons. These have to do with its social composition and the kinds of ideological themes which characterize it.

The current group of student activists is predominantly upper middle class, and frequently these students are of elite origins. This fact is evident as soon as one begins to learn the personal histories of activist leaders. Consider the following scene at a convention of Students for a Democratic Society a few years ago. Toward the end of several days of deliberation, someone decided that a quick way of raising funds for the organization would be to appeal to the several hundred students assembled at the convention to dig down deep into their pockets on the spot. To this end, one of the leadership, skilled at mimicry, stood on a chair, and in the style of a Southern Baptist preacher, appealed to the students to come forward, confess their sins and be saved by contributing to SDS. The students did come forward, and in each case the sin confessed was the social class or occupation of their fathers. "My father is the editor of a Hearst newspaper, I give $25." "My father is Assistant Director of the —————— Bureau, I give $40." "My father is dean of a law school, here's $50"!

These impressions of the social composition of the student movement are supported and refined by more systematic sources of data. For example, when a random sample of students who participated in the anti-Selective Service sit-in at the University of Chicago Administration Building was compared with a sample composed of non-protesters and students hostile to the protest, the protesters disproportionately reported their social class to be "upper middle." their family incomes to be disproportionately high, their parents' education to be disproportionately advanced. In addition, the protesters' fathers' occupations were primarily upper professional (doctors, college faculty, lawyers) rather than business, white collar, or working class. These findings parallel those of other investigators (3). Thus, the student movement represents the disaffection not of an underprivileged stratum of the student population but of *the most advantaged* sector of the students.

One hypothesis to explain disaffection among socially advantaged youth would suggest that, although such students come from advantaged backgrounds, their academic performance leads them to anticipate downward mobility or failure. Stinchcombe, for example, found high rates of quasi-delinquent rebelliousness among middle class high school youth with poor academic records (Stinchcombe, 1964). This hypothesis is not tenable with respect to college student protest, however. Our own data with respect to the anti-draft protest at Chicago indicate that the grade point average of the protesters averaged around B-B+ (with 75 percent of them reporting a B- or better average). This was slightly higher than the grade point average of our sample of nonprotesters. Other data from our own research indicate that student activists tend to be at the top of their high school class; in general, data from our own and other studies support the view that many activists are academically superior, and that very few activists are recruited from among low academic achievers. Thus, in terms of *both* the status of their families of origins *and* their own scholastic performance, student protest movements are predominantly composed of students who have been born to high social advantage and who are in a position to experience the career and status opportunities of the society without significant limitations.

Themes of the Protest

The positive correlation between disaffection and status among college students suggested by these observations is, I think, made even more paradoxical when one examines closely the main value themes which characterize the student movement. I want to describe these in an impressionistic way here; a more systematic depiction awaits further analysis of our data.

Romanticism. There is a strong stress among many Movement participants on a quest for self-expression, often articulated in terms of leading a "free" life—i.e., one not bound by conventional restraints on feeling, experience, communication, expression. This is often coupled with aesthetic interests and a strong rejection of scientific and other highly rational pursuits. Students often express the classic romantic aspiration of "knowing" or "experiencing" "everything."

Anti-authoritarianism. A strong antipathy toward arbitrary rule, centralized decision-making, "manipulation". The anti-authoritarian sentiment is fundamental to the widespread campus protests during the past few years; in most cases, the protests were precipitated by an administrative act which was interpreted as arbitrary, and received impetus when college administrators continued to act unilaterally, coercively or secretively. Anti-authoritarianism is manifested further by the styles and internal processes within activist organizations; for example, both SDS and SNCC have attempted to decentralize their operations quite radically and members are strongly critical of leadership within the organization when it is too assertive.

Egalitarianism, populism. A belief that all men are capable of political participation, that political power should be widely dispersed, that the locus of value in society lies with the people and not elites. This is a stress on something more than equality of opportunity or equal legal treatment; the students stress instead the notion of "participatory democracy"—direct participation in the making of decisions by those affected by them. Two common slogans—"One man, one vote"; "Let the people decide".

Anti-dogmatism. A strong reaction against doctrinaire ideological interpretations of events. Many of the students are quite restless when presented with formulated models of the social order, and specific programs for social change. This underlies much of their antagonism to the varieties of "old left" politics, and is one meaning of the oft-quoted (if not seriously used) phrase: "You can't trust anyone over thirty".

Moral purity. A strong antipathy to self-interested behavior, particularly when overlaid by claims of disinterestedness. A major criticism of the society is that it is "hypocritical." Another meaning of the criticism of the older generation has to do with the perception that (a) the older generation "sold out" the values it espouses; (b) to assume conventional adult roles usually leads to increasing self-inter-estedness, hence selling-out, or "phoniness." A particularly impor-tant criticism students make of the university is that it fails to live up to its professed ideals; there is an expectation that the institution ought to be *moral*—that is, not compromise its official values for the sake of institutional survival or aggrandizement.

Community. A strong emphasis on a desire for "human" relation-ships, for a full expression of emotions, for the breaking down of interpersonal barriers and the refusal to accept conventional norms concerning interpersonal contact (e.g., norms respecting sex, status, race, age, etc.) A central positive theme in the campus revolts has been the expression of the desire for a campus "community", for the breaking down of aspects of impersonality on the campus, for more direct contact between students and faculty. There is a frequent counterposing of bureaucratic norms to communal norms; a testing of the former against the latter. Many of the students involved in slum projects have experimented with attempts to achieve a "kibbutz"-like community amongst themselves, entailing communal living and a strong stress on achieving intimacy and resolving tensions within the group.

Anti-institutionalism. A strong distrust of involvement with conventional institutional roles. This is most importantly expressed in the almost universal desire among the highly involved to avoid institutionalized careers. Our data suggest that few student activists look toward careers in the professions, the sciences, industry or politics. Many of the most committed expect to continue to work full-time in the "movement" or, alternatively, to become free-lance writers, artists, intellectuals. A high proportion are oriented toward academic careers—at least so far the academic career seems still to have a reputation among many student activists for permitting "freedom."

Several of these themes, it should be noted, are not unique to student activists. In particular, the value we have described as "romanticism"—a quest for self-expression—has been found by observers, for example Kenneth Keniston (13), to be a central feature of the ideology of "alienated" or "bohemian" students. Perhaps more important, the disaffection of student activists with conventional careers, their low valuation of careers as important in their personal aspirations, their quest for careers outside the institutionalized sphere—these attitudes toward careers seem to be characteristic of other groups of students as well. It is certainly typical of youth involved in "bohemian" and aesthetic subcultures; it also characterizes students who volunteer for participation in such programs as the Peace Corps, Vista and other full-time commitments oriented toward service. In fact, it is our view that the dissatisfaction of socially advantaged youth with conventional career opportunities is a significant social trend, the most important single indicator of restlessness among sectors of the youth population. One expression of this restlessness is the student movement, but it is not the only one. One reason why it seems important to investigate the student movement in detail, despite the fact that it represents a small minority of the student population, is that it is a symptom of social and psychological strains experienced by a larger segment of the youth—strains not well understood or anticipated heretofore by social science.

If some of the themes listed above are not unique to student activists, several of them may characterize only a portion of the activist group itself. In particular, some of the more explicitly political values are likely to be articulated mainly by activists who are involved in radical organizations, particularly Students for a Democratic Society, and the Student Non-violent Coordinating Committee. This would be true particularly for such notions as "participatory democracy" and deep commitments to populist-like orientations. These orientations have been formulated within SDS and SNCC as these organizations have sought to develop a coherent strategy and a framework for establishing priorities. It is an empirical question whether students not directly involved in such organizations articulate similar attitudes. The impressions we have from a preliminary examination of our data suggest that they frequently do not. It is more likely that the student movement is very heterogeneous politically at this point. Most participants share a set of broad orientations, but differ greatly in the degree to which they are oriented toward ideology in general or to particular political positions. The degree of politicization of student activists is probably very much a function of the kinds of peer group and organizational relationships they have had; the underlying disaffection and tendency toward activism, however, is perhaps best understood as being based on more enduring, pre-established values, attitudes and needs.

Social-Psychological Roots of Student Protest: Some Hypotheses

How, then, can we account for the emergence of an obviously dynamic and attractive radical movement among American students in this period? Why should this movement be particularly appealing to youth from upper-status, highly educated families? Why should such youth be particularly concerned with problems of authority, of vocation, of equality, of moral consistency? Why should students in the most advantaged sector of the youth population be disaffected with their own privilege?

It should be stressed that the privileged status of the student protesters and the themes they express in their protest are not *in themselves* unique or surprising. Student movements in developing nations—e.g., Russia, Japan and Latin America—typically recruit people of elite background; moreover, many of the themes of the "new left" are reminiscent of similar expressions in other student movements (16). What is unexpected is that these should emerge in the American context at this time.

Earlier theoretical formulations about the social and psychological sources of strain for youth, for example the work of Parsons (20), Eisenstadt (8), and Erikson (6), are important for understanding the emergence of self-conscious oppositional youth cultures and movements. At first glance, these theorists, who tend to see American youth as relatively well-integrated into the larger society, would seem to be unhelpful in providing a framework for explaining the emergence of a radical student movement at the present moment. Nevertheless, in developing our own hypotheses we have drawn freely on their work. What I want to do here is to sketch the notions which have guided our research; a more systematic and detailed exposition will be developed in future publications.

What we have done is to accept the main lines of the argument made by Parsons and Eisenstadt about the social functions of youth cultures and movements. The kernel of their argument is that self-conscious subcultures and movements among adolescents tend to develop when there is a sharp disjunction between the values and expectations embodied in the traditional families in a society and the values and expectations prevailing in the occupational sphere. The greater the disjunction, the more self-conscious and oppositional will be the youth culture (as for example in the situation of rapid transition from a traditional-ascriptive to a bureaucratic-achievement social system).

In modern industrial society, such a disjunction exists as a matter of course, since families are, by definition, particularistic, ascriptive, diffuse, and the occupational sphere is universalistic, impersonal, achievement-oriented, functionally specific. But Parsons, and many others, have suggested that over time the American middle class family has developed a structure and style which tends to articulate with the occupational sphere; thus, whatever youth culture does emerge in American society is likely to be fairly well-integrated with conventional values, not particularly self-conscious, not rebellious (20).

The emergence of the student movement, and other expressions of estrangement among youth, leads us to ask whether, in fact, there may be families in the middle class which embody values and expectations which do *not* articulate with those prevailing in the occupational sphere, to look for previously unremarked incompatibilities between trends in the larger social system and trends in family life and early socialization.

The argument we have developed may be sketched as follows:

First, on the macro-structural level we assume that two related trends are of importance: one, the increasing realization of student life in high schools and universities, symbolized by the "multiversity," which entails a high degree of impersonality, competitiveness and an increasingly explicit and direct relationship between the university and corporate and government bureaucracies; two, the increasing unavailability of coherent careers independent of bureaucratic organizations.

Second, these trends converge, in time, with a particular trend in the development of the family; namely, the emergence of a pattern of familial relations, located most typically in upper middle class, professional homes, having the following elements:

(a) a strong emphasis on democratic, egalitarian interpersonal relations

(b) a high degree of permissiveness with respect to self-regulation

(c) an emphasis on values *other than achievement*; in particular, a stress on the intrinsic worth of living up to intellectual, aesthetic, political, or religious ideals.

Third, young people raised in this kind of family setting, contrary to the expectations of some observers, find it difficult to accommodate to institutional expectations requiring submissiveness to adult authority, respect for established distinctions, a high degree of competition, and firm regulation of sexual and expressive impulses. They are likely to be particularly sensitized to acts of arbitrary authority, to unexamined expressions of allegiance to conventional values, to instances of institutional practices which conflict with professed ideals. Further, the values embodied in their families are likely to be reinforced by other socializing experiences—for example, summer vacations at progressive children's camps, attendance at experimental private schools, growing up in a community with a high proportion of friends from similar backgrounds. Paralleling these experiences of positive reinforcement, there are likely to be experiences which reinforce a sense of estrangement from peers of conventional society. For instance, many of these young people experience a strong sense of being "different" or "isolated" in school; this sense of distance is often based on the relative uniqueness of their interests and values, their inability to accept conventional norms about appropriate sex-role behavior, and the like. An additional source of strain is generated when these young people perceive a fundamental discrepancy between the values espoused by their parents and the style of life actually practiced by them. This discrepancy is experienced as a feeling of "guilt" over "being middle class" and a perception of "hypocrisy" on the part of parents who express liberal or intellectual values while appearing to their children as acquisitive or self-interested.

Fourth, the incentives operative in the occupational sphere are of limited efficacy for these young people—achievement of status or material advantage is relatively ineffective for an individual who already has high status and affluence by virtue of his family origins. This means, on the other hand, the operative sanctions within the school and the larger society are less effective in enforcing conformity.

It seems plausible that this is the first generation in which a substantial number of youth have both the impulse to free themselves from conventional status concerns *and can afford to do so*. In this sense they are a "liberated" generation; affluence has freed them, at least for a period of time, from some of the anxieties and preoccupations which have been the defining features of American middle class social character.

Fifth, the emergence of the student movement is to be understood in large part as a consequence of opportunities for prolonged interaction available in the university environment. The kinds of personality structures produced by the socializing experiences outlined above need not necessarily have generated a collective response. In fact, Kenneth Keniston's recently published work on alienated students at Harvard suggests that students with similar characteristics to those here were identifiable on college campuses in the Fifties. But Keniston makes clear that his highly alienated subjects were rarely involved in extensive peer-relationships, and that few opportunities for collective expressions of alienation were then available. The result was that each of his subjects attempted to work out a value-system and a mode of operation of his own (13).

What seems to have happened was that during the Fifties, there began to emerge an "alienated" student culture, as students with alienated predispositions became visible to each other and began to interact. There was some tendency for these students to identify with the "Beat" style and related forms of bohemianism. Since this involved a high degree of disaffiliation, "cool" non-commitment and social withdrawal, observers tended to interpret this subculture as but a variant of the prevailing privatism of the Fifties. However, a series of precipitating events, most particularly the southern student sit-ins, the revolutionary successes of students in Cuba, Korea and Turkey, and the suppression of student demonstrations against the House Un-American Activities Committee in San Francisco, suggested to groups of students that direct action was a plausible means for expressing their grievances. These first stirrings out of apathy were soon enmeshed in a variety of organizations and publicized in several student-organized underground journals—thus enabling the movement to grow and become increasingly institutionalized. The story of the emergence and growth of the movement cannot be developed here; my main point now is that many of its characteristics cannot be understood solely as consequences of the structural and personality variables outlined earlier—in addition, a full understanding of the dynamics of the movement requires a "collective behavior" perspective.

Sixth, organized expressions of youth disaffection are likely to be an increasingly visible and established feature of our society. In important ways, the "new radicalism" is *not* new, but rather a more widespread version of certain subcultural phenomena with a considerable history. During the late 19th and early 20th century a considerable number of young people began to move out of their provincial environments as a consequence of university education; many of these people gathered in such locales as Greenwich Village and created the first visible bohemian subculture in the United

States. The Village bohemians and associated young intellectuals shared a common concern with radical politics and, influenced by Freud, Dewey, etc., with the reform of the process of socialization in America—i.e., a restructuring of family and educational institutions (14, 5). Although many of the reforms advocated by this group were only partially realized in a formal sense, it seems to be the case that the values and style of life which they advocated have become strongly rooted in American life. This has occurred in at least two ways: first, the subcultures created by the early intellectuals took root, have grown and been emulated in various parts of the country. Second, many of the *ideas* of the early twentieth century intellectuals, particularly their critique of the bourgeois family and Victorian sensibility, spread rapidly; it now seems that an important defining characteristic of the college-educated mother is her willingness to adopt child-centered techniques of rearing, and of the college educated couple that they create a family which is democratic and egalitarian in style. In this way, the values that an earlier generation espoused in an abstract way have become embodied as *personality traits* in the new generation. The rootedness of the bohemian and quasi-bohemian subcultures, and the spread of their ideas with the rapid increase in the number of college graduates, suggests that there will be a steadily increasing number of families raising their children with considerable ambivalence about dominant values, incentives and expectations in the society. In this sense, the students who engage in protest or who participate in "alienated" styles of life are often not "converts" to a "deviant" adaptation, but people who have been socialized into a developing cultural tradition. Rising levels of affluence and education are drying up the traditional sources of alienation and radical politics; what we are now becoming aware of, however, is that this same situation is creating new sources of alienation and idealism, and new constituencies for radicalism.

The Youth and Social Change Project

These hypotheses have been the basis for two studies we have undertaken. Study One, begun in the Summer of 1965, involved extensive interviews with samples of student activists and nonactivists and their parents. Study Two, conducted in the Spring of 1966, involved interviews with samples of participants, nonparticipants and opponents of the tumultuous "anti-ranking" sit-in at the University of Chicago.

Study One—The Socialization of Student Activists

For Study One, fifty students were selected from mailing lists of various peace, civil rights, and student movement organizations in the Chicago area. An additional fifty students, matched for sex, neighborhood of parents' residence, and type of college attended, were drawn from student directories of Chicago-area colleges. In each case, an attempt was made to interview both parents of the student respondent, as well as the student himself. We were able to interview both parents of 82 of the students; there were two cases in which no parents were available for the interview, in the remaining cases, one parent was interviewed. The interviews with both students and parents averaged about three hours in length, were closely parallel in content, and covered such matters as: political attitudes and participation; attitudes toward the student movement and "youth"; "values," broadly defined; family life, child-rearing, family conflict and other aspects of socialization. Rating scales and "projective" questions were used to assess family members' perceptions of parent-child relationships.

It was clear to us that our sampling procedures were prone to a certain degree of error in the classification of students as "activists" and "nonactivists." Some students who appeared on mailing lists of activists organizations had no substantial involvement in the student movement, while some of our "control" students had a considerable history of such involvement. Thus the data to be reported here are based on an index of Activism constructed from interview responses to questions about participation in seven kinds of activity: attendence at rallies, picketing, canvassing, working on a project to help the disadvantaged, being jailed for civil disobedience, working full-time for a social action organization, serving as an officer in such organizations.

Study Two—The "Anti-Ranking" Sit-in

In May, 1966, about five hundred students sat-in at the Administration Building on the campus of the University of Chicago, barring the building to official use for two and a half days. The focal issue of the protest, emulated on a number of other campuses in the succeeding days, was the demand by the students that the University not cooperate with the Selective Service System in supplying class standings for the purpose of assigning student deferments. The students who sat-in formed an organization called "Students Against the Rank" (SAR). During the sit-in, another group of students, calling themselves "Students for a Free Choice" (SFC) circulated a petition opposing the sit-in and supporting the University Administration's view that each student had a right to submit (or withhold) his class standings—the University could not withhold the "rank" of students who requested it. This petition was signed by several hundred students.

Beginning about 10 days after the end of the sit-in, we undertook to interview three samples of students: a random sample of 65 supporters of SAR (the protesters); a random sample of 35 signers of the SFC petition (the anti-protesters); approximately 60 students who constituted the total population of two randomly selected floors in the student dormitories. Of about 160 students thus selected, 117 were finally either interviewed or returned mailed questionnaires. The interview schedule was based largely on items used in the original study; it also included some additional items relevant to the sit-in and the "ranking" controversy.

Some Preliminary Findings

At this writing, our data analysis is at an early stage. In general, however, it is clear that the framework of hypotheses with which we began is substantially supported, and in interesting ways, refined, by the data. Our principal findings thus far include the following:[2]

Activists tend to come from upper status families. As indicated earlier, our study of the Chicago sit-in suggests that such actions attract students predominantly from upper-status backgrounds. When compared with students who did not sit-in, and with students who signed the anti-sit-in petition, the sit-in participants reported higher family incomes, higher levels of education for both fathers and mothers, and overwhelmingly perceived themselves to be "upper-middle class." One illustrative finding: in our dormitory sample, of 24 students reporting family incomes of above $15,000, half participated in the sit-in. Of 23 students reporting family incomes below $15,000, only two sat-in.

Certain kinds of occupations are particularly characteristic of the parents of sit-in participants. In particular, their fathers tend to be professionals (college faculty, lawyers, doctors) rather than businessmen, white collar employees or blue-collar workers. Moreover, somewhat unexpectedly, activists' mothers are likely to be employed, and are more likely to have "career" types of employment, than are the mothers of non-activists.

Also of significance, although not particularly surprising, is the fact that activists are more likely to be Jewish than are non-activists. (For example, 45 percent of our SAR sample reported that they were

Jewish; only about one-fourth of the non-participants were Jewish). Furthermore, a very high proportion of both Jewish and non-Jewish activists report no religious preference for themselves and their parents. Associated with the Jewish ethnicity of a large proportion of our activist samples is the fact the great majority of activists' grandparents were foreign born. Yet, despite this, data from Study One show that the grandparents of activists tended to be relatively highly educated as compared to the grandparents of non-activists. Most of the grandparents of non-activists had not completed high school; nearly half of the grandparents of activists had at least a high school education and fully one-fourth of their maternal grandmothers had attended college. These data suggest that relatively high status characterized the families of activists over several generations; this conclusion is supported by data showing that, unlike non-activist grandfathers, the grandfathers of activists tended to have white collar, professional and entrepreneurial occupations rather than blue collar jobs.

In sum, our data suggest that, at least at major Northern colleges, students involved in protest activity are characteristically from families which are urban, highly educated, Jewish or irreligious, professional and affluent. It is perhaps particularly interesting that many of their mothers are uniquely well-educated and involved in careers, and that high status and education has characterized these families over at least two generations.

Activists are more "radical" than their parents; but activists' parents are decidedly more liberal than others of their status. The demographic data reported above suggests that activists come from high status families, but the occupational, religious and educational characteristics of these families are unique in several important ways. The distinctiveness of these families is especially clear when we examine data from Study One on the political attitudes of students and their parents. In this study, it should be remembered, activist families were roughly equivalent in status, income and education because of our sampling procedures. Our data quite clearly demonstrate that the fathers of activists are disproportionately liberal. For example, whereas forty percent of the non-activists' fathers said that they were Republican, only thirteen percent of the activists' fathers were Republicans. Only six percent of non-activists' fathers were willing to describe themselves as "highly liberal" or "socialist," whereas sixty percent of the activists' fathers accepted such designations. Forty percent of the non-activists' fathers described themselves as conservative; none of the activists' fathers endorsed that position.[3]

In general, differences in the political preferences of the students paralleled these parental differences. The non-activist sample is only slightly less conservative and Republican than their fathers; all of the activist students with Republican fathers report their own party preferences as either Democrat or independent. Thirty-two per cent of the activists regard themselves as "socialist" as compared with sixteen per cent of their fathers. In general, both nonactivists and their fathers are typically "moderate" in their politics; activists and their fathers tend to be at least "liberal," but a substantial proportion of the activists prefer a more "radical" designation.

A somewhat more detailed picture of comparative political positions emerges when we examine responses of students and their fathers to a series of 6-point scales on which respondents rated their attitudes on such issues as: US bombing of North Vietnam, US troops in the Dominican Republic, student participation in protest demonstrations, civil rights protests involving civil disobedience, Lyndon Johnson, Barry Goldwater, congressional investigations of "unAmerican activities," full socialization of all industries, socialization of the medical profession.

Figure 1 presents data on activists and non-activists and their fathers with respect to these items. This table suggests, first, wide divergence between the two groups of fathers on most issues, with activist fathers typically critical of current policies. Although activists' fathers are overwhelmingly "liberal" in their responses, for

Figure 1. Students' and fathers' attitudes on current issues

Issue	Activists		Nonactivists	
	Students	Fathers	Students	Fathers
Percent who approve:				
Bombing of North Vietnam	9	27	73	80
American troops in Dominican Republic	6	33	65	50
Student participation in protest demonstrations	100	80	61	37
Civil disobedience in civil protests	97	57	28	23
Congressional investigations of "un-American activities"	3	7	73	57
Lyndon Johnson	35	77	81	83
Barry Goldwater	0	7	35	20
Full socialization of industry	62	23	5	10
Socialization of the medical profession	94	43	30	27
N	34	30	37	30

the most part, activist students tend to endorse "left-wing" positions more strongly and consistently than do their fathers. The items showing strongest divergence between activists and their fathers are interesting. Whereas activists overwhelmingly endorse civil disobedience, nearly half of their fathers do not. Whereas fathers of both activists and non-activists tend to approve of Lyndon Johnson, activist students tend to disapprove of him. Whereas activists' fathers tend to disapprove of "full socialization of industry," this item is endorsed by the majority of activists (although fewer gave an extremely radical response on this item than any other); whereas the vast majority of activists approve of socialized medicine, the majority of their fathers do not. This table provides further support for the view that activists, though more "radical" than their fathers, come predominantly from very liberal homes. The attitudes of nonactivists and their fathers are conventional and supportive of current policies; there is a slight tendency on some items for nonactivist students to endorse more conservative positions than their fathers.

It seems fair to conclude, then, that most students who are involved in the movement (at least those one finds in a city like Chicago) are involved in neither "conversion" from nor "rebellion" against the political perspectives of their fathers. A more supportable view suggests that the great majority of these students are attempting to fulfill and renew the political traditions of their families. However, data from our research which have not yet been analyzed as of this writing, will permit a more systematic analysis of the political orientations of the two generations.

Activism is related to a complex of values, not ostensibly political, shared by both the students and their parents. Data which we have just begun to analyze suggest that the political perspectives which differentiate the families of activists from other families at the same socioeconomic level are part of a more general clustering of values and orientations. Our findings and impressions on this point may be briefly summarized by saying that, whereas nonactivists and their parents tend to express conventional orientations toward achievement, material success, sexual morality and religion, the activists and their parents tend to place greater stress on involvement in intellectual and esthetic pursuits, humanitarian concerns, opportunity for self-expression, and tend to de-emphasize or positively disvalue personal achievement, conventional morality and conventional religiosity.

When asked to rank order a list of "areas of life," nonactivist students and their parents typically indicate that marriage, career and religion are most important. Activists, on the other hand, typically rank these lower than the "world of ideas, art and music" and "work for national and international betterment"—and so, on the whole, do their parents.

When asked to indicate their vocational aspirations, nonactivist students are typically firmly decided on a career and typically mention orientations toward the professions, science and business. Activists, on the other hand, are very frequently undecided on a career; and most typically those who have decided mention college teaching, the arts or social work as aspirations.

These kinds of responses suggest, somewhat crudely, that student activists identify with life goals which are intellectual and "humanitarian" and that they reject conventional and "privatized" goals more frequently than do nonactivist students.

Four Value Patterns

More detailed analyses which we are just beginning to undertake support the view that the value-patterns expressed by activists are highly correlated with those of their parents. This analysis has involved the isolation of a number of value patterns which emerged in the interview material, the development of systems of code categories related to each of these patterns, and the blind coding of all the interviews with respect to these categories. The kinds of data we are obtaining in this way may be illustrated by describing four of the value patterns we have observed.

Romanticism: Esthetic and Emotional Sensitivity

This variable is defined as: "sensitivity to beauty and art—appreciation of painting, literature and music, creativity in art forms—concern with esthetic experience and the development of capacities for esthetic expression—concern with emotions deriving from perception of beauty—attachment of great significance to esthetic experience. More broadly, it can be conceived of as involving explicit concern with experience as such, with feeling and passion, with immediate and inner experience; a concern for the realm of feeling rather than the rational, technological or instrumental side of life; preference for the realm of experience as against that of activity, doing or achieving." Thirteen items were coded in these terms: for each item a score of zero signified no mention of "romanticist" concerns, a score of one signified that such a concern appeared. Figure 2 indicates the relationship between "romanticism" and

Figure 2. Scores on selected values by activism (percentages)

	Activists	Nonactivists
(a) *Romanticism*		
High	35	11
Medium	47	49
Low	18	40
(b) *Intellectualism*		
High	32	3
Medium	65	57
Low	3	40
(c) *Humanitarianism*		
High	35	0
Medium	47	22
Low	18	78
(d) *Moralism*		
High	6	54
Medium	53	35
Low	41	11
N	34	37

Activism. Very few Activists received scores on Romanticism which placed them as "low"; conversely, there were very few high "romantics" among the nonactivists.

Intellectualism

This variable is defined as: "Concern with ideas—desire to realize intellectual capacities—high valuation of intellectual creativities—appreciation of theory and knowledge—participation in intellectual activity (e.g., reading, studying, teaching, writing)—broad intellectual concerns." Ten items were scored for "intellectualism." Almost no Activists are low on this variable; almost no nonactivists received a high score.

Humanitarianism

This variable is defined as: "Concern with plight of others in society; desire to help others—value on compassion and sympathy—desire to alleviate suffering; value on egalitarianism in the sense of opposing privilege based on social and economic distinction; particular sensitivity to the deprived position of the disadvantaged." This variable was coded for ten items: an attempt was made to exclude from this index all items referring directly to participation in social action. As might be expected, "humanitarianism" is strongly related to Activism, as evidenced in Figure 2.

Moralism and Self Control

This variable is defined as: "Concern about the importance of strictly controlling personal impulses—opposition to impulsive or spontaneous behavior—value on keeping tight control over emotions-adherence to conventional authority; adherence to conventional morality—a high degree of moralism about sex, drugs, alcohol, etc.—reliance on a set of external and inflexible rules to govern moral behavior; emphasis on importance of hard work; concern with determination, "stick-to-itiveness"; antagonism toward idleness—value of diligence, entrepreneurship, task orientation, ambition." Twelve items were scored for this variable. As Figure 2 suggests, "moralism" is also strongly related to Activism; very few Activists score high on this variable, while the majority of nonactivists are high scorers.

These values are strongly related to activism. They are also highly intercorrelated, and, most importantly, parent and student scores on these variables are strongly correlated.

These and other value patterns will be used as the basis for studying value transmission in families, generational similarities and differences and several other problems. Our data with respect to them provide further support for the view that the unconventionality of activists flows out of and is supported by their family traditions.

Activists' parents are more "permissive" than parents of nonactivists. We have just begun to get some findings bearing on our hypothesis that parents of Activists will tend to have been more "permissive" in their child-rearing practices than parents of equivalent status whose children are not oriented toward activism.

One measure of parental permissiveness we have been using is a series of rating scales completed by each member of the family. A series of seven-point bipolar scales was presented in a format similar to that of the "Semantic Differential." Students were asked to indicate "how my mother (father) treated me as a child" on such scales as "warm-cold"; "stern-mild"; "hard-soft";—10 scales in all. Each parent, using the same scales, rated "how my child thinks I treated him."

Figure 3 presents data on how sons and daughters rated each of their parents on each of four scales: "mild-stern"; "soft-hard"; "lenient-severe"; and "easy-strict." In general, this table shows that

Figure 3. Sons and daughters ratings of parents by activism (percentages)

Trait of parent	Males		Females	
	Hi Act	Lo Act	Hi Act	Lo Act
mid-stern				
per cent rating mother "mild"	63	44	59	47
per cent rating father "mild"	48	33	48	32
soft-hard				
per cent rating mother "soft"	69	61	60	57
per cent rating father "soft"	50	50	62	51
lenient-severe				
per cent rating mother "lenient"	94	61	66	63
per cent rating father "lenient"	60	44	47	42
easy-strict				
per cent rating mother "easy"	75	50	77	52
per cent rating father "easy"	60	44	47	37
N	23	24	27	26

Activist sons and daughters tend to rate their parents as "milder," "more lenient," and "less severe" than do nonactivists. Similar data were obtained using the parents' ratings of themselves.

A different measure of permissiveness is based on the parents' response to a series of "hypothetical situations." Parents were asked, for example, what they would do if their son (daughter) "decided to drop out of school and doesn't know what he really wants to do." Responses to this open-ended question were coded as indicating "high intervention" or "low intervention." Data for fathers on this item are reported in Figure 4. Another hypothetical situation presented to the parents was that their child was living with a

Figure 4. Father's intervention—"If Child Dropped Out of School" (percentages)

Degree of Intervention	Activism of Child	
	High	Low
Low	56	37
High	44	63
N	30	30

Figure 5. Father's intervention—"If Child Were Living With Member of Opposite Sex" (percentages)

Degree of Intervention	Activism of Child	
	High	Low
None	20	14
Mild	50	28
Strong	30	58
N	30	30

member of the opposite sex. Responses to this item were coded as "strongly intervene, mildly intervene, not intervene." Data for this item for fathers appears in Figure 5. Both tables show that father of Activists report themselves to be much less interventionist than fathers of nonactivists. Similar results were obtained with mothers, and for other hypothetical situations.

Clearly both types of measures just reported provide support for our hypothesis about the relationship between parental permissiveness and activism. We expect these relationships to be strengthened if "activism" is combined with certain of the value-patterns described earlier.

A Concluding Note

The data reported here constitute a small but representative sampling of the material we have collected in our studies of the student movement. In general, they provide support for the impressions and expectations we had when we undertook this work. Our view of the student movement as an expression of deep discontent felt by certain types of high status youth as they confront the incongruities between the values represented by the authority and occupational structure of the larger society and the values inculcated by their families and peer culture seems to fit well with the data we have obtained.

A variety of questions remain which, we hope, can be answered, at least in part, by further analyses of our data. Although it is clear that value differences between parents of activists and nonactivists are centrally relevant for understanding value, attitudinal and behavioral cleavages among types of students on the campus, it remains to be determined whether differences in family status, on the one hand, and childrearing practices, on the other, make an independent contribution to the variance. A second issue has to do with political ideology. First impressions of our data suggest that activists vary considerably with respect to their degree of politicization and their concern with ideological issues. The problems of isolating the key determinants of this variation is one we will be paying close attention to in further analysis of our interview material. Two factors are likely to be of importance here—first, the degree to which the student participates in radical student organizations; second, the political history of his parents.

At least two major issues are not confronted by the research we have been doing. First, we have not examined in any detail the role of campus conditions as a determinant of student discontent. . . . The research reported here emphasizes family socialization and other antecedent experiences as determinants of student protest, and leads to the prediction that students experiencing other patterns of early socialization will be unlikely to be in revolt. This view needs to be counterbalanced by recalling instances of active student unrest on campuses where very few students are likely to have the backgrounds suggested here as critical. It is possible that there are two components to the student protest movement—one generated to a great extent by early socialization; the second by grievances indigenous to the campus? At any rate, the inter-relationships between personal dispositions and campus conditions need further detailed elucidation.

A second set of questions unanswerable by our research has to do with the future—what lies ahead for the movement as a whole and for the individual young people who participate in it? One direction for the student movement is toward institutionalization as an expression of youth discontent. This outcome, very typical of student movements in many countries, would represent a narrowing of the movement's political and social impact, a way of functionally integrating it into an otherwise stable society. Individual participants would be expected to pass through the movement on their way to eventual absorption, often at an elite level, into the established institutional order. An alternative direction would be toward the development of a full-fledged political "left," with the student movement serving, at least initially, as a nucleus. The potential for this latter development is apparent in recent events. It was the student movement which catalyzed professors and other adults into protest with respect to the Vietnam war. Students for a Democratic Society, the main organizational expression of the student move- ment, has had, for several years, a program for "community organizing," in which students and exstudents work full-time at the mobilization of constituencies for independent radical political and social action. This SDS program began in poverty areas; it is now beginning to spread to "middle class" communities. These efforts, and others like them, from Berkeley to New Haven, became particularly visible during the 1966 congressional elections, as a wave of "new left" candidates emerged across the country, often supported by large and sophisticated political organizations. Moreover, in addition to attempts at political organizations, SDS, through its "Radical Education Project" has begun to seek the involvement of faculty members, professionals and other intellectuals for a program of research and education designed to lay the foundations for an intellectually substantial and ideologically developed "new left."

At its convention in September, 1966, SDS approached, but did not finally decide, the question of whether to continue to maintain its character as a campus-based, student organization or to transform itself into a "Movement for a Democratic Society." Characteristically, the young people there assembled amended the organization's constitution so that anyone regardless of status or age could join, while simultaneously they affirmed the student character of the group by projecting a more vigorous program to organize uncommitted students.

The historical significance of the student movement of the Sixties remains to be determined. Its impact on the campus and on the larger society has already been substantial. It is clearly a product of deep discontent in certain significant and rapidly growing segments of the youth population. Whether it becomes an expression of generational discontent, or the forerunner of major political realignments—or simply disintegrates—cannot really be predicted by detached social scientists. The ultimate personal and political meaning of the student movement remains a matter to be determined by those who are involved with it—as participants, as allies, as critics, as enemies.

Footnotes

1. The research reported here stemmed from a coalescence of interests of the author and of Professor Bernice Neugarten of the Committee on Human Development of the University of Chicago. The author's interests were primarily in the student movement and the families and social backgrounds of student activists. Professor Neugarten's interests have been primarily in the relations between age-groups in American society. The plan to gather parallel data from students and their parents accordingly provided a welcome opportunity for collaboration. The research has been supported in part by grant #MH 08062,

National Institute of Mental Health; in part by grants from the Carnegie Fund for the Advancement of Teaching and the Survey Research Center of The University of Michigan. I wish to thank Professor Neugarten, Charles Derber and Patricia Schedler for their help in preparing this manuscript; its flaws are entirely my own responsibility.

2. A more detailed report of the procedures and findings of these studies is available in Flacks (9).

3. For the purposes of this report, "activists" are those students who were in the top third on our Activism index; "nonactivists" are those students who were in the bottom third—this latter group reported virtually no participation in any activity associated with the student movement. The "activists" on the other hand had taken part in at least one activity indicating high commitment to the movement (e.g., going to jail, working full-time, serving in a leadership capacity).

References

1. Aaron, Daniel. *Writers on the left.* New York: Avon, 1965.
2. Bell, Daniel. *The end of ideology.* New York: The Free Press, 1962.
3. Braungart, R. G. Social stratification and political attitudes. Pennsylvania State University, 1966, (unpublished ms.).
4. Bronfenbrenner, U. The changing American child: A speculative analysis. *Merrill-Palmer Quarterly,* 1961, 7, 73-85.
5. Coser, Lewis. *Men of ideas.* New York: The Free Press, 1965.
6. Erikson, Erik. Identity and the life-cycle. *Psychological Issues,* 1959, 1, 1-171.
7. ————. *Childhood and society.* New York: Norton, 1963, 306-325.
8. Eisenstadt, Samuel N. *From generation to generation.* Glencoe: The Free Press, 1956.
9. Flacks, R. The liberated generation. University of Chicago, 1966. (mimeo)
10. Goldsen, Rose; Rosenberg, Moris; Williams, Robin; and Suchman, Edward. *What college students think.* Princeton: Van Nostrand, 1960.
11. Jacob, Philip. *Changing values in college.* New York: Harper, 1957.
12. Keniston, Kenneth. *The uncommitted.* New York: Harcourt Brace, 1965.
13. Keniston, Kenneth. Social change and youth in America. In E. Erikson (Ed.) *The challenge of youth.* Garden City: Doubleday Anchor, 1965.
14. Lasch, Christopher. *The new radicalism in America.* New York: Knopf, 1965.
15. Lipset, Seymour. *Political man, the social bases of politics.* Garden City: Doubleday Anchor, 1960.
16. Lipset, Seymour. University students and politics in underdeveloped countries. *Comparative Education Review,* 1966, 10, 132-162.
17. Lipset, Seymour and Altbach, P. Student politics and higher education in the United States. *Comparative Education Review,* 1960, 10, 320-349.
18. Miller, Daniel and Swanson, G. E. *The changing American parent.* New York: Wiley, 1958.
19. Newcomb, Theodore and Flacks, R. *Deviant subcultures on a college campus.* US Office of Education, 1963.
20. Parsons, Talcott. Youth in the context of American society. In E. Erikson (Ed.), *The challenge of youth.* Garden City: Doubleday Anchor, 1965.
21. Shils, Edward. The intellectuals in the political development of new states. *World Politics,* 1960, 12, 329-368.

22. Stinchcombe, Arthur. *Rebellion in a high school.* Chicago: Quadrangle, 1964.
23. Trow, Martin. Student cultures and administrative action. In Sutherland, R. *et al.* (Eds.), *Personality factors on the college campus.* Austin: Hogg Foundation for Mental Health, 1962.
24. Veblen, Thornstein. The intellectual pre-eminence of Jews in modern Europe. In B. Rosenberg (Ed.), *Thorstein Veblen.* New York: Crowell, 1963.

REVOLUTION, REFORMATION, AND REEVALUATION

James W. Trent

In 1964, the student demonstrations at the University of California's Berkeley campus startled the world. Now, five years later, demonstrations of this kind have become commonplace the world over, and in the United States they are becoming prevalent in high schools and junior colleges as well as in four-year colleges. Although no campus appears immune to them, they are no less disquieting than they were a few years ago. They have shattered the administrative structure at numerous major universities, and their reverberations have affected governments both regionally and nationally.

Discussion of what has become "The Movement" of student activists is proliferated in the news and professional publications. Many reasons, from a Communist conspiracy to a castration complex, are seriously and unstintingly offered for the activists' behavior; many characteristics, from irredeemable to heroic, are attributed to the activists; many solutions to the activists' confrontations, from the fiercely repressive to the indulgent, are offered.

Behind the conglomeration of reasons, characteristics, and solutions there exists a consistent need to cut through the unceasing rhetoric on the issue and to examine the few facts that are known about activists and their movement. These are especially important to examine in the face of daily opinion that passes as fact. With

Edward E. Sampson, Harold A. Korn & Associates, *Student Activism and Protest: Alternatives for Social Change,* (San Francisco: Jossey-Bass, 1970) "Revolution, Reformation, and Reevaluation" by James W. Trent, pp. 24-59. Reprinted by permission.

enough facts and enough sifting of good implications and opinions from bad, there may exist a solid basis for suggesting positive alternatives for dealing with the present presses on the American college. Never has there been a greater need for research and evaluation of the system of higher education than under the present circumstances; thus, the proper method of evaluation also becomes a matter of concern.

The greater substance of this chapter comprises, first, a summary of several past and recent surveys pertaining to the characteristics of student activists; second, the implications the data have for the nature and roles of contemporary higher education in this context; and, third, problems of evaluating the context.[1]

Our theses are (1) that the intense activism observed in higher education is growing but remains representative of only a small proportion of students in the United States; (2) that the majority of students today largely manifest the apathy and conformity that have characterized students of the past, rather than the kind of commitment and autonomy that leads to political activism or serious intellectual involvement; (3) that, nonetheless, a considerable and growing number of nonactivists are sympathetic to causes advocated by the activists; (4) that students are increasingly affected by activists' causes and activities, regardless of their sympathies; (5) that, although activism can be destructive, it has great potential as a catalyst for improvements in higher education; (6) that the system of higher education can be reformed in the ways that activists and others are urging without having first to be destroyed; and (7) that new and consistent forms of evaluation are necessary for appropriate reformation.

Student Activism

There is endless argument over what has contributed to the new student spirit which appears in such contrast to the silent generation of a decade ago. Any one or combination of factors may be involved: permissive child rearing, reaction to dehumanizing technocracy, sophistication derived from mass media, improved education leading to unprecedented critical thinking, affluence no longer making the seeking of security a dominant concern, reaction to anachronistic middle-class mores and parents, disenchantment over the war whose validity could no longer go unquestioned in the name of patriotism, equal disenchantment over the increasing manifest disenfranchised in society, or other factors. Whatever its source, however widespread, there is a new spirit. What matters now is what forms it takes and with what effects on society.

Activism implies dissent from the status quo. But more than one form of dissent is apparent on the American college campus. There are the dissidence and general unrest found among many students who manifest an often unarticulated and uncomprehended anxiety in the face of a rapidly changing, complex, and threatening world. There is the "rebellion for the hell of it" among the few who argue that they want to be left entirely free from social and educational constraints so that they may simply "do their own thing." There is the show of contempt for any social order found in a very few anarchistic students who have disaffiliated themselves from society and who want devastating confrontation for its own sake. There are rationally motivated intellectual dissenters who are not interested in bringing down the social order but in probing it, testing it, and changing it. Added to this group in the last several years are the black and Mexican-American—or Chicano—militants who want not so much to change the educational establishment but more to rid it of racism and to gain a greater share of its benefits.

The activists who wish to change society may sometimes be impulsive, noisy, and belligerent. Sometimes they even may be naive and wrong, depending upon the standards used for judgment. They may attract followers who find it faddish or fun to thumb their noses at any authority. But their motives are not to be confused with those of individuals who complain about their own uneasiness, play at independence, or disdain society out of displaced hatred.

Two hundred students interviewed by *Fortune* in 1968 explained "Our most wrenching problem is finding a place for ourselves in society."[2] To solve the problem means to change society, a common cry evident in the sampling of criticisms reported in the *Fortune* survey. The young critics view society as perverted, tolerating "injustice, insensitivity, lack of candor and inhumanity." Too big and "numbered by boredom," society needs to be infused with a "human scale" whereby the individual can participate in the decisions that affect him. It must become an open system, no longer controlled by engulfing, anonymous, and immoral big business. The profit motive is questionable, and competition a "social blight" that perverts people's values. In a world of hunger and want there is immense waste, particularly the economic and human waste of the war. Education is not blameless; rather than a sanctuary of free expression and thought, the university has become a grade-race factory controlled by trustees or regents who are actually remote from the university and whose views reflect economic and political pressures. The government, too, is ridden with apathy, hoards power, and is remote from those most affected by its decisions. Still, the critics urge:

We are not a generation of text book revolutionaries . . . nor are we dupes, as some people suspect, of "the communist conspiracy;" the Soviet Union, with its own repressive establishment, has no appeal for us. We come to our convictions through practical experience. . . . Viewing these conditions, some of us think that the whole social system ought to be replaced by an entirely new one; the existing structures are too rotten for repair. And so, some of us advocate a revolution.[3]

There are scholars such as C. Robert Pace (in speaking to the faculty of the UCLA Graduate School of Education) who argue cogently that a cultural revolution has been under way for some time, in part beginning with the personalization of man and stress on his individual psyche launched by men like Freud. Reaction to the post-industrial depersonalization of man may be an important part of the revolution. And revolution in various forms is undoubtedly being urged.[4] This fact is substantiated in the summary of the *Fortune* survey and in many other sources. For example, Jerry Farber, a former faculty member of California State College at Los Angeles, argues in "The Student As Nigger" that the American student, like the black man, is powerless, subservient to an exploitative academic establishment, and that he must, therefore, stop prostituting himself before that establishment.[5]

Michael Rossman, formerly a member of the Free Speech Movement's steering committee at Berkeley, asserts that the entire community is divided by conflicts of interest which are also questions of power and powerlessness. In this context political advance and educational reform develop through confrontation. To Rossman it is a matter of both personal identity and violence:

To be is to confront . . . to confront in any style—by action or rhetoric—is to encounter in yourself and to awaken in those confronted those emotions which are involved with doing violence: anger, fear, guilt, creation. Thus, the act of confrontation, of articulation—of identity, is psychologically very similar to the act of violence. Liberals will not deal consciously with the terrifying violence within them. They act it out in indirect ways, the results of which they think they can continue to ignore, though now America is cracking. It won't work, Charlie; you've got to let yourself get angry; you've got to watch yourself get angry—and maybe violent as well—before you can find out who you are.[6]

Michael Vozick, formerly a founder of San Francisco State's 1965 Experimental College and currently the head of the Center for Educational Reform at the National Student Association, rejoined Rossman that to be is not to confront but to be. Yet he does believe in revolution and reform of a certain type; indeed, he pointed out to Rossman that:

You and I know that the revolution has to be lived in order to believe in it with integrity. We find it, if only as a tone of voice, on every campus. Students are into the beginning of the next culture. The question is how.[7]

Vozick offers answers to his question: by teaching consciousness through the demonstrations of the creative possibilities seen and lived, by working for the voluntary abdication from destructive power roles of university and other leaders, by working "to learn the ingenuity and allow the awareness with which we can penetrate, with revolutionary sincerity, the whole of this culture," by asking which act will empower, best train, and best help everyone to learn what is really going on before each situation with a choice of confrontation versus non-confrontation.

Here, then, is revolution of complex and far-reaching dimensions. It does not center on one or a few issues; it does not take a single form. Whether regarded as necessarily leading to the violent overthrow of the Establishment or the Establishment's reform from within, it cannot be explained simply or dismissed as an ephemeral phenomenon with no legitimate basis. Certainly the revolution has been prompted by far more than either sexual or generational conflict as proposed by either Farber or Feuer.[8]

Extent of Activism

To say that the revolution reaches deep and far is not to say, however, that it directly involves a majority of students. The results of several studies and data from our study of high school graduates across the nation all lead to the same conclusion: that up to 1966, student activism, however defined, involved a very few select students in a very few select colleges and universities.

Peterson found that at most, only 9 per cent of any student body was reported as involved in protest movements and that protests occurred disproportionately often at select institutions of high quality. In Peterson's survey of the state of activism as viewed by deans of students and equivalent officers at 85 per cent of the country's four-year colleges, only 38 per cent of the deans reported student activism over civil rights, the issue which has evoked the most activism. Twenty-eight per cent of the deans reported student activism over living group regulations, 21 per cent over United States involvement in the war in Vietnam, 18 per cent over student participation in campus policy-making, 9 per cent over rules regarding "controversial" visitors to campus, 7 per cent over curriculum inflexibility, and 4 per cent over academic freedom for faculty.[9]

Heist observed that "strong political advocacy" has taken place since 1960 on a few campuses where this activity would least be expected but then added:

The fact that a few institutions have had a fairly continuous manifestation of such student activity and involvement, often centered in social problems or political issues, is not generally known. On several campuses in the United States, conflict and a degree of turmoil seem to be taken as a matter of course; these may even be defended as part of the "design" of an effective educational program. The truth is that the colleges or universities which witness considerable and frequent student activity and committed support of off-campus causes tend to draw a student clientele that is measurably different from the student bodies in the great mass of institutions. In these schools a notable concentration of students of high ability and nonconservative values often tends to set a pattern for activism or some degree of protest.[10]

Even at schools of this kind, however, the proportion of activist leadership was very small. In his survey of three liberal arts colleges renowned for their liberal, aware, and activist students, Heist found that the combined key leadership groups of the three schools comprised only eleven students. At Berkeley, no more than 3 per cent of the student body was committed enough to the Free Speech Movement to risk arrest. Moreover, the Berkeley group was selective in background as well as in numbers. Heist found that half of the group had transferred from the select colleges and universities identified by him and Peterson as the few institutions whose students were noticeably involved in activism.

Baird analyzed American College Survey data obtained from sophomores in 1965 in thirty-one institutions. Even though he defined the term comprehensively and did not focus exclusively on radicals, he found that less than 3 per cent of the students were activists.[11]

Finally, our research on a sample of nearly 10,000 high school graduates in sixteen communities across the United States shows that of those graduates who went on to persist in college over a four-year period, very few were concerned with any of the current political, social, or educational issues that might disturb student activists. Rather, their responses to questionnaire and interview items dealing with these areas of concern indicated that most of them had a kind of uncritical acceptance of, and contentment with, the *status quo* not unlike that of the silent generation of the past.[12]

A February 1969 issue of *Time* would suggest that there has been a virtual avalanche of activism since 1965. Figures charted without reference to any statistical source state that 2 per cent of American college students are "The Wreckers," 6 per cent "The Militants," and 20 per cent "The Protesters." Substantial evidence indicates otherwise.

Beginning in 1966, data obtained from a random sample of entering college freshmen, who were taken to be representative of entering American college students generally, revealed that 15 per cent of the women and 16 per cent of the men had participated in any sort of demonstration, activist or not. Of the Anglo students, 12 per cent had participated occasionally and 2 per cent frequently. The rate of participation was higher among the black students: 24 and 11 per cent respectively.[13]

In 1968, a Harris poll indicated that only 2 per cent of college students were activists; in the same year a Gallup poll indicated that only 20 per cent of students engaged in any protest activity whatsoever, whether or not they were activists.[14]

Again in 1968, Peterson repeated the same sort of survey of student protest that he conducted in 1965. As viewed by college deans or equivalent officers, there were signs in the three-year interval that students had shifted much of their protests over civil rights to the war, educational relevancy, and governance. Also, more institutions reported student protest. However, there was no wide-scale dispute over the nature of undergraduate teaching. (Fifteen per cent of the institutions reported protests over curricular rigidity, compared with 8 per cent in 1965.) And, although more institutions reported protests and leftist groups (primarily SDS Chapters) in 1968 than they had in 1965, *proportions of activists within student bodies did not change.* This fact, however, does not belie the influence of the activists. Peterson considers an additional 8 to 10 per cent of students to be sympathetic with the "movement for social change" and "capable of temporary activation depending on the issues."[15]

The data reviewed so far refer to students who were enrolled in college. Information pertinent to the issue of activism is also available on recent college graduates compared with those who graduated around 1950 and 1935. We conducted an intensive interview study of approximately 125 college graduates of three age groups selected to be representative of the San Francisco Bay and Los Angeles metropolitan regions; the age groups were composed of men and women primarily in their twenties, forties, and sixties. Few graduates of any age were really involved in political or community action; only a negligible number could be considered activists, even in attitude. Just over 3 per cent of the men and just over 1 per cent of the women felt they were either very liberal or radical in their political and social attitudes. Roughly 25 per cent of the men and 30 per cent of the women represented themselves to be conservative. Proportionately, the youngest graduates were no more liberal and no less conservative than the older graduates. This was also reflected in their reading habits: 10 per cent of the men said they read magazines of liberal persuasion, regardless of age group; 5 per cent of the youngest women reported this, compared with roughly 20 per cent of the women in their forties and sixties.

Of the three groups, the youngest graduates indicated the least social concern and responsibility for others. And, although they did indicate some awareness of the nature of the needs and the basis for the behavior of today's college students, in some ways they were the least sympathetic. For example, only 4 per cent of the youngest graduates approved of college student demonstrations, compared with 18 per cent of the graduates in their forties. None of the oldest graduates approved of demonstrations, but they felt in far greater proportion that contemporary students show serious, concerned thinking about and involvement with the community.[16]

The evidence is, therefore, that there is very little activism manifested by recent college graduates who live in California metropolitan areas. In this context there certainly is no evidence of conflict of opinions and values between generations. This corroborates Keniston's interview-based conclusions and Glazer's observations that there is generally a warm rapport between radicals and their parents, and that in some cases the parents have actually encouraged radicalism in their children and others through the examples of their moral, ethical, and humanist values.[17] The only difference between the generations is that the parents think their children have gone too far and the young radicals think that their parents have not gone far enough. Again, Feuer's and Farber's parent-child conflict theories of radicalism gain no credence here; and even if they are ever demonstrated, indications are that they will not be widely applicable.

Student Characteristics

But if the underlying dynamics of activism have not been clearly demonstrated, a number of personality and other characteristics have been found to distinguish student activists from college students at large. Before delving further into the important personality characteristics that distinguish the activists from other more representative college students across the nation, we offer a brief portrait based on responses to questionnaire items in 1963 by our national sample of what this more typical college student is like or at least was like in the early sixties.

The large sample of high school graduates will hereafter be referred to as the national sample. However, it can be considered national only in the sense of its geographical spread (across California, the Midwest, and Pennsylvania) and not in the sense of being a statistically representative sample of that age group throughout the United States. At the same time, it is assumed representative of a large segment of young adults in the country, especially those living in cities with a population of between 30,000 and 100,000; and it is composed of all or almost all graduating high school seniors in the sixteen communities originally surveyed in 1959. The scope, sampling, and findings of this research are reported elsewhere.[18]

Of the original national sample, 40 per cent entered college full time in 1959 and attended approximately 700 colleges throughout the United States; about half of this group persisted for four years. When the original sample was again surveyed in 1963, over 72 per cent of the persisters, most of whom had reached senior standing, responded to the questionnaire administered to them and to scales from the Omnibus Personality Inventory.[19]

The questionnaire items inquired into the students' vocational, social, and personal values. When asked to check a list of self-descriptions applicable to themselves, 23 per cent of the students considered themselves "nonconformists"; a significantly greater proportion, 28 per cent, described themselves as a "common man" ($\chi^2 = 9.17$; P < .01); and a little over 1 per cent considered themselves "radicals." It is not clear what these terms meant to the students or whether the terms had the same connotations for the respondents that we intended them to have. Furthermore, a majority of the students rejected the list of self-descriptions offered them altogether. But within the limits of these data, a greater tendency toward commonality was implied than toward any nonconformity or radicalism.

By 1963, a majority of the young adults in the national sample had registered or intended to register in the same political party as their father, which in largest proportion was the Republican party. Ten students in the sample considered themselves socialists. Over 500 of the youths, representative of the entire sample, were interviewed personally and for the most part were found to have very little political interest and astuteness. Typically, the interviewed subjects felt their choice of political party was prompted by the fact that it was their parents' choice, and very few could articulate any political beliefs. Unlike the activists considered later in this paper, most of the youths reported a belief in formal organized religion. But here again, in most cases their religious beliefs were ascribed to their parents, and only in rare instances were the subjects articulate about their faith or able to evince any real understanding of it.

The two factors deemed most important to a satisfying life for almost all of the subjects were job and family; and, predictably, a majority of the college persisters regarded the main purpose of college to be the development of vocational skills or talents. Forty-three per cent of the persisters saw the gaining of knowledge and appreciation of ideas as the main goal of attending college. Of this group, 11 per cent expected to get their greatest life satisfactions from interests in community and world problems, science, humanities and the arts, and scholarly pursuits.

When asked about specific issues relating to their college experiences, a majority (70 per cent) of the persisters declared that "most of the faculty are intellectually stimulating"; that "existing rules and regulations regarding student behavior are sensible and necessary" (68 per cent); and that "the faculty and administration are quite successful in developing responsibility among the students" (56 per cent). Half of the students, however, felt "too much bound by course work"; over 40 per cent felt that rules and regulations should be "more permissive"; and over 30 per cent felt that "the administration and faculty generally treat students more like children than adults."

Some students voiced some criticism of their college experience, but most, including those who had some criticism, found college basically satisfying. There was no evidence of general dissension. A utilitarian orientation toward college seemed to prevail over intellectual and social commitment. Concern over social or religious issues was seldom mentioned by the students, and political interests, awareness, and involvement were lacking in almost all of them. Very few stressed the importance of scholarly endeavor or interest in the arts and sciences. It is not yet completely known how discerning the questionnaire items are, nor therefore how valid are the data they elicited, but these data at least seem to indicate that these students had little of the intellectual, social, or political interest and involvement that concern the student activists of this generation.

Activist Characteristics

Various appellations, ranging from "dirty beatniks" to "Communist conspirators," have been given to student activists. This name-calling has never been based on objective appraisal of the student, and it might bring surprise to some quarters responsible for this labeling to learn that many of these students are the brightest and most able students found on the nation's campuses. For example, research showed that the students in Berkeley's Free Speech Movement at the University of California at Berkeley were exceptionally high in measured intellectual disposition, autonomy, flexibility, and liberalism, as well as in level of ability, and that they exhibited marked qualities of individuality, social commitment, and intellectuality not observed among more representative samples of college students. They were, in fact, atypical Berkeley students and represented some of the university's most able and intellectually dedicated students.[20]

The Free Speech Movement which erupted at the University of California was one of the most notorious and long-lived of current student activist movements. And since its composition was such that it was probably similar in nature and dynamics to student movements elsewhere, certain comparisons based on Omnibus Personality Inventory data are pertinent: (a) between a sample of representative Free Speech members who risked arrest and a representative group of Berkeley seniors who were their peers at the time of the demonstrations and (b) between the Free Speech sample and those more typical college students in the national sample who persisted in college for four years. From these comparisons, it becomes apparent that few college students in general can match the positive development of those personality characteristics that distinguish student activists from their college contemporaries.

The standard mean scores obtained on the Omnibus Personality Inventory scales by the three groups are shown in Figure 1. The 1965 seniors were drawn from a random sample of seniors of that year. The members of the Free Speech Movement, surveyed by Heist[21] two months after their arrest in December 1964, were considered representative of the entire group of arrested students with the exception of a slight overrepresentation of sophomores and an underrepresentation of graduate students.

The highly reliable scales on which these groups are compared measure the students' sensitivity and openness to ideas, beauty, and their general environment, together with their freedom from constriction of thought and overt anxiety. The scores were standardized on the basis of a large sample of public college and university freshmen. For all scales the normative freshman mean is 50, and the standard deviation is 10.

The scores of the Free Speech members on all the traits measured

Figure 1. Omnibus personality inventory scores

Scale	National Persisters ('63) (N = 1385)	Berkeley Seniors ('65)* (N = 92)	FSM Arrested* (N = 130)
Thinking Introversion	52	55	63
Complexity	51	54	66
Estheticism	51	52	61
Autonomy	53	61	67
Impulse Expression	51	54	64
Religious Liberalism	48	58	64
Lack of Anxiety	52	51	48

*Source of Berkeley Senior and FSM data: Heist, *op. cit.*

by the Omnibus Personality Inventory were clearly distinguishable from the scores of their own Berkeley classmates and those of the national sample of college persisters (with differences generally significant at the 1 per cent level). With the exception of the Anxiety scale, the mean scores of the activist group exceeded the 1965 Berkeley senior scores by at least 6 standard points and also exceeded the scores of the national sample by at least 10 standard points. All differences between the Free Speech Movement sample and the other samples were considerably beyond the 1 per cent level of significance.

The highest scores obtained by the Free Speech members were on the Complexity and Autonomy scales, indicating they had far more interest in intellectual inquiry, tolerance for ambiguity, objectivity, and independence of thought than the members of the other groups. But the Free Speech members compared with the other students were also marked by their much greater interest in reflective abstract thinking in the areas of art, literature, music, and philosophy (Thinking Introversion), concern with esthetic matters (Estheticism), and freedom and imaginativeness of thinking (Impulse Expression). Their high Religious Liberalism score indicated independence from long-established religious tradition and corroborated Watts' and

Whittaker's finding that formal religion was not important or even relevant to the lives of most of the activists.[22]

The Anxiety scale is composed of the twenty most discriminating items selected by Bendig from the Taylor Manifest Anxiety Scale.[23] The lower scores indicate more anxiety than the other groups of students, perhaps a natural reflection of the stress imposed by the legal predicament the Free Speech students were in at the time they were tested. Or it may represent a price paid for the greater intellectual and social commitment they demonstrated in contrast to other college students of their generation.

Regardless of the reason for the greater manifestation of anxiety among the Free Speech members, their unusually high scores on the intellectual disposition and autonomy scales indicate their involvement with educational as well as political activism. One last point to be made in all fairness to the national sample, however, is that this group was not so much lacking in intellectual orientation, perhaps, as in the student activists' high degree of intellectualism. When viewed separately they might be regarded as manifesting the average degree of intellectuality one would expect in a college group. However, there is no formula at present which can determine objectively just what the "average degree of intellectuality" is, actually or ideally.

Activism and Major Field

There is evidence that a majority of today's students attend college principally to gain professional competence. Keniston has pointed out that what this kind of student prizes above all is "the expertness of the man rather than the man himself" because this is what really counts in the "bureaucratized and organized society" in which he lives.[24] The implication is that most students adhere to this belief regardless of their field of study, but this attitude must be particularly persuasive among that large segment of students who major in applied professional or preprofessional fields, since from the outset they presumably are less intellectually oriented than the more academic students. In the national sample, a majority of the persisters majored in such applied subjects as business, engineering, and education. It was found that most of these students had little deep involvement in intellectual pursuits or concern with social and political reforms and tended to be the most authoritarian and intellectually restricted of all college students observed in the sample.

This finding was first observed in a comparison of the proportion of students at different levels of intellectual dispositions who majored in the liberal arts, education, and technology. For purposes of this comparison, the students' scales on the Omnibus Personality Inventory's Thinking Introversion, Complexity, and Estheticism scales were combined into a single standard scale taken as a comprehensive measure of intellectual disposition. On the basis of the Omnibus Personality Inventory norms, the persisters were then categorized at three levels of intellectual disposition: high—upper 30 per cent of the distribution: middle—middle 40 per cent of the distribution; and low—lower 30 per cent of the distribution.

The representation of the liberal arts majors at the three levels of intellectuality approximates that which would be expected of the normative sample (Figure 2). The technical majors (mostly business and engineering) and education majors were consistently lower on all measures of intellectual disposition than the liberal arts majors. Since it is probably fair to say that the low level of intellectual disposition reflects a certain amount of anti-intellectualism, a majority of the technical and education majors who attended college from 1959-1963 must be described accordingly.

From questionnaire responses it is also known that these students in applied fields were, and very significantly so, the least interested in education for the sake of knowledge, ideas, and creative development; the least interested in such cultural activities as the theater, book-browsing, and artistic activities; and the least concerned about human relations and justice.

In addition, other analyses showed that the technical and education majors were the lowest in autonomy of all the groups

Figure 2. Students in the national sample in various curricula

Level of Intellectual Disposition	Major (*percent*)		
	Liberal Arts (N = 1096)	Education (N = 572)	Technology and Business (N = 899)
High	28	11	7
Middle	37	34	25
Low	35	55	68
Total	100	100	100

$\chi^2 = 273.96$; p $<.001$

under consideration on the three scales of the Omnibus Personality Inventory which purport to measure independence, openness, and flexibility in thinking. For example, on the Autonomy scale, the liberal arts majors obtained a standard mean score of 54.0, compared with a score of 48.4 obtained by the education majors, and a score of 48.7 obtained by the technology majors. The liberal arts groups differed significantly from the education and technology majors (beyond the 1 per cent level), and this fact generally held true in separate analyses which controlled for level of ability and socio-economic status.

In contrast to these findings, student activists were found to possess a high degree of autonomy and intellectual disposition and to come from the fields of the humanities and especially the social sciences in disproportionately high numbers.[23] As the data above indicate, students in these fields in our sample scored higher in these traits than the students in technical and educational fields. But that is not to say they were all activists. Very few were, and the activists were most likely to be students at a few select liberal arts colleges and universities. Moreover, the liberal arts students in the national sample, considered separately, did not reach nearly the level of autonomy and intellectualism of the activists, as indicated by the Omnibus Personality Inventory scores obtained by the Free Speech members (Figure 1). To conclude, then, student activism was associated with curriculum, type of college attended, and a uniquely high level of intellectual disposition and autonomy not shared by the vast majority of students.

Activist Characteristics Since 1965

The situation apparently has not changed essentially in the last few years between 1964 and 1969. Baird, referred to earlier, considered the sophomores he studied in the spring of 1965 as activists if they checked three of the following activities: having organized a political group or campaign, having worked actively in an off-campus political organization, having worked actively in a student movement to change institutional policy and practice, or having participated in one or more demonstrations over political or social issues. Although the activists did not score differently on the Dogmatism scale than the other students and did not achieve a significantly higher grade-point average, they were significantly higher than the other students on such purported self-concept measurements as Leadership, Speaking Ability, Understanding of Others, Sensitivity to the Needs of Others, Originality, Expressiveness, Independence, and Intellectual Self-confidence. On the whole, the activists "conceived themselves as confident, inter-personally capable, sensitive, driving, and talented."[26]

The activists also scored significantly higher on scales having to do with competency and potential in the arts, sciences, leadership, originality, and identification with the intellectual concerns of the faculty. They had a broader range of experiences, had achieved in nonacademic areas, and had participated more in such programs as honors and independent studies. They were much more likely to be engaged in social service and leadership activities.

The life goals they checked reflected their significantly greater desire to be leaders and decision-makers, to be politically involved and helpful to others, and to receive recognition. They did not, however, give significantly lower ratings to being financially secure, making their parents proud of them, following a religious code, or being successful in their own business, as might have been expected. Security, respect, religious codes, and success can be defined broadly; and these terms may have been interpreted broadly by the activists. Also, had the left-oriented radical activists been singled out specifically, they might have shown more rejection of ties to family, religion, success, and security.

As the matter stands, it cannot be said that all activists reject all the traditional values of society; but it is evident that Baird's sample of activists, like those studied previously, are more autonomous, questioning, creative, talented, intellectual, open-minded, and altruistic than other students.

Comparable secondary analyses of the representative sample of freshmen in 1966 studied by Astin, Panos, and Creager[27] reflect most of the findings of previous research. The activists (those who had demonstrated) were involved in more activities; they were more aggressive, out-going, and involved in a variety of ways. They were significantly more likely to perceive themselves as being characterized by leadership ability, speaking ability, social self-confidence, political liberalism, and originality. There was a greater proportion of activists among the students who noted themselves in the top 10 per cent of the intellectually self-confident. They indicated greater concern with becoming involved in the arts in college, with participating in humanitarian endeavors such as the Peace Corps or Vista, and with becoming a community leader.

These traits of social awareness and involvement, openness, esthetic interests, autonomy, and altruism continued to be characteristics of the activistically oriented in 1968 as revealed by the *Fortune* survey of October of that year.[28]   The *"Fortune*-Yankelovich" survey consisted of interviews of 718 college and noncollege men and women between eighteen and twenty-four years old, a sample taken to be representative as to race, sex, marital status, family income, and geographical region.

Two groups of college students were identified: (1) the "practical-minded," consisting of students who felt that education is "mainly a practical matter," providing money, career, and position in society, and, conversely, (2) the "forerunners," reflecting the attitudes toward career and college that *Fortune* believes will become prevalent in the years ahead and consisting of students who chose the statement that they were less concerned with the practical benefits of college than with the opportunity to "change things rather than make out well within the existing system." The forerunners were not necessarily activists, but presumably activists would have their sympathy. The third group, of course, consisted of those individuals who had not entered college. The survey report presented the percentage of the three groups who took specific positions on items having to do with current issues, social norms, prominent figures in society, parents, and values and attitudes toward themselves, technology, business, and their careers.

Compared with the "practical-minded" students and their noncollege peers, the "forerunners" exhibited the most independence from family and middle-class norms; the most activistic orientation, autonomy, and esthetic values; the greatest altruistic orientation; and the most individualistic and humanitarian attitudes toward work. More specific consideration of the data is warranted by their currency and the importance of their implications.[29]

Divergence from Family and Societal Norms. None of the three groups manifested an outright rejection of the family, but the forerunners were proportionately least likely to respond that they identified with their family—65 per cent compared with 78 per cent of the practical-minded and 82 per cent of the noncollege group. Rejection of middle-class values was much more apparent among the forerunners, 35 per cent of whom identified with such values, compared with approximately 67 per cent of both other groups. A large generation gap was reported by 69 per cent of the forerunners, compared with 56 per cent of the practical students and 48 per cent of the young adults who had not entered college. For many students, therefore, and particularly for the forerunners, the generational conflict theory seems pertinent. But this becomes questionable on the basis of another item: only 24 per cent of the forerunners and an average of 13 per cent of the other young adults felt that there was any great difference between their values and those of their parents. The gap may exist in ways other than beliefs and values. Yet it may also be in great part a myth perpetuated in press, text, and treatise and finally subscribed to as truth by each new generation of college students.

Less than half of any of the three groups felt that they could identify with people of their religion; and, again, this was especially true of the forerunners. Yet, 75 per cent of the noncollege group felt that "living a good Christian life" was important, compared with 54 per cent of the practical-minded and 36 per cent of the forerunners. This is not to say the forerunners lacked idealistic values. As will be seen in subsequent discussion, they were by far the most humanitarian in outlook; and it is in these terms that they may show their "religious" beliefs rather than in the traditional, fundamentalistic ethic connotated by the phrase "good Christian life."

In the meantime it is not clear just what the reference group is for the forerunners, a situation which applies to the liberals of the past or present. Eight per cent of the forerunners felt that they could identify with the Old Left; 19 per cent felt they could identify with the New Left, compared with less than 5 per cent of the others. "Doing their own thing" may preclude the label of belonging to any particular social, religious, or political camp.

Tendency Toward Activism. The individualism noted in the last point above does not preclude acceptance of overt activism, however. Sixty-six per cent of the forerunners considered civil disobedience justified, compared with 32 per cent of the practical-minded college students and 18 per cent of their noncollege peers. Sixty-four per cent of the forerunners said that they would welcome more nonviolent protests by black and other minorities, compared with 41 per cent of the practical-minded and 35 per cent of the young adults who did not enter college. Obviously, most of the forerunners were sympathetic to major activist causes.

Autonomy. The forerunners exhibited the greatest degree of autonomy by far in a variety of ways. They were the most open-minded toward themselves and others: in greatest proportion they reported themselves honest with themselves, interested in the different ideas and experiences of the world around them, acceptant of others' peculiarities, and tolerant of others' views. They were least interested in civil regulation in that only a minority of them felt that there should be more emphasis on "law and order" in contrast to most of the other young adults. They showed the greatest need for self-responsibility in that in least proportion could they easily accept having little decision-making power early in their careers. They placed far more stress on independence and individualism: in greatest proportion they felt that there should be more freedom for the individual to do what he wants, that there should be more emphasis on self-expression, and that "doing your own thing" is important; in least proportion could they easily accept outward respect for the sake of career advancement or conformity in clothing and grooming. Generally, a minimum of 15 percentage points distinguish the forerunners from the practical-minded college students on these items; the differences were even greater between the forerunners and those who did not enter college.

Esthetic Values. The forerunners did not express an interest in beauty in any greater proportion than the other young adults. They did, however, welcome more emphasis on the arts in far greater proportion, and they were more predisposed to careers involving the arts. Though beauty in some fashion was important to most of the young adults, the forerunners expressed the greatest interest in the widest variety of esthetic experience.

Altruism. The forerunners' great altruism and social concern were reflected in the fact that a greater proportion of them expressed concern with what is happening in the country, concern with bringing about needed change in society, and the belief that genetic control is not good.

Individualism and Humanitarianism in Work. The greater autonomy and altruism of the forerunners were indicative of their attitude toward work. Again on the basis of considerable percentage differences, the forerunners were decidedly the least likely to feel that hard work always pays off or keeps people from loafing or getting into trouble. They were much more likely to feel that business requires conformity and least likely to feel that it allows for creativity or self-development. In contrast to the others, family and the money to be earned had relatively little influence on the career choices of the forerunners; rather, influencing factors on the forerunners were the opportunity to make meaningful contributions and the ability to express themselves. Their autonomous, humanitarian, even self-actualized values were also reflected in the forerunners' career choices: 64 per cent of these students were predisposed to the teaching arts and helping professions (such as social welfare and psychology), compared with 33 per cent of the "practical-minded" students and 5 per cent of those who did not enter college (and who ordinarily would not be expected to enter these professions).

There are a few scattered expectations on specific points, but the data obtained on college-aged samples from 1963 through 1968 are for the most part consistent on the differences between the activistically oriented students and the others. Activists, or those most likely to be sympathetic to activism, now, as in the recent past, are marked by traits of leadership, autonomy, intellectual-esthetic interests, social awareness, and involvement with social issues. Other dimensions may be involved in the rising number of protests among minority students, and some protests among blacks and whites alike have led to violence and vandalism. The protests are increasing to the extent that they occurred on 35 campuses in April 1969. Some protesters are no doubt dogmatic and little concerned with altruism. But considerable evidence indicates that it is probable that surveys cited above and that they are protesting for the reasons mentioned at the outset of this paper. Regardless of excess, the activists may be distinguishing themselves by coming closer than most members of society to realizing the goals of a democratic society.

Role of the College

By now it should be clear that activism involves the development of intellectual disposition, autonomy, and social awareness among college students. The implications of the data are that the relatively small but growing number of student activists and their sympathizers are seeking changes in society, beginning with its institutions of higher education, that will reflect and fulfill their ideals and goals. Given the active leadership, dissatisfaction with the status quo, intellectual disposition, autonomy, humanitarianism, and originality found among so many activists, it is evident that the changes that they seek in higher education cannot—and should not—go unheeded by the educational and legislative establishment. Concerted, concerned response from the college is necessary.

The contention here is that student political activism could act as a catalyst and supplement for the kind of educational activism which we view as a crucial part of the learning process. Student activists need not be alienated from the educational establishment but can bring enriched meaning to it. Our further contention is that it is the proper function of the college to activate intellectual and social commitment in its students, rather than resist this function when it is urged by the activists. At least college should make students consciously aware and critical of their own values and beliefs in important areas of concern to themselves and society, even when political activism may not be the final outcome of this increased awareness.

If the function of the college is viewed in this context, its role might then be conceptualized as an activating, facilitating, and mediating agency for students and as a catalytic agency of social change for society. It might activate important learning and personal behavior by stimulating intellectual awareness and growth and an understanding of and concern over social issues. It might facilitate learning and personal development by providing the conditions most conducive to optimum student development. It might mediate between the student and society by providing a moratorium so that students could be free to act in an attempt to draw meaning from and bring meaning to life without fear of reprisals from a more conforming society. In so doing, the college would be providing a catalyst for social change through its graduates. But under present conditions it may have to concentrate all its resources on changing and solving the social problems beyond simply studying them or encouraging its students to deal with them.

That education, and especially higher education, should act as a stimulating and challenging agent for students seems an idea so indisputable that it hardly appears to invite examination. Yet, what is purported in principle often remains unaccomplished in fact. Many graduate from college without ever becoming aware, for example, of the satisfactions that dedicated intellectual endeavor can bring; and, at least on the basis of the data presented in this paper, what is largely missing among current college graduates is the thinking, critical man, deeply aware of his cultural and intellectual heritage, alert to the contemporary problems existing in society, and able to bring historical perspective to present-day difficulties.

Of course, the gaining of such wisdom is a lifelong process, but for that very reason its nurture should begin early, and college should activate and aid, rather than hinder, its development. With our industrial society's emphasis upon narrowly skilled and professional training, however, such an ideal of what college should begin to develop is being lost except by a very few schools and people. Instead, there continues the training of generations of professionals whose major goals are directed primarily to home, job, family, and "getting ahead." Such goals in themselves are not to be criticized, but a danger exists when they are the *only* goals seen as worthwhile. Then people too commonly become egocentric, narrow, and restricted.

In contrast, the minority of student activists seems to be providing a healthy, if sometimes extreme, departure from commonly accepted goals and norms. Whatever point of view one may take about the methods of some of their activities, at least these young people are concerned with the major social issues arond them and are earnestly engaged in trying to remedy the ills they see in society. According to the 1968 *Fortune* survey, the majority of students are still the practical-minded, professionally oriented. But the proportion of forerunners most concerned with understanding and improving society is larger than the proportion that would have been expected from our national sample of data obtained five years previously. If the proportion of militant activists has not increased, there is indication of a larger proportion of students sympathetic with many of the activists' concerns. This is important since the influence of the activists is magnified when they rally sympathizers who are anxious to cope with society's problems such as those posed by the activists.

Often coinciding with this concern about social ills is a growing dissatisfaction among students with the type and kind of education they are receiving. There is evidence that the great majority of students are generally satisfied with their education but that a small though growing minority is seriously critical. These critics believe the university has lost its autonomy from the society around it and has become part of the "system." Perhaps the most overt expression of this disenchantment is directed against the new professionalism—a sign of the growing discontent with the trend of higher education in the United States in some of today's more able and valuable students. Speaking for them, Mario Savio, probably the most renowned student leader of the Free Speech Movement, has said, "The futures and careers for which American students now prepare are for the most part intellectual and moral wastelands."[30]   Once again, there is Farber, among others, who considers the plight of the student as no better than that of the exploited "nigger."[31]

The important question is what can be done to stimulate both those already highly developed and those so eager to receive a vocational certification in the form of a college degree that they seem impervious to any degree of intellectual stimulation or social awareness. A few answers to this question have come from some of the more able students themselves.

In a 1966 conference sponsored by the National Student Association, the discussion focused on the need to redefine a good education for today's youth. The participating students concluded that any viable definition should embrace at least these three elements: (1) relevance to a world of rapid social change, (2) commitment to the individual as the focus of value in the educational process, and (3) readiness of the educational system to explore diverse and changing needs of the current college population in order to meet the highly diversified developmental opportunities many of these students require. In regard to the last point, it was emphasized

that at least a significant segment of current student bodies are demanding a voice in the shaping of their own education—not as a right and not because they feel themselves necessarily wiser than their elders, but because they profoundly believe that exercising this responsible privilege is itself educative. A major challenge to many institutions is precisely that of devising the conditions under which students may properly test this condition.[32]

Other answers are coming from the evaluations, innovations, and educational experimentation proposed or taking place on many campuses.[33] Frequently these innovative efforts involve the collaboration of students, faculty, and administration, as exemplified in the student-organized special courses and the experimental college initiated at San Francisco State College, and now found nationwide. Sometimes these efforts involve collaboration between colleges, at least at the level of sharing ideas and resources, as is the case in the Union of Research and Experimentation in Higher Education. More recently the innovations are beginning to involve collaboration between colleges and their surrounding community as exemplified by urban centers such as those found at the University of Southern California and the proposed urban-centered, urban-oriented college in the Bedford-Stuyvesant area of Brooklyn.[34]

But whatever the nature of the innovation—whether it involves collaboration of colleges, elimination of grades in order to promote learning for the sake of learning, more flexible and widespread use of seminars and field techniques, emphasis upon independent study, student-oriented and student-taught courses, urban-oriented curricula and colleges, the creation of special colleges within a large collegiate complex, or the restructuring of the format of a college—it is hoped that the innovation will activate a new spirit of learning and social awareness among the many students previously not disposed to this kind of educational activism. Such activism might provoke the student professionalist to think more critically from new reference points even if his basic values have not changed. If college should not necessarily liberalize students in this respect, it should at least make them more libertarian.

It is equally important that these kinds of educational experimentations should also facilitate personality development and growth for those already predisposed to liberal humanistic learning. Data have shown that colleges do seem to serve this facilitating function much more than does the workaday world.[35] Perhaps if students were given a more innovative college program than many educators have yet envisioned, students might begin to reach that level of development and concern for society that is characteristic of the more able activist students at present. At least, colleges should do their utmost to promote this kind of positive growth and welcome it when it manifests itself on the campus scene.

If the concept of a liberal education were applied to the meaning behind every college degree, then the idea of the college or university as a mediating agency in the society might also be adequately fulfilled. Here too, then, the student might have an opportunity to develop personally. There are several aspects to the mediating role of the college, but in this sense perhaps its first and most important function is to preserve its autonomy as a way of maintaining academic freedom. In this way the college can serve the spirit of truth and free inquiry—ideals which may often, although not necessarily, clash with the more partisan pressures of the rest of society and even with established elements within the college. In making new discoveries, the college must subsequently act as a mediator between new truths and knowledge and the older established values still dominant in the larger society; it does so by providing in a way for society to understand, evaluate, and eventually accept new findings despite the resistance of the status quo.

Another way, then, in which the college or university could serve as a mediating agency in society is by providing its students a moratorium to rethink their values critically and constructively in light of what they learn. Traditionally, college has served the function of a "rite of passage" for young adult entrance into society. For many young people, the period spent in college provides one of the last opportunities to devote all their time to their own intellectual, social, and moral development before the pressures of adult society and responsibilities turn their attention in other directions. This kind of extended moratorium contains several possibilities: it can give students a chance to insure and expand the ways in which they have developed and to establish more firmly the new identities they are trying to forge; it can provide the opportunity for the opening of proper channels for the free expression of students' ideas about their education and the problems of the society around them, and offer students the opportunity to deal with these ideas and problems; in the process, it can encourage students to assume contributive adult responsibilities; and it can enable many students who are professionally oriented to have a better chance to benefit from a liberal education.

It may well be true, as Kerr maintains,[36] that one of the major functions of college is to prepare people for professional jobs in society, but it is also true that society is frequently in need of revision and change as new knowledge and new ideals arise. Therefore, one of the most important things a student can bring to society is not conformity to its values but rather an open, free, critical, thinking mind, dedicated to truth and human development. If the college can act as mediator for the introduction of the spirit of free inquiry into the community, through both its own va'ues and the values of its students, then society can look forward to seeing an enriched humanistic perspective brought to it, beyond that which is evident from our survey of recent and previous college graduates.

The college that encourages its students to become involved with social problems inevitably will itself become involved with these problems and with the community burdened by them. But there is another reason why the college must become involved. It seeks to research and understand urban problems and sources of human development in our technocratic urban settings. But it is not sufficient only to analyze these elements in academic, ivory-tower fashion. Society depends upon the knowledge and expertise concentrated in the college in order to become systematically aware of its problems and subsequently to solve them.

To think, as does Barzun,[37] that higher education can be reduced to a glorification of the three R's is controvertible. In fact, the three R's, the development and communication of knowledge, and our whole cultural heritage might well be best taught and implemented through the innovations proposed. Moreover, there is evidence that colleges following the traditions advocated by Barzun have actually been unsuccessful in realizing these objectives.[38] It is equally controvertible to think, as does John Millett, the Chancellor of Ohio Board of Regents, that the college should remain free from radical criticism or from radically criticizing society on the ground that it is the product of the American affluent majority.[39] The college is not merely a product of society. Its functions are such that it has a key role in delineating and developing society's products. In these complex, changing days when technology frequently leaves large segments of society unprepared for and cut off from technology's benefits, the college cannot magically remain a quiet conscience, as Millett would have it, while remote from and yet subservient to society. Rather, the function of higher education necessitates that it bring its insights, knowledge, and skills to the attention of the community for the sake of the community's own improvement. While maintaining (and improving upon) traditional academic functions, higher education must at the same time be a catalyst and, indeed, a vehicle for social change.

Conditions for Reformation

Wallerstein sees this expanded role of higher education resulting inevitably in a certain amount of tension not unlike that implied in the above conceptualization of the functions of the college in the face of the many who are resistant to all but the status quo in society. There is agreement here that the tension is essential, particularly given Wallerstein's conclusion that:

The newer role envisaged for the urban university, one deeply integrated into its immediate environs, subject to a rational societal allocation of priorities, a planning in which the university but also the rest of the community participates is perhaps less familiar in the traditions of the great universities. Such a role has, of course, been played by many rural state institutions, especially in American history. The research and the curricula of many of the land-grant colleges were long geared to the needs of the agricultural community. Today it is precisely the urban problems of advanced industrial society that require the urban university to take on new tasks, and in a new way. Again the demand fits in not only with the ideals of the left but with the rhetoric of service of many representatives of established values and institutions. To fight for democratic and mutually planned rather than aristocratic and bestowed service is surely a legitimate objective within the framework of what are presumably American traditional values.[40]

We would only add that the university so integrated with its environs would probably be best able to serve all its functions, including—through feedback of knowledge—its function centered primarily on pure research and dissemination of knowledge.

Reform of this kind would offer constructive avenues for the strengths of the activists and assure attention to their legitimate demands without the necessity of devastating confrontations. Those few radicals who are as relentlessly close-minded as the most reactionary within the establishment may never be satisfied without total confrontation regardless of the rapidity and extent of reformation. But without radical changes in higher education (and society at large) there will be no possibility of sufficient satisfaction for anyone. The changes, of course, can occur effectively only under certain conditions. As we view the situation we would include conditions that may be summarized under the headings of diversification, innovation, democratization, socialization and reevaluation.

Diversification. For years educators and government officials have urged universal higher education. Many activists are now insisting that this insistence be more than rhetorical. Yet what is intended by and what will result from higher education for all is not clear. Higher education cannot feasibly be all things for all people. Neither can it extend expectations only to dash them with limited opportunity and undue curricular and parietal constraints. The nature and needs of those who seek higher education differ greatly, and the college must be sufficiently diversified in its programs and modes of education and service to respond to the needs of the different individuals comprising its clientele. The diversification must go beyond the current distinction between private and public, select and general, liberal arts and professional, two-year and four-year, or undergraduate and graduate institutions. There must be diversification across institutions and within separate institutions in a coordinated, programmatic way that will make education personally relevant to the creative, to those not attracted to or not ready for college as it now exists, to those who find it easy to come to college, and to those who are dismayed by it. This may well mean rethinking the whole notion of college and how it is to operate. It may also mean putting a college in an educational park, a tenement house, a factory, or a tent. The important thing is to find ways to diversify college effectively beyond the traditional stereotypes.

Innovation. The needed diversification of higher education as we are discussing it implies the necessity for innovation. A perpetual attempt must be made to improve educational programs by examining what programs are to be offered and how they may be offered and evaluated to assure that they are more effective than past programs. Innovation can easily become a cliché in higher education. The addition of an audio-tutorial laboratory in a college may represent a minimum of innovation if it is handled as electronic gadgetry made to fit in the long-established curricular mold. The innovation that is needed involves more than just a new device or even a new idea. There probably are very few really new ideas in education. What is most needed is a consistently fresh approach to education—an open, flexible search for superior substance and presentation of that substance. Useful precedent and tradition should not be ignored, but it is just as important that the educational process not be confined to precedent, the effectiveness of which has almost never been demonstrated.

Democratization. The innovative search for "relevance" in higher education is not possible when it is frustrated by intellectual dogmatists or other reactionaries who possess inordinate power in the faculty, administration, or governing board. The paradigm of the past, such as that described by Woodring,[41] has been the faculty aligned against the trustees, the administration arbitrating in between, some students having an occasional say in recent years, and each group concerned primarily with its own vested, exclusive interests. One of the most needed innovations in the college is a system of organization that will promote open communication and flexible responsiveness among these groups in place of their collision. The college may best be governed by congress where there exists an intercommunication and balance of power among the faculty, students, administration, trustees, and, at least in some cases, community representatives. A preconceived notion is that students are too transient and immature to participate in campus governance. In reality, they often are no more transient than the faculty, and they have shown themselves to be quite capable of making momentous decisions affecting their own education and the college in general. As examples, students have been involved in the selection of faculty at Antioch College for some time; at the 1969 annual meeting of the American Personnel and Guidance Association a consistent characteristic of the dozen or so successful college programs for cultural minorities described was that the involved students shared in the decision making of the programs at all levels. In governance, as well as teaching, students have been a wasted power. A rewarding collaboration between students and the other factors of higher education may be possible; otherwise there likely will result a power struggle even more intense than that so far observed on American campuses.

Socialization. The position here has been that the college is no mere reflection of the affluent majority. It has many roles to fulfill for many publics. As a result, the college must be more concerned than traditionally it has been with socialization in that it must relate more often and more effectively to the different factors of society. As an agent of social change it must be sensitive to the needs of society and must deal personally with its members to achieve collaboration in changes devised to meet the needs. In order to carry out this and other important functions. For instance, the college cannot implement an educational moratorium when student protests are met only by repressive retaliation from both legislators and the immediate community. Citizens and civic leaders alike are in great need of an education whereby they will gain an understanding of the meaning of a college education (including social consciousness and intellectual development apart from professional training) and of the problems and issues this involves currently. This education of the public cannot be accomplished unless large numbers of the college see to it consistently and systematically. The opinions of the established constituency and policy-makers cannot be disregarded or flaunted; instead, they must be opinions that follow from a comprehension of the college.

Reevaluation. Implied throughout this discussion is the position that the viability and development of higher education is dependent upon proper evaluation. Many studies of the past, such as those contained in *The American College,*[42] are important, but they are not sufficient for the present in design or content. Many of these studies bear replication, but there must be a reevaluation of higher education of yet a different sort. Research must go beyond the assessment of the effectiveness of a particular program or an institutions's impact on the personality development of its students. There must be a systematic and comprehensive evaluation of the whole system of higher education. Moreover, to accomplish this purpose, the evaluation itself must be innovative. A thorough explanation of the nature of this type of research and evaluation must be withheld until it can be treated at length. For the moment the essential issue is to note the critical functions of the research. It must delineate the input, process, and outcome variables and the effects of their interactions within and across institutions in reference to discerned criterion variables. It must thereby provide research models that will result in the identification and understanding of the dynamics of higher education from student attitudes to administrative styles, so that decision making and implementation of programs in the college can be made on an informed basis, with a clear notion of the relevant issues, the alternatives available, and what to expect of the different alternatives. It must provide a constant, sweeping monitoring and subsequent evaluation of the system and its different components. In the light either of "the normal" state of affairs or changing situation, there is no other way to respond rapidly to legitimate protest, to deal with problems before they become insurmountable or otherwise to implement adjustments and improvements in the system. We may anticipate evaluative research and research models of this nature from work done at Berkeley's Center for Research and Development in Higher Education; the Carnegie Foundation's national assessment of higher education under Clark Kerr's direction; programs under way at the American College Testing Program, American Council of Education, and the Regional Educational Laboratory for the Carolinas and Virginia; and the nationwide evaluation of higher education now under way at the Center for the Study of Evaluation at the University of California at Los Angeles. The actual development of research and evaluation along these lines is a major thrust of the Center for the Study of Evaluation. But it is crucial to have a much broader participation in the evaluation of higher education.

These observations are no doubt obvious to many; they are surely debatable to others. Any debate, however, must consider the alternatives the college has before it. It may maintain its present status, revert to a Barzunian model, and repress resultant criticism and confrontation from student activists. Under the circumstances it will run the risk of being shut down or of becoming ineffectual as it ignores instead of leads the cultural revolution that is evident. Or it may seek additional roles, meanings, and methods that will make its major functions relevant to the needs and natures of its students and other clientele in this period of cultural revolution.

The latter alternative cannot be accomplished easily or immediately. It probably will not satisfy the few activists who are determined on total confrontation with the college, whatever its response. It will, however, probably satisfy most of the activists who will have rendered an incalculable service to higher education by insisting upon being satisfied only through positive changes in the college. In any event, the college and the rest of society must be prepared to absorb and heed a good many activists for some time to come.

The qualities found among student activists suggest that many of them are not merely banner-wavers of the moment who will live out their lives in comfortable suburban homes, forgetting what they were once so excited about on the steps of Berkeley's Sproul Hall or Harvard's yard. Many of them will probably become involved with professional and family life and will doubtless become more mellowed and patient in outlook as they meet their obligations and the kind of responsibilities that come with the attainment of true adult autonomy. But it is probable that the qualities they bring to their meaningful dissent in college will be enduring, positive, and influential and that they will continue to initiate intellectual dissent and social awareness. They are likely to be heard from, in conversation, in printed word, and in public address. The time is surely right and the need urgent for the college not only to stimulate activism among its students but to provide the circumstances under which it can flourish without negative excesses on the part of the activists or reprisals from society.

Footnotes

1. Judith Craise assisted with portions of an article that appeared in the July 1967 issue of the *Journal of Social Issues,* parts of which have been incorporated.

2. G. H. Wierzynski, "A Student Declaration: 'Our Most Wrenching Problem . . . ,' " *Fortune,* 1969, *79*(1), 114 ff. This comment and those that follow in this paragraph actually represent a synthesis of the students' statements.

3. *Ibid.,* p. 116.

4. Two major revolutions are apparent in higher education. Predominantly white middle-class activists are seeking to change higher education from what they see as negative aspects of the affluent, established society. As noted above, minority militants are seeking not so much to change higher education as to assure that they receive more of it. This chapter concentrates on the white activists' protest.

5. Jerry Farber, "The Student as Nigger," in J. Hopkins (Ed.), *The Hippie Papers: Notes from the Underground Press* (New York: Signet Books, 1968), pp. 160-168.

6. Michael Rossman and Michael Vozick, "Dear Michael: Two Letters on Confrontation," *Change in Higher Education,* 1969, *1*(1), 40-43.

7. *Ibid.,* p. 43.

8. Farber, *op. cit.;* Lewis S. Feuer, *The Conflict of Generations: The Character and Significance of Student Movements* (New York: Basic Books, 1969).

9. Richard E. Peterson, *The Scope of Organized Student Protest in 1964-1965* (Princeton, N.J.: Educational Testing Service, 1966).

10. Paul Heist, "Intellect and Commitment: The Faces of Discontent," in O. W. Knorr and W. J. Minter (Eds.), *Order and Freedom on the Campus: The Rights and Responsibilities of Faculty and Students* (Boulder, Colo.: Western Interstate Commission for Higher Education, 1965), p. 62.

11. L. L. Baird, *A Study of Student Activism* (Iowa City: American College Testing Program, 1968), mimeographed.

12. James W. Trent and Leland L. Medsker, *Beyond High School: A Psychosociological Study of 10,000 High School Graduates* (San Francisco: Jossey-Bass, 1968).

13. A. W. Astin, R. J. Panos, and J. A. Creager, *National Norms for Entering College Freshmen* (Washington, D.C.: American Council on Education, 1967).

14. D. Seligman, "A Special Kind of Rebellion," *Fortune,* 1969, *71*(1), 68.

15. Richard E. Peterson, *The Scope of Organized Student Protest in 1967-1968* (Princeton, N.J.: Educational Testing Service, 1968).

16. James W. Trent and J. H. Ruyle, *The Educated American* (Berkeley: Center for Research and Development in Higher Education, University of California, in preparation).

17. Kenneth Keniston, *Young Radicals: Notes on Committed Youth* (New

York: Harcourt, 1968); and Nathan Glazer, "The Jewish Role in Student Activism" *Fortune*, 1969, *70*(1), 112.

18. Trent and Medsker, *op. cit.*

19. Center for the Study of Higher Education, *Omnibus Personality Inventory—Research Manual* (Berkeley: Center for the Study of Higher Education, University of California, 1962); and Paul Heist and George Yonge, *Omnibus Personality Inventory Manual* (New York: Psychological Corporation, 1968).

20. Heist, *op. cit.*; R. H. Somers, "The Mainsprings of the Rebellion: A Survey of Berkeley Students in November, 1964," in Seymour M. Lipset and Sheldon S. Wolin (Eds.), *The Berkeley Student Revolt: Facts and Interpretations* (New York: Anchor Books, 1965), pp. 530-532; and William Watts and David Whittaker, "Some Social-Psychological Differences Between Highly Committed Members of the Free Speech Movement and the Student Population at Berkeley," *Journal of Applied Behavioral Science*, 1966, *2*(1), 41-62.

21. *Op. cit.*

22. Watts and Whittaker, *op. cit.*

23. A. W. Bendig, "The Development of a Short Form of the Taylor Manifest Anxiety Scale," *Journal of Consulting Psychology*, 1956, *20*, 384.

24. Kenneth Keniston, "Faces in the Lecture Room," *Yale Alumni Magazine*, April 1966, *35*(7), 20-34.

25. Heist, *op. cit.*; Somers, *op. cit.*; Watts and Wittaker, *op. cit.*

26. Baird, *op. cit.*; p. 11.

27. *Op. cit.*

28. "What They Believe: A *Fortune* Study," *Fortune*, 1969, *79*(1), 70.

29. The grouping and interpretation of these items are my own.

30. Mario Savio, "An End to History," in H. Draper (Ed.), *The New Student Revolt* (New York: Grove Press, 1965), pp. 179-182.

31. Farber, *op. cit.*

32. Edward Joseph Shoben, Jr. *Students, Stress and the College Experience* (Washington, D.C.: Council Press for the United States National Student Association, 1966), p. 19.

33. See S. Baskin, *Higher Education: Some Newer Developments* (New York: McGraw-Hill, 1965); W. M. Birenbaum, *Overlive: Power, Poverty, and the University* (New York: Delta Books, 1969); Educational Facilities Laboratory, *A College in the City: An Alternative* (New York: Educational Facilities Laboratory, 1969); and B. L. Johnson, *Islands of Innovation Expanding: Changes in the Community College* (Beverly Hills, Calif.: Glencoe Press, 1969).

34. See Birenbaum, *op. cit.*

35. See Trent and Medsker, *op. cit.*

36. Clark Kerr, *The Uses of the University* (Cambridge: Harvard University Press, 1963).

37. Jacques Barzun, *The American University: How It Runs, Where It Is Going* (New York: Harper, 1968).

38. Philip E. Jacob, *Changing Values in College* (New York: Harper, 1957).

39. John Millett, *Reconstruction of the University* (Cincinnati: Institute for Research and Training in Higher Education, University of Cincinnati, 1968).

40. I. Wallerstein, *The University in Turmoil: The Politics of Change* (New York: Atheneum, 1969), p. 143.

41. Paul Woodring, *The Higher Learning in America: A Reassessment* (New York: McGraw-Hill, 1968).

42. Nevitt Sanford (Ed.), *The American College* (New York: Wiley, 1962).

MULTIVERSITY, UNIVERSITY SIZE, UNIVERSITY QUALITY, AND STUDENT PROTEST: AN EMPIRICAL STUDY

Joseph W. Scott and Mohamed El-Assal

Introduction

Berkeley and Columbia (2, 29) have become symbols of a militant generation of college students and of student activism. Student activism, characteristic of the 1960's has become a defined "social problem." Since the Berkeley demonstrations of 1964, such activism has increased in number of incidents and in the degree of militancy. Recently students have not only employed the "sit-in," but also have captured buildings and held administrators as hostages, sometimes until they agreed to demands of the students or until the police arrived.

There is ample evidence that current student protest movement in the U.S. had its origin in the 1950's (11). Widespread anti-ROTC demonstrations occurred largely in the late '50's, indicating that the students were not as "silent" and as contented as some writers would have us believe (23). Yet, notwithstanding such signs of the future, no forecast was made of the activism and militancy of students present today on U.S. campuses.

Very few systematic studies on the student movement have been reported (15, 26, 31, 4, 30, 32, 25, 17, 20, 22). Even after Berkeley, few, if any, studies on student protest have appeared in the major sociological journals.[1] Many journalistic accounts and commentaries

From the *American Sociological Review*, Vol. 34, No. 5, October 1969, pp. 702-709. Reprinted by permission of the American Sociological Association and the authors.

on student activism were written, but these have not been based on methodical and empirical research. In the absence of such research, the nature of the protest movement is a matter largely for speculations and opinions.

Although the general subject of student demonstrations stands in need of research, some aspects are more deserving of concentration than others. To date, most authors have dealt with the personal characteristics of the activists themselves. These authors have compared student activists with other college groups, with national samples of college students, and with non-college samples. In some of these studies, the student activists have been given personality inventories and have been questioned on their private values and political ideologies. In addition, some parents and grandparents have been interviewed. Yet, these studies still leave a significant gap in our knowledge. University structures themselves have been studied, but few reports have been discovered by the writers; one report found is by Peterson (17). The apparent scarcity of published material is somewhat inconsistent with the importance of university administrative structures as a factor in student grievances. Specifically, the increasing social heterogeneity of the student bodies and bureaucratization of the administrative structures are of crucial importance because they are two principal conditions stimulating student unrest and moving student activists to protest demonstrations. For these reasons the university structures in relation to their environments should be intensively studied. What has been reported about the relationship of structures to their environments has been written largely by behavioral scientists (12, 7, 19, 8, 27, 24, 1, 3).

Since so many speculations have been advanced, we believe that systematic research is required to determine which speculations are best supported by empirical data. For example, permissive family socialization (4, 5, 32), selective university recruitment and socialization (6, 11, 13), university size and heterogeneity (17, 18), university opportunity structures for protest (28, 18), and university bureaucratization (16, 9) have all been subjects of speculation as causes of student unrest and rebellion. Our study tries to sort out the strength of some of these variables.

The Problem

Since 1960, most American universities have changed structurally and socially, and some of these changes have given rise to conflicts between students and administrators. During the time that many of these schools have grown structurally from simple teachers colleges to complex universities, their number of mature graduate and undergraduate students have greatly increased. Such students do not want their campus activities and classwork dictated, regulated, managed or rigidly preplanned. But paradoxically, as a larger percentage of college and university students are married, mobile, financially independent, and more insistent on personal freedoms, many administrations have become more bureaucratic, and regimentation of the educational process has increased. Thus, many administrators have unwittingly been drawn into conflict with the activist students. The issues and rhetoric of student protest demonstrations as reported in the mass media lend support to this conclusion. The nature of this conflict has been noted by Clark Kerr (10), former president of the University of California who spoke of an incipient revolt against multiversity as follows:

If the alumni are concerned, the undergraduate students are restless. Recent changes in the American university have done them little good—lower teaching loads for the faculty, larger classes, the use of substitute teachers for the regular faculty, the choice of faculty members based on research accomplishments rather than instructional capacity, the fragmentation of knowledge into endless subdivisions. There is an incipient revolt of undergraduate students against the faculty; the revolt that used to be against the faculty in *loco parentis* is now against the faculty *in absentia*. The students find themselves under a blanket of impersonal rules for admissions, for scholarships, for examinations, for degrees. It is interesting to watch how a faculty intent on few rules for itself can fashion such a plethora of them for the students. The students also want to be treated as distinct individuals.

Continuing in the same vein, Kerr held that the typical state university had become large, complex, and diversified; teaching had become less important than research; faculty members had become less members of the particular university and more colleagues within their academic disciplines; teaching had become minimal for the most highly paid faculty members; classes had become generally larger; the students themselves had become so vast in number and so heterogeneous that the campus for them often seemed confusing, full of dilemmas, fraught with problems of belonging and security.

Kerr in the statement above offers us a research proposition which may be tested. First, let us postulate that the more complex the formal structure is, the more likely is the administration to be bureaucratic as opposed to primary and patrimonial. Accordingly, the more bureaucratic the educational institution, the more structurally separated are the students from administrators, faculty, and students; and the more the students are personally separated from administrators, faculty members, and other students by structural complexity and social heterogeneity, the more likely the students will feel separated, neglected, manipulated, and dehumanized to the extent that they will engage in protest activities. Given these premises, we hypothesize that the more nearly a university constitutes a "multiversity," the higher the rate of protest demonstration. To test the stated research hypothesis, we had to correlate the degrees of formal complexity and social heterogeneity with the number of student demonstrations, introducing at various points the intervening variables of institutional size, institutional quality, and size of community in which the educational institution is located.

Method

First, we select a *purposive sample* of 104 state-supported non-technical and non-specialized colleges and universities that reflect the diverse (1) sizes of such institutions, (2) sizes of resident communities, and (3) geographic parts of the United States. Secondly, we compiled separate sociodemographic profiles for each school (college or university) using secondary sources, namely, *The College Blue Book: American Universities and Colleges,* and *The Digest of Educational Statistics,* and other documents published by the U.S. Department of Health, Education, and Welfare. Thirdly, we gathered a list of the number and types of demonstrations occurring at each school from January 1, 1964 to December 31, 1965. Each dean of students and each editor of the school newspaper was then sent a questionnaire containing the following categories of information to which they were to reply: (1) the issues over which any demonstrations occured, (2) the duration of each demonstration, (3) actions of demonstrators, i.e., violent or peaceful, (4) organizations involved, (5) actions taken by the administration, (6) the total number of demonstrations.

These questionnaires were mailed to the representatives of the schools in our sample. The receipt of one or more questionnaires from the same school was considered as a single report for the school. When one dean and one student editor were diametrically opposed in their reporting, we wrote to them for clarification. The mail-back rate was as follows:

Schools not Responding	Schools Reporting no Demon-strations	Schools Report-ing some Demon-strations	Total
35	25	44	104

Compared with other studies requiring mail-back questionnaires, the ratio of questionnaires returned was quite favorable. The mail-back rates were nearly equal when schools with an enrollment over ten thousand were compared to those under ten thousand. The questionnaire responses came from schools in 42 states from all geographical sections of the United States, namely, New England, Middle Atlantic, North Central, Southwest, Rocky Mountain, and Far West.

The *independent variable* in this study was "multiversity"—an index combining structural complexity and social heterogeneity. The *dependent variable* was the number of demonstrations. The *intervening variables* were the size and quality of the institution, and the size of the community in which the institution was located.

"Multiversity" was operationalized as composite index based on these factors: (1) the number of departments granting doctoral degrees, (2) the number of departments granting masters degrees, (3) the number of departments granting bachelors degrees, (4) the number of departments offering first professional degrees, (5) the ratio of dormitory to non-dormitory students, (6) the ratio of outstate to instate students, (7) the ratio of foreign students to native born students, (8) the ratio of students to professors, and (9) the ratio of undergraduates to graduate students. The first four variables were clearly indicators of administrative complexity: span of control, horizontal and vertical specialization, the number of hierarchies of authority, the degrees of segmentation and coordination, and the number of rules, regulations, and lines of communication. The second five variables were indicators of administrative complexity and social heterogeneity of the student body. These variables not only indicate the diverse human elements which must be administratively allocated, integrated, and managed daily in order for the university to carry on, but they also indicate socially the extent of secondariness in the daily interpersonal contacts among the students themselves.

The multiversity index was derived by first recording the scores and ratios for each school using these nine dimensions. Secondly, we arrayed scores and ratios from high to low. Thirdly, we reduced each array to dichotomized categories using the medians as cutting points. Fourthly, we ran a Guttman scale analysis using these dichotomous scores for the nine variables. The result was a quasi-scale with a coefficient of reproducibility of .84 and a minimal marginal coefficient of reproducibility of .51. No items were eliminated in order to raise the coefficient of reproducibility, since we were interested only in reliably ranking schools from complex to simple by our composite index. The quasi-scale scores varied from ten to one. The arrayed scores resulted in a bimodal distribution with about 30% of the cases receiving a score of one and about 38% receiving a score of ten. The other scores were evenly distributed between these extremes. Finally, using the median of this array of scores, we divided the schools into two categories: "complex" versus "simple" schools. This dichotomy will be our short way of designating "multiversities" versus "non-multiversities" respectively.

Abstractly a "complex" school would be above the median in numbers of departments granting doctoral, masters, bachelors and professional degrees, and in numbers of non-dormitory, outstate, foreign, and graduate students, as well as in numbers of professors to students.

Definitions

Size of school in this study was the number of full-time equivalent students. The schools were categorized as follows: 15,000 or more; 10,000-15,000; 7,000-10,000; 4,000-7,000; and 2,000-4,000. *Quality* of school was computed by summing the schools' positions in three arrays: the ratio of the number of library books to all students, the percent of full-time faculty with doctoral degrees, and the percentage of graduates receiving national scholarships and honors. When a school was above the median, it received a score of one; if it was below, it received a score of two. The quality index varied from three (high quality) to six (low quality). Finally, *size of community* was defined as the total population of the community according to the official census of 1960. We began with four categories: 500,000 or more; 50,000-500,000; 15,000-50,000; and 15,000 or less.

With the schools categorized as "simple" and "complex," we analyzed the relationship among the variables: complexity, size, and quality of schools, size of community in which the schools were located, and number of student demonstrations.

Findings

Complexity

The great majority of the complex schools reportedly had some demonstrations, while the great majority of the simple schools reportedly did not have demonstrations. The gamma coefficient representing this association was .80. Complex schools had 2.44 demonstrations per school reporting, and simple schools had .75 demonstrations per school reporting. (See Figure 1.)

Figure 1. School characteristics and schools reporting
student demonstrations

School Characteristics	Intervening Variables	Schools Reporting Demonstrations	Schools Reporting No Demonstrations	N
Complex institutions		87%	13%	32
				G=.80
Simple institutions		43	57	37
School size				
Large (10,000+)		96	4	26
				G=.94
Small (10,000−)		44	56	43
Community size				
Large city (50,000+)		74	26	27
				G=.36
Small city (50,000−)		57	43	42
High quality institutions		85	15	33
				G=.69
Low quality institutions		44	56	36
School size				
Mostly complex	10,000+	96	4	23
	10,000−	67	33	9
				G=.82
Mostly simple	10,000+	100	0	3
	10,000−	38	62	34
Community size				
Mostly complex	50,000+	94	6	16
	50,000−	81	19	16
				G=.66
Mostly simple	50,000+	42	58	26
	50,000−	45	55	11
School quality				
Mostly complex	High Quality	89	11	27
	Low Quality	80	20	5
				G=.75
Mostly simple	High Quality	67	33	6
	Low Quality	39	61	31

Size of School

Generally, the schools with ten thousand or more students had the most demonstrations. Over 90% reported having had some demonstrations. The medium-sized and small schools usually reported no demonstrations. The gamma coefficient for this association was .94. The large schools had 2.89 demonstrations per school, and the small schools had .72 demonstrations per school.

Size of School and Complexity

The schools with enrollments of 10,000 or more students fell disproportionately in the complex category, and the schools of fewer than 10,000 students fell disproportionately in the simple category. However, *regardless of complexity, all the large schools, except one, reported having had some demonstrations.* But, among the smaller schools, complexity exerted an appreciable influence: the great majority of small schools in the complex category had demonstrations whereas the great majority of the small schools in the simple category did not have demonstrations. The gamma coefficient representing this association was .82.

Size of Community

All in all, the schools in large- and medium-sized communities had disproportionately more demonstrations. The great majority of schools in small-sized towns did not have demonstrations. The gamma coefficient representing this association was .36.

Size of Community and Complexity

The great majority of the complex schools in both large and small communities had demonstrations. However, a substantial majority of simple schools had not had demonstrations, especially when they were located in communities of fewer than 50,000 persons. The gamma coefficient representing this association was .66.

Quality of School

By and large, the schools of highest quality (as defined) had disproportionately more demonstrations than schools of the lowest quality. A great majority of high quality schools had demonstrations, while a majority of low quality schools had no demonstrations. The gamma coefficient representing this association was .72. There were 2.36 demonstrations per high quality school and .75 demonstration per low quality school.

Figure 2. Stepwise multiple correlation coefficients, beta coefficients
and zero-order coefficients for school, size, complexity,
school quality, community size and number of demonstrations

Dependent Variables	Number of Demonstrations	% Variance Explained
	R	
School size	.580	33.6
School size and complexity	.591	34.9
School size, complexity, and quality	.593	35.2
School size, complexity, quality, and community size	.594	35.3

Dependent Variables	Beta Coefficients
School size	.430
Complexity	.119
Quality	.080
Community size	.038

Matrix of Zero-order Correlation Coefficients

Variables	(1)	(2)	(3)	(4)	(5)
(1) Complexity	...	.73	.72	.27	.50
(2) Quality	...	...	.58	.17	.42
(3) School size	...	...	...	.46	.58
(4) Community size	...	...	...	...	.28
(5) Number of demonstrations	...	...	...	...	...

Quality of School and Complexity

The great majority of complex schools regardless of quality had demonstrations. By contrast, among the simple schools, two-thirds of the high quality schools had demonstrations; very few simple, low quality schools had demonstrations. In sum, high quality and complexity increased greatly the probability of schools having demonstrations but low quality and simplicity reduce greatly the probability of schools having them. The gamma coefficient representing this association was .75.

Introducing all the intervening variables at the same time did not give us enough cases in some cells to indicate all interactive effects. This multivariate table, however, did indicate that 100% of the complex, large, high quality schools had demonstrations, while only

34% of the simple, small, low quality schools had them. Half of these small schools had only one demonstration each during the period surveyed.

Our hypothesis that *as an institution becomes more like a multiversity the rate of demonstration also becomes higher appears to have been supported.* School size seems to give rise to those structural and social features which lead us to term an institution with such characteristics "a multiversity." School size was, therefore, found to be the most consistent predictor of student demonstrations.

In terms of predictive power, our non-parametric analysis revealed that school size was first; complexity was second; quality was third; and size of community was fourth. To get some indication of their relative numerical weights as predictive variables, we completed another analysis of our data.[2]

In Figure 2 we have presented the results of a stepwise regression analysis. The table contains the multiple correlation coefficients, the beta coefficients, and simple zero-order inter-correlations coefficients. From this analysis, the ordinal relationships among the independent variables are clarified. School size accounted for almost all the explained variance. Complexity was heavily dependent on school size and thus accounted for only a small part of the total variance. School quality and community size accounted for almost none of the variance. Although these data do not meet all the assumptions of this regression analysis, we nevertheless believe the results to be suggestive. In the next section we present a paradigm to explain these findings.

Increasing Size and Bureaucratization of Universities

In becoming large, high quality, and heterogeneous, many schools had to expand and to formalize their administrative structures in order to coordinate large diverse numbers of communication activists and people in the massive educational enterprises of teaching, research, and public service. Accordingly, they expanded their administrative staff personnel such as vice-presidents, deans, associate deans, department chairmen, associate department chairmen, administrative assistants, secretaries, executive secretaries, clerks, clerical helpers, and consultants. Simultaneously, they formalized and routinized their administrative procedures in order to coordinate and to regulate the granting of examinations, of degrees, of stipends, of scholarships, research on human subjects, teaching and research facilities, housing, extracurricular organizations, teaching schedules, speakers, sports activities, and hiring, termination, promotion and evaluation of personnel.

This routinization by formalization "caused" students, faculty, and staff alike to be treated more and more as impersonal and processable categories of people characterized by some "common factor." When such personnel (the students in particular) had grievances, these grievances were routinely "processed" by administrative assistants, IBM cards, letters, or standardized forms and the like, thereby effectively closing off these people from the top of the university hierarchy. For students to receive some direct *personal* contact from higher administrators when they had grievances for which they sought redress, they sometimes had to engage in illegal or extralegal protest actions, e.g., collective demonstrations and disorders, which were not easily processed by daily routines, not easily mediated by impersonal mediators or communication, not easily ignored, and finally not easily delegated to lower-level bureaucrats by the top-level university administrators. Large, complex, high quality schools, being more likely to provide little or no opportunity for the concerned students to directly vote on the outcome of their grievances, encouraged and increased the likelihood of student protest demonstrations (11, 16). The probability of demonstrations was also increased because at the same time that these particular schools heightened the experience of administrative autocracy, administrative regimentation, and social alienation, they also attracted, recruited and socialized more radicalized and politicized students who were inclined to change these very structural conditions wherever they found them in society (6, 9, 17, 21).

Conclusions

Large, complex, high quality schools had a much higher rate of demonstrations per school than small, simple, low quality schools. These large schools did not, however, produce more demonstrations per 1,000 students than the small schools, indicating that demonstrations are not a result of number alone. The interaction effect between school size, administrative complexity and social heterogeneity was found to be fundamental to understanding some social conditions associated with student unrest and student protest in the U.S. today.

Footnotes

1. The authors could find no studies on the student revolution in the American Sociological Review, American Journal of Sociology, Social Problems, Sociometry, Social Forces, Social Science and Social Research and others, during the period of 1950-1967.

2. One of the ASR referees raised the question of whether or not larger schools (10,000+) really have a higher rate of demonstrations per 1,000 students than what would be normally expected. In calculating the rate of demonstrations per 1,000 students for each school, we learned that more large schools had demonstrations than the small schools, but they were on the whole not higher rates per 1,000 students. Large size does not produce a higher rate of demonstrations than small size; large size is simply more likely to be associated with the occurence of student protest demonstrations. Complexity is positively associated with student protest demonstrations among both large schools (10,000+) and small schools (10,000-). The relationship is more definitive among small schools than among large schools. Of the 26 large schools reporting, 23 were clearly complex, and 3 were clearly simple. Since all large schools but one had demonstrations, complexity does not stand out as vividly among large schools as it does among small schools where there is a sharp increase in demonstrations as small schools become more complex.

References

1. Brown, Donald R. "Social changes and the college student: A symposium." *The Educational Record* (October 1960):329-358.
2. Draper, Hal. *Berkeley: The New Student Revolt.* New York: Grove, 1965.
3. Fishman, Jacob R., and Soloman, Fredric. "Youth and social action: Perspectives on the student sit-in movement." *American Journal of Orthopsychiatry* 33 (May 1963):872-82.
4. Flacks, Richard. "The liberated generation: Explanation of the roots of student protest." *The Journal of Social Issues* 23 (July 1967):52-75.
5. Heist, Paul. "Intellect and commitment: The facts of discontent." Berkeley: Center for the Study of Higher Education, 1965.
6. Kaplan, Samuel. "The revolt of the elite: Sources of the FSM victory." *The Graduate Student Journal* 4 (Spring 1965):27-29.
7. Katz, Joseph and Sanford, Nevitt. "Causes of the student revolution." *Saturday Review* (December 1965):64-79.
8. Keniston, Kenneth. "American students and the political revival." *The American Scholar* 32 (Winter 1962):40-64.
9. ————. "The sources of student dissent." *The Journal of Social Issues* (July 1967):108-137.
10. Kerr, Clark. "Selections from *the Uses of the University*." pp. 38-60 in S. M. Lipset and S. S. Wolin (eds.), *The Berkeley Student Revolt.* New York: Doubleday, 1965.
11. Lipset, Seymour M. "Student opposition in the United States. *Government and Opposition* (April 1966):351-374.
12. Lipset, Seymour M. and Altbach, Philip G. "Student politics and higher education in the United States." *Comparative Education Review* (June 1966):321-49.
13. Lipset, Seymour M. and Seabury, Paul. "The lesson of Berkeley." *The Reporter* (January 1965):36-40.
14. Lipset, Seymour M. and Wolin, Sheldon S. *The Berkeley Student Revolt.* New York: Doubleday, 1965.
15. Lyonns, Glen. "The police car demonstration: A survey of participants." pp. 519-530 in S. M. Lipset and S. S. Wolin (eds.), *The Berkeley Student Revolt.* New York: Doubleday, 1965.

16. Nelken, Michael. "My mind is not property." *The Graduate Student Journal* (Spring 1965):30-34.
17. Peterson, Richard E. *The Scope of Organized Student Protest.* Princeton: Education Testing Service, 1966.
18. —————. "The student left in American higher education." *Daedalus* (Winter 1968):293-317.
19. Reisman, David. "The college student in an age of organization." *Chicago Review* 12 (Autumn 1958):50-58.
20. Sasajima, Masa, Davis, Jonius A. and Peterson, Richard E. "Organized student protest and institutional climate." Princeton: Educational Testing Service, 1967.
21. Savio, Mario. "An end to history." pp. 216-219 in S. M. Lipset and S. S. Wolin (eds.), *The Berkeley Student Revolt.* New York: Doubleday, 1965.
22. Schiff, Lawrence F. "The obedient rebels: A study of college conversions to conservatism." *The Journal of Social Issues* 20 (October 1964):75-94.
23. Scott, Joseph W. "ROTC recruitment, student protests, and change in the military establishment." University of Toledo, 1968. Mimeographed.
24. Seabury, Paul. "Berlin and Berkeley." *Comparative Education Revew* (June 1966):350-58.
25. Solomon, Frederic and Fishman, Jacob R. "Youth and peace: A psychological study of peace demonstrations in Washington, D.C." *The Journal of Social Issues* 20 (October 1964):54-73.
26. Somers, Robert H. "The mainsprings of the rebellion: A survey of Berkeley students in November 1964." pp. 530-537 in S. M. Lipset and S. S. Wolin (eds.), *The Berkeley Student Revolt.* New York: Doubleday, 1965.
27. Springer, George P. "Universities in flux." *Comparative Education Review* (February 1968):28-38.
28. Starobin, Robert. "Graduate students and the FSM." *The Graduate Student Journal* (Spring 1965):25.
29. The Graduate Student Society. "The Columbia student strike." New York: Columbia University, 1968.
30. Trent, James W. and Craise, Judith L. "Commitment and conformity in the American College." *The Journal of Social Issues* 23 (July 1967):34-51
31. Watts, William and Whittaker, Dave. "Free speech advocates at Berkeley." *The Journal of Applied Behavioral Science* 2 (Winter 1966):41-62.
32. Westby, David L., and Braungart, Richard G. "Class and politics in the family backgrounds of student political activists." *American Sociological Review* 31 (April 1966):690-92.

Part 5

The External Environment

THE MASS COLLEGE

Burton R. Clark

Organization character is a complex matter, often hidden from public view.[1] It may be identified in part by obtaining answers to the following questions: Is the organization independent of or dependent upon its environment; and if the latter, on whom is it dependent? What is the general orientation of the organization's programs and relationships? Does the organization have a distinctive way of life? What can the organization do? What degree of competence can be expected in the performance of tasks? What general roles does it assume within a larger scheme?

Administrative Dependency

No organization is free of environmental influence, but a highly independent firm, agency, or school can be inner-directed for the most part. The placement of San Jose Junior College within a unified district of the California public schools renders it an administratively dependent organization. In key policy matters its administrators are subordinate to the central authorities of the district. Financial control, personnel selection, and other basic operational matters of a junior college in a unified or high school district may be handled by the district or delegated to the college at the district's discretion. In San Jose the district chose to exercise considerable control, and in

This selection appears in *The Study of Academic Administration*, published by the Western Interstate Commission for Higher Education and the Center for the Study of Higher Education in Berkeley in 1963. It has been reprinted in *Professionalization* edited by Vollmer and Mills, Prentice-Hall, 1966, pp. 282-291.

respect to many means of developing an organizational orientation, the college was clearly not its own boss. Then, in addition to dependency on the local district, the administrative placement of the college also rendered it dependent on certain fundamental provisions of the state public school system. Central here was the *state* definition of junior college clientele, because this determined that the college would have little discretion in building its social base. The choice of selecting certain kinds of students for admission, for example, was not open to the college.

The relationship of the college to the local district, and at a second remove to the state public school system, is permanent in its general form. The specific degree of dependency is more problematic and subject to change. Compared with the time of its origin, the college gained some strength a few years later in certain areas of authority. Its ever-growing enrollment meant that as an administrative unit the college was the largest component of the district, approaching in size the combined enrollment of all San Jose high schools. With this, its voice in district affairs could hardly remain subdued. Its sizable staff began to make itself heard, and the directorship of the college became a position of some importance. Eventually, the college could also hope to gain some support from local business as it became more widely known as a source of trained personnel. Besides, in a rapidly growing metropolitan area, there is always some interest in more college facilities.

But all these changes did not remove the college from the unified district. Within this structure, the controlling board must continue to consider the interests of the other departments of the system and bring the college into a system-wide equilibrium. Barring a virtual breakdown in district administration, members of the superintendent's staff remain the ultimate arbitrators among the professional personnel. Their control of personnel assignment and budget allocation insures that the district will be unified in operation as well as in name. Thus the dependent relationship of the college to local public school officials remains intrinsic to its administrative location. It would be changed only by a drastic move that would pull the college out of the district and place it in a different type of control structure. Only one alternative is provided in California—a separate local district for the junior college alone. This form of school government clearly reduces administrative dependency and hence is generally desired by junior college personnel. But such a change is not likely in San Jose and in the metropolitan areas of the state generally. Where the tax base (assessed valuation) of existing city districts readily supports a junior college, the integration of junior college management with that of the elementary schools and high schools is highly probable.

Dependency on Unselected Base

Administrative dependency is common for subordinate units within an organization. While frequently overlooked in the consideration of educational problems and its meaning not always understood, it can be readily identified. The control of a headquarters over a field office is relatively easy to see, partly because the relationship is highly structured. Not so apparent, however, is the influence on an organization from an unorganized source. The relationship is diffuse and likely to escape participants as well as outsiders. A second dependency pattern of San Jose Junior College is of this kind and is of primary importance in its character. The principal features of the college's student body were beyond its control. Membership in the student body is completely open to the general public. Once within the doors, students choose courses and majors within wide ranges, although the college attempts to exercise some control through counseling and guidance. But overall the college is directly shaped by virtually unlimited student choice of admission and participation. As a result, the size and composition of the student body and the shape of the college's programs are not in an important sense controlled or consciously determined by anyone. Effects of the self-selecting student body go past the curriculum to shape the formal structure and the instructional staff. Few features of the organization escape some determination by attributes of the student body as a whole.

Decisive in establishing dependency on this kind of student base was the organization's lack of discretion in being able to decide whom it would serve and what kind of education it would offer. This authority rested with the state and the district, and through their definition of the open door, the student body was made an active force. Direction by students occurs most completely when a junior college is new. Once a character is formed it has a momentum of its own, and later generations of students do not find the organization so open to influence by student choice. Orientations of a college, such as its emphasis on certain programs, become built-in and somewhat resistant to change. But the exposure of a college to a nonselected pool of students will always entail a relatively high degree of adaptability, compared with colleges based on selected, constructed constituencies, because the college is placed in a reacting rather than initiating position.

Secondary School Orientation

Related to the college's twofold dependency on district and students was its emerging secondary-school perspective. To tend in outlook more toward the high school than to four-year colleges and universities is natural in the college's setting, because its administration places it in a public school "society" and at the same time removes it from the direct impact of other kinds of colleges. It has been seen that the college is controlled and operated by a local board and financed by local and state funds in ways virtually identical to that of the public high school. Its administrative and instructional staffs were largely trained in secondary education and are expected to follow public school procedures. It is open to everyone and serves as a comprehensive school, incorporating, in a sense, "noncollege" students as well as those normally defined as college students. As a result, its student body has the heterogeneity of ability and interest found in the public high school. Besides, the college is geared to local conditions. For the San Jose area it is assuming tasks that were previously and still are partly performed by the public high school: providing terminal occupational training at home, preparing and filtering candidates for study in four-year colleges, and counseling on occupational choice and academic promise. Its terminal work includes curricula shifted to it from the local high schools. In operation as well as in formal existence, it is the "capstone," a term used by junior college advocates, of the local public school system.

The contrast with the university and four-year college concerning these features is striking. As mentioned in the introduction, the "higher" public colleges are controlled by state-wide boards and financed by state funds. The public junior college is the only unit of public higher education appearing in large number which is locally governed. The instructional staffs of the senior colleges are recruited from their own realm, and training in the public schools is more likely to be held against a senior college teacher than considered a virtue. Similarly, administrative training and experience are of a different order in the two types of colleges, with preparation in a school of education differently valued. In respect to admissions, four-year colleges and universities are generally selective and hence not open to everyone. They do not embrace the notion of being comprehensive schools for all. Besides, they do not normally commit themselves to vocational programs of less than four-year's duration as alternatives to the traditional definition of attending college. Then, too, their student bodies are generally recruited from the state and the nation rather than from the local neighborhood alone.

Such differences between a junior college and the other better-known forms of college organization are bound to create a basic difference in total orientation. In common with many other junior colleges, the San Jose Junior College avoids the university man, the instructor oriented toward research and scholarship and considered impatient with the poor student. On this score, the college finds the four-year-college teacher also too much influenced by the traditional image of college as a place for selected students. Along with other public junior colleges, the San Jose Junior College does not pretend to approximate a "community of scholars." It aspires to have personnel oriented to teaching, counseling, and local affairs, and personnel sympathetic to student bodies in the thirteenth and fourteenth grades of the public schools. It more closely reflects a public school emphasis on the instructor as teacher-counselor. How far removed it is from the image of the educational enterprise acclaimed in universities, and somewhat in colleges, may be suggested by two statements of ideals by university administrators. The first is a definition of the university by James B. Conant: "A university is a community of scholars, with a considerable degree of independence and self-government, concerned with professional education, the advancement of knowledge, and the general education of the leading citizens."[2] "Community of scholars," "considerable degree of independence," "advancement of knowledge," "general education of the leading citizens"—such conceptions are indeed alien to the place and nature of the junior college. Junior colleges do not talk this language, nor do the public schools generally, of course.

A second statement is by Theodore C. Blegen, from his analysis of problems of the State University of New York: "A teaching institution that affords no place to research and gives research no encouragement and support defeats itself. It defeats itself because in effect it denies the need for self-education by its own faculty."[3] Such a statement helps to highlight similarities and differences in definitions of the work of the teacher. The importance of research is generally accepted in the state university, debated in four-year colleges, and little if ever considered in the junior college and the public schools. The self-image of the San Jose Junior College is far from such ideals. In the college, the tasks and symbols of scholarship and research have only peripheral relevance to what is expected of the organization.

Nevertheless, the San Jose Junior College has some orientations not characteristic of public schools and some university-type procedures. Teachers are freer than in high school, because they may fail students rather than having to put up with them. There is a tendency for teachers to identify "upward" toward the four-year college and university, claiming parallel work, rather than "downward" toward the high school. This amounts at times to an attempt to think of the school as a college-preparatory academy. Some staff members are interested in high academic standards and scholarly publication. But these tendencies can wax only within the limits of the situation, as set by the clientele, the rules for relating to them, the public school system, and the fact that the college administration must largely operate as an arm of district management. Notable is the limitation on scholarly study and research set by the time investment in teaching and counseling. The work with students tends to be a total work performance for the teacher.

Diffuse Commitment

Organization character may vary greatly in degree of distinctiveness, which is generally gained by selective commitment and special symbols. A private college may combine a particular history of denominational support with a special constituency, take pride in specific campus buildings and noted graduates, and claim a type of undergraduate life not possessed by any other college. Above all, distinctive character is based on selective work and special competence.

The emerging character of San Jose College is relatively indistinct. Like most other public schools, its commitments are diffuse rather than selective. The college depends financially on the local tax-paying public and serves a broad-base clientele. Hence its social bases are diffuse compared to colleges that lean on more narrowly defined supports. As a public school, the college is expected to provide many kinds of services for many kinds of people, particularly tailoring its curricula to the needs of diverse students. It rapidly became part of its character to think in broad comprehensive terms about multiple functions. Some of its operations, such as terminal vocational education and part-time adult education, are undefined in limit, expandable according to demand, and hence especially subject to diffusion. The character of the college has been moving toward that of a community college.

The character of the college is also relatively "unspecial" in the sense of sharing many attributes with other junior colleges of the state system and with locally controlled junior colleges in many parts of the country. It is one of a kind among sixty-odd colleges in the state, for example, and, like a public high school, it can hardly maintain that it is very different from the other members of its tribe, especially when it aspires to provide the array of services typical of the others. It is different in its area of location and somewhat different in being near to a state college, but not on other grounds. In public education the bases for distinctiveness are not readily available to most organizations. They are expected to be reasonably standardized units.

By its diffuse nature, San Jose Junior College is somewhat freer to adjust purposes and programs within wide limits than it would be if it were a specialized school. It is not selectively tied to an academic program alone, or to a completely vocational one, or to a particular class of students. It is free to move within an open range of activities as a changing environment indicates. More readily than the narrowly committed school, it can be in succession primarily a vocational school, an adult center, and a preparatory college. Each function is already a part of its comprehensive activity, and no unalterable selective commitments exist to bar a shift in emphasis. Nationally, the public junior college has demonstrated this flexibility; "special and adult students" reached 60 percent of the total enrollment in the nation's junior colleges in 1944, at a time of shortage of regular students.[4] This aspect of flexibility in the character of comprehensive schools, not always apparent from the outside, is one to which school administrators are generally sensitive. This flexibility in the public schools is perhaps somewhat analogous to the policy of diversification in plant and product practiced by American business firms to enhance security in a changing environment.

The character of San Jose Junior College may be summarized in these terms: It is a relatively dependent organization, coming under direct control of a superior educational authority and compelled to react to a clientele not of its making. Its unselected student body determines the nature of its work and the evolution of its programs. It is oriented by context toward the outlook and operating modes of American secondary education and has taken on the multiplicity of commitments expected of a comprehensive school. Its tasks are diffuse and flexibly organized, producing an indistinct character when compared to schools that specialize in clientele and curricula. Its ability to react to an unselected social base is particularly noteworthy.

The characteristics of dependency on unselected base and diffusion in commitment may be widely observed in other public junior colleges, especially in the California system. Administrative subordin-

ation varies elsewhere according to the control structures in which
junior colleges are located. The integrated forms of district control,
where the junior college is administered together with other public
schools, are most likely to parallel the San Jose findings. Separately
administered junior college districts are at a first remove from this
degree of administrative dependency, subordinating the junior college only to its own lay board. The characteristic of secondary school
orientation, in turn, should be strongest in the integrated colleges
and somewhat less strong, typically, in the more independent
colleges. But in all control systems that represent local authority
there is likely to be a strong tendency toward a secondary school
orientation. In contrast, junior colleges directly administered by state
educational systems will probably be relatively autonomous from
local influences, with less secondary school orientation. Furthest
removed from public school influence, of course, is the junior college
administered as part of a university or state college, where formal
dependency will tend to result in a traditional college orientation. It
is the forms of local control that predispose toward a common-
school model.

Clearly the problem of where to locate junior colleges administratively is more than a question of efficient, economical ordering of
educational effort, of a logical structuring of school government.
Since administrative place shapes the character of schools, it affects
educational values. A particular type of location, such as the local
school district, will accentuate certain programs and play down
others, instill one outlook while obstructing another. The logical
place for junior colleges, therefore, depends on the values that one
wishes to implement.

The characteristics mentioned above as least likely to vary among
public junior colleges were (1) unselected base and (2) diffuse
commitment. These are also the organizational features which suggest classification of the public junior college under a general
organizational type, the mass enterprise. There are schools other than
the junior college, and organizations in other fields, that are also
diffusely related to unselected, relatively undifferentiated clienteles.

A Special Ability

The character of an organization enables it to engage in certain
tasks and disqualifies it from engaging in others. The San Jose Junior
College tends toward the need of ability to manage a heterodox,
self-selecting student body. It is in the business of exposing a large

student body of below-average college aptitude to some education beyond the high school. This exposure prepares a minority of the students to transfer after one or two years to a four-year college or university, principally the nearby state college. Some of these students are persons of ability who had poor academic records in high schools and were thus "salvaged"[5] for higher education by the junior college. But since most students terminate, and do so largely against their original hopes, the college particularly needs skill in disabusing students of their notions of transferring and in inducing them to accept a two-year alternative.

One competence which a junior college develops, therefore, is a general ability to react to an heterogenous free-forming clientele with diverse programs. The ability to handle diversity, however, militates against a high degree of competence in any one educational effort, such as the vocational or the college-preparatory alone. San Jose Junior College cannot be a highly intellectualized academy or a first-rate technical school, because its trade school commitment will not allow it to be an academy and its college-preparation work will not permit a full flowering of a technical orientation. In short, ability lies not in a distinctive educational specialty; competence lies in balancing disparate operations and in providing the means of student movement from one operation to another.

This brings us to the college's operational specialty, its most important feature: the specific operation of transforming transfer students into terminal students. Since the movement of students in the college must be principally away from the transfer work, the efficacy of the college is especially defined by its ability to reassign the student from a transfer to a terminal major without losing him in the process. Junior colleges in general have found this difficult. Four-year colleges and universities do not have this task, because they do not include short-term terminal alternatives. High schools do not overlap the college years, hence do not have the problem either.

When the question is asked, what can a junior college do that other schools cannot do, one answer is that it can manage the latent terminal student who wants to embark on a college education, but who would not, at the most, get past the first two years. For this type of student, the junior college provides short-term vocational and general educational programs as alternatives to the usual curricula, as well as two years of college work per se. Besides, the junior college provides an inexpensive two years of college-credit work for the few students who will proceed to other schools and short-term programs for the students who always had terminal intentions.

The Social Base of the Mass College

The intriguing feature of San Jose Junior College and the public junior college generally is the relationship to an outside base of operations composed of a large, undifferentiated aggregation of potential students or clients. This characteristic, central to what will be called the mass enterprise, meaningfully differentiates organizations in education from one another, and also serves as a way of understanding some organizational similarities between such common distinctions as political, economic, and educational organization. The student constituency of San Jose Junior College showed itself as an active force in determining the practices of the college; it showed itself as such to a degree not normally anticipated when one considers who determines policies in American schools and colleges. This active nature of a student body seems to be related to the college's dependency on an amorphous social base. How? We are used to organized pressure, to intervention, and to direction by professional staff, but how does an unorganized influence operate? What happens when the students collectively and without intention, heavily condition the college?

A matter of first importance for the influence of the student body on the policies of any educational institution is the extent and kind of selection of students exercised by the institution. Selectivity makes possible a structuring of clientele. Selection is a control device, allowing participation only within certain limits. Such control is evident in private colleges, which selectively cultivate a social base and structure their clientele. They establish ties with certain families, social groups, and feeder schools. Selectivity in such cases reduces the need of the institution to adjust to undifferentiated constituencies, and gives to participation a certain distinction. In general, then, the form and content of an aggregation of students entering a college is determined largely by the extent to which the college itself can select. Is the student body to be of low, medium, or high social status? Strongly or weakly motivated? Of high or low aptitude? The selective school can tailor a constituency that supports the self-imposed ideals of the school authorities. Even a college that is temporarily unselective can affect the nature of its student body if it has a strong self-image to bring to bear.

But the educational organization that is permanently unselective has little choice in defining a student body and depends on the fortunes of its environment. With nonselection comes a weakening of control and an enlarging of the discretion of potential students.

Participation is "open." The form and content of an entering student body are then free-forming, as far as organizational control is concerned. Nonselection is the most essential condition under which students impose their collective will on a junior college.

Secondly, the extent to which participation is voluntary affects the influence of the student body on the character of a college. Older students are more often voluntary than younger ones. When students pass the age of compulsory school attendance, usually at sixteen, the relation between students and the school changes. Past this age and especially past high school graduation, the student is set free, granted greater choice in attending, and made less subject to the control of school personnel. He can give, change, or withhold his participation. If he also has the right to enter a nonselective college, then his voluntariness becomes an active force. He can decide for himself whether and when he will enter and actively contend for his own version of the ends and means of his education. The conjunction of nonselection and age above compulsory schooling in the public junior college gives maximum thrust to the choices and characteristics of students.

One consequence of these conditions is the college's vulnerability to the competition of attractive alternatives. In the lower grades students are usually not free to shift from one school to another; student bodies are nearly always fixed by the jurisdiction of school districts. But after high school, competition enters. The voluntary students are mobile, allowed to choose among schools and programs. The nonselective college faces specialized, selective competitors, drawing off good students from the local population and from the college's own student body. The other colleges are generally free to manipulate their own admission standards in the light of their own interests; they may attempt to take only the most promising students if there are many such students available, or they may go to the bottom of the barrel when the supply of students is low. The nonselective school must passively take what comes to it. The junior college competes in other ways, however, by inexpensiveness, convenience of location, and an adaptive array of programs. Programs can be manipulated from year to year, and the pressure of competition on the mass college is to be adaptable and attractive to the diversity of students who make their appearance. The result, again, is to enhance student impact on the college.

A third major consideration in the influence of the student clientele is the nature of the processing of people in a junior college. Like other schools and like such institutions as the social agency, hospital, and prison, the junior college works on people rather than on objects. Students *flow through* the organization; they are not sold a product or given a service, as in a business firm and in most public and private service organizations. The students are acted upon in the work of the school, and the students, in turn, shape the tasks of work; they are organizational participants, intervening from within. We should expect such a people-work organization to be extensively affected by attributes of its clientele, including their intentions. But decisive for the character of the organization is the extent to which the client participants are controlled. How to control a clientele that is always within the doors is a general problem faced by all organizations that work on people. One answer is the asserting of professional authority and the defining of the client participant as incompetent to decide what treatment he should receive. The hospital patient is defined as sick, the prison inmate is labeled as criminal; both are defined as having something wrong with them, hence are placed in special roles and withdrawn from normal activities. Their choices are narrowed and the authority of an organizational staff is extended over them. The extent of control varies greatly but there is no doubt about who knows best.

In schools, the participation of the student is a normal social role; there is no deviant status attached to the student as a basis for the school staff to assert control. Control over students is strong in many societies, however, as it was earlier in American education, on the ground that the educator, adult and experienced, knows better than the student what is proper for the student to learn and to do. Where the student is defined as immature and the teacher is seen to have the responsibility of instilling cultural principles and bodies of knowledge, then the desires and attributes of students are not likely to affect the character of schools. But tendencies of modern society change these assumptions. Even in the elementary school, the teacher becomes a more responsive agent, turning toward the needs and verbalized desires of students of diverse background for cues as to what shall be taught.[6] By the time the student enters secondary education, major choices as to avenues and forms of participation in school are open to him. The further he goes, the more the comprchensive school assumes a servicing role. The public junior college is at the point in educational structure where professional dictation is likely to be minimal. The students are not only unselected and voluntary participants, but they are older than those in the high schools and possess more of the rights of adults. Their needs go off in all directions: preparation for a number of diverse colleges, job training for a varied array of occupations, sophistication in such personal concerns as the responsibilities of marriage. The spectrum of possible concerns is wide and the comprehensive school is oriented to do as much as possible for all students. The student is granted much choice; student processing needs then to be responsively and flexibly organized, without regard to academic tradition and staff conceptions of the ultimate purpose and shape of the organization. Processing in a junior college is student-oriented in more than a superficial sense of the term.

An important feature of the flow of students through a junior college is the shortness of their stay. The in-and-out flux is always on a large scale in the two-year school. The vast majority do not remain even two years, earlier transferring to other colleges, going off to jobs, or just dropping out. This means the junior college must take on some of the coloration of a short-stay institution. Somewhat like such military units as the basic training post, the classification center, and the replacement depot, the junior college processes batches of people who are here today and gone tomorrow. Unlike the military establishment, however, the college does not have firm control. Besides, the handling of large numbers who have a short stay cannot help but promote some mass-processing tendencies, such as classroom counseling, in order to get the job done. The student is not around long enough to allow for the slow development of identification with the college or gradual assimilation into a set of values different from what he has known before. The task is to do something for large numbers relatively quickly, in the first place to get them on a track appropriate to their ability. Proper classification is uppermost in importance. Then the students can be given some training in whatever time remains before they move out, a week to two years later. Since the leaving is voluntary, the college has no control over it. The self-selection in and out makes the college a "service" version of the classification and distribution center, doing what it can for those who will come to it and in the time they will grant. The need is to build processing systems for the major types of entrants, the latent terminal student being the most difficult type.

This exploratory review of the relationship of the junior college to its students, actual and potential, leads to a general conclusion. As a consequence of dependency on an unselective-voluntary clientele, such a college will be extensively shaped by characteristics of the multitude. Of all types of schools, the unselective-voluntary type will be most open to wide clientele influence.[7] It has little opportunity to shape a social base and it has a strong organizational need to adapt to self-selective students.[8] The hands of its constituents are not tied by a compulsory status; the opposite might almost be said: the school is compelled by the kinds of students who elect to appear. The school can neither force students to attend, as in the early grades, nor choose a particular type of student as in the selective colleges. Being neither compulsory nor selective, the junior college faces a large educational market of free buyers, all or none of whom can choose to avail themselves of the opportunity.

In an earlier study, a similar kind of school was analyzed and termed "service enterprise."[9] This conception highlighted the adaptive response of the public adult school to changing clientele interests and the tendency of the adult education administrator to look to environment for direction rather than to self-determined purpose. Typical of American adult education is the transitory quality of participation of the part-time adult student and the immediacy of the organizational attempt to "service the demand." The concept of service enterprise connotes these features. The junior college, too, has attributes of a service enterprise, but it has a student body that is somewhat more involved and less changeable than that of the adult school. It has greater steadiness because it is part of an educational sequence for the young; hence, it does not need to be so immediately adaptable in insuring its survival. The notion of service is relevant but needs extension in order to point to other aspects of character and to be applicable to a wide class of organizations.

The concept of the mass enterprise, as developed in this study, appears to serve these requirements better. In the strictest sense, a mass enterprise is an organization whose character is defined by dependency on a large, nonselected, voluntary clientele. In this sense, the term applies in its purest form to the junior college and the adult school. In both we find the faculty adapted to a mass character. The constraint of organization character in these schools begins with the unsolicited social bases on which they rest.

This definition of mass organization is different from the common use of "mass" to connote sheer numbers. It is also somewhat different from, although related to, the definition of mass organization in the sociological literature on "mass society."[10] In the latter, the mass organization is one in which a relatively unstructured membership participates weakly and without influence; with this goes a susceptibility of the membership to mobilization by leadership groups that know how to play upon emotional adherence. Such an organization is highly susceptible to totalitarian control. This sociological definition emphasizes an advanced or acute state of "mass-ness," where the membership leads itself to manipulation and is ready to take on new ways of behaving. Typical here is the *activist* mass organization, one readily deployed by its leadership. The present study emphasizes a more *passive* form of mass organization, one controlled *by* the multitude rather than vice versa. Membership is relatively unstructured and participation is segmental, as in the activist organization, but mobilization by leadership is absent. Instead, leadership adapts to membership in a service fashion, induced to passivity by conditions that promote dependency.

In this sense many business firms and public bureaus are mass organizations, steered by the desires of a heterogeneous public. But generally such agencies do not purport to have a "nonmass" role and are not traditionally conceived to have broad social and cultural functions. Their adaptive responsiveness gives issue to no special social problems. But the attempt in modern democratic societies to adapt schools to the multitude is of a different order. Here core cultural values are at stake, because the schools have traditionally been defined as agents of the general society, transmitting a heritage and helping to bring the young to adulthood. The impact of mass organization on the role of the school needs extensive exploration. The mass enterprise in higher education contributes to a vast democratization, but it also entails a lowering of standards of admission and attainment. Its existence may be essential to the welfare of "nonmass" colleges, but at the same time it may change the nature of higher education by blurring its meaning and encouraging a sovereignty of the poorly qualified. Value judgments on the "worth" of the public junior college need to be made on complex grounds, weighing the pros and cons, for much more than money and administrative convenience are at issue.

Footnotes

1. For a general discussion of the concept of organization character, see Philip Selznick, *Leadership in Administration*, Row, Peterson & Company, Evanston, Ill., 1957, pp. 38-55.

2. James B. Conant, *Education in a Divided World*, Harvard University Press, Cambridge, Mass., 1948, p. 158.

3. Theodore C. Blegen, *The Harvests of Knowledge: A Report on Research Potentials and Problems in the State University of New York*, The Research Foundation of State University of New York, Albany, N. Y., 1957, p. 8.

4. Jesse P. Bogue, *The Community College*, McGraw-Hill Book Company, Inc., New York, 1950, p. 35.

5. Junior college advocates refer to a "salvage function" in enumerating advantages of the public junior college. Salvaging lost talent is a claim that links the work of the junior college to several national concerns, e.g., the full utilization of manpower and equality of opportunity.

6. For a discussion of changes in the role of the teacher, see David Riesman, *The Lonely Crowd*, Yale University Press, New Haven, Conn., 1950, chap. 2.

7. Using the two variables of selectivity and voluntariness of participation, three other major types are suggested: selective-voluntary membership (the private college, selective state universities); unselective-captive (the public elementary school and high school); selective-captive (the private elementary and secondary school). These broad categories offer a crude comparative framework and the examples are illustrative only. Only the type in which the public junior college falls is here discussed.

8. On the need of the public schools generally to be increasingly adaptable as they undergo "democratization," see David Riesman, *Constraint and Variety in American Education*, University of Nebraska Press, Lincoln, Nebr., 1956, pp. 108-112.

9. Burton R. Clark, *Adult Education in Transition: A Study of Institutional Insecurity*, University of California Press, Berkeley, Calif., 1956, chap. 4.

10. General discussion of mass society may be found in Karl Mannheim, *Man and Society in an Age of Reconstruction*, Harcourt, Brace and Company, Inc., New York, 1950, pp. 79-107; Emil Lederer, *State of the Masses*, W. W. Norton & Company, Inc., New York, 1940; C. Wright Mills, *The Power Elite*, Oxford University Press, New York, 1956, chap. 13; and Philip Selznick, *The Organizational Weapon*, McGraw-Hill Book Company, Inc., New York, 1952, chap. 7, which also offers a definition of mass organization, p. 286.

THE VULNERABILITY AND STRENGTH
OF THE SUPERIOR COLLEGE*

Paul F. Lazarsfeld and Wagner Thielens, Jr.

Let us take time for a brief review. In Chapter 3 an index of apprehension was developed, permitting the characterization of each social science teacher in our sample according to the level of apprehension he felt at the time of the study. The items in the index were originally chosen, on common-sense grounds, as typical expressions among teachers of what might ordinarily be meant by this term. Then, to determine more precisely the meaning of the classification, in Chapter 4 we cross-tabulated the apprehension index against other characteristics of our respondents, including their interest in matters of civil liberties and their experiences in the realm of academic freedom. We concluded that the apprehension we

*This article is taken from Chapter 7 of Lazarsfeld and Thielens' book, *The Academic Mind*, a study of the political pressures on social scientists in colleges and universities during the McCarthy era of the 1950's. The study analyzed the amount of political pressure, the forms it took, and the colleges' response to political interference. Several thousand social scientists were interviewed in a national sample, and their perceptions of the political forces are summarized in the book. The section included here deals with the characteristics of the colleges which made them vulnerable to political pressure. In the first part of the article the authors briefly review some of the themes in *The Academic Mind*, then they go on to discuss the organizational features of the colleges under political pressure.—Ed.

measured was a combination of fear for one's own professional security and an objective concern with the state of academic freedom in general. For most professors it was not a paralyzing apprehension, since it left room for a considerable readiness to defend their rights and to express their own opinions, especially in the confines of the campus. We postponed for later chapters an analysis of the more subtle ways in which academic morale and freedom had been corroded during the difficult years.

Keeping still to the overall statistical picture, the causes of teachers' apprehension were then considered. To organize our material we followed the well-established idea that all human experiences are determined by two broad groups of elements: the characteristics of the people themselves and those of the environment in which they live and work. In the two preceding chapters, the pivotal attribute of the social science teacher turned out to be his permissiveness. We discussed the professional significance of this trait. And the data showed that permissive respondents were more likely once to have engaged in activities which, during the difficult years, became controversial in the larger community. They were also more interested in the free flow of new ideas on social matters. These were the two main personal reasons for the apprehension of permissive teachers.

We shall now take up the college, and attempt to find out whether its characteristics affect faculty apprehension. When we look again for a pivotal variable, the quality of schools moves to the fore. Discussed in the first chapter, it now appears as a basic characteristic around which many of our findings about colleges can be fruitfully organized. It is also something more. The quality of education is surely in itself a vitally important matter. Its preservation, in fact, may provide the main reason for caring about academic freedom. Thus the findings of the present chapter acquire heightened significance.

A great philosopher once made an observation which describes very well the way in which college quality came to hold a central position in our study:

Not until we have unsystematically collected observations for a long time to serve as building materials, and indeed only after we have spent much time in the technical disposition of these materials, do we first become capable of viewing our idea in a clearer light and of outlining it architectonically as one whole.[1]

Our building materials were various characteristics of college organization, some of them already reported, others to be added now. The technical disposition shows that they are in various ways statistically related to the quality rating we have presented in Chapter 1. Its architectonic importance begins to appear when we discover the closeness of its link with the pivotal variable on the personal level, professors' permissiveness. The social significance of the whole, we hope, will become evident.

We shall proceed in four steps. First, from our preceding data it appears probable that there are more permissive social scientists in the colleges of higher quality. We shall document that this is indeed the case.

Second, knowing that permissive teachers were more likely to be under attack, we shall then want to know whether this was only an individual experience, or whether it was the superior college as an entity which came under pressure during the difficult years.

Third, if this too is the case, then a third question becomes crucial: How did the administrations in the more distinguished institutions handle this situation? They were under obvious cross-pressures: Precisely because they had a more distinguished social science faculty, the community at large might be expected to attack their institutions more vigorously. Which way did the administrations side?

Finally, having given what evidence we have on this crucial point, we shall then try to explain our findings. And we shall show how all this affects the level of apprehension among social scientists.

College Quality and Individual Permissiveness

The first point in our outline is easily settled. In Chapter 1, an index was set up to distinguish colleges according to their quality, using objective data obtained from independent sources not connected with our survey. It now turns out that the quality of a college is highly related to the permissiveness of its social science faculty. This can be clearly seen in Figure 1.

The better a college, the larger the proportion of permissive social scientists included in its faculty. The reasons for this are apparent from the data given in the previous chapter. Colleges which have larger resources and more desirable working conditions attract more distinguished social scientists. These teachers in turn are more likely to be permissive. The original and creative minority among them will often have analytical minds which do not automatically accept current beliefs, minds willing to entertain unorthodox ideas as to how a modern society can best function.[2] Next to the creative leader comes the competent teacher and productive research scholar. Even

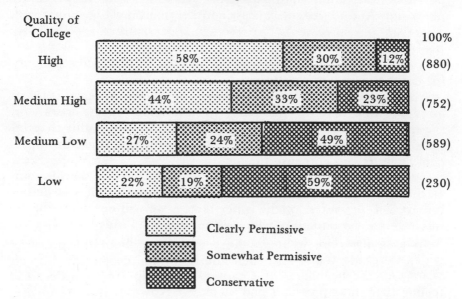

Figure 1. The better a college, the more of its social
scientists are permissive

Clearly Permissive

Somewhat Permissive

Conservative

if he might be by nature more amenable to the general currents of
public opinion, he is more directly in communication with the
leaders of his profession, and his thinking is shaped by the process of
mutual interaction among primary groups which we have described
above. Thus he too will add to a permissive climate when appointed
to a distinguished institution.

Next we want to gauge the pressures which the larger community
brings to bear on colleges of differing quality.

Clouds over the Campus

Was the stream of accusations during the difficult years heavily
directed toward the more distinguished colleges? We turn first to one
of the questionnaire items which furnished material for the description of incidents in Chapter 2:

Has any group or person accused anyone on this faculty here of being subversive
or of engaging in any un-American activities in the past few years?

To guard against bias, the answers need to be tabulated separately for
more and less apprehensive respondents. For there is the danger that
the apprehension of our respondents distorted the descriptions of

events in their colleges; the more apprehensive teachers were likely to paint a darker picture, partly because they were more attuned to potential difficulties and partly because they were simply more observant. And in this special case another point must be considered. There are, of course, more professors in larger colleges, and therefore the numerical chance that at least one teacher on the campus was accused is greater. So in Figure 2 the findings are reported separately for larger and smaller institutions.

Irrespective of the size of the school or the respondents' state of mind, we find that the frequency of accusation reports arises with the quality of the school. For the remaining Figures in this chapter, we shall not separate the judgment of apprehensive and non-apprehensive professors, because the picture is always the same: apprehensive professors are more pessimistic when they describe the situation at their college, but when it comes to comparing schools—whether for attacks, pressures, or the other factors we will consider—the result is the same regardless of which segment of the faculty we listen to.

In a similar vein, what do the teachers say about the pressures which were directed against their administration during the difficult years? At the beginning of Chapter 2, we reported a widespread feeling that these pressures had increased. Now our interest focuses on quality differences. Figure 3 reports for each of the four quality groups the proportion of respondents who thought that their administration has been under increased pressure in the last six or seven years from at least one of the four sources—politicians, alumni, trustees, or the community at large.

In general, as with accusations, the pressure reports increase markedly as we move up the quality rating of institutions. There is, however, a small but interesting break in this trend. The lowest quality level does not have quite the lowest frequency of pressure accounts. A more detailed study shows that this irregularity can be traced to the five secular institutions in this group. Two of these are tax-supported Negro colleges in the South, where the integration issue has recently become acute. The other three are relatively large private schools, each of which serves a big industrial city and is completely dependent for support on local money, either from industry or some other interest group. With no tax support and little private endowment, they appear to have been especially at the mercy of their local sponsorship. [3]

Having its administration under pressure and its faculty under attack necessarily makes for a definite strain on a college. Probably our best concrete measure of this strain is the prevalence of the

Figure 2. Accusations against teachers occur more
frequently in superior colleges

Proportion of *apprehensive* respondents who report accusations

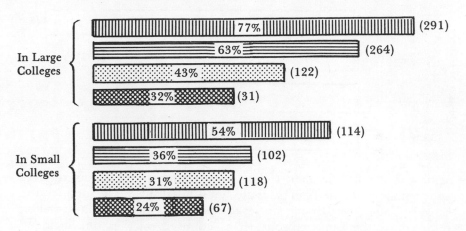

Proportion of *non-apprehensive* respondents who report accusations

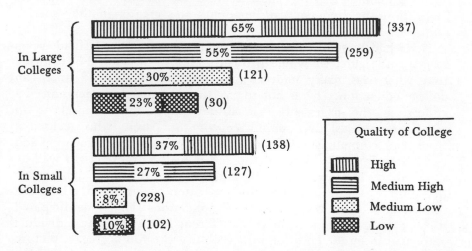

incidents described in Chapter 2: episodes ranging from long-drawn-
out Congressional investigations to an attack by a student group on
an individual professor. A count of these incidents has an important
advantage over the data given in Figure 2. There our percentages
pertained to the proportion of professors who reported an accusation

Figure 3. Proportion of respondents reporting
increased pressure on the administration

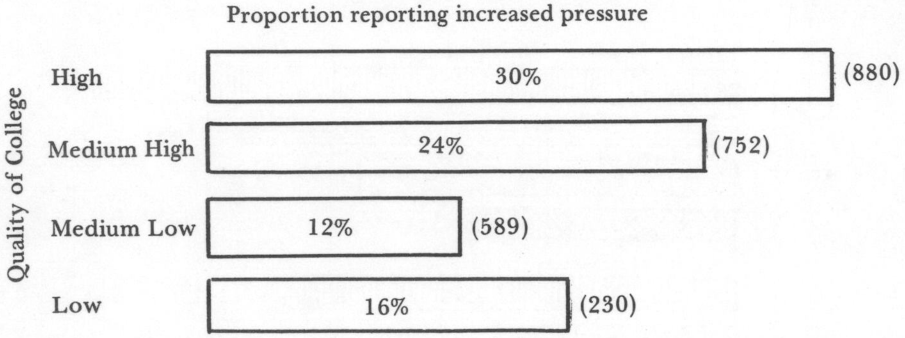

Proportion reporting increased pressure

against a faculty member. If many respondents in a school referred to the same case, the figures would be inflated. In the incident count, however, such overlapping stories are pooled; however many teachers referred to the same episode, it is counted only as one incident. Therefore, Figure 4 has an especially probative value for the point we are now making. It shows that, without exception, in every type of institution the frequency of incidents was greater in the superior colleges.

If we had to summarize the problem created by the difficult years in just one figure, we would probably choose this one. For it shows that what was really under attack was the quality of American college education. This is not to say that the man who denounced a college in the pages of a local newspaper, the counsel of an investigating legislative committee, or the parent who accused a teacher of communism, was hostile to superior college education and wanted to lower it. Many of the actors in the drama might well be shocked if they saw this figure, and would, with much right, stress the purity of their motives. Such is often the difference between individual acts and their collective implications. Their unanticipated social consequences can be very different from what the individual actor had in mind. To bring into visibility the full aggregate picture which is usually inaccessible to the individual observer is one of the main functions of a study like the present one.

The college professor is in a peculiar situation. When attacks and accusations are made against a teacher, before they can have an ultimate effect upon him they must be refracted by an intervening medium: the administration. The president of the school can act as a

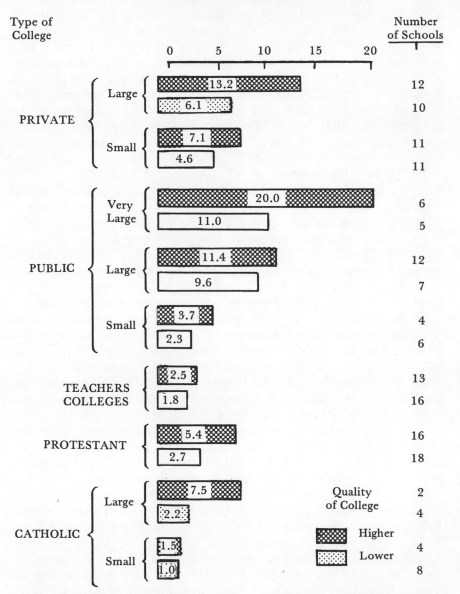

Figure 4.* The difference which quality makes in the average
number of incidents in nine groups of colleges

*For this figure each of the nine types of colleges is divided as evenly as possible into two groups of higher and lower quality schools. The dividing line, of course, varies from one type to the next.

conductor for the hostile sentiments, or as an insulator protecting the faculty. He must, of course, contend with the trustees, who themselves can vary in the role they choose to play; they can consider themselves called upon to police the college, or alternatively to interpret and defend it to challengers. But whatever their role, in most cases the officials of the college administration have considerable latitude. They can try diplomatically to placate an irate trustee body, or prevent their displeasure by initiating stern measures against controversial faculty members. The president can make full use of his legal prerogatives, or defer to the majority judgment of the faculty. The actual role of the administration is therefore a matter very much at issue; and so we come to the third step in our program.

Administrative Performance

It is not easy to pinpoint the factors that make up the central ingredients of administrative performance on issues of academic freedom. According to general thinking on such matters, at least three aspects are important. As a minimum, clearly defined standards are needed, providing a policy which is understood and accepted by the faculty and which will be predictably adhered to in specific cases. Secondly, a machinery for the making of individual decisions is required. There is probably widespread agreement that the faculty as a whole should play an important role at some stage of an issue involving the rights and obligations of teachers, even though the final decision will, according to American tradition, generally remain with an administrative authority. Finally, in any organization a good administration must be willing to protect its staff. This means more than just fair procedure in handling accusations. Every occupational group develops certain norms for which an outsider will have little understanding. A capable college administrator must be alert to the traditions of the professoriate; if they come into conflict with the oscillating moods of the larger community, he will, if at all possible, give the edge to the enduring needs of the academic man.

There was insufficient time in our interviews to ask teachers for a detailed picture of the philosophy and behavior of their administrative officials. And even at best the pooled judgments of professors could not give a really complete picture; for this, interviews with administrators and trustees, investigation of documentary evidence, and so on, would be necessary. Nevertheless, we did obtain at least some information on each of the three aspects of administrative performance just sketched: clarity of policy, adequacy of procedural machinery, and protective orientation.

On the first point two simple and direct questions seemed appropriate. One read:

Do you feel the administration of the college has taken a clear stand on matters of academic freedom, or not?

In the whole sample 59 percent reported a clear stand, and 29 percent the absence of one; the remaining 12 percent could not make up their minds. The other item required a report rather than a judgment:

Has the faculty and the administration discussed questions of academic freedom in joint meetings within the last year or not?

Thirty-six percent of the respondents reported such meetings, 53 percent said they had not occurred, and 11 percent could not remember. On both items, Figure 5 shows, the administrations in high quality schools get a better verdict from their social scientists.

A detailed picture of procedural adequacy would have required questions about the school's formal regulations for the handling of cases involving academic freedom, as well as concrete examples of how they were carried out. But there was time during the interview for only one question. We therefore started with a double assumption: it is desirable that the faculty play a considerable role in educational matters; trustees, since they are relatively most remote from the academic scene, should exercise great restraint in this connection. Against this background we asked the following question:

If you had to choose one, who would you say has the most powerful voice here on this campus, in determining the degree of academic freedom that exists here—the trustees, the president, the deans, the heads of departments, the faculty, the students, or who?

Each school was separately characterized by summarizing the answers of all interviewed teachers. A value of 2 was given to each response giving the faculty the most important voice, of 1 if the administration (president and deans) was considered paramount, and of 0 to a choice of the trustees. For each college the scores were then added together and averaged. Values for the resulting school index vary from about 0.5, indicating a dominance of the trustees in the handling of academic freedom matters, to about 1.5, attributing a considerable role to the faculty.

Dividing the schools as nearly as possible into two equal groups according to this index, we can compare procedural adequacy in

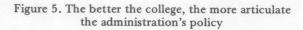

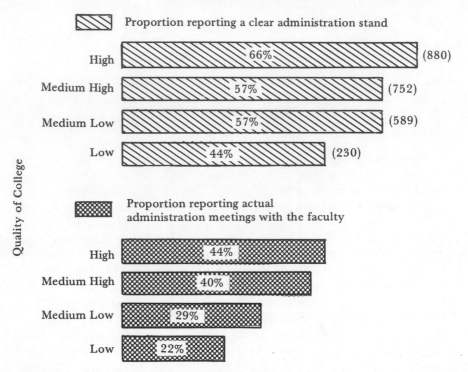

Figure 5. The better the college, the more articulate
the administration's policy

colleges of different objective quality ratings. Results are reported, in Figure 6, only for the seventy-seven schools with more than thirteen interviews.

Under the assumption that faculty participation is the most desirable and trustee dominance the most inadequate administrative device, on the whole the superior colleges have a much more desirable record.

The third element of administrative performance, protectiveness, should in many ways be most important of all. General standards and procedural rules so often don't quite fit a concrete case. It is then that the motivation and understanding of the administration comes to the fore. But how may the situation be gauged through the eyes of the faculty? One set of data, while inferential, has a rather convincing ring. It will be remembered that respondents were asked at one point if any of their colleagues had been accused of subversive activities. A second item in the questionnaire read:

Have there been any cases here in this college where you feel the academic freedom of any member of the faculty has been threatened?

In answering the two questions, 46 percent of the respondents reported accusations, but only 28 percent stated that someone's academic freedom was threatened. In a rough way the difference between these two figures can be used as an indicator of the readiness of an administration to absorb attacks without passing them on to the teacher—to build, so to speak, a security wall for him behind which he can do his professional work. (We are, of course,

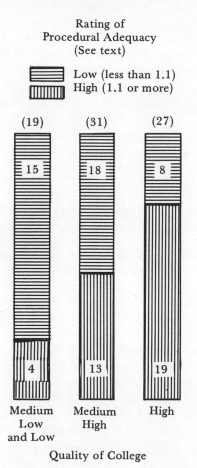

Figure 6. Superior colleges give the faculty a
greater voice in academic freedom matters

aware of other factors which could enter into this difference of 18 percent; we want to use this figure only for comparative purposes.) It turns out that the protective element in good administration is indeed the more frequent, the higher the quality of a college. The inferential evidence is offered in Figure 7.

The line representing the proportion reporting accusations is only a summary of Figure 2 in this chapter. The figures for threats provide new, but by now not unexpected information: Threats to academic freedom are reported by an ever larger proportion of respondents, the higher the quality of their college. Our main interest at this point is with the four enclosed percentages inside the shaded area. Representing the difference between accusations and threats, they provide a rough index of administrative absorption. In the low quality colleges there are few accusations, but they seem to be readily converted into actual difficulties for a faculty member; the difference is only 3 percent. In the best colleges both accusations and difficulties are more frequent, but the difference is 28 percent; at these schools the administration is much more likely to shield the professor and not to pass on accusations which come to their attention.

This interpretation is strengthened by the top line of Figure 7. About half of our respondents, it will be remembered, report accusations against faculty members. Those who did were asked a second question:

Do you feel the administration handled the incident in a way which protected the rights of the faculty?

In almost two-thirds of the cases reported the respondents testified to the fairness of their administration. And again, as shown in the top line of Figure 7, the affirmative answers are more frequent in colleges of higher quality. Here we no longer deal with an inference, but with the direct reports of teachers who had occasion to watch what happened in concrete incidents at their schools. Another consideration makes this increase from 58 percent to 69 percent all the more impressive. The superior colleges have a considerably larger number of permissive professors who are likely to apply rather strict standards to the performance of their administration: inversely, it will be remembered from Chapter 5 that the conservative teachers, who are more numerous in the low quality schools, are in general likely to approve of constituted authority. Nevertheless, testimonies to fair treatment increase in frequency with the quality of the school.

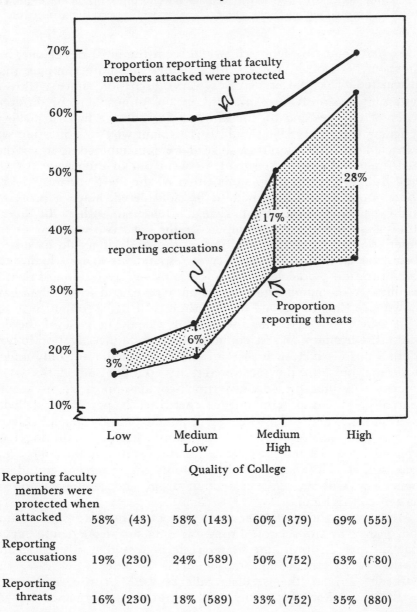

Figure 7. School quality as related to accusations of subversion, threats to academic freedom, and the administration's treatment of accused professors

	Low		Medium Low		Medium High		High	
Reporting faculty members were protected when attacked	58%	(43)	58%	(143)	60%	(379)	69%	(555)
Reporting accusations	19%	(230)	24%	(589)	50%	(752)	63%	(?80)
Reporting threats	16%	(230)	18%	(589)	33%	(752)	35%	(880)

One more approach to the topic of protection by the administration remains. The following questionnaire item was intended to meet the issue head-on.

If someone accused you of leftist leanings, do you think the administration of the college would support you wholeheartedly, with reservations, or hardly at all?

At first sight this approach would seem the most direct one, but interestingly enough, the resulting figures are more complex than anticipated. The matter deserves some discussion, since it throws light simultaneously on variations in the atmosphere of different types of colleges and on the kind of decision we had to make in designing this study. We should first explain why this question was restricted to leftist leanings. It will be remembered that another question asked whether respondents went out of their way to show they had no extremist opinions either of the "left" or the "right." There, both possibilities had to be considered, since a professor might be concerned about giving offense to either the liberal atmosphere prevailing on campus, or the conservative mood of the larger community. But at the time of the study it would have been absurd for all but a tiny minority of respondents to ask whether the administration would lend support against an accusation of rightist leanings. As common sense would anticipate, and as the data have shown (see Chapters 2 and 6), accusations of being too much to the right were very rare during the difficult years. The issue of the day was leftist leanings, and we could safely limit an investigation to how administrations met such accusations. Respondents not only understood the question, they answered it in a confident mood. Sixty-two percent said that the administration would support them "wholeheartedly," the top term on our checklist; 20 percent said "with reservations," and only seven percent said "hardly at all." Eleven percent felt unable to say what the administration would do. If we remember that 40 percent indicated that pressures on the college had increased, it is impressive to see that only seven percent considered themselves without any protection from the administration in matters of this kind.

What about the relation between protection by the administration and quality of the school? From our data so far one could expect that the professors in the better colleges would testify to greater protection by the administration. This is indeed the case, and markedly so, in the secular colleges (the private and public institutions). For these, the administrative performance of the superior college is confirmed in Figure 8.

In the traditional schools (teachers colleges, Protestant, and Catholic schools) the trend is just the opposite. This might possibly be due to a special interpretation of this questionnaire item by conservative teachers in a conservative school. There the reaction is likely to be as follows: "Of course the administration would support me if someone accused me of leftist leanings, because they would consider him crazy; who in his right mind could ever call me such a thing?" However, there are more significant implications in Figure 8, to which we shall return presently. For the moment, because the secular schools furnish the large majority of social scientists, we add their feelings of protection to the other findings in this chapter, which now permit a clearcut summary:

The higher the quality of a college, the larger its proportion of permissive social scientists.

The higher the quality, the stronger the pressures and attacks from the off-campus community.

The higher the quality of a school, the better the performance of the administration in defending the academic freedom of its social scientists.[9]

The first of these three findings reinforces the idea that if permissiveness is a pivotal characteristic of the social science profession at large, then it is not surprising that it is also a prevailing property of the superior college.

The second finding is the one which calls most for contemplation. The fact that the difficult years put the superior college under especially heavy strain shows that the problem goes considerably beyond the realm of the rights of individual teachers. It was the very quality of social science teaching and of inquiry as a whole which was put into jeopardy.

The third finding requires some further speculation. At first glance we have here a paradoxical result. If the more distinguished colleges are more subject to pressure and more frequently the scene of controversial incidents, how is it, nevertheless, that their administrations perform better by all of our criteria, including the protection given to social scientists?

Some Speculations on the Superior Administrator

In American colleges the trustees and their appointee, the president, have great power. If it is true that power corrupts, one

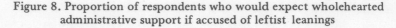

Figure 8. Proportion of respondents who would expect wholehearted
administrative support if accused of leftist leanings

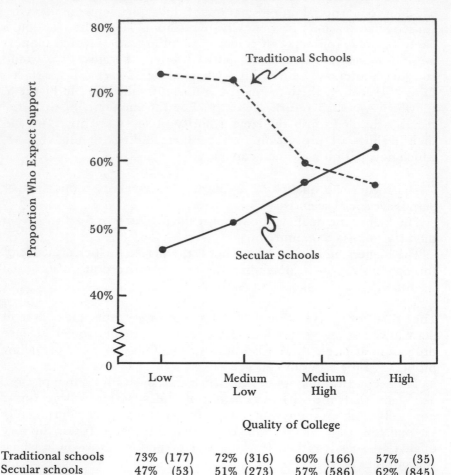

Quality of College

Traditional schools	73% (177)	72% (316)	60% (166)	57% (35)
Secular schools	47% (53)	51% (273)	57% (586)	62% (845)

would expect that when the temper of the times brings the
permissive social scientist into distrust, a strong college president
would be tempted to exercise his power and curb the faculty.
Actually, the better the college, the less frequently does this occur.
We have here another example of a rather curious feature in the
American scene to which Harold Laski has drawn attention in
discussing the American system of mass communications. He
considered it a rather bad one, because it was not conducted in the

public interest but for private profit. Still, he wondered why it wasn't even worse. By mere economic mechanics there should be no limit to how much a low cultural level of broadcasting and a sensational handling of printed news could be made ever more marked and ever more profitable. Laski concluded that there must be a self-corrective in the American system which makes for a tolerable level of performance. We seem to face such a self-corrective device in the management of colleges. Offhand, one might expect that college administrations in America should behave very badly in academic freedom matters. They are appointed by the board of trustees and are responsible to them rather than to the faculty. The trustees and regents themselves are representatives of the community, and in most cases of its wealthy and conservative sector. It is probably here that the unexpected safety device comes in. For the most part the individuals chosen as trustees are selected because they are successful in their own enterprises. Many of these men have undoubtedly acquired respect for efficiency and intrinsic success. If they are responsible for a college, they want it to have prestige, so they appoint presidents whom they hope will make their regime "successful," without going too deeply into the existing academic implications of the idea. The president, in turn, will build up a staff whose men and women command the respect of their peers and live up to the prevailing norms of the teaching profession. We have shown that a permissive atmosphere is a part of these norms. In quiet times, undoubtedly, this system works without much friction, because the external prestige and success of the institution is paramount for everyone concerned: the trustees, administration, and professors. Ideological differences seldom come to the fore.

But suppose a crisis develops, in which the trustees, together with other agencies in the community, become very conscious of and desirous of a conservative temper. How easily can they enforce this mood upon their school? As we have seen, the answer depends partly upon the control system, which in turn is already related to the type of president the trustees will have appointed. But to a certain degree the matter is not in their hands. Even if they themselves have conservative attitudes, it will be exactly those administrators who have built up successful colleges who will have the strongest personal and professional involvement in the prestige of their institutions, and be least willing to sacrifice good teachers in the interests of possibly temporary cycles in ideological mood. At such a moment the professional pride of the college administrator can take on an autonomy of its own. The more successful he has been in building up the prestige of his college, the more likely he will be to protect it now against the pressures upon it. In such a crisis, the better colleges, even if under more attack, will be better protected by their administration.

This interpretation is limited on one repect. It assumes that trustees and administrators were not originally inclined to protect permissive teachers. Actually this whole social mechanism often places men in important positions who defend a permissive faculty because they genuinely believe in its worth. Many institutions, especially those which are privately endowed, draw trustees from families greatly concerned with the intellectual inheritance of the nation. These, in turn, are likely to appoint as administrators distinguished professors who belong to the permissive tradition we have described. A cursory review of recent appointments shows how many university presidents indeed come from the ranks of the social scientists nowadays. Our speculations thus suggest that a more careful analysis of the recruitment of trustees and university administrators would be important for the study of academic freedom. Meanwhile, we can make one contribution, by giving some findings which compare the reports of teachers in tax-supported and privately-endowed schools.

Some Differences Between Types of Schools

In Chapter 2 various pressures on schools, as judged by their faculties, were described. We return briefly to these data, concentrating on the public and private schools among the 77 which have enough interviews to provide usable rates. A college is classified according to the proportion of teachers who say that in their impression, "the administration of this college is under more pressure to avoid controversy than it was six or seven years ago." A number of sources for these pressures were mentioned in the question. We focus here on two of these: politicians and trustees. Three observations are provided by the figures, which are shown in Figure 9. Both of these pressure sources impinge more often upon tax-supported than on privately endowed schools. This simply confirms for the seventy-seven colleges what was shown in Chapter 2, Figure 2b, to be true of all. (It is also worth recalling from that table that not all pressures were felt more widely in public than in private schools; the reverse is true of those from alumni.) Secondly, in both types of schools politicians appear more often than trustees. And, finally, the prominence of politicians as sources of high pressures is noticeably more pronounced in the public schools.

Figure 9. The privately-endowed schools are less subject to
pressures from politicians and trustees than tax-supported institutions

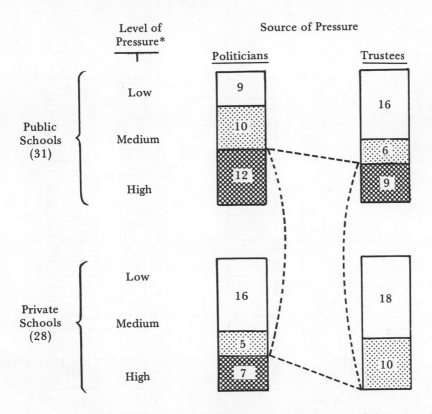

*A low pressure level is indicated if less than 20 percent of the respondents
report increased pressures, a high level if 40 percent or more do.

The interplay between politicians and trustees in public institutions can be suggestively traced if the 31 larger schools are
tabulated according to whether each source appears to create a high
or a low pressure level. In Figure 10a we find a clear tendency for
trustees (often called regents) and politicians to take the same
position. From a survey taken at one time only, one cannot tell
whether the trustees follow the policies of legislators and governors
or whether they take the lead themselves. Common observation,
however, strongly suggests that their general tendency is to be guided
by the initiative of political forces.

Figure 10. Pressures follow different patterns in public
and private schools

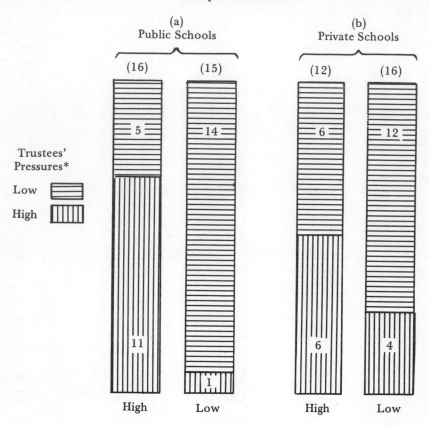

*Because the pressure rates in private schools are lower to begin with (Figure 9), the dividing line in the present table between high and low pressure is 30 percent for the public and 20 percent for the private schools.

In private schools (Figure 10b) the trustees appear to act more independently. In half the schools they remain aloof even if the level of political pressure is high. And in a few colleges the trustees independently initiate pressure—perhaps to forestall the politicians' interference.

From the faculty point of view the position of the administration matters most, and here the difference between the two types of schools is also the most marked. We know from previous tables that about two-thirds of all social scientists feel the administration would support them wholeheartedly in case of attack. Thus a rate of 40 percent or less indicates a relatively low, and 70 percent or more a high, level of protection. In these terms the difference between tax-supported and privately endowed schools looms high indeed. Figure 11 gives the evidence.

Political pressures, to begin with, are lighter on the private schools. The trustees are then less inclined to pass them on. And the administration is often prepared to follow a policy of interposition. This last step can be inferred from Figure 12, which relates political pressures to the level of protection attributed to the administration.

The situation actually reverses in the two types of schools. In tax-supported schools, the higher the political pressures, the lower the administrative protection. But in privately endowed schools our figures indicate an impressive example of countervailing powers: the higher the political pressures, the more ready the administration to protect its faculty.

One could say that in a private school a more pluralistic system of power prevails. Our data suggest that all three elements considered here, political authorities, trustees, and administration officials, are likely to make decisions independently of each other. Under such circumstances there are checks and balances which serve to give the faculties more breathing room in times of crisis. The tax-supported institutions are more monolithic. All components of the system move together and the full brunt of pressure is likely to fall directly on the teacher.

The findings also throw some light on the role of the private trustee as compared to the politically-appointed regent. Both are often chosen from the conservative sector of the community. But when a man becomes a trustee of a private institution he is more free to absorb the atmosphere of the academic tradition. Though he represents the business community, he isn't directly accountable to it, and can change his beliefs in the light of his experiences on the campus. The regent, if he wants to keep his position, must in most cases be reappointed by some political body. He cannot, therefore, deviate too much from the spirit in which he was initially chosen. This need not be a conscious process; it is quite possible that his perception of academic life will be limited and colored from the start by this commitment. Thus in times of crisis the private trustee is more likely to become a mediator between the community and the college than is the regent of a tax-supported institution. Some data

Figure 11. In private schools faculties had much better
administrative protection than in public schools

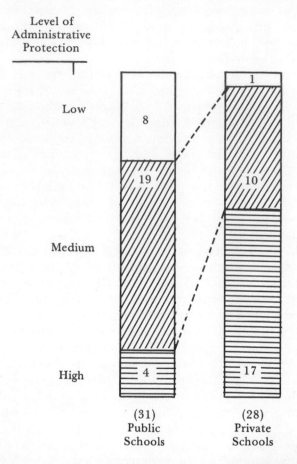

Level of
Administrative
Protection

Low

Medium

High

(31)   (28)
Public   Private
Schools   Schools

from the study by Beck corroborate our findings.[4] There are more
public officeholders and twice as many lawyers—potential office
holders—among the trustees of state universities. And while they
have somewhat less conservative views on economic affairs, being
also less wealthy, they have less respect for academic freedom. What
was a casual observation in the 1930's emerges from our study as a
major issue today. How can trustees of tax-supported institutions be
made more independent in their decisions? Several possible ideas
come to mind: broader representation of other professions besides
lawyers; limits on the number of trustees who hold or have held
public office; preference for men and women who participate in

Figure 12. The relation between pressures from politicians
and administrative protection

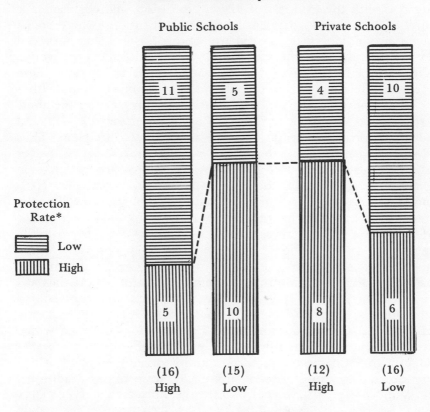

*Here the pressure levels are again separated by a rate of 30 percent in public
and 20 percent in private schools. The protection rate division is at 50 percent
and 65 percent respectively, because it is generally lower in tax-supported colleges (Figure 11). It will be remembered that in low quality traditional schools,
the question on administrative protection seemed differently interpreted. But
these figures deal only with the secular public and private schools.

other cultural or philanthropic activities. Only a more detailed study
of present-day trustees could determine whether these or any other
solutions are promising.

Finally, one more word about the traditional schools. All through
the analysis of our data we realize how little has been written about
these colleges. Authors who deal with higher education in this
country are almost always concerned only with the larger and
superior institutions. Even those who are alarmed about the

standards of these schools seem to feel that they are the places where the intellectual destiny of the country is forged. The prevailing concern is with the frontiers of higher education, and cognizance is hardly taken of what happens in those institutions where social analysts are rare, either as students or professors. Our data call attention especially to the traditional schools with higher objective quality ratings. In Figure 8 it was shown that social scientists at these schools feel relatively unprotected by their administrations. Other signs of discomfort can be added: relations among faculty members are reported as less good, turnover in teaching personnel is high, and incidents involving academic freedom are relatively frequent. Thus while in secular schools objective quality makes for a better atmosphere all around, this is less or sometimes not at all so in traditional schools, where the administration presumably wants to maintain a specific ideological climate. The institution has the material means to attract productive and correspondingly permissive professors. But their permissiveness, when it is brought into the limelight by an accusation or a climate of suspicion, may come almost as a shock to the administration. Giving priority to considerations apart from formal academic standards, its officials will have little impulse to protect them. Between the professional orientation of the faculty and the traditional norms of the administration an imbalance of mutual expectations develops which leads to the kind of anomalies we have mentioned.

One might also see the picture in an historical context. Not too many decades ago most American colleges were of the traditional type. Many of them have evolved into the fully secular type. They appoint teachers distinguished for their research, and see their main task as the training of students who later will perform specific intellectual functions either in the professions or in specialized managerial roles throughout the community. Many smaller schools remained wedded to the earlier function of improving the educational level of the population at large. The traditional colleges of high quality rating are, so to speak, in a transition stage. They are beginning to have resources and teaching personnel like those of the larger secular institutions. But in many cases their administrators, to all appearances, do not yet favor the newer and more specialized academic functions. Objective quality, therefore, is not paralleled by a greater acceptance of the concepts of academic freedom.

Apprehension and College Quality

The essential points of the last two chapters can be pulled together into a schematic presentation.[5] Figure 13 indicates that the

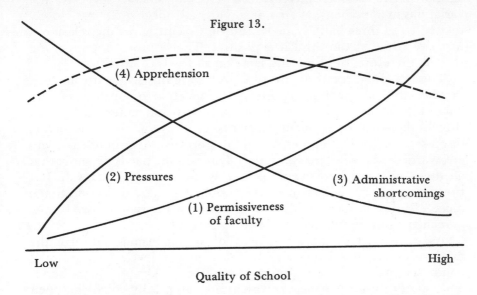

Figure 13.

(4) Apprehension

(2) Pressures

(3) Administrative
shortcomings

(1) Permissiveness
of faculty

Low   High

Quality of School

proportion of permissive professors (1) at a college, and the amount
of pressures (2) impinging on it, increase as we move from less to
more distinguished institutions. A third line refers to the performance of the college administration regarding the management of
academic freedom issues. In order to emphasize a specific point, this
line does not indicate positive performance of the administration,
but rather the inverse: its shortcomings (3). We found that such
shortcomings are less frequent in the superior colleges.

To these three lines in Figure 13 we have added a fourth,
indicating approximately what we should expect the results concerning apprehension to be like on the basis of what we know so far. In
superior colleges (to the right in the figure) the pressures are
great and so is the vulnerability of the faculty; but at the same time
the administration has fewer shortcomings and is more likely to
protect its social scientists. On the left side of the graph the
professors are less vulnerable and, as a result, the outside community
has less of an inclination to create difficulties for the college; but at
the same time the administration is less likely to help the faculty if
trouble does arise. In both these situations, then, we have compen-
sating factors, and this should make for approximately the same level
of apprehension (4). Somewhere in the middle range, we expect to
find a relative maximum of apprehension, because the two contributing factors—permissiveness of the faculty and pressures from the
outside—outweigh the factor which protects against it—excellence of

administrative performance. All in all, the scheme suggests that variations in apprehension are not too great. College quality is closely related to all three basic variables. But in two instances the relation is negative while in the third it is positive. The resulting apprehension should, therefore, be about the same on all levels of quality.

The actual figures of Figure 14 corroborate this schematic analysis quite well. The top line reports the proportion of professors who have a score of 2 or more on the apprehension index. Below are shown the two component elements of the apprehension index, discussed earlier in Chapter 3: the proportions of respondents who are worried and who are cautious.[6] This is done partly to show that all these measures lead to approximately the same general result. But the two auxiliary indices of worry and caution give us an additional piece of information: the difference between the two, shown by the percentages inside the shaded area of Figure 14.

As we expected, there is a peak of apprehension—although the differences are not large—on the third quality level. This group is composed mainly of large (but not very large) tax-supported schools, and of Protestant colleges which are atypically high in their socio-academic resources. The more distinguished Protestant colleges experience conflict between their orthodox traditions and the more secular-minded faculty they can afford. The tax-supported schools in this group can afford a more distinguished faculty, but are not large enough to impress the legislatures, and therefore are subject to greater political pressures.

In addition to this general trend, Figure 14 reveals a somewhat unexpected finding: apprehension does not trail off on the lowest quality level. The schools in this group are mainly teachers colleges and very small denominational institutions. Careful reading of the interviews suggests a psychological interpretation. The teachers in these institutions seem to be especially timid, and it is likely that they feel apprehensive under circumstances in which the average social scientist would still be relatively at ease.

The differences between worry and caution in Figure 14 lead us back to the complexity of apprehension. As we move toward higher quality schools the component of worry in the apprehension index increases as compared to the caution element. In view of all the preceding evidence, we are inclined to make the following interpretation. In the more distinguished colleges apprehension is relatively less determined by fear about one's own job, and more by general concern with the status of academic freedom. Precautionary moves in particular are less necessary, but the whole matter is more on

Figure 14. The relation between quality of college and apprehension

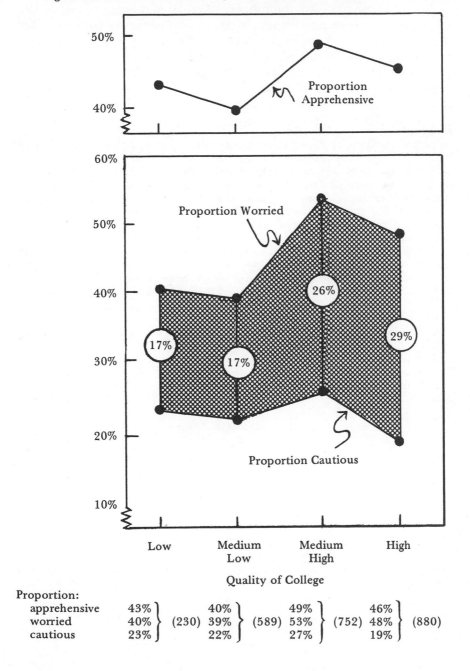

Quality of College

Proportion:								
apprehensive	43% }		40% }		49% }		46% }	
worried	40% }	(230)	39% }	(589)	53% }	(752)	48% }	(880)
cautious	23% }		22% }		27% }		19% }	

professors' minds and so the expressions of worry are relatively more frequent.

Our two pivotal variables have given us a general view of the whole situation. Permissiveness of the individual professor makes for high apprehension in a variety of ways. The quality of his college is a redeeming factor, because the better schools have a more protective administration. With this basic structure in mind, we can now explore in greater detail significant aspects of the way some teachers in our sample experienced the impact of the difficult years.

Footnotes

1. Kant, *Critique of Pure Reason*, quoted from Michael Polanyi, *The Logic of Liberty* (Chicago: University of Chicago Press, 1951). Preface, p. v.

2. The question was previously raised as to whether teachers who are permissive in terms of this report would protect conservative colleagues when the latter were under attack. A similar issue comes up here: does the analytical training of the more qualified social scientists enable them to scrutinize leftist stereotypes more closely? It is possible that a general hospitality for social improvements might make one less critical toward programs of political reform, regardless of their real merit. This too is a question our study can only raise, not answer.

3. According to impressions reported by Professor Riesman, direct pressure by parents also occurred more frequently in these "streetcar colleges."

4. Hubert Park Beck, *Men Who Control Our Universities* (New York: King's Crown Press, 1947).

5. This was suggested by Professor S. A. Stouffer during a discussion of our findings.

6. A teacher is considered "worried," for purposes of the present discussion, if he answered "yes" to two or more of the six worry items in Table 3-1; he is "cautious" if he answered "yes" to two or more of the five caution items in Table 3-2.

ENVIRONMENTAL PRESSURE, PROFESSIONAL AUTONOMY, AND COPING STRATEGIES IN ACADEMIC ORGANIZATIONS

J. Victor Baldridge

Organizational theorists have recently become increasingly concerned with the impact of the external environment on complex organizations. (For example, see 27, 28, 10, 30, 9, 13). For decades the prime focus has been on the internal operation of bureaucracies, but in the last few years more attention is being paid to the social context within which an organization functions. Nowhere is this concern more pronounced than among sociologists who study academic organizations, for in colleges and universities throughout the nation it is increasingly obvious that many of the life and death decisions for the organization are being made outside—in the halls of Congress, in the meetings of the New Left radicals or right-wing extremists, in the Pentagon, and in the governor's office. Anyone who has watched academic decision-making in the last decade can see that powerful external forces are impinging on the university from all sides, tearing at the fabric of the academic community, and threatening to destroy much of the autonomy that academic institutions have so painfully built up over the years.

Colleges and universities provide an excellent setting for the study of environmental pressure on an organization, not only because this is a timely topic, but more especially because they are important "professional" organizations, a subject that has now grown to be a major subsection of organizational theory in sociology. One of the critical demands made by professional workers, whether they are working in a hospital, college, industry, or law firm, is for "professional autonomy," i.e., the right to make critical task decisions based solely on the good of the client and on the expertise of the professional. Of course, there are always counterforces that undermine professional autonomy, such as the heavily studied area of conflict between "bureaucrats" and "professionals."

However, some of the most important types of counterforces that undermine professional autonomy come from pressures *outside* the organization as suggested by research on the public schools (2,4), voluntary social service agencies (22) and colleges (1,8). In the literature that is slowly emerging in this field there is a constant theme: If the professional organization is well "insulated" from environmental pressure then professional norms, task definitions, and work routines dominate the activities of the organization. Under that circumstance professionals are key power wielders within the organization. Major universities, hospitals, and law firms usually exhibit this kind of professional domination. On the other hand, if the insulation between the organization and the environment is weak, then nonprofessional values dominate, and frequently the professionals are reduced to the role of hired employees doing the bidding of bureaucratic managers. (For the same basic thesis in traditional work organizations, see 31). Public school teachers, social workers, and nurses often complain that this is an accurate description of their plight. Thus a basic theoretical proposition emerges from the literature: *The higher the social insulation of professional organizations, the higher the professional autonomy within them. Conversely, the greater the environmental pressure, the lower the professional autonomy.*

Broadly conceived, this proposition seems very sound but it presents rather difficult research problems. It seems reasonable to establish a crude continuum of environmental pressure on professional organizations, with social work agencies and public schools at one end, and universities and hospitals at the other. However, as soon as this is done, the obvious problem arises of confounding variables besides environmental influences: the level of staff training, the nature of financial support, the task itself, and numerous other factors. How can we control for these intervening factors in order to test the major thesis of environmental pressure? One option is to focus on a single type of organization—colleges and universities—and seek variation on environmental pressure *within* that category of organization. This effectively controls for most of the variables above, and still allows a clear test of the thesis. This article uses that strategy and reports on theoretical propositions that elaborate the environmental pressure thesis for colleges and universities. The Stanford Center for Research and Development in Teaching is supporting a major study of the issue, and this article constitutes one of the background arguments elaborated for that research. Since the field research is scheduled to take several years, the theoretical propositions are offered at this point, with future reports due on the actual empirical results.

This article offers propositions about three major factors:

1. *Professional autonomy* is the ability of the principal task-oriented professionals—in this case the faculty—to determine the major goals of the organization and to establish operating systems that support those goals. Lack of autonomy implies that there are other critical goal-setting groups that have significantly more influence than the faculties.

2. *Environmental pressure* is a global concept that might cover a huge variety of impinging factors, but three major types of pressures have been chosen for analysis: financial dependency, clientele base, and direct political pressure. While these three factors certainly do not exhaust the many possible types of environmental pressures, they are among the most important, and there is a body of organizational research dealing with each.

3. *Coping strategies* are devices used by professionals to protect themselves from environmental pressures. On one hand, coping mechanisms are ideological claims,—the demand that professionals have power because their expertise gives them the "right" to hold influence. On the other hand, coping strategies take the form of structural and organizational devices that protect the professional's influence. These include tenure rights, professional organizations, unions, control of governing boards, and other organizational structures that enhance professional power.

In the following sections a number of propositions are offered about the interlocking relationships between professional autonomy, environmental pressure, and coping strategies.

Professional Autonomy—The Dependent Variable

Professional autonomy is the ability of professional staff members to set goals and structure the organization to maximize their concerns. (For a number of papers on this issue see 33). Unfortunately the concept of "goal setting" is extremely ambiguous, so professional autonomy must be translated into more concrete operational factors. At least four issues seem critical: (1) control over core tasks, (2) work evaluation by peers, (3) work standardization, and (4) departmental antonomy.

Control Over Core Technology

First, there is *central task control*, the process by which the professional staff exercise control over the basic organizational tasks, the "core technology" in James D. Thompson's terminology. We always expect that any fairly complex organization will have a central administrative structure that deals with "support functions," i.e., obtaining money, coordinating diverse activities, and maintaining physical facilities. Professional autonomy is not so much control over these support facilities as it is control over more central academic tasks, i.e., setting the curriculum, defining the nature of the student body, setting graduation requirements, and specifying research goals. If the environment impinges on the college to the extent that these central professional functions are not handled by the faculty, but are instead defined by law or set by the administration, then the faculty has low professional autonomy.

Operationally, control over the central task could be measured in at least two ways. First, we might use a list of "influence spheres." In a school with high professional autonomy, we would expect both faculty and administration to rate the faculty influence as very high on the curriculum, research goals, admissions criteria, and subject-matter content. In short, there would be high central task control *perceived* by staff people. In addition, we would expect structural arrangements to reflect this professional autonomy. Alongside the administrative structures of the college or university there would be well-developed faculty decision mechanisms, including committees, academic councils, senates, and the like. Moreover these structural mechanisms would be rated as having high influence over the critical core technologies. Of course, the exact structural arrangements would vary considerably. For example, we would not expect as elaborate a committee system or faculty senate in a small college as we might in a major university. Nevertheless, in a school with high professional autonomy there would be "parallel hierarchies" with effective, respected faculty mechanisms that parallel the administrative structures. In some cases these may be almost entirely informal, but generally formal mechanisms appear even in rather noncomplex colleges. In short, faculty influence and professional autonomy have to be protected and empowered by effective, strong structural decision mechanisms. Consequently, one measure of professional control over the core technology would be the existence of faculty decision mechanisms and a high rating of their effectiveness. .

Peer Evaluation of Work

Because of their expert knowledge the professionals maintain that only expert peers should have the right to evaluate their work. This has been one of the persistent arguments and empirical findings in the literature on professionalization (See 33). The physician demands that only other physicians monitor his work; the lawyer looks only to other legal experts for evaluation; the professor feels that only another professor can make meaningful assessments of his teaching and scholarly research.

W. Richard Scott, Sanford Dornbusch, et. al. (24), have proposed that the effective, operational authority in any organization may be found in its *evaluation systems*. In short, authority is the right to set tasks, determine effectiveness criteria, and evaluate work performance. (For a study of this theory applied to university faculty, see Hind's article in Part 3 of this book). In this sense the true professional always demands that operational authority be lodged with the professional group itself, not with administrators, clients, or outside groups. Thus, faculties with high professional autonomy demand and receive the right to evaluate performance, grant tenure, and make promotions.

The intrusion of outside forces often undermines the claim for peer evaluation and "professionally irrelevant" criteria are often imposed by interest blocs outside the university. The whole concept of "academic freedom" is an attempt to provide insulation against these outside encroachments and to ensure professionally defined criteria of evaluation. In many ways the right to determine who is hired, promoted, and granted tenure is at the very heart of the academic freedom and professional autonomy issues, for the faculties only have true operational "authority" over their own activities when they can control evaluation practices. The right to peer evaluation is central to professional autonomy and the surest sign of external interference is a breakdown in the evaluation system and the imposition of external, nonprofessional criteria.

Work Standardization and Professional Autonomy

One of the major demands of a professionally autonomous faculty member is simply that he be left alone. With his expert knowledge and his internalized training he believes that the greatest gift of mankind is the splendid freedom of doing more or less as he pleases, without the interference of administrators, pressure groups, or (particularly) students. Of course, power groups both inside and outside the university are not so sure that this is the best of all possible worlds. There are nagging suspicions that left to his own devices the professor might neglect his students, take many "consulting" trips, or perhaps even be a little lazy. Consequently, as groups other than the faculty gain power they tend to impose work schedules, reporting devices, and standardized procedures to insure that the faculty is performing its work properly. Anyone who has moved from the relatively protected, insulated position of a major private university to the externally vulnerable public college has tasted the flavor of standardized work procedures in the endless accounting for pennies, the virtual time-clock schedule, the loss of freedom over course scheduling, the standardization of contracts that specify work activities in detail, and the endless streams of bureaucratic red tape that state agencies use to control faculty behavior. Thus, one of the best measures of professional autonomy is the freedom from standardization, the freedom to make one's own work times and schedules, and the freedom from outside-imposed red tape. Operationally, this would be one of the easiest variables to measure, for a series of questions about financial accounting, control of time, and the detail of contract work specifications would reveal great differences between colleges with different environments.

Departmental Autonomy

As a professional group, academics are splintered into disciplines and departments. In the university or college, departments are not only administrative arrangements for coordination (as they are in most governmental or industrial organizations), but also the center of one's professional career, the location of one's significant peers, and the base from which one learns particular methodologies, theories, and scientific views of the world. Indeed, one of the most critical features of the academic profession and the academic organization is the nature of its fragmented, insulated departments that divide the scholarly world into hostile little tribes, speaking different languages and worshiping different gods. (For an excellent discussion of this, see 6). The academic professional has roots deep in the soil of his department and his life revolves around it to a significant degree.

If the department is so critical to the academic professional, both as a center of his discipline and as an administrative structure within his school, it is no wonder that academics are extremely jealous about their departments' freedom from "outside" control-"outside" being defined as other departments, administrators, students, or groups outside the university.

If we view the departmental structure as a strong enclave of professional expertise and as the structural system that supports a particular professional world view, then one of the major ways of protecting professional autonomy is to have strong, insulated, independent departments. Consequently, one way to measure professional autonomy is to determine how much freedom the department has to set goals, hire faculty, arrange departmental academic standards, and control significant parts of the budget. Operationally, this would be fairly simple to measure, for department chairmen can readily respond to questions about the degree of autonomy that their departments have in certain specified areas.

Unfortunately the departmental autonomy thesis may be complicated by the size of the college or university, because as an organization grows larger more and more decisions may be turned over to departments simply because the central administration cannot handle all the details. (For a discussion of the size variable, see Part 1). As a result, the general thesis that the higher the environmental pressure the lower the departmental autonomy must be considered with size factors controlled. It is difficult to predict the interaction between size, environmental pressure, and departmental autonomy, so this is a critical question we hope to answer in future research.

In summary, *professional autonomy* is a complex of several factors, including (1) the right to control critical "core technology" decisions, (2) the availability of decision mechanisms to protect that right, (3) the ability to control the evaluation and reward system, (4) the freedom to avoid standardization of work imposed by nonprofessionals, and (5) the protection of professional values in relatively autonomous departments. With these factors in mind, let us turn to the environmental pressure variable and see how its various components affect professional autonomy.

Propositions Linking Professional Autonomy and Environmental Pressures

Just as professional autonomy is an umbrella hiding several factors, "environmental pressure" is also a composite variable. While dozens of pressures could be singled out, only three will be considered here in order to show their effect on professional autonomy.*

Resource Pressures

All organizations must have adequate resources if they are to survive and carry out their tasks. Control over acquisition of resources, setting of priorities, and allocation of funds is of course a critical factor that determines much of the destiny of an organization. In academic organizations the faculties, as an assembled group, rarely make budgetary decisions. Nevertheless, the professional corps does exercise an enormous influence on the academic priorities of an institution, and indirectly over the administrators that make the critical resource allocation decisions. The degree of environmental control is a major factor in determining whether administrators are responsive to professional faculty demands rather than the demands of other groups.

Proposition 1: The greater the external control of resources, the lower the professional autonomy.

This first proposition, while rather obvious, is nevertheless critical, for it separates schools with strong internal resources, such as endowments, from those that depend on outside funds, such as government support, gifts, or foundation grants. Obviously schools with huge endowments or other internally controlled resources should be expected to display much more professional independence than those that must continuously seek outside aid.

However, the simple "external/internal" distinction tells little of the story, for it is not only the external nature, but the *configuration* of those sources that determines professional autonomy. At first

---

*The following propositions about the effect of enviornmental pressure on professional autonomy are global. That is, we have not tried to specify how each subtype of pressure affects each subtype of professional autonomy, i.e., control over core technology, mechanisms for decisions, peer evaluation, departmental autonomy, and work standardization. We have not done this because it would be extremely tedious to go through all five subtypes of professional autonomy with each subtype of environmental pressure, and because in almost every case all the effects would run in the same direction. That is, if the environmental pressure caused lower control over the core technology, it would almost always cause less effective internal faculty decision mechanisms, more work standardization, less peer evaluation, etc. In effect, each of the professional autonomy subtypes are only operational ways of measuring the variable, not factors to be considered individually.

glance it may seem that the more groups a college is dependent on, the less its professional autonomy, for those external groups make their own unique demands about the goals and activities of the institution. On closer examination, however, this simply is not the case, for many—even most—of the more independent, professionally dominated universities have numerous sources of funds. A revision is suggested:

Proposition 2: The more concentrated *external resources are in the hands of a few contributors, the lower the professional autonomy.*

It is the concentration of resources in a few powerful hands, not the mere existence of many groups, that really gives external forces enormous power over the destiny of a college or university. (For an examination of this thesis, see Evan (10)). The concentration of funds in the state legislature makes state colleges dependent on the desires of the state; the control of major funds by a religious body can make a school a vassal of the church; dependence on a local school board exposes the community college to powerful local interests.

It is important to see that some types of "concentration" are different from others. The most important case is when it appears that resources are "concentrated" in the hands of students (through tuition) or in the hands of donors (through a large number of small individual gifts). This type of concentration is likely to show up in an annual financial report of an institution, especially a private one. At first it seems that such an institution would be very dependent on concentrated external resources, but this masks the fact that, while they are major fund sources, small gifts and individual tuition payments are actually the accumulations of hundreds of individual decisions—aggregative, accumulated resources, not direct, concentrated resources controlled by a few people. To illustrate this point, if a million dollars is listed in one line of the income budget for student tuition, and another million from a thousand different donors, this is certainly not the same kind of "concentration" as if the two million dollars came from the Ford Foundation. While this point seems clear, it nevertheless poses serious research problems. For example, our research team was at first fooled into considering a school as having concentrated resources if most of its funds came from tuition, but later we began to see that this type of "aggregated" concentration of funds was radically different from the "direct" concentration that comes when only a few people hold the funds, even if those aggregated funds do show up in a budget report as one source. Consequently, the following corollary is offered to accompany the second proposition:

> *Corollary 2a: The more "direct," instead of "aggregated" a single source is, the more concentrated is that source; hence, less professional autonomy is associated with direct control.*

The above three propositions about resource control are very helpful in explaining why some types of schools have more professional autonomy than others. Clearly this is not the only factor, for a number of state schools have great amounts of professional autonomy in spite of their dependence on the state legislature; many religious schools have been able to develop strong professional faculties; and many junior colleges have devised means of warding off external pressure. Of course, there are exceptions, but the general rule seems to stand: All other things being equal, the more dependent a school is on the environment for resources, the less autonomy the professionals have. In general, then, community colleges with a local school board as their source of funds will have very low professional autonomy; a liberal arts college with strong financial ties to a church but some measure of independence because of its tuition base probably will have a medium level of professional autonomy; and schools with major endowments or constitutionally empowered taxing rights would display the most professional autonomy. (For a confirmation of this point, see 14.)

Coping mechanisms. How does the academic profession attempt to protect itself from environmental intrusions that come with financial dependence? A number of coping mechanisms are available.

> *Coping Strategy 1: Professional organizations attempt to maintain autonomy by seeking alternative sources of income.*

Just as some large industries attempt to decrease their dependency on a single market by diversifying their products, academic organizations work hard to diversify their sources of income. (See 28, p. 32). The current movement among private universities to secure state aid, as in Pennsylvania, is clearly an attempt to gain more money and at the same time diversify the resource base. In addition, there is a continued effort to maintain "aggregate" sources, i.e., to maintain a wide variety of alternative sources instead of a few concentrated ones. For example, some schools (such as Stanford) have learned that heavy dependence on federal research grants can seriously affect the financial stability of the university when those funds fluctuate. Consequently these federally dependent schools are trying to spread out to other, less concentrated, resource bases. In addition, many state schools (such as Berkeley) have recently undertaken major campaigns to raise more *private* funds in order to diversify some of their financial inputs.

Coping Strategy 2: Professional organizations attempt to maintain resources autonomy by stockpiling resources.

One way to ensure that current resource suppliers do not get a strangle-hold over professional autonomy is to save for a rainy day by storing away resources. (For an excellent discussion of stockpiling in industrial organizations, see 28, p. 20). The endowment is the cushion that many schools fall back on when they need independence from environmental pressure. In this sense, then, the endowment system is not only a financial device, but also a significant contributor to professional autonomy, a buffer that protects the integrity of the school.

Coping Strategy 3: Professional organizations attempt to buffer the direct influence of financial dependency by pooling and sharing of limited resources.

Resource pooling occurs in at least two different ways. On one hand there is pooling *among* different colleges and universities as they share computer facilities, libraries, and talented faculty. The other major strategy is to pool resources *within* an institution, buffering areas that are resource-poor by giving them funds from areas that are resource-rich. Every major university, for example, supports many of its humanities programs with money drawn from the overhead on scientific research projects. Internal shifting to eliminate some of the cruder impacts of the commercial market helps give vulnerable professional groups more autonomy.

Client Dependency
The second major type of environmental pressure is the dependency that comes from particular types of client relations. Burton R.

Clark's study (8) of the "open door" community college is an important analysis of a school that was highly dependent on its environment. Part of Clark's analysis concerns the formal external control that resulted from the close link between the college trustees and the community. Another part, however, deals with the environmental dependency arising from the fact that admissions policies were set by the community, not by the college. In effect, the professional staff had no control over the "inputs," the raw material coming in from the environment. Consequently, Clark argues, the goals of the college were largely determined by the marketplace of student course selection rather than by the faculty's professional judgment about the curriculum. Clark's discussion leads to another proposition about environmental influence:

Proposition 3: The lower the professional control over client characteristics, the lower the amount of professional autonomy.

The inability of the professionals to control client characteristics usually comes from one of two factors. On one hand, the faculty may not have high control because there is some external influence group that has the legal right to set admissions policies, as in Clark's community college and the City University of New York. The client control issue thus has a specifying corollary:

Corollary 3a: The more legal power to set admissions policies is vested in an external group, the lower the professional control of clients; hence, the lower the professional autonomy.

The second major factor that influences the control of professionals over client characteristics is the size of the recruiting base. Obviously schools that have a large, well-stocked recruiting pool will be more able to select carefully and use a professionally imposed set of standards, while schools that have a small recruiting base must be satisfied with what they can get. Consequently:

Corollary 3b: The larger the recruiting pool relative to the needed student body, the more the professional staff can exercise discretion; hence, the greater the professional autonomy.

Coping strategies. There are several coping strategies that help the professionals maintain control over the client base.

Coping Strategy 4: Professional staffs try to formulate and project an appropriate "public image" to (1) enlarge the client recruitment pool, and (2) predefine the nature of the client group.

A "public image" serves a dual purpose. On one hand it helps attract a larger recruitment pool, simply by virtue of the school's being well-known. On the other hand, the articulated public image serves as a screening device that eliminates most of the "undesirable" applicants in advance. Most high-prestige schools, for example, have very few unqualified applicants (even though they still may have to select a smaller group because of limited space), and this is largely due to the image that the school projects. Colleges and universities often go to great expense to proclaim their unique role, and "public relations" staffs have become a major component of many administrations. Baldridge (1), for example, shows how New York University deliberately tried to change its public image through intense propaganda and information spreading. Faced with competition from other universities that were stealing its traditional clientele, NYU shifted the recruitment strategy, concentrating more on high ability students and emphasizing "urban" education. NYU's experience is not unusual, for schools constantly work to project a favorable, selective public image. By thus controlling the nature of the client base and the recruitment pool, the public image projection becomes one effective coping strategy against environmental pressure. In effect, the public image becomes a way for the professionals to reach out and manipulate the environment.

Coping Strategy 5: Professionals use their claim to expert knowledge to argue against the imposition of external standards of admission for students.

"We are the only ones who really know what standards make sense; any other nonprofessional standards are merely 'political' pressures"—so goes the fundamental argument of the faculty against anyone who tries to impose external standards. This kind of argument does carry a great deal of weight, for the expert knowledge of the faculty is generally respected; nevertheless the "open door" admissions policy is a strong contemporary movement that often overrides professional opposition.

Coping Strategy 6: Having failed at controlling admissions, the

.faculty will attempt to control the client base by heavy pressure on lower ability students to "counsel out" of school.

Even in situations where the faculty cannot control who *comes* in—and they usually do—they certainly have a great deal of influence over who *stays* in. Clark (8) reports on the heavy emphasis that was given counseling services in the open door community colleges where many of the students were academically unprepared and vocationally unsure. The faculty felt that it was their job to test severely the students in their first years. In this way, professors tried to "cool out" many students who would have been eliminated if the faculty had held control over admissions. What the professionals could not gain over admissions, they made up for by constant pressure on "undesirable" students.

Countervalues as Environmental Pressures

The two basic types of environmental pressure listed above, control of resources and control of clients, are normal activities in the day-to-day life of a college or university. The third type of environmental pressure involves the deliberate imposition of hostile values on the professional faculty by outside groups. In its extreme case this kind of "countervalue" pressure tends to be dramatically hostile to the fundamental fabric of the professional values. The shrill attacks on university faculties during the McCarthy era of the 1950's—the subject of Lazarsfeld's and Thielen's research in the *Academic Mind* (14)—is a clear example of this kind of pressure. Of course, in more subtle forms this pressure goes on all the time, in the "suggestions" offered by a trustee that a controversial faculty member should not be rehired; the veiled threat by a donor that funds will be withheld if the faculty continues on its "liberal" course; and a thousand and one other small incidents that arise in daily activities. The following proposition opens the discussion.

Proposition 4: The greater the consensus between the school and its significant surrounding environment, the greater the professional autonomy of the faculty, and vice versa.

It is important to specify the qualifications under which this type of pressure will be effective in decreasing professional autonomy. The mere existence of countervalues in the environment is not enough to undermine professional autonomy; there must be effective methods for translating those countervalues into political clout. Consequently, the following corollaries are offered to specify more carefully the conditions under which countervalues might impinge on professional autonomy.

Corollary 4a: The more control over resources held by groups with countervalues, the lower the professional autonomy.

Corollary 4b: The more control over client characteristics by groups with countervalues, the lower the professional autonomy.

Corollary 4c: The more control over the formal governing board by groups with countervalues, the lower the professional autonomy.

The first two corollaries are direct sequels to earlier discussions, and the third is so obvious as to need no further discussion. The impact of right-wing political groups during the McCarthy era (see Lazarsfeld and Thielens (14)) provides a vivid example of this kind of countervalue pressure, but there are of course many other cases of countervalues. One of the most persistent is that of religious devotion versus academic inquiry, a theme of value conflict that permeates a vast segment of the academic system in the United States. Faculties in religion-dominated schools almost by definition have some degree of conflict between objective, scientific "truth" and a different kind of religious, nonscientific "truth." If strong religious bodies control clients through church-based student recruitment, control governing boards through church-selected boards of trustees, and control financial support through church contributions, there are strong possibilities of value conflict between the demands of scholarly objectivity and the demands of religious adherence. Among the other types of value conflicts that now affect the campus are the antiscientific mood of the youth counterculture, the leftist radical movements that perhaps correctly feel that the academic community has prostituted its knowledge in the service of "imperialistic" economic and political policies, and resurgent conservative movements in opposition to "campus violence."

It is generally true that the more hostile values are forced on a college or university the lower the professional autonomy of the faculty, especially if those hostile groups control the resources, clientele, and the formal trusteeship. However, the impact of value-oriented interest groups is more complex than this, for there are parallels with the earlier discussion of financial control. If hostile interests are concentrated on one side of an issue—let us say all the major environment pressures are politically conservative and are aligned against a liberal faculty—the impact of these forces is likely to be more influential than when they are fragmented into opposing groups. Earlier we noted that it was not merely the number of financial power groups, but their configuration that influence professional autonomy. In parallel fashion, it is the configuration of value-oriented interest groups, not their absolute number, that determines the autonomy of the college or university.

The relationship between interest group configurations and professional autonomy is probably curvilinear. Other things being equal, *high concentration* of interest groups on one side of a value issue leads to low autonomy. *Medium fragmentation* of groups on many sides of an issue leads to freedom-giving "cross-pressures" in which the professionals can maneuver by playing off one group against another. However, *extreme fragmentation* of interest groups leads to a kind of war of all against all, with the resultant hostilities and controversies becoming so disruptive that the professionals are caught in the middle of a massive assault that leaves them very little autonomy.

Obviously the relationship between professional autonomy and environmental value-pressures is a very delicate one. Ideally, college faculty would want its values to be shared by its supporting environment, thus eliminating the direct value-pressure. However, barring that fortunate configuration, professional autonomy is most threatened by either of two extremes: (1) *extreme concentration* of interest groups as a power bloc, or (2) *extreme fragmentation* that leads to the faculty's being caught between vicious interest groups on all sides of the issue. Given any pressure at all, the most comfortable situation is to have a *medium fragmentation* level so that various groups can be played off against each other and areas of freedom between the groups established. Of course, this discussion is dependent on the prior argument that outside groups can only have major impact when they can translate their pressure into effective control over resources, client characteristics, or formal trusteeship.

In light of this discussion we can now offer the last proposition about value-pressures.

Proposition 5: Other things being equal, high concentration of value-pressure groups on one side of an issue leads to low professional autonomy; medium fragmentation of value-pressure groups leads to cross-pressures and higher professional autonomy; high fragmentation of value-pressure groups leads to intense conflict and lower professional autonomy.

Coping strategies. Over the years academic professionals have experienced many different kinds of value-pressures: political, religious, scientific, and edeological. In response, academics have developed a rather elaborate set of defense mechanisms that help ward off those impinging forces. One of the most critical is the development of a tight "professional culture" in which the professionals support each other and fight against the intrusion of alien values. We normally call this the quest for "academic freedom" and normative frameworks have been developed to articulate and protect that value. Although the norms by themselves do not insure that academic freedom will be protected, they do provide a basic intellectual undergirding that can stir the public conscience against intrusions. A strong, protective academic culture serves as a wall to shut out the external interference that otherwise might impose countervalues on the academic community. It is interesting to note that in the *Academic Mind* Larzarsfeld and Thielens (14) report that schools with highly developed academic cultures—strong feelings of professional idenity, and high academic "quality" in the traditional sense—were the most resistant to interference from right-wing pressure blocs. The administrations in those schools took strong stands in order to protect their faculties, and they justified their action by appeals to professional standards and academic freedom. Thus, the first coping strategy in the face of countervalues may be stated:

Coping Strategy 7: In the face of countervalues, faculties develop strong normative protective positions, commonly known as "academic freedom," and use this value as a legitimation behind which they can hide.

However, articulating a value such as academic freedom is not enough, for without structural and organizational protections the value can be easily undermined. Consequently the normative value is supported by some tough organizational strategies, the most important of which is the tenure system. The tenure mechanism has long been used as an organizational protection of cherished values, of course, and it is coupled with a "trial by peers" in which only competent professional colleagues have the right to say when a man has overstepped the bounds of admissible behavior.

Coping Strategy 8: Professional faculties use tenure and trial by peers as a protection against external interference.

Of course, tenure, academic freedom norms, and trial by peers are the result of power: They do not simply happen but have been won in hard fights by generations of professional faculties. Thus, to talk of normative structures and procedural safeguards is to talk, one step backwards, of power that has been successful in wresting control from both the external environment and the trustees of institutions. Hard strategic bargaining accomplished those victories over a long period of time. In fact, Clark (6), Mayhew (19), and Reisman (21) have all argued that one of the longterm developments in American higher education has been the gradual accumulation of professional power by faculties, to the point that in the present decade most of the major universities are dominated by the faculties in a guild-like, syndical fashion.* This control was gained by power plays, both inside a given institution and outside in professional organizations and unions.

The power element must assuredly be brought into the equation as a protective mechanism against external intrusion; a number of power strategies are used. First, there are the professional organizations that have been developed around each discipline. These organizations insist that only they have the right to judge the competency of their disciplines, and in many cases they are able to ward off incursions by nonprofessionals. They bring many types of sanctions to bear on schools that do allow external intrusions, including public censure, withdrawal of accreditation, and refusal to supply personnel.

---

*The syndical, guild-like control of the faculty—if that is an accuarate description—raises an important value question that we unfortunately do not have time to comment on extensively. This is the question of whether faculties *should* have strong professional autonomy. Throughout this paper the analysis has been rather one-sided: It should be obvious that I feel that in general faculties as professional groups should have autonomy. However, there is a real question whether in some cases professional autonomy has not lead to unfortunate consequences. Students and outsiders alike are charging that faculties have become *too* autonomous, that students are neglected while autonomous faculty members play with esoteric research, that ivory-tower mentalities separate the professor from the "real" world, that research is petty, uninteresting and, worst of all, not useful. The experience of other professions, notably medicine, is that when the professional group becomes *too* autonomous it becomes self-serving, insensitive to social needs, and intolerant of legitimate claims on it by the larger society. Under these circumstances the value issue must be sharply focused, and nothing in this article should be construed as saying that professional autonomy is always a good thing. In fact, there are many cases where it assuredly is not.

Coping Strategy 9: Disciplinary professional organizations use power to counter value pressure groups in the external environment.

The professional organizations for each discipline are paralleled by a number of organizations that claim to speak for the entire academic professional community, including the AAUP and various teachers' unions. The AAUP in particular has always been deeply involved in protecting the academic professionals from external interference, or, as they more often put it, "upholding academic freedom." While unions have typically been more concerned with bread-and-butter issues, they too have been aware that countering external value-pressures is a critical issue for any faculty. All these groups are willing to use sanctions when schools are obviously violating academic freedom principles.

Coping Strategy 10: National agencies for the entire academic profession work to elaborate and protect academic freedom values, thus helping insulate faculties from external value-pressures.

While the disciplinary and national professional organizations are working outside the college or university, the faculties are also trying to work internally to protect their domains from external pressures. Primarily this takes the form of developing faculty senates and strong faculty decision bodies to ensure faculty dominance in the "core technology" areas of student selection, research policies, and academic requirements. Moreover, the faculties constantly seek to control the appointment of key administrators—presidents, deans, provosts—in order to insure a protective aegis under which they can work. Forming a strong protective boundary network of officials over whom the faculty has great control is of course a critical function that trustees are reluctant to hand over to faculties, but this is one of the constant goals of faculties who need environmental protection.

Coping Strategy 11: Internally, faculties try to gain power over the "boundary roles" in order to have a protective buffer between themselves and external pressures.

In summary, value-pressures are one of the most critical issues for a professional group that is intimately involved in the world of ideas, values, and norms—with the transmission and transformation of cultural ideas and ideals. Consequently, a number of coping strategies are used simultaneously to fight the almost inevitable pressures that come from the surrounding environment.

Conclusion

The basic task of this article has been to specify the types of professional autonomy and the types of environmental pressures, to show the impact of environmental pressure on autonomy, and to outline some of the coping strategies used to counter the pressures. The principal thesis of the paper has been that much can be learned about the autonomy and organization of the academic profession by examining its context rather than by focusing on the internal nature of either the profession itself or the particular academic organization.

If the thesis is correct, we would expect that much of the variation in the internal operation and structure of colleges and universities can be predicted from a knowledge of their relation to their outside environment. At one end of a continuum we would find colleges and universities with *high environmental pressure and consequently low professional autonomy*. The local community colleges are clearly at this extreme of the continuum, because they are financially dependent on a local school district, have their student clientele entirely defined by law, and are faced with pressures toward vocational training and community service instead of the more traditional academic values.

At this end of the continuum the faculty has extremely low autonomy as measured by the variables outlined in the first part of the article. Work is highly standardized, with formal contracts that usually specify not only the exact number of teaching hours but even the precise courses to be taught. Office hours are specified and checked; absences require permission from department chairmen; and there is very little freedom over financial matters. The faculty has very little control over major decisions, and there are few effective decision mechanisms for faculty input. In many ways the decision process is centralized in the administration, and departmental autonomy over hiring, promotion, and tenure is very limited. Peer evaluation is not nearly as strong as in other types of schools, and these evaluations are not as much a part of the promotion and tenure scheme. In fact, promotions are usually based on standard time schedules, not on quality of performance, much as in the public schools. Certainly it would be senseless to attribute all these characteristics to environmental pressure, for other factors, such as the nature of the faculty itself and the overall goals of the college are active determinants. Nevertheless, the "captured" nature of the community college vis-á-vis its environment is a critical issue in the faculty's lack of autonomy.

At the other end of the continuum is the large private university with heavy endowments and high insulation from its environment. Depending on its tuition, endowments, and individual research grants for financial support, the major private university has a great measure of freedom from its surrounding environment. The client pool is usually large, and control over it is in the hands of the faculty who determine admissions criteria. In addition, while the major university is most likely to have value-pressures placed on it because of its liberal professors, it nevertheless has the strongest commitment to academic freedom, the most articulate support from professional guardians outside the organization, and the most protective administrators manning the boundary roles.

At this end of the continuum—in the Yales, Harvards, and Stanfords—the faculty has an amazing amount of autonomy. There is almost no standardization of work: The teaching hours, course loads, office hours, contractual relations, and other symbols of standardization are deliciously ambiguous and vague, allowing the professor the greatest amount of the supreme right to be left alone. Control over major decisions is very decentralized, and the faculty has great input through committees, faculty senates, and autonomous departments. Hiring, promotion, and evaluation of faculty are reserved to the faculty itself. Any intrusion of the realm is strongly and usually successfully resisted. The freedom from environmental influence allows enormous freedom for the faculty in such universities.

Of course, there are countless variations between the community college at one extreme and the major private university at the other end. However, it would be decidedly tedious to cover all the bases, so that task will have to go undone. The basic principles are here, but the application to each specific situation would be a task beyond this article. Of course, not all of the variations between schools can be explained by the environmental pressure variable, but it seems to have real explanatory power in unraveling the various configurations of professional autonomy that we find in colleges and universities.

References

1. Baldridge, J. Victor. *Power and Conflict in the University.* New York: John Wiley & Sons, Inc., 1971.
2. Bidwell, Charles E. "The School as a Formal Organization." In James G. March, *Handbook of Organizations.* Chicago: McNally, 1968, pp. 972-1022.
3. Boland, Walter. "Size, Organization, and Environmental Mediation." In

Academic Governance, ed. J. Victor Baldridge. Berkeley: McCutchan, 1971, Chapter 3.

4. Carlson, Roland O. "Environmental Constraints and Organizational Consequences: The Public School and its Clients." In *Behavioral Science and Educational Administration*. Chicago: National Society for the Study of Education, 1964, Part 2, pp. 262-276.

5. Clark, Burton R. *Adult Education in Transition*. Berkeley, California: University of California Press, 1956.

6. Clark, Burton R. "Faculty Organization and Authority." In *The Study of Academic Administration*, ed. Terry Lunsford. Boulder, Colorado: Western Interstate Commission on Higher Education, 1963.

7. Clark, Burton R. "Interorganizational Patterns in Education," *Administrative Science Quarterly*, Vol. 10, No. 2 (1965): pp. 224-237.

8. Clark, Burton R. *The Open Door College*. New York: McGraw-Hill, 1960.

9. Dill, William R. "Environment as an Influence on Managerial Autonomy," *Administrative Science Quarterly*, Vol. 2, No. 4 (March 1958): pp. 409-443.

10. Evan, William M. "The Organizational Set: Toward a Theory of Interorganizational Relations." In *Approaches to Organizational Design*, ed. J. D. Thompson. Pittsburgh: University of Pittsburgh Press, 1966, pp. 173-191.

11. Hind, Robert R. "Analysis of a Faculty: Professionalism, Evaluation, and the Authority Structure." In *Academic Governance*, ed. J. Victor Baldridge. Berkeley: McCutchan, 1971, Chapter 13.

12. Lawrence, Paul R. and Lorsch, Jay W. "Differentiation and Integration in Complex Organizations," *Administrative Science Quarterly*, Vol. 12, No. 1 (1967): pp. 1-47.

13. Lawrence, Paul R. and Lorsch, Jay W. *Organization and Environment*. Boston: Division of Research, Graduate School of Business Administration, Harvard University, 1967.

14. Lazarsfeld, Paul and Thielens, Wagner. *The Academic Mind*. Glencoe: Free Press, 1958, Chapter 8.

15. Levine, Sol and White, Paul E. "Exchange as a Conceptual Framework for the Study of Interorganizational Relationships," *Administrative Science Quarterly* 5 (1961): pp. 583-601.

16. Litwak, Edward and Hylton, Lydia F. "Interorganizational Analysis: A Hypothesis on Coordinating Agencies," *Administrative Schience Quarterly* 6 (1962): pp. 395-420.

17. Maniha, J., and Perrow, Charles "The Reluctant Organization and the Aggressive Environment," *Administrative Science Quarterly*, Vol. 10, No. 2 (September 1965): pp. 238-257.

18. March, James G. and Simon, Herbert. *Organizations*. New York: John Wiley & Sons, 1958, Chapters 5, 7.

19. Mayhew, Lewis B. *Arrogance on Campus*. New York: Jossey-Bass, 1970.

20. Messinger, S. L. "Organizational Transformation: A Case Study of a Declining Social Movement," *Administrative Science Quarterly* 20 (1955): pp. 3-10.

21. Reisman, David and Jenks, Christopher. *The Academic Revolution*. New York: Doubleday, 1968.

22. Rose, Arnold. "Voluntary Associations Under Conditions of Competition and Conflict," *Social Forces* 34 (1955): pp. 159-163.

23. Schelling, Thomas. *Strategy of Conflict.* Cambridge: Harvard Press, 1960.

24. Scott, W. Richard, Dornbusch, Sanford M., Busching, Bruce, C. and Laing, James D. "Organizational Evaluation and Authority," *Administrative Science Quarterly*, Vol. 12, No. 1 (June 1967): pp. 93-117.

25. Simpson, R. and Gulley, W. H. "Goals, Environment, Pressure, and Organizational Change," *American Sociological Review* 27 (June 1966): pp. 344-351.

26. Stinchcombe, Arthur L. "Social Structure and Organizations," In *Handbook of Organizations*, ed. G. S. March. Chicago: Rand McNally, 1965, pp. 142-193.

27. Terreberry, Shirley. "The Evolution of Organizational Environments," *Administrative Science Quarterly*, Vol. 12, No. 4 (March 1968): pp. 590-613.

28. Thompson, James D. *Organizations in Action*. New York: McGraw-Hill, 1967.

29. Thompson, James D. "Organizations and Output Transactions," *American Journal of Sociology* 68 (November 1962): pp. 309-324.

30. Thompson, James D. and McEwen,W. J. "Organizational Goals and Environment: Goal-setting as an Interaction Process," *American Sociological Review* 23 (February 1958): pp. 23-31.

31. Udy, Stanley, Jr. *Organization of Work*. New Haven: Taplinger Press, 1959.

32. Vollmer, Howard and Mills, Donald, eds. *Professionalization*. Englewood Cliffs, N.J.: Prentice-Hall, 1967.

33. Watten, R. L. "The Interorganizational Field as a Focus for Investigation," *Administrative Science Quarterly*, Vol. 12, No. 3 (December 1967): pp. 396-419.

Part 6

Conflict
and the
Dynamics of
Policy Making

IMAGES OF THE FUTURE AND ORGANIZATIONAL CHANGE: THE CASE OF NEW YORK UNIVERSITY

J. Victor Baldridge

This paper deals with problems of policy planning in formal organizations, especially as these policies relate to the long-range goals and future strategies of an organization. It is essentially a study of one type of organizational change, a type that is deliberative and purposive rather than simply a reaction to nonplanned factors. The present study attempts (a) to specify some of the forces that cause an organization to plan deliberate changes and (b) to follow the planning process through its inception and elaboration stages.

A growing body of literature in political sociology and political science discusses social change on a national scale, most of which deals with the political development of underdeveloped countries. One major branch of this research, dealing with future-oriented ideologies as impetuses for social change, is generally called research on "images of the future" (e.g., the work of Wendell Bell, (2); Charles Moskos, (7); James Mau, (6); and Ivar Oxaal, (9)).

However, when we turn from the societal level to the organizational level, we find that there has been almost no research on ideology and future planning as a source of change in complex organizations. Most studies on organizational change have focused on

Originally issued as Research and Development Memorandum No. 58, Stanford Center for Research and Development in Teaching, January 1970. The research reported herein was supported in part by Contract No. OEC-6-10-078 with the U.S. Office of Education, Department of Health, Education, and Welfare. The opinions expressed do not necessarily reflect the position or policy of that Agency and no official endorsement should be inferred. Available through the ERIC Document Reproduction Service, LIPCO, 4827 Rugby Ave., Bethesda, Maryland 20014. The document should be cited as ED 037184.

"rational planning" as it is implemented in business organizations, but this approach usually ignores ideological factors and certainly does not fall within the same tradition that guides the studies of developing nations. One exception was Philip Selznick's (11) work on the Tennessee Valley Authority in which he devoted considerable attention to the "image of the future" as articulated by the Authority, and the consequences that resulted when the image was put into practice. Similarly, Charles Perrow (10) and others have dealt with the problem of goal setting in organizations, but the systematic analysis of future images was not an important feature of their work. All in all, organizational theorists have devoted little attention to ideological elements as they affect organizational change.

The present report attempts to focus attention on this neglected area by showing how ideological positions are critical in organizational change. The research grows out of an analysis of change processes in organizations that is being funded by the Stanford Center for Research and Development in Teaching. This is a long-term project that is developing some theoretical framework and empirical support for a theory of organizational change.

In addition, this paper depends heavily upon research on organizational change the author conducted at New York University in 1967 and 1968 (1). This was an intensive case study of three major changes in the university, one of which will be reported here. The study's techniques included (a) study of documents, (b) observation of decision-making bodies, (c) interviews with 93 faculty and administrators, and (d) a questionnaire sent out to all the full-time faculty and administration of the university, of which 693 (40 percent) were returned and usable.

Organizational Change: Forced Necessity or Planned Change

In order to outline some of the theoretical background it is necessary to touch briefly on one of the most persistent arguments cutting through study of social change, for there seem to be two dominant answers to the question of how change is caused.* On one hand, a Marxist school argues that social change is provoked by constraining factors that force some type of adaptation. This might be called a theory of "adaptation to necessity." Marx, for example, analyzed one historical case by arguing that social change was pro-

---

*For a review of these two positions and some of their major proponents, see Etzioni (5, pp. 6-9) and Birnbaum (3).

moted by the economic features of the British society, quite apart from
the value positions or ideological stances of the people involved. Marx
suggested that material and structural features of the society were the
bases of social change, and that value positions and ideological
statements were only an intellectual superstructure for justifying and
explaining that material base. This is a persistent theme in sociological change analysis, and it argues that change is promoted by
external conditions, material factors, or structural frameworks. From
this perspective change is largely a question of adaptation to
necessity, not of rational planning or goal-oriented behavior. Most
organizational change theorists seem to fall within this school for
they emphasize the importance of technological advances, the
unintended consequences of bureaucratic structure, and the un-
planned and unintended features of informal groups processes. From
this perspective change is not planned or goal directed, but is instead
dictated by the necessity of adapting to some structural condition,
be it economic, organizational, or technological.

A second explanation for the causes of social change grows out of
the work of Max Weber (14). Rather than focusing upon Marx's "real
factors," Weber focused upon the "ideal factors." Where Marx had
focused upon the technological, economic, structural, and materialistic base as the prime agent of social change, Weber stressed the role
of future orientations, ideological components, and value positions.
His classic study of *The Protestant Ethic and the Spirit of Capitalism*
(14) attempts to show how value orientations promoted social
change in the Puritan society. This strand of sociological analysis
emphasizes the importance of planning and the critical role that
images of the future play in promoting social change. It is from this
tradition that the research on images of the future in developing
nations is drawn.

Thus, there is a constant debate about the causes of social change,
with some authors following Marx by emphasizing structural features
of the organization, technological innovation, and economic necessity, and others following Weber by stressing the importance of
rational planning, future orientations, and ideological stances. The
battle between the "realists" and the "idealists" continues, although
it becomes more and more obvious that they are actually complementary approaches.

This paper will emphasize one side of the debate, for it concerns
particularly the role of ideal factors, ideological positions, and images
of the future as they affect organizational change. However, it will be
necessary throughout the paper to point out the interrelationships

between these two strands of argument, for ideal factors are always framed and supported by structural features and pressures that come from the external environment. Much of the discussion will attempt to show how "images of the future" and "constrained necessity" dovetail in an adequate interpretation of organizational change processes.

The following are some of the critical questions that guided the study of change processes at New York University:

1. How do constraint factors and images of the future interact in the empirical situation as the organization changes? In other words, how can we weave back together the insights derived from Marx and Weber?

2. What is the role of critical organizational elites and interest groups in change?

3. How do groups in the organization interact to set the content of the image of the future?

4. How do abstract images of the future become operationalized into concrete policy?

5. Once the image has been operationalized what kinds of political debate and activity surround its implementation?

6. How are structural adjustments made in the organization to protect the new goals and images?

7. What kinds of consequences, intended and unintended, flow from the implementation of the image?

We will return to these questions at the end of the paper after presenting the New York University case material in the next section.

Case Study: The Change Process at NYU

The role that a university plays in society is both planned and accidental, both deliberate and a whim of fate. The role of NYU as an institution of higher education is a strange mixture of historical events, deliberate planning, and pressure from many sources. This paper will examine some critical changes in NYU's role that have occurred over the last few years.

Pressures for Changing NYU's Traditional Role

For many years NYU had a consistent interpretation of its role in New York higher education. From its founding the university offered educational opportunities to all types of people, including under-privileged minority groups and students of relatively low academic ability. This was all part of a consistent philosophy about the university as a "school of opportunity," and in this sense, NYU was in the best tradition of the great "American dream." Generations of NYU students and faculty testify to the importance of this philosophy to their lives, and many a Wall Street businessman or New York teacher will give credit to the change that NYU afforded him. Large groups of the faculty were strongly dedicated to this ideal and were willing to fight when that image of the university was threatened.

Times were changing, however, and not all the members of the university community were happy with a philosophy that accepted large numbers of relatively poor students and then failed many of them. As one professor said:

Sure, we were the great teacher of the masses in New York City. In a sense this was a good thing, and we undoubtedly helped thousands of students who otherwise would never have had a chance. But we were also very cruel. We had almost no admission standards, and a live body with cash in hand was almost assured of admission. But we *did* have academic standards, and we were brutal about failing people. There were many years in which no more than 25-30% of an entering class would graduate. Sure, we were the great "School of Opportunity" for New York, but the truth of the matter is that we were also the "Great Slop Bucket" that took everybody and later massacred them.

From the inside, then, there was mounting opposition to the "school of opportunity" philosophy with its low admission standards and high failure rates. In particular, professors from liberal arts and graduate units objected to standards that lowered the university's student quality. Internal pressure for change was slowly building up.

External events were also pressing the university toward a reevaluation of its goals and image. Organizations are seldom the sole masters of their fates for external forces of various kinds impinge upon them, shaping, remaking, and molding them in many ways. NYU exists in an environment in which other universities are competing for resources, students, and social influence. For many years NYU was the major "service university," while the City University of New York and Columbia maintained extremely high standards, and did not serve the bulk of the student population. In the early 1960's, however, the picture changed, as the state and city assumed more responsibility for educating the masses. An extensive network of junior and senior colleges was opened and expanded and the public university enrollments shot up dramatically, partly because the public schools charged very small tuition rates, while privately supported NYU was forced to charge extremely high fees. In short, the competitive position of NYU *vis à vis* student enrollment was severely threatened by the rise of the public institutions.

The results were rapid and dramatic. In 1956 NYU published its

Self-Study, a major attempt at long-range planning which fore-shadowed many of the changes that were to occur shortly. The authors of that farsighted document were at least aware of the threat the public institutions held for NYU, but it is doubtful that they understood how close that threat was. In fact, they state with some confidence,

Even the enormous expansion of the tuition-free city college system with its excellent physical plant has not as yet substantially affected the character of NYU ... (8, p. 11).

The *Self-Study* went on to predict increasing enrollments for NYU over the decade from 1955 to 1966. By the early 1960's, however, it was obvious that the expected growth patterns were simply not materializing. Figure 1 compares the *Self-Study* projections and the actual enrollments for the period 1955-1966. By 1966 the actual figures were running a full 20% behind the predictions. As one administrator viewed it, "We certainly anticipated pressure from the public universities, but frankly the pinch came ten years ahead of our expectations."

NYU was seriously threatened by the competition of the public universities, for not only were they losing students but the financial stability of the institution was being undermined by loss of vitally

Figure 1. Comparison of enrollment figures:
self-study projections and actual figures

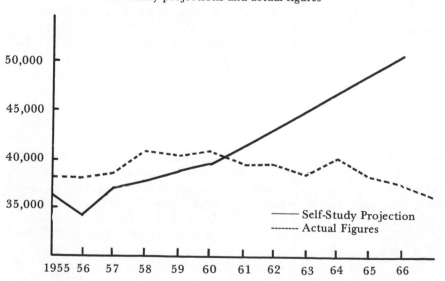

needed tuition. The question was how to frame a new image of the university that would serve the educational needs of the people and the organizational needs of NYU.

The Political Struggle for a New Image of the Future

From a sociological perspective it is critical to see that the resultant plans for the future were framed by a political context, and pressures were impinging on the decision makers from numerous sources. On one hand, there were the internal pressures for change from the liberal arts groups and from the graduate schools. On the other hand, the external challenges from the public universities made a confrontation virtually inevitable. The forces for change were great, but there were also groups that had strong vested interests in the *status quo*. At least three major units of the university—the School of Education, the School of Commerce, and influential alumni—were strongly committed to the school of opportunity image. However, it was this image that was being challenged as the university searched for a new educational role.

By the end of 1961 a debate about the future of the university was quietly raging behind closed doors. The discussion went far deeper than the mere question of how to recruit more students, for the essential issue was really about NYU's total educational role. Could NYU continue with business-as-usual, or was this a critical turning point? Many of the top administrators felt that the time was ripe for a deep-rooted and sweeping evaluation of NYU's future destiny. This was particularly true in light of the financial crisis that was facing the institution.

In terms of an images-of-the-future analysis, the debate at this point involved the goals and long-range commitments of the university. The assessment at this stage was not that the university should adopt some type of management techniques to solve its financial crisis, but that it would have to develop new goals and new orientations to the future if it was to survive as a significant element of American higher education. Confronted with pressures from many sides, the leaders of the university deliberately started to "tinker with the future." NYU was consciously changing its goals and deliberately projecting a new self-image, a new institutional character. In essence a strange paradox was developing, for the "constraint" factors were forcing the university into an examination of its future goals and ideological commitments—Marx and Weber were joining hands!

At this time several events pushed the changes even faster. First,

James Hester, who had been Executive Dean of the liberal arts units for two years, was selected to be president in 1962. The new president was acutely aware of these problems and made it his first order of business to confront them. Second, the Ford Foundation invited NYU to make an application for a comprehensive development grant. This opportunity was seized as a critical element of financial support for changes that would soon be instituted. In early 1962 several committees were appointed to formulate plans for the Ford request. Many questions about NYU's future educational role came under scrutiny, and numerous faculty bodies were invited to prepare proposals. How those discussions eventually reached the decision stage is a debatable question. On one hand many faculty members complained that the critical decisions were really made by a small group of administrators without much consideration of the faculty. On the other hand, some administrators claim that the faculty's contribution was limited because of their constant inability to look beyond the needs of their individual departments or schools to the needs of the entire university.

In any event, it is fascinating to note how deliberately and consciously the university began to plan its future. The debate, fact finding, and committee work for the Ford request went on for more than a year. Rather than responding impulsively to the pressures of the moment, the university was attempting to plot its future course realistically after a careful study of its needs.

By the fall of 1963 the Ford Report was completed and the implementation of future policies awaited the Foundation's decision. Ford responded generously, expressing strong confidence in the plans. NYU was challenged to raise 75 million dollars from other sources to match Ford's 25 million dollars. Financial resources for the changes were now at least possible, although securing the 75 million dollars did not look easy.

There was no single plan that emerged from the Ford Report evaluation, but instead there was a complex interconnected series of changes for promoting NYU's new image of the future. They included:

1. Undergraduate admissions standards would be raised substantially.
2. The fragmented undergraduate program (Education, Commerce, Washington Square College, Engineering, and University College had separate programs) would be unified.
3. An "urban university" orientation would be developed.
4. More full-time faculty and students would be recruited, with more on-campus residences.

5. More energy would be directed toward graduate and professional training, so that direct undergraduate competition with the state university would be avoided.

Not all these decisions were implemented at the same time, but over a period of months these moves began to gain momentum. It is important to note several things about these decisions. First, they represented important, far-reaching changes for the very nature of NYU. In a sense, the old NYU was being significantly transformed. Second, the relation to the external social context is particularly critical, for NYU was under serious attack from competing institutions that were undermining its traditional role. In large measure these decisions represented a "posture of defense" for NYU, for without them it is quite probable that the institution would have been forced into severe retrenchment and stagnation as the public institutions assumed its traditional role and captured its traditional student population. Third, however, the posture of defense allowed a realistic development of new images of the future that could well turn potential disaster into a vital new educational role. The "constrained necessity" interpretation for organizational change interlocks here with the "image of the future" approach.

The Role of Critical Elites in Shaping the New Image

Almost all studies of future images as impetuses for social change have to confront the question of *whose* image is accepted, and this raises the question of powerful elites and political interest groups. From the point of view of most people at NYU the new decisions "came down from the top." Without doubt it was a small group of top administrators who made the critical decisions, and there were strong complaints that they were sometimes made arbitrarily with little consultation with the faculty, or even with most administrators. The overwhelming sentiment of the persons interviewed was that these decisions were carried out with a firm hand.

To be sure, the University Senate was consulted about most of the plans, but at that time the Senate was relatively weak and many people believe that it merely rubber-stamped a series of decisions that had already been made. As one Senate member put it,

We were "informed" about these matters, and we were asked to vote our approval, but I wouldn't say we were actually "consulted" in any meaningful way. It was a one-way street—they told us what they were going to do and we said "OK."

Of course, many faculty committees were working on the Ford

Report, but few of the critical decisions came from these commit-tees. The first time most of the faculty knew about these decisions was when they were publicly announced. As one rather bitter professor in the School of Commerce commented,

The School of Commerce was about to have its throat cut and we didn't even know about it until after the blood was flowing! Sure, Hester came over and gave us a little pep talk about how much this was going to improve things, but he didn't really ask our advice on the issue. He didn't exactly say it was going to be his way "or else," but we got the point.

On the other side of the issue, the administration clearly saw the threats facing NYU as the public universities challenged them. It was clear that something radical had to be done, and had to be done quickly. Several administrators expressed strong dissappointment in the faculty's contribution to the Ford report, declaring that most of their ideas were conservative and bound by entrenched loyalties to departments and schools. In effect, many administrators felt—probably correctly—that they had a broader perspective from which to view the problem than most of the faculty, and therefore it was their duty to move into the situation as the key "change agents." Further, they knew some of the moves would be violently opposed, and extensive consultation might arouse enough hostility to defeat the whole matter. As President Hester explained in an interview:

The university was confronted with critical conditions. We had to undertake action that was radical from the standpoint of many people in the university. Some of these changes had to be undertaken over strong opposition and were implemented by administrative directives. In two of the undergraduate schools a number of faculty members had accepted the "school of opportunity" philoso-phy as a primary purpose of their school. This had been justifiable at one time, but no longer. Many faculty members simply did not recognize that circum-stances had changed and did not accept the fact that the service they were accustomed to performing was now being assumed by public institutions at far less cost to the students.

At this point the administration had to be the agent for change. It was incumbent upon us to exercise the initiative that is the key to administrative leadership. In the process, we did interfere with the traditional autonomy of the schools, but we believed this was necessary if they and the university were to continue to function.

It might be helpful to examine some of the factors that enabled the administrators, as a critical elite, to execute this change so successfully.

First, the power of the central administration was greatly en-hanced following a decade of centralization which had been initiated under the strong leadership of President Henry Heald in the early 1950's. Before Heald's administration NYU had been a very loose collection of essentially autonomous schools. His tenure, however, brought much power to the central administration. President Hester's success very much depended on President Heald's success several years earlier. If the same moves had been made a decade earlier, they might well have failed.

Second, Hester was a new, popular president who could still rely heavily on the "honeymoon effect" to carry the day for him without too much threat. The trustees were obviously going to back their new man, even if a substantial part of the faculty opposed the move—which they did not. Moreover, as one Commerce professor noted, "Hester is as close to a popular president as any you'll find, and that makes him a hard man to beat on most issues." The general faculty appears to have agreed, for when they were asked to indicate their "general confidence in the central administration of the university" on a questionnaire, they indicated a high degree of confidence. Figure 2 compares responses to this question in 1968 with a 1959 Faculty Senate Survey.

Figure 2. Degree of confidence in central administration
(all faculties combined)

	N	High	Medium	Low
1958	580	40.3%	17.6%	42.1%
1968	693	47.4%	32.0%	20.6%

Thus, the popularity of the central administration and Dr. Hester's newness to the presidency were major assets as the administration struggled to implement its decisions.

Third, support for these changes came from large segments of the faculty. Cross-pressures from interest groups on either side of an issue often allow decision makers more freedom, and allow them to press for changes that would be impossible if most groups lined up in opposition. This is exactly what happened in this particular case. Many liberal arts professors were strongly in favor of the rise in admissions standards, especially since the new standards hurt the nonliberal arts units the most. In addition, many graduate level professors felt that raised standards in the undergraduate levels would indirectly improve the graduate programs and would certainly give them better undergraduates to teach. Thus, there were powerful interest groups supporting the change, as well as opposing it.

Fourth, the decisions were successful because of the obvious bureaucratic weapons which the central administration controls. There is a centralized admissions office at NYU and the central administration could achieve some of its new goals simply by instructing the admissions office to raise standards, thus effectively by-passing the opposition that centered in some schools. In addition, the twin powers of the budget and personnel appointment were often brought to bear in the struggles that followed the decisions.

Finally, one of the most important reasons that these dramatic changes could be introduced was the external threat NYU faced from the public institutions. It is one of the most common findings of sociological research that groups threatened by external forces will tolerate many internal changes that they otherwise would fight to the death. The administration was willing to fight for changes that would save the university and the trustees, convinced that these changes were imperative, stood solidly behind the administration.

Translating an Image into Action

The new program was implemented during 1962-63 and 1963-64. The effects were dramatic and had repercussions throughout the university. First, admissions of undergraduates dropped 20 percent in the period from 1962 to 1965, as can be seen in Figure 3. The sharp dip is largely due to the increased admissions standards. This drop in enrollment cut off vitally needed tuition funds at the very moment when approximately ten million dollars above normal costs were needed to carry out other aspects of the quality up-grading. By 1967, however, the new policy was successful, for enrollment rose again as the university attracted large numbers of better students.

A second indicator of the impact of the changes was the rise in the test scores of entering freshmen. Figure 4 shows the Scholastic Aptitude Test scores of entering NYU freshmen from 1961 to 1966 (from 4). Arnold Goren, the Director of Admissions, is probably doing more than exercising his public relations duties when he calls this a "fantastic" increase for this short time.

A third indicator of the changes is related to student housing. As part of the new role for NYU more emphasis was placed on attracting students from outside New York City, and upon drawing

Figure 3. Undergraduate enrollment, New York University, Fall 1960 through 1967-68

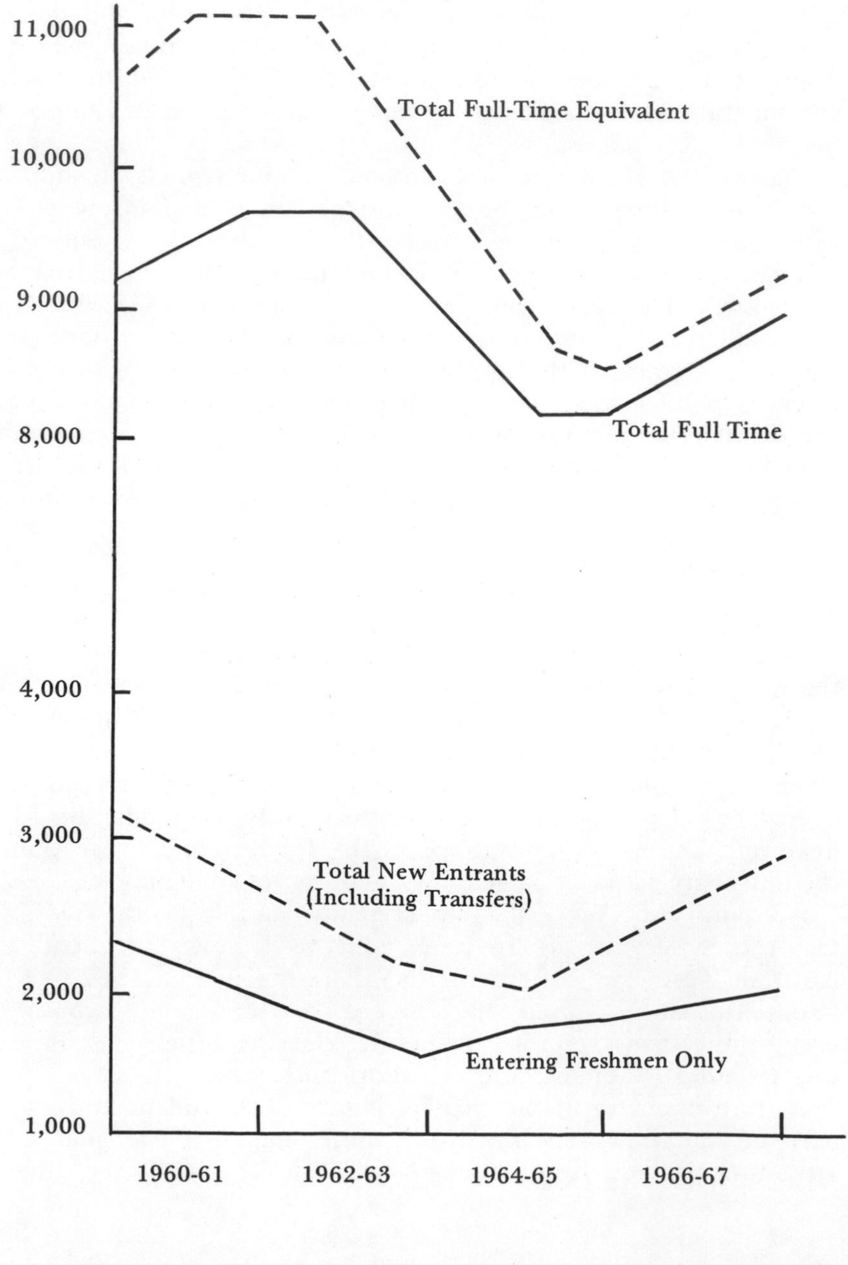

11,000

Total Full-Time Equivalent

10,000

9,000

8,000

Total Full Time

4,000

3,000

Total New Entrants
(Including Transfers)

2,000

Entering Freshmen Only

1,000

1960-61   1962-63   1964-65   1966-67

Figure 4. Percentage of Freshmen with SAT Scores Above 600: 1961-66

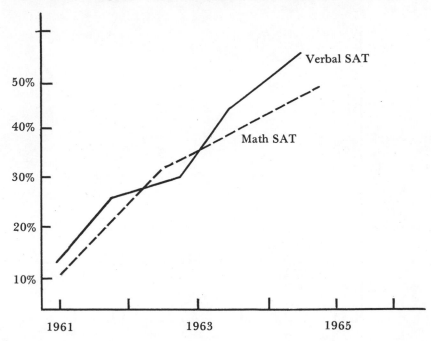

more full-time resident students. In order to do this the university was forced to go into student housing on a large scale. Moreover, the recruitment of a full-time faculty also demanded more housing, and the university added faculty residences almost as rapidly as it did student housing. Figure 5 shows the increase in students who are housed directly by the university.

A fourth change was in the composition of the graduate student enrollment. There has been a major shift in emphasis toward more full-time graduate students in the arts and sciences, while students in the professional schools have remained relatively constant. Figure 6 (data derived from Cartter, 4) shows this very clearly. In 1960 only 23 percent of the graduate enrollment was full time, while by 1967 the full-time graduate students had *tripled* in only seven years. In fact, NYU's commitment to graduate and professional education is shown by the fact that of the 6,908 degrees granted in 1967, nearly two-thirds (4,549) were either graduate or professional.

A fifth change was the development of the Coordinated Liberal Studies Program. NYU had undergraduate programs in Washington Square College, in University College, in the School of Engineering,

Figure 5. Students in university housing: 1960-67

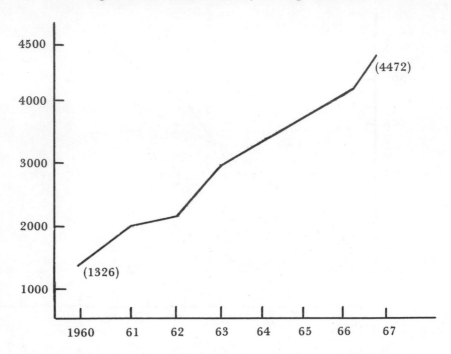

in the School of Commerce, and in the School of Education. Many of these programs were almost exact duplications resulting in administrative overhead, inefficient use of faculty, and ineffective utilization of space. In addition, segregation of the courses into schools meant that students were often isolated and could seldom have the intellectual stimulation that comes with diversity in the classroom. In the mid-1950's a Gallatin College concept was proposed by Chancellor George Stoddard. This college was to consolidate all the undergraduate units for the first two years. The plan seemed reasonable and would eliminate much duplication while lowering educational costs and expanding the horizons of the students. However, at that time the plan was politically premature and was quickly killed by the opposition of the various schools with vested interests in the fragmented pattern.

Although Hester, coming from outside the university to assume his deanship in 1960, was amazed at the administrative duplication in the undergraduate program, he was then unable to change anything. But in 1962, when he became president of the university, he renewed the battle for coordination. A commission was set up in February 1963 to make plans for some type of compromise coordination system. Eventually plans for the Coordinated Liberal Studies Program were included in the Ford Report. In September 1964, the program was officially launched, over the strong opposition of the same groups that had previously been opposed to the Gallatin College idea. This time, however, the plan was much less radical, for it involved only the combination of the first two years of study for Washington Square College, Education, and Commerce. Thus, the battle was not completely lost by the opponents, and the strength of the resistance is obvious from the fact that it took all the power of the president's office to insure that it even got a trial run. The plan has been in operation several years now, and most of the political controversy has abated.

Figure 6. Enrollment in graduate and advanced professional education: 1960-67

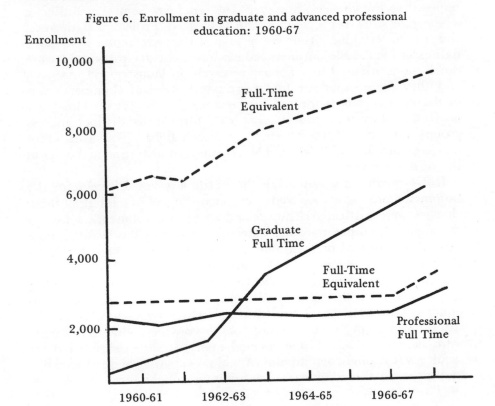

When Images of the Future Clash: The Impact
on the School of Commerce

The previous section dealt with the implementation of the new goals for the whole university, but this section will focus in closer on one unit that resisted those changes. Increasing admission standards, moving to full-time students and faculty, and a general upgrading in quality changed the School of Commerce dramatically. Commerce was one of the schools most fully dedicated to the "school of opportunity" image and it had a large core of professors who fought strongly for this value when it was threatened. The officials in the central administration had made the critical decisions, but vested interest groups in Commerce were determined to fight it all the way.

Not all the faculties of business education in the university were opposed to the changes, however. The Graduate School of Business, a separate unit for graduate and advanced professional degrees, wanted to establish itself as a major research center and as a nationally reputable business education unit. Its professors were much more oriented to scholarly research on industry and business, and they feared that the undergraduate School of Commerce was damaging the reputation of business studies at NYU. Thus, the professors of business education at NYU formed two distinct interest groups with two different emphases, each fighting for a different image of the future of NYU. The central administration had allies in the GSB professors.

However, this did not make the battle any less difficult, for the Commerce professors believed they might be out of a job if all these changes were instituted. They feared reduced enrollments, a loss of the night school program, decreases in the size of the faculty, and a general lowering of their influence in the university. And the things they feared most happened in a short time!

Probably the majority of the Commerce faculty was opposed to major changes in their basic philosophy and to changes in admissions policies. Moreover, the administration's chief representative on the scene, Dean John Prime, was not totally convinced that the changes were desirable. Dean Prime resisted many of the changes, and his faculty was strongly behind him. A real power struggle developed but in this battle the administration had most of the weapons. As one professor put it:

I guess now that it's all over these changes were good for us. But we fought it all the way; there was a fantastic battle. Actually, I'd say it was rammed down our throats. Several foundations made reports which suggested we were too "provincial," and we needed to upgrade standards and eliminate the duplication in our undergraduate programs. But remember, this was done by academic types, who really didn't understand a professional school and were prejudiced against us. This would not have happened a few years ago when the whole university lived off Commerce's surplus money. It is only our growing weakness which made this change possible. The various schools are always competing, and at this moment we are in a bad relative position.

For many months the task of implementing the new changes went on against strong opposition. Finally, two major changes in Commerce leadership were announced. In April 1962 Commerce was placed under an Executive Dean who was over both Commerce and the Graduate School of Business. Then in 1963 Dean Prime resigned, and Dean Abraham Gitlow was appointed as local dean at Commerce. Both Executive Dean Joseph Taggart and Dean Gitlow favored the administration's plans for upgrading quality in the School of Commerce. About that time the major breakthrough came in faculty cooperation.

By almost any yardstick the School of Commerce is radically different from what it was a few years ago. The most dramatic example is what might be called the "X" effect. The following chart shows how SAT scores went up and how enrollment figures went down.

As mentioned before, many Commerce professors feared they might lose their jobs if enrollments were drastically cut—and they were right. A faculty of nearly 300 in the late 1950's dropped to 61 in 1967-8. Many part-time members were dropped, nontenured people never were tenured, and even a few senior men were "bought off" to retire early. Very few new people were hired during that time, and many left for one reason or another.

Without a doubt the changes hit Commerce very hard. A resisting faculty was cut to the bone; a dean retired; the autonomous School of Commerce was placed under an "executive dean" who was also in charge of the Graduate School of Business; many courses were wrested from Commerce and put in the Coordinated Liberal Studies program; the student enrollment decreased radically. On the other hand, the quality of the students, faculty, and program was vastly improved. Most people at NYU now feel that these changes were necessary—even present members of the Commerce faculty. Nevertheless, the old School of Commerce died in the political struggle, and one of the most powerful organizational interest groups on campus was hobbled. As one Commerce professor put it, "We lost

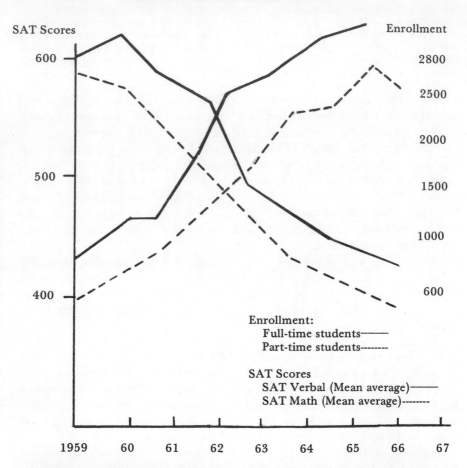

Figure 7. The "X" effect. Changes in the School of Commerce.
Enrollment and SAT scores: 1959-67

the fight, and now we have less influence in the university than we
have had in 50 years."

NYU's New Image of the Future: A Summary Chart

Figure 8 provides a summary of the changes at NYU. It is
obviously oversimplified, for many more factors went into these
changes than these that have been discussed. Moreover, the interest
groups that were supporting or opposing the changes are not
monolithic masses, and there were many shades of opinion within
each one. The issues were complex and the groups were often
subdivided among themselves. However, this chart describes the
general picture.

Figure 8. Developing a new image of the future for NYU

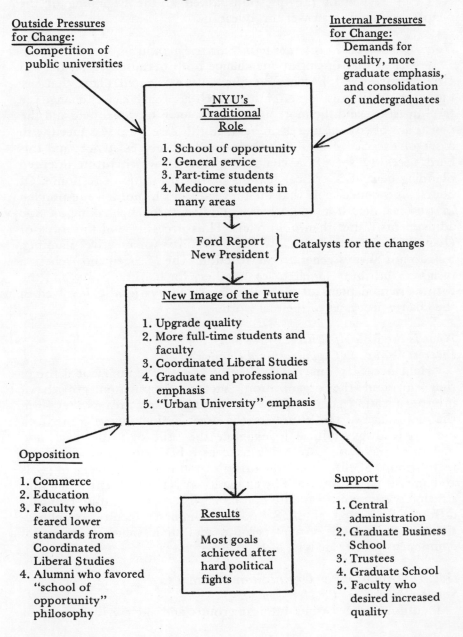

Outside Pressures
for Change:
    Competition of
    public universities

Internal Pressures
for Change:
    Demands for
    quality, more
    graduate emphasis,
    and consolidation
    of undergraduates

NYU's
Traditional
Role

1. School of opportunity
2. General service
3. Part-time students
4. Mediocre students in
   many areas

Ford Report
New President } Catalysts for the changes

New Image of the Future

1. Upgrade quality
2. More full-time students and
   faculty
3. Coordinated Liberal Studies
4. Graduate and professional
   emphasis
5. "Urban University" emphasis

Opposition

1. Commerce
2. Education
3. Faculty who
   feared lower
   standards from
   Coordinated
   Liberal Studies
4. Alumni who favored
   "school of
   opportunity"
   philosophy

Results

Most goals
achieved after
hard political
fights

Support

1. Central
   administration
2. Graduate Business
   School
3. Trustees
4. Graduate School
5. Faculty who
   desired increased
   quality

Conclusions

What generalizations can be made from the case study material on NYU? A review of the questions asked at the beginning of the chapter will help to answer this question.

How Does Necessity Interact with Future Planning?

It is clear that organizations change both because of the force of circumstances and because of the future-oriented plans that are made. In a real sense determining which approach causes change is a false question, and the more interesting issue is how planning and the constraint of circumstances interact. In this case NYU was faced with a set of external events that threatened its very existence, and this hard necessity set off a chain of events in which future-oriented planning became a critical feature of the institution's response. Of course, it is conceivable that the university might not have responded in this manner, but could have muddled through, making *ad hoc* adjustments rather than bold plans. Thus necessity and the force of changing circumstances allow the possibility for creative planning, but do not always generate the reaction. The Marxian and Weberian insights contribute much to each other, for hard necessity and the future-oriented plans of men are almost always jointly involved in the change processes of the real world.

What Is the Role of Critical Elites and Interest Groups in Organizational Change?

"Hard necessity" may well develop out of the impersonal forces that surround the organization, such as population growth or interorganization competition, but the ideas and dreams that form the new image of the future for the organization always come from men. It is always critical to examine the issue of *whose* goals and images of the future are being used as a basis of action. There are many groups of elites in a large organization that have divergent goals and images of the future. For example, at NYU the central administration was one critical elite that had a vision of the future radically different from that of the School of Commerce faculty. A delineation of the various interest groups and their values is a critical component for the analysis of change processes.

How Do Groups in the Organization Interact to Set the Content of the New Image?

Identifying the various interest groups and their values is a first step, but the analysis must push further to determine how these groups interact, and how one set of organizational interest groups is able to impose its image of the future on the organization. This, of course, is the classic question of politics, and a political framework is extremely helpful for the organization theorist concerned with change processes. In fact, the book on the NYU study deals extensively with building a "political model" for studying organizational change (See 1). A political analysis of elite interest groups must include a discussion of the differences in values held by the groups, the tactics they use, the nature of coalition formation between the groups, and the kind of decision-making mechanisms used to settle the dispute. Setting the new image for the organization is essentially a political process by which "dominant coalitions" (13, Chap. 9) impose their values on the organization and plans are articulated in light of the compromises that emerge from the political debate.

How Do Abstract Images of the Future Become Concrete Policy

The political goal-setting process emerges with a set of future-oriented plans, but these must always be translated from abstract images into concrete policy that guides the organization's action. In the NYU situation the abstract concept of "quality" has translated into concrete policies about higher admissions standards, more full-time students, and more emphasis on urban education. In the process of translation from the abstract to the concrete images of the future often undergo subtle and important changes, so the analyst must always be alert to the degree of overlap between abstract idea and concrete action.

What Kinds of Political Debate and Activity Surround Attempts to Realize the Image?

Concrete policy articulates the abstract goal but is rarely enough to insure that it is completely carried out. One of the persuasive features of political systems is that the very act of implementing a goal often results in changes of that goal. Even after policy has been stated the political battle goes on, for those elites and interest groups that lost the original round of battle will struggle to recoup some advantages as the policy is being implemented. For example, the stated policies of the university were vigorously opposed by the School of Commerce faculty long after the original decisions and policies had been set. Thus, the analyst of change in organizations must be sensitive to the continued controversy over an image—it is not a static thing that once-and-for-all settles issues, but instead is a living encounter between the dreams and goals of conflicting interest groups and elites.

How Are Structural Adjustments Made to Protect the Goals and Images?

Organization theorists, in particular, are sensitive to the issue of structural arrangements for carrying out human goals. Selznick (11) argued that values and goals are not self-sustaining, but instead require the protection of interested elites and structural frameworks. In fact, organizations are the ingenious technique of modern man for translating his images of the future and his values into stabilized structures that work to actualize them. At NYU, for example, there were many structural changes in the organization that were designed to advance the new image, including the creation of a new Coordinated Liberal Studies Program and the restructuring of the relations between the School of Commerce and the Graduate School of Business. Values and images must be translated into protective structures if they are not to wither and die on the organizational vine.

How do New Controversies Flow from the Implementation of the Image?

The best-laid plans of mice and men often go astray but remarkably enough they also work out right sometimes. The image of the future defines a course of action and often this is the outcome that actually occurs. NYU was taken out of direct competition with the state university, succeeded in attracting higher quality students, and began to build a much stronger image of quality in many areas. But this is only part of the story and it is only fair to mention the high cost of such an enterprise, both in financial commitment and in terms of the human cost that unavoidably accompanied such a major readjustment. One of the most pervasive outcomes of the implementation of any image is the continued political controversy and readjustment which eventually builds up to the point that new images of the future are proposed and new battlelines are drawn—and the process of image building and image articulation begins again. So it goes with changing dynamic organizations as they struggle to implement the images and goals of men.

References
1. Baldridge, J. V. Power and Conflict in the University. New York: Wiley, 1971.
2. Bell, W. Jamaican Leaders. Berkeley: University of California Press, 1964.

3. Birnbaum, N. "Conflicting Interpretations of the Rise of Capitalism: Marx and Weber." *British Journal of Sociology* 4 (1953): 125-141.
4. Cartter, A. M. *An Analysis of New York University*. New York University: Unpublished manuscript, 1968.
5. Etzioni, A. (ed.). *Social Change*. New York: Basic Books, 1964.
6. Mau, J. *Social Change and Images of the Future*. Cambridge: Schenkman Press, 1968.
7. Moskos, C. *The Sociology of Political Independence*. Cambridge: Schenkman Press, 1967.
8. New York University. *A Report from the School of Commerce*. Internal House Publication, 1968.
9. Oxaal, I. *Black Intellectuals Come to Power*. Cambridge: Schenkman Press, 1967.
10. Perrow, C. "The Analysis of Goals in Complex Organizations." *American Sociological Reivew* 26 (1961): 854-866.
11. Selznick, P. *TVA and the Grass Roots*. Berkeley: University of California Press, 1948.
12. Selznick, P. *Leadership in Administration*. Evanston: Row, Peterson, 1957.
13. Thompson, J. *Organizations in Action*. New York: McGraw-Hill, 1967.
14. Weber, M. *The Protestant Ethic and the Spirit of Capitalism*. Translated by Talcott Parsons. New York: Scribners, 1958.

THE DYNAMICS OF CONFLICT ON CAMPUS:
A STUDY OF THE STANFORD "APRIL THIRD MOVEMENT"

James Stam and J. Victor Baldridge

In the spring of 1969, Stanford University experienced a rash of student activism unprecedented in the history of the university. During this period a partisan interest group known as the April Third Movement dominated the pages of the *Stanford Daily* and completely captured the attention of the university community.

The movement began on April 3 when some 800 people gathered in a university auditorium to discuss plans for the control of the Stanford Research Institute. SRI, formed in 1946 as an applied research affiliate of the university, had been in the center of controversy for months because of its alleged involvement in war-related research, including research in counterinsurgency and chemical-biological warfare. Under considerable student pressure, the university trustees seemed to be on the verge of selling SRI. At this point, however, student opinion shifted considerably, and fearing that an independent SRI would actually do more war-related research than a university-owned SRI, the student group that had assembled on the night of April 3 voted nearly unanimously to demand that the Stanford Trustees, "discontinue all plans for severance of the Stanford Research Institute from the University . . . that instead SRI be brought under tighter control by the University and that guidelines be established for socially acceptable research."[1] On the following day a noon rally was held, demands were formally presented to President Kenneth Pitzer and a few committees were formed. The April Third Movement was under way.

The goal of this article is to analyze the conflict over the Stanford

Research Institute, primarily focusing on the A3M as the critical student pressure group. This paper deals with a series of critical sociological questions about the crisis at Stanford:

1. What was the nature of the *policy decision* and how did it affect the controversy?
2. What were the *background factors* that caused the April Third Movement to attack SRI?
3. What were the characteristics of the *group dynamics* that held the A3M together and made it such a strong political force?
4. What *tactics* did the A3M use in its fight against the trustees, the administration, and SRI?
5. What *responses* did the authorities make, and how did this affect the A3M?
6. What did the whole *cycle of conflict* look like, and what were the consequent decisions?
7. What factors contributed to the *breakup* of the A3M?

The reader will note that these are essentially sociological questions concerning group dynamics, organizational decision making, and conflict dynamics. This is in marked contrast to the majority of research on student revolutions that focuses on the social-psychological characteristics of the students and their personal dissatisfactions with the society. (See Part 4 of this book). We were frankly concerned with the processes of conflict and the nature of the policy-making system in the university.

This research starts with the fundamental premise that policy making in a complex organization like the university is often a political process, not merely a bureaucratic procedure.[2] The university is splintered into many interest groups. They have different goals for the community, different life styles, different career channels, and different levels of interest in university policy. This splintered community is naturally prone to conflict, and it is normal that this volatile situation should occasionally explode over policy issues. Given a critical policy decision, many interest groups with different values, and a wide variety of tactics available for pressure, the critical analysis concerns the dynamics of conflict that finally result in a decision.

Let us turn now to the analysis of the A3M and the Stanford conflict. In order to collect data on the events a case study was conducted during the spring and summer of 1969. Three basic sources of data were used.

1. Participant observations continued throughout the life of the movement and included nearly all meetings and activities of the group.

2. Documentary study included an examination of all available news releases on the movement; all issues of the movement periodical *Declassified;* many position papers and leaflets published by the A3M; and a wide variety of administrative and faculty memoranda, communications and position papers.

3. Interviews were held with a large number of active participants in the movement, and many hours of discussion and group meetings gave valuable insight into the nature and goals of the group. Key administrators and faculty members also provided vital information.

Using the case study techniques we will try to answer in turn each of the above questions about background factors, the nature of the policy, and the cycle of conflict. Throughout this article the same format is used. First, a series of abstract propositions is made about specific variables that affect the conflict. This is critically important, for we are trying not only to study A3M as one case but also to develop an analysis scheme by which similar events can be studied. After the abstract propositions are discussed, they are used as a conceptual screen through which the Stanford events are sifted. Figure 1 shows the five stages in the analysis. Each of these stages will be discussed in turn.

Stage One: A Potential Decision

In order for conflict to occur there must be a catalyst condition, a potential decision that inflames the community. There are basic characteristics that the potential decision must possess in order for conflict to be generated. Without these conditions the probability of a conflict spiral developing is low.

Figure 1. The five stages of conflict development

Stage 1	Stage 2	Stage 3	Stage 4	Stage 5
Introduction of a stimulus event— a potential decision	Background factors affecting conflict development	Mobilization of partisans	Cycle of Conflict	Policy Formulation

First, there must be *action possibility*. That is, the strain can be alleviated by human action, and be within the control of the organization. The members of the A3M were well informed on the charter of SRI and knew that the trustees of Stanford University had the power to take action and make the binding decision on the issue.

Second, the potential decision must have a *differential effect* on members of the organization. This differential effect may arise solely from a difference in value systems. That is, a given decision might have the same objective effect on all members of an organization, but divergent value systems might give rise to considerable conflict over the issue. The decision about the disposition of SRI certainly had differential effects for the various parties involved. At one point the president of SRI stated that the majority of the SRI employees would walk out if research restrictions were imposed. Certainly this statement would produce far greater concern for a trustee of the university than it would for a student activist. Furthermore, the cash value of SRI to the university would have a vastly different effect on the trustees than it would on the radical students. Finally, the ongoing problem of implementing controls over the type of research done at SRI would be a concern of the trustees long after the present crop of students had left campus. Clearly, the potential decision would have a differential effect on the two groups.

Third, the potential decision must be of *importance* to at least two groups within the organization that have different goals or desires regarding the issue. Both groups might be partisan groups who seek to influence the authorities in favor of their respective positions, or the conflict might rage between a group of partisans and the organizational authorities. It hardly seems necessary to labor the point that the issue of war-related research at Stanford and SRI was a matter of importance to many in the University community. After weeks of conflict, some 1,300 signed a complicity statement and over 3,000 voted to commend the A3M for their action. Furthermore, an all campus "day of concern" received widespread participation from both students and faculty. Clearly, the issue was a matter of considerable importance on the Stanford Campus.

Finally, group action occurs only when a partisan group perceives that the authorities might act contrary to their wishes. In this case the students had a long history of distrust toward the trustees, and they were fairly certain that their demands would not be met.

Stage Two: Background Factors Affecting the Conflict Development

Certain specific background factors in the organization help determine the type of conflict that will result in any given situation.

The clarification and definition of these factors is critical.

The Normative Variable Trust

William Gamson[3] suggests that one major determinant of conflict is trust—the basic attitude that partisan groups hold toward decision-making authorities. The trust dimension is based on a group's perception of the "efficiency" of the authorities in achieving collective goals and their "bias" in handling conflicts of interest.

Three levels of trust are specified: *confidence, neutrality,* and *alienation. Confidence* means that the group identifies with the authorities and perceives them as the group's agents. The group believes that the political institutions will produce favorable decisions, and that the basic authority structure is valid and worthy of confidence. *Neutrality* means that the group feels the authorities are not biased for or against them. *Alienation* means that the partisan group regards the authorities as incompetent to achieve collective goals and biased against the group. Authorities are not only failing to serve the group's interests, but in addition are serving some rival set of interests. In short, trust is the belief by partisans that the authorities can and will give them their preferred outcomes on a given policy decision.

The April Third Movement was clearly an alienated partisan group. Months of participant observation and many hours spent listening to speeches and discussions gave some feeling for the depth of the alienation. Documentary evidence is certainly inadequate to convey this feeling, but the following quotations from movement publications give examples:

The men who govern the University have a vested interest in continuing counter insurgency. Some are directors of defense oriented firms which benefit from the performance of defense related research at Stanford and SRI. Since we are asking the Trustees to make a decision which will be detrimental to their own concerns, they will not make that decision willingly; they will make that decision only in response to very strong pressure from the Stanford community . . . The Trustees are men of death and oppression. We reject this and call for life and love. Join us in creating a new community and a new world.

We should understand then that the Trustees and President Pitzer (himself a member of the Board of Directors of the Rand Corporation, a larger version of SRI that does much counter-insurgency research, war games, and mega-death planning also) have their positions, their military and economic power at stake. Given a choice these men would rather close down Stanford than lose SRI to the community. They will never willingly allow the research programs at SRI to come under the control of people who wish to stop American military and economic penetration of the third world.[4]

These brief quotations give some indication of the high degree of the A3M's alienation, an alienation that helped create the proper atmosphere for severe conflict.

The Internal Group Variables: Involvement and Cohesion

Political involvement is the degree to which partisan groups are actually interested in influencing organizational policy. For most people politics is a remote and unrewarding activity and usually the "law of apathy" prevails: Most of the time, on most issues, most people don't give a damn. Political involvement is the exception rather than the rule. On the other hand, high involvement means that the group can sustain high interest for influencing a given policy decision at the same time. *Cohesion* means that once involved the members of partisan group are able to agree on basic goals and tactics; they are not torn apart by internal strife to the extent that their influence attempts are ineffective.

The A3M's involvement, of course, varied a great deal with the fortunes of war and with the pressures of such things as exams. Nevertheless, the A3M did manage to capture the attention of the entire university community and the participation of a substantial number of that community. During one sit-in some 1,300 signed a complicity statement, admitting their participation in the sit-in. Over 1,500 Stanford students indicated that they would participate in another sit-in if need be, and about 3,000 students voted to commend the A3M for "helping to focus the attention of the campus upon the nature of the research being conducted at the University and SRI."

Student involvement varied substantially, but there was always a deeply dedicated core of student radicals at the center of the movement. They gave countless hours of labor to the cause and were able consistently to involve about 400 people in militant actions. Some of the later rallies and planning meetings ran well over a thousand in attendance. Clearly, the A3M was able to maintain a relatively high level of involvement from April 3 until the end of the spring quarter.

Turning to the cohesion variable, the A3M represented a considerable spectrum of values and interests. However, the movement could always rally around one common goal, namely, the end of war-related research at Stanford and SRI. In addition, that cohesion was fostered by the group's decision style, organization, and propaganda. "Participatory democracy" was the general style of decision-making employed by the group. Major decisions were always made by the group as a whole, and the coordinating committee generally offered voting privileges to anyone interested in coming to the meetings. This feeling of freedom and openness did much to contribute to the cohesiveness of the group. In general there was little overt pressure for conformity to any single line of thought, and thus partisans with somewhat divergent viewpoints could work together for a common goal. As an organizing tactic, the development of small "affinity groups" contributed a great deal to group cohesiveness. The groups were small and intimate, the atmosphere was always friendly, and they were generally conducive to the building of personal friendships. Propaganda was a third factor that contributed to group solidarity. The A3M was a prolific publisher and obtained extensive coverage from the *Stanford Daily* and the Stanford radio station. Rallies, carnivals, speeches, theatrics, posters and a political evangelism called "rapping" were important propaganda techniques, that helped hold the group together and helped politicize the uncommitted. The level of cohesion remained high enough even to sustain intense conflict which resulted in about 100 arrests at various times.

Access Variable

Access refers to the openness in the lines of communication and influence between partisan groups and key authorities. The degree of access can range from a very low level where partisans have absolutely no control or influence over the decision, to the other extreme where the partisans are actually given the authority to make the decision. The degree of access tends to affect the trust dimension of partisan groups with low access leading to low trust and vice versa. High access in which the partisans have open channels of communication and a voice in decision-making will often result in high levels of conflict, but the conflict will be formalized and directed through the legitimate legislative channels. Extremely low access will often act as a damper on interest articulation because the authorities seem so isolated that partisans see little value in an influence attempt. When it does occur, however, conflict generated by partisans with extremely low access is likely to be very unrestrained.

In the case of the A3M, the issue centered around one question. Was SRI to be retained by Stanford University, and were controls to be placed over the type of research that went on there or not? On this issue there was only one final authority, the Board of Trustees, and the students had low access to this decision-making body.

The Resource Variable

Resources are the weapons that a group may use to pressure authorities on an issue, and they largely determine the effectiveness of the partisan group's influence attempts. Three basic types of resources are suggested by Gamson. *Constraint resources* add disadvantage or difficulty to the opposed authorities. The ability to withdraw support is a constraint resource, as are the use of propaganda, demonstrations, sit-ins, disruption, violence, or threats. *Inducement resources* add some new advantage or benefit to the authorities. There is always the exchange or promise to exchange some specific good or service in return for desired actions by authorities. The use of inducement resources need not require any immediate return. Often inducements are offered in order to accumulate political obligations that may be drawn on in the future. *Persuasion resources* do not add anything new in the way of advantages or disadvantages to the authorities. Instead, they generally convince the authorities that the influencer's argument is correct.

The relationship between conflict and resources is a simple one: For high conflict of any type, both partisans and authorities must have high resources; otherwise one group will dominate, and high conflict will not occur. It is important to note that high resources alone do not necessarily result in high conflict. Resources are necessary, but not a significant cause of conflict.

Turning to the A3M at Stanford, it was obvious that they were very restricted in the kinds of resources they might use to influence the SRI decisions. As for "persuasion," the arguments presented by the student radicals had little appeal for the trustees who were charged with the financial welfare of the university and could not help but be impressed by the money that the sale of SRI would add to the University coffers. "Inducement" resources were also in short supply, for the students really had very little that the Trustees needed. If an alienated partisan group has no persuasion or inducement resources, it must begin with "coercive" tactics. This was largely the case with the A3M.

To begin with, the movement had enough student support to effectively close parts of the university for nine days and gain national attention, including the attention of a Senate investigating committee. Student disruptions had caused widespread concern in high places, and there were rumblings that Congress was pondering some federal sanctions on the universities. In addition to the fears of federal sanctions, there was also the question of what serious disruptions do to the image of the university and what effect they have on alumni and other private giving. University officials and trustees are aware of the hidden costs and disadvantages that can result from serious disruptions on a campus, and hence these militant tactics become an extremely powerful constraint resource when the students finally acted.

Stage Three: Mobilization of Partisans and Modes of Interest Articulation

Now the stage is set. Background conditions within the student group have combined to make it ripe for action, and a significant policy decision on SRI has been raised—a policy decision that is important, has differential effect, on which there are action alternatives available, and on which the students feel that the decision makers will be biased against the student position. Under these circumstances the *mobilization of partisans* occurs; the real question now is how the partisans will get organized and what they will do to influence policy. We call this activity to influence decisions *interest articulation*. In general, four types of interest articulation are suggested. Let us discuss each type briefly, then return to the A3M and show how its unique background variables combine to produce one unique type of interest articulation.

Apathy

One possible course of action that can be taken by partisans is to ignore the whole issue and make no attempt to influence the decision. This is by far the most typical response. On most issues, most of the people do not become actively involved and authorities are allowed to act without interference. It is the exception rather than the rule for partisans in an organization to become involved in the process of policy formation.

Formalized Conflict

In formalized conflict the interest articulation is carried on through the formal channels of the system. The partisan group appeals to the existing formalized ajudication bodies, observes the established decision rules, and abides by the eventual decisions of the legitimatized decision-making body. There may be intense conflict over an issue, but the influence pressures are constrained by the legitimated methods of decision making as defined by the organization.

Strategic Conflict

In the strategic mode of interest articulation the partisans do not resort to serious extralegal tactics, but neither do they follow formal political procedures for conflict resolution. As a rule, they are excluded from the formal channels of decision making and, hence, they organize to use pressure tactics, which may not be sanctioned by the organization, but are nevertheless sanctioned by the larger society. Partisans in the strategic mode might use intense lobbying, the circulations of petitions, and the formation of unions.

Anomic Conflict

The final mode of interest articulation is used by those who are excluded from the formal decision-making channels and who lack the resources for or confidence in strategic actions. In this case, the normal legislative channels are rejected and pressure is applied through means that are entirely extralegal, both from the organization's point of view and from that of the larger society. Tactics are often highly coersive and include such elements as propaganda, threats, demonstrations, arson, bombings, and violence. Student protest movements give us a prime example of this type of interest articulation.

Earlier, we discussed three basic types of resources that groups may use. They were termed *constraint resources, inducement resources* and *persuasion resources.* These three types of resources parallel the three types of tactics that partisan interest groups will use. Once again, the conflict mode under which the group is operating has an effect on the type of tactic employed. Groups acting in the formalized mode will use persuasion as their primary tactic. Groups using the strategic conflict mode will use persuasion and escalate quickly to inducements. Finally, groups operating in the anomic mode will escalate their tactics as high as constraints and these will constitute their primary tactic.

A sort of "principle of economy" seems to operate in the use of tactics. The tactic of persuasion is the least costly, hence, this tactic is usually attempted first. The tactic of inducements is more costly than persuasion and is seldom resorted to until partisans are convinced that persuasion will not work. The use of constraints or coersion, particularly as seen in anomic interest group activity, can often lead to physical violence, injury, legal action, and incarceration. These tactics are often outside the sanction of the larger society and, hence, can carry with them severe costs in terms of social disapproval and punitive action. There are times, of course, when a particular interest group may be totally lacking in one type of resource and, hence, may be forced to omit that type of tactic.

With these four types of interest group activity available, what determines which activity a given partisan group will select to use? This is a critical question, for here we want to link the *background variables* (trust, involvement, group cohesion, access, and resources) with the *interest articulation* variables (apathy, formalized, strategic, anomic). The following five propositions suggest the connection:

1. High trust promotes conflict which is restrained and formalized; neutral trust promotes strategic conflict; and low trust promotes anomic conflict.

2. All types of high conflict situations require high involvement on the part of at least some partisans. Low involvement promotes apathy.

3. High group cohesion promotes high levels of conflict and allows for effective influence. Low cohesion tends to render the group ineffectual and promotes apathy.

4. High access promotes high trust and formalized conflict; medium access promotes neutral trust and strategic conflict; and low access promotes low trust and anomic conflict.

5. Resources are necessary for conflict of any type and low resources lead to inaction. High resources do not necessarily lead to high conflict, however. Resources are necessary, but not a sufficient cause of conflict.

These five propositions suggest how each background variable by itself affects the mode of conflict, but we are really much more interested in the *combination of factors*. It is only when we put them all together that we can predict with some assurance what a group will do. Let us assume, then, that available resources and high involvement are "threshold" factors, that is, no group is going to get involved in the conflict if it does not have high involvement and some resources. Then let us ask about the various combinations of access, trust, and cohesion. Figure 2 suggests what groups might do if they have different scores on each of these variables.

Now let us see where the Stanford A3M fits in that picture. With low trust and access, and high cohesion, involvement, and resource potential the A3M is clearly a case of a group ripe for anomic types of action, a classic case of the Number 18 combination in Figure 2. A highly unhappy group, distrustful of the decision makers, sure that the decisions would be biased against the wishes, and organized into a cohesive group, it is no wonder that the A3M began to use coercive tactics: Sit-ins began, windows were broken, police were called, and hundreds of hours of negotiations were undertaken.

On April 3, 1969, about 800 people met and formulated a series of demands regarding research activities at Stanford and at SRI. At this point the group was still relatively unstructured and unstable. During the next few days, however, the group developed into an effective interest group with articulated goals, symbolic expressions, common life styles, a high rate of interaction, and a name of their own. While a great deal of informality prevailed, there was nevertheless a degree of organization and an array of standing committees to handle everything from legal defense to the publication of a periodical. The partisans were now mobilized and the cycle of conflict was under way.

Stage Four: The Cycle of Conflict

Once the conflict has begun our analysis suggests succeeding rounds or cycles of conflict over potential decisions. The rounds of the battle include the following elements: (1) a partisan attempt to influence a potential decision; (2) a response by authorities; (3) an evaluation of that response by partisans; and (4) a decision by partisans to stop the conflict or go on to a new round. Thus, the action of the authorities is the critical cycling point in the conflict development.

In this case, conflict over research at Stanford had already been going on for some time when the April Third Movement came on the scene. As early as May 1966 there was some student picketing of administrative offices at Stanford over the question of university acceptance of classified research contracts. In October 1968 the SDS had posted demands for the control of research at Stanford and SRI on the door of the Board of Trustees' office. In January 1969, the SDS disrupted a meeting of the trustees and called for the resignation of certain members either from that board or from the positions they held in defense-related industry.

Round One

For the A3M itself, round one consisted of a show of force at the public meeting on April 3 and a series of demands presented to the trustees. In reaction to these demands, the trustees decided to give a

Figure 2. The impact of combinations of the background variables on the modes of interest articulation

Possible Combinations: Read Down

Background Variable Names	1	2	3	4	5	6	7	8	9	10	11	12	13	14	15	16	17	18
Trust	+	+	0	-	+	0	0	0	0	0	-	-	-	-	-	0	0	-
Cohesion	+	0	-	+	+	+	0	+	+	-	+	0	-	-	0	+	0	+
Access	+	0	+	+	0	+	+	0	0	0	0	0	0	-	-	-	-	-
Mode of Interest Articulation — Prime Possibility	F	F	F	F	F	F	F	S	S	S	S	An	An	An	An	An	An	An
Secondary Possibility			S	A		S	S		An	A	An	S	A	A		S	S	

Possible Combinations: Read Down

Background Variable Names	19	20	21	22	23	24	25	26	27
Trust	-	-	0	+	+	+	+	+	+
Cohesion	0	-	-	0	-	+	0	-	-
Access	+	+	-	+	+	+	-	-	0
Mode of Interest Articulation — Prime Possibility	A	A	A	A	A	A	A	A	A
Secondary Possibility				F	F				

LEGEND

1. Values of Independent Variables

+ equals high
- equals low
0 equals medium

2. Modes of Interest Articulation

F equals Formalized
S equals Strategic
An equals Anomic
A equals Apathy

token response and stall for time. They requested the Board of Directors of SRI not to take any new contracts in chemical and biological warfare pending completion of a committee study on the relationship between Stanford and SRI. They also voted to hold a hearing on SRI-university relations following the publication of the committee report.

Round Two

On the evening of April 9 about 900 students gathered in the auditorium for nearly 3½ hours of discussion, debate, and evaluation of the trustees' actions. The group voted overwhelmingly to reject the Trustees' response to their demands and to stage a sit-in at the Applied Electronic Laboratory (AEL), a two-story building near the inner campus. The students moved immediately to the building and about 400 students occupied it shortly before midnight.

The next day (April 10) the demonstrators received written notice from President Kenneth Pitzer informing them that they were violating university policies and requesting them to leave. About 500 attended a meeting that evening and voted to continue the sit-in. The vote included a demand that the trustees act decisively to meet their demands by Monday, April 15.

On the following day, President Pitzer again requested the demonstrators to leave the building and formally notified the Stanford Judicial Council that the students occupying AEL were in violation of the university policy on campus disruption. But the sit-in continued, sometimes in an atmosphere that was almost carnival-like. Large numbers of students spent each night in the building sleeping in the corridors, offices, or even on the roof. During the day, great crowds joined the group particularly for the noontime or evening rallies, which featured lengthy discussions of issues and tactics. Over 1,300 people signed a "complicity statement" which read, "I am sitting at AEL wish you were here."

On Monday, April 14, the trustee committee on relations between the university and SRI released its report. The majority of the Scott Committee recommended that SRI be sold, with nine of the 12 members agreeing with this majority position. Seven of these favored sale with a restrictive convenant that would prohibit certain types of war-related research for a period of 20 to 25 years. Three members of the committee (one professor and two students) supported closer ties between SRI and the University with control over the type of research to be accepted.

On April 16 the Stanford Judicial Council held hearings on the

AEL sit-in to determine whether the campus disruption policy was being violated. After eight hours of testimony and two hours of deliberation, the Judicial Council concluded that the sit-in at AEL was indeed a disruption of an approved activity of the university. The council recommended that President Pitzer take action in accordance with the section of the charter dealing with "extraordinary circumstances" and declare the Applied Electronics Laboratory closed to all persons from Friday, April 18, 1969, to Friday, April 25, 1969. Meanwhile the demonstrators occupying AEL voted to end the sit-in voluntarily.

Following the close of the sit-in, Student Body President Denis Hayes called a mass meeting of the Stanford Community. Some 5,000 students and faculty gathered in Frost Amphitheater to discuss the issues. At this meeting some 3,000 ballots were distributed to students and faculty. More than 1,500 Stanford students indicated that they would participate in "another sit-in or similar action of protest" unless the Board of Trustees responded positively to concerns about the research at the University and SRI by mid-May. In addition, students at the meeting voted 3,073 to 203 to commend the April Third Movement for "helping to focus the attention of the campus upon the nature of the research being conducted at the University and SRI." The A3M was at a turning point: It could either stop its action or go on to more radical tactics. The next section lays out the theoretical considerations that determine a group's further tactics at such a turning point.

Re-evaluation by the Partisans

Thus far, we have noted that the cycle of conflict involves (1) an influence attempt by the partisans, and (2) a reaction by the authorities. Earlier, however, we also noted that after each authority response there was (3) an evaluation of strategy by the partisans, to see whether they must continue to pressure for a different decision. What determines whether they quit or escalate their tactics?

Four sets of variables determine what partisans will do: (1) they evaluate their goals to see whether the authorities' decisions are congruent with their goals; (2) the group examines its own internal processes to see if it has the commitment and cohesion to undertake a new round of action; (3) there is an analysis of resources and tactics to see if they are adequate, or whether the authorities have effectively cut off some tactics (for example, a new court order may short-circuit a planned sit-in); and (4) the group unconsciously evaluates its trust toward the authorities. If their goals have not been met it is unlikely that their trust toward the authorities has changed, but it is at least possible that the authorities have somehow convinced the partisans that the best possible decisions were being made, even if these are not what the partisans want. The role of persuasion and propaganda is critical as the authorities try to raise the trust level of the partisans.

Figure 3 shows how various moves could be made by the partisans, depending on their evaluation of their goals, cohesion, resources, and trust. (1) With negative goals outcomes, high internal cohesion, continued resource availability, and low trust the partisans are likely to escalate tactics, hoping to make it too expensive for the authorities to ignore them. (2) If they have won their point, but still have low trust and high cohesion and resources they are likely to simply escalate their goals, as many a harassed administrator has learned after a group won a point and he had sighed relief too quickly—only to find a new set of demands tacked on his door! (3) With unfulfilled goals, low trust, and available resources, a group that has found its commitment and cohesion falling apart will try to regroup, build new cohesion, and seek new recruits. (4) If the group is still prone to act, but has lost its resource capacity it is likely to build coalitions with other groups to increase the resource base. (5) If all the factors are negative then stop is really the only option that a group has. Finally, (6) with an increase in trust the group is likely to slack off its efforts in the hope that authorities will eventually favor them. Figure 3 summarizes these various options.

The Encina Hall Sit-in

Turning back to the A3M, the first round had proven inconclusive. The trustees had made token gestures. At that point the A3M's cohesion was strong, its trust was low, its goals were still unmet, and its resources were strong, (a combination like Column 1 in Figure 2). The logical move was to escalate tactics.

On April 30 a five-man committee of the trustees held a public hearing on the SRI issue. After the trustee hearing about 800 students gathered in the Student Union. Following lengthy discussion and debate the group voted to stage a sit-in at Encina Hall, the "nerve center" of the university administration. The students moved immediately to the building and at 1:05 a.m., after a brief scuffle with a group of right-wing students who were blocking the front door, the activists broke the glass doors and about 300 students entered the building. The students were repeatedly warned by the Dean of Students, by faculty members, and finally by the Deputy

Sheriff that if they did not leave the building they would be arrested. At 7:00 a.m. the demonstrators in the building called a meeting to decide what action they would take.

At 7:15 a.m. three buses arrived and discharged about 125 officers. One group of police quickly entered the building. Moments earlier the student meeting had ended in a vote to leave the building. A faculty member was immediately informed of the vote and he shouted at the police to stop. The police did so and waited for ten minutes while the demonstrators gathered their belongings and left the building. No arrests were made that morning. At 9:30 a.m. the university obtained from the superior court an injuction and temporary restraining order to prohibit further action.

That evening (Thursday, May 1) about 900 people gathered in a University auditorium for a meeting of the April Third Movement. Moments after the meeting began a university policeman stood up and read the court injunction against the A3M leaders. Shortly thereafter it was disclosed that four process servers were serving papers just outside the doors of the auditorium. The reading of the injunction changed the entire structure of the meeting, and angry discussion continued until 2:30 in the morning. Finally the assembly ended by demanding that the Academic Senate recommend that the administration withdraw the injunction order. However, the senate did not act on that demand at their Friday meeting.

A Struggle For Survival

On Monday evening, May 5, a general meeting of the A3M was held on the Old Union courtyard. A thousand people were expected; about 150 attended. It was generally conceded that the Encina sit-in was a mistake and had cost the movement its "broad base of support." Several stressed the need to "return to the original goals" and to rebuild support for the movement. In essence, a tactical error had been made, and the badly splintered group decided to regroup and build new coalitions. (See Figure 3, Columns 3 and 4).

The following Thursday evening, at a general meeting of the A3M, the group voted to stage a class boycott on Monday and Tuesday in order to emphasize "the extraordinary importance of the issues." The affinity groups spent the weekend in planning and organization. Red arm bands, rallies, discussion groups, guerilla theater and a colorful political carnival marked the first day of the boycott on Monday, May 12. Forty-seven faculty members announced plans to postpone their classes, and Stanford's Council of Presidents endorsed the boycott.

Figure 3. The excalate/de-escalate chart. Partisan re-evaluation
of tactics after each round of conflict

Areas Re-evaluated	Possible Changes					
	1	2	3	4	5	6
A. Goals — Received Preferred Outcome?	-	+	-	-	-	+ or -
B. Internal Resources — Cohesion maintained?	+	+	-	+	-	+ or -
C. Transactional Resources — Tactical Weapons still available?	+	+	+	-	-	+ or -
D. Trust — Has it increased?	-	-	-	-	-	+
Type of Action for Future Rounds	Escalate Tactics	Escalate Goals	Regroup	Coalition Action	Stop	Stop or De-escalate Tactics & Goals
Explanation	Have resources Hope tactics may win next round	If tactics worked and trust still low, then try for more goals	Consolidate internal resources, hope for new round	Unite to gain more resources	Disintegration of group	Trust increased Conflict becomes more formalized.

Over 1,100 students participated in the carnival, which included a wide variety of political games sponsored by the various affinity groups. The second day of the boycott climaxed with a meeting to hear the trustees' expected decision on SRI. The decision was released about 6:00 p.m. from the ninth floor of the Pacific Mutual Life Insurance Building in San Francisco. The Trustees decided unanimously to sever formal ties between the university and SRI.

Apparently the students had won. The obvious thought was now the conflict would be over. However, we earlier predicted that a win, accompanied by strong group cohesion and continued basic distrust, would actually result in new demands rather than a cessation of activity. (See Figure 3, column 2). This "goal escalation" is exactly what happened. Although the students had gotten most of their demands, they simply upped the ante, demanding that the decision to sever SRI relations be reversed so that the university would retain tight control and root out unpopular research.

In short, by this time the conflict had generated a life of its own, and an upward spiral was sucking everyone on to more radical confrontations. The partisan students were expanding their sources of support by building coalitions with other partisans; the goals were being escalated and more severe demands were made; the tactics were becoming more radical all the time; the authorities were moving up the power hierarchy drawing in more powerful officials to deal with the crisis; and the authorities were mounting ever more severe counterattacks against the partisans. This was the mounting cycle of conflict that Stanford faced after the trustee decision on SRI.

The Next Round: Attack on SRI at Hanover Street

On May 13, the day after the trustee's severance decision, about 1,000 persons gathered for a meeting of the A3M. Several proposals for action were considered. Discussions continued throughout the afternoon and into the evening. Finally, the group decided to disrupt a nearby facility of SRI located on Hanover Street. The following morning students marched to Hanover Street and set up picket lines under the watchful eyes of about 50 police. The students began blocking traffic at a nearby intersection, and a massive traffic jam was created. Demonstrators distributed leaflets to the stalled motorists and attempted to engage them in conversation to explain the demonstration. The traffic jam lasted until about 11:00 a.m. and was finally cleared as cars maneuvered around the barricades or drove over open fields to other streets.

Finally, about 11:00 a.m. the police began their long-awaited move. About 150 police officers using tear gas swept down the street clearing the area of demonstrators and forcing them into open fields. Sixteen arrests were made as students and police engaged in brief scuffles. Most of the demonstrators left as a group shortly before noon. Damage to the building and grounds was estimated at $10,000.

Round Two at SRI-Hanover

It was Monday, May 19, and the day began as it had on Friday, with demonstrators gathering into affinity groups in front of the Student Union and moving off toward Hanover Street. This time, however, the police were on hand in force. About 225 policemen had been stationed at Hanover Street, and a helicopter was circling over head. The demonstrators were dispersed quickly and roadblocks were removed almost as soon as they were placed. After about an hour of "cat and mouse" with the police, the demonstrators retreated to campus. They eventually decided to spend the afternoon in "peaceful picketing" at the main SRI facility in Menlo Park. About 450 demonstrators gathered there shortly before noon, forming picket lines on the sidewalk and distributing leaflets to nearby homes while some 175 policemen looked on.

The Momentum Slows Down

That evening, at a general meeting of the A3M it was decided to "move on SRI when the police are not there in force." The following day featured a "phone-in" at SRI calculated to tie-up the switchboards and disrupt normal activity. On May 22, about 130 A3M demonstrators picketed peacefully for an hour and a half in front of the Hanover Street Facility of SRI. There were no arrests and no serious confrontations with the 17 police officers present.

The following Sunday, May 26, a planning meeting was called for 7:30 p.m. in a University auditorium. Unfortunately, this was also the evening of Spring Sing, and only about 20 people were on hand for the meeting. The assembled group laid plans for the movement's next action. This included a noon rally on Tuesday, May 27, followed by a march to the Hoover Institute to talk to Director Glen Campbell who is a University of California regent. This really was the last gasp of the dying movement, and a burning of Campbell's effigy topped the dwindling meeting. Toward the end of the semester the pressure of examinations did much to curtail the activities of the April Third Movement.

A Quiet Death for the A3M

During the summer the A3M announced two meetings. The first

was held at 7:30 p.m. on Wednesday, July 23. About 40 members were present. The meeting began with a discussion of the current legal entanglements stemming from the various SRI demonstrations. The number of arrests was steadily rising and the bail fund was nearly depleted. Movement members were urged to sign up for the fund-raising committee.

The second meeting of the summer took place on July 30. Fifteen movement members were present. At this meeting, plans were laid for six movement members to gather the following Friday evening for the purpose of making sandwiches to be sold at a rock concert in order to bolster the bail fund. The meeting adjourned after about 45 minutes of discussion. This was the last official meeting of the April Third Movement; however, the legal defense committee did continue to function into the next academic year during a period of arrests and trials stemming from the SRI demonstrations.

Warrants were issued for a total of 99 persons, most of them Stanford students, and arrests continued into the fall quarter. A variety of charges were listed and trials began on August 18, 1969 in the North Santa Clara County Superior Court. Several defendants pleaded no contest to the charges against them, and jail sentences were meted out in some instances.

Stage Five: Mediation and Conciliation, the Formation of Policy

The conflict had run its course. Battles had been won and lost. There remained only the dynamics of mediation and conciliation. Here negotiations were undertaken, compromises were forged and a politically feasible policy was hammered out. This policy represented the official climax of the conflict.

In the Stanford events the decision that emerged was a jerry-built compromise that really made no one happy, but neither did it violently offend everybody. The final decision was to sell SRI outright. This was some solace to those who wanted Stanford free of the burden of SRI's war-related research, but it certainly did not meet the demand for closer relations with Stanford and restriction of war research.

All in all, the decision was a delicate compromise. Many students were still upset, but the faculty, through the University Senate, backed the trustee's decision. With the oncoming summer the student opposition died and the crisis was over.

Summary

Let us review for a moment. The essential task of this article has been to analyze policy formation under conditions of high conflict, a situation that is all too common on campuses today. Taking the April Third Movement at Stanford we have tried not only to describe what happened, but to explain regularities in behavior—to construct a primitive theory of conflict in organizational policy situations.

Following William Gamson's lead we suggested that much of the conflict can be understood as the attempt of partisans to influence the decisions of authorities. In this case the partisans were the A3M students, while the authorities were the trustees and administration of the university. There were five stages in the analysis.

First, we suggested that certain decisions have more potential for producing conflict than others. Decisions that are seen as important, have action possibilities, affect large numbers of people, and have differential consequences for different interest groups are the ones most likely to cause intense conflict.

In stage two we examined the background factors that make a group ripe for conflict. A group is likely to try to influence policy if it is directly affected by the outcome of the decision, of course, but only if it is simultaneously low in trust (feeling that the authorities are biased against them), high in cohesion (able to form and organize a group of partisans), and high in available resources (able to effectively use a resource that cannot easily be countered by the authorities.) With these factors making the background ripe for conflict it is likely that partisans will mobilize to fight for a favorable policy decision.

Stage three dealt with the mobilization of partisans. Figure 2 showed how the unique combination of low trust, high cohesion, and high resource potential led the April Third Movement to select anomic behavior as an appropriate "interest articulation" behavior, thus rejecting apathetic, formalized, and strategic modes. Anomic interest articulation is the most radical from the tactical perspective, for partisans who feel that they are excluded from the formal channels of decision and who have few "legitimate" tactics naturally turn to forceful, nonlegitimate procedures—the sit-in, rock-throwing, and violence.

Once the partisans have been mobilized, the cycle of conflict is begun. The conflict cycle consists of (1) an influence attempt by the partisans, (2) reaction by the authorities, (3) re-evaluation by the partisans, and (4) either a stop or escalation of tactics depending on the new situation. If there is a tactic escalation, it is likely to be accompanied by both an escalation of goals with more severe demands being made, and an authority escalation with increasingly higher levels of the admininstrative hierarchy being brought into the struggle and increasingly severe countertactics being used. Figure 3 showed how the various reevaluations by the partisans might lead either to a cessation of the conflict or an escalation. Any number of rounds might be fought at this stage, and the level of conflict may vary in a number of ways.

Finally, at stage five there is mediation and negotiation. It is rare indeed that any one group wins completely, and the more usual case is a negotiated compromise that partially meets the needs of many groups. A decision that pleases everyone is just as infrequent! Consequently, the end of one round and one decision is likely to bring up a new topic, a new battle, and a new cycle of conflict. So it goes in dynamic organizations, and particularly in that newly politicized institution, the university.

Footnotes
1. *The Stanford Daily*, April 4, 1969.
2. J. Victor Baldridge, *Power and Conflict in the University* (New York: John Wiley & Sons, Inc., 1971).
3. William A. Gamson, *Power and Discontent* (Homewood, Ill.: The Dorsey Press, 1968), pp. 39ff.
4. April Third Movement, *Declassified* (Stanford, California, April 11, 1969), p. 5.